BUILDINGS OF IOWA

SOCIETY OF ARCHITECTURAL HISTORIANS

BUILDINGS OF THE UNITED STATES

Buildings of

IOWA

DAVID GEBHARD

GERALD MANSHEIM

New York   Oxford

OXFORD UNIVERSITY PRESS

1993

Buildings of the United States is a series of books on American
architecture compiled and written on a state-by-state basis. The primary objective
of the series is to identify and celebrate the rich cultural, economic, and geographical diversity
of the United States as it is reflected in the architecture of each state. The series has been commissioned
by the Society of Architectural Historians, an organization devoted to the study, interpretation,
and preservation of the built environment throughout the world. People who share
these interests are invited to join the society.

OXFORD UNIVERSITY PRESS

Oxford   New York   Toronto
Delhi   Bombay   Calcutta   Madras   Karachi
Kuala Lumpur   Singapore   Hong Kong   Tokyo
Nairobi   Dar es Salaam   Cape Town
Melbourne   Auckland   Madrid
and associated companies in
Berlin   Ibadan

Published by Oxford University Press, Inc.
200 Madison Avenue, New York, New York 10016

Oxford is a registered trademark of Oxford University Press

Photography Credits:
Introduction, pages 22, 23, 24 (top), Iowa State Historical Department, Iowa City.
ME353, page 140, Loren Horton. CE224, page 233, Art Wittern. MW058, page 478, Jerri McCombs.
All other photographs were taken by the authors.

Buildings of Iowa has been supported by grants from the National
Endowment for the Humanities, an independent federal agency; the Pew Charitable
Trusts, and the Graham Foundation for Advanced Studies in the Fine Arts.

LIBRARY OF CONGRESS CATALOGING-IN-PUBLICATION DATA
Gebhard, David.
Buildings of Iowa / David Gebhard and Gerald Mansheim.
p.   cm.—(Buildings of the United States)
At head of title: Society of Architectural Historians.
Includes bibliographical references and index.
ISBN 0-19-506148-9
1. Architecture—Iowa—Guidebooks.   I. Mansheim, Gerald, 1931–.
II. Society of Architectural Historians.   III. Title.   IV. Series.
NA730.I8G43   1993
720′.9777—dc20   92-38791

Printing (last digit): 9 8 7 6 5 4 3 2 1
PRINTED IN THE UNITED STATES OF AMERICA
on acid-free paper

Dedicated to Tom Martinson

Foreword

It is with pride and pleasure that the Society of Architectural Historians presents this volume to the public. It is among the first in the monumental series, Buildings of the United States, undertaken by the society.

Buildings of the United States is a nationwide effort, indeed a national one. Heretofore, the United States was the only major country of the Western world that had not produced a publication project dealing with its architectural heritage on a national scale. In overall concept, Buildings of the United States is to a degree modeled on and inspired by The Buildings of England, the series of forty-six volumes conceived and carried out on a county-by-county basis by the eminent English architectural historian Nikolaus Pevsner, first published between 1951 and 1974. It was Pevsner himself who—years ago, but again and again—urged his American colleagues in the Society of Architectural Historians to do the same for this country. In method and approach, of course, that challenge was to be as different from Buildings of England as American architecture is different from English. Here we are dealing with a vast land of immense regional, geographic, climatic, and ethnic diversity, with an architectural history—wide-ranging, exciting, sometimes dramatic, as it is—essentially compressed into three hundred years; Pevsner, on the other hand, was confronted by a coherent culture on a relatively small island with an architectural history that spans over two thousand years. In contrast to the national integrity of English architecture, therefore, American architecture is marked by a dynamic heterogeneity, a heterogeneity woven of a thousand strands of originality, or, actually, a unity woven of a thousand strands of heterogeneity. It is this quality that Buildings of the United States will reflect and record.

Unity born of heterogeneity was a condition of American architecture from the very beginning. The buildings of the English, Spanish, French, and Dutch colonies not only differed according to national origin, but in the transformation process they also assumed a special scale and character, qualities that were largely determined by the aspirations and traditions of a people struggling to fashion a new world in a demanding but abundant land. Diversity even marked the English colonies of the Eastern Seaboard, though they shared a common architectural heritage. The brick mutations of the English prototypes in the Virginia Colony were very different from the wooden architecture of the Massachusetts Bay Colony: they were different because Virginia was a plantation society dominated by the Anglican church, while Massachusetts was a communal society totally nurtured by Puritanism. As the colonies became a nation and developed westward, similar radical contrasts became the way of America's growth. The infinite variety of physical environment, together with the complex origins and motivations of the settlers, made it inevitable that each new state would have a character uniquely its own.

This dynamic diversity is the foundation of Buildings of the United States. The primary objective of each volume will be to record, to analyze, and to evaluate the architecture of the state. All of the authors are trained architectural historians who are thoroughly informed in the local aspects of their subjects. In developing the narrative, those special conditions that shaped the state, together with the building types necessary to meet those conditions, will be identified and discussed: barns, silos, mining buildings, factories, warehouses, bridges, and transportation buildings will take their place with the familiar building types conventional to the nation as a whole—churches, courthouses, city halls, and the infinite variety of domestic architecture. Although the great national and international masters of American architecture will receive proper attention, especially in those volumes for the states in which they did their greatest work, outstanding local architects, as well as the buildings of skilled but often anonymous carpenter-builders, will also be brought prominently into the picture. Each volume will thus be a detailed and precise portrait of the architecture of the state that it represents. At the same time, however, all of these local issues will be examined as they relate to the architectural developments in the country at large. When completed, therefore, the series will be a comprehensive history of the architecture of the United States.

The series was long in the planning. Indeed, the idea was conceived by Turpin Bannister, the first president of the Society of Architectural Historians (1940–1942). It was thirty years, however, before the society had grown sufficiently in strength to consider such a project. This happened when Alan Gowans, during his presidency (1972–1974), drew up a proposal and made the first of several unsuccessful attempts to raise the funds. The issue was raised again during the presidency of Marion C. Donnelly, when William H. Jordy and William H. Pierson, Jr., suggested to the board of directors that such a project should be the society's contribution to the nation's bicentennial celebration. It was not until 1986, however, after several failed attempts, that a substantial grant from the National Endowment for the Humanities, which was matched by grants from the Pew Charitable Trusts and the Graham Foundation, made the dream a reality. The activities that led to final success took place under the successive presidencies of Adolf K. Placzek (1978–1980), David Gebhard (1980–1982), Damie Stillman (1982–1984), and Carol H. Krinsky (1984–1986). Development and production of the first books has continued under those of Osmund Overby (1986–1988), Richard J. Betts (1988–1990), and Elisabeth Blair MacDougall (1990–1993). And all the while, there was David Bahlman, executive director of the SAH at the headquarters of the society in Philadelphia. In New York was Barbara Chernow of Chernow Editorial Services, Inc., who, with her husband, George Valassi, was a valuable resource during the initial stages of the project. A fine board of editors was established, with representatives from the American Institute of Architects, the Historic American Buildings Survey, and the Library of Congress. These first volumes have now been seen through production thanks to the very able work of the managing editor, Susan M. Denny, who joined the project in 1991. Buildings of the United States is now part of the official mission of the Society of Architectural Historians, incorporated into its bylaws.

In the development of this project, we have incurred a number of obligations. We are deeply indebted, both for financial support and for confidence in our efforts, to the National Endowment for the Humanities, the Pew Charitable Trusts, and the Graham Foundation for Advanced Studies in the Fine Arts. We also express our gratitude to a number of individuals. First among these are Dorothy Wartenberg, formerly of the Interpretive Research Program of the NEH, who was particularly helpful at the beginning, and our current program officer, David Wise. The dean of the College of Arts and Science at the University of Missouri–Columbia provided a graduate research assistant to the project. We also express our gratitude to three groups of individuals. First are the current members of the editorial board, listed earlier in this volume, and the following former members: the late Sally Kress Tompkins, the late Alex Cochran, Catherine W. Bishir, John Freeman, Alan Gowans, Robert Kapsch, and Tom Martinson. Next are our present and former project assistants—Preston Thayer, Marc Vincent, and Robert Wojtowicz. Next are the two previous executive directors of the society, the late Rosann Berry and Paulette Olson Jorgensen. Finally, thanks are due to our loyal colleagues in this enterprise at Oxford University Press in New York, especially Ed Barry, Claude Conyers, Marion Osmun, Leslie Phillips, and Stephen Chasteen.

The volumes, state by state, will continue to appear until every state in the Union has its own and the overview and inventory of American architecture is complete. The volumes will vary in length, and some states will require two volumes, but no state will be left out!

It must be said, regretfully, that not every building of merit can be included. Practical considerations have dictated some difficult choices in the buildings that are represented. There had to be some omissions from the abundance of structures built across the land, the thousands of modest but lovely edifices, often rising out of a sea of ugliness, or the vernacular attempts that merit a second look, but which by their very multitude cannot be included in even the thickest volume. On the other hand, it must be emphasized that these volumes deal with more than the highlights and the high points. They deal with the very fabric of American architecture, with the context in time and in place of each specific building, with the entirety of urban and rural America, with the whole architectural patrimony. This fabric, of course, includes modern architecture, as, on the other end of the scale, it includes pre-Columbian and Native American remains.

As to architectural style, it was our most earnest intent to establish as much as possible a consistent terminology of architectural history: the name of J. A. Chewning, mastermind of our glossaries, must be gratefully mentioned here. The *Art and Architecture Thesaurus,* a comprehensive publication and database compiled by The Getty Art History Information Program and published by Oxford University Press, has also become an invaluable resource.

Finally, it must also be stated in the strongest possible terms that omission of a building from this or any volume of the series does not constitute an invitation to the bulldozers and the wrecking ball. In every community there will be structures not included in Buildings of the United States that are clearly deserving of being preserved. Indeed, it is hoped that the publication of this series will help to stop at least the worst destruction of architecture across the land by fostering a deeper appreciation of its beauty, richness, and historic and associative importance.

The volumes of Buildings of the United States are intended as guidebooks as well as reference books and are designed to facilitate such use: they can and should be used on the spot, indeed should lead the user to the spot. But they are also meant to be tools of serious research in the study of American architecture. It is our earnest hope that they will not only be on the shelves of every major library under "U.S." but that they will also be in many a glove compartment and perhaps even in many a rucksack.

ADOLF K. PLACZEK
WILLIAM H. PIERSON, JR.
OSMUND OVERBY

Acknowledgments

The writing of this guide would have been impossible without the active aid and encouragement of the following individuals: Larry Adams; Randy Alexander; Keith Arrington; Steve Caldwell; S. Allen Chambers, Jr.; Lyndon D. Crist; Harold Eastman; Bruce Ehrich; Gloria Hafner; Charles Herbert, FAIA; Loren N. Horton; James Jacobsen; William Keck, FAIA; Karen L. Laughlin; Barbara Beving Long; Monica Moen; Molly Myers Naumann; Patrick N. Nefzger; Floyd Pearce; Winifred Rhoades; Stephen L. Rhodes; June Samspon; Wesley Shank; Gary Smith; Judy Sutcliffe; Myrna Ver Hoef; Elizabeth Voss; and Peggy Whitworth. Carol Betts provided the excellent copyediting of *Buildings of Iowa*.

Records and research materials have been provided by the Historic American Buildings Survey, Washington, D.C.; the Historic American Engineering Record, Washington, D.C.; the State Historical Society of Iowa, Des Moines; the Iowa State Historical Department, Division of the State Historical Society, Iowa City; and the Iowa Chapter, American Institute of Architects, Des Moines.

Maps for this book have been prepared by the Geographic Resources Center in the Department of Geography of the University of Missouri–Columbia, with Christopher L. Salter as its director, Timothy L. Haithcoat, program director, and Karen Stange Westin, project coordinator.

DAVID GEBHARD
GERALD MANSHEIM

Contents

SOUTH (SO), 308

NORTH (NO), 348

MISSOURI RIVER—WEST (MW), 455

List of Maps

Guide for Users of This Volume

For the convenience of the users of this guide, the authors have divided it into five parts, corresponding to five geographic areas of the state of Iowa: Mississippi River—East; Central; South; North; and Missouri River—West. Within each part, sections on towns and cities are arranged alphabetically. It should be possible for anyone possessing this book, an official state highway map, and a little patience to find each of the properties listed. Each part opens with a map of the area. Cities and towns covered by the guide are shown on these maps. Larger cities and towns are shown by a dot within a circle, indicating to the user that a more detailed map accompanies the section for that city or town, and several cities are covered by even more detailed inset maps. Buildings are indicated on maps by the identifying codes used to mark corresponding text entries. Rural buildings and structures are included in the sections on nearby towns and cities, and specific road directions are given to each of these locations.

Each text entry begins with an identifying code, which is a two-letter abbreviation of the name of the area and the number of the property. The name of the property, and alternate names, if appropriate, follow the code. On the next line appear the date or dates of construction, the name of the original architect (if known), and the location. Finally, there is a narrative description of each property.

Road and highway numbers, from county roads to interstates, are provided in directions to rural sites. We have used the abbreviations that commonly appear on road maps; that is, "route J40" refers to the state secondary road or county road designated J40; "Iowa 136" refers to state route 136; "US 30" denotes federal highway 30; and "I-80" refers to interstate highway 80. Those roads prefixed with "X" are county roads. While street and avenue names are provided for almost every listed community, we have found that actual street signs are sometimes missing, and in many cases the address of a building is not visible. In these cases we have attempted to provide more general directions. Since many of the communities covered in this guide are not large, a visitor should encounter little difficulty in locating the structure or building mentioned.

The index includes the names of architects and builders, cities and towns, and major buildings. Since many of the buildings described in the volume are not well known, it is often easiest to locate a building description by browsing through the entries for a specific geographic section. In the index, some structures are grouped by type, so that a reader interested in barns or mills, for example, can find them easily.

Some of the geographic areas covered in this book were visited and surveyed as far back as 1981; thus, a visitor should be prepared to find that a few buildings mentioned in the guide may no longer exist or that others have been substantially remodeled.

Almost all of the structures described in this book are visible from public roads. If not, "not visible" follows the property address or location. Buildings that are open to the public are identified at the end of the appropriate entries. Of course, we know that the readers of the volume will always respect the privacy and property rights of others.

BUILDINGS OF IOWA

Introduction

FROM THE FIRST YEARS OF EUROPEAN SETTLEMENT DOWN TO the present moment, Iowa has symbolized the heart of America. John Plumbe, Jr., writing in 1839, spoke of the state as "this blooming belle of the American family."[1] One hundred years later, during the Great Depression of the 1930s, Grant Wood noted, "Thomas Benton returned to make his home in the Middle West just the other day, saying, according to the newspapers, that he was coming to live again in the only region of the country which is not 'provincial.' "[2]

Benton, as an exponent of American regional painting, was acting on an ideology reaching back to Thomas Jefferson—the belief that the core of American life should be rural, not urban. Though Iowa has, in fact, continually been an important contributor to the economy of the country in such areas as mining and manufacturing, the image it projects is that of the agricultural center for the nation. That it would emerge as such a center was anticipated in the early years of its settlement. In his 1856 volume, *The Garden of the World, or the Great West,* another Thomas H. Benton asserted that "the future farms of Iowa, large, level, and unbroken by stump or other obstruction, will afford an excellent field for the introduction of mowing machines, and other improved implements calculated to save the labors of the husbandman."[3] This is, of course, exactly what has come about; the mechanized farming technology embraced by the farmers of the state has made Iowa not only the breadbasket of the nation, but also a supplier of food to the world.

The pervasive sense of Iowa as a rural, agricultural place has been sustained by the dispersal of its urban environments. Although Des Moines is a moderate-sized city (pop. 190,800), it is not the dominant urban center for the state—as Chicago is for Illinois, Milwaukee for Wisconsin, or Minneapolis-Saint Paul for

3

Minnesota. Cedar Rapids, Iowa City, Waterloo, Sioux City, Dubuque, and Burlington are contenders in many ways, both locally and outside of the state. In contrast to America's "great" urban environments, the cities of Iowa are of a size and intimacy that make them both livable and governable. The high productivity of the average farm has meant that the typical Iowa farm family is of the middle class. Thus the historic division between city resident and farm dweller does not exist. In a sense, the farms of Iowa have emerged, in their relation to adjoining towns and cities, as a form of low-density suburbia.

The unity of urban and rural in Iowa is, as one would expect, effectively mirrored not only in the artifacts of buildings and groups of buildings, but also in the general transformation of the landscape. It is this landscape, in the broadest sense of the term, which reveals the built environment of the state. While many elements of the landscape have remained as constants, others have been radically modified; and it should be borne in mind that some of these alterations may have been the result of Native American activities that preceded the white incursions of the 1830s and later.

"With the exception of some high hills in the northern part," wrote Benton of Iowa in 1856, "the surface is nowhere mountainous, but consists of table lands, prairies, and gentle swelling eminences covered with timber."[4] Plumbe pointed out the advantage of this type of terrain, its being "divided into prairies and woodland, so as almost wholly to dispense with the labor of clearing, which was and still continues to be so material a draw-back upon most of the Western States."[5] Another characteristic of the state of Iowa is its waterways. The Mississippi River forms the eastern boundary of the state, and to the west the Missouri River defines that state border. Projecting like fingers from these two major waterways are innumerable smaller rivers and streams, of which the main ones are the Des Moines, Iowa, Cedar, and Wapsipinicon rivers. These rivers had been used as transportation corridors by the Native Americans, and the settlers followed suit. To the utilization of the rivers for transportation, the settlers added the potential for generating power for milling operations.

Early maps, sketches, and descriptions illustrate the remarkable play between open prairie land and the groves and tongues of forests. It was only in the extreme northwest corner of the state that the open prairie almost completely dominated the scene. Elsewhere the wooded lands spread along the larger streams and rivers, and in many cases extensive groves existed between the waterways. The general proximity of timber in most places meant that wood was available for fuel and for construction ranging from fences to buildings. Other natural assets commented on quite early were the excellent limestone, which could be used as cut stone or burned to make lime; clay, which could be utilized to produce bricks and terracotta products; coal, which could produce energy; and lead, with its many uses.

The Transformation of the Land

It is reasonable to suppose that there was some transformation of the environment between the "two great rivers" by Native Americans, but to what extent remains an open question. Agriculture would seem to have appeared at Middle Woodland sites along the Mississippi and its major tributaries some time between 500 B.C.E. and C.E. 1.[6] In western Iowa, agriculture is associated with the Glenwood, Mill Creek, and Oneota cultures, and was probably introduced around 1200 C.E.[7] Whether any of this agricultural activity affected the environment, other than by transient depletion of the soil, remains unknown at this time.

There can be no question, however, that the moment the European immigrants entered the Iowa scene, changes took place. The view held nearly universally throughout the nineteenth century and much of our own era is that the land was a commodity to be revamped and organized to serve man's needs. The writer-geographer J. B. Jackson has pointed out that the ideology that viewed land as a commodity led to specific ways of looking at and experiencing the landscape.[8] The regularizing and transforming of the landscape began on a grand scale with the use of the United States rectangular survey system, with its origins in the Land Ordinance of 1785, which in turn was expanded in 1796.[9] These and other ordinances laid the framework for imposing a tight grid system on the landscape.

The United States rectangular survey system was based upon the six-mile-square township, which in turn could be divided into sections, and plots of 640 acres, 320 acres, 160 acres, and 80 acres. The townships themselves could be compiled to form counties, and the counties then grouped to form the individual state. This multiple-grid system was advantageous for dealing with land ownership and proved a convenient geographic boundary device for local government; but it also made possible the creation of artifacts that would make apparent people's transformation of the environment. Once a survey had been made, the visual tokens of the grid system slowly began to appear: roads, hedges, fences and planted clusters of trees. Buildings themselves, whether a lone schoolhouse or church, a farm complex, or an entire town (in most instances), responded to the grid.

Native Americans: The Land and Architecture

The dating of the earliest Native American occupation of Iowa is anything but firm, yet present evidence points to an antiquity of around 10,000 B.C.E. (the Paleo-Indian phase).[10] From this period on, various Native American groups lived within the current boundaries of the state. These earliest groups were nomadic and relied on the hunting of animals, augmented by the gathering of local berries, seeds, and nuts. Beginning around 500 B.C.E., first eastern Iowa and later the west absorbed the ideas and traits of the Woodland cultures. Initially, subsistence was still achieved by hunting and food gathering, but later this was supplemented by agriculture. The cultivation of crops meant, of course, that places of habitation, the villages, became larger and more permanent. Some of the low burial mounds found in the state may have been built during the Early Woodland period.[11]

It was during the Middle and Late Woodland periods that the Native American left more lasting marks on the landscape. Excavations, especially in northeast Iowa and to the far west, have revealed the forms of their dwellings and the layouts of their villages. Along the Mississippi and its major tributaries, the Woodland peoples lived in villages usually constructed on the high bench or terrace overlooking a river or stream.[12] The villages were composed of wigwams (wikiups), dwellings constructed of a frame of bent saplings which were covered with bark and reed mats.[13] The usual wikiups, in both prehistoric and historic times, were accompanied by conical wigwams as well as by gable-roofed, bark-covered houses.[14] Generally these latter dwellings were small and round in form, though some were elongated, somewhat akin to the eastern longhouses. The dwellings were laid out in an informal fashion, often close to one another, but not according to any recognizable geometric scheme.

To the west in Iowa, along the Missouri, the Native American dwellings were like the earth lodge forms (often referred to as pit houses in archaeological literature)[15] associated with various pre-European and post-European houses of the Native Americans of the Great Plains. These houses were constructed by excavating a rectangular depression in the ground, usually only 3 feet deep and ranging from 18 to 45 feet square. Four large tree trunks were placed near the center, marking the corners of a square, and horizontal log beams were placed upon these posts. Then, small saplings were fixed in the ground around the rectangular pit, and these were bent over to join the horizontal log beams. Smaller branches were woven in and out of the saplings, and finally everything was covered by mud and sod. A rectangular ramp led down into the dwelling, and in many cases this was also roofed. As was the case in the villages to the east, the individual earth lodge dwellings were informally sited within the village compounds.[16] Some of these earth lodges built by the Great Oasis people (c. 900–1300 C.E.) ranged up to 40 feet in length.[17]

Mounds and enclosures are associated with various phases of the Native American Woodland cultures in Iowa. These have been categorized into eight types, ranging from the simple burial mound type to the later linear mound and effigy mound types.[18] The principal concentration of these examples of earth sculpture are found along the Mississippi River and a few of its tributaries. The earliest of these mounds, used for burial purposes, were made sometime immediately after 1000 B.C.E. The last of the mounds (conical, linear, and effigy) were built around 1250 C.E. Almost all of these mounds have been attributed to the Woodland cultures (including the Hopewell), although a few may have been constructed by peoples representing the later Middle Mississippi culture.

The largest number of these mounds are conical in form, and are usually found in groups. A typical conical mound will be 20 to 30 feet in diameter (although some are 60 or more feet in diameter), and normally only 2 to 6 feet high. Many of the mounds contain single or group burials, although a number have not revealed any burials whatsoever. The methods of construction varied considerably. In many instances the ground upon which the mound was to be built was carefully cleared down to a sterile level, then a floor of clean sand was usually laid over this clay, and finally a layer of earth was added. Actual burial pits were provided within some mounds, and in a few cases, more elaborate stone slab burial chambers can be found.

Viewed as earth sculpture, the linear and effigy mounds have attracted the attention of present-day Americans. Linear mounds are of two types: chain mounds constructed by connecting individual small mounds together to form a line, and linear mounds designed as a single form.[19] Occasionally accompanying the linear mounds, or occurring as separate affairs, are earth and stone enclosures. Some of these are rectangular or square, while others are more elaborate, such as those near New Albin.[20]

Native American ceremonial enclosure, near New Albin

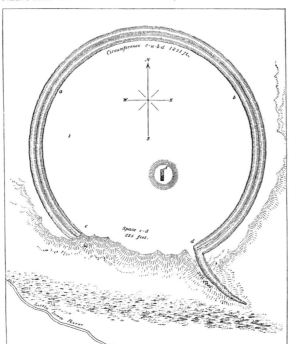

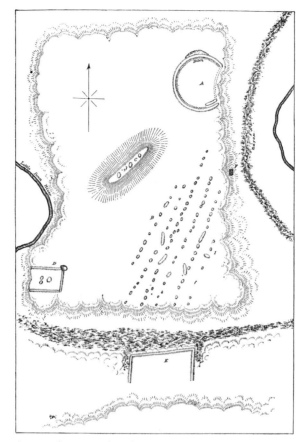

Native American mounds and ceremonial enclosure, near New Albin

In some instances linear mounds accompany effigy mounds, but in many cases the two types of mounds exist independently.[21] As with the conical and linear mounds, the groups of effigy mounds are located on benches, terraces, or hills overlooking waterways. Generally, effigy figures are composed as a group, not singly (although in most instances, it is not known whether they were all built at once or sequentially, over a period of time). Most of the figures depicted are recognizable, though it is not always easy to "read" them from a single vantage point. The most frequently encountered forms are birds with outspread wings and bears. Other figures include panthers, turtles, wildcats, lizards, and probable depictions of humans. There are also other examples which are not readily identifiable, including several which have been referred to as elephants. While a few of the effigy mounds have revealed burials (including intrusive burials), this does not seem to have been their primary use. Surprisingly, with all of the recording of mounds and the archaeological research that has taken place in Iowa, the examples of linear and effigy mound complexes have not been conclusively attributed to any single or specific group of the Woodland peoples.

The existence of these mounds in Iowa, and the occurrence of similar mounds to the east and south, was noted early in the nineteenth century. Between 1880 and 1895 Theodore Hayes Lewis, under the tutelage of Alfred James Hill, made an extensive survey of the mounds of the Midwest, including those in Iowa.[22] Also, in the 1880s the United States Bureau of Ethnology sponsored a study by Cyrus Thomas of the mounds throughout the country.[23] What these and other surveys pointedly reveal to us are the tremendous numbers of mounds and mound complexes in Iowa and elsewhere which have disappeared. Most of these have simply been plowed under; others occupied sites where villages, towns, and cities have been built. Fortunately, a few remaining mound sites have been preserved, and in several cases these are part of the national or state park systems—such as Effigy Mound National Monument, Toolesboro Mounds National Historic Landmark, and Pikes Peak State Park.

The Late Woodland peoples were succeeded in Iowa by the Oneota culture—a far northern extension of the flourishing Mississippian cultures to the south of Iowa. The house types and the informal layout of Oneota villages were similar to those of the Late Woodland peoples, but there is no evidence that the Oneota engaged in any extensive campaign of mound building. When French traders first entered Iowa in the late seventeenth century, the Native Americans they encountered were the Ioways, whom archaeologists and ethnologists consider to be a historic continuation of the pre-European Oneota.

Toolesboro Mounds, 500 B.C.E.–300 C.E., in autumn

Toolesboro Mounds, 500 B.C.E.–300 C.E., in winter

By the early 1800s the Ioways' hold on the state had been superseded by that of the Sauk and Mesquakie tribes. These tribes had come into Iowa from present-day Wisconsin and Illinois in the eighteenth century. They were joined by the Sioux, to the north, and, to the far west and along the Missouri River, by the Omaha, the Oto, and the Missouri. The house types of these peoples ran the gamut from bark dwellings with pitched roofs to the many forms of the wigwam, the tipi, and, in the opening years of the nineteenth century, the earth lodge. During the decades from 1830 through the opening of the 1850s, all of the Native American groups then living in Iowa ceded their lands to the settlers.

European Settlement and Planning

The first truly permanent settlement in Iowa took place in 1788, when the French Canadian Julien Dubuque obtained a lease on some 21 square miles in and around the present Mississippi River city that bears his name. He was interested in the area because of its lead deposits, and he engaged in both mining and fur trading there until his death in 1810. At the time Dubuque arrived, Iowa was a part of the Louisiana Territory and was governed by Spain. In 1800 Iowa and the Louisiana Territory were acquired by France, and in 1803 the territory was purchased by the United States. Five years later, in 1808, the United States Army founded Fort Madison on the Mississippi River.

After being part of two adjoining territories, Iowa itself officially became a territory in 1838; surveys of the land were undertaken, and the federal government established land offices. Within two years the new capital, Iowa City, was established and work began on the state capitol building. In 1846 Iowa was admitted to the Union, and in 1857 the capital was moved to Des Moines, where it has remained.

The initial settlement of Iowa, from the 1830s up until the Civil War, tended to be river-oriented. Thus the first sequence of the platting of large towns and small cities occurred along the west bank of the Mississippi River: Burlington in 1834, Muscatine and Davenport in 1836, Keokuk and Dubuque in 1837, and Clinton in 1855. This was paralleled by the laying out of the future major cities of central Iowa in the midst of what was hoped would be highly productive farmland: Iowa City, Des Moines, Cedar Rapids, Marshalltown, Cedar Falls, and Waterloo, all of which were platted between 1839 and the early 1850s. Sioux City and Council Bluffs developed on the Missouri River as early as the 1830s and 1840s, and, further north, Mason City was platted in 1854. These dates of the establishment and platting of communities across the state reveal the rapidity and tempo of settlement.

Generally, at least before 1860, the founding and platting of most Iowa towns was in the hands of one individual or a small group of entrepreneurs who actually "set up shop" on the site. Elkader, as a case in point, "was laid out by Thompson, Davis and Sage, who also erected the first mill in 1847."[24] A similar pattern occurred in Waterloo: "The first settlement in Waterloo was made by Charles Mullan, who, moving with his family from Illinois arrived here June 24th, 1846. . . . He surveyed and laid out the original town plat in the fall of 1853, and with Geo. W. Hanna and J. H. Brooks was one of the proprietors."[25]

A second type of founder of new towns in Iowa was the settlement society. The site and lands surrounding Guttenberg were "sold and conveyed by the county commissioners to the Western Settlement Society of Cincinnati, Ohio, and the society entered several hundred acres of land contiguous to the town, and employed John M. Gray, County Surveyor, to lay out a much larger town."[26] Similar in certain ways were the settlement and platting of towns by religious groups. The Amana Society, founded in Germany, established a group of adjacent villages in central Iowa in the 1850s. The Mormons established a number of communities in western Iowa in the late 1840s and early 1850s before they moved on to Utah. And there were other sects: a group of French Fourierists attempted to establish themselves near Oskaloosa, and the French Icarians did likewise with their settlement of Icaria, near Corning, in the southwestern part of the state.

There were also a number of towns established or platted by the federal government (as the administrator of the territories), and also by the state and

Bellevue, view from the south

by the counties. Bellevue, on the banks of the Mississippi, was "laid out by Commissioners appointed by the United States."[27] The site of Iowa City, which was planned as the capital of the state, was selected by a state-appointed commission, and this commission was also responsible for the plat plan and for the sale of lots. One of the typical episodes of governmental founding of cities includes the communities established to house the county seats. In several towns, such as Bedford, the seat of Taylor County, the site was selected by a commission appointed by the state through an act of the general assembly; in other cases locations were chosen by the county commissioners, by individual judges, or by popular vote.

Compared to the states west of the Missouri River, throughout the Great Plains area and on the West Coast, the railroad companies' direct participation in establishing towns in Iowa was minimal until after the Civil War.[28] Iowa's first railroad, the Rock Island, began building tracks out of Davenport in 1853, and the first locomotive arrived in 1855.[29] By 1860 five of Iowa's towns on the Mississippi River—McGregor, Clinton, Dubuque, Davenport, and Burlington—enjoyed direct passenger and freight connections to the Atlantic Coast.[30] The total mileage of railroad tracks laid within the state by 1860 was modest, 679.77 miles, compared to 2,867.9 miles within neighboring Illinois to the east. This meant that three-quarters or more of the principal towns and cities of Iowa were established before the railroads traversed their areas (though it should be noted that a number of towns were platted in anticipation of the coming of a railroad). The arrival of the railroad had a pronounced effect on towns that had already been platted and settled. With only a handful of exceptions, all of the towns platted in Iowa from the 1830s on were based upon the grid system. Yet the path of the railroad tracks into, through, and out of a community seldom mirrored the grid. In some towns, such as Newton, the right-of-way of the Chicago, Rock Island, and Pacific Railroad followed a diagonal path through the grid added later by the city. In the case of other communities, for example, Cedar Rapids, one of the existing city streets was transformed into the right-of-way. Often the solution was to build the tracks at the edge of the original plat, and then to lay out a new addition of the grid to encompass the tracks, the station, and, eventually, grain elevators and other businesses.

Then there are those cases where the settlement was revamped to respond to the arrival of the railroad. The town of Cherokee in the northwest section of the state illustrates this wait-and-see attitude: "It was not until August, 1870, that the village was located, though a few small buildings had been put up prior to that date, but only of such character that they could be removed to whatever point the railroad might locate their depot."[31] The west-central town of Creston, founded in 1869, is an example of a railroad-sponsored community. "The town was laid out by the railroad company [Chicago, Burlington, and Quincy Railroad] and it has always taken an active interest in its growth and prosperity. It has erected a very fine depot here at the cost of about $75,000 and has taken much pains in improving the grounds it has reserved for railroad use."[32]

Since the founding of towns was essentially a private business affair, it should not be surprising to note that there were by far more towns founded within the state than currently exist. David C. Mott, in a long series of articles, "Abandoned Towns, Villages and Post Offices of Iowa," lists 2,807 names (not all of which represent abandoned communities); and he conjures up the demise of these towns: "The blasted hopes of many an ambitious village brings regret. Many a 'Sweet Auburn, loveliest village of the plain,' is now a meadow or a cornfield, with no trace of its former busy life."[33] Mott suggests some of the reasons for the demise of these towns: failure of water power, "the waning of navigation of some inland rivers, the coming of the railroads which so often missed these towns, the coming of the automobile which made travel and transportation speedier and easier, the coming of rural mail service."[34]

The system of blocks of streets, laid out at a 90-degree angle to one another, on which the towns and cities were organized was simply a miniaturization of the larger-scale division of the land into townships and sections. In a typical Iowa town the individual block measured 300 by 300 feet; streets varied in width from 60 feet for the smaller, to 100 feet for the larger. Each block was generally bisected by a narrow alley. While it might have been advantageous to vary the size of the blocks according to use—for instance, business versus residential—this was seldom done. Leaving them all the same size meant that it was easier to expand the business and industrial corner of a town into what had originally been residential.

While the prevailing approach throughout the nineteenth century in Iowa was to orient the grid system to the cardinal points of the compass, a number of the cities responded to other considerations. Many of the earliest towns platted along the Mississippi, from Guttenberg in the north to Burlington and Keokuk in the south, were laid out in regard to their riverside location. This was also true for inland river towns like Keosauqua on the Des Moines River, or Wapello on the Iowa River.

With the advent of the railroad, there was a group of towns whose grids mirrored the direction of the tracks, rather than the cardinal points of the compass (though it should be noted that most of the railroad-sponsored towns in Iowa were oriented north-south and east-west). In the towns that were not oriented to the cardinal points of the compass, this "grievous" error was corrected by reorienting later additions.

Except for the notable example of Iowa City, which was planned as a capital city for the state, there were very few towns platted in the nineteenth century which exhibit any variation on the grid scheme. Denison reveals a number of innovations, ranging from an oval formed by a pair of streets laid out around Prospect Hill, to a set of parks laid out as an octagon and as a circle. Shenandoah platted a ten-block crescent, only part of which (the South Crescent) was carried out.

If there was a glimmer of a hope that the newly platted town might become a county seat, a square block would almost always be set aside as a site for a courthouse. This "Public Square" or "Courthouse Square," as it was often labeled on the plats, was in most instances placed at or close to the center of the layout of blocks and streets. In addition to the courthouse square, a number of communities provided an adjoining square block for a pleasure park. Examples of such adjoining public open spaces occur in the plat plans for Atlantic in Cass County, for Eldora in Hardin County, and for other communities.

In the published plats of nineteenth-century Iowa cities, some of these central squares are depicted as assuming different shapes, ranging from squares with their corners rounded off, to circles and ovals. In most instances it is unlikely that such shapes were ever built, or if they had been initially constructed in this fashion, their shapes were later returned to the configuration of right-angle blocks. Osceola's "Public Square" is shown with 45-degree cut-off corners; and Indianola's central square has radically cut-off 80-degree corners. In a handful of towns the square was sited as the terminus of a major street; Des Moines and its Polk County Courthouse form the most widely known example of such a scheme.

Either within the first plat or included in the plat of a later addition, there was usually a lot or a full block designated as a site for a public school. More often than not, one of the early public buildings to be constructed in a town would be the public high school or normal school. (Iowa would long have the highest literacy rate in the country.) Because of Iowans' strong faith in education—and progress tied to education—a good number of towns set aside sites for institutions of higher learning such as colleges and academies. These were almost always situated outside of the downtown, in residential areas.

By the end of the nineteenth century the larger towns and cities had acquired a variety of public open spaces. These included parks (usually sites given to the community by private individuals), county fairgrounds, and cemeteries; and if a railroad was present, the station would sometimes be set within a well-landscaped park. Other sources of open landscaped space were state institutions built near or adjacent to towns. These hotly contested "prizes" were of course looked upon more for their economic implications than for the amenities of public space. But the asset of their open space was generally commented on in the nineteenth century. The Iowa Hospital for the Insane built at Mount Pleasant and the one at Independence provided extensive acreage, as did other state institutions such as the Iowa Institute for the Deaf and Dumb at Council Bluffs and the Iowa Soldiers' Orphans Home at Cedar Falls.

Planning and Parks, 1890s to Present

Many of the towns and cities of Iowa, like their counterparts elsewhere, were passionately caught up in the Beaux-Arts City Beautiful movement which came to the fore after the 1893 World's Columbian Exposition in Chicago. Charles Mulford Robinson, one of the pioneer city planners of America, was engaged by a surprisingly large number of communities in Iowa between 1907 and 1913. He was joined over the years by other "stars" of the national planning profession: John Noland, Edward H. Bennett, and Harland Bartholomew. After World War II, national planning firms, such as Victor Gruen and Associates, were engaged to revamp downtowns or to plan suburban developments and shopping centers.

Pre-World War I planning in Iowa, as was generally true throughout the country, was concentrated on laying out Beaux-Arts-inspired civic centers, systems of public parks, and boulevard schemes that connected the parks with the downtowns and the civic centers. The three most striking episodes of such Beaux-Arts planning were in Des Moines, Cedar Rapids, and Davenport. In each of these cases the proposals entailed building parks, boulevards, and a civic center which took advantage of the community's riverfront. Post-1900 planning in Des Moines typifies what was experienced throughout the state. Shortly after the turn of the century the Des Moines Commercial Club formed a Town Planning Committee, and it subsequently engaged Charles Mulford Robinson. The plan, as it developed, called for the Des Moines River to form one axis for the civic center, with the cross axis made up of streets which led to the area of the state capitol and other state buildings.[35]

Both Charles Mulford Robinson and Edward H. Bennett (representing the Chicago firm of Daniel H. Burnham and Company) were involved in the civic-center scheme for Cedar Rapids, where a plan imaginatively utilized Mays Island, in the middle of the Cedar River as the location for the principal public buildings of the city.[36] In Iowa, as in other states, those individuals who were concerned about planning established a planning association, the Iowa Town Planning Association, which sought to encourage not only local planning and its realization but also statewide planning.

Other ingredients of pre- and post-World War I planning developed within the state. Almost every Iowa community in the nineteenth century installed a street railroad system, at first horse-drawn, and later electrified. After 1900 a number of these systems were extended far out into the country, forming interurban rail systems. It was in the same years that suburban residential development took place, based upon the Picturesque garden tradition, as espoused earlier by Andrew Jackson Downing, Frederick Law Olmsted, and others. Thus cities such as Des Moines, Iowa City, Cedar Rapids, and Davenport exhibit informally laid-out suburban schemes characterized by curved streets and the dominance of nature, achieved through open spaces and abundant vegetation.

In the 1920s and later, the planning efforts of Harland Bartholomew and Associates of Saint Louis for Des Moines (1925–1940) and Cedar Rapids (1931), or of John Noland and Justin R. Hartzog for Dubuque (1936), became less poetic and more down-to-earth, dealing generally with questions of zoning and transportation. After 1945, as one can see in Victor Gruen's plan for Dubuque, most planning dealt with pragmatic aspects of urban renewal and other problems related to the economy. Planning in Iowa in the 1970s and 1980s still seemed committed to the world of economics, though some of the romance of the past reappeared in schemes for further improvement of riverfronts and parks.

In his 1928 article "The State Parks of Iowa," Thomas P. Christensen cited the "inspired" writings and activities of Theodore Roosevelt, John Muir, and Gifford Pinchot as the touchstone for the development of a statewide park system in Iowa.[37] Agitation for such a system came to the fore in the mid-1890s, and in 1901 the Iowa Park and Forestry Association was organized in Ames. In 1917, through the efforts of this association and others, the state legislature passed, and the governor signed, an "act to authorize the establishment of public parks."[38] In the following year the act was expanded, making it possible for counties to raise money and purchase land for parks. Also, making 1918 a landmark year, the state purchased its first lands for parks.[39]

By the end of the 1920s there were more than 31 state reserves and parks. Almost all of these had been "improved" through the designs of professional landscape architects. Many of these early parks, such as those at Clear Lake, and Ledges Park in Boone County, were designed by John R. Fitzsimmons, a landscape architect trained at Harvard University.[40] In the 1930s Iowa parks were the target of a wide range of improvements within one or another of the various federal relief projects, especially the Works Progress Administration (WPA), the Public Works Administration (PWA), and the Civilian Conservation Corps (CCC). The road systems, picnic and camping areas, shelters and recreation buildings constructed of indigenous materials, such as stone and wood, constitute some of the outstanding examples of planning and architecture within the state. After World War II, the state and county parks systems were considerably expanded, but as seen in planning in general during these years, the poetry and romance of the earlier work was lacking.

Two intriguing landscape architecture projects in Iowa were the 1910 design of the Chicago landscape architect Jens Jensen for Luther College in Decorah, and the 1930s scheme of Alfred Caldwell for Eagle Point Park in Dubuque. Jensen's approach to the beautiful hilly site of Luther College, overlooking the Upper Iowa River, was to make more vivid the prairie landscape of the place (in the fashion of the eighteenth-century English landscape architect Capability Brown). Some twenty years later, Caldwell adopted Jensen's prairie theme in landscape architecture and strongly mixed it with Frank Lloyd Wright's early Prairie style of architecture. The result of this nearly perfect melding of architecture and the landscape easily equals Wright's own wonderful essay at Taliesin, in Spring Green, Wisconsin, or Jensen's designs for parts of the Chicago public park system.[41]

Iowa and Its Architecture

The common belief that as one travels west, one finds there was an ever-increasing time lag in the occurrence of architectural fashions, is simply not the case. As Iowans grew out of the log cabin and sod house (in the far western parts), they got "right up and at 'em" in mirroring what was going on in the East. The characteristic Iowa county courthouse of the 1840s, or the typical rural or urban dwelling, was designed in the style of the moment, ranging from the late Federal-Greek Revival mode to the Romanesque and Gothic revivals, to the Italianate. Such styles might indeed be a bit old fashioned for the few major urban centers of the East—Boston, New York, or Philadelphia—but it was exactly what was being built at that moment in cities, towns, and rural areas of upstate New York, western Pennsylvania, or central Ohio and Kentucky. This up-to-date quality of Iowa architecture continued throughout the nineteenth century, and it should be no surprise that it has characterized the architectural scene in the state up to the present moment.

The romantic image of the first settlement of the western American frontier as typified by the pioneer's log cabin is beautifully fulfilled in Iowa. From the very first settlements in newly platted towns, or on homesteads in the country-side, the first buildings were generally log cabins. The usual cabin was a two-room single-story structure built of split logs, though there were a fair number of one-and-a-half-story and even two-story cabins built. Either at the moment the cabin was built or soon afterward, a masonry fireplace with its accompanying chimney was provided, and factory-built, double-hung windows were purchased and used. The log cabin was not simply an on-the-spot, do-it-yourself affair. It was a house type presented in pattern books of the mid-century. Daniel Harrison Jacques of New York, in his 1859 *The House: A Pocket Manual of Rural Architecture,* opened his presentation by stating, "As our first design, we present a log cabin—a kind of dwelling which must continue to be common for a long time to come, in parts of the west and south."[42]

Whether such a log structure was the first county courthouse, a store, or a dwelling, it was always regarded as temporary, to be replaced as soon as possible by an acceptable masonry or mill-framed and sheathed wood building. Again, as was true of the general pattern of settlement of the state, the replacement of the log structure by a permanent one usually happened quickly. In most instances the log structure was not discarded or torn down, but was simply moved and used for another purpose. There are a number of examples where the initial log county courthouse was replaced by a permanent building, and then the first building was sold and transported off the site, either within the town or out into the country. On the homesteaded farm the log cabin often assumed a second life as a barn or storage building.

Although the Iowa log cabin was almost always the work of the settler, it is interesting to note how it often reflected elements of high-style architecture. Its proportions (especially the relationship of width and height of a facade) were quite classical, so too the pitch of the roof and also the general symmetry of windows and doors. In many examples, if the building was sheathed in clapboard, louvered shutters were added to the windows, and the cornice-entablature was cleaned up, so that the building could easily pose as a late Federal design.

Sod houses appeared relatively late in the settlement of the Iowa, after 1850.[43] As with the log cabin, the sod dwelling and the even more primitive dugout were viewed as impermanent structures. These were built almost exclusively in the western areas of the state, where there was a lack of timber. They continued to be built as dwellings through the 1870s; after this decade, sod-walled structures were almost exclusively used as small utilitarian farm buildings.

By the time sod houses were built, pre-milled house components—doors, windows, and the like—were cheap and easily available, as were cast-iron stoves and sheet-metal chimneys. These sod houses were constructed of rectangular blocks of prairie sod, whose shape, size, and method of construction were similar to those used in southwestern or California adobe buildings. Generally the floors were of packed earth; the low-pitched, gabled, or shed roofs were formed of log beams, log rafters, a sheathing of prairie grass or willow brush, and then several layers of sod and dirt.

Almost from its earliest years of settlement, Iowa (as well as other midwestern states) attracted individual socioreligious groups that established colonies. A wide range of ethnic groups—Norwegians and Swedes, Germans and Czechs, and the Dutch—were also drawn to the rich lands of the state. While some of these groups consciously sought to retain aspects of their ethnic identity in language and culture, they almost instantly assumed whatever was the prevailing imagery and method of construction found in the architecture of their adopted land. If one searches diligently, one discovers a few instances here and there that could be looked upon as elements taken from the architecture of foreign homelands, but these are scarce and scattered. There are certainly those examples, such as one finds among the people of the Amana Colonies, where there was a strong tendency to the simple and puritanical, but the basic forms and fenestration of the buildings of these and other groups were an obvious reflection of the typical frontier image of the time. The ethnic qualities one finds in a number of Iowa communities, such as Pella with the Dutch windmills and half-timbered buildings, are purely an invention of the middle to late twentieth century.

There are two striking aspects of early domestic settlement architecture in Iowa, in addition to its up-to-date quality. The first is how speedily permanent masonry or milled-wood houses were constructed; the second, how large—in some case how grand—many of these dwellings were. Pre-1875 written descriptions and early drawings and prints of the Mississippi River landscape between Burlington and Dubuque note numerous hilltop Italianate villas, matching in miniature what one would have then encountered along the Hudson River.

These dwellings were not only large and built quickly, they were often of brick or stone and elaborately detailed, both within and without. A look at the individuals and families who built these houses reveals that a large number of settlers came to Iowa after they had sold their farms or businesses in upstate New York, Vermont, or elsewhere in New England. In a sense, these were not the ordinary homesteaders one usually envisions as settlers of the west. They were drawn to settle in Iowa because of its agricultural and trade possibilities, and they came with a reasonable amount of capital, enough to organize their farms or business activities and to build themselves stylish dwellings without delay.

The farmers, businessmen, and professionals were joined by carpenters and masons who could construct the houses and other buildings. Sawed lumber and prebuilt components were at first imported into the state, but sawmills and woodworking establishments came into existence very quickly. These first buildings, whether they comprised business blocks, churches, schoolhouses, or dwellings, almost always derived their designs from their builder (often working in a traditional fashion with the owner) or from pattern books. The studies that have so far been made of pre-1860 Iowa architecture have not revealed how many and which pattern books had been used (one was advertised as early as 1839 in Davenport). We are aware of specific houses, such as the Silas W.

Gardner house at Lyon, which were designed by Palliser and Palliser of New York and illustrated in their *Palliser & Palliser's American Architecture* (1878 and 1888). It would seem likely as well that there were a good number of Iowa dwellings derived from plans presented in the pages of such magazines as the *American Agriculturalist* (especially during the 1840s and 1850s) or *Wallace's Farmer* (published between 1879 and 1929).

That pattern books were used seems most likely, as the mid-nineteenth-century publication of Orson S. Fowler's *Home for All, or the Gravel Wall and Octagonal Mode of Building* indicates. This little volume, advocating the glories and ethical virtues of the octagonal dwelling, was first published in 1848, and by the beginning of the 1850s Iowa had acquired its first batch of octagonal dwellings. The brief popularity of the octagonal mode all across the country provides a clue as to how extensively pattern books were used, before 1850, as well as their striking influence in the later nineteenth century and in the twentieth century.

Octagonal houses in Iowa ran the gamut from large, sumptuous examples of the mode, such as the 1857 Langworthy house in Dubuque, to the more austere versions, an example of which would be the Logan House of about 1854 in Decorah. The octagonal mode was also utilized for other building types such as the Grundy County Courthouse at Grundy Center (1870, demolished), and for barns from the mid-1870s on.[44]

The principal public buildings of Iowa during most of the nineteenth century were public schools, churches, and county courthouses. Public school, academy, and college buildings were often the first permanent masonry buildings constructed within a newly established town. While there are a few examples of early schools utilizing the Greek Revival style, most of them were within the Italianate mode, exhibiting segmental arched windows, bracketed entablatures or cornices, and central cupolas.

Within a few years after the establishment of a new town, churches began to be built. Along with schools and possibly courthouses, churches were always considered to be the emblems indicating that a community had become a town, and, it was hoped, a civilized one. Generally, most of the earliest churches were either late Greek Revival buildings, or were Greek Revival structures with some proportions, details, and fenestration that might point to the Gothic, the Romanesque, or the Italianate. By the late 1850s and on into the 1860s, denominational differences were increasingly expressed in the buildings' images.

The Roman Catholic church tended at first to think of itself garbed in a simplified Romanesque Revival style, part Italian, part French. In the years after the Civil War, the Catholic church turned increasingly to the French Gothic, though a certain number of Romanesque-inspired churches were still built. Before and after the turn of the century, there was an increased tendency for church builders to look at the Italian or French Baroque (Beaux-Arts) as a possible source.

From its introduction into the state, the Episcopal church held tightly to the image of the small-town or rural English Gothic church, responding to the edicts of the Ecclesiological movement. With the fewest of exceptions, these Episcopal churches were small, almost dollhouselike in overall size and fenestration; at the same time, their designs were sophisticated, and the buildings were richly detailed with elaborate woodwork, carved stone, and stained glass windows.

The Congregationalists, following the national precepts of design laid down by their denomination, opted for an abstracted version of the Romanesque. The Quakers built their interpretation of the simple brick or clapboard-sheathed meetinghouse, while the Presbyterians maneuvered between the Romanesque (eventually taking over the Richardsonian Romanesque beginning in the late 1880s), and an urbane Gothic image.

The county courthouse, as a building type, provides a historical view of the succession of images employed for public buildings throughout the nineteenth and twentieth centuries.[45] In Iowa the first permanent masonry courthouse was built in 1839–1840 for Henry County at Mount Pleasant (demolished). In essence this brick two-story building, with its low, hipped roof and four end-wall chimneys, appeared more as a large residence in the Federal style than as a public building. Following the construction of this courthouse, there was a spate of them built throughout Iowa, and they were made in the Greek Revival image. These buildings were usually gabled rectangular brick structures, two stories high, and often surmounted by a cupola or tower placed either at the center of the roof ridge or directly over the entrance pediment. The sides of these buildings were usually presented with pilasters supporting a wide entablature and cornice. The principal fronts varied, some with pilasters, others with columns providing a two-story portico. Most of these early Greek Revival courthouses are now gone, but one can gain a sense of what they were like from the few surviving examples, such as the 1861 Allamakee County Courthouse at Waukon (now a museum), and the Lee County Courthouse of 1841 at Fort Madison, which is still in use.

Surprisingly, though variations of the Italianate mode were extensively used for schools, business blocks, and dwellings, it was generally not a style that was used often for the county courthouses of Iowa. The tendency was to mix Italianate features, first with the late Greek Revival, and then, into the 1860s, 1870s, and 1880s, with the French Second Empire style, the new rage. The 1857–1859 Greek Revival Poweshiek County Courthouse in Montezuma exhibits numerous Italianate details, while the Howard County Courthouse of 1879–1880 in Cresco has an Italianate body with some French Second Empire detailing.

In the late 1870s and into the 1880s the French Second Empire was the modish image for county courthouses across the country. The most impressive contribution to this rich, exuberant style in Iowa was the Davis County Courthouse (1877) in Bloomfield. The French Second Empire mode gave way in the mid to late 1880s to the Richardsonian Romanesque, and the state fortunately

Corn Palace, Sioux City, 1891

Coal Palace, Ottumwa, 1890

still possesses a good many examples of this profoundly American imagery. Since most of these buildings were constructed of brick with limestone trim, they tend to convey the banded coloristic qualities associated with the Ruskinian Gothic. The 1883–1884 Ringgold County Courthouse (demolished) was in fact a rather energetic example of the Victorian Gothic, similar in spirit to the contemporary work of Frank Furness in Philadelphia. Typical of the Victorianized Richardsonian Romanesque is the Washington County Courthouse of 1885–1887, the body of which was built around a massive corner tower.

A revealing and vivid clue as to how Iowans viewed architecture can be seen in their late nineteenth-century exposition buildings. The wildest of these, verging on Victorian madness, comprised the group built for in-state exhibitions meant to celebrate local industry and production. All of these, like the famous Ice Palaces of Minnesota, are gone, but we can still experience them through illustrations and written descriptions. Sioux City, with its aggressive campaign to sell itself, initiated its first Corn Palace in 1888. This was followed by a second in 1889, and the third and final one in 1891.[46] Contemporaneous with these corn palaces were Ottumwa's 1890 Coal Palace (built, of course, with blocks of coal), Creston's Bluegrass Palaces of 1889, 1890, and 1892, and the 1892 Flax Palace in Forest City.[47] All of these structures featured accretions of almost unbelievably rich Victorian architectural elements—these were indeed palaces one might encounter in the fairy tales of Hans Christian Andersen. Iowa's self-image can also be glimpsed in the buildings that the state constructed at various

Bluegrass Palace, Creston, 1890

Flax Palace, Forest City, 1892

Iowa State Building, Centennial Exhibition, Philadelphia, 1876

Iowa State Building, Louisiana Purchase Exposition, Saint Louis 1904

national and international expositions of the late nineteenth and early twentieth centuries. For the Centennial Exhibition held in 1876 in Philadelphia,
Iowa presented itself through an Eastlake dwelling that had a few references
to the post-Civil War Italianate style; the building was described as "a neat
tasteful frame cottage."[48] For the 1893 World's Columbian Exposition in Chicago, the state of Iowa leased an existing Richardsonian Romanesque park pavilion, and the architectural firm of Josselyn and Taylor of Cedar Rapids made
some additions and alterations.[49] The image chosen for the Iowa pavilions at
the smaller exhibitions at Omaha (1898) and at New Orleans (1884–1885) was
loosely Colonial Revival. At the two great American expositions of the early
1900s, at Buffalo (1900) and at Saint Louis (1904), the state represented itself
in terms of a knowing, sophisticated version of Ecole des Beaux-Arts Classicism.

Following the ins and outs of fashion, the designers of Iowa courthouses
turned to the classical Beaux-Arts mode in the 1890s and on through the 1920s.
The first phase of the Beaux-Arts looked to the liveliness of the French Baroque tradition and its revival in the nineteenth century. Thus the 1893 Dubuque County Courthouse in Dubuque can be thought of as a Victorian interpretation of the Beaux-Arts. By the early 1900s, Beaux-Arts classicism had
become more "correct" but often still retained its former richness of form and

details, beautifully summed up in the 1906 Polk County Courthouse in Des Moines.

The one and only exception to the dominance of the Beaux-Arts tradition for the design of Iowa courthouses between 1900 and 1920 was the well-known Woodbury County Courthouse (1915–1917), designed by William L. Steele, and Purcell and Elmslie. This is the only example of a large public building designed by the exponents of the Prairie school. The general format, a public-oriented building capped by a tower devoted to the business of the court, was similar to that of the later Beaux-Arts style Veterans' Memorial and City Hall of 1927–1928 in Cedar Rapids. A comparison of these two buildings well illustrates how in architecture "the clothes make the man."

The teens and twenties brought even more simplification and refinement to courthouse architecture. Frequently the building form was a rectangular three-story box, with a rusticated basement and a surface above composed of inset loggias accompanied by the suggestion of end pavilions. The O'Brien County Courthouse (1917) at Primghar and the post-World War I Pocahontas County Courthouse (1923) at Pocahontas sum up this approach. The path of abstraction of the Beaux-Arts Classical tradition continued on through the later 1920s and the 1930s up to the opening of World War II. Those courthouses designed during the Coolidge and Hoover administrations tended to be traditional classical buildings that had been brought up to date; those in the depression years of the Franklin D. Roosevelt administration (the PWA Moderne) were to be perceived as efficient office buildings. The Louisa County Courthouse of 1928 at Wapello would characterize the former approach; the Jones County Courthouse (1937) at Anamosa, the latter.

After World War II a number of the older county courthouses of Iowa were replaced by larger, more "efficient" buildings. Until the 1970s, two approaches characterized the design of these buildings. One of these was to continue on with the Beaux-Arts tradition but to water it down, so that the building would be responded to more as a modern building than a classical one; an example of this would be the 1958 Emmet County Courthouse, in which the architect seems to have played a visual game between the theme of narrow classical engaged piers and the theme of machine repetition signaling the modernist architectural image. The second approach, as seen in the Clarke County Courthouse (1955–1956) at Osceola, was to commend the building fully to the modernist image by suspending a rectangular box above the landscape. In recent years the modernist imagery of the International style has been replaced by the masonry cut-into box, which presents the building as a piece of minimalist sculpture; the Butler County Courthouse (1975) in Allison is a case in point.

If one looks into who designed these county courthouses one can begin to understand how the practice of architecture developed within the state. With only a few exceptions, the designers of the first permanent buildings remain unknown, which usually means that the structures were designed by their builders in consultation with the clients. An exception would be Stephen B. Brophy, who designed the first Muscatine County Courthouse (1839–1941). Brophy provided a simple Greek Revival design of sophisticated proportions which would have been at home anywhere in the East.[50] By the 1860s and later, the professional architect was definitely on the scene. Iowa courthouses of the years 1860 through 1900 were designed by both out-of-state and in-state individuals who advertised themselves as architects. A good number of designs for county courthouses in Iowa were obtained through public competitions. Of the winners of such competitions, well over half were out-of-state architects. Eckel and Mann of Saint Joseph designed the Pottawattamie County Courthouse at Council Bluffs (1885–1888, demolished); T. Dudley Allen of Minneapolis designed three of the county courthouses in Iowa, and was an unsuccessful competitor in two other competitions; John C. Cochrane, one of the architects for the Illinois State Capitol, designed the Marshall County Courthouse (1884–1886) in Marshalltown; and there are numerous other architects from Chicago, Milwaukee, Cleveland, and elsewhere that ended up designing one or more of the county courthouses of the state.

While competitions continued to be held to obtain architects for these courthouses, after 1900 there was a marked tendency to engage architects who practiced within the state. Thus after 1900 the Des Moines firm of Proudfoot and Bird obtained a good number of commissions for county courthouses, and such patronage of in-state architects has continued to the present day.

Iowa's two major public commissions of the nineteenth century, the first Iowa State Capitol (1840–1842) at Iowa City, and the later capitol building at Des Moines (1871–1886), were produced by talented professionals. John Francis Rague designed the earlier building, Cochrane and Piquenard the latter. Professionalism also dominated other prominent public building types, including libraries and post offices. The Chicago firm of Patton and Miller designed some 100 Carnegie libraries throughout the Midwest, and of these, 19 were built in Iowa.[51] The remaining 80-plus Carnegie libraries within the state were designed by both local Iowans and out-of-state architects, with the general tendency increasingly to engage in-state architects.[52]

Post office buildings, along with county courthouses, churches, bank buildings and motion picture theaters, are among the most memorable building types encountered in almost all of Iowa's towns and cities. As was true throughout the country, the earlier post offices, from the 1890s through 1920, were almost always designed in Washington, D.C., by the Office of the Supervising Architect for the Treasury Department. In the 1920s and 1930s a number of the designs were by local architects working within the specifications set by the Washington office.

The styles of these post office buildings in Iowa followed the pattern generally found elsewhere in the country. The first were Beaux-Arts Classical; from the twenties on they were designed according to variations on the Georgian and Federal themes and were meant to be read as Colonial. In contrast, the public library buildings were far more varied, ranging from the Beaux-Arts Classical to the medieval and, in the teens and twenties, to the Craftsman (Arts and Crafts) and Prairie modes. One would find it difficult to point to even one example of a federal post office building constructed since 1945 which has contributed substantially to the aesthetic quality of any Iowa city or town; on the other hand, especially in the 1970s and 1980s, a remarkable number of public libraries were built which represent some of the best designs of these decades.

Turning to the commercial architecture constructed in Iowa from the early 1860s on, it would seem quite certain that most of these buildings were designed by architects. The *Directory of 19th Century Iowa Architects,* compiled by Alan M. Schroder,[53] indicates that almost every Iowa community of some size had one or more architects. This continued to be the case into the early 1900s.[54] One can play all sorts of games in trying to answer the question of who was the first practicing architect to live and work in Iowa. Certainly the first strong designer to emerge was John Francis Rague, who designed the State Capitol at Iowa City and later (1854) established himself in Dubuque.[55] Rague, however, was hardly alone in pursuing architecture in the state in the 1850s. Josiah P. Walton was located in Muscatine in 1854, George Edwards (of Edwards and Carroll) was established in Davenport by 1856, J. B. Graham was practicing in

Commercial Buildings on the west side of Main Street, south of the town square, Malcom, Iowa

Keokuk by 1857, and J. Stover was listed in Burlington in 1859. There were a number of others. By the 1860s there were a few figures, such as William Foster of Des Moines, whose practice extended around the entire state.[56]

These architects, and those who followed, furnished their clients with a sequence of styles that were popular on the national scene. As in public architecture, the round-arched, bracket-corniced Italianate style merged into the French Second Empire; and this in turn was replaced by the turreted Queen Anne, the Rusticated Richardsonian Romanesque, and finally, before the turn of the century, the Beaux-Arts Classical. In designing these commercial buildings of the late nineteenth century, the architects of Iowa relied on ordering an impressive array of prefabricated parts from catalogues, ranging from cast-iron piers and lintels to pressed metal entablatures and cornices, as well as doors, windows, and other components. Some of these were produced quite early within Iowa; others were ordered from Chicago, Cleveland, and other points to the east.

By the late 1850s, Iowa architects found themselves involved also in domestic architecture, though to what extent remains unknown. Only in recent years have research and historical surveys begun to pin down who designed Iowa's middle- and upper-middle-class houses. It is also becoming apparent that designs derived from pattern books proliferated in the years after 1880. The architect George F. Barber of Knoxville, Tennessee, provided inspiration through the many editions of his *The Cottage Souvenir #2* (1891), and his *New Model Dwellings and How Best to Build Them* (1895). Historical studies are revealing an increased number of homeowners who ordered sets of his working drawings.

Domestic designs that came from Barber or others, from in-state or out-of-state architects, or from carpenter-builders, methodically followed national trends throughout the nineteenth century. By the 1860s the earlier Federal-Greek, Gothic Revival, and Italianate styles were replaced by (or in some instances combined with) the French Second Empire mode. In the seventies the Eastlake mode entered the scene, its features often combined with one of the earlier styles, or with the emerging Queen Anne. Though brief, the predilection for the masonry monumentalism of the domestic Richardsonian Romanesque was a vigorous trend within the larger cities, especially in Sioux City and Dubuque. The final decade of the century witnessed the gradual triumph of the Colonial Revival, first combined with the Queen Anne, and then on its own.

Whether it be a skyscraper of the 1910s, a suburban house, or a farm dwelling, the Iowa buildings realized after 1900 simply illustrate how far-reaching was the American scene. Most businessmen wished to see themselves and their warehouses in exactly the same garb as those of their compatriots in Chicago and New York. While a few of these buildings were designed by non-Iowa architects—for instance, some of the commercial buildings by Daniel H. Burnham and Company of Chicago—most were designed by the larger Iowa firms, such as Liebbe, Nourse and Rasmussen and Proudfoot and Bird,[57] both of Des

Moines, or by Josselyn and Taylor of Cedar Rapids. The products of these and other Iowa firms were, in fashionability and quality of design, well the equal of what one would have found elsewhere in the country.

The architecture of Iowa directly related to agriculture forms a significant chapter on both the regional and national scene. Drawings and written descriptions indicate that the classic, continually repeated organization of the Iowa farm complex was established at the very beginning of settlement. The farm complex was approached via a dirt or gravel driveway usually laid out perpendicular to the public road. This driveway penetrated to the center of a group of buildings. The formal front of the house faced the public road, although the everyday entrance—usually through a porch—looked out onto the driveway between the dwelling and the farm buildings. Often a fenced lawn, perhaps with a few flower beds, was placed in front of the farmhouse, and a gate from the farm driveway led up to the formal entrance—an entrance that was seldom used. The barn, smokehouse, corncribs, ice house, and other utilitarian buildings would be located on the other side of the driveway. This classic farm complex, with its right-angle relationship to the public road, has continued to be used to the present day.

In addition to the changes in architectural fashions over the decades, which are beautifully revealed in the farm dwellings, there have been other changes as well. The earlier small barns with gable roofs were replaced around the turn of the century by much larger octagonal barns and gambrel-roofed barns; high cylindrical silos made of hollow tiles or reinforced concrete became a common sight by 1910. The latest elements are the new high-tech, large-scale, and brightly painted metal silos one now finds all over Iowa.

Rural barns throughout America (and it is certainly the case in Iowa) form a fascinating chapter within the history of nineteenth- and twentieth-century architecture. The advantages and disadvantages of the various forms for the barn were endlessly discussed in farm journals, and in such pattern books as W. E. Frudden's *Farm Buildings, How to Build Them.*[58] As Lowell J. Soike has pointed out in his *Without Right Angles: The Round Barns of Iowa,* a good number of these barns built before 1918 were designed and constructed by companies and contractors who specialized in this building type.[59] While there is no question that these round barns are impressive objects on the landscape, one should remember that their popularity was just one more indication that the midwestern farmer looked at agricultural production as a business entailing the latest technology. The round barn, with its central round silo, was adopted by the farmers because it was considered to be the latest technological device for sheltering and feeding livestock. Like the short-lived rage for the octagonal house, the popularity of the round barn was relatively brief, lasting from around 1910 through 1918. The form was discarded when it was demonstrated that it had as many disadvantages as advantages.

As nineteenth-century agriculture on the plains evolved, a variety of more

Farm complex near Waukon, c. 1910.

specialized building forms came to be associated with the typical farm complex. One of these was the corncrib, which started out as a small gable-roofed log structure, often in the form of a keystone or V-shape.[60] While the roofs and floors of these structures were tight, the walls were left with air spaces between the logs or milled, sawed sheathing, so that the interiors would be well ventilated. Plans for such buildings were published in the *American Agriculturalist* in the 1860s.[61] By the end of the century, with the increased need to store larger quantities of corn, the form of the double crib with a central drive-through evolved. By 1916 W. E. Frudden provided readers of his *Farm Buildings, How to Build Them* with schemes for a central-gabled tower for elevating machinery, and even a cylindrical model realized in terracotta tile.[62] Prefabricated perforated steel cribs were produced and marketed from 1910 to the present, as were cribs of concrete block or reinforced concrete. These twentieth-century cribs run the gamut from those with gambrel roofs, to those with semicircular ends, to structures that are purely circular. The corncrib remains a very important feature of the farm scene, and in recent years, with the general increase in the size of farms, the cribs have been getting ever larger, and their images, high-tech.

Equally dominant on the agricultural scene were the grain elevators which thrust themselves upward near rail lines, like skyscrapers of the plains.[63] The first of these were tall, vertical wood buildings (often sheathed in sheet metal) surmounted by a pair of shed roofs from which shot up an even narrower gabled roof monitor. Rows of reinforced concrete grain elevators began to appear on the landscape after 1900, and by the twenties almost every town with a railroad connection displayed these sentinels of the plains; in larger cities they even appeared downtown. Accompanying these elevators were other utilitarian buildings used for processing grain. These often sprouted tubes, pipes, gangways, and pieces of machinery that frequently created the type of small-scale industrial world one might find in 1920s and 1930s paintings by Charles Sheeler or Charles Demuth. This factorylike aspect of agriculture accelerated in the late 1950s and afterward with the introduction of processing facilities, which, with their machine image, match the high-tech imagery of current architecture.

A blend of technology and our image of Iowa's picturesque rural scene is reflected in silos associated with farm complexes. The earliest of these were low, small, rectangular structures of wood; circular forms, also in wood, began to appear in the later nineteenth century. Just after the turn of the century, silos began to be built of hollow terracotta tile, of concrete block, or of reinforced concrete. Generally, the silo was placed adjacent to the principal barn, but in some instances (as in a number of the round barns), the silo was incorporated within the barn. After 1945 the silo emerged as a high-tech form, beautifully summed up in the bright blue "glass fused to steel" silos built by the A. O. Harvestore Products, Inc., of DeKalb, Illinois. The Harvestore silos were first introduced in 1949, and continue to be installed on farms. The earliest were 14 feet in diameter; today the most common diameter is 20 feet. The silos range in height from 40 to 89 feet. Generally they are plain, monochrome, but they can be "customized" with the date or the farmer's name, or they can display the flag of the United States or Iowa.

Another utilitarian form that dramatically announced the location of a town or city is the water tower. The earliest of these were usually of wood, occasionally of cast and wrought iron. The classic hemispherical-bottom metal tanks on steel legs which we so closely associate with the towns of the Middle West were introduced into Iowa at Fort Dodge in 1894 by the Chicago Bridge Company.[64] This early water tower is no longer standing, but similar ones can be found at Urbana (between Waterloo and Cedar Rapids), Independence, West Union, Algona, Hampton, and in many other communities. In the years since 1945 many of the older water towers have been replaced by an inverted teardrop-shaped tank that melts into its thin, enclosed, curved stem.

In both the nineteenth and twentieth centuries, bank buildings constituted one of the dominant building types in Iowa towns. In the early twentieth century several firms emerged which specialized in this building type. One of these was A. Moorman and Company of Saint Paul, Minnesota (1918); another was the Lytle Company of Sioux City (1921). The usual imagery they employed was that of the Beaux-Arts Classical, sometimes pointing to the Greek, sometimes to the Roman, and in some instances to the Renaissance. There are a few additional examples by these firms that utilized the Prairie school image, as well as the Colonial Revival. Generally the buildings provided by these two firms were sophisticated, well-detailed designs; and although the buildings appeared traditional, they were often highly innovative in structure, layout, and mechanical equipment.

Turning to, public architecture in Iowa after 1900, one finds that the most impressive buildings were public schools, small city halls, and on a number of occasions churches. The group of schools designed in the 1920s in Des Moines by Proudfoot, Bird and Rawson took the Elizabethan image and re-created the romantic feeling of an English country house set within a picturesque garden. In the later 1930s the PWA and WPA programs of the federal government helped to finance a large number of school buildings and auditorium-gymnasiums, almost all of which expressed the Streamline Moderne image. In the twenties, and above all in the depression years of the 1930s, numerous small Iowa towns built tiny street-side buildings that contained all of the municipal functions, from the city-hall council meeting room to a garage to house the community's fire truck. A few of these in the teens were Prairie-esque; in the twenties they leaned toward the Georgian and Federal styles, and in the 1930s the style was that of the Streamline Moderne. The quality of good design in this earlier work continued in the decades after World War II, especially in the numerous "finger-plan" single-floor schools built all over the state. These schools, with a corridor to one side and classrooms to the other, generally demanded large suburban sites at the edges of a community.

As one would expect of a center of American Scene painting, Iowa has public buildings of the twenties and thirties that contain an impressive number of murals.[65] Grant Wood's importance in the 1930s is directly revealed in his many murals, and his influence appears in post offices and school buildings in murals produced by artists working in the American Scene tradition.[66] These murals, as well as the earlier Beaux-Arts murals in the state, show us how painting could successfully be related to architecture, and vice versa.

The commercial architecture of Iowa followed the usual national pattern of the 1920s and later: first Beaux-Arts Classicism, with an occasional look to the medieval; then the Art Deco and Streamline Moderne in the later twenties and thirties. With only a few minor exceptions, International style modernism seized hold of the commercial scene after 1945. Mies van der Rohe designed one building in Des Moines, and some years later Gordon Bunshaft of Skidmore, Owings and Merrill designed a small office building, also in Des Moines. The swing in fashion has in recent years brought Postmodernism to the state, and in the 1980s almost every major commercial building—whether the image be high-tech or abstracted classicism—indicated how Iowa architects kept up with the latest trends.

Because of slow replacement of some of the older structures, Iowa has retained an appreciable number of older roadside buildings, especially service stations. Some of these form wonderful roadside ruins. There are abandoned double-pier stations, and even some in the Mediterranean mode. There are still many Art Deco service stations that have continued in use or have been converted to other uses. Although Iowa never had an abundance of roadside programmatic buildings or sculpture, there are a few highlights, such as the 1958 statue of Pocahontas on the outskirts of the town of Pocahontas.

The state has also contributed to the inventory of twentieth-century architectural follies. These whimsical structures include the Grotto of the Redemption (1912–1954) at West Bend; "The World's Smallest Grotto" (1946–1976) in Iowa City, and Frederickus Reinders's scattering of follies in Hospers (1921, 1945).

Iowa architectural firms and individual architects designed a wide array of houses for the middle and upper middle classes of the state. The preference during the first two decades of the century was for the Colonial or English Tudor styles. In the realm of the American Arts and Crafts movement, Iowa did indeed realize an assortment of Craftsman dwellings and California bungalows, plus a small number of public and commercial edifices reflecting the influence of Gustav Stickley and his *Craftsman* magazine. At least for domestic architecture, many of these designs were derived from pattern books published in Iowa or elsewhere, and probably a good number of houses were built from working drawings ordered from lumberyards or from regional and national home and farm magazines.

Iowa is a place that for many people personifies the rich productivity of the prairie, so it is to be expected that the state participated to the fullest in the early episode of American modernism, the Prairie movement.[67] The high point of the Prairie school approach to suburban development is found in Walter Burley Griffin and Marion Mahoney Griffin's Rock Crest-Rock Glen development of 1912 in Mason City. Within the development are a number of the Griffins' most significant designs, including one of the most romantic and picturesque of American Prairie houses, the 1912 Melson house. Louis H. Sullivan's design for the Merchants National Bank in Grinnell (1913–1914) is unquestionably one of the gems of his late Prairie banks; and William L. Steele and Purcell and Elmslie's Woodbury County Courthouse at Sioux City (1915–1917) embodies the summation of approach of the Prairie school architects to the design of a public building.

In addition to Sullivan, the Griffins, and Purcell and Elmslie, a good number of the principal advocates of the Prairie mode designed and built within the state of Iowa. These included George W. Maher, Francis Barry Byrne, Dwight Perkins, and William Drummond. The homegrown Prairie exponents of Iowa were dominated by William L. Steele of Sioux City, and Einar Broaten of Mason City. However, a majority of the Prairie houses built in the teens and early 1920s in Iowa were designed by local architects who, it would seem, treated the Prairie mode not as a crusade but simply as one of the available fashionable images.[68] When one travels throughout Iowa, one is surprised by the number of these Prairie houses that were built, not just in the larger towns and in the cities, but also in very small towns, and even out into the country. There is no question that there was a sizable clientele within Iowa for the Prairie dwelling, as well as for the Craftsman house and the California bungalow. Most of the Prairie houses were based either on Frank Lloyd Wright's Prairie box—derived from his 1906 project for the *Ladies Home Journal*—or from more classical-oriented houses of George W. Maher.

The number of prefabricated houses that were erected and purchased within Iowa in the years after 1900 is also surprising. Studies of prefabricated housing in Iowa are only beginning, but even now it is apparent that some Iowans must have thought of this form of housing as a viable one. There are a few clues indicating that Iowans did purchase prefabricated houses from Sears, Roebuck and Company.[69] Aladdin Homes of Bay City, Michigan, and Hodgson Portable Houses of Boston and New York advertised extensively in such regional and national Iowa magazines as *Successful Farming* and *Better Homes and Gardens*, both published by the Meredith Publishing Company of Des Moines. Within Iowa itself was the Gordon-Van Tine Company of Davenport, which advertised itself as the "World's Largest Specialist in Home Building Since 1865." It sold not only "plan-cut houses," but also barns and other farm buildings.

That Iowans had not lost an interest in the potential of prefabricated housing is indicated pointedly by the number of houses bought from the Lustron Corporation of Columbus, Ohio. These prefabricated porcelain-enameled steel houses were built between 1949 and 1951. As was the case with the Prairie houses of the teens and early twenties, Lustron houses were erected all over Iowa, from the smallest towns to the largest cities. Considering the brief period of time in which they were produced, it is amazing how many were built within the state.

In the years immediately after World War I, Iowans continued to build Craftsman and California bungalows, though these later examples tended to be more sedate in fenestration and detailing. By the end of the twenties and into the thirties the smaller bungalows and dwellings began to reflect one or another of the period revivals, especially the Colonial and the English Tudor. A fitting termination of the period revival for the small Iowa house is notable in the wonderfully romantic, almost dollhouselike dwellings that were designed by the builder Howard F. Moffitt and built in Iowa City at the end of the 1930s and the beginning of the 1940s. Larger, upper-middle-class homes and houses for the wealthy followed a similar course, only there was an added sprinkling of the French Norman and the Mediterranean-Spanish styles. Compared to the residents of New York, Chicago, San Francisco, or Los Angeles, Iowans did not build many grand suburban or country houses in the opulent decade of the 1920s. There are a few exceptions in and around Cedar Rapids, Iowa City, and Des Moines. Salisbury House (1923–1928), the suburban estate of Carl Weeks in Des Moines, with its assemblage of medieval parts imported from England, could easily match similar Tudor houses built elsewhere in the country.

One influence of Iowa on the national architectural scene occurred through the production of architectural components by the Curtis Company of Clinton, and the Pella Company in Pella. The heyday for the Curtis Company was in the 1920s and 1930s when national figures such as Royal Barry Wills and Dwight James Baum designed entrances, fireplace mantels, and other woodwork components for the company. The influence of the Meredith Publishing Company on the national scene has been strong since the mid-1920s, whether it be through the popular middle-class magazine *Better Homes and Gardens* or the more recent *Metropolitan Home*. Under the editorship of the architect John Normile, this company published pattern books and offered a mail-order-plan service for its "Builtcost Gardened Homes." As did the Curtis Company, Meredith engaged a number of nationally known architects—Royal Barry Wills and Verna Cook Salomonsky among them—to provide the drawings for houses.

Although the effect of the Great Depression of the 1930s was a devastating one for the construction of single-family houses, a good number were built in Iowa, especially after 1935. While the Colonial style predominated among them, a remarkable number of Art Deco-Streamline Moderne houses were built within the state. As would be expected, most of these are encountered in the larger cities, but still a tour of the smaller cities and towns will almost always reveal one here or there. If a list were made of a dozen major examples of pre-World War II Moderne houses, the Streamline all-concrete Butler house (1935–1937) in Des Moines would be right at the top.[70]

In the years following World War II, the newly expanded suburbs of Iowa cities and towns sprouted forth with mildly Colonial Revival dwellings and versions of the California ranch house. There were a few episodes of important period revival houses built after 1945, especially those designed by the Chicago architect Jerome Robert Cerny. Frank Lloyd Wright dotted the Iowa landscape with a number of his low, single-story late Usonian houses, and the Modernist Richard J. Neutra and Keck and Keck of Chicago illustrated how the glass post-and-beam dwelling could be related to the woods and hills of the state. By the mid-1950s a number of local architects had taken up the imagery of the post-World War II Modern with real understanding. This was especially the case with the houses designed by Crites and McConnell, as it was with the late Modern and Postmodern in the domestic designs of Charles Herbert and Associates (now Herbert Lewis Kruse Blunck Architecture) of Des Moines.

A perusal of the awards issues of the *Iowa Architect* from the 1980s reveals how closely these architects have been involved with the current imagery—ranging from high tech, to late Modernism, to Postmodernism—and it equally reveals the general high level of design found throughout the state. Along with the intensified programs of historic preservation and historic renovation, Iowa buildings of the late 1980s, through siting, scale, and contextualism, accomplished much to create a sense of the specificity of place, whether within an existing downtown or on new sites reaching out onto the prairie.

Mississippi River— East (ME)

T HE REGION SPREADING WESTWARD SOME ONE HUNDRED miles from the west bank of the Mississippi River was the first area settled in Iowa by Europeans and Anglo-Americans. The topography of this area is that of rolling hill country penetrated by a pattern of rivers and streams that generally flow southward along a northwest-southeast line. A few of the rivers—the Des Moines, Iowa, Wapsipinicon, Maquoketa, and Turkey— were sufficiently deep, and their summer flow great enough, to encourage water transportation.

This region was well forested to the east, and as one traveled west, one found that areas of open prairie began to break in between the river and stream valleys. From the time of the first settlement, the rich lands situated in the river valleys were cleared for agriculture (just as they had been much earlier by the Native American cultures). By the 1870s most of the hilly parcels of land had also been cleared, both to open them up for pasturage and for their timber. During the territorial years and on into the period of early statehood, river transportation was supplemented first by an extensive pattern of state-sponsored roads (including plank roads), and later—from the middle to late 1850s—by an increased number of railroads.[1] Although much of eastern Iowa conveys the atmosphere of a rural, untrammeled countryside, what one encounters today is in fact an almost completely transformed environment.

A glance at the statistics listed in Alfred Theodore Andreas's 1875 *Illustrated Historical Atlas of the State of Iowa* reveals that almost all of the larger and smaller villages that one can visit today in this region were established in the 1840s and 1850s. The earliest were quite naturally located adjacent to or close by rivers (both for reasons of transport as well as for power); only later, with the advent of the railroad, were larger, nonriver towns platted and developed.

37

Mississippi River - East

1. Anamosa (Jones Co.)
2. Andrew (Jackson Co.)
3. Bellevue (Jackson Co.)
4. Bennett (Cedar Co.)
5. Burlington (Des Moines Co.)*
6. Clinton (Clinton Co.)*
7. Davenport (Scott Co.)*
8. DeWitt (Clinton Co.)
9. Dubuque (Dubuque Co.)*
10. Durant (Cedar Co.)
11. Dyersville (Dubuque Co.)
12. Elkader (Clayton Co.)
13. Elkport (Clayton Co.)
14. Fairport (Muscatine Co.)
15. Fort Madison (Lee Co.)
16. Franklin (Lee Co.)
17. Garnavillo (Clayton Co.)
18. Guttenberg (Clayton Co.)
19. Holy Cross (Dubuque Co.)
20. Keokuk (Lee Co.)*
21. Lansing (Allamakee Co.)
22. Lowden (Cedar Co.)
23. Lowell (Henry Co.)
24. Luxemburg (Dubuque Co.)
25. McCausland (Scott Co.)
26. McGregor (Clayton Co.)
27. Manchester (Delaware Co.)*
28. Maquoketa (Jackson Co.)
29. Massillon (Cedar Co.)
30. Mechanicsville (Cedar Co.)
31. Mediapolis (Des Moines Co.)
32. Monona (Clayton Co.)
33. Monticello (Jones Co.)
34. Montrose (Lee Co.)
35. Morning Sun (Louisa Co.)
36. Mount Pleasant (Henry Co.)*
37. Mount Union (Henry Co.)
38. Muscatine (Muscatine Co.)*
39. New Vienna (Dubuque Co.)
40. Nichols (Muscatine Co.)
41. Oxford Junction (Jones Co.)
42. Petersburg (Delaware Co.)
43. Postville (Allamakee Co.)
44. Saint Donatus (Jackson Co.)
45. Salem (Henry Co.)
46. Strawberry Point (Clayton Co.)
47. Tipton (Cedar Co.)
48. Toolesboro (Louisa Co.)
49. Wapello (Louisa Co.)
50. Waukon (Allamakee Co.)
51. Welton (Clinton Co.)
52. West Branch (Cedar Co.)
53. West Liberty (Muscatine Co.)
54. West Point (Lee Co.)
55. Wilton (Muscatine Co.)

A detailed map of site locations has been provided for cities indicated by ⊙ on the map and by * in the list at left.

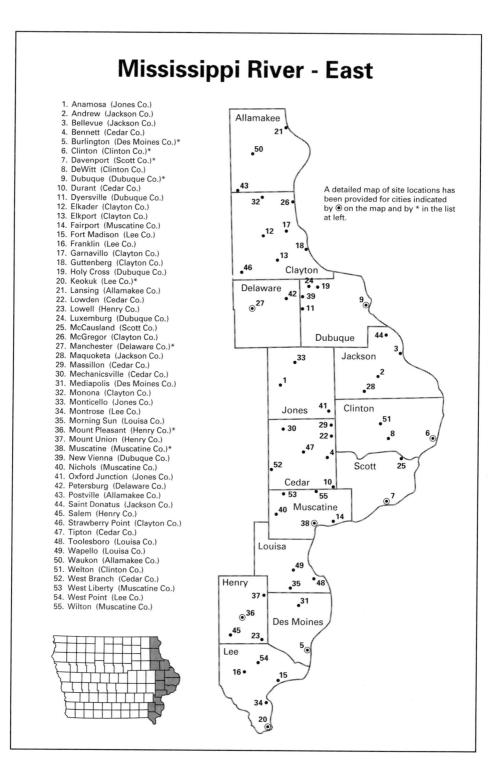

38

Anamosa

The community was laid out in the mid-1840s on rolling land north of the Wapsipinicon River. Its economic future was assured when the county seat and the state penitentiary were located there, and later when it became a junction point for the Iowa Midland Railroad and the Dubuque and South Western railways. Though close to the Wapsipinicon River, the city is not oriented to it, except for some hilltop residences on its southern border. Across the Wapsipinicon River is the Wapsipinicon State Park, a 251-acre park begun in 1921. Local limestone was used for the gateposts and other structures within the romantic, well-laid-out park.

ME001 Jones County Courthouse

1937, Dougher, Rich and Woodburn. W. Main St. between N. High and N. Jackson streets

The style of this courthouse is PWA Moderne, here rendered in pale brown brick with cast-stone trim. The design is that of a three-story block flanked by two small one-story wings. On the entrance facade there is a pattern of a row of pilasters with windows set between which was often repeated in other courthouses. There is a sparse sprinkling here and there of Moderne ornament (including a pair of bronze lanterns by the entrance); otherwise the building conveys the feeling of grimness characteristic of the depression years.

ME002 Iowa State Reformatory

1872 and later, L. W. Foster and Company. N. High St., at end of Broadway

This is a reformatory posing as a nineteenth-century castle: it has towers, crenellation, and all the expected attributes. The soberness of its purpose is countered by the playfulness of the overall image. When construction began in the 1870s, it was described as "one of the finest buildings in the state, and among the best arranged and magnificent prisons in the west."[2] The central section was finished in 1880, the women's section in 1881, and the administrative building in 1889.[3]

ME003 Cottage

c. 1875. 406 N. Davis St.

The gable ends with their patterned wood detailing are the features that capture one's attention. The story-and-a-half cottage has brick walls and a moderately pitched roof; its first floor is placed right on ground level.

ME004 Edgar M. Condit House

c. 1870. 102 E. Pine St.

This two-story, side-hall Italianate house has a small side porch to the left and a bay to the front; the windows within the clapboard siding have segmental arches. The present entrance porch is of a later date. Now missing from the dwelling is the original cast-iron railing that was sited above the front bay window and at the crown of the roof.

ME005 House

c. 1878. 323 W. Main St.

A much added to and remodeled, largely Eastlake dwelling, the house includes a tower displaying the characteristic four-gabled roof one so closely associates with the style. On the other hand, the roundheaded windows and other details look back in fashion to the earlier Italianate style.

ME006 U.S. Post Office Building

1940, Louis A. Simon, Neal A. Mellick. West side of Ford, south of Main St.

The architects created the usual Colonial Revival image for this post office, but they also tried to absorb the newfangled modern style. On the whole, they succeeded. The gable roof helps, as does the cast-stone entrance screen with its pilasters, slight gable, and central cupola.

ME007 Anamosa Public Library

1902, Dwight Perkins. Northeast corner S. Ford St. and First St. E.

ME008 Col. W. T. Shaw House

The Chicago architect Dwight Perkins was associated with the Sullivanesque Chicago school and with Frank Lloyd Wright and the Prairie school. In this library Perkins looked back to the Richardsonian Romanesque as it had been classically reordered in the late 1880s by McKim, Mead and White. The beautiful limestone walls convey the tactile quality of stone but they are not picturesque; the same is the case with the symmetrical, balanced composition found on the building's principal facade. The library is situated in a residential area, and its appearance is definitely suburban.

ME008 Col. W. T. Shaw House

c. 1855. South end of Oak St.

The banker W. T. Shaw selected a magnificent hilltop site overlooking the city and the Wapsipinicon River valley. Upon this he con-

structed a large brick Italianate house. Its high square tower, placed within an ell, not only commands a wonderful view but dominates the house and site as well. With its extensive landscaped grounds and secondary buildings, this house constitutes one of the great country estates of Iowa. While a few changes have been made in the house (a Colonial Revival entrance porch replaces the original one, and the brick walls have been painted), it all remains beautifully intact.

ME009 Stone City

3 miles west of Anamosa on route E28

The first limestone quarry was established at Stone City in 1852; by the late 1870s, the limestone industry was supporting a thriving community.[4] Later, with the increased use of portland cement for reinforced concrete walls and concrete block, the economic base of the community all but disappeared. In 1932 the community experienced a brief reawakening as a summer art colony under the direction of Grant Wood. Many of Stone City's buildings have disappeared, including John Aloysius Green's 1883 Second Empire-style mansion (it burned down in 1963) and the large three-and-a-half-story Columbia Hall (torn down for its stone in 1936), yet a number of structures remain that have architectural merit.

Among these is the two-story rusticated ashlar block Henry Dearborn and Sons Building of 1897, located on the south side of Main Street (route E28), just before the Wapsipinicon River. Across the river, south of Main Street and the former railroad tracks, is Saint Joseph's Catholic Church designed in 1913 by the Dubuque architect Guido Beck. It goes without saying that the church is of native stone (rusticated ashlar); in style it is a version of the Gothic mode featuring a corner entrance tower, a style often built throughout the United States in the late nineteenth and early twentieth centuries. The gabled front of the church is corbeled, the sidewalls are buttressed, and the three-story tower is crenellated. The most impressive and handsome building still to be found within Stone City is the Old Stone Barn of 1888. This three-story structure stands west of the church and south of Main Street. It is of stone and measures 124 feet long, 50 feet wide, and 40 feet high. The two narrow walls are buttressed, and secondary buttresses continue along each of the long sidewalls. A low-pitched hipped roof with very little overhang sits lightly atop the heavy masonry walls. A two-story arched entrance occupies one end of the building, its large scale played off against the three rows of small double-hung windows.

ME010 Riverside Cemetery

1854 and later. Southeast edge of town, E34, just east of Wapsipinicon

Within the Riverside Cemetery is the grave of Grant Wood. The compound for the Wood family is announced by a sleeping stone lion; Grant Wood's own marker is a modest, simple granite block, with a single polished surface. The surface of the block is raised only from the surrounding ground. Within a wooded hilly section of terrain is located this very early cemetery. It was from the beginning treated in the "natural" fashion of the picturesque English garden. This was enhanced under the guidance of the painter Ossian Simonds, who added more winding roads and planted trees with contrasting open glades.

Andrew

ME011 Butterworth Tavern

1852. .5 miles north of Andrew on route 62

This building could easily be exchanged with scores of handsome stone or brick Greek Revival houses one can find in upstate New York and on into the Ohio River valley. The tavern is a two-story, gable-roofed structure, with balanced pairs of windows on each side of the entrance. The entrance itself is deeply sunk into the exposed limestone walls, its sides reading as pilasters supporting an entablature and cornice. The recessed front door is accompanied by side lights and a horizontal transom. The house exhibits an appropriately wide entablature below the cornice of the main roof. Each end gable has a pair of chimneys. The building was occupied for some time by Ansel Briggs, Iowa's first elected governor.

Bellevue

The riverside community of Bellevue was laid out initially in 1835 and was resurveyed in the 1840s. Though it had a number of operating mills by mid-century, its economy was that of a shipping point, first as a Mississippi River port and then later as a railroad stop. Other than the fact that the town's grid followed the north-northwest course of the river, and that its east-west streets were platted to plunge into the river, there is nothing singular about its layout. Over the years, parks and school grounds have been added, and increasingly, its waterfront is being treated in a parklike fashion.

ME012 **Potter's Mill** (Dyas Mill)

1843. South end of 2nd St.

This six-story restored mill is situated on the north shore of Mill Creek. The design of the building looks back to the late Federal style. In the center of the main facade are loading doors on each floor, finally terminating in a dormer unit in the roof with its own door. There are pairs of double-hung windows to each side of the doors. A large monitor extends across the entire roof. The mill was initially designed to grind flour, but after 1900 it was used to process feed. The building has recently been restored.

ME013 **Commercial Building**

c. 1860. Northwest corner Riverview St. (US 52) and Spring St.

The two-story brick building still exhibits an iron balcony with railings and bracketed supports. Below, thin cast-iron columns support the various display windows and the entrance. The windows on the upper floor have segmented curved lintels of stone.

ME014 **House**

c. 1870. 301 State St.

A number of remarkable features are gathered together in this grand-scale brick dwelling. Its third floor is encased in a dormered mansard roof, as in a French Second Empire house. A "correct" tower rises where the two wings join, but the entrance porch at the base of the tower is really Eastlake. Instead of being elevated on a raised basement, the building sits directly on the ground. These aspects and later additions have created an unusual building.

ME015 **House**

c. 1893. Southwest corner Franklin and 3rd streets

The handsome late Queen Anne-Colonial Revival design of this house exhibits all the prerequisites of the mode: a three-story corner bay tower, a horizontal band of fishscale shingles, Palladian windows in the third-floor dormer, and an extensive veranda with a roof supported by clustered columns. A semicircular projection of the porch at one corner

ME012 Potters' Mill (Dyas Mill)

has its own low-pitched conical roof and extravagant finial on the crown.

ME016 **Baker House** (Mount Rest)

1893. Northeast corner Spring and 3rd streets

If one's predilections are for the startling and dramatic in design, then the Baker house is a must to see. It is situated on a flattened pad with a steep wooded hill rising in back. The approach is dramatic, via a narrow staircase leading up from the street corner. The two-story rectilinear block of the house is continued at each end by two rectangular towers. The right angle of the walls meeting above the entrance steps has been rounded. Above this is a rounded tower. The building is sheathed in shingles, and it has a wide, heavily decorated entablature and cornice. Some of the design ingredients are derived from the Queen Anne, some from the Colonial Revival, but the overall image of the house is neither of these.

ME017 **Wynkook House** (Springside)

1848. North end of Bellevue, unsigned road beyond end of Washington St.

The Wynkook Villa, as it was referred to, is one of the largest remaining Italianate/Gothic Revival houses in Iowa. Between two broad projecting wings of the house, with their sawed and carved bargeboards, is a square tower surmounted by an Eastlake roof of four wall dormers. An overscale Gothic window looks out of the front of the tower's third floor. The rooflines are broken by paneled chimneys and finials. The walls of the building are of stone laid in a horizontal random pattern. The house now has a romantic, lonely quality to it as it sits high on its hillside location at the north edge of Bellevue, looking down over the Mississippi.

ME018 **Elbridge Gerry Potter Farm** (Paradise)

1842 and later. 4 miles west of Bellevue on route D57

Elbridge Gerry Potter was a wealthy atheist who made his original fortune through a distillery and flour mill in Illinois. His extensive establishment was more than just a large farm; it was really a small village unto itself. Before his death the complex consisted of a three-story main house plus seven other good-sized buildings laid out in a narrow valley on the 1,400-acre farm. The house, which is still standing, is a large rectangular three-story box surmounted by an eight-sided cupola. Along the front of the house was a two-story porch, covered at its second level by a shed roof. Also still standing are a two-story stone dormitory building and a structure designed to house wagons.

ME019 **Mathias Furtz (Spruce Creek) Chapel**

1852. 5 miles northeast of Bellevue on Spruce Creek Rd.

This small stone-walled, gable-roofed chapel was built by an emigré from Luxembourg, Mathias Furtz. The altar and crucifix within were carved by the builder. The size of the chapel and its play of scale come close to making it an out-and-out folk folly.

ME020 **Bellevue State Park**

Southwest of Bellevue, just off US 52

The first 66 acres of this park were acquired in the early 1920s. Additions have been made over the years, and the park now contains 547 acres. The design of the park, part of which is on top of the high cliffs overlooking the river, was made to respond sensitively to the topography and plant forms. Numerous features—lookouts, picnic areas, camping areas—have a rustic look provided by native stone and wood.

Bennett

Bennett, in eastern Cedar County, possesses a fine example of a Prairie school brick bank building, now used as the community's town hall and public library. Constructed in 1919 on the corner of Main and Sixth streets, the structure has an entrance somewhat reminiscent of Louis H. Sullivan's bank at Sidney, Ohio. The entrance on the narrow side of the building has a lunette in cast stone above the door. The lintel of the doorway is extended to each side and terminates in squared geometric ornamentation. On the sides of the building, the sills of the large windows rest on projecting bands that conclude in a square. Below the cast-stone cornice is a series of three bands.

Burlington

The city, named after Burlington, Vermont, since its earliest settlers came from there, was laid out along the Mississippi in 1834[5] on a site selected by Zebulon Pike nearly thirty years earlier. Its grid, placed at the junction of the river and Hawkeye Creek, essentially parallels the riverfront. As often commented on, its site was indeed picturesque due to the steep rise of two hills directly adjacent to the river, followed by a series of hills rising to the west. During its first years the city's economy was primarily derived from shipping on the river and on merchandising for the developing farms to the west. In 1855 the railroad reached the Mississippi on the Illinois side, opposite Burlington. A year later, work commenced on a railroad running west from Burlington. However, it was not until 1868 that a "splendid iron bridge" was built across the Mississippi. The iron and stone-piered bridge was of nine spans, and in length it was 2,000 feet. In the late 1880s Glazier observed that "the smoke stacks of manufactories are seen in all parts of the city."[6] Among these industries were the Murray Iron Works, the Burlington Plow Company, Wolfe's Furniture Factory, and the Burlington Wheel Works. Trade carried out via the railroads and the river and manufacturing continued to fuel the city's economy through the 1920s.

One of the assets of the community is Crapo Park, situated among the hills and bluffs overlooking the Mississippi. This 100-acre park was established in 1895–1896 and was designed in that year by Ernshaw and Punshaw. The park was a gift of a local philanthropist, Philip M. Crapo. It contains a selection of trees indigenous to this region and features winding roads and paths, formal gardens, and pools. Another important open space within the city is Dankwardt Park, just north of Crapo Park (both are off South Main Street). As so often

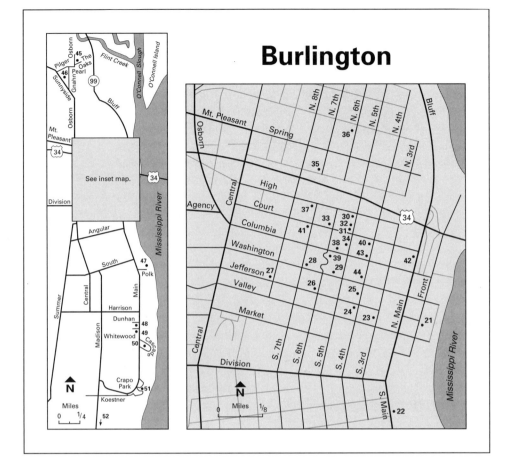

occurs, a highway (US 34), which extends west from MacArthur Bridge, has plowed its way through the town, not only dividing it in two but destroying a good number of historic buildings. Fortunately, most of the highway is set down into the ground between the hills, so that it is not seen, nor does it impinge excessively on the adjacent buildings. As with other river towns, civic leaders of the city make a continual effort to develop much of the waterfront into a parklike setting.

ME021 **Memorial Auditorium**

1938, Robin B. Carswell. Front St., east of Jefferson St.

This gleaming white concrete structure is set within the park that runs along the river. The building is a splendid example of the late-1930s PWA Moderne. Its several connected volumes are purely classic in their propor-tions and the general symmetry of their fen-estration. But the classic has taken on a vari-ety of Moderne features—concrete walls, glass bricks, doors with portholes—which must have made any Burlington citizen of the time re-spond to the building as a Moderne structure. The most formal facade is reserved for the entrance to the auditorium, where five doors are placed below a cantilevered balcony; above

ME021 Memorial Auditorium

this balcony five windows continue the pattern of the door below. At ground level, near the corners, are box-framed windows, with perforated openings at each floor level above. As with many public buildings of the 1930s, the auditorium was funded by the federal government (Treasury Department).

ME022 Burlington Railroad Passenger Station

1944, Holabird and Root. 300 S. Main St.

Because of the importance of the Burlington Railroad within the national railway system, the new station was allowed to be built during World War II. The structure of the station was reinforced concrete, sheathed in stone. The limitation of materials available at the time partially explains its design. The building was planned as a combined railroad and bus station, its most important spaces being a large waiting room and an adjoining restaurant. The lobby was designed as a comfortable, living-room-like space with both movable and built-in furniture. The restaurant had a C-shaped low counter, paralleled by seating. The design of the station was essentially Streamline Moderne, but Streamline Moderne working its way into post-World War II Modern. The restaurant wing has a dramatic

curved facade, à la Eric Mendelsohn, the German modernist of the 1920s and later; other Moderne elements are the horizontal band windows and the enlarged porthole windows. The great Chicago firm of Holabird and Root designed a number of small railroad stations in Iowa in the late 1930s; in Burlington itself, in 1938–1939, they also designed the James S. Schramm house (ME050).

ME023 Capitol Theater

1937, Wetherell and Harrison. 213 N. 3rd St.

This shimmering gold, orange, and black glazed terracotta motion picture theater asserts its presence on the street with great force. The use of such brilliant colors and reflective surfaces meant, of course, that the 1930s facade and marquee would grip one's attention as firmly during the day as they would at night when everything was lighted by neon and incandescent lights. The design theme of this Streamline Moderne theater is established by the play between the narrow, emphatically vertical banding of the terracotta facade against the horizontality of the wedge-shaped marquee. The Des Moines firm of Wetherell and Harrison designed a number of theater buildings during the 1930s in Iowa.

ME024 Hedges Block

1880–1882, Charles A. Dunham. Southwest corner of Jefferson and 4th streets

Here we have one of those instances of vigorous, brittle angularity of design that so troubled both traditionalists and modernists of the first decades of this century. We asso-

ME024 Hedges Block

ME026 "Hamburgers"

ciate this mode with such nineteenth-century figures as William Butterfield and Charles Eastlake in England; in America it reached its height in the Philadelphia work of Frank Furness. In the three-story Hedges building, the Burlington architect Charles A. Dunham introduced this hefty primitive quality primarily in the cut-stone detailing on cornices, entablatures, pediments, and around windows and doors. Characteristic of the mode are squat columns, V-shaped arches, and small roof pinnacles. The general flavor is medieval, somewhat Romanesque as well as Gothic; but designs such as these are so original in their uses of precedent that they can be treated as pure nineteenth-century architecture.

ME025 First Congregational Church

1869–1870, Charles A. Dunham. 313 N. 4th St.

A corner crenellated tower with angled corner buttresses is folded into the gable-roofed body of the church. The entrance to the church is through a pair of doors in its main gabled front, above which is a large tripartite lancet window. The base of the building is of rusticated limestone, while the masonry surfaces above are more finely cut. The windows of the church exhibit a variety of late nineteenth- and early twentieth-century art glass. In style, it revives the English Gothic.

ME026 "Hamburgers"

1936, Charles B. Moore. 600 Jefferson St.

This little Moderne square box is sheathed in white vitrolite, with black trim. The sign "Hamburgers" is so dominant that the entrance facade really ends up as a sign, and

nothing more. The building was planned by its owner. Its original name was "Dinty's Snappy Service."

ME027 Burlington Produce Company Building

c. 1870. Northwest corner of Jefferson and 8th streets

The rough limestone walls together with the crenellated parapet suggest that here we have encountered a fragment of an English medieval castle, not a nineteenth-century commercial block. The center portion of the parapet has been raised to give emphasis to the main facade. All of the doors and windows are topped by segmental arches. Other than the crenellation, no other purely decorative feature occurs in the building. Instead, the rough masonry surface alone imparts a strong sense of character.

ME028 Saint Paul's German Methodist Church (now the Art Guild of Burlington, Inc.)

1869–1870, Charles A. Dunham. Northeast corner of 7th and Washington streets

The historical references made in this church are to the French Romanesque, coupled with an Eastlake spire and such Italianate features as bracketed gables. The walls are of rubble limestone quarried from the site, while the tower and south facade are regularly coursed cut limestone. In various rebuildings and repairs, the tower's spire, which rises 148 feet from the base of the building, has lost its small intermediate dormers and its metal cap, ball, and cross at its pinnacle. Because of its steep hillside location, the church is cut into the hill, and on its south or entrance front a high, terraced stone podium has been provided.

ME029 **Fordney House**

c. 1845, 1870. 516 Washington St.

The Fordney house began as a late Federal side-hall house. In 1870 the house was extensively revamped into the Italianate mode. Heavy projecting pediments were added over the two first-story windows and the entrances; above, cornices project over the second-floor windows. The roof's cornice acquired appropriate paired brackets, a cupola was added, and a two-story porch was built onto the side. Because the house is located on a hill, a half basement is revealed at the front, and the entrance is approached by a long flight of stone steps.

ME030 **Christ Episcopal Church**

1884, Charles A. Dunham. Southwest corner of High and 5th streets

What immediately catches one's eye in this stone church is the corner tower. It stands out as a cylinder for the first two floors and then suddenly becomes an elongated rectangle surmounted by a high-pitched gable roof. While towers of this type are found in England, their source is French and Flemish. In 1973 the church was almost completely destroyed by fire. It was rebuilt following the original design with a few changes; the north side dormer was eliminated, and buttresses were introduced on the side walls to stabilize the older walls.

ME031 **Hedge House** (Hedge Hall)

1859. 609 5th St.

At first glance one would think of this two-and-a-half-story yellow brick house as an example of Beaux-Arts Classicism at the turn of the century. Instead, we have here a building in what we can loosely label as the highly fashionable Renaissance Revival style. The entablature is elaborately ornamented with a vine-and-leaf pattern, and is occasionally broken by small round windows. The wide, projecting cornice is supported by a continuous row of brackets. The principal windows exhibit projecting lintels, and the corners of the building are deeply quoined. Equally rich in form and detail is the entrance porch supported by paired columns that are set on a high base.

ME032 **Ellery-Kratz House**

1869. 613 B 5th St.

The thin, elongated form of the Ellery-Kratz house conveys the feeling that it is a two-story town house waiting around for others to be built on each side. In style it is French Second Empire, with a concave mansard roof. The pediments above the windows, some segmental and others curved, with the hint of a consoled keystone, are boldly carved and project from the brick walls of the house. The present wide entrance porch across the front of the house, with its thin columns, is a Colonial Revival addition of a much later date.

ME033 **Carson-Tracy House**

c. 1888, c. 1906. 601 N. 6th St.

Often the late Queen Anne and the Colonial Revival styles were mixed together; in the case of this house, most of the "Colonializing" was the result of an extensive series of additions and remodelings that probably came about shortly before the second owner took possession of the house around 1906. The first floor of the house is sheathed in rough limestone that conveys a primitive feeling. The second floor and attic are covered with patterned shingles. The tour de force of the house is the wide octagonal corner bay tower. Its base is stone, the next level is shingled, and the third-floor walls are decorated with plaster relief sculpture. The tower is terminated by a faceted S-shaped dome.

ME034 **Russell House**

1855, 1870. 521–527 N. 5th St.

The right half of this two-story brick town house was built in 1855; in 1870, the original owner duplicated the original house to the right, creating one of Burlington's few row houses. The style of these town houses is late Federal with Italianate features, particularly the low-pitched gable roof crowned by pairs of projecting chimneys. The building's owner, Simeon Russell, who operated a brickyard, continually enlarged the house to the rear.

ME035 House

c. 1885. 809 N. 7th St.

Facing out over this house's extensive garden is a dramatic octagonal tower. On its third floor a gabled wall dormer projects upward into the spirelike roof. The dormer window is enclosed on each side by a pair of thick stepped brackets that support its gable ends. At the other side of the house is a round bay tower, cantilevered out from the second floor. In style this brick house is Queen Anne. One suspects that the two-story porch overlooking the garden, as well as the entrance porch, are later Colonial Revival additions.

ME036 Manson House

1869–1870, attrib. Louis Lloyd and David Reid. 931 N. 6th St.

Charles Manson, the Iowa jurist for whom this house was built, seems to have had a fondness for bay windows; there are four of them on the first floor, including one on a grand scale toward the garden side of the house. The mansard roof of this Second Empire house is so close to the horizontal that it reads as a roof only because of its shingle sheathing, its pattern of abbreviated gabled dormers, and the cornice below. The house is of the central hall type, with an extension to one side to accommodate a secondary entrance from the side street. The brick walls of the house are stuccoed; the trim is in cut stone.

ME037 MacMillan House

c. 1903. 611 N. 7th St.

A midwestern two-story box, this dwelling is sparsely clothed in Colonial Revival detail. The strong design element in the house is the play between the hip-roofed box and the semicircular entrance porch with large Tuscan columns. Other Colonial details are the front entrance with side lights, and the simple but sophisticated narrow keystone (in wood) above each of the second-floor windows. These

keystones terminate at the roof soffit, extend down over the plain lintel, and then penetrate the wood window frame.

ME038 Charles E. Schramm House

c. 1893. 512 Columbia St.

The Richardsonian Romanesque served as a point of reference for this coursed ashlar limestone block dwelling, but the picturesque medievalism of the Romanesque has been all but eliminated. The roofscape is calm and sedate; the rectangular openings and the great Richardsonian arches seem to refer to the world of geometry, rather than directly to a romantic past. On the first floor a rectangular groove cuts into the solid stone balustrade of the porch. The headers of the windows are directly adjacent to the roof soffits.

ME039 Garrett-Phelps House (Phelps House Museum)

c. 1851, 1871. 521 Columbia St.

Burlington possesses a number of houses that were built in the mid-nineteenth century and were radically revamped either later in the century or in the early twentieth century. The Garrett-Phelps house started life as a mildly Italianate dwelling; in the 1870s it acquired a mansard roof, an Italianate bracketed roof, and a hip-roofed entrance tower. If one were to catalogue its style today, one would probably label it as French Second Empire. Alongside the house to the west is the upper entrance to Burlington's well-known landmark, Snake Alley, a narrow winding street descending steeply down to Washington Street.

ME040 YWCA Building

1912, Shattuck and Shussey. c. 1948. 409 N. 4th St.

Until the advent of modernism after World War II, the image employed for YWCAs was generally quite different from that for YMCAs. Designers of YWCA buildings tended to look to domestic images that at the time were thought to be more "feminine" than the more institutional look usually reserved for the YMCAs. Burlington's YWCA, with its Palladian-like round-arched windows, rows of dormers directly above the cornice, and columned, arched entrance, looks to the English Georgian town house for its inspiration. The building was erected in two stages, the northern section built after 1945. This later stage was remarkable for the time because it basically carried on the domestic theme of the earlier red brick and stone-trimmed structure. To evaluate the different approaches to the Ys, one might go to 712 North Fourth Street to compare the YMCA building of 1912.

ME041 **Walker House**

1937. 615 Court St.

The Colonial Revival house with pedimented wall dormers was a popular image created for domestic architecture in the 1930s. Usually, designs such as the one for the Walker house were referred to as the "Colonial farmhouse type." Though the house was two stories high, the lowering of the roof eave around the windows and the use of a horizontal wood band to connect the second-floor window sills suggests that the dwelling was a modest story-and-a-half house. Sparse but delicate detailing often occurs in the 1930s Colonial Revival houses; here it can be seen in the linear quality of the side-lighted entrance and in the horizontal band of carved Adamesque swags placed below the eave.

ME042 **Des Moines County Courthouse**

1939, Keffer and Jones. Southwest corner of Court and Main streets

This PWA Moderne design is a little on the grim, dry side. The central four-story section projects out just slightly from the two sides. A characteristic composition of the wall surface is created with four recessed vertical panels, each containing soffits and windows. There is relief decoration within the spandrels separating the second level from the third and fourth floors. Below the second-floor windows are spandrels with circular shieldlike devices that are more geometric than classical. The corners of the building are carved and treated with cut vertical lines suggesting fluting or the rounded corner of a 1930s refrigerator. The parapet of the central pavilion contains an abstract rendering of dentils, minus any cornice.

ME043 **Burlington Free Public Library**

1896–1898, W. T. S. Hoyt; J. C. Sunderlind. 501 N. 4th St.

The stone Burlington Public Library building with its open tower was described in 1896 as "Italian Renaissance." One would guess that the projecting hipped roofs and quoined corners were deemed Italian, but the building really reads as a late-1890s version of picturesque Beaux-Arts Classicism. The interior is well preserved and includes two fireplaces, mosaic floors, and a great deal of polished oak woodwork, as well as oak furniture.

ME044 **Burlington City Hall**

1923, Washburn and Weibley. Northwest corner of 4th and Washington streets

George H. Washburn, who had opened his own architectural office in Burlington in 1898, turned to full-fledged Beaux-Arts Classicism for the city hall. Three-story-high engaged Corinthian columns declare the principal entrance front of the building. The suggestion of a portico is accentuated by paired Corinthian pilasters placed on each side. Except for a narrow planting strip in front of the building, its place within the downtown streetscape is identical to that assumed by any bank building.

ME045 **Van Bennett House**

1941, Dane D. Morgan. 1 The Oaks St.

The Burlington architect Dane D. Morgan, a graduate of the Carnegie Institute and the Illinois Institute of Technology at the end of the 1930s, brought his view of the modern to

bear on what is one of Iowa's most impressive pre-World War II Modern houses. The house is beautifully situated with a broad expanse of lawn stretching toward the semiprivate street. Trees enclose the house on each side, and on the garden side emerges an extensive view of the city and the Mississippi Valley. The low rectangular volumes of the house are clothed in an ashlar block stone. The large stones, though roughly cut, maintain (in good Modernist fashion) the continuity of the wall, reading as a thin skin, not as structure. Several of the windows in the two-story section are arranged in vertical bands, with recessed spandrels between the first- and second-floor windows. These spandrels of a metallic green color contain a vertical repeated "V" pattern. One enters the house via the driveway, then through a porch to the side of the garage which leads to the entrance.

ME046 **House**

c. 1870, c. 1905. 1846 Sunnyside

A late Italianate brick house has been transformed into a real "mansion" by the addition of a large two-story porch, with a smaller one-story porch tucked in under it. The larger porch is treated as a rotunda with its center open to the sky as an oculus. The four Roman Ionic columns are immense, as are the entablature and the roof balustrade. The rotunda space is maintained and accentuated by the first-floor porch, which curves inward toward the facade underneath the larger porch. All in all, these porches represent a remarkable design, and they are of such strength that

one does not sense that they are additions to an older house.

ME047 **Carpenter House**

1877, later, Dunham and Jordan. East end of Polk St.

The Burlington architectural firm of Charles A. Dunham and Thomas Jordan created in the Carpenter house a highly personal interpretation of the Eastlake style. The individuality of this house is due in part to the architects' use of limestone for the first floor and parts of the second floor, to the general horizontality of the design, and to the extensive utilization of porches to capture views of the river from the house's blufftop location. There is a suggestion of half-timbering on the wood-sheathed walls. The infill between the timbering is arranged in horizontal or angular patterns. Shed roofs and gabled hips abound.

ME048 **Lustron House**

c. 1950. 2223 S. Main St.

From 1947 through 1951, the Lustron Corporation of Cicero, Ill., and Columbus, Ohio, manufactured and marketed their all-steel houses throughout the Midwest. It is surprising to note how many of these porcelain-enameled single-floor houses were bought and built throughout Iowa during these years. Though somewhat more expensive than built-on-the-site, wood-frame houses, they had the advantage of being constructed with great machine precision. With only a few exceptions, the Lustrons built in Iowa have held up well, and as is the case with this example, they look as if they have just come from the showroom floor.

ME049 Cottage

c. 1870. 2415 S. Main St.

A modest little single-floor cottage sports a finely detailed front entrance porch. Twisted columns support the roof, and sawed and turned work adorns the gable above the entrance.

ME050 James S. Schramm House

1938–1939, Holabird and Root (Helmuth Bartsch). 2690 S. Main St.

The design of the Schramm house seems poised somewhere between the popular Streamline Moderne of the time and the emerging mode of European high-art Modernism. The walls of this flat-roofed house are of whitewashed brick that from a distance reads as concrete. The building is composed of one- and two-story volumetric boxes that have been carefully integrated with one another. There are curved forms in the wall of the staircase and in the studio to the rear, and these appropriately use glass brick. A gently curving driveway leads down to the motor court that forms the entrance to the house. To the rear, overlooking the river, is a screened porch and accompanying terrace. Like the 1941 Van Bennett house (ME045), the Schramm house is one of Iowa's important pre-1941 Modern/Moderne houses. To the south of the Schramm house, hidden

within a small wooded ravine, is another Schramm house, designed in 1964 by George Fred Keck and William Keck of Chicago. The second Schramm house is a characteristic, well-carried-out version of the 1950s modern home, with delicately detailed volumes, flat roofs, and extensive walls of glass. Like the earlier house, this one takes full advantage of its location overlooking the Mississippi River. In addition to the Paul Kuenzle house (ME052), Keck and Keck designed three other modernist houses in Iowa during the post–World War II years: the G. P. Schroeder house (1948) in Independence, and the Donald Bruser house (ME150) and the Kirk Fowler house (1962), both in Bettendorf.

ME051 Hawkeye Log Cabin

1909–1910. East side of Crapo Park

In a long article written in 1960, William J. Peterson, superintendent of the Iowa State Historical Society, noted, "Every community, large or small, might well erect a log cabin."[7] Here is Burlington's much-needed moment in history, a 1909–1910 replica, created in the same year that Theodore Roosevelt was laying the cornerstone of the Lincoln Memorial Building (which enclosed a log cabin) in Hodgenville, Kentucky. Burlington's competing version is of split logs and has a long porch on one side which overlooks the river valley. The Hawkeye Log Cabin was built by the Hawkeye Native Association. Also within Crapo Park, to the south of the log cabin, is the 1844 stone Schneider cottage, built by Rudolph Weingert.

ME050 James S. Schramm House

ME052 Kuenzle House

1969–1970, George Fred Keck and William Keck. South of Crapo Park on Madison Ave., turn east on Nikonha Pl.; house lies to the east after Nikonha Pl. turns to the south. Not visible from road

This post-World War II Modernist house is situated within dense vegetation, on a spectacular blufftop site with extensive views of the Mississippi River valley and beyond into western Illinois.

From the entrance drive one can see a low brick-sheathed rectangular volume, its fenestration balanced around a wide recessed glass entrance. There is an assertive white band at the top of the walls, and above this is the narrow, thin projecting slab of the flat roof. One can just catch a glimpse of the careful composition of round chimney stacks and of the many skylights on the roof. To the rear, as the roof slopes, the house becomes a two-story dwelling centering on a large two-story porch. The porch and this entire side of the house look out over a lawn with modern sculpture, and then on to a remarkable view of the river valley far below.

ME053 Nealley-Prugh House

1872, Harry W. Jones; c. 1905. Madison Ave., .5 mile south of city limits on old Iowa 61

The original stone house has been so enshrouded by the extensive remodeling (c. 1905) that the whole now reads as a turn-of-the-century Colonial Revival home. This later design was by the gifted and fashionable Minneapolis architect Harry W. Jones. Jones provided a highly visible two-story Ionic portico as the new entrance to the house, and then injected numerous other changes and additions, inside and out.

ME054 Gasoline Service Station

1929. East side of US 61, on the Great River Rd., 11 miles south of the Burlington city limits

The Mediterranean or Spanish theme was frequently employed for gasoline service stations throughout the country from the mid-1920s through the 1930s. This example is sheathed in cream-colored brick with touches here and there of red Mission-style tile roofs. The central office is treated as a tower, with arched windows below and round windows above.

ME055 Malchow Mounds

9 miles north of Burlington on Iowa 99; 1 mile north of Kingston; west side of route 99

The Malchow Mounds and the adjacent Poisel Mounds total over 55 mounds, erected between 200 b.c.e. and 200 c.e.. The groups of conical mounds on these two sites constitute the most extensive mounds still remaining within Iowa.

Clinton

In 1836 a town named New York was platted at the present site of Clinton, but the projected town did not develop. In response to the prospect of a railroad bridge being built across the Mississippi at this point, Clinton was platted in 1855, and its grid developed parallel to the Mississippi River.[8] A second, later grid north of First Avenue South bends to the north-northeast to follow the banks of the river. The breadth of the river plain at this location meant that the commercial downtown, the industrial/railroad section, and much of the residential area could be accommodated on flat land. Several railroad projects were launched in the 1850s, and the city was finally connected by the Chicago Northwestern Railroad across the Mississippi to Illinois (the first bridge was completed in 1864) and to Council Bluffs on the Missouri to the west. By the 1870s there were two railroad bridges across the Mississippi, and a rail line extended along the river, first to Lyons and then further north. During that

Clinton

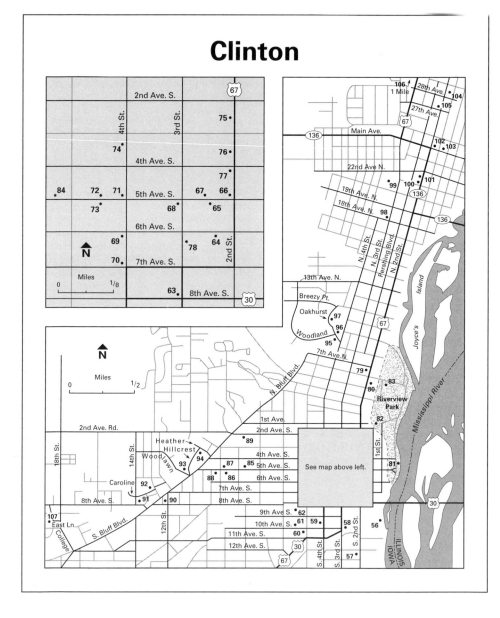

decade Clinton was glowingly portrayed as a thriving city: "Nestling among a young growth of artificial shade trees are many beautiful white cottages and stately brick residences, and towering above them all are noble business blocks that are the result of a rapid and healthy growth."[9]

Clinton's two principal industries throughout the latter part of the nineteenth century were lumbering and the railroad. To this was added the economic advantage of the city's having acquired the county seat in 1869. The most influential of Clinton's industries was the Curtis Woodworking Company (founded in 1866), which supplied architectural parts and millwork to the whole of the country and in the process both mirrored and encouraged architectural taste, especially during the years 1910 through 1940. The Curtis Company had its own local impact on the architectural scene by its development of Castle Terrace, a beautifully conceived enclave of period revival houses (1926–1930) set within wooded hills. In the nineteenth century, Curtis's major local competition was the Disbrow Company (founded in 1856) in nearby Lyons.[10] This company provided exterior and interior Eastlake, Queen Anne, and early Colonial Revival architectural details to builders all over the state. The lumber industry (primarily sawmills) was so extensive and the companies so successful that Clinton early on had its own contingent of local millionaires, many of whom built substantial houses along South Fifth Avenue and elsewhere. By the mid-1890s, with the depletion of timber, the city experienced a severe depression. Slowly, in the early 1900s, new industry was introduced to the community, but its growth in the remainder of this century has been slow and modest.

In addition to its wide, tree-lined suburban streets, the city developed River View Park, between the railroad and the river's edge, and to the north, Eagle Park. Within the city itself is Mount Pleasant Park (to the west of South Bluff Boulevard at Second Avenue) which from 1883 on was the site for the local Chautauqua meetings. The park contains a number of small cottages, some of which date back to the 1880s.

The city of Lyons, platted north of Clinton in 1877, was annexed in 1895; two years previously, Chancy had been annexed to the southwest. The joining of the two cities of Clinton and Lyons accounts for the second small "downtown" one encounters on Main Avenue, north of Twenty-third Avenue North.

ME056 Chicago and Northwestern Railroad Swing Bridge

1909; SE 2nd St. and 8th Ave. S.

This swing bridge gives the delightful appearance of a child's Erector set that had been enlarged, and it was put together like one. It is a handsome and above all a playful-looking object. This is the third bridge on the site. The first bridge was a wooden Howe truss structure built during the years 1864–1865.

ME057 Curtis Woodworking Company Buildings

Southwest corner 2nd St. S. and 12th Ave. S.

The brick two- and three-story factory buildings on this industrial site date from the late 1870s through the 1920s. The original small two-story office building is mildly Italianate; the buildings of the years 1910–1930 refer in passing to Beaux-Arts Classicism. The Curtis Company, along with Morgan Woodwork of Baltimore (founded in 1855), was one of America's principal suppliers of wood architectural parts, such as doors, windows, and cabinets. The company's products were most closely associated with the Colonial Revival. Curtis was started in 1866, and by the 1920s it had branches throughout the Midwest. It was one of the first producers of architectural parts to establish an extensive national advertising campaign, and it was also one of the first to engage nationally known architects to design its products. Among these architects were Russell Whitehead, Dwight James Baum, and the firm of Trowbridge and Ackerman. The company developed an ideal suburb, Castle Terrace, in Clinton. The company ceased production in 1966.

ME058 Milwaukee Passenger Station

1915–1917. 317 11th Ave. S.

The central section of the cruciform-plan station announces through its height, large arched windows, and doors that this is the main waiting room of the station. The two somewhat lower wings to each side have a pattern of arched openings. In style the station's precedent is the French and Italian Romanesque. The terracotta band of corbeled arches below the eaves and gable ends and the brickwork are particularly impressive.

ME059 Pierson Block

1888. 920–926 S. 4th St.

The glory of this three-story brick block rests in its thin cornice centering on the large decorated plaque giving the building's name and date. On the street level the center storefront remains basically intact.

ME060 Sisco-Hiubek House

c. 1868. 505 10th Ave. S.

This two-story brick Italianate house has a later (c. 1910) Colonial Revival porch.

ME061 Weston House

c. 1869. 538–540 10th Ave. S.

The two-and-a-half-story entrance tower of this French Second Empire house has an unusual vertical diamond window that plunges into the mansard roof. To the right is a lower bay tower with a curved segmented roof and small oval dormer windows. The wood shingle pattern and the ironwork on the cross of the tower are still in place. Later modifications and additions have been made to the house, but its picturesque roofscape remains.

ME062 Saint Mary's Roman Catholic Church

1884–1888, Josiah L. Rice. 520 9th Ave. S.

The interpretation of the Gothic here seems to be composed of three or more layers piled on one another. This layered effect, emphasized by horizontal stone banding placed in the brick walls, is countered by the verticality of the numerous windows and recessed panels. Next door, at 516 Ninth Avenue South, is the rectory, designed by Josiah L. Rice in 1896. Its image is that of the Queen Anne style, with a few Richardsonian Romanesque elements touched in.

ME063 Clinton Public Library

1903–1904, Patton and Miller. 306 8th Ave. S.

Here the Beaux-Arts cause is stated without restraint. The atmosphere of the building is like that of the classically inspired buildings of the 1893 World's Columbian Exposition at Chicago, or the 1904 Louisiana Purchase Exposition at Saint Louis which was being planned at the same time as this library building. Balustraded stairs lead up to a grandly scaled entrance defined by two pairs of Tuscan columns. The gray color of the smooth, finely cut limestone surfaces of the building has weathered into a mellow tone, suggesting great age. Some insensitive post-World War II changes have been made to the building—aluminum entrance doors were added, a metal railing now appears on the side of the entrance steps—but the strength of the original design overcomes these intrusive elements.

ME064 National Guard Building

c. 1947, E. Bert. 213 6th Ave. S.

This two-story 1930s Moderne building was finally constructed after World War II. A protruding curved molding meanders up and down the marble facade, connecting all the windows and the entrance. A dramatic eagle with outstretched wings appears on top of the central door molding, and six standing figures of warriors occupy the recessed spandrels between the first- and second-floor windows.

ME065 Wilson Building

1912–1914, John Morrell and Sons. 217 5th Ave. S.

The Wilson Building is Clinton's one skyscraper, a six-story commercial building clothed in a creamy white terracotta. The architects have contained the windows within a frame from the second to fifth floors. The vertical sections of this frame have been articulated by fluting to suggest that they are piers.

ME066 Van Allen Department Store

1913–1915, Louis H. Sullivan. 200 5th Ave. S.

This is Louis Sullivan at his best. He took the theme of horizontality which he had used on the earlier Carson, Pirie, Scott Department Store building in Chicago (1899–1904) and applied it in a simplified fashion to the upper three floors of this building. As in the Carson, Pirie, Scott store, Sullivan treated the sidewalk-level first floor as a wide open space with large showcase windows. He penetrated down through the horizontal banded windows of the fourth through the second floors with three theatrical explorations of rich terracotta ornament. They seem to have been conceived as stylistic flowers: their stems grow from a stylized brick segment suggesting earth, and flowers burst forth at the top. The building exhibits an array of fascinating details, such as the surface play between the projecting horizontal band connecting the window sills and the flat, horizontal surface band that serves as a continuous header for the windows. In the upper window pattern on the Fifth Avenue side, Sullivan altered slightly the basic balanced symmetry of the repeated openings by using only one double-hung window on the left and then a single sheet of glass on the right.

As with Sullivan's late Prairie banks, the Van Allen Store indicates the vigor and inventiveness of the architect during his late years. The play of the rich projecting terracotta ornament (particularly the three flowerlike cartouches above the fourth-floor windows) against the plain horizontal brick surfaces of the building was a design theme that he utilized in a good number of his late buildings. A similar relationship of ornament to the building surfaces—reminiscent of the Churrigueresque—is found in his Merchant's National Bank at Grinnell (1914), in his Home Building Association Bank (1914) at Newark, Ohio, and in his People's Savings and Loan Association Bank (1917–1918) at Sidney, Ohio.

The exterior of the Clinton building remains essentially intact. A few changes have come about, including the elimination of the small square Luxor Prism windows above the showcase windows, and the introduction of repeated dark signage within the lower sections of the upper three floors of windows. Plans are currently being made by the architect Crombie Taylor and others to adapt the building to some type of new community use.

ME067 First National Bank Building

1911–1912, John Morrell and Sons. 226–228 5th Ave. S.

This is a lively Beaux-Arts design that strongly establishes its presence on the street. The architects have achieved this success by creating strong accents of highlighted surfaces played against dark shadows and recessed areas. At the center is a Roman temple with columns in antis, the two Ionic columns flanking the entrance. Above is a deep tympanum in the pediment with a dramatic eagle that catches fragments of sunlight. The modernists were at it; in this case they broke the verticality of the temple front and the entrance with a V-shaped marquee, which fortunately has been removed.

ME069A Clinton High School (Roosevelt School)

ME068 United States Post Office Building

1901–1902, James Knox Taylor, Louis A. Simon. 301 5th Ave. S.

The post office building is a polished, sophisticated exercise in the Beaux-Arts mode. The smooth, finely cut limestone has accentuated horizontal joints; the entrance, composed of three arches, is set behind a pair of engaged Ionic columns. The entablature, projecting cornice, and roof balustrade tie everything together and effectively terminate the structure. To the rear is a sympathetic addition of 1934.

ME069 Clinton High School (Roosevelt School)

1888–1889, Josiah L. Rice. 600 S. 4th St.

One could well drive by this two-and-a-half-story Romanesque Revival building and assume it was a county courthouse rather than

ME069B Clinton High School (Roosevelt School), detail

a school building. The architect produced a square box and then through a slight play of surfaces and the injection of a corner tower, roof gables, and dormers, he was able to produce a picturesque form. The usual Richardsonian ornament is present, including the sunflower motif.

ME070 First Baptist Church

1870, 1887, Josiah L. Rice. 620 S. 4th St.

The style of this church is loosely Romanesque, but not of the Richardsonian variety. The composition of the entrance facade of this church works around the theme of walls with vertical recessed panels and gable roofs. The long, narrow wing to the right has a deeply cut arched opening balanced on each side by two shallow panels. The open wood-shingled tower was added in 1887 during a rebuilding of the church after a fire.

ME071 First Presbyterian Church

1917–1919, Coolidge and Hodgdon. 400 5th Ave. S.

Churches of the 1920s, and period revival designs in general, have an ease about them, as if everything were accepted and effortless. Limestone Gothic churches such as this were built all over the country in the decades of the twenties and on into the thirties. The upper-middle-class Presbyterians almost seem to have created their own recognizable version of the rural English Gothic. Their church complexes were more often than not placed on large, well-landscaped sites; the buildings were low in scale, and rambling. While they were authentic in their use of Gothic sources, there is a pronounced modernity about the resulting buildings. The Clinton church presents a gable-roofed entrance front to the street; it is dominated by a window surmounted by a wide pointed arch. The walls to the side are treated as three receding layers of buttresses; the entrance door has a strong domestic scale about it.

ME072 George W. Curtis House (now Clinton Women's Club)

c. 1880. 420 5th Ave. S.

What would have been aptly labeled a "substantial" dwelling of the decade of the 1880s, the George Curtis house is a textbook Queen Anne design in brick, stone, stucco and half-timbering, and fishscale shingles. On the east side an adventuresome third-floor porch projects out, supported by large consoles. All of the picturesque gable ends have varied patterns of half-timbering. The house also contains some excellent examples of leaded stained glass. The present entrance porch, slightly Craftsman in feeling, was added in the teens to replace the original wood porch. The adjoining coach house (now used as the Carriage House Theater) to the west of the house was designed around 1885 as a calmer version of the Queen Anne style by the Clinton architect Josiah L. Rice.

ME073 Charles F. Curtis House

c. 1885. 417 5th Ave. S.

This house reveals the Queen Anne style as seen through the eyes of a Richardsonian Romanesque architect. The usual complexity of surfaces and details has been replaced by the plainness of masonry walls of brick and sandstone. Compared to his brother's house across the street, Charles Curtis's dwelling bespeaks reserve and confidence. As with the George Curtis house, this dwelling still has its carriage house, also by Josiah L. Rice, c. 1885.

ME074 Universalist Church (Apostle Church of God; Sacred Heart Roman Catholic Church)

c. 1875, W. Pahley, architect and builder. c. 1893. 316 S. 4th St.

The church as we see it today is the result of extensive remodeling of the building in the early 1890s. The church's front main gable seems randomly punctured with several sizes of pointed-arched windows, and the walls of the tower have Gothic windows and quatrefoil windows above. While the design is Gothic, it is hardly a traditional one.

ME075 The Hair Stable

1905. 216 S. 2nd St.

The designer of this two-story brick commercial building was obviously interested in getting as much as possible into his 20-foot-wide street frontage. On the street level are two entrances, one to the store, the other to the stairs leading to the second floor. Between them is a large glass shop window, separated from the two entrances by slender cast-iron columns. A large-scale metal-roofed bay projects from the second level; above is a pressed metal entablature, cornice, and pedimented finials. Without the date placed in the pediment one would normally have assumed that a design such as this would have been produced in the 1880s or early 1890s.

ME076 Roehl/Phillips Furniture Store

1960, Phil Feddersen. 308 S. 2nd St.

In the decades of the 1950s and early 1960s, modernism, especially related to small commercial buildings, was remarkably varied. In the Roehl/Phillips building the architect has gone back to the early-twenties Modern style closely associated with the Dutch designer Willem Dudok. The front conveys a well-thought-out composition, which together with the company's lettering becomes a sign. On the ground level, Feddersen created a low, domestic scale with overhanging canopy and thick piers. Attached to the ends of the canopy are projecting stucco balconies with windows behind; a louvered rectangle of vents continues to the pencil-line cornice.

ME077 Pahl Building

c. 1916, Gus Ladehoff, designer/builder. 402–406 S. 2nd St.

Terracotta sheathing used to face commercial buildings enjoyed great popularity during the years 1900 through 1930. A creamy white glazed terracotta has been employed in the two-story Pahl building. This surface has been delicately enriched by three narrow horizontal bands of Sullivanesque ornament. The cornice has another band together with a cartouche that projects above the parapet. The design of this cartouche seems directly derived from the designs of Sullivan's associate, George Grant Elmslie. Another, smaller two-story commercial building with Sullivanesque ornament is the Charles Koons Building (c. 1919) situated at 512 South Second Street. Both buildings have suffered from modernization on their ground floors.

ME078 First United Methodist Church

1902–1903, Sidney J. Osgood. 621 S. 3rd St.

The Grand Rapids architect of this building was active in producing designs for county courthouses and churches in the Midwest. His church in Clinton is a small, romantic, medieval pile. The street corner works around a round bay tower; at the opposite end of the recessed gabled facade is an octagonal tower. The lantern that stood at the peak of the highest roof is now gone, and metal-and-glass doors now provide entrance into the building.

ME079 Clinton County Courthouse

1892–1897, G. Stanley Mansfield, Josiah L. Rice. 612 N. 2nd St.

The design is that of a red sandstone Romanesque square block, articulated by round towers at each corner. From the center of the building rises a low, Romanesque-inspired tower clad in green patinated copper. The Freeport, Illinois, architect G. Stanley Mansfield was one of eight architects who competed for the project. According to Ronald E. Schmitt,[11] the tower as built differs from the original design, being a more abstracted version of the Romanesque. It was most likely the product of the local architect Josiah L. Rice. The exterior of the building remains basically as built; however, numerous changes have occurred in the interior.

ME080 Schall's Candy Store

1917. 501 N. 2nd St.

The feature that immediately captures one's attention on the street facade of this two-story commercial building on a raised basement is the central, colored terracotta decoration. The design of the ornamentation is Sullivanesque, but modified and more literally within the Gustav Stickley-Craftsman tradition. The curvilinear Sullivanesque patterns read as the foliage of a pair of trees. To the sides of the main terracotta panels are two small vertical shieldlike motifs with the company's initials on them.

ME081 Lighthouses

c. 1935. Leo F. Hannaher. Riverview Park, opposite the east ends of 4th and 5th avenues S.

Three miniature ornamental towers take the form of lighthouses. Their masonry faceted shafts are topped by open metal lanterns with metal domed roofs. They were constructed during the depression years by the WPA.

ME082 Municipal Swimming Pool

1929, Walter E. Bort. Riverside Park, east of S. 1st St., east of 1st Ave.

A popular image for recreational buildings throughout the country from 1900 through the 1930s was the Mission Revival style or the later Spanish Colonial Revival style. The composition of this stucco-sheathed building with its paired low, hip-roofed towers and central loggia is Mission rather than Spanish Colonial Revival, although the proportions of the three-arched loggia are reminiscent of the Spanish Colonial Revival.

ME083 **Riverview Stadium**

1936–1937, A. H. Morrell. Riverview Park, east of 2nd St. and S. 6th Ave. N.

This outdoor baseball stadium of brick and stucco was styled in a combination of late-1920s Art Deco verticality and 1930s Streamline Moderne horizontal stripping. The principal ticket booth and adjoining gateposts are particularly effective, posing as miniature buildings. The project was one of those in Clinton sponsored by the WPA. Also in Riverview Park is the Memorial Flag Pole (1930); its base displays cast bronze figures designed by Leonardo Runcelle. It is located in the park off the east end of Fifth Avenue South.

ME084 **Seaman House**

1904, John Morrell and Son. 516 5th Ave. S.

What was meant to be read as a substantial "mansion" was realized within the Beaux-Arts tradition. Its first-floor base is rusticated, and the upper two floors of smooth-surfaced brick and terracotta are held in place by a broad overhanging "Italianate" tile hipped roof. Other classical motifs are the entrance porch with its four Ionic columns and roof balustrades and the central Palladian windows and door above the entrance. The building has been converted into apartments.

ME085 **Sherman Seaman House**

1909. 746 5th Ave. S.

The two-story, hip-roofed Prairie-style box has its living porch to the front and entrance to the side. The headers of the second-floor double-hung windows are directly below the stucco roof soffit, and a horizontal wood band ties the window sills together.

ME086 **T. J. Hudson House**

1914, John Morrell and Son. 823 5th Ave. S.

This is another Prairie-style house with side entrance and living porch across the front. Large, squat, "primitive" columns have been used on both the entrance and living porches. The adjacent garage would appear to be original to the house.

ME087 **Fred Van Allen House**

John Morrell and Son. 844 5th Ave. S.

A tiled hipped roof and an entablature with windows crown this two-and-a-half-story stucco-sheathed box. Everything seems over-scaled on the front elevation except for the pair of bay windows that seem to belong to a smaller, less formal house. This dwelling, with a few nods to the Chicago work of George W. Maher, was designed for one of the owners of the Van Allen Department Store, who in 1913 engaged Louis H. Sullivan for its design (see ME066).

ME088 **Walsh House**

1893–1897. 915 5th Ave. S.

The silhouette of this dwelling, with its segmented domed bay and tower, is Queen Anne; but the simplified details, the Tuscan columns, and the flowing shingle-and-stone surfaces point to the rising popularity of the Colonial Revival style in the 1890s. The house was originally designed and built for G. L. LeVeille, the first contractor for the courthouse. Because of difficulties with the courthouse construction, he left town, and Walsh purchased and completed the house.

ME089 **Washington Junior High School**

1933–1935, Karl Keffer and Earl E. Jones. 751 2nd Ave. S.

This two-story school in brick with stone trim is an example of the late-twenties Art Deco Moderne. In the entrance pavilion the architects have played on the theme of verticality, with the whole of the entablature composed of deeply shadowed vertical bands. Two panels with stylized eagles project above the central parapet. Later, unrelated additions were made in 1952 and 1957.

ME090 **Walter E. Bort's Stone Tower Studio**

c. 1923–1953, Walter E. Bort. 722–732 S. 12th St.

For his own studio and house, the architect Walter E. Bort took an existing brick farmhouse and through the years added stone and wood components, producing the wonderful poetic effect of a medieval Cotswold village.

ME090 Walter E. Bort's Stone Tower Studio

The village quality is enhanced by stone walls that seem to flow from the building and by the thick plantings of trees and shrubs on the half-acre site. This interpretation of the English medieval beautifully sums up the elusive element of charm that the period revival architects of the 1920s sought to realize.

ME091 House

c. 1928. 1354 8th Ave. S.

The curvilinear, picturesque pattern of streets in the suburban enclave of Castle Terrace was platted in 1892, but the area was not extensively developed until the 1920s. Many of the upper-middle-class period revival houses of the late twenties were built by the Curtis Woodworking Company. The image most frequently used was the medieval English or French. This particular stone and half-timber house is English Tudor, and it commands its wooded hilltop location.

ME092 Cottage

c. 1928; 1332 Caroline Ave.

This is another of the period revival houses of Castle Terrace. In this case the mode is that of a Colonial cottage that centers on a tall divided chimney; low to the side is the suburban necessity of an attached garage.

ME093 Charlton House

1910, John Morrell and Son. 1100 Woodlawn

The Charlton house is a Colonialized Craftsman bungalow in which attention is centered on a wide pedimented open porch supported by four columns in an order that seems related to the Doric. The porch has been successfully glassed in with narrow transomed casement windows.

ME094 Eugene J. Curtis House

1921, Trowbridge and Ackerman. Hillcrest Dr., S. Heather Lane

The Curtis family engaged the New York firm of Alexander B. Trowbridge and Frederick Lee Ackerman to design this large-scale country house. Its character is established by a steeply pitched hipped roof, immense chimneys, and lower bay windows that tie the building to its site. The building is similar to work produced in England in the teens and twenties by Ernest Newton and M. H. Bailey Scott. The design could be thought of as a rationalized medievalism. In this version the ground floor opens up extensively to gardens and terraces through numerous bands of casement windows and doors and through several wide bay windows.

ME095 McGauvran House

1963, Phil Feddersen. 405 Oakhurst Dr.

The Clinton architect Phil Feddersen designed several well-carried-out interpretations of Frank Lloyd Wright's single-story Usonian schemes of the 1930s through the 1950s, of which this house is one. The Mc-Gauvran house is sheathed in brick. A hipped roof with a wide fascia/entablature seems to hold the house to the ground. Another example of this architect's Usonian designs is the Vandiren house (1961, 3800 Lakewood Drive). In that house the architect used limestone for the walls, again contained by a low, wide overhanging hipped roof.

ME096 House

c. 1930. Northeast corner Oakhurst Dr. and 4th St. N.

A romantic twenties composition, this rough limestone-sheathed two-story French Norman suburban house peeks out of a thick, heavy forest of conifers. In the ell of the two wings is a round tower surmounted by a high conical roof.

ME097 **Gates House**

1902–1903. 500 Oakhurst Dr.

Here is one of those exotic instances of California's Mission Revival reaching into the Midwest. The white stucco surfaces of the scalloped, parapeted cowls of the various gable ends contrast with the dark red tile roof.

ME098 **Cotton House**

1853. 316 18th Ave. N.

This is a textbook example of the Gothic Revival cottage, right out of one of the works of A. J. Downing. The one-and-a-half-story cottage has heavily molded, pointed windows and doors, a porch supported by delicate wood piers with sawed work above their capitals, and board-and-batten walls. The major external change in the house is the replacement of the original steeply pitched roof by a lower gambrel roof, in the aftermath of a fire in 1943.

ME099 **Lyons Female College** (now Our Lady of Angels Seminary)

1858. 407 22nd Ave. N.

The central three-and-a-half-story brick building is Italianate. At the center of the building is a large, high cupola, and above its bracketed, extended eaves is a small drum and bulbous dome. The later south building is Romanesque Revival with some detailed wood touches of the Queen Anne.

ME100 **Grace Episcopal Church**

1856. 2100 N. 2nd St.

This is a mid-nineteenth-century interpretation of the tradition of the rural or village

ME100 Grace Episcopal Church

English church. The scale is small, as is generally the case with Episcopal churches, and the fineness of detailing is well carried out. In plan, this church has a corner entrance tower and buttressed side walls. In 1898 two bays were added to the church; in 1904 the ceiling was removed and the beamed roof was exposed.

ME101 **United Methodist Church**

1856, 1893. 2118 N. 2nd St.

Parts of the first church building, which was partially destroyed by fire in 1892, are visible on the side. The "new" 1893 front is an intriguing interpretation of the Richardsonian Romanesque. The low stone-and-brick entrance tower (perhaps originally planned as a bay) has a split band of deep grillelike windows above the door; a similar deeply set group occurs well below the Roman arched window; and a third group crops up on the right tower. Certainly a spire must have been planned for the right-hand tower. All in all, the front of the building has the adventurous sprawl of a planned ruin.

ME102 **Iowa Savings Bank Building**

1914, Harry R. Harbeck. 122 Main Ave.

This tall, thin Sullivanesque bank is, when one stops and carefully looks at it, a surprisingly original design. The architect has employed the Sullivanesque scheme of a pier with terracotta capital as a repeated motif on both sides of the building. Then, in a different color and laid brick, he has suggested that each wide vertical panel contains a stylized Doric pilaster. Each of the four repeated bays is covered by a terracotta gabled cornice, with a curvilinear cartouche at the peak. The small entrance that originally stood in the center of the narrow south facade is now gone. A simple but sympathetic addition was made to the rear of the building in 1931; in 1967 a new arched wing was projected off to the east. The building has now acquired a revolving sign at the corner.

ME103 **Lyons High School** (Nee-Hi Hall)

1905. 96 Main St.

Semicircular wall dormers, filled with ornament, terminate each of the end portions of this two-story school building on a raised basement. The detailing, such as the highly contrasting stone quoins, is classical, with a somewhat mild Georgian Revival quality.

ME104 **Saint Irenaeus Catholic Church**

1864–1865. 2811 N. 2nd St.

From its high, hilltop location, this double-towered stone church looks down on what was once the river town of Lyons. The pointed-arched windows of this Gothic Revival church are finely cut into the walls of beautifully dressed light-colored limestone. A rosette window appears in the east gable. The twin belfry towers support thin spires above; the north one is 136 feet high, the south one 30 feet higher.

ME105 **Silas Gardiner House**

c. 1878, George Palliser and Charles Palliser. 2700 N. 2nd St.

In style, this house is Eastlake with a few Queen Anne overtones. The building was designed by the New York firm of Palliser and Palliser and was illustrated on plate 26

in their 1878/1888 publication *Palliser's American Architecture*. The architects described the Gardiner house as being of the "Jacobite Period." They noted that in this house, "the roofs are shingled and painted black; the exterior walls are painted—body of the work Venetian Red and trimmed in Indian red, and cut work in black: each cut in with yellow; panels under veranda floors yellow." Palliser and Palliser published a number of pattern books between 1876 and 1893, and in them they advertised not only their professional services but also plans from their books, which could be ordered for a modest sum. The fact that the Gardiner house was illustrated and under the client's name would strongly suggest that he commissioned the design from the architects.

ME106 **Eagle Point Park**

North end of N. 3rd St. at N. Stockwell Lane

Within the park situated on a cliff overlooking the Mississippi River are three structures of note. These are, first, a stone lookout tower (1937), a 35-foot-high double-tiered circular tower with crenellated walls. It poses like a folly in an eighteenth-century English garden, as a fragment of a ruined castle. The second is a lodge (c. 1913, c. 1935, and 1967), a stone and wood-clad recreation building situated on a stone podium. The single gabled roof with an extension at the lower pitch covers the entire building. The 1966–1967 changes designed by Phil Feddersen, like the WPA alterations of the thirties, have both respected and added to the lodge's successful rustic image. The third noteworthy structure is a foot bridge (c. 1937), a narrow, graceful stone pedestrian bridge that spans a small ravine. The walkway gently slopes down to the arched sections and then slowly rises on the opposite bank.

ME107 **Warburg College** (now Glenwood Apartments)

1893–1894. West on 8th Ave., south to S. 18th St., south on S. 18th St. to East Lane, north on East Lane to campus

Here we have the Collegiate Romanesque in brick with stone trim. The main building, which was built as a student dormitory, is three and a half stories high; over this tall mass of masonry is a high central tower with a segmented spired roof. Close by the main building is another dormitory building, Cotta House (now an apartment building). The designer of this 1922–1923 building looked to the seventeenth-century Queen Anne period in England for a source.

Davenport

The early history of Davenport was closely tied to that of Rock Island in the Mississippi River (between Iowa and the Illinois shore where the river curves to the west).[12] In 1816 the federal government established Fort Armstrong on the island. Two prominent figures who later were to be involved with the founding of Davenport were Col. George Davenport, a fur trader, and Antoine Le Claire, an early landowner. In 1836 a six-by-seven-block grid was laid out on the Iowa shore. Since a segment of the river at this point runs east-west, the grid was oriented parallel and perpendicular to the river. The area adjacent to the riverbank was reserved as "public grounds," and three additional sites were reserved within the grid for public uses. It was noted in the mid-1850s that the city was "delightfully situated on the west bank of the Mississippi, with a bluff 100 foot high skirting its back, and extending for miles up and down the river."[13]

From its beginnings Davenport was both fortunate and aggressive in its economic development. Very early, levees were built at the river's edge so that steamboats could tie up directly at the shore. The city was also the site of the first bridge across the Mississippi (1856). This was a complex wood truss bridge (called the White Bridge because of its paint color) placed on a series of large stone piers. By the seventies, the city was a major railway center for both east-west and north-south traffic. From its earliest years the city also profited by its proximity to the industrial cities of Moline and Rock Island across the river in Illinois. In the late 1880s, Willard Glazier observed of Davenport that "handsome houses dot the bluffs. River views for residences have been extensively occupied by the well-to-do citizens, and the scope of the country brought within range of the eye from some of these hill-top dwellings is scarcely to be excelled for beauty as anything I have seen on the river."[14]

The residential areas for the middle class and the wealthy tended to extend toward the hills west of the downtown and especially to the northwest, where in many cases they did indeed encompass the views Glazier mentioned. Several of the more prestigious of these developments were Prospect Park (1894), laid out around Prospect Rock, and McClellan Heights (1906) to the north. McClellan Heights was laid out in a rolling wooded section, and its street patterns were accommodated to the terrain.

During its early years the city saw a number of Greek Revival structures built.[15] These included the 1842 Scott County Courthouse, the Mount Ida Female College (1857), and the two-story columned house of Dr. E. S. Barrows (c. 1853). More modest Federal and Greek Revival structures were built also

Davenport

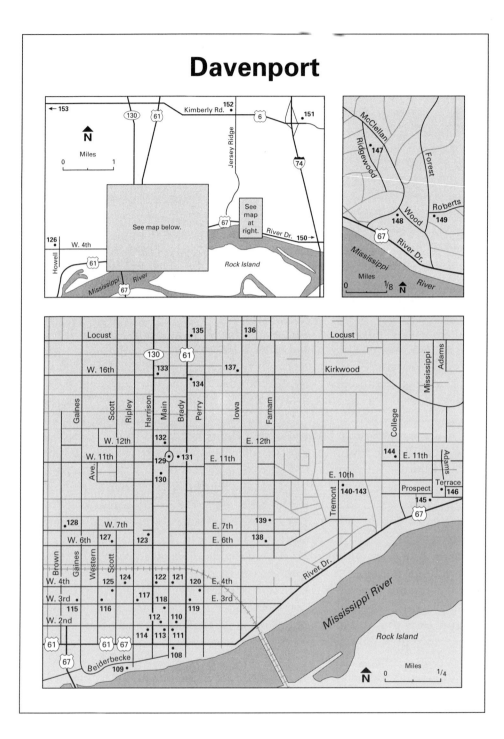

for commercial and residential use. Few of these classically inspired buildings remain. One exception would be the Shick Apartments of 1852 (at 201–314 Gaines Street). These two-story row houses on raised basements were constructed of local limestone. Contemporary with these classical modes were versions of the Italian or bracketed style. Early, extant examples of this style would be the Mario Clare Dessaint House (c. 1865–1870), an Italianate villa (at 4807 Northwest Boulevard), and the John Littig house (c. 1867) which, as so often happened, combined the Italian and the Gothic into a single composition. The most stately of these early Italianate houses was the Antoine and Marguerite Le Claire residence (1855), which fortunately is still standing (at 630 Seventh Street).

Along with continual and at times repeated changes within the city, transformations were taking place by way of major engineering projects associated with the river. In 1872 the earlier wood truss bridge was replaced by a new iron bridge. This bridge was provided with two levels, an upper one for trains and a lower one for wagons; it also housed a lift span, so that steamboats could easily pass through. In 1895 this bridge was in turn replaced by the all-steel "Government Bridge." In the mid-1930s, Dam and Lock 15 were completed. This metal roller-gate dam and lock projects a strong Streamline Moderne image, appearing almost like a 1930s futurist vision from Buck Rogers.

In 1911 the city formed the Levee Improvement Commission, a body that became the prime vehicle for initiating the City Beautiful movement within Davenport. It projected three blocks between Bradley and Scott (designed by the landscape architects Reeves and Ramsey in 1912), which would contain public buildings and a union railroad station, all in a parklike setting. Adjacent to the river, an English-style park was laid out between the railroad and a levee, and a small boat basin was planned. Extensive stone walls were constructed as a levee along the river, and a balustraded walkway ran along the top of much of it.

Architecturally the community mirrored what was going on elsewhere in the Midwest during the years after 1900.[16] There were occasional sallies into the more avant-garde styles. At 902 Cole Avenue, William Radcliff built himself an impressive Craftsman California bungalow (1911). A few years later a mild Prairie-style house was built at 2207 Brady Street (1912–1914).

The 1920s marked a high point for Davenport. It was during these years that the downtown sought through its skyscrapers to project the image of a major urban center. These were also the years of the construction of a good number of impressive period revival houses. The Great Depression of the thirties brought all of this to an end, and it was not until the end of the 1950s that there was a new surge of building. The thirties in Davenport is, in many ways, beautifully summed up in Helen Hinrichson's American Scene mural of 1936, *Davenport Marches On*. This was painted for one of the walls of the downtown

Walgreen Drug Store. The 30-foot-long mural can now be seen at the Davenport Art Gallery.

Post-1960 changes entail a new library building designed by Edward D. Stone (1967–1968, at 704 Brady Street) and a group of new buildings for the Davenport Museum (at the east edge of Fejervary Park, off Division St). This latter group includes the Putnam Museum (1962–1963; Palmer Wing, 1966) and the Davenport Municipal Art Gallery (1966; Wiese Wing, 1971). In the downtown area in and around Perry Street the city and private developers have since 1983 been creating River Center, which not only has linked a number of business and performing arts activities but also has combined old and new buildings (especially the Orpheum Theater and the Mississippi Hotel Building). The architect for this project was Roman Scholtz.

Much of the building from 1970 to the present has taken place north of the city in and around Interstate 80. One of the largest of these complexes is Northpark Mall (1973, 1981). Within this one-million-square-foot completely enclosed mall are 160 shops and five department stores. Since the mid-1970s there has been an intensified interest in historic preservation in Davenport. This has led to the funding of detailed historical studies and the establishment of historic districts.

ME108 Dillon Memorial Fountain

1918–1919, Franklin B. Ware and Arthur Ware, Paul Schulz. South end of Main St., south of River Dr.

The site for the fountain was determined by the Davenport landscape architectural firm of Reeves and Ramsey in their 1912 design for Water Front Park. The designers' Beaux-Arts plan, sponsored by the city's Levee Improvement Commission, envisioned a monument placed in the center of Main Street flanked on each side by public buildings in parklike settings. A national competition was held for the memorial fountain and it was won by the New York firm of Ware and Ware, and Paul Schulz. They provided a suave, sophisticated design with a fluted column set in a wreath-encircled base placed in the center of the fountain. On top of the column is a bronze lamp, well proportioned to the capital and column below.

ME109 Petersen Memorial Music Pavilion

1924. Southwest corner Ripley Ave. and Beiderbecke Dr.

The music pavilion is modeled rather clearly on Harrison Albright's design for the organ pavilion built for the 1915 Panama California International Exposition in San Diego, California. The California building, described as being based upon the Spanish Plateresque, is like the Davenport pavilion, a mixture of Hispanic Plateresque and late Renaissance elements. The designer of the Davenport pavilion nudged the building further toward the "correct" Beaux-Arts by simplifying the arched facade and by placing a freestanding Corinthian column on each side.

ME110 Putnam-Parker Buildings

1909–1910, Daniel H. Burnham and Company. 1920. 104 W. 2nd St.

The eight-story steel-frame Putnam Building (the westernmost section) was constructed first. It was designed as a modern multifloor department store by one of America's greatest turn-of-the-century architectural firms, the Chicago-based Daniel H. Burnham and Company. The exterior image was one often repeated at that time: the base consisted of the ground-floor show windows and entrances, above which was a mezzanine floor; above this was the simple brick shaft with its arrangement of paired windows. The capital of the building consisted of a projecting cornice, below which was a terracotta decorated band with oval and horizontal windows. In 1920 the seven-story Parker Building was constructed on the opposite corner, and the space between the two buildings was left as a large light court, with a single-story building as an infill. The newer Parker Building essentially followed the design pattern of the earlier one, with the exception of the shaft windows, which are wide Chicago windows.

ME111 **J. H. C. Petersen's Sons Company** (now Petersen, Harned, and Von Maur)

1892, Frederick G. Clausen. 219 W. 2nd St. / 131 W. 2nd St., southeast corner of Main St.

The Davenport architect took the late Richardsonian Romanesque as his theme for this four-story retail department store building. He used stone for the base and red brick above; he carried out the ornamentation in terracotta. Clausen attracted attention to the two street entrances by treating them as slightly projecting pavilions with a round-arched window above; the third and fourth floors exhibit curved bay window units. The store's name in terracotta within the entablature is akin to the letterhead of business stationery.

ME112 **Row of Retail Commercial Buildings**

c. 1937–1940. North side of W. 2nd St., between Main St. and Harrison Ave.

This remarkably well preserved streetfront of Streamline Moderne retail store buildings starts at one end with Grant's (1939–1940) and ends at the other with Walgreen's (c. 1937). Between these is a Lerner Shop, with its usual recessed center with narrow bands of glass brick, and three additional stores, including a Woolworth's. Some of the integral signage remains. The most impressive of these is for Grant's, where the two sets of letters appear on the corner curved parapet; they are realized in the same dressed limestone as the rest of the building.

ME113 **First National Bank Building** (now First Bank)

1923, Frank A. Childs and William Jones Smith. Southwest corner W. 2nd St. and Main St.

Both of the principals of this Chicago firm attended the Ecole des Beaux-Arts in Paris. Their nine-story Davenport Bank Building is a forceful testimony to their ability to carry on the classical tradition. Though they applied the usual design principle of base, shaft, and capital to the two street facades, they refined the building's finely cut limestone surfaces so that the plain walls dominate, and they laid on the usual classical detailing in a light, linear manner. On the recessed surfaces around the main entrance are eight panels of standing figures in relief. The entrance and lobby were "influenced by the Italian Renaissance and by the metal compositions in the Rejas of the Spanish Renaissance."[17] The ground-floor windows which light the main public banking room were divided into a horizontal window grouping below, then a paneled soffit, and finally an upper lunette window, with all of this detailing carried out in metal.

ME114 **Davenport Transportation Center**

1984–1985, Solomon Cordwell Buenz and Associates. Southwest corner W. 2nd St. and Harrison Ave.

A horizontally banded second floor projects out over a recessed columned loggia below. The center of the building exhibits a gentle curved bay that is almost Regency in feeling. The loggia and the curved glass-and-masonry wall above create a low pedestrian scale. This well-designed modern structure would be enhanced by the introduction of much more landscaping, especially good-sized trees and evergreen shrubbery.

ME115 Mass Building

1901. 702–704 W. 3rd St., northeast corner of Gaines Ave.

This is a three-story brick commercial building with a metal-clad corner bay tower and two angular bays that are also sheathed in metal. The design format is really taken from the nineteenth century, but the detailing leans toward the classical. The street floor has been appreciably modified.

ME116 Charles F. Ranzow and Son Paint Company Building

1875. 528–532 W. 3rd St., northeast corner of Western Ave.

An excellently preserved two-story brick commercial building, this structure is still occupied by its original tenants. Cast- and wrought-iron columns and storefronts appear on the first floor, where pressed metal was utilized for the cornice and for the central projecting pediment.

ME117 Kahl Building / Capitol Theater

1919–1920, Arthur Ebeling / Rapp and Rapp. 326 W. 3rd St., northeast corner of Ripley Ave.

The size and height of the Kahl Building indicate how aggressively the community was trying to create the aura of a big-city downtown. The ten-story building was delicately clad in white terracotta over a steel frame. The design was inspired by classical architecture, but its lightness hints at the Gothic or the Hispanic Plateresque. The building houses a restaurant in the basement, a 2,400-seat theater, and additional space for offices. The theater, designed by the well-known Chicago-based theater specialists Cornelius W. Rapp and George L. Rapp, is luxuriously classical, including the landscape murals within the three half-bays. (These murals were restored in 1968.) Missing from the theater's entrance is its original curved roof marquee with incandescent lights and its five-story vertical sign.

ME118 American Commercial and Savings Bank (now Davenport Bank and Trust)

1927, Weary and Alford. 203 W. 3rd St., southwest corner at Main St.

There has been a time-honored tradition for financial institutions to create the impression that they are a segment of the government, if not the government itself. This bank building of the late twenties carries out this illusion with great force. The 11 floors of the building are encompassed within a shell that alludes to the Greek; the layered domed bell tower could be an Athenian monument, while the ground floor takes one into the Hellenistic and Roman realms of the classical world. Equally Roman and Imperial is the three-story-high public banking room on the lower level. As is true with the nearby First National Bank Building (ME113), the limestone sheathing has been detailed to read as a thin skin, with the detailing carried out in a linear manner. As a skyscraper, the building functions well; at street level the treatment is that of a rusticated basement which is carried up to the second and third floors with pilastered walls and arched openings. The roofscape is highly effective, its central pedimented roof surmounted by the narrow, tall clock tower.

ME119 RKO Orpheum Theater and Mississippi Hotel (now Adler Theater)

1931, 1935–1936, A. S. Graven. 110 E. 3rd St.

This ten-story downtown theater and hotel block was the last major building completed in Davenport before the advent of the Great Depression. In style, the structure is Art Deco that has been highly simplified to express a sense of down-to-earth rationalism. The brick facade with metal spandrels is articulated by slightly recessed vertical bands containing paired windows. Two solid brick pavilions project out ever so slightly suggesting a Beaux-Arts Classical composition. The 2,700-seat theater (which is strongly Art Deco) was restored in 1985 and was reopened in 1986 as a performing arts center. It now forms part of the adjacent River Center.

ME120 United States Post Office and Federal Building

1932–1933, Seth J. Temple. Southwest corner of E. 4th St. and Perry Ave.

Although it was designed before the New Deal, this two-story stone-sheathed box seems to be of the PWA Moderne style. All of the elements of the building are kept close to the smooth stone surface; there is neither great depth nor any projections. The light-colored stone body of the building sits on a dark granite base. Two entrances with elaborated surrounds and accompanying light posts occur within the principal facade. The architect, Seth J. Temple (a graduate of Columbia University who had also attended the Ecole des Beaux-Arts in Paris), was following a course of abstracting the classical tradition, similar to that of the Philadelphia architect Paul Cret.

ME121 **Saint Anthony's Roman Catholic Church**

1850–1853, attrib. Father Samuel Mazzochelli. 407 Main St.

The tactile ashlar limestone walls of this church, with their corner quoining, effectively convey a sense of the primitive, of a beginning for the city. The plan of this Greek Revival church is that of a Latin cross, covered with low-pitched gable roofs. The windows are surrounded by finely cut stone and are round arched. The center arched entrance door is balanced on each side by doors with flat entablatures. Within, the sanctuary has side aisles and a nave covered by a barrel vault.

ME122 **Davenport City Hall**

1894–1895, John W. Ross. 226 W. 4th St., northeast corner with Harrison Ave.

This Richardsonian Romanesque city hall was designed by the Davenport architect John W. Ross after he won a national competition for the building. Ross employed the usual array of design features that had come to be associated with the style: a central open tower (more Spanish Romanesque than French) that works into the side of the principal gable; a round bay tower at one corner; a square hip-roofed tower at the other end; and, of course, the familiar wide arched openings. The building's steel frame is clad in horizontal blocks of rough and smooth sandstone. The building was "restored" during 1979–1981. Regrettably the new metal-framed windows have been brought out close to the adjoining masonry walls, thereby destroying the quality of the original design.

ME123 **Raphael Building**

1875, attrib. Jacob Raphael, builder. 628 N. Harrison Ave.

This two-story brick Italianate commercial block was meant to be experienced as two separate structures. The narrow one on the left has a gable roof, while the one on the right is parapeted with a metal projecting cornice. The segmental-arched second-floor windows are the same in both sections, as are the thin, elongated cast-iron Corinthian columns that articulate the two first-floor storefronts.

ME124 **Scott County Jail**

1897, Frederick G. Clausen and Parke T. Burrows. W. 4th St., between Ripley and Scott avenues

At the end of the nineteenth century, Italian architecture, particularly that of Tuscany and Lombardy, increasingly became one of the sources for American architecture. Often, as is the case with the Scott County Jail, there is a Romanesque rather than a Renaissance feel to these American interpretations. The hip-roofed tower of the jail building, with its row of three arched windows on each face, is just the sort of image one associates with the smaller cities and rural architecture of northern Italy. In this three-story building with a raised basement, the architects have employed roughly surfaced masonry up to the sills of the third-story windows and then introduced a band of finely surfaced masonry that continues up to the roof soffit.

ME125 Fraternal Order of Eagles Lodge

1923–1924, Rudolph Clausen and Walter O. Kruse. 324 Scott Ave.

The English Georgian style, with its association with London clubs and town houses, was frequently employed in the United States from the late nineteenth century on through the 1930s. Clausen and Kruse employed this image for their three-story club building. However, instead of using stone for trim in contrast with the variegated color and matte face of the brick, they used a mottled, buff-colored terracotta. Unusual for this building type is the devotion of the ground floor to the automobile: a garage and an auto showroom. A ballroom occupies the second floor, and a clubroom and other lodge space is on the third floor.

ME126 Monroe Elementary School

1939–1940, Childs and Smith; Kruse and Parrish. 1926 W. 4th St.

In the fall of 1940, Davenport opened up the six new school buildings. In imagery, three of these school buildings were English Tudor (see, for example, the Madison Elementary School, ME135). One was Georgian/American Colonial, and two (including the Monroe School) were Art Deco/Streamline Moderne. Of these six buildings, the Monroe School was without question the most impressive in quality of design. Its architects were also the most flagrant in their use of the Moderne image with its bands of windows, corner windows, glass brick, and curved walls.

ME127 Lambrite House

1855–1856, John C. Cochrane. 510 W. 6th St.

A wood-sheathed Italianate villa with a high tower placed within the front ell, the building has low-pitched roofs that are gabled, their eaves supported by brackets reinforced at each corner by additional pairs of heavy brackets. Numerous additions have been made to the house, but its Italianate qualities are so strong that these porches and two-story additions seem simply ready to be peeled off, so that the building could really reassert its full presence.

ME128 Wiese House

c. 1895, Gustav H. Hanssen. 709 Brown Ave.

Designs with an Islamic flavor began to enter the American scene in the 1880s, first as interior spaces (such as a "Turkish smoking room") or as garden pavilions. By the 1890s the image began to be used on exteriors, especially in Florida and California. The Islamic atmosphere of the Wiese house is primarily conveyed through its central three-story tower, modeled on examples from Moorish Granada in Spain. Other Moorish innuendoes are expressed in the columns, their capitals, and the tile roof.

ME129 Soldier's (Civil War) Monument

1880–1881, R. F. Carter. 1100 block of Main St., between 10th and 11th streets

Like the 1918 Dillon Memorial Fountain (ME108), the Soldier's Monument interrupts Main Street and forces the roadway to go around either side. The monument is also the center of the adjacent open spaces, with the high school on one side and the cathedral on the other. The monument itself has a dual base and an obelisklike shaft; on top of the capital is the statue of a Civil War soldier.

ME130 Davenport High School Building (now Central High School)

1904–1907, J. Temple and Parke T. Burrows. 1120 Main St.

In the central pavilion of this three-story building on a raised basement the architects provided a screen of Ionic columns and pilasters. The verticality of the columns and piers was carried up to the parapet through pairs of bold consoles. Though Beaux-Arts in design, the building's sandstone and brick walls tie it into the Richardsonian Romanesque of the late nineteenth century.

ME131 Grace Trinity Episcopal Church

1867–1873, Edward T. Potter. 1121 Main St.

The well-known architect of this church, Edward T. Potter of New York, was the brother of the Bishop of New York, and as such he received a number of commissions for Epis-

ME131 Grace Trinity Episcopal Church

copal churches. His design for the Davenport church was based upon English Gothic precedent, but he was highly inventive in his interpretation of this style. The narrow central nave of the church drops down slightly and then continues out over the side aisles with shed roofs. Buttresses along the side aisles bring the yellowish limestone walls right down to the ground. Within, "the aisles are divided from the nave by a row of slender and widely spaced iron columns, from which spring the arching timbers supporting the high roof."[18] Light enters the nave not only through a rose window and gabled dormers but through a thin continuous band of glass between the eave of the nave roof and the spring of the shed roofs of the side aisles. Foundations for a tower were laid at the time of construction, but it was never built.

ME132 **Parker-Ficke House** (now Delta Sigma Chi House)

1881–1884, attrib. Benjamin W. Gartside. 1208 Main St.

The French Second Empire style appears here in its most exuberant phase. The design was built around numerous pavilions and bays, each of which asserts its own identity primarily through separate mansard roofs. Each of these bays or pavilions is really quite small, so the general effect is that of seeing a French country chateau from some distance. Close up, the effect is that of a charming, somewhat enlarged (and unbelievable) dollhouse. This fragmented quality is enhanced by the highly contrasting trim of stone, wood, and cast iron which is played off the darker brick body of the building. The roofscape with its projecting tower and dormered mansard roofs is further enriched by metal rail crests and variously patterned and colored shingles.

ME133 **North Harrison Trust Company** (People's Trust and Savings)

c. 1915. 1601 Harrison Ave.

A small-scaled street-corner bank building conveys the needed aura of financial stability through its staid Beaux-Arts Classical imagery. The facade of the building, with its engaged Tuscan columns, has been realized in a light cream-colored terracotta.

ME134 **Miller House**

1981, Willett L. Carroll. 1527 Brady Ave.

In the Miller house, the architect has begun with an Italianate box and then elaborated its roof with Eastlake-inspired gambrel roof gables. The solidity of the brick walls and the heavy wood brackets contrast strikingly with the Gothic filigree of the Eastlake features of the design. Combinations of this type occur in several of the designs of the New York architect E. C. Hussey, in his 1876 pattern book *Home Building*. He writes that a "general disposition began to show itself in the part of designers to mix up French with the Swiss, and especially the Gothic, introducing gables, dormers and hoods of a decided Gothic character."[19]

ME135 **Madison Elementary School**

1939, Childs and Smith; Arthur H. Ebeling. Northeast corner Locust St. and Brady Ave.

In contrast to the contemporary Monroe Elementary School, which utilized the latest fashion, the Streamline Moderne style, the Madison School continues the English Tudor tradition. However, here the Tudor is not only simplified compared to the use of this style in the teens and twenties, it is also somewhat miniaturized, as if the architects wished to bring it all down to the scale of the child. The principal devices used to convey the medieval are second-floor oriel and bay windows that terminate the two low projecting wings.

ME136 **Retail Building**

c. 1940. Northeast corner of Locust St. and Iowa Ave.

The Streamline Moderne style was used here to provide a shell for a two-story corner commercial block. The street corner of the building on the second floor is curved and is accompanied by a pair of narrow vertical glass-brick windows. Toward the right side the parapet of the two-story section of the building curves down to the adjacent single-floor storefronts. The present storefronts appear to be later modifications of the original design, but the block still reads as a white Moderne object that seeks to project one into the new age.

ME137 **First Presbyterian Church**

1898–1899, Frederick G. Clausen and Parke T. Burrows. 316 Kirkwood Blvd.

In this reddish-brown sandstone church, the architects seemed to be looking back some fifteen years to the then-fashionable Richardsonian Romanesque. However, in contrast to Richardson, their interest appears to have been in the arena of richness and elaboration. Projecting from an octagonal sanctuary is the main entrance tower, a smaller octagonal tower to the left, and in front of this a broad porte-cochère. The surfaces are treated in alternating bands of smooth and rusticated masonry. The windows, doors, and balconies abound with coupled columns, cornices, and a wide array of ornamentation in low and high relief. The Presbyterian church is one of the most impressive Richardsonian Romanesque buildings still standing in Iowa.

ME138 **Smith-Murphy Octagon**

1854, Willett L. Carroll. 516 E. 6th St.

"Since, then, the octagon form is more beautiful as well as capacious, and more consonant with the predominant or governing form of nature—the spherical—it deserves consideration." So argued Orson S. Fowler in his little volume (1849 and 1852) *A Home for All; or, the Gravel Wall and Octagon Mode of Building* (p. 87). Within a few years after the publication of Fowler's ode to the octagon, owners and architects took up the form, and the Smith-Murphy house was one result. In general outline and plan, it would appear that the Davenport architect Willett L. Carroll studied the plates in Fowler's volume that illustrated the William Rowland house. Like the Rowland house, the Smith-Murphy octagon looked stylistically to the Italianate in its details, for example, the bracketed roof and multiple thin paired columns. The house now is devoid of much of its earlier wood detailing, but its basic form remains intact.

ME139 **Sharon House**

1891. 728 Farnam Ave.

This French Second Empire-style house, with its central Italianate tower and vertical windows, was stylistically late on the scene. The lower two floors of this brick dwelling, with their great bay windows, are relatively simple compared to the crescendo of activity that occurs within the mansard roofs and the tower. The angled front bays are treated as pavilions, and their concave roofs are dotted with dormers and surmounted by wrought-iron cresting. The tower, detailed with great brackets and roof crest, is almost entirely of glass.

ME140 **Saint Katherine's School**

1884, later. 901 Tremont Ave.

Saint Katherine's School for Girls was established in 1884 by the Episcopal Diocese, which at that time purchased the John L. Davies house (c. 1872). New buildings were erected and existing nearby houses were acquired on into the 1920s. Those of note follow.

ME141 **Davies House** (Cambria Place)

c. 1872. John Cochrane

This Victorian version of the Italianate Villa style is not only large and grand in size but it has acquired a variety of wood Eastlake details in sawed, turned millwork. Some changes and additions have been made to the two-and-a-half-story brick dwelling, but its essential character still remains.

ME142 **Renwick House**

1877; John C. Cochrane; H. G. Bramlick, landscape architect. 901 Tremont St.

The tower of the Italianate Villa-style Renwick house is even more elaborate in its detailing than that of the nearby Davies house. A Colonial Revival porch (c. 1900) has replaced the earlier system of porches that encompassed much of the ground floor of this limestone-walled "mansion."

ME143 **Classroom and Dormitory Building**

1884–1885, Edward S. Hammatt. 901 Tremont St.

The easiest answer to the question of style in this building is to revert to the popular term "Victorian." The French mansard roof is extensive and is supported by brackets. The narrow vertical windows and the gabled dormer have a Queen Anne flavor.

ME144 **Shaw House**

1901, Gustav A. Hanssen. 1102 College Ave.

The Shaw house not only commands a fine view of the river from its bluff location, it also bespeaks a calmness and assurance, qualities often found in these Queen Anne/Colonial Revival houses of the late nineteenth and early twentieth centuries. A three-story bay tower with curved corner gently disappears into the wide veranda below. The horizontality of that veranda, together with the breadth of the house itself, helps to tie the building to its extensive grassy site. The details of the house, ranging from the paired Roman Doric columns to the classical entrance, result from part of the intense interest in Colonial architecture during the decades after the United States centennial in 1876.

ME145 **Shuler House**

1905–1906, Frederick G. Clausen and Rudolph J. Clausen. 1 Prospect Terrace

Houses such as this were usually thought of as Georgian at the time they were built. In truth they really are a domestic version of the Beaux-Arts, for there is in fact very little that is either English or American Georgian about them. In the two-and-a-half-story Shuler house, one's attention is centered on the two-story Ionic columned porch with the first-floor veranda carefully tucked underneath it. The brick walls are appropriately quoined, and the third floor, which lies above the principal cornice, has round-arched dormer windows.

ME146 **Davidson House**

1896. 204 Prospect Ave.

In contrast to the Shuler house (ME145), the white clapboarded Davidson house reveals a classical vocabulary used to express the American Colonial Revival. The building's two-story pedimented entrance porch with Ionic columns suggests the earlier Greek Revival of the 1830s and 1840s. The wide entrance doorway is crowned by a Federal-inspired lunette window, and bracket-supported balconies appear below each of the principal windows on the front facade. The second-floor balcony within the portico has now been enclosed.

ME147 **Haas House**

1928. 129 Ridgewood Ave.

For a brief moment in the 1920s, the Spanish Colonial Revival and the Mediterranean (Italian) stucco house were the stylistic rage. Middle- and upper-middle-class home magazines abounded with these designs, as did the professional journals of these years. While everyone admitted that the style was eminently logical for Florida, Texas, and above all California, there were also arguments about the rationale for using this mode throughout the country. The Haas house would seem to look directly to examples from Southern California. As with the best examples in California, the Haas house plays off a few openings within its broad, rather abstract stucco walls. In truth, Spanish-inspired houses such as this work well in the Midwest and elsewhere. They seemingly become a part of the landscape through their earthy red tile roofs, and their white walls play off against the intensity of dark green foliage.

ME148 French House

1912–1914, Seth J. Temple and Parke T. Burrows. 2625 Wood Lane

The French house could be considered an excellent display of the design methods of the Ecole des Beaux-Arts, i.e., to analyze rationally the problem and then proceed without any specific stylistic image in mind. The French house thus is classical in its plan and proportions, and above all in its overriding principles. A central two-story pilastered pavilion projects forward from the mass of the house, which has a low hipped roof. On each side of the pavilion are two single-floor porches; together with the accompanying terrace, they offer a view to the Mississippi River. The house is built of reinforced concrete with hollow tile work as an infill. Decorative portions include half-timbering details at the gable ends and leaded glass (the leaded stained glass window at the stair landing depicts an idyllic woodland scene). The importance of the automobile is recognized in the important location of the garage building, toward the front of the house.

ME149 Bechtel House

1931. 9 Roberts Ave.

Along with the Spanish image, the French Norman enjoyed widespread popularity during the 1920s. In the Bechtel house, forms from Normandy and Brittany are piled together to form a wonderful, playful, and romantic country chateau. On one side of the wide Gothic-arched entrance is a circular stone tower with a conical roof. A second, smaller round tower at the other side provides transitions between the low left wing and the main two-story portion of the house. High-pitched slate-covered hipped roofs, tall chimneys, and even a small glass lantern present as picturesque a roofscape as one could ask.

ME150 Bruser House

1959, George Fred Keck and William Keck. 62 Elmhurst Lane (Riverdale)

Two rectangular volumes of the Donald Bruser house are sited right at the edge of a hill overlooking the Mississippi River valley. The house is two stories high on its garden facade, with views over the river. The usual array of materials associated with the Kecks is employed here: thin, brick-sheathed walls, wood, and glass. Another Keck and Keck house in the Davenport area is the similar Kirk Fowler dwelling of 1962. It is located at 2317 Washington Street, Bettendorf.

ME151 Jumer's Castle Lodge

1973–1974, Don Gullickson; Jumer's Construction / Gordon Burns and Associates. 1983–1984, tower. Northeast corner Hwy. 74 and US 6 (Bettendorf)

One can't easily miss this more than seven-story version of a Bavarian half-timbered building. The earlier part of the building was a modest three-story section, but it is the gabled and mansard-roofed tower that really announces the building to motorists on the highways. One enters the lodge through a sumptuously planted forecourt, crosses a heavy timbered bridge, and eventually ends up within an appropriate banqueting hall. The rooms are decorated according to someone's idea of the bedrooms of a Bavarian house.

ME152 Paul Revere Square

1984. Northwest corner US 6 (Kimberly) and Jersey Ridge Rd.

The time-honored American Colonial Revival was used here for a U-shaped retail center. Each of the three- or four-story brick buildings presents itself as an abstracted form, with major emphasis on the smooth, extensive brick walls. Within the central court is an open hip-roofed pavilion, which serves as a visual centerpiece. The open side of the court is approached by stairs that penetrate the terraced walls.

ME153 Schumacher House and Pharmacy (The Castle)

1905. 222 E. Bryant in Walcott

The small town of Walcott is situated 6 miles west of Davenport on US 6. Once in town, prepare yourself for a medieval scene, for the Schumacher building is indeed a castle. Across an open lawn is a medieval fortress with cornice turret towers, towers, and corbeled parapets. If you go closer you will find that all of this has been realized in pressed sheet metal.

ME154 **Nebergall Round Barn**

1914, Benton Steele. Near Blue Grass

The community of Blue Grass is situated 5 miles west of Davenport on US 61. The Nebergall round barn is on Telegraph Road, 2.5 miles east of route Y40 at Blue Grass. The architect/builder, Benton Steele, designed and constructed round barns throughout the Midwest from 1907 to 1923. The Nebergall barn is the only example of his work still standing in Iowa. The design is realized in terracotta bricks and board-and-batten wood siding; the barn has a double-pitched gable roof, topped at the center by a conical cupola.

DeWitt

The site of DeWitt on the high prairie was selected as the seat of Clinton County in 1840 because of its central location. Within the town's north-south, east-west grid, the public square was placed one block east of Church Street (the main street). By the 1870s DeWitt had become a junction point for the Chicago and Northwestern Railway and the Saint Paul Railroad. In fact the north-south line of the latter ended up running right up Church Street.

ME155 **United States Post Office Building**

1936, Louis A. Simon and Neal Melick. 510 9th St.

It is remarkable how many subtle variations on the Colonial Revival theme were worked out in the thirties by Simon and Melick. Here we have the usual brick box with a gable roof, but its point of difference is the entrance. It is recessed within a rectangle, and then it culminates in a high lunette window. In the public space inside is a 1938 WPA mural by John Bloom; the subject, farmers and a cornfield.

ME156 **House**

c. 1875. Northeast corner of 5th St. and 5th Ave.

This two-story Italianate house has a wrap-around Eastlake porch and a gable roof. The sawed work adjoining the porch piers and the paired brackets underneath the gable and the soffit are on the elaborate side.

ME157 **House**

c. 1908. 1204 6th Ave.

The two-story rectangular block, usually covered with a hipped roof, was a popular building type in the years 1900 through 1915. In this house the general feeling conveyed is that of the classical tradition: there are broad, wide window openings accompanied by a wraparound piered porch. This house is constructed of concrete block in a pattern that imitates ashlar stone blocks.

Dubuque

In the 1850s, before the Civil War, Dubuque was described as "one of the largest and most densely populated [cities] in the state." The city was "handsomely situated upon a natural terrace," and it was noted that "this city is more compactly built, and contains a greater portion of fine building than any other place in the state."[20] Dubuque's history of settlement is one of the oldest in Iowa, going back to 1788, when the Frenchman Julien Dubuque crossed over the Mississippi River to begin to mine lead. Mining operations were expanded

Dubuque

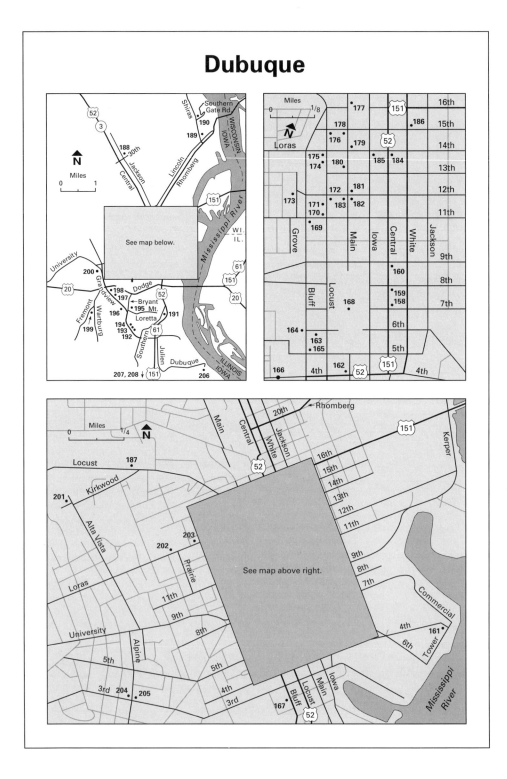

in the 1830s by the Langworthy brothers and thereafter by others. The first permanent settlement of Dubuque occurred in 1833, and the first platting of the town took place that year and was formalized in 1837. In the mid-1840s the federal government appropriated funds for a harbor improvement. In 1865, a 1,760-foot-long iron-and-stone bridge was completed across the Mississippi River, connecting the city to the Illinois Central Railroad. A few years later, in 1868, the Dubuque and Sioux City Railroad was completed west to the Missouri River. The 1865 railroad bridge was joined in 1887 by the Dubuque High Bridge, a bridge for wagons.

The first section platted for the city lay on a relatively flat field parallel to the river and its plain. This grid was laid out on a north-northwest by south-southeast axis. A large public square was provided at the base of the bluff, on Bluff Street between Sixth and Seventh streets. Later additions to the city adapted all sorts of different "paths" due in part to differences of ownership, the existence of the steep bluff, and other irregularities of the terrain. The steep bluffs and hills of the city encouraged the introduction in 1868 of horsecar service on a number of the streets. Electricity was introduced in 1889, and by 1917 the lines were extended in all directions. Buses were introduced in 1925, and the last of the streetcars ran in 1930. Unusual transportation systems within Dubuque were the two funicular railroads; one of these, the Fenelon Place Railroad, is still in existence.

In 1907 the nationally known city planner Charles Mulford Robinson made a number of City Beautiful proposals for the city. These entailed improving existing streets, providing new parks, and looking to the "improvement of the riverfront" as a public open recreational space. These proposals, as was usually the case, remained on paper. They were followed by a much more thorough and detailed Beaux-Arts city proposal by the Cambridge, Massachusetts, planners John Noland and Justis A. Hartzog. Among the recommendations contained in the 1932–1933 volume, *City of Dubuque, Iowa, Regional Plan,* was a new civic center to be located between Third Street and Seventh Street, and Locust and Bluff streets. The center of this composition was to be a city hall looking down the axis of Fifth Street to the river. It was to be balanced on the left by a new county courthouse and on the right by a new federal post office and courthouse building, but only the latter was built (1932).

As with other Iowa communities situated on the Mississippi, Dubuque acquired an impressive dam and lock set (No. 11). The dam and lock, located below Eagle Point Park, were started in 1933 and completed in 1937. Like the others on the river, this dam and lock convey a Streamline Moderne image in concrete and steel. In contrast, the housing and central office building constructed by the locks are Colonial Revival in style.

The economic foundations of the community have over the decades been varied. The initial basis was the mining of lead accompanied somewhat later by the city's involvement with steamboats and shipping. Once introduced, the railroad became an important industry. With the influx of central Europeans, breweries assumed importance in the city. By the early 1920s, a wide variety of manufacturing establishments were operating from Dubuque. Another "industry" of the city has been and remains its numerous institutions and schools run by the Catholic church, the Lutheran church, and other groups.

Like other early Iowa communities established on the west bank of the Mississippi River, Dubuque had even before 1850 acquired a number of major buildings, especially churches. The earliest, Saint Raphael's Roman Catholic Church (c. 1835), was a Greek Revival box with a front screen wall, a low-pitched gable roof, and round-arched windows. The uptown Catholic Cathedral (1847) and the church buildings for the Congregationalists and the Centenary Methodists were Greek Revival designs. The Episcopal and the Methodist Episcopal churches were Greek Revival structures modified by entrance towers, spires, pointed-arched windows, and crenellations so that they would read as Gothic. These early church buildings were either drastically enlarged in the following decades or were replaced entirely by new buildings; none of these first churches is still standing today. One of the pre-1860s churches still in use is the First Congregational Church at 255 West Tenth Street. It was designed by a local architect, David Jones, and was built between 1857 and 1860.[21] The style was Romanesque, though its telling features of a tower and spire were never built as designed.[22] The church has been appreciably modified, both internally and externally, but a close, careful look will reveal the original fabric of the building.

Certainly compared to most American cities, Dubuque has been able to retain a remarkable number of its earlier buildings and monuments.[23] Still, there have been major losses, many of which have occurred since 1945. The First Town Clock Building (1864) collapsed in 1872; earlier, in 1858, the five-story (Italianate) Saint Cloud Hotel, "The Largest Building in the Entire West," burned to the ground. Gone now are some of the city's "grand" houses of the nineteenth century: James Langsworthy's Greek Revival two-story house of 1849; James March's and John Emerson's houses, two impressive examples of the Italianate Villa mode; and F. E. Bissell / R. A. Babbages's Gothic Revival extravaganza of c. 1857. Losses also include the city's first octagon house, the 1857–1866 Federal Customs House and Post Office (designed by Ely S. Parker), and finally the splendid 1894–1895 Richardsonian Romanesque Central High School building (demolished in the 1980s).

The Islamic-style building that housed Catherine Beecher's Dubuque Female Seminary (1853–1859) still stands at the head of Iowa Street, but it was drastically remodeled in 1907, effectively stripping it of its oriental exoticism (it is now the Lady of Lourdes Nursing Home). On the endangered list at the time of writing this guide are the Madison Street Steps (1918), a fantasy of cantilevered and suspended stairs, platforms, and bridges climbing the limestone bluff. The steps are located on Madison Street, just off North Main and Seventeenth streets, but because of the deterioration of the steps they were closed to public use in 1956.

Since the early 1970s Dubuque has plunged into various approaches to historic preservation, contextualism, and urban design. This has led to the restoration of a number of important historic houses, many of them converted into restaurants and bed-and-breakfast hotels. The Egyptian Revival Dubuque County Jail has been rescued and converted into an art gallery. The town's second clock tower now is a centerpiece for the Town Clock Plaza, and Washington Park has been redesigned and now houses a new "Victorian" white gazebo. Though the usual shopping centers have developed to the west (such as Kennedy Mall off US 20), the downtown is still very much alive and vital.

ME158 Dubuque County Courthouse

1891–1893, Fridolin J. Heer and Son. 720 Central, northeast corner with 7th St.

As with many Iowa municipal buildings, the first courthouse in Dubuque was a two-story log structure, built in 1836. Three years later a brick courthouse was erected. It was a two-story building with a gable roof, essentially Greek Revival in imagery. In 1857 the architect John F. Rague added three more bays to the front of the building. He also added a few touches to its gabled front—a deep two-story arched entrance, and Gothic hoods for the windows to the side. Considering the city's size and aspirations, it is surprising that it was as late as 1891 before a new, really proper courthouse was built. This was designed by the Swiss architect Fridolin J. Heer and his son, Fridolin Heer, Jr. The older Heer came to the United States in 1864, and the follow-

ing year set up an office in Dubuque. His son studied architecture in Germany and later worked in Chicago in the Adler and Sullivan office. Though the 1891 courthouse is indeed Beaux-Arts in its detailing, it reads as a "Victorian" building rather than as an example of the "new" French Classicism. The reasons for this have to do with its vertical massing, the relationship of individual details to one another, and the strong contrast between dark brick walls and light limestone trim. The design entails a two-story basement section surmounted by a two-story section of piers, pilasters, and intertwined arches. Above the entrance porch, drawing dramatic attention to the principal facade, is a deep arch that reaches into a pedimented attic. When built, the central tower rose into a segmented dome, and below on each of the corners was a large-scale figure. The dome was removed, as were the figures, and the tower now has a tall narrow lantern. In 1932, as part of John Nolen's City Beautiful civic center for Dubuque, it was proposed that the building be demolished. Fortunately (for the building) the depression intervened, and it was left standing and in use. In the early 1970s, it was restored and its dome was gilded.

ME159 Dubuque County Jail

1857–1858, John F. Rague. Southeast corner of Central and 8th streets

The feeling that incarceration was a form of death and burial led in the nineteenth century to the use of Egyptian architectural forms for prisons and jails. Iowa's only example is this small two-story jailhouse designed by John Francis Rague. Rague, who designed the Il-

ME159 Dubuque County Jail

linois and Iowa capitol buildings, normally showed a predilection for the Greek Revival. Having lived in New York, the architect most likely knew of the "Tombs" prison (1835–1838), which may have been his inspiration. Essentially Rague's building is a Greek Revival house detailed with a few convincing Egyptian details: a pair of Egyptian "bundle papyriform" columns within the recessed entrance, carved heads for the windows, and a bold and wide "gorge" cornice, a type of cornice that is deeply indented. A few of the original window lintels still reveal winged-sun disks in the form of lion's heads. The walls of the jail are of a rough limestone; in strong contrast, the frames of the doors and windows are in cast iron. Within, there are tiers of cells, each of the cells measuring only 4 feet 4 inches wide by 10 feet long.

ME160 Two Commercial Blocks

c. 1880, 1885. Southeast corner of Central and 9th streets

These two buildings that housed stores and offices still manage to convey a sense of what was the nineteenth-century streetscape in this section of the downtown. On the second floor of each structure, above the cast-iron and glass storefronts, are rows of arched windows. The southern building is Richardsonian Romanesque, while the northern building has a mild Italianate flavor.

ME161 Shot Tower

1856. East end of 4th St., at Commercial St.

Early panoramic views of Dubuque show the 150-foot-high limestone-and-brick shot tower

"posing" on the banks of the Mississippi River like an Egyptian obelisk overlooking the Nile. It was the presence of lead that encouraged Julien Dubuque to come to the place and begin his mining operations. The production of lead shot for guns was, briefly, an important industry for the city. Melted lead was poured from the top of the tower, and it formed perfect spherical balls as it dropped and cooled. At the bottom was a large receiving tank of water. The tower was actually used for production only from 1852 through 1862. In 1874 an equestrian statue of Andrew Jackson (by John J. Kavanaugh) was placed on top of it, but this remained only through 1881. After suffering from general neglect for many years, the tower was stabilized in 1959, and it remains one of the city's major landmarks.

ME162 Majestic Orpheum Theater

1910, Cornelius W. Rapp and George L. Rapp. Northwest corner of Main and 4th streets

The designers of this French Second Empire-inspired theater, Rapp and Rapp, emerged in the 1920s as the architects for opulent theater buildings in Chicago, New York, and elsewhere. The street elevation of the Majestic was that of a richly organized Beaux-Arts design: a large central arched opening flanked by pilasters, and a dormered curved roof with a suggestion of a central pavilion. Originally a discreetly lighted sign hung above the arch and a thin metal marquee extended out to the curb on the street. The auditorium of the theater had two balconies, box seats, and a dress circle gallery. The stage was planned for vaudeville, but later it was used for motion pictures. In the early 1970s the building was rescued from possible demolition and became part of the adjoining Five Flags Center, with its large indoor arena. In 1974 the exterior and interior of the theater were restored.

ME163 United States Post Office and Federal Building

1932–1934, James A. Wetmore; Proudfoot, Rawson, Souers, and Thomas; Herbert A. Kennison. 350 W. 6th St.

This four-story PWA Moderne post office is reminiscent of the work of Paul P. Cret in the late 1920s (e.g., the Folger Shakespeare Library, Washington, D.C., 1928–1932). The central four-story pavilion, dominated by smooth masonry surfaces and sculptured eagles which "grow" out of the parapet corners of the building, looks back to the mid-twenties designs of Bertram G. Goodhue. Within, one will find two Grant Wood-inspired murals of the 1930s: Bertram Adam's *Early Settlers of Dubuque* (1936–1937) and William E. L. Bunn's *Early Mississippi Steamboats* (1936–1937). Of the three buildings that John Noland projected in his 1932 civic center design, the post office was the only one realized. The post office was to have been connected by an arcade to a new city hall to the south, and to the other side of the city hall was to be the courthouse.

ME164 Mary of the Angels Home

1879, 1899, 1911, 1929; Franklin D. Hyde, Guido Beck; Fridolin Heer and Son. 605 Bluff St.

The south portion of this institution was designed by F. D. Hyde in 1879 as a private residence for Jesse D. Farley, who controlled river shipping and railroad interests. The house was a good-sized brick two-story building with a mansard roof, and was a French Second Empire design. Because of financial losses, Farley was forced to sell the house in 1892 to the Sisters of Saint Francis. From 1879 through 1929, additions were continually made to the former house, all in the original French Second Empire style. Fridolin Heer and Son's addition included a new entrance pavilion with an Ionic columned porch and a central gabled wall dormer.

ME165 Cooper House (Redstone)

1888, Thomas T. Carkeck. 504 Bluff St.

Redstone, a house named for the color of its walls of red Georgian stone and brick, was built by A. A. Cooper, a wealthy manufacturer of buggies, for his daughter Elizabeth. Though certainly thought of as a "mansion," the house in fact was designed as a duplex. It is an excellent illustration of how architects of the time could pull together several different architectural traditions, yet have the amalgam read as one. The format of the large dwelling is that of a classicized version of the Queen Anne style, modified by a close look at the Richardsonian Romanesque and accompanied by detailing we associate with the Colonial Revival. As is usually the case with "mansions" of this sort, the interior is far more openly "posh" than the more puritanical exterior. Inside, one finds marble fireplaces, leaded stained glass windows, and finely carved, turned, and routed woodwork. In 1976 and in 1984, the house was restored, and is now an inn.

ME166 Fenelon Place Elevator

1882, 1893, 1916, J. W. Graves. 4th St. west of Bluff St.

Small inclined railroads were built in several American cities in the late nineteenth century; needless to say, almost all are now gone. This short incline was built for private use of a banker, J. K. Graves, so that he could travel from the lower town up the bluff to his home in suburbia. The first railroad was powered by steam, which was replaced in 1893 by electricity. A second inclined railroad, now destroyed, existed at the west end of Eleventh Street (from 1887 to 1927). The Fenelon Place Elevator is still in operation and is a major tourist attraction in the city.

ME167 Saint Raphael's Roman Catholic Cathedral

1857–1859, John Mullany. 1878, tower. 231 Bluff St.

Saint Raphael's church is the third cathedral church by this name in Dubuque. It was designed by John Mullany, an Irishman who was trained in Augustus Welby Pugin's office in London before he came to the United States in 1847. He arrived in Dubuque in 1859, and immediately commenced the design and supervision of this Gothic Revival church. The building enjoys a dramatic location, right at the west end of 90-foot-wide Second Street. In design, the central tower is of the Gothic form. The building's most unusual feature is the lancet window at the base of the tower. There are two entrances at the side of the tower within the body of the building. In Mullany's original scheme these two entrance walls were to have terminated in their own gables, with high pinnacles at each of the corners. Mullany also had projected a tall, thin spire roof, but a more abridged 243-foot-high square tower was eventually added in 1878. The stained glass windows, imported from England, were added in 1866, and the stations of the cross in 1890. The interior murals are by an Italian artist whose name is recorded as Gregori.

ME168 Town Clock Plaza

1873, Barton-Aschman Associates (clock and tower, Fridolin Heer, Sr.; relocated 1971); 1967 and later. Main St., below 5th and 9th streets

Dubuque has long been fascinated with the public clock. Its first town clock (1864) rose from a simple Greek Revival building, but in contrast to the plainness of the building, the clock tower was exuberantly Italianate. This first clock tower collapsed in 1872. It was replaced the following year by an equally exuberant French Second Empire design by Fridolin Heer, Sr. Before the three-story Ruskinian Gothic building upon which the tower had been placed was demolished, the tower itself was moved to Town Clock Plaza, where it became the centerpiece of the park's de-

sign. The tower now sits on a high arched brick base and functions as would a folly in an English Picturesque garden. The only major item missing is the original rooftop weather vane with an immense cast-iron "key to the city."

ME169 Carnegie Stout Library

1901, Williamson and Spenser. Southeast corner of Bluff and 11th streets

A robust Roman temple front, composed of six Corinthian columns, provides the entrance to this Beaux-Arts-style building. The internal circulation is organized around a central rotunda, lighted from above; another set of eight Corinthian columns encircles the second level of the rotunda. An addition was built to the east in 1979–1981. The visual language of the addition harks back to the classicized PWA Moderne of the 1930s with a row of vertical openings cut into the wall to suggest classical piers.

ME170 F. D. Stout House

1890–1891. 1105 Locust St.

As the Richardsonian Romanesque continued into the 1890s, it became less picturesque and more ordered. The F. D. Stout house illustrates this classicizing trend. The usual rusticated red sandstone was still used for the walls. However, while a few round-arched openings, a corner tower, and the roofscape are varied, the fenestration of the house, with its emphasis on repeated rectangular openings, reveals none of the playfulness and romance one associates with the earlier forms of the style at the beginning of the 1880s. The result is a strong urban design of real authority, a design which could easily have been in fashion and built contemporaneously in Chicago or New York.

ME171 H. L. Stout House

1892, Fridolin Heer and Sons. 1145 Locust St.

Victorian architects of the late nineteenth century had a remarkably nonchalant attitude when it came to exuberant combinations of architectural images. Seemingly, Heer had several premises that he wished to try out in the H. L. Stout house. The first was to create a contrast between the solidity of masonry and the fragility and lightness of wood. The stone base and first floor of the house are almost monumental; opposed to this quality is the lightness of the wood surfaces and detailing of the second floor, the attic, and the wide-based tower with its row of Moorish windows and curved roof. A second "game" played by the architect is in the realm of images: parts of the building are pure Queen Anne, others are Colonial Revival—and then there are the Richardsonian Romanesque elements, all held more or less in place by the Islamic tower.

ME172 Masonic Temple

1931–1932, Raymond E. Moore. Southwest corner of Locust and 12th streets

The architectural form traditionally favored by the Masons in America during the first decades of this century was the classical Beaux-Arts temple. By the twenties an abstracted medievalism began to be used. The Dubuque temple approaches its medieval theme by way of a close look at the designs of Bertram G. Goodhue and others. Turrets, buttresses, rough masonry surfaces, and other picturesque medieval details are present, but equally apparent is the classical basis of the design, with a slight overlay of Art Deco details.

ME173 Harger House

1890. 1207 Grove Terrace

The brick Harger house enjoys a commanding location atop the bluff and overlooking the city and river beyond. The date of 1890 for the large one-and-a-half-story Gothic house is remarkably late for the fashion. Its original owner, Benton M. Harger, was a dealer in books, stationery, and wallpaper, and one suspects that his literary interests may account for his choice of a medieval image. The most telling Gothic features of the design are the steeply pitched gabled roof, the highly visible bargeboards, and the piered porch running across the front of the house. The shed-roofed second-floor balcony-porch over the entrance harks back to the Eastlake style of the 1870s.

ME174 Thompson-Ryan House

1866, John M. Van Osdel. 1375 Locust St.

The Thompson-Ryan house has been aptly described as one of Iowa's most outstanding examples of the Italianate/French Second

ME174 Thompson-Ryan House

Empire mode. Its two-story brick base is crowned by a dormered mansard roof, and atop this is a curved cupola with a mansard roof. The cupola's scale would be appropriate in a public building. The walls of the brick dwelling are treated as recessed panels, set behind brick corner piers and below a wide entablature. All of the stone-and-wood detailing is carried to the height of elaboration. This is particularly evident in the recessed entrance, the first-floor bay, the long side porch, and finally on the pilaster-encrusted square cupola. The house was originally built for John Thompson, one-time mayor of Dubuque; it was purchased in 1888 by the meat packer William Ryan. It was designed by Chicago's "first" architect, John M. Van Osdel. From the 1840s through the 1860s Van Osdel designed a number of Chicago's "palatial" mansions, many of which, like the Thompson-Ryan house in Dubuque, combined the Italian Villa with the French Second Empire style.

ME175 Ryan House

c. 1870, John M. Van Osdel. 1389 Locust St.

A classic, sumptuous example of the Italian villa style in brick, this house boasts all the characteristics one associates with late versions of this form. A square four-story tower with a concave mansard roof sits between two wings of the house. Segmental- or round-arched windows occur throughout the building, each beautifully emphasized by exaggerated stone heads. Missing are a few cast-iron details: the metal balustrade atop the roof and a projecting balcony once situated above the entrance door. If the assumed date of 1870 is correct, it is peculiar that Van Osdel would have produced a house in an earlier style than that of the 1866 Thompson-Ryan house next door.

ME176 **Richards House**

1882–1883, Franklin D. Hyde. 1392 Locust St.

The wood detailing and perpendicular emphasis of the Richards house places it squarely within the Eastlake style. All of the many gable ends are filled with open medieval timberwork, the best being the high north roof gable, which exhibits a pattern of squared work. The architect has, in a manner particularly typical of the Eastlake style, played with contrasts. The tall, thin verticality of the volumes of the building, the steeply pitched roofs, and the gables are contrasted with the horizontal banding of the building, which starts at the stone raised basement and is repeated in a band of clapboard, a thin curved band of fishscale shingles, and finally the upper surface covered with a different pattern of shingles. Missing from the house now (as is often the case in these buildings) is the delicacy of the metalwork that starts and terminates designs such as this: a cast-iron fence at its base and then a ridgecrest and finials.

ME177 **Robinson-Lacy House**

1878, Fridolin Heer, Sr. 1640 Main St.

The French Second Empire style enjoyed great popularity in Iowa (as it did throughout the country) in the decade of the late 1860s and on through the 1870s. In this example, a side-hall plan, Fridolin Heer used the solidity of masonry to suggest permanence and presence. The mansard roof is heavily divided into individual planes by molding on the edges and eaves. The roof springs from a sizable bracketed entablature and cornice; the dormers within the roof, whether rectangular or circular, are surrounded by heavy moldings. The structure of the house consists of double brick walls, with an airspace between. The architect provided two separate heating systems, one using hot water, the other gravity flow hot air.

ME178 **Young House**

c. 1875, Fridolin Heer, Sr. 1491 Main St.

This is another of Heer's elegant French Second Empire-style houses. The walls in this instance are sheathed in finely cut Indiana limestone with the addition of an incised design to suggest smooth ashlar blocks. The impressive design element of this house is its north wall, facing Fifteenth Street, where the architect has created a series of angular geometric patterns that seem to pour across the surface. Equally exciting is the three-dimensional pattern he created using chimneys and dormers within the mansard roof.

ME179 **Saint John's Episcopal Church**

1875–1878, Henry Martyn Conger. 1410 Main St.

The architect of this church, Henry Martyn Conger of New York and Brooklyn, specialized in the design of religious buildings, especially for the Episcopal church. In style he moved between interpretations of the Gothic and the Richardsonian Romanesque. He designed numerous Episcopal churches in New England, New York, and on into the Midwest. At the time he was designing Saint John's in Dubuque he was working on similar churches in Portland, Connecticut, and in Germantown, Pennsylvania. A few years earlier he had designed the Chapel of the Good Shepherd at Faribault, Minnesota (1873). His largest church in the Upper Midwest was Grace Church Cathedral at Topeka, Kansas (1889). The scheme of Saint John's Episcopal Church is pure nineteenth-century English Gothic Revival: cruciform in plan with rough limestone walls, smooth stone trim, and a large rose window at the front. The low, square tower, now crenellated, was meant to have a tall upper tower and spire, as in the work in England of Augustus Welby Pugin and others. Within the church are five windows from the studio of Louis Comfort Tiffany.

ME180 **Eighmey House**

c. 1892. 1337 Main St.

When first built, the Eighmey house presented the usual blend of the Queen Anne and the Colonial Revival styles current in the early nineties. The building's most pronounced feature was the pair of circular corner bay towers, one topped with a conical spire roof, the other with a concave/convex metal roof. In the early 1900s the house was made more up-to-date and respectable (and of course even more Colonial) by the addition of not one but two two-story porches with Corinthian columns.

ME181 **Red Cross Building**

c. 1941; 1200 Main St.

By the end of the 1930s, the Streamline Moderne had become increasingly less exuberant. The two-story Red Cross building in Dubuque still retains a few hallmarks of this popular style—the curved central parapets and the marquee faced with stainless steel, as well as the glass brick panel on the central bay. Also very much in the style is the yellow tile sheathing.

ME182 **Strand Theater**

c. 1941. Southeast corner of Main and 12th streets

Modernity of image was of great importance for motion picture theaters. Many began as legitimate theaters and were later transformed into movie houses to show silent and then talking films. Even after they became motion picture houses, most theaters were updated from time to time. The Strand has an even more varied history for it started out as a Baptist church in the late nineteenth century, and it later was transformed into a theater. (The brick walls of the original church are visible on its north side, on Twelfth Street.) What we now see is a facade remodeling of around 1940. The designer has used two highly contrasting colors of vitrolite—shimmering black and cream—to establish the presence of the theater. The smaller cream-colored volume projects out of the rectangular geometric form of what was the body of the church and its two towers. On the ground level on each side of the entry marquee are two curved bays of black vitrolite and glass brick.

ME183 **Saint Luke's United Methodist Church**

1896–1897, George W. Kramer. 1199 Main St.

The present church building represents the fourth Methodist church built in Dubuque; the first was of logs, the second was a Greek Revival design (1839), the third was Gothic Revival (1853), and the 1896–1897 church is Richardsonian Romanesque. Kramer enjoyed a national reputation as a designer of churches; his preferred images ranged from the Italian Romanesque to the French Gothic. In this church, Kramer utilized the Richardsonian Romanesque but simplified it and added across the face of the building an entrance loggia with an Italian flavor. The sanctuary space within is decidedly horizontal, reinforced by a segmental hooped ceiling. The ceiling, sheathed in sawn quarter oak in 1916, adds a low-key, mellow quality. The windows of the church are indeed its crowning glory. They were produced by the Tiffany studio and are of Favrile glass. The Good Shepherd window was exhibited by Tiffany at the World's Columbian Exposition of 1893, and was later purchased and installed in the church. Also from the Tiffany studios are the chandeliers and the brass altar railings.

ME184 **German Trust and Savings Bank** (now Dubuque Bank and Trust Company)

1922. Southeast corner of Central and Loras Blvd.

As it progressed into the 1920s, the Beaux-Arts Classical tradition tended to become abstract; often, as in the case of this bank building, the classical ornamentation simply seemed to glide over the surfaces of the building. Emphasis was placed on the fluted pilasters as the principal decorative device. Externally and internally the materials used were meant to convey a low-key opulence. In this Dubuque bank the exterior is sheathed in cream-colored terracotta set on a base of light-gray Minnesota granite. Inside, the walls are covered with a smooth surface of Italian marble.

ME185 **Dubuque City Hall**

1857–1858, John F. Rague. Southeast corner of Iowa and 13th streets

Dubuque's three-story city hall of 1857–1858 was somewhat unusual for the Midwest, for it combined a number of commercial activities with public usage. The basement was divided in an unlikely fashion between the police station and two saloons, and the ground floor was occupied by market stalls which were rented out. The second floor housed the council chambers, courtroom, and the city offices. The third floor was a large, open "town hall." Dubuque's market/city hall was modeled after the Fulton Market in Brooklyn, a building certainly known to Rague during his residence in New York. In its general proportions and its detailing the brick city hall in Dubuque is similar to many utilitarian buildings, especially mill buildings. Each of the bays on its three floors is treated as a recessed panel covered with a segmental arch. Originally the first-floor openings on the two long sides of the structure contained French doors, so that each market stall opened both to the central interior corridor and to the street outside. The only strongly public aspect of the building was its French Second Empire/Italianate bell tower (designed by John D. Abry).

ME186 Saint Mary's Roman Catholic Church

1864–1867, John Mullany. Northeast corner of 15th and White streets

The 236-foot-high steeple of this Gothic Revival church has dominated downtown Dubuque since the late 1860s. In plan the church is an entrance-tower type. Alongside the soaring tower are two chapel-like appendages in a contrasting dollhouse scale. Victorian in its splendor is the upper portion of the tower, with steeply pitched wall dormers and the zigzag pattern on the roof of the spire. The interior is equally rich with carved, painted, and gilded reredos, and wall surfaces painted in maroon and gold.

ME187 Lustron House

c. 1951. 887 W. Locust St.

Here is a turquoise and cream-colored Lustron house, in this case with a central entrance and enclosed porch.

ME188 Dubuque Brewing and Malting Company

1894–1895, Louis Lehle; Fridolin Heer and Son. 3000 Jackson St.

This immense Richardsonian Romanesque pile covers some three acres. It was designed by Louis Lehle of Chicago, who became widely known throughout the Midwest for the design of breweries. The local firm of Fridolin Heer and Son supervised its construction. The first floor of the building is in stone, the upper floors in brick. Appropriate to the style are the numerous towers with steeply pitched roofs and corner pinnacles.

ME189 Mathias Ham House

1839, 1857. 2241 Lincoln Ave.

ME189B Louis Arriandeau Log Structure

The original 1839 house was a one-and-a-half-story Greek Revival cottage constructed of stone. With his rise in fortune, Ham built his new "mansion" in front of his modest cottage. The new house was a square block constructed of smooth-faced limestone ashlar. In style the house is Italianate and features a gable on each face. At the center of the roof is a high octagonal cupola; pairs of large brackets support the overhanging roof. In addition to the Italianate front entrance porch, there is a wide veranda to the side. An unusual feature of the house is the placement of four dormers within the roof valleys. The house is now a museum and open to the public.

Next door to the Ham house, within Eagle Point Park, is the 1833 Louis Arriandeau (William Newman) log cabin. This was originally located at the corner of Locust and Second streets. It was moved to Eagle Point Park in 1915; then, in 1967, it was taken down and re-created at the present site within the park. The form of this log cabin is that of two rooms separated by a covered "dog-trot." Cabins of this plan were built over many years in the south, the lower Mississippi Valley, and on into the west. The Newman cabin has two chimneys (one for each room), with the fireboxes constructed of stone and the flues built of logs. The present double-hung windows may or may not be original.

ME190 Eagle Point Park Pavilions

1934–1936, Alfred Caldwell; Wendell Reffenberger. Eagle Point Park off Shiras Ave.

Two of the most memorable examples of the Prairie school landscape architecture are situated in Iowa. One of these is the Rock Glen development in Mason City, designed by Wal-

ME190 Eagle Point Park Pavilion

ter Burley Griffin; the other is Eagle Point Park in Dubuque. Neither of these Iowa landscape designs is situated within a characteristic midwestern prairie landscape. Instead, both are placed within highly picturesque rocky glens; they have far more to do with the eighteenth-century English sense of the sublime than with the horizontality of the prairie.

The designer of Eagle Point Park with its "nature-aiding" park structures was the Chicago-trained landscape architect Alfred Caldwell. Caldwell was appointed park superintendent in 1933, and he devised a plan that he named "The City in a Garden." With a large WPA crew funded through the federal government's relief programs of the depression years, Caldwell built his own version of Frank Lloyd Wright's Taliesin at Spring Green, Wisconsin. In lookouts, pavilions, shelters, stone circles, pools, and pathways he brought together the "organic" sensitivity of Wright in architecture and of Jens Jensen in landscape architecture. Native limestone was the fundamental building material, and he treated it so that the structures read as manmade, but at the same time their layered horizontality reflected the character of the nearby native limestone outcroppings. Just as William Steele and Purcell and Elmslie's Woodbury County Courthouse in Sioux City represents the high point of public architecture for the Prairie school, Caldwell's work at Eagle Point Park is a near-perfect summation of "organic" landscape architecture. A further indication of Caldwell's approach to the Prairie style can be seen in a house he designed for Ward F. Donovan. This two-story house (1941) is located in Dubuque at 1721 Plymouth Court. Within Eagle Point Park is a later version of the Prairie mode, a band-stand designed around 1957 by Rossiter and Ham.

ME191 Kelly House

c. 1855, Henry Kelly. 274 Southern Ave.

A house type used extensively throughout the United States during the decades of the 1830s through the 1850s was a two-story rectilinear dwelling with an exterior two-story porch, usually with an exterior staircase. Houses of this type were built quite early in French Canada, in the Caribbean, and in the lower Mississippi Valley. In California such dwelling are called Monterey, and in New Mexico, the two-story Territorial. The Kelly house is an excellent example of this mode in the upper Mississippi Valley. The first-floor walls of the house are of stone, the upper walls of board-and-batten. Though the form of the house is very late Greek Revival in style, the board-and-batten walls, plus the use of barge-boards, give a hint of the Gothic.

ME192 McCoy House

1925, design, Karl F. Saaur; 1928–1930, construction. 1160 Grandview Ave. S.

Grandview Avenue possesses a number of well-designed period revival houses of the 1920s and 1930s. The one-and-a-half-story McCoy house is French, more "Provincial" than Norman. Dark-colored brick is used as an accent against the background of light-tan brick walls. The composition of the roof is particularly successful: it works down from the higher wall-dormer section to the left, to the gabled dormer above the entrance; finally the hipped roof is brought down to and terminated by the large chimney.

ME193 House

c. 1935. 1144 Grandview Ave. S.

Here the Moderne and the Regency Revival styles are combined, all centering on a wide first-floor bow window.

ME194 House

c. 1928. 1130 Grandview Ave. S.

An English period revival house in brick, this dwelling's centerpiece is the composition of interlocking entrance-gable chimney and the roofs. The gable and the chimney have been tied together further by diagonal pattern-work in their brick surfaces.

ME195 Villa Raphael

1909. 1235 Mount Loretta

The Villa Raphael was originally built as a mother house of the Sisters of Presentation. While this four-story brick building with octagonal bay towers at the ends hints at the Romanesque, its character is established by the two-story entrance porch in the Doric order. An unsympathetic addition (at least it is sheathed in brick) has been built to the right of the older complex.

ME196 House

c. 1939. 535 Grandview Ave. S.

This stark, hygienically clean version of the thirties Streamline Moderne is sheathed in light cream-colored brick and, of course, glass bricks. The spare, tightly clipped landscaping perfectly matches the house.

ME197 House

c. 1917. 160 Grandview Ave. S.

This brick and stone-trimmed house conveys a slight feeling that it was in the avant-garde for its time. A few of its details are reminiscent of the Prairie style, but others seem to lead back to Secessionist modes in Vienna. Its principal organizational device is the center pavilion with its entrance, curved roof, and large second-floor window that extends up into the shed-roofed dormer.

ME198 House

c. 1939. 120 Grandview Ave. S.

This would appear to be a duplicate of the house at 535 Grandview, only in this case the landscape is more wild and informal.

ME199 Wartburg Theological Seminary

1914–1916, Perkins, Fellows and Hamilton. 1981–1982, Brown, Healey Block. 333 Wartburg.

The Chicago firm of Perkins, Fellows and Hamilton developed a strong reputation for the design of schools and other types of educational institutions in the Midwest. In this instance the style used is English medieval carried out in stone. The six-story crenellated tower with its small, set-back spire has been reduced to a minimum so that it appears, as the architects wished, as "modernized Gothic." The site plan is that of a basic U-shape, centering on the tower building and then informally meandering off to the side. The architects of the new construction to the north and west, Brown, Healy and Block of Cedar Rapids, have sought "compatibility" in relating their new structures to the old, and they have succeeded admirably in their use of scale and materials.

ME200 University of Dubuque

University Ave., past Algona St.

The two most interesting pieces on the campus are the old chapel (now Alumni Hall, 1907) and the new Blades Hall (1980–1981, designed by the Durrant Group). The chapel is a small Gothic Revival structure of brick with stone trim. An open screen-wall tower projects from the center of the chapel's front gable end. Blades Hall occupies the site of the 1907 three-and-a-half-story Steffins Hall, and its designers have utilized several fragments from the older building: the two former loggias and the central entrance in the Doric order form the screen wall beyond which is centered the Gothic Revival chapel. The new Blades Hall with its heavily emphasized roof and large round windows is highly sympathetic to the older architecture.

ME201 Kuehnle House

1924. Northwest corner of Kirkwood and Alta Vista streets

A reasonably good-sized house has been maneuvered through its roofs, gables, and dormers to read as an English cottage. The lower floor and the gable ends are sheathed in stone and brick; the dormers are half-timbered; and the roof is rolled over the eaves, suggesting medieval thatching.

ME202 Loras Academy

1854, 1873, 1878, 1882. Loras Blvd. at Prairie Ave.

The academy is an impressive pile of brick and stone-trimmed buildings that range in style from Victorian Gothic to French Second Empire. It is the latter that predominates, with its emphasis on entablatures and cornices above which rise the dormered mansard roofs.

ME203 House

597 Loras Blvd.

A square two-story Italian villa in wood, this house has a steep hipped roof that terminates in a cupola with windows. One side, on ground level, has a pair of angled bays, while a porch, partially open and partially closed, occupies the adjacent side of the house.

ME204 Lewis-Adams House

1854, 1904. 325 Alpine St.

When built in the mid-1850s, the house of General Warner Lewis was a quiet, rather modest version of the late Federal style. In 1904 he transformed it into something much more magnificent. Essentially he "Colonialized" the house by pulling the entrance forward, and by adding a columned porch; above, he created a curved balustraded balcony, behind which was a wall with Ionic columns and a new central gable. But he also added several features one would normally associate with the nineteenth-century Italianate: bracketed eaves and a central, large-scale cupola with round-arched windows. What is remarkable is that because this all works together so well, one is not really aware of the varied background of the house when one first encounters it.

ME205 Edward Langworthy House

1857, John F. Rague. 1095 3rd St. W., at northeast corner of Alpine St.

The Langworthy house is in many ways characteristic of the approach taken to the 1850s fad for Orson S. Fowler's "Octagonal Mode of Building." While the house is indeed an octagon, it has a characteristic central hall plan. The architect seems to have gone to great lengths to squeeze his rectangular plan within an octagonal form. The resulting battle between the octagon and the rectangle has

ME205 Edward Langworthy House

produced some delightful and at times surprising results. The entry hall is T-shaped, giving entrance to a central double staircase hall with a living room on one side and a library on the other. Except for two of the six bedrooms on the second floor, all of the rooms have angled walls. On the first floor this complexity of walls has been augmented by angular bay windows: the living room has three bays and the dining room, two. As often occurs with octagon houses, a utilitarian two-story wing containing the kitchen, pantry, and general service area has been thrust to the rear. The Langworthy house has the usual large-scale central cupola, which also encloses the upper portions of the chimneys. The walls of the house are of double brick, and the two long interior walls that define the long side of the stair hall contain the fireplace and lower parts of the chimneys. The Langworthy house was the second of two octagonal houses built in Dubuque. An early, smaller example built on Central Avenue was torn down in 1932.

ME206 Julien Dubuque Monument

1897, Alex Simplot. South end of Julien Dubuque Dr.

One encounters what would appear to be a folly in an eighteenth-century English garden 180 feet above the Mississippi River. It is a limestone tower built in 1897 to honor the French founder of Dubuque. The romantic crenellated tower was meant to be experienced as a "castle on the Rhine,"[24] and indeed it has some of that quality.

ME207 New Melleray Trappist Abbey

1867–1875, John Mullany, 1975, remodeling; Frank Kacmarick, Hammel, Green, and Abrahamson, Inc. Southwest of Dubuque on US 151, approximately 7 miles; right on county road D41 1.5 miles

The monastery was established in 1849. Temporary wooden buildings were first constructed, but in 1865 the Dubuque architect John Mullany, who had designed a number of churches in the area, was engaged to design permanent buildings in stone. During a period of ten years, the monks quarried the local limestone and built their new monastery. The main complex consists of two-, three-, and four-story sections arranged around a completely enclosed cloister. In style it is Puginesque Gothic, featuring rough stone walls with finely cut stone for window and door frames and other details. In 1975 a two-story wing containing a chapel below and a dormitory above was revamped to provide a large single space for the chapel. The second floor was removed and the walls were stripped of their plaster. The resulting space is an impressive one, and surprisingly it seems as if it had been designed as a two-story gabled chapel from the very beginning.

Across the road from the abbey-monastery is the Church of the Holy Family. This Gothic Revival brick church with a central entrance tower (1889) presents a near-perfect picture of a rural Iowa church. An open field leads up to the cemetery in front of the church building. A thick, dark-green grove of coniferous trees forms a backdrop to the red brick building with its tall, thin white spire. Though the composition is impressive during the summer months, its best moments are on a sunny winter day with gleaming white snow, the red brick church, and the shadowing green trees in the background.

ME208 Mount Saint Bernard College and Seminary

1850–1851. South of Dubuque on US 61, 2.5 miles to Key West; the college building is situated at the southwest end of town

This is a three-story building of rough stone walls and cut stone trim, with a gable roof. It is loosely Federal/Greek Revival in style, with a symmetrically fenestrated front. The large double-door entry and fanlight above are enclosed in a recessed arched opening.

Durant

Within the small railroad town of Durant is Saint Paul's Episcopal Church (c. 1875), located on Sixth Street, south of Third Street. Its low-pitched roof, bracketed eaves, and general proportions are late Italianate, but the windows with pointed arches are obviously meant to read as Gothic. It is the belfry of the entrance tower that really establishes the personality of this wood clapboard building. Eight tall, elaborately decorated Italianate wood columns together with a rich cornice support the low spire roof. Between each of the pair of columns is a balustrade composed of X's, devoid of the usual coping; thus this reads simply as a horizontal row of X's.

In downtown Durant one will come across two commercial monuments. One is a former bank building (c. 1917) on the north side of Fifth Street, between Seventh and Eighth; the other is a former service station (c. 1925) at the northwest corner of Fifth and Tenth streets. The former bank building (now occupied by the American Legion) is a small brick Georgian structure, almost domestic in scale. Between four pilasters are two side windows, with the entrance in the center. All three openings have lunette windows within their arches. The double-piered canopied former service station lightly suggests that the world of the auto in the twenties must somehow be related to the land of play— California or Florida. The Durant service station is sheathed in white stucco, and it has just the needed touches of red tile roofs here and there.

Dyersville

ME209 Saint Francis Xavier Roman Catholic Basilica

1887. Southwest corner of First Ave. N. and Second St. S.W.

This structure is one of the best-known nineteenth-century Gothic Revival churches in Iowa. The body of the church measures 70 by 175 feet; flanking the entrance are paired towers 212 feet high. Both externally and internally the detailing points to the French High Gothic style as a source, though the strong contrast between the light stone detailing and the brick walls conveys the fla-

vor of a multicolored Ruskinian Gothic Revival building. Inside, the church has a 70-foot-high vaulted nave, accompanied by high side aisles. The altar is of onyx and marble and is situated under a tall baldacchino. The two side altars, crafted of wood, were installed in 1897. The ceiling over the main aisle is painted, as are other sections of the interior. The frescoes and the "Gothic" stenciling, based directly on European examples, were added in 1905. The stained glass windows have been added over the years, one of the most recent being the rose window above the organ which was put in place in 1959.

Close by, at the southwest corner of Third Street Southwest and Second Avenue Southwest, is the Roman Catholic School (1907). The design reference here is to the classical; there is an entrance porch with Ionic columns, and an open domed tower with arched openings. The materials, stone and brick, match those of the nearby church.

Elkader

Elkader perfectly fits one's image of a small, prosperous midwestern community. The name for the town was coined after the romantic nineteenth-century Algerian leader Abd-el-kader. The surrounding country is hilly and covered with trees; through this winds the Turkey River. The river is the dominant feature of the town, breaking it in two with the business district to the southwest side and the county courthouse opposite. The history of the community follows a typical pattern of mid-nineteenth century settlements in Iowa. The town was laid out in 1847, and a flour mill was erected at that time. The town grid of streets runs southeast-northwest and southwest-northeast, following the course of the river at this point. The earlier mill was replaced in the 1860s by a larger one that stood just northwest of the county courthouse.

Some effort was made to use water transportation by steamboat on the Turkey River, but this did not prove feasible. In the early 1870s, a narrow gauge railroad was built which connected the town to the line of the Milwaukee and Saint Paul Railroad.

ME210 Clayton County Courthouse

1867, 1877, 1896. Northwest corner of E. Bridge and S. High streets

The competition among communities to be awarded a county courthouse was often fierce. In the instance of Clayton County, the first courthouse was built at Guttenberg in 1839.

In 1844, the designation was moved to Garnavillo (originally named Jacksonville), and it came to Elkader for a single year in 1856, then returned to Guttenberg. In 1860, it was back again in Elkader where it has remained. The present building was started in 1867, constructed with a temporary flat wood roof. A decade later, the building was completed with a hipped roof and a flat crown designed to receive a low cupola. In 1896 the cupola was extended upward to include a clock (which is still running) with four faces. The square two-story building, set low to the ground, rests upon a stone base, with hollow brick walls above. The detailing of the building, with its arched front windows, arched windows of the cupola, and bracketed hipped roof, places it stylistically within the Italianate mode. The configuration of the building—consisting of a rectangular box with a tall cupola—is often referred to as the "coffee mill" type of midwestern courthouse. The interior has been somewhat remodeled, but the central hall with its double staircase is still present. The building's siting on an open block overlooking the Turkey River gives it an impressive civic presence.

ME211 **Keystone Bridge**

1889, Mathias Tschirgi. Bridge St., over the Turkey River

Along with the adjacent courthouse, this double-span stone bridge constitutes one of Elkader's major civic monuments. The center piers of the bridge are pulled forward and suggest the towers of a medieval castle. The rusticated blocks laid on a regular ashlar pattern are massive in form, refined in detail. The bridge's designer, Mathias Tschirgi, also designed the high truss bridge over the Mississippi at Dubuque (1887). The keystone bridge was constructed by the firm of Byrne and Blade of Dubuque. At 346 feet in length the Elkader bridge is often billed as the longest keystone bridge west of the Mississippi.

ME212 **Carter-Reimer House**

1850. Southeast corner of E. Bridge and S. High streets

Often mentioned as the classic example of the Greek Revival style in Iowa, the Carter-Reimer house is unusual in that it was built for the occupancy of two brothers, Ernest and Henry Carter, and the balanced symmetry of the design accurately reflects that it is a double house. The two-story center block with a piered entrance porch is balanced on each side by one-story dependencies. Each of these dependencies in turn has an inset four-pier porch that helps to create the illusion that the far flanks of the dependencies are separate pavilions. Heavy entablatures and cornices dominate both the two-story and one-story sections of the house.

ME213 **Opera House**

1903. 207 N. Main St.

Here, the western false front is raised to a large scale. This three-story stage-set screen of brick has thin detailing of pilasters and arched windows that slightly hint at the Richardsonian Romanesque. The interior, painted in white and silver gray with gold and red trim, was sensitively restored in 1967.

ME214 **House**

c. 1887. 401 N. 1st St.

This is a commodious Queen Anne dwelling whose glory resides in its sumptuously detailed porches. The ground-floor veranda swings around the house and provides horseshoe entrances for both street fronts. On the second floor a wide corner porch was worked out with its own variation on the horseshoe arch theme, and on the third floor, pedimented miniaturized balconies are suggested. Classical lunettes and decorations of classical garlands indicate that the Colonial Revival was beginning to enter into fashion in Elkader.

ME215 **Davis (Witt-Kramer) House**

1845–1850. 405 N. 1st St.

The early nineteenth-century Federal style tradition lingers on through the middle of the century in this house. Much of its interior detailing and its front piered entrance porch are Italianate. In plan it is the classical side-hall scheme; its structure is of brick with wide stone lintels over the windows.

ME216 McTaggart-Price House

c. 1876. 206 Cedar St.

In style this is one of those nineteenth-century designs that is nearly impossible to pin down. The arched openings, pavilion with central gable, and hipped roof are reminiscent of the Italianate, but the detailing and vertical feeling of the design have more to do with post-Civil War Victorian architecture. An unusual feature of the design is the use of white brick for the arched windows and quoining of the walls. Though the house has sixteen rooms, the scale of its walls and openings conveys a dollhouselike appearance.

ME217 Marmann-Stemmer House

1889. 113 N. Oak Ave.

This house is one of the gems of the Queen Anne style in Iowa. J. C. Stemmer, the original owner-builder, was a lumberman, and he equipped his two-story brick house with a rich variety of band-sawed and turned woodwork. The front veranda with its patterns of curved arches and spandrels was matched by the elaborate open trusswork of the third-floor gables on the side of the house. The elaborate interior woodwork is enriched by numerous stained glass windows.

ME218 Kramer-Schmidt House

1867. S. Oak St., end of W. Bridge St.

This is another of Elkader's double houses, in this case a simple two-story gabled building of red brick. The street facade of the house seems all windows: there is a row of eight in the second floor and six below. The present porch is not original to the house.

ME219 Saint Joseph's Roman Catholic Church

1856, first church. 1897–1900, second church, Guido Beck. 330 S. 1st St.

The first church building (now used as a parish hall) was of Gothic Revival design. The structure was of stone; its plan was cruciform with an entrance tower and spire. During 1897–1900 Guido Beck replaced this church with a version of a late Gothic Revival church.

This latter church building was inspired by French Gothic design, which is most tellingly stated in the 142-foot-high entrance tower and spire. Within the sanctuary, two rows of thin clustered Corinthian columns create a traditional nave and side aisles, and above is a groin-vaulted ceiling.

ME220 Motor Mill

completed 1867. 12 miles southeast of Elkader on route X30, parallel to the Turkey River

This stone mill set alongside a flowing river within a hilly forest projects a romantic image. The limestone gristmill is six stories tall and covered by a single gabled roof. It was designed by John Thompson, who was responsible for the design and the construction of a number of mills in this section of the state. The mill was to have been the center of the new town of Motor, which was laid out in 1845. Also still in existence nearby and dating from these early years are a livery stable, tavern, and two-story cooperage.

ME221 Osborne Conservation Center

5 miles south of Elkader on Iowa 13, near Osborne

This site is of interest for two reasons: it houses a 260-acre demonstration area of trees and plant material that can be used successfully in erosion control, and it is a place where several historic folk buildings have been relocated. These include a log cabin (c. 1840), a one-room schoolhouse, a railroad depot, and a blacksmith shop.

ME222 **Saint Peter's German United Evangelical Lutheran Church** (Pioneer Rock Church)

1858. North on Iowa 13, west on Iowa 128, south on US 52, through Garnavillo, near Osterdock Rd. (route X47)

Saint Peter's is the very picture of a mid-century Greek Revival church, romantically situated in wooded open country. The walls rising two stories are of rough limestone; the two-tier tower and steeple are of wood. The church is classically severe, with a single door with lunettes at the ground level, a pair of windows above, and finally a small lunette window in the gable. The church is currently maintained by the nearby Garnavillo Historical Society and is open to the public.

ME222 Saint Peter's German United Evangelical Lutheran Church (Pioneer Rock Church)

Elkport

Sited on the banks of the Turkey River, Elkport houses a little gem of a building, the Elkport Savings Bank (c. 1895) on Main Street near the center of town. The building (now deserted) is tiny, but the architect made the most of its narrow street elevation. The front facade was divided into two parts. To the left is a large semicircular window, its inner wood mullions repeating the arch form; the arch defining this window exhibits a decorative keystone. The theme of this central arch is repeated at the parapet, and this arch contains the name of the building carved in stone. The smaller section of the front, set back on the right only inches from the other, contains a tall, elongated arched opening, with glass above and the entrance door below. The walls of the building are in a fine light-tan brick, and the trim is in smooth stone.

Fairport

Three miles east of Fairport on Iowa 22, near Montpelier, is the 417-acre Wildcat Den State Park. This heavily wooded, hilly, and stream-cut terrain was acquired by Emma and Clark Brint in 1925. Their desire was to protect this wild, romantic place from any encroachment. In 1927 they presented 67 acres to the state for a park. The state acquired an additional 141 acres for the park, and other additions were made later. The initial planning of the park took place in the late 1920s; most of the construction of roads, paths, and picnic areas occurred in the thirties as a Civilian Conservation Corps project. Within the park is the Pine Creek Gristmill and Dam and a Pratt truss iron bridge dating from around 1883. Nye platted a town at the mouth of Pine Creek in 1833–1834, but it never materialized.

ME223 **Pine Creek Gristmill**

1848, Benjamin Nye, builder. Wildcat Den State Park

This mill originally relied exclusively on water power; later this energy source was supplemented by steam power. The mill continued in operation through 1927. Fortunately the machinery remained intact, making it possible for present-day visitors to gain an understanding of the operation of one of Iowa's mills. The 1848 mill building is a three-and-a-half-story wood structure with gable roof and it is set solidly on a stone foundation. A two-and-a-half-story shed addition was built later, and numerous interior changes have occurred over the years. The heavy wood post-and-beam frame of the building was constructed using the traditional method of mortised joints, and the exterior was sheathed in clapboard. The mill building and its accompanying raceway and dam were restored

ME223 Pine Creek Gristmill

in the 1930s by the CCC. Additional restoration took place in the late 1970s and early 1980s.

Fort Madison

ME224 **Fort Madison**

1808–1813. 1980s, later, reconstructed

This Mississippi River community is the site of the 1808–1813 Fort Madison, the first American fortification built in Iowa. The fort was abandoned near the end of the War of 1812, and only one chimney remained as a monument. In 1908 a replica of this chimney, "The Lone Chimney Monument," was erected to mark the site of the fort. The fort itself was excavated in 1965, and in 1986 work commenced on rebuilding the entire fort in the city's Riverside Park; much of the construction has been accomplished by prison inmates from the State Penitentiary.

The first settlement at Fort Madison took place in 1832, and it was incorporated by an

act of Congress in 1836.[25] An unusual feature of its north-south, east-west grid was the inclusion of three public squares between E and F streets, the center one designated as the site for a courthouse. The town's earliest industry consisted of lumber and planing mills, supplemented by extensive river trade. In the late 1870s and 1880s, the railroad and a bridge across the Mississippi added to the economic base of the city. Other industries developed in the twentieth century; certainly one of the most widely known is the W. A. Sheaffer Pen Company, started in 1913. Another "industry" of the community is the Iowa State Penitentiary (the first section was erected during 1838–1841).

Although both the railroad and the highway (US 61) intervene between the river and the city, the development of the ten-block-long Riverside Park ties the city to the riverbank in an effective manner. A museum center—the former railroad passenger station—and the reconstruction of Fort Madison fit in well with the public openness of the park area.

ME225 **Lee County Courthouse**

1841–1842, attrib. Father Samuel Mazzochelli. 701 F St.

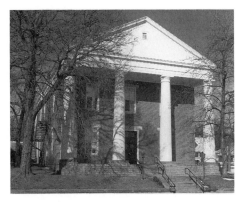

long building was planned to be read as three blocks (including a central portion flanked by two somewhat lower balanced sections). The designer has used the rhythm of fenestration to differentiate these sections. In the center the ground floor is an arcade; on the second floor there are rectangular openings, and on the third floor, arches reappear. The sections on each side have a pattern of rectangular openings at top and bottom, with arches on the second level. The important corner location of the bank is emphasized by a corner bay tower with an S-curved roof.

The Lee County Courthouse is one of several buildings (including the first Iowa State Capitol building) that have been attributed to Father Mazzochelli. The myth that he was the architect for the Lee County Courthouse is romantic, but hard-core evidence is hardly present. The design of the courthouse is that of a quite late version of the Greek Revival temple as a public building. Four somewhat massive Tuscan columns support the entablature and pediment. The deep entablature and cornice are carried around the remaining three sides of this two-story brick structure. On the roof ridge above the front entrance was a square base upon which was an octagonal domed cupola. Interior changes were made within the courthouse in 1876, and at that time a new wing was added to the north. In 1895 additional space was added to the building to house rooms for the supervisors and judges, and for a new boiler/heating room. The building was destroyed by fire in 1911. Surprisingly there was a strong contingent in the city and community that wished simply to rebuild the building as it had existed (with some interior modifications). Since the building was insured, this in the end seemed the most sensible course of action (for both sentimental and financial reasons). What we see today then is the rebuilt (1911) structure, minus its domed cupola and the row of chimneys that projected above the roof on both sides of the building.

ME226 Lee County Savings Bank Building

1883. Northwest corner of 8th St. and G St.

A three-story Richardsonian Romanesque commercial block realized in sandstone, this

ME227 The Fort Cafe

c. 1940. Northwest corner of 8th St. and Ave. H

This is a Streamline Moderne restaurant consisting of a small box with rounded corners that is equipped with horizontal mullioned windows and a projecting canopy over the window. The cut-out letter sign is carried along the edge of the roof.

ME228 Fox Theater

1951. 831 Ave. G

Here the Streamline Moderne is being slowly transformed into the more "respectable" Modern style that one associates with the years after 1945. The roof of the marquee curves up from below and is held in place by angled rectangles at each side. Above the marquee is a rhythmic pattern of U-shaped fins containing windows. The letters of the sign are brittle in their angularity, in contrast to the curved sign base upon which they are placed. As one would expect, the whole is brilliantly lighted at night with fluorescent tubes, rows of incandescent lights, and back-lighted panels. The 1951 design was, as in many theaters, a remodeling of an earlier theater, built in 1919.

ME229 Santa Fe Railroad Passenger Station (now Lee County History Center)

1910. South of Ave. H at 9th St.

If this long, low, red brick station with a hip-roofed tower were stuccoed, it would read as a Mission Revival building. Having been built in red brick, its references seem to be to the earlier Richardsonian Romanesque, coupled with an intense look at northern Italian rural architecture. Its 1975 conversion to museum use has been well carried out.

ME230 **W. H. Atlee House**

1895. 903 Ave. E

This stone-sheathed Richardsonian Romanesque dwelling presents a series of ornamented projecting gable ends. The entrance is a deep arched porch that leads off on one side to a walled terrace. The wide bay on the left is balanced on the other side by an octagonal three-story corner tower. The design, while romantic and picturesque, is highly controlled and contained.

ME231 **Union Presbyterian Church**

1884–1885, Lawrence B. Valk. 719 Ave. F

The design of this church was referred to as "Modern Gothic," i.e., Eastlake Gothic in this instance. The recessed corner tower is covered by a steeply pitched gable roof which is broken into on two sides by gabled wall dormers. In good Eastlake fashion, the peaks of the main gable roof are carried out from the walls and are supported by brackets. For the time, the brick walls and openings of the church are effectively plain, even puritanical. The architect of the building, Lawrence B. Valk, was the author of *Church Architecture*, published in New York (Holt Brothers) in 1873.

ME232 **Dierker House**

1931, Morton Geis. 1102 A St.

Poised on a hilltop location is the Dierker house. Its version of the popular white stucco Moderne style lies midway between the earlier Art Deco and the later Streamline Moderne. The street facade, consisting of a central two-story block and two one-story projecting wings, is symmetrical, except that this balance is countered by the second-floor balcony that extends to the right. On the garden side of the house, with its view over the Mississippi Valley, are bands of corner windows, an exterior stair leading to a living deck, and a Moderne wall fountain. Other Moderne touches are the steel ship railings, a projecting semicircular canopy, and angled and arched openings. The architect of the house, Morton Geis, practiced out of Quincy, Illinois.

ME233 **Samuel Atlee (Walden) House**

c. 1865. 804 Ave. E

One assumes that this commodious two-story brick house started out as Italianate, and at some point in the late 1890s or early 1900s changes were made. One of the principal additions was an elaborate wood porch which was pulled across the face of the house. At its left end, the cross gable declares the house's main entrance; at the right, the gable extends out to the side street. The terminal points of the porch are groupings of three columns, set on a high base, with their entablatures extended far down from the roof.

ME234 **House**

c. 1890. 621 Ave. E

This two-story Queen Anne dwelling asserts its presence almost entirely through its varied applied surface patterns. The central gable end facing the street has at its base a large, centrally placed window; this is connected to a pair of second-floor windows by a wood pattern (a central rectangle, surrounded by two curved shapes); and finally, in the gable end, is an overscaled lunette window and a horizontal band of paneling. The design may have come from one of the pattern books popular at the time, but whoever carried it out exercised great sensitivity.

ME235 **Beck House**

1860. 630 Ave. E

A T-shaped two-story Italianate dwelling, this house has been transferred into the Gothic mode by an emphasis on vertical mass, steeply pitched roofs, and pronounced bargeboards. All of the usual Italianate features are here— round-arched windows, brackets supporting the eaves, segmental arched porches, and so on—but the building's height and the roof overcome these references to assert the Gothic.

ME235 Beck House

ME236 **Cottage**

c. 1865. 614 Ave. E

This cottage displays an even more complex play of images than does the Beck house (ME235). This one-and-a-half-story cottage with a mansard roof should read as French Second Empire, but it does not. The central steeply pitched wall gable with its cut-out bargeboards takes over, and it becomes Gothic Revival. Other wonderful contradictions occur in the dormer windows, where the round-top windows and bracket-supported gables are Italianate. Also Italianate is the segmental arched entrance porch and the wide entablatures and brackets supporting the main roof.

ME237 **Saint Joseph's Roman Catholic Church**

1886. Near southwest corner of 5th St. and Ave. F

Saint Joseph's is a translation of the French Gothic in brick with stone trim. The plan is that of the central tower type. In this instance the two doors to the side of the tower have been brought forward, and each has its own gable roof. To the side of each of these doors are two small octagonal towers with crenellated parapets and a spire behind the crenellation. The scale of all of these elements in the entrance front strongly suggests miniaturization. Within, the church is divided into traditional side aisles and a nave, all covered by a series of light plaster groin vaults.

ME238 **Sacred Heart Roman Catholic Church**

1899. Northeast corner of 23rd St. and Ave. I

The French Romanesque style takes precedence in this building, though the corner tower plan and the high pitch of the main roof seem more Gothic. Compared to smaller Saint Joseph's (ME237), the design of this church is correct, but on the dry side. The glass in the entrance gable facade, in the rose window, and in the wide lunette above the entrance is far more open than one usually experiences in a church that looks back to the Romanesque. The six-story tower with a spire is strongly reminiscent of the Romanesque in the south of France. Following French precedent, there is a series of three domes over the nave.

ME239 **Schroeder House**

1865. 1 mile northeast of Fort Madison on US 61

This is a beautiful and ideally situated Italianate farmhouse. A gabled entrance pavilion projects from the main mass of the two-story building; on the first floor, within the canopied porch, is an unusual design for a door, side lights, and transom-lunette. The door has a semicircular top—a form repeated in the transom-lunette—and the sides of the sash are taken down and joined to the edge of the side lights. Another fascinating detail is found on the left side of the house, a small open porch with segmental arches. Within the porch on the wall of the house is a pair of twin-sashed double-hung windows. The sense of this composition is that it is not a porch as such, but rather the symbol of a porch.

ME240 **Louis Wilmesmeier "Bank" Barn**

1859. 1.5 miles northeast of Fort Madison on US 61

This really immense board-and-batten wood barn was built into the hillside so that easy access could be gained on two levels. The principal louvered windows are round arched as is each of the windows in the three ridgetop cupolas. The effect of these windows is sufficient to suggest that the Italianate style was

ME240 Louis Wilmesmeier "Bank" Barn

most likely being considered by the barn's builder.

ME241 Lauther Cottage

c. 1875. 2.5 miles north of Fort Madison on route X32

In this small brick farm dwelling, the Gothic Revival style has been combined with the Italianate. The scheme is that of a one-and-a-half-story cottage with a central entrance and gable that projects slightly from the face of the building. The roofs are steep, and the tops of the upper windows in the gable ends all have pointed arches. The entrance porch, on the other hand, is Italianate. Limestone has been used for the foundation, and the first-floor windows have decorated stone lintels.

Franklin

The town of Franklin, as well as much of the surrounding area, is one of the sections of the state that abounds with stone buildings—commercial blocks, houses, cottages, and barns. Most of these date from the 1860s and early 1870s. Two examples within Franklin include the schoolhouse (1872) at the west end of town, and the former "Old Inn" (1867) at the south end. The two-story school building has a hexagonal tower with a small onion dome that is situated on the ridge of its front gable end. The "Old Inn" is a one-and-a-half-story building; its most unusual feature is the suggestion in stone of pediments over the principal windows. Both of these buildings would loosely fall into the Greek Revival mode.

Southeast of Franklin is a stone dollhouselike Gothic cottage (take the gravel road at the southeast corner of the town, .4 miles; the house lies north of the road). This is the 1873 Charles Cabainer house. A balanced arrangement of a central entrance with paired double-hung windows comprises the front elevation of the cottage. Above the entrance door is a small, steeply pitched gable with a single tall pointed-arched window. Over the entrance is a horizontal stone lintel supported by small stone brackets. Carved within this is the owner's name and the date.

Garnavillo (see also Elkader)

Within Garnavillo's downtown, close to the junction of US 52 and route C17, is the Farmers State Bank Building (1915, now the Garnavillo Savings Bank). The small brick-clad elongated box reads as a Prairie-style bank building, primarily because of its cast-stone Sullivanesque ornament. Two piers divide the central window into three parts, and the capitals and impost blocks of these piers bear Sullivan-inspired ornament. The wide lintels over the balanced composition of the entrance to the left and a window to the right also display variations on this ornament.

On Washington Street one will come across the former First Congregational Church of 1866. The style of this brick building is Greek Revival. Since 1966 the building has been used as the Garnavillo Historical Museum. It is open to the public. Also on Washington Street, facing the town square, is the 1949 High School Gymnasium, a brick Streamline Moderne building that should have been built a decade earlier.

Two miles southeast of Garnavillo, on US 52, is the 1877 William Reinhardt house. Its design is that of a simple one-and-a-half-story brick cube, covered by a low-pitched gable roof. The balanced placement of the windows and doors, which have segmental-arched heads, and the return of the roof at the gable eaves convey the feeling that this is a late Federal-style dwelling, which one would have supposed had been constructed in the 1850s.

Guttenberg

The community's original name was Prairie La Porte, reflecting its early settlement by people of French extraction. Later (from 1845 onward) the town was colonized by Germans sponsored by the Western Settlement Society of Cincinnati, Ohio. The first platting of the town site took place in 1837, followed in 1843 by a second, more extensive survey. The first surveyed section, running parallel to the river, has a north-northwest, south-southeast axis; the new sections were oriented north-south, east-west. The site of the town is on a low terrace overlooking the wide Mississippi. Directly behind, hilly bluffs rise steeply. Unusual for a river town, the railroad tracks in Guttenberg were laid three blocks away from the river's edge, and much of the river bank was retained as a "public landing." In later years this land was formed into a riverside park. Architecturally the principal interest within the town consists of the numerous commercial buildings and houses built in stone by the German settlers. A few of the more important of these are listed below.

ME242 The "Albertus" (Marble Front Building)

1852; 222 River Park Dr.

This three-story stone building has windows and doors with slightly pointed arches. Over the central entrance on the second and third floors are projecting iron balconies. Within, the building's most interesting features are the two stone vaults in the basement.

ME243 Two Stone Warehouse Buildings

c. 1860s. Southeast corner of River Park Dr. and Lessing St.; northeast corner of River Park Dr. and Chiller St.

These two buildings with gambrel roofs were constructed to receive goods delivered by steamboat. The limestone has been left rough, creating a handsome tactile surface. The eavelines are low, so that the buildings really hug the ground.

ME244 Friedlein Building

c. 1850s. 370 Priam St., southwest corner of Priam and 3rd streets

This mellow yellow-tan limestone building was constructed as the town's first hotel. The two-and-a-half-story, gable-roofed form and the placement and proportions of the windows indicate a vernacular continuation of the Federal tradition. Next door is a small two-story stone building which was planned as the bakery for the hotel.

ME245 Junk Brewery

c. 1865. West end of Goethe St. at Bluff St.

Nestled into the base of the bluff and surrounded by trees is this former brewery building. Its two-story stone mass was located at this site to take advantage of the cool caves of the limestone bluff.

ME246 Dam and Locks 10

1936–1937. Just above Guttenberg, extending east across the Mississippi River

This is one of 26 dam-and-lock projects undertaken by the federal government during the depression years to increase the navigability of the river. The concrete forms of the locks and dam are treated in a mildly Streamline fashion characteristic of the 1930s. The low profile of the dam does not disrupt the sense of the north-south flow of the river.

ME247 Turkey River Mounds State Park

500–1000 C.E., mounds. South approximately 4.5 miles on US 52, east on county road

A group of conical and linear Indian mounds is arranged along the top of a ridge overlooking the Mississippi River.

ME248 True-Round Barn

1915–1916, Xavier Jacque, designer and builder. South of Guttenberg on US 52, just north of Millville

This is one of four round barns with dome-shaped roofs that still exist in the state. Sheet metal covers both the walls and the roof of this example. Centered inside is a silo that is 12 feet in diameter; it extends up through the peak of the roof.

Holy Cross

Just east of Holy Cross is the 1849–1850 Western Hotel (Pin Oak Tavern). The street front of the building has a shed-roofed porch across the entire first floor. Because of the slope of the ground to the rear, the stone basement opens onto a porch on that level. The main section of the building is one-and-a-half stories high, but at the rear the roof is brought down, forming the effect of a saltbox. Within, there is a central stairway, and the fireplaces and chimneys are on the inside of the end gable walls. If one were to suggest a style source for this vernacular building, it would be the late Federal style. The building is located on the south side of US 52, .8 miles east of Holy Cross's main street.

ME249 **Harvestore Grain Elevators**

1980s. Across US 52 from Pin Oak Tavern

The high-tech image of these grain elevators contrasts markedly with the mid-nineteenth-century atmosphere of the tavern across the road.

Keokuk

Willard Glazier noted when he visited the city in the 1880s that Keokuk had "broad thoroughfares, handsome and substantial buildings, [and] occupie[d] a beautiful locality." He also mentioned the advantageous location of Keokuk, "The Gateway City," at the confluence of the Mississippi and the Des Moines rivers, and at the lower end of the 12-mile-long Keokuk Rapids on the Mississippi: "The situation of Keokuk" he observed, "at the foot of the Rapids has made her a port of considerable importance for steam boats which carry large quantities of grain and other freight every season to St. Louis and southern ports on the river. Steamers touch here daily, some bound through from St.

Keokuk

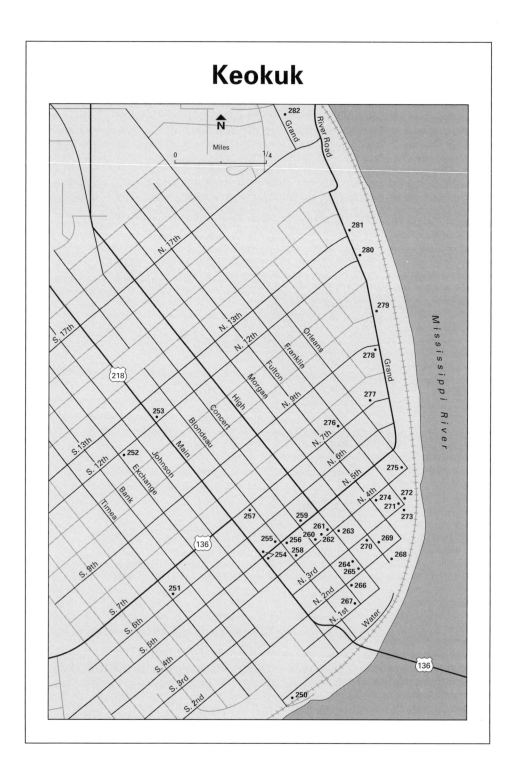

Lock and Dam, plus Powerhouse

Paul, and others stopping at Keokuk to discharge and take on freight and passengers."[26]

The city's grid was laid out in 1837 by Dr. Isaac Galland, an agent for the New York Land Company. Its north-northwest by south-southwest orientation of streets was a response to the large bend in the Mississippi which opened up to its juncture with the Des Moines River. By 1857 a railroad extended from the city, and in 1871 a large iron bridge was built across the Mississippi, constructed to accommodate the railroad, a carriageway, and a walkway for pedestrians. In 1877 the federal government constructed a canal and accompanying locks so that steamers and barges could bypass the Keokuk Rapids. This was supplanted in 1910–1914 by the 4,696-foot-long reinforced concrete Keokuk Dam, which contains locks and a hydroelectric power plant. Hugh L. Cooper, who designed the dam, became one of the world's leading designers of hydroelectric plants and dams.

Like other Mississippi River towns in Iowa, Keokuk was initially established on a flat terrace raised above the river. It then grew along the river and upward into the hills northwest of the downtown. Henry Lewis's drawing of the community indicates that as early as 1849 it spread into the hills and along the river. At first, public open space consisted of three centrally located public squares and Kilbourne Park, an open space given to the city by the family that developed Keokuk's first planned addition to the original city. In the 1850s an extensive cemetery was laid out within the northwestern hills. Later, three large parks were added: Rees Park for softball, Bluff Park for scenic views, and Rand Park for culture and recreation "in the Victorian manner." Rand Park, on the northeast side of town overlooking the Mississippi, contains a 10 1/2-foot-high bronze statue of the Sac Indian chief Keokuk. This sculpture of 1913 was designed by Nellie Verne Walker. In addition, Rand Park contains a round classical temple composed of eight Tuscan columns and a fountain within (1901), and there is also an openly romantic "witch's hat" pavilion.

On the whole, Keokuk has been fortunate that so many of its nineteenth- and early twentieth-century buildings have been preserved.[27] Grand Avenue, which extends along the north bluff of the Mississippi, contains a remarkable array of large-scale houses from the late nineteenth century and later. Several of these, such as the Rich house and the Green house, are of both regional and national significance. One of the city's greatest architectural losses was the Female Seminary building (c. 1855), an impressive stone octagon with cupola. Another was the Iowa Medical College building, later used as a courthouse, which was built in 1859 and finally torn down in 1976.

ME250 **Keokuk Union Depot**

1890–1891, Burnham and Root. Water St., foot of Bank St.

This picturesque brick-and-stone railroad station consists of a central pavilion and two end pavilions with circular links. It is the roofs which dramatize the composition; they seem to wander over the buildings in one direction or another, even curving down over the gable ends. In front of the station on the passenger platform is a long metal canopy supported by wrought-iron members arranged almost Art Nouveau-like in a pattern of sprouting plants. This is one of the few stations in the state which is still in use.

ME251 **Wells House**

c. 1860. Northeast corner of 6th and Timea streets

A powerful, bold statement of two vertical cubes is here realized in stone. The taller of the rectangular volumes has a bracket-supported hipped roof, a recessed entry, and to the side, an elongated window which lights the stair. In style, it is Italianate.

ME252 **Emmanuel United Methodist Church**

c. 1910. Southeast corner 12th St. and Exchange St.

The precedent here is that of the Italian High Renaissance and the centralized church building. The center of this church is a square with its corners cut off. Above this rises a drum with windows, and a low dome. Two grand temple fronts with pediments face out into the two streets. Each of these fronts has four Corinthian columns set in front of a triple-arched loggia. The auditorium within is a square lighted principally by the drum.

ME253 **Conoco Service Station** (Super Oil Company)

c. 1925. Northeast corner of 12th St. and Main St.

Two piers project upward and support the mansard roof covering the pump area. To each side are bays for serving the auto. What effectively captures one's attention is the sheathing of the complex in glassy glazed white brick, accentuated by rectangular geometric designs in dark-green glazed brick. The roof adds to the building's colorful presence with its bright green glazed Mission tile covering.

ME254 **Keokuk National Bank (now Northwest Bank) and Keokuk Savings Bank**

c. 1924, 1920. Northeast corner 5th and Main streets; northwest corner 5th and Main streets

These two limestone-sheathed classical bank buildings of the early 1920s face Keokuk's Main Street. Both speak strongly with the authority of the classical tradition, and as usually happens with bank buildings in American towns and cities, they suggest by their siting and classical image that these financial institutions are as public as city hall or the county courthouse. The Keokuk National Bank has a recessed, pedimented entrance; its side flank has a series of high windows set behind a row of Roman Ionic columns. The Keokuk Savings Bank is more openly a cubic block. The front is slightly recessed behind four engaged Corinthian columns. Projecting between these columns is the central entrance with a curved pediment; to each side are windows with their own gabled pediments.

ME255 **Wooley Building**

1888. 28–30 N. 5th St.

A fairly straightforward two-story brick and stone-trimmed building displays an energetic pediment with two fanlike devices over the main entrance. The street corner of the building is treated as a two-story rectangular bay which was originally designed to have a major entrance at its base.

ME256 **YWCA** (now Lee County Office Building)

c. 1910. Southeast corner of N. 5th St. and Blondeau St.

The underlying concept of the building, and its proportions, symmetry, and balance, are purely classical, but the building is detailed in a fashion one associates with the Midwest Prairie school. The Prairie-style features are found in part in the light cream-colored terracotta which sharply contrasts with the surrounding dark brick surfaces. The recessed entrance with a segmental curve carried above the upper window is a design device often used by the Chicago architect George W. Maher. The suggestion of engaged piers with horizontally banded capitals on the two side pavilions, together with the design of the terracotta panel on the building (consisting of four small squares and the sign between), is another set of devices frequently used in the Prairie style.

ME257 United States Post Office and Federal Building

1887–1890. 25 N. 7th St.

As the use of the Romanesque Revival style developed on into the 1890s and later, the general tendency was to turn away increasingly from French examples and to look to Italy. This predilection for things Italian was bound up with the popularity of Italy as a place to visit and with people's willingness to accept the authority of the classical tradition. The United States Post Office and Federal Building in Keokuk reveals some holdovers of the Richardsonian Romanesque, particularly in the arcade on the main floor. The most assertive Italian feature of this stone, brick, and terracotta building is the seven-story campanile attached at the corner. In a characteristic Italian fashion, it is layered with repeated entablatures and cornices, and its top level is an open arched loggia.

ME258 Fraternal Order of Eagles

c. 1910. 405 Blondeau St.

This is another classical composition (slightly Georgian) with Prairie-style ornamentation. The scale of this building and its delicate detailing are what one generally associates with an urban club house. The first floor has a row of five deeply set openings articulated by a pair of square terracotta blocks at the spring of the arches, each with a projecting keystone at the top. The upper floor has tall window units divided between a wide transom and a pair of casements below. The character of the letters on the building sign, as well as much of the ornamentation, really has more to do with design in Vienna at the turn of the century than with the Prairie mode.

ME259 Keokuk Public Library

1962, Frank W. Horn and Associates. Northeast corner of N. 5th and Concert streets

A modernist building of the 1960s, this library has a central entrance section with glass walls and wedge-shaped roof that perfectly mirror the popular modern style of the decades of the 1950s and 1960s. The two drum-like brick forms to each side, with a narrow vertical group of metal bay windows, seem to go back to the Scandinavian modern style of the 1930s. The building's low scale and the landscaped space around it carry on the traditional approach to library buildings of the nineteenth century.

ME260 Saint John's Episcopal Church

1883–1888, Appleton and Stephenson. Northeast corner of N. 4th and Concert streets

Saint John's Church was specifically modeled after an Episcopal church at Jamaica Plain, a suburb of Boston, Massachusetts. The Boston architectural firm of Appleton and Stephenson was engaged to prepare plans. Work on the church started in 1884 and it was completed in 1888. The church almost seems to be a small-scale afterthought to its great four-story crenellated tower. The style of this stone church revives the late English Perpendicular Gothic. The interior, as is usually the case with Episcopal churches, is modest in size, but luxuriously and tastefully carried out. This is especially evident in the woodwork of the roof and in the many leaded and stained glass windows. With the open, parklike space around the building, the church assumes even more strongly the image of an English village church.

ME261 Roman Catholic Church

1873. Northwest corner of N. 4th and High streets

The sources for this brick and stone-trimmed Roman Catholic church, one assumes, were French Gothic—not the original thirteenth- or fourteenth-century Gothic, but rather the French Gothic Revival of the mid-nineteenth century. Each face of the principal tower exhibits a round window whose surrounding stone molding seems to be a ship's wheel. Above, the cornice with its gable-roofed wall dormer (created when the wall surface continues up and through the eaves of the roof) is closely akin to the contemporary Eastlake style.

ME262 Harrison House

1857. 220 N. 4th St.

When built in the late 1850s, this house was described as being in the "French style of architecture." The most telling French Second Empire feature is the concave metal-sheathed mansard roof, broken by semicircular pedimented dormers. While the two first-floor porches and the entrance canopy are close to the Italianate in style, other detailing is quite classic, almost like something from the Renaissance. This is especially apparent in the window frames of the front two-story curved bay and on the entablature/cornice with a pronounced row of dentils.

ME263 Francis de Sales Church
(demolished)

1898. Northeast corner N. 4th and High streets

Across the street from the earlier Roman Catholic Church stood this later, more correct version of the French Gothic style. The building's gabled facade with central rose window was quite flat. A tower with a spire projected slightly from the building. The side aisles were lighted by pointed windows placed within gabled wall dormers, and each dormer was enclosed by its own pair of buttresses. The rusticated limestone walls contrasted with the finely cut surface trim. Both the stone decoration and the windows were kept close to the surrounding surface plane.

ME264 House

c. 1878. 218 High St.

A good-sized dwelling with Eastlake ornamentation, this house tries as much as possible to pose as a cottage. The main roof sways down and joins a low shed-roofed porch. The first floor is of brick; above, over a dozen horizontal bands of different shingle patterns decorate the surfaces. The gable and bargeboards are typically Eastlake, their lower edges sawed in a gentle wavelike pattern, and groups of round holes occur here and there.

ME265 Curtis House

1849, 1857, 1900–1901. 206 High St.

The original late Federal-style house has been revamped so that it now reads as a two-story hip-roofed cube with vigorous turn-of-the-century Colonial Revival elements, the strongest of which is the entrance porch. Soft, almost primitive Ionic columns support the wide entablature and cornice of the porch. To emphasize the entrance to the house, the central section of the porch has been pulled forward and extended upward. This section has an entablature with garlands, wreaths, and brackets supporting the cornice. Similar brackets support the main roof cornice. Other Colonial Revival elements are the dormers with gable roofs and the entrance with side lights and transom. All of these wood details contrast with the ashlar block masonry walls of the house.

ME266 Sample House

c. 1860. 205 N. 2nd St.

A tall, lean Italianate brick house, this dwelling has contrasting wood and stone detailing in white. The low-pitched gable roofs have been raised up on a high entablature that contains horizontal oval windows between pairs of brackets. The ground-floor windows have been brought down to the floor, and the arched windows in some areas contrast with the flat-topped windows elsewhere. There is a classic Italianate second-floor balcony with cantilevered hood on the northwest side of the house. The base for what must have been (one assumes) a cupola exists where the ridges of the cross-gabled roofs converge.

ME267 McGavic House

1852. 116 Concert St.

This is a sophisticated, refined brick Italianate Villa design, due in part to later remodelings that added a rich array of details. The building's form is out of the ordinary, consisting of two gable-roofed wings projecting forward, with the entrance between them. Behind the entrance and rising three floors is the hip-roofed tower. The entrance, which is new, has two narrow Tuscan columns supporting a classical entablature. The roof edges have been cut back, again most likely due to a twentieth-century remodeling. All of the changes, which have to a marked degree "Colonialized" the house, have been carried out with taste and understanding.

ME268 Meigs House

1910. 123 Morgan St.

The reference in this house—a two-story Colonial Revival dwelling in stone, with a shed roof carried across the lower floor above the first-floor windows—is to the Pennsylvania Colonial. There is an entrance porch with a wide pediment and Doric columns, and a large screened living porch to the side. The house was built by the federal government as the official residence for Montgomery Meigs, the engineer-in-charge of the lock and drydock on the river immediately below this site.

ME269 McQuoid House

c. 1920. 211 Morgan St.

This modest-sized upper-middle-class period revival house of the 1920s was carried out in ashlar block stone of highly varied colors. The historic theme followed in the design is the English Tudor. The garage at the rear of the property, also in stone, is carried out according to the same medieval image.

ME270 Weess House

1880–1881. 222 Morgan St.

The Weess house, a large, somewhat urban version of the French Second Empire style, was described in the 1880s as a "Palatial Residence." The *Daily Democrat* for August 1, 1897, noted that "the noble dwelling cost $24,000 and is as pleasant a habitation as the most fastidious and luxuriously inclined could demand."[28] One assumes that a house three stories in height, measuring 79 by 73 feet and containing 17 rooms, would indeed fill at least the basic requirements of its occupants. As with a number of structures that were labeled "French" in the nineteenth century, many details of this house are what one would normally expect in an Italianate house. What is specifically French is the concave mansard roof, the classically carried out quoining at the corners of the wall, and the front entrance with its high pediment.

ME271 Scrogg House

c. 1855. 524 N. 3rd St.

This Italianate French Second Empire-style dwelling could appropriately be called a mansion. The entablature of the house is of brick that has been paneled in wood, with pairs of wood brackets springing upward to support the overhanging roof. Sometime in this cen-

tury the house was "Colonialized" by the addition of a broad porch with Ionic columns which curves around two sides of the house.

ME272 McCune House

1848, c. 1910. 307 Franklin St.

What appears at first glance to be an elegant 1900s Colonial Revival house is in fact a stone Greek Revival house of the late 1840s. The house was built to overlook the Mississippi, and originally it faced on Third Street. In the early 1900s, the house was "Colonialized" with a new imposing two-story Ionic portico facing onto Franklin Street. Other additions were a front entrance with side lights and fanlight, a dormer with a wide broken pediment centered on the new porch, and another porch on the river side of the house.

ME273 Curtis Cottage (Port Sunshine)

c. 1863. 523 N. 3rd St.

This small Italianate one-and-a-half-story cottage was carved out in finely cut, monumental limestone ashlar block. The scale of the block is what one would expect to encounter in a larger house or in a commercial building. The result of this play of scale between the stone of the wall and the cottage size of the house transforms the dwelling nearly into a dollhouse. The only elaboration on the cottage is the bracketed hood over the entrance and the porch to the side (which has had its wooden pillars replaced). The stone voussoirs over each arched window are highly abstract, the arches kept parallel to the same plane as the surrounding walls.

ME274 **Chittenden House**

1855. 507 N. 4th St.

A classic towered Italianate villa, this dwelling looks like it is right out of one of the numerous popular pattern books of the 1840s and 1850s. The three-story tower is placed just where it should be, between a projection of one wing of the house to the left and another wing further back to the right. The entrance is in the base of the tower; the third floor of the tower has bracketed cast-iron balconies. There is a porch to the right of the entrance, and to the left is a large tripartite window whose sashes are carried down to the floor. Above this window is another projecting iron balcony.

ME275 **Baker House**

c. 1900. 404 Orleans St.

Dwellings with numerous classical references were responded to in different ways in the 1890s though the 1910s. Most people termed them "Colonial" or "Georgian." Designs such as these not only represent an ideological return to eighteenth-century America, but also are in their own way another expression within the increasingly popular Beaux-Arts tradition of the time. The Baker house, which is grand in scale and in abundance of details, could be thought of as Georgian Colonial. The walls are of ashlar block limestone, while almost all of the exterior detailing is in wood. At the street front is an ample semicircular balustraded porch supported by pairs of Ionic columns. To the side is a wide veranda, treated in a similar fashion. The entablature is terminated by bold dentils, and above, dormers with wide lunette windows dot the roof.

ME276 **Sheppard House**

c. 1885. 712 Franklin St.

The Sheppard house is a Queen Anne dwelling held in place by a horizontal Colonial Revival veranda that winds its way across the front of the house. The dominant porch with its splayed base covered in narrow clapboard, small Tuscan columns, wide entablature, and balustraded railing on top would seem to be a later addition.

ME277 **Stripe House** (Rose Villa)

1856. 710 N. 7th St.

This two-story brick-and-stone Gothic Revival "cottage"—a building reminiscent of the work of A. J. Downing—has a symmetrical facade. The central gable, with its lush bargeboards, contains a large-scale pointed window seemingly taken directly from a church. Now missing is the original first floor front porch with its Gothic-style center balustrade.

ME278 **Joy House**

c. 1897. 816 Grand St.

Impressively situated in a parklike setting, the Joy house brings together a variety of late nineteenth-century architectural images. The format of this stone, brick, stucco, and wood dwelling is picturesque Queen Anne—there is an extensive veranda, a varied, steeply pitched roofscape, and an assertive three-story corner bay tower. But the detailing goes off in two directions. The half-timbering apparent in the principal front gable is more "correct" Tudor Revival than Queen Anne, while other details, such as the columns and entablature, are Colonial Revival.

ME279 **Green House**

c. 1910, Ernest W. Wood. 1001 Grand Ave.

The Green house is unquestionably one of the principal landmark houses not only of Keokuk, but of Iowa. The viewer of the house is confronted with a two-story, hip-roofed volume similar in design approach to the concurrent work of the Chicago architect George W. Maher. In the Green house, the substan-

ME279 Green House

tial, classic restraint of Maher is presented in rough-cut stone, the horizontal joints of which cast deep shadows. The most remarkable feature of the house is the entrance porch. Here we have a broad arched opening springing directly from the terrace platform. The sides of the entrance arch spill off to each side almost like buttresses. The effect is that of a fragment of a medieval castle set down in front of a dwelling.

ME280 **Rich House**

1916, Barry Byrne. 1229 Grand Ave.

Generally we associate the designs of the Chicago architect Barry Byrne with Frank Lloyd Wright and the Midwest Prairie school. But even Byrne's Prairie-style houses do not perfectly fit the mode, and much of his work after 1920 could be more aptly thought of as

Expressionist. The Rich house is a fascinating design exercise. The principal garden facade has a two-story segmental curved portico with a gabled section above, which relates not to Chicago but to the turn-of-the-century Viennese Secessionists (particularly the work of Josef Hoffmann). Other sections of the Rich house, especially the tile roof ends which are treated as a sloped roof interrupted by recessed dormer windows, anticipate Byrne's Expressionist designs of the 1920s and later. The stucco walls, tile roofs, terrace walls, and roofed corridors convey a Mediterranean/ Hispanic feeling, but a close look shows that Byrne's reference to that tradition is slight. Corydon M. Rich, who engaged Byrne to design the house, was president of the American Rice and Cereal Company, and he built his new house on the site of an earlier extravaganza, the John Carl Hubinger "castle." Although Rich transformed some of the earlier landscaping, including filling in an artificial lake created by Hubinger, he still was able to take advantage of the site's mature vegetation.

ME281 **Weissenberger House**

c. 1938. 1307 Grand Ave.

This is a Dutch Colonial Revival house; its lower floor is sheathed in rough limestone, and there are two wide bay windows on each side of the central entrance. The house provides an ideal picture of the suburban Colonial house, set far back from the street amid trees, shrubs, and an extensive lawn.

ME280 Rich House

ME282 Logan House

c. 1936, Morton Geis. 1813 Grand Ave.

The two-story block of this suburban Colonial Revival house is Georgian; projecting forward on each side are one-story wings with large tripartite windows. Off the central section to the right is the service wing, its fenestration comprised of a central window balanced on each side by round windows. The rear wing plus the two projecting front wings feature a roof balustrade, solid in part but with occasional latticework openings. The one-story wings read as Regency or Federal in style and are in subtle contrast to the Georgian-inspired central section of the house.

Lansing

At 509 Center Street in Lansing one will encounter an elegant two-story Greek Revival building. This cruciform structure was built during the years 1863–1864 as a public school (it is now called the Stone School). The walls are of local limestone, 2 feet thick. Within, there are eight schoolrooms with 12-foot-high ceilings. The open wood bell tower over the main entrance has arched openings on each of its eight sides.

At 611 Dodge Street is a substantial two-and-a-half-story French Second Empire house (c. 1875). Its presence on the street is established by its square three-story tower with mansard roof; below, a porch wraps around the front of the house.

About 6 miles north-northwest of Lansing on Iowa 26 is Fish Farm Mounds State Park. Here on the crest of a ridge running parallel to the Upper Iowa River are thirty conical Indian mounds, which were first fully surveyed in 1890 by Cyrus Thomas. Thomas recorded another group of larger mounds on a lower terrace below, one of which contained a circular stone burial vault roofed over by stone in a corbeled fashion. These were built during the Hopewellian phase of the Woodland Culture.

Northeast of Lansing the country is hilly and sprinkled with beautiful groups of farm buildings. One of these, which makes a near-perfect rural picture, can be seen off Iowa 26 on the north side of Allamakee County Road X6A. The farm consists of a red-painted barn with dominant gabled roof, plus four other small outbuildings; to one side, next to a grove of trees, is the white clapboard farmhouse (c. 1900). Further north on Iowa 26, 1.5 miles south of the Iowa-Minnesota border, is a 12-sided red barn (c. 1900). Its double-pitched gambrel roof is sheathed in metal, and at the pinnacle is a small metal cupola.

Lowden

The commercial block in Lowden, described in ME283, is one of Iowa's most important late nineteenth-century landmarks. Looking to the twentieth century, those interested in prefabricated houses can find a gray Lustron house (c. 1950) at 108 Hall Avenue.

ME283 **Commercial Block**

1878. Southwest corner of Main St. and McKinley Ave.

Here is a single-story commercial block (1878), each of its three ground-floor stores occupying a bay set between paneled masonry piers. Steps lead up to each of the store's entrances, and there are large showcase window areas on each side of the double entrance doors. A delicate band of dentils has been placed within the span between the piers; and above, a bracketed cornice springs into a gable formed in the center bay.

Lowell

Located 3.4 miles east of the town of Lowell on route J20 is the Melcher house and adjacent pottery workshop. The house is given an early date of 1842, but certainly what one sees today most likely was built in the mid-1850s and later. The handsome square two-story house is a Federal type which has been updated with Italianate features. These include the usual bracketed roof and a double-piered entrance porch. The basic proportions of the house are Federal, as seen in elements such as the widow's walk at the summit of the low-pitched hipped roof. The pottery workshop is in a two-story building with a gabled roof; its walls are of thick native limestone. Vertical boards sheath the gable ends, and timber was used for the lintels of the doors and windows.

Luxemburg

As one approaches Luxemburg from the east on US 52/Iowa 3, one can see the tall steeple (172 feet high) of Holy Trinity Roman Catholic Church. Like a number of other Roman Catholic churches in northeast Iowa, Holy Trinity looks to the late Gothic tradition for its inspiration. But the version expressed in this 1874 church is pure "Victorian" in the apparent thinness of the masonry walls and in the truly linear quality of all of its details, both inside and out. The church is noted for its 14 elaborate hand-carved Stations of the Cross (imported from Europe) and its statue of Saint Isidore in front of the building. The church is located in the center of town, just off the highway.

McCausland

Three miles southwest of McCausland is the Isaac Cody Homestead. The two-story stone house represents a late continuation of the Federal tradition. The interior was quite elaborate for the time (it was constructed in 1847), having built-in closets and walnut doors and fireplace mantels. At a later date (c. 1860) a two-story clapboard addition was made to the original house. This addition became the principal entrance to the house. Isaac Cody was the father of Buffalo Bill Cody, and the younger Cody spent his early years at this homestead. The house is now a museum and is open to the public. It can be reached by traveling south on the gravel road that leaves McCausland at its southwest corner; proceed 1 mile to the first gravel road to the right (west); follow this road 1 mile, then take the gravel road to the left (south); the Homestead is about a mile further.

McGregor

Situated at the base of the high river bluff some distance from the river itself, is a splendid, exuberant example of the Queen Anne style, the Huntting house (ME284).

The Hartwick House (1886) is 5.2 miles west of McGregor on the north side of US 18. This large-scale dwelling is an animated version of the Queen Anne style. The three-story tower displays an array of shingles in a variety of shapes, and the porches extend the house out into the landscape. Additions made to the house in 1903 and other changes somewhat "Colonialized" its design.

South of McGregor, east off Iowa 340, are two state parks that adjoin the Mississippi and provide dramatic views of the river valley. These are McGregor State Park and Pikes Peak State Park. Both parks provide excellent examples of the evolution of park planning over a number of decades, and they also contain a number of rustic park facilities. Within Pikes Peak State Park (named for Zebulon Pike) is an impressively designed stone-and-timber shelter (c. 1938). Thick limestone piers with just a suggestion of capitals march across the front of the building. These support what seem to be very light header beams and roof rafters above. The feel of the building is that of the 1930s: it is rustic, but with a tinge of modernity about it. Walking trails lead the visitor to four concentrations of Indian mounds. Two of these are composed of elongated oval mounds arranged in a line almost perpendicular to the Mississippi River. A third group of similarly formed mounds (at the far southern end of the park) runs parallel to the river. Finally, north of the shelter is an effigy mound in the form of a bear.

Effigy Mound National Monument is 3.4 miles north of McGregor. The first acquisition of land at the site took place in 1949. A Visitor and Museum Center opened in 1960 and additional acreage was added the next year. Within the national monument are 191 prehistoric mounds, 29 of which are effigy mounds in the form of either bears or birds. The largest of the effigy mounds is the Great Bear Mound, which measures 70 feet wide and 137 feet long. The Marching Bear group consists of ten bears, accompanied by three birds with outstretched wings, and two linear mounds. The nonrepresentational mounds are either conical or linear. The mounds in this area were surveyed by Theodore H. Lewis and Alfred J. Hill during the years 1881–1885; an examination of their records indicates how many mounds no longer exist. The mounds within the monument were built over many centuries and by several different Native American groups. The various mounds date from the eighth through the fifteenth centuries.

ME284 Huntting House

1882–1886. 322 Kenny Ave.

The Huntting house displays many vigorous Queen Anne features. There is a broad splayed veranda-porch on the first floor; above is a recessed porch with curved sides made of latticework. The two-story corner bay to the left merges upward into an octagonal tower, the front half of which is an open porch. The picturesque roofscape is augmented by wide dormers, gables with bays, and narrow chimneys.

Manchester

The village site was initially surveyed in 1855, and it was resurveyed the following year by the Iowa Land Company. The location of the north-south, east-west grid pattern was on high, rolling terrain overlooking a wide S-curve of

Manchester

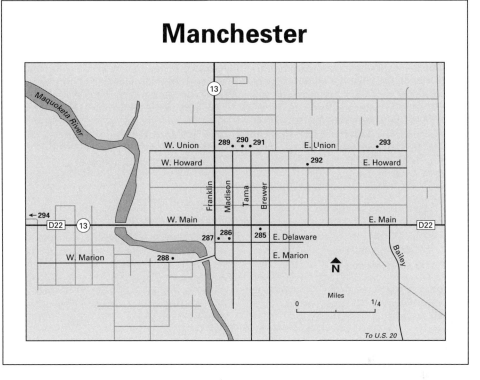

the South Fork of the Maquoketa River. Early in its development the community was traversed first by a stage route and then in the 1850s by the Illinois Central Railroad.

ME285 Delaware County Courthouse

1894–1895, Charles E. Bell. E. Main between S. Tampa and S. Brewer streets

The usual battle occurred in Delaware County pertaining to the location of the county seat. It wasn't until 1880 that the courthouse was finally situated in Manchester, and it was some 15 years later that a permanent building was erected. The building was designed by the Council Bluffs architect Charles E. Bell, who advertised "School Houses and Courthouses a Specialty." For his design of this red brick, stone-trimmed building, Bell brought together two fashionable images of the 1880s and 1890s, the Richardsonian Romanesque and the French Châteauesque. Essentially the upper portions of the building—the steeply pitched roof, wall dormers, corner pavilions, and the main tower—look to the Château-

esque; the body of the building below, with its deep sandstone arch, is Richardsonian Romanesque.

ME286 United States Post Office Building

1938, Louis A. Simon and Neal Melick. Northwest corner of Delaware St. E. and Madison St. S.

The usual low, single-story brick-sheathed box makes an appropriate nod to the Colonial Revival style via a central pediment, a slight hint of supporting pilasters, and an entrance composed of a fanlight and engaged Doric columns and piers. In the interior public space is a WPA mural by William E. Henning. The subject is rural farm life: milking, barn, cow, kitchen, and dinner table.

ME287 **Commercial Blocks**

1876, 1879. East side Franklin Street between E. Main and E. Delaware streets

The Masonic Temple building of 1879 is the tallest of these three contiguous commercial blocks. The designer of the Masonic Temple block has employed a high, semicircular gable to emphasize the distinct entrance to the temple. He has suggested that this is a distinct entity by pulling pilasters forward from the walls of the building and then providing a separate pediment. The smaller two-story commercial building at the end of these three buildings still retains a cast-iron railing atop the cornice.

ME288 **Bungalow Court**

c. 1935. 213–215 Marion St. W.

Oneupmanship on the traditional California-inspired bungalow court takes place here. The "bungalows" are former railroad passenger cars, sheathed in clapboard and transformed into dwellings which face the usual central grassy court.

ME289 **House**

1872. 120 Union St. E.

This house is an Italianate villa designed on a side-hall plan; its cupola exhibits a rather steeply pitched hipped roof. A "new," sophisticatedly detailed Colonial Revival porch (c. 1910) has been added across the front, and other changes have occurred. The newer porch—distinguished by a thin cornice line, an entablature with dentils, and fluted wood piers—has been successfully worked into the much earlier design.

ME290 **House**

c. 1905. 204 Union St. E.

The street elevation of this two-story Colonial Revival house is entirely correct; there is a balanced arrangement of windows and entrance with a broken pediment above. But the "real" entrance to the side (for the automobile) is something else. Here is a truly grand, overscaled entrance: two piers with oddly piled-up moldings support a pediment, and the entrance is recessed with a small second-floor balcony above.

ME291 **Cottage**

c. 1875. 300 Union St. E.

This is a wonderful variation on the theme of a French Second Empire cottage. To the side of the entrance is a wide bay; above, in the mansard roof, the bay emerges along with dormers as a pavilion tower. The dormers in the tower have curved tops and pronounced keystones; those over the body of the house are left plain.

ME292 **Cottage**

c. 1870. 516 Howard St. E.

The charming proportions and wood detailings of this one-and-a-half-story Gothic Revival cottage make it one of the most impressive in the state. The sawed bargeboards within the gable ends are indeed like lace. The small entrance pavilion as well as the bay window on the right side are equally luxurious, with paneled walls and bracketed roof.

ME293 **Lustron House**

c. 1950. 828 Union St. E.

Here is another of the side-entrance enameled metal prefabricated houses. As is almost always true of these post-World War II Lustron houses, this one is in pristine condition.

ME294 **Coffin's Grove Stagecoach House**

1855. 3.5 miles west of Manchester; west on route D22, 2 miles, then north .5 miles on route W69; the house is on the north side of road

In design, this two-story brick structure indicates a late continuation of the Federal tradition, accompanied by several more contemporary details. The double-row overlapping cornice of dentils and brackets suggests the Italianate, and in the attic gables are pointed

ME294 Coffin's Grove Stagecoach House

Gothic-style windows. The stagecoach house was on the principal route of the Western Mail Stage Company, running from Independence to Dubuque.

Maquoketa

Maquoketa, the seat of Jackson County, was laid out on the south bank of the Maquoketa River, a site selected because of the availability of water power and large stands of trees for lumbering. When the water was high it was possible for small steamboats to navigate the river as far as Bridgeport, some two miles west-northwest of Maquoketa. The town's traditional grid was laid out in 1850, with the courthouse square located one block west of Main Street. By 1870 the city was connected to the Davenport and Saint Paul Railroad and to the Midland Railroad. In the seventies the city was cited for being planned with "great taste and liberality," and these qualities still predominate today. The downtown is pleasant and well used; the suburban area, particularly to the west, has wide tree-lined streets, and the accompanying houses generally have extensive sites.

ME295 **First National Bank Building (now Hawkeye Bank and Trust); The Lytle Company**

1920. West side of S. Main St. between W. Platt and W. Pleasant streets

A Beaux-Arts composition was used here for a small-town bank. The entrance and windows are situated between a row of Ionic columns. The columns as well as the walls of the building are sheathed in glazed white terracotta. The design was produced by an architectural company from Sioux City that planned many banks in the Midwest in the teens and twenties.

ME296 **Commercial Block**

1896. 207 Main St. S.

A pair of two-story bays projects from the brick wall at the second- and third-floor levels. These bays as well as the entablature and cornice above are made of pressed metal.

ME297 Cottage

c. 1875. 210 Second St. S.

Toward the street this one-and-a-half-story cottage boasts two lavishly detailed gable ends, one of which is an odd gambrel-roof type. The house is slowly losing its wood detailing, but nonetheless, the two gables alone place it stylistically within the Eastlake mode.

ME298 House

c. 1875, later. 209 Pleasant St. W.

The two-story gabled brick block of this house eludes any stylistic designation. The porch to the side is early Queen Anne, while the corner porch with its semicircular bay is Colonial Revival (c. 1910).

ME299 House

c. 1880. 401 Pleasant St. W.

The Eastlake was merging into the Queen Anne when this two-story wood-sheathed house was built. The wall patterning on this house is especially impressive. The design begins with a vertical board skirt, then come clapboards, a curved roof of fishscale shingles, two large panels composed of four patterns of boards laid diagonally, then a horizontal band with clapboard set in rectangles; finally there is a return in the gable end to fishscale shingles.

ME300 Christian Reformed Church

1900. Southeast corner of Locust St. W. and Niagara St. S.

This is a small-scale late Queen Anne/Shingle-style church, realized in brick and shingles. Gothic arches penetrate each of the principal gable ends, and a low, sloping wall tower is tucked between two wings of the building.

ME301 House

c. 1897. 209 Locust St. E.

A grand-scaled Queen Anne/Colonial Revival house, this building is set in wide, spacious grounds. The extensive ground-floor veranda runs around an open pavilion to a side carriage entrance. The form of the house, with its round corner bay tower and picturesque roofline, is Queen Anne, but all the detailing is derived from the Colonial Revival.

ME302 House

c. 1875. 215 Locust St. E.

A substantially sized two-story brick Eastlake dwelling has been picturesquely sited at the summit of a hill. The tall chimneys with narrow panels and the several steeply pitched roofs add an accentuated Gothic verticality to the house. The original entry porch has been successfully replaced by a Colonial Revival one (c. 1910).

ME303 Seneca Williams Mill (Oakland Mill)

1867. 1.5 miles west of Maquoketa

This two-story stone mill has been rescued from neglect and has been restored (from 1976 on). Water from the adjacent Mill Creek enters the base of the building and once powered two 25-horsepower turbines. The building, which has a symmetrically fenestrated facade, now houses an art gallery, and it is open to the public.

ME304 Hurstville

1871. 1 mile north of Maquoketa

One mile north of Maquoketa, just west of the Maquoketa River, is the now-deserted company town of Hurstville, founded by Alfred Hurst in the 1870s to service his nearby lime quarries. The town and its lime kilns were active from 1871 through the 1920s. Remaining structures include four lime kilns, the company store/offices, Alfred Hurst's own house, and a few other structures and dwellings. All of the buildings are relatively simple structures clothed either in shiplap or board-and-batten. Much of the site is now overgrown, and today it conveys a picture of romantic melancholy.

Massillon

On the north side of this community is Massillon Park, within which is the Benjamin Fraseur Log Cabin (1842), which was restored in 1976. Behind the cabin is the Diamond Community Church (1869). This clapboard church with tall narrow windows was originally located to the north in Jones County and was moved to Massillon in 1894.

Mechanicsville

On the north side of Main Street within the two-block downtown area is the Mershon and Rhodes Building (c. 1879). Though some changes have taken place, the metal front of this building remains intact. The second floor has a small central bay, and the surface is virtually paneled in Corinthian pilasters.

Some 6 miles south of Mechanicsville is the large and impressive Alexander Buchanan farmhouse (1883). Buchanan, who came to Iowa in 1841, was a successful farmer (as well as a developer who laid out the town of Buchanan), and his dwelling reads more as a suburban "mansion" than a rural house. The two-story house is of brick, with extensive stone trim carried as horizontal bands across the facade. The square tower held within the fold of two wings, and its angular, brittle quality place it within the Eastlake style. The various gable ends exhibit elaborate designs in open and closed woodwork, and small gabled dormers dot the roof surfaces. Although the plans for the house exist (they are in the collection of the Iowa State Historical Society in Iowa City), they do not bear the name of the architect. The house can be reached by traveling south from Mechanicsville on route X40, 5.5 miles; the house is on the east side of the road.

ME305 Amos Miller House

c. 1870. 616 E. Main St.

The architectural jewel of the town is the Amos Miller house. The Miller house is unquestionably one of Iowa's most original domestic designs of the nineteenth century. It is a one-and-a-half-story house with a mansard roof. The walls are of brick with strongly accentuated corner quoining; the second-floor windows begin in the brick wall, project through the wide entablature and cornice, and are covered by flat roofs supported by short wooden piers. When originally built, the ground floor at the front had a small entrance porch with a square bay to one side. Sometime around 1910, the front was remodeled and a substantial Colonial Revival porch with Ionic columns was added; a new fireplace chimney was attached to the side wall.

ME306 McNee House

1847, William Rate, builder. Route X40 south for three miles; then go one mile west on route F14, then south

on the gravel road, the house can be seen on the west side of the road

An unusual, quite early exercise in cut limestone is the Duncan McNee house, 4 miles south of Mechanicsville. Heavy layered masonry cornices project into a low-pitched central gable; below, the central entrance is given an arched opening. This two-story house has the flavor of the Federal style, with some suggestions of the Greek Revival. The structure conveys a highly abstract quality through its sparse fenestration and masonry walls. The house was constructed in 1847 by a local builder, William Rate.

Mediapolis

On Main Street, between Orchard Street and the railroad tracks, is the International Order of Odd Fellows (IOOF) Hall (c. 1875). While some changes have been made in its two storefronts, the remainder of the building's metal facade remains intact. Paired columns on high bases are placed between each of its second-floor windows, and there is the usual wide entablature with projecting cornice above. At the center of the roof is a single gable bearing the lettering "IOOF."

The First United Methodist Church (c. 1900) at the northeast corner of North and Orchards streets, represents a fascinating version of the turn-of-the-century Colonial Revival. The two street facades are dominated by three large Palladian windows, each of which has been placed within a projected frame. The keystones of the central arched windows are strongly emphasized, and each of these windows has semicircular headers. There is colored art glass within each of these Palladian windows. In one of the windows, the grain elevator complexes at Mediapolis are depicted almost as a medieval castle, with cylindrical towers at each of the corners, and a central volume topped by a cross-gable top floor. This elevator complex is situated on North Street, west of Orchard Street.

Monona

The community of Monona, some 25 miles west of the Mississippi River in northeastern Iowa, contains one of Frank Lloyd Wright's 1915 American Ready-Cut System houses.

ME307 Delbert Meier House

1915, Frank Lloyd Wright. 402 N. Page St.

Wright entered the prefabricated-house industry through a series of designs that he produced for the Richards Company of Milwaukee, Wisconsin. These designs ranged from duplex units to two-story houses and single-floor cottages. The prefabrication system was composed of sandwiched panels that utilized the conventional system of stud construction. The system was actually only par-

ME307 Delbert Meier House

tially one of prefabrication, for exterior and interior walls were stuccoed and plastered on site. The units built in Milwaukee, and probably the Meier house as well, were assembled according to written instructions, but without the architect's on-site supervision.

The Meier house is a two-story version of the prefab scheme; essentially it is a variation on Wright's prairie box, which he had designed for the *Ladies Home Journal* in 1906. Underneath the cantilevered low-pitched hipped roof are groups of six casement windows which go around all four corners of the second floor. On the first floor, thin projecting slabs and bands of wood connect all of the headers and sills of the groups of casement windows. Other thin wooden banding occurs on the walls of the building, forming a rectangle on each facade, connecting the window sills of the second floor together, and acting as a horizontal line to separate the basement from the first floor. There is an open entrance porch at the front (extended in the late 1950s to form a carport), and an enclosed sun porch is situated at one corner.

Monticello

As with nearby Anamosa, Monticello was located south of the Maquoketa River. The initial grid plat of 1850–1851 was oriented so that Main Street was on a north-northeast by south-southwest line; later additions went in a variety of other directions, including a railroad addition that simply paralleled the tracks (which ran in a north-northwest by south-southeast direction). The Dubuque and Southwestern Railroad was completed through the community in 1859. It was later met by the Davenport and Saint Paul Railroad at the south edge of town.

ME308 Monticello State Bank Building

c. 1895. Northwest corner of 1st St. W. and Cedar St. N.

This two-story building is of a somewhat rusticated Beaux-Arts design realized in brick and stone. The corner entrance with its stubby granite columns is at a 45-degree angle to the rest of the building and succeeds in visually commanding this important junction of two major downtown streets. Large glass areas were introduced on both floors of the building between the supporting piers.

ME309 Monticello Public Library

1903–1904, Patton and Miller. Southeast corner of Grand St. and Cedar St. S.

One suspects that the historical precedent used here was the supposed Dutch vernacu-

lar. The walls are stuccoed, and gabled parapets project above the tile roof. The central entrance gable is scalloped, but the door below is slightly Gothic in flavor.

ME310 Central Block

1881. North side of 1st St. E. between Maple and Sycamore streets

Most two- and three-story commercial blocks such as this elude any style designation based on specific historic precedent. The bold, brittle angularity of parts in a design like this reflects an approach similar to the one taken by the Philadelphia architect Frank Furness and other "major" designers in the East. The Central Block has gained or suffered, depending on one's opinion, by the remodeling of the two storefronts; the one on the left has acquired a wood-shingled roof above its display window, while the one on the other side is newly sheathed in cast stone.

ME311 House

321 3rd St. E.

Without question, the Eastlake mode of the 1870s led to some delightful and inventive interpretations of Gothic design, and this house is one of them. Amid a virtual forest of gables on this one-and-a-half-story house, a classic Eastlake tower rises. Sometime around 1910 the house acquired a Colonial Revival porch with concrete block below and Tuscan columns above. An even later remodeling consisted of a resheathing of the building in large cement-asbestos shingles.

ME312 Cottage

c. 1875. 218 2nd St. W.

A lacy floral-patterned bargeboard decorates the steeply pitched gables of this one-and-a-half-story Gothic Revival cottage. The two principal openings on the front have Gothic U-shaped headers; above, on the second floor, round-arched windows contrast sharply with the brick walls. The present porch was added later, as were many of the windows.

ME313 House

c. 1910. 324 Gill St. N.

Two high gabled roofs run parallel to each other in this Craftsman house. An extensive porch wraps around the base, and the upper floors read almost as second and third houses. The walls at the base are brick, with stucco and half-timbering above. A long, low, shed-roof dormer breaks out of the main roof just above the porch. Entrance to the house is at the side, directly off the driveway.

ME314 Bungalow

c. 1910. 511 1st St. W.

This one-and-a-half-story Craftsman bungalow nestles into a forested suburban site. The central gabled dormer has small square windows on each side, and flower boxes below. The chimney was constructed of rough river stones and brick.

ME315 Agricultural Storage Building

c. 1910. North side of US 151, approximately 7 miles east of Monticello

Vernacular structures often provide highly sophisticated compositions, as in this board-and-batten farm storage building. The wood building has a main roof that is gabled at one end and hipped at the other. This roof is joined at right angles to another gable roof with unequal slopes. On top of the main roof are two little gable-roofed "houses" set at right angles to one another and at different levels.

Montrose

Montrose, sited at a deep western bend of the Mississippi River, was the location of a French-Canadian trading post of 1799. Later, in 1834, the first Fort Des Moines was established there. In 1837, after the fort was abandoned, the town's grid was platted. Two other events that took place here are historically important, the establishment by Dr. Isaac Galland of the first schoolhouse in Iowa in 1830, and the planting of the first orchard (apples) in Iowa. The actual location of both the schoolhouse and the orchard now lies under Lake Keokuk (created by the construction of Keokuk Dam in 1914). The small one-room log Galland schoolhouse was in use for only three years; eventually it was cut up and used for firewood. In 1940 a replica of the Galland school was erected and now some fifty years later the replica has all the appropriate appearance of age, and its location on a hillside backed up by a thick grove of trees conveys the atmosphere of Iowa in the 1830s. The actual building is located on the Mississippi River Road, three miles south of town at the site of Galland.

Within Montrose is Saint Barnabas Episcopal Church (1867–1872) situated at Third and Chestnut streets. Romantically sited in an open, parklike setting, it conveys the atmosphere of an English painting. As is generally the case with Episcopal churches, Saint Barnabas seems to pose as a dollhouse-scaled English village church, with a square entrance tower and buttressed side walls. The style of the church is Gothic Revival; the rough limestone walls have weathered to an ancient appearance.

Morning Sun

ME316 **Morning Sun City Hall and Library**

1937, James Troup, engineer. Southwest corner of Main and Division streets

The Morning Sun City Hall and Library building is unusual for depression-era public designs in Iowa, although not for other areas of the country. The precedent for this design is the early nineteenth-century English Regency and its offshoot, the American Federal style. What appealed to clients, the public, and architects about these styles derived from classical architecture was that, reduced to basic geometric volumes and simple, often undecorated surfaces, the buildings seemed somewhat modern, as well as traditional. Also, the mode conveyed a sense of urban sophistication, of high fashion.

The combined city hall and library at Morning Sun (what an enjoyable name for a town) is a brick structure on a raised basement, the high point being a four-story square

entrance tower topped by a low rectilinear block containing four clock faces. The tower is defined by a linear stone edge at each corner, and the stone block containing the clock faces has fluted pilasters at the corners and a low hipped roof. The two windows on each side of the tower are coupled vertically with the windows of the raised basement. The upper windows have stone lintels with keystones projecting through them.

ME317 **Floyd Tisor Standard Oil Company**

c. 1925. Northwest corner of S. Main St. and Manor Rd.

This prefabricated steel service station was moved to Morning Sun in 1940. Except for the rear portion, this little hip-roofed building is almost entirely glass, the walls made up of factory sash windows. The establishment's original name was the Central Oil and Grease Company.

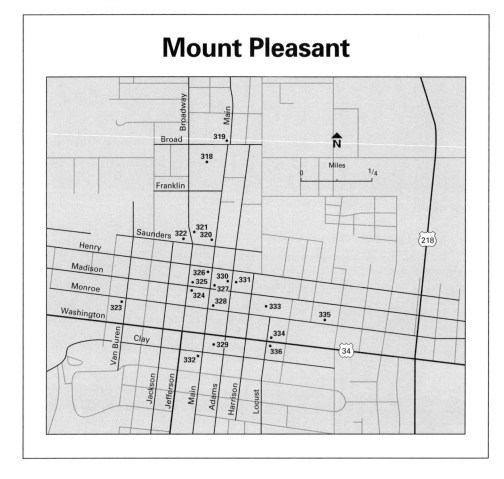

Mount Pleasant

Mount Pleasant

The city, which early acquired the title of the "Athens of Iowa," was described by Andreas in 1875 as having "long enjoyed a reputation abroad for its liberal support for educational institutions and churches, and the high standard of morality maintained by its citizens generally."[29] The community was established on the open high prairie approximately in the center of Henry County, and it thus was selected to be the site for the county courthouse. An informal platting of the site of the future city took place in 1835, but it was not officially surveyed until 1837 when a grid of 35 blocks was recorded. Though the grid was supposedly oriented to the cardinal points of the compass, it was in fact askew, the principal streets running west-northwest and east-southeast. A public square was provided in the center of the grid (it now contains an Art Deco WPA bandstand of 1937). The educational institutions for which the community became known, Iowa Wesleyan University, the Female Seminary, and the German College, were situated at the edges of the town. In 1851, Mount Pleasant was joined to Burlington to the east by a wood plank road. By 1860 the city was connected to the east and west by the Chicago, Burlington, and Quincy Railroad.

Mount Pleasant's economy has to a considerable degree been geared toward its educational institutions, supplemented by serving the surrounding rich farmlands. It has retained a large number of original 1850s and 1860s business blocks. The residential architecture boasts three of the state's outstanding examples of the towered Italian Villa mode, and it exhibits a number of excellent examples of the late Queen Anne style.[30] Gone now is the original 1855–1865 building for the Iowa Hospital for the Insane, an elongated structure of three and four stories with five pavilions, designed in the Italianate style by Jonathan Preston.

ME318 Iowa Wesleyan College

1844. N. Main, between Franklyn and Broad streets

This institution is credited (in error) as being the "first college west of the Mississippi." Originally named Mount Pleasant Collegiate Institute, it became Iowa Wesleyan University in 1849, and in 1911 it assumed its present name. The sparse number of buildings and their low scale means that it is the parklike quality of the 25-acre site which dominates.

ME318.1 Old Pioneer

1843–1845

This small collegiate building seems more like a house than a public institution. It is two stories high, with a gable roof and red brick walls. The style is late Greek Revival, though the double-hung windows have been changed to four-light units and a porch has been added at the front.

ME318.2 Old Main

1854–1855

Old Main is an excellent contrast to the Old Pioneer building. Here the scale has been shifted over into the public realm by the three stories and central domed cupola/tower. In style it has moved from the Greek Revival to the Italianate. The windows are treated as doubled narrow vertical units; the hipped roof is supported by brackets; and a perfect piered Italianate porch serves as an entrance.

ME318.3 University Chapel

1889–1893

The chapel building is appropriately Gothic, in this case what would loosely but aptly be labeled Ruskinian Gothic. The red brick walls are set high on a raised stone foundation. Light stone trim appears in a highly contrasting fashion throughout the building. An impressive play is enacted in each of the facades between tight balance and symmetry, and elements that seem purely random, accidental, and, of course, picturesque. According to the college records, the plans for the building were drawn by a "Mr. Snider of Akron, Ohio."

ME318.4 The PEO Library

1927

This late-1920s Beaux-Arts design was carried out with restraint. The two-story walls are organized around wide pilasters; the recessed entrance is set behind four two-story-high Ionic columns. The national PEO Sisterhood was established at Iowa Wesleyan College in 1862.

ME319 Harlan-Lincoln House

pre-1854. 101 W. Broad St.

An essentially Greek Revival house has merged into the Italianate through its bracketed eaves, the verticality of its windows, and its porch with thin wooden piers. A low monitor unit with four small horizontal windows crowns the center of the hipped roof. To the side, on the first floor, is a side-by-side pair of rectangular bays. Old photographs of the house show a veranda that extended across the entire front and along the left side of the building.

ME320 Bereman House

1865–1869. 401 N. Main St.

By breaking down the volumes of a house into readable separate parts and then highly elaborating them, an architect could suggest that a modest-size dwelling was a "mansion." The Bereman house reveals this approach carried out with great success, for it reads as a very large Italian villa, but in fact the interior rooms are of modest dimensions. The house is built up from lower bays and porches to the central section, which is itself almost a tower, and then on to a towering octagonal cupola. The pattern of the roof brackets and the extent of the projection of the roof is particularly dramatic.

ME321 Penn House

c. 1867. 408 N. Broadway

Three trends that occurred in the 1870s are exemplified in the design of the Penn house. The first of these was the increased use of details derived from the French Second Empire style, particularly the mansard roof. The second was the desire to emphasize the vertical, whether in interior space, in volumes, or in detailing. The third was the treatment of ornamental detail in a brittle, angular fashion. Many of the principal features of the

Penn house are Italianate—the bracketed eaves, the angular bay windows, and the wood pillared porches with segmental arches. But these elements are here dominated by one single feature, a mansard roof with a concave surface broken by numerous dormers and chimneys.

ME322 Ambler House

pre-1869. 405 N. Broadway

The design of this house is one often found within the Italian Villa mode: a central tower with the entrance at its base and a plan which is essentially a variation of the central hall scheme. On the third floor of the tower, Romanesque triplet windows are set within an arched framework on each face. The same motif is repeated on the front of the tower at the second level. When the house was built there was a porch to the right of the entrance tower. This is now gone, and some time after 1870 bracketed hoods were placed over the front door and over the tower's second-floor triplet window. A delightful element is the tiny, narrow, octagonal two-story bay which projects from the garden corner of the house.

ME323 Ball House

1894. 500 W. Monroe St.

This is a late Queen Anne-style house at its best, with a varied roofscape, an elongated bullet-roofed corner bay tower and, of course, a proliferation of Moorish arches, moon windows, and spindles. Modern additions and the infill of porches have taken place on the first floor. Still, the design is so assertive that

ME323 Ball House

these later additions recede far into the background. This house presents many points of similarity to the Crane house (ME334) which was based on designs taken from George F. Barber's *New Model Dwellings and How to Build Them* (1891).

ME324 **Harlan Hotel**

1857, 1875, 1895. Southeast corner of Madison and Jefferson streets

The first section of this brick hotel building (built originally as a residence) is the center section, built in 1857. This section is French Second Empire in style: it has a mansard roof with a wide and sumptuous grouping of dormers. In 1875 a three-story section was added on the left; another narrow three-story addition was built on the right in 1895. Both additions adhered to the details used in the original house; the only difference was in their roof forms. The 1895 wing housed the new main entrance, which was deeply recessed within an arched opening. In front of the entrance is a porte-cochère with paired columns and balustrade. The house has now been turned into a hotel.

ME325 **United States Post Office Building**

1935, Wyatt C. Hedrich. Northeast corner of Madison and Jefferson streets

This small PWA Moderne post office building was constructed of light tan brick. The re-

cessed layers of the brick around the long windows creates strong shadow patterns.

ME326 **Sargent House**

1862–1864. Southwest corner of Main and Henry streets

One of three classic examples of the Italian Villa mode in Mount Pleasant (for the others, see above), the Sargent house presents the central three-story tower scheme, the peak of the tower roof still bearing a finial supported on a tripod. The system of the entrance porch on the ground level is unusual; the entrance is covered by a projecting hood (as is the tower window above), and to each side, projecting forward, are two pavilionlike arched porches. The sides of the house boast angled bay windows, and the wrought-iron fence with its cast-iron posts still separates the grounds from the public sidewalk. The foundation of the house is Bedford limestone; above are solid brick walls 14 inches thick.

ME327 **Carnegie Public Library**

1903–1904, Patton and Miller. Northeast corner of Main and Madison streets

Patton and Miller went back to H. H. Richardson's 1880–1883 Crane Memorial Library in Quincy, Massachusetts, for their inspiration for this building. They have detailed the central round tower and the adjacent round arch in limestone; the remainder of the building is sheathed in brick, with a limestone foundation and trim. Instead of placing the front gable over the entrance, as Richardson did at Quincy, the architects have located it to the left of the tower. Though Romanesque in intent, the arrangement of the windows and the brick walls suggests the Colonial Revival. This touch of the Colonial is just enough to make the design seem up-to-date for the early 1900s.

ME328 **Brazelton Building**

1855. Northeast corner of Main and Monroe streets

The four-story Brazelton building was constructed as a hotel combined with retail stores. The hotel was large for the 1850s, containing 46 rooms, plus a ballroom. In style the building is Italianate, with round-arched and Palladian windows, plus the usual wide entablatures and bracketed cornice. Several of the ground-level storefronts with their simple piers and continuous entablature above are still in place.

ME329 Henry County Courthouse

1914, J. W. Rower. Southeast corner of Washington and Main streets

The citizens of Mount Pleasant built the first brick-and-stone courthouse in Iowa between the years 1839 and 1840. It was a handsome late-Federal-style building which conveyed the feeling that it was a large dwelling rather than a public building. Its walls were of brick and its low-pitched hipped roof was broken at the wall edge by four chimneys. In size it was 24 feet square and two stories in height. It was to have had a cupola, but this was never built. This building was demolished in 1871, and a nearby commercial building was remodeled for county governmental purposes. In 1914 a new courthouse was erected, designed by the Urbana, Illinois, architect J. W. Rower. In style, it is Beaux-Arts Classical, appreciably simplified. The principal pedimented entrance was set between four engaged Tuscan columns. The two-story building on a raised basement is sheathed in smooth surfaced limestone, with the exception of the basement podium, where the horizontal joints of the masonry are deeply cut.

ME330 Conaway-Mills-Tickenberg Cottage

c. 1865. 205 N. Adams St.

The proportions and modest roof pitch of this one-and-a-half-story cottage are essentially Greek Revival. The designer sought to make it Gothic Revival by adding sawed, open bargeboards running entirely around the house, a central wall gable, and finials at the gable ends. The front porch also is Gothic Revival, with latticework used to cover the pillars and as a horizontal band under the eaves. The windows in the gable ends became pointed by the addition of a louvered section above the normal double-hung window.

ME331 Schliep House

c. 1866. 206 N. Adams St.

The Schliep house is a variation of the two-story Italianate cube house. A porch with piered supports runs across the front of the house; to the right, a two-story wing with a bay projects from the main block, and this wing has its own small entrance and porch.

ME332 Singer-Pitcher House

c. 1865. 301 S. Main St.

The Greek Revival and Italianate are brought together in this two-story hip-roofed dwelling. There are narrow pilasters at the corners of the building and pronounced pediments are present above each of the second-floor windows. The Italianate flavor enters in the general verticality of the design and in the emphasis placed on the main roof cornice with paired brackets. The present cast-iron supports for the front porch are a later addition.

ME333 Mount Pleasant High School Building

1932, Karl Keffer and Earl E. Jones. Monroe at Locust St.

This PWA Moderne school displays an especially strong entrance, composed of a single heavy block articulated by the suggestion of wide fluted piers at each of its corners. The white color of the smooth limestone of the entrance pavilion contrasts dramatically with the tan brick of the surrounding walls. The entrance was made of aluminum, and is deeply recessed; the corners of the windows above are cut off at a 45-degree angle. The building's name appears within two horizontal bands between the corner pilasters. The rest of the building is divided into narrow vertical brick bands with an infilling of windows.

ME334 **Crane House**

1892. 401 E. Washington St.

According to a letter written in 1892 by Anna Kurtz, the niece of the owner, Hervey N. Crane, the design for this house was taken from the Knoxville architect George F. Barber's widely used pattern book, *The Cottage Souvenir, No. 2.* Anna reported, "Uncle Hervey says he knows enough to pick out a popular plan."[31] Barber also designed the Isaac P. Van Cise house (ME335), and there are a number of design features of the J. O. Ball house (ME323) that suggest that Barber may have designed that house as well. All of these dwellings are in the Queen Anne style at its liveliest. In the Crane house, the gable-roofed entrance porch has been projected forward on consoles with dramatic drop panels. Above the entrance is a design device often employed by Barber, a single central pillar branching out at the top and supporting the entire gable above. Next door to the Crane house, at 407 East Washington Street, is a somewhat later Queen Anne dwelling (c.

1900), now encumbered by classical (Colonial Revival) details.

ME335 **Van Cise House**

1892, George F. Barber. 603 E. Monroe St.

This is a somewhat calmer version of the Queen Anne than either the Crane house (ME334) or the Ball house (ME323). The centerpiece of the Van Cise house is the corner bay tower, which starts out as a rectangular volume covered by a shed roof; above this is a five-sided window bay and finally a high conical roof. The architect provided the client with a full set of working drawings for this house.

ME336 **Stall House**

early 1840s. 400 E. Washington St.

This full-fledged Greek Revival house is credited with being the oldest house still standing in Mount Pleasant. Its plan is that of a central-hall type; there are two rooms on each side, each with its own fireplace. The dwelling is a two-story gable-roofed design with brick walls that are now painted white. The pediments at each end are open, with a slight return, and the entablature beneath the eaves is quite wide. Behind the entrance porch with double Doric columns is a broad door flanked by side lights, with a transom above. The center window on the second floor has small pilasters on each side and is crowned by its own entablature.

Mount Union

Along the nearly deserted Main Street of Mount Union are several well-preserved late nineteenth-century commercial buildings, Johnson Harness Shop and Smith Drugstore and Ice Cream Parlor, on the south side of the street, and to the west on the north side of the street, the H. R. Williams General Store building (c. 1880). On the Williams General Store, pressed metal that imitates masonry has been used to sheath the entire two-story building. These three buildings provide an excellent sense of what a main street in a small Iowa town was like in the early 1880s.

ME337 **Johnson Harness Shop and Smith Drugstore and Ice Cream Parlor**

1877. Main St., 2 blocks west of route X23

The designs of each of these tiny retail buildings utilize pressed metal; in fact the harness shop is sheathed in the material. The original fronts are basically intact.

Muscatine

Phillipe Ronde's 1858 illustration of Muscatine depicts a thriving community oriented to the river and railroad.[32] The buildings in his view seemingly meander along the river and then are scattered upon the surrounding hills. Several decades later, in the mid-1870s, views of the city convey a much more orderly scene tightly held in place by the city's grid system of streets. The situation of Muscatine was an advantageous one. It was located on a deep westward bend of the Mississippi River, which meant that it brought the potential of river transportation far into Iowa. To the northwest of the city, adjacent to the west bank of the Mississippi, was Muscatine Island with its very rich alluvial soil. As Glazier remarked in 1892, the city was built "on a rocky bluff, the scenery from which in all directions is very charming to the lover of nature."[33]

The grid of the city, which runs parallel and perpendicular to the river (along northeast-southwest and southeast-northwest axes) was laid out in 1836. The community was first named Bloomington; in 1849 it assumed its present name (after the Mascoutin Indians). The year following its founding, Muscatine became the seat for the county of the same name. In 1854 the Muscatine and Oscaloosa Railroad was organized, later to be joined by other lines. The economic base of the community was derived from river and rail transportation. The lumber industry was strong in Muscatine, and by the 1890s the production of pearl buttons (manufactured from the river's mussel shells) commenced. In the twentieth century, light manufacturing and food processing were the city's principal industries. The Lock and Dam 16, constructed in the thirties, is one of a series built on the Mississippi by the Army Corps of Engineers.

Muscatine

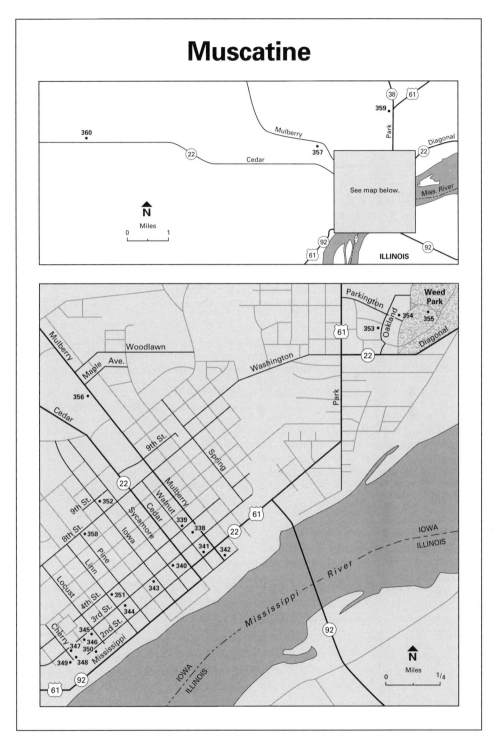

The riverfront of Muscatine developed in a classic fashion. It was first devoted exclusively to dockage for the riverboats; then the railroad ran parallel to much of the riverfront, and the accompanying commercial and warehouse buildings sprang up. Eventually parks were added, Riverview Park (c. 1925, at the foot of Oak Street) and Mussen Park (off Peal Avenue and Oregon Street). Kent-Stein Park was developed (west of League Street) along the former Muscatine slough; and in the northern part of Muscatine, Weed Park was deeded to the city by one of Iowa's foremost horticulturists, James Weed. Even before the High Bridge over the Mississippi was built in 1891, the city had become a center from which radiated wagon and later automobile roads. Today, the principal river highway (Iowa 61), the Inland Route (22), and the bridge route east converge on and utilize the city streets. Only when one gets out into the northwest section of the city—into the world of post-World War II suburbia and the mall shopping center—does one encounter a freeway system.

The community possesses a remarkable number of nineteenth-century commercial and domestic buildings. The city has been carefully surveyed as to its historic places and structures, and many of the buildings have been impressively restored.[34]

ME338 **Muscatine County Courthouse**

1909–1910, Joseph E. Mills and Sons. 401 East 3rd St.

Joseph E. Mills and Sons of Detroit provided the city with two Beaux-Arts public buildings: the county courthouse and the city hall. The limestone-sheathed courthouse conveys more of a late nineteenth-century version of the classical tradition rather than that of the twentieth century. The volumes of the building read vertically, as does the fenestration; there is little in the way of solid walls to play against the opening. The central open tower complex, topped by a clock dome with dormers, also projects a pre-1900 atmosphere. The strongest purely classical element is the pedimented entrance, supported by two pairs of Corinthian columns. The 1909–1910 courthouse replaced a remarkable 1867 building that centered attention on a high drum, a hatlike dome, and, high atop the dome, a standing figure.

On the courthouse grounds is an 1875 stone Civil War memorial consisting of a soldier atop a column which in turn is set on a high base. Interestingly, the top of the base has four pediments with semicircular dormers remarkably similar to the dome of the courthouse, built some 35 years later.

ME339 **Muscatine County Jail**

1856–1857. 411 E. 4th St.

A Federal/Greek Revival dwelling is employed here as a jail. The brick building is two stories high with the suggestion of piers at each corner and the gabled ends articulated as classical pediments. The entrance is strongly treated with substantial pilasters and a double-layered entablature with cornice. The main cornice is also quite wide, and a pattern of bricks suggests classical dentils. The building has recently been restored.

ME340 **Muscatine City Hall**

1915, Joseph E. Mills and Sons. 204 E. 3rd St.

The architect devised an L-shaped plan for the two-story building on a raised basement. At the juncture of the two wings, he placed a quarter-circular portico. This splayed plan works well, for this entrance portico faces the street corner at a 45-degree angle. Compared to this architect's work on the courthouse, he has in this case brought Beaux-Arts Classicism into the twentieth century. As often encountered throughout Iowa, a miniature Statue of Liberty greets visitors as they walk up to the building's main entrance.

ME341 Trinity Episcopal Church

1851–1855, Frank Will. 411 E. 2nd St.

The designer of this church, Frank Will, was an English emigré who became a leading member of the New York Ecclesiological Society. He designed many small Ecclesiological churches across the country. On this church's gable end facing the street, Will placed a wall tower, stepped in design, and terminated the roof above with an arched opening and a gable roof. Short buttresses define the sides of the sandstone Gothic Revival building. As with most Episcopal churches, the building is not only small in size, but all of its features are miniaturized. The design is dominated by the slate-covered roof which descends close to the ground. Sympathetic additions were made to the building during 1912–1915 and in 1955.

ME342 Judge Woodward House

1848, c. 1874. 501 E. Mississippi Dr.

This brick house started out as a late Federal-style design. Around 1874 it was substantially enlarged and remodeled, transforming it into an Italianate/French Second Empire dwelling. A narrow third floor was added; bays were projected off various elevations, a heavy classical cornice was added, and the side bay emerged above the roof with a segmented concave roof.

ME343 Welch Apartments

c. 1900. 220–228 Iowa Ave.

The designer of this four-story building has set down a plain red brick block, and then dramatically played off one- and two-story bay windows, together with an elaborate pressed tin entablature, cornice, and gables. Atop the cornice, somewhat pushed back, are gabled monitor windows that provide light to the top floor. Although the street-level storefronts have been blandly remodeled, the upper portions of the building are still highly assertive. As with so many turn-of-the-century commercial buildings, it is quite impossible to categorize the style of this building. It has the flavor of nineteenth-century classicism, realized through strongly angular, brittle details.

NE344 Funck House

1884. 310 W. 3rd St.

It would seem that the architect of the Funck house began with the idea of refining the much earlier Italianate style. He quickly added a series of much more fashionable details of the mid-1880s. To the left on the second floor, the building was angled and a tiny arched corner porch was injected. Below, the columns of the wood porch boast capitals that are a reflection of the interest at the time in Egyptian art and architecture.

ME345 George Stone House (West Lawn Terrace)

1852. 606 W. 3rd St.

The George Stone house is another of Iowa's impressive contributions to America's Italian Villa mode. The editors of *The American Agriculturalist*, in an article titled "An Italian Villa" (January 1850), observed that, "Houses in the Italian Style are most appropriately placed up the side or on top of a hill" (p. 25). The Stone house appears in just this fashion;

from its large-scale belvedere one could look out over the city and the river beyond. The house is in fact a two-and-a-half-story dwelling with small windows tucked into the entablature between the paired brackets. At the front, the center of the roof is lifted up into a curved wall dormer, while to the sides of the building there are similar low curved dormers within the low-pitched gable roofs. This theme of the segmental curve then is repeated in wall dormers on each facade of the belvedere. There is an extensive porch on the ground floor. The posts for this porch are thin and tall and are connected to a curved band that suggests, in a linear fashion, arches between the posts. The brick walls are now stuccoed and painted so that they contrast with the building's dark trim.

ME346 **Fred Stone House**

c. 1856. 614 W. 3rd St.

One version of the Italianate style was based on the late eighteenth-century Federal house, and upon this was grafted a bracketed roof, porches, and bays. Sometimes, as is the case in the Fred Stone house, these wood details are fragile and thin, seemingly having as much to do with the concurrent Gothic Revival style as with the Italianate. In this house the paired, very narrow wooden brackets move along the eaves and gable ends without having any entablature. From the porch columns spring thin wooden double arches; and an arched hood covers the central second-story windows above the entrance.

ME347 **Moore House**

1851–1856. 716 W. 3rd St.

The boxlike form, proportions, and much of the fenestration of the Moore house indicate its essential derivation from the Federal style. Elements of the Italianate style enter in the usual places: a balustraded porch across the first-floor front, angled bay windows, an emphasized entablature/cornice with paired brackets, and a rooftop widow's walk with a central belvedere. In comparison to the nearby Fred Stone house (ME346), the wood details of the Moore house have thickness and weight, coming close to suggesting their ultimate source in stone.

ME348 **Ward House** (Ward's Folly)

1852. 205 Cherry St.

In the 1850s there were several large Greek Revival "mansions" built within one or another of Iowa's Mississippi River towns. The Ward house, though never completed, is Muscatine's contribution to this imagery. A grand two-story pedimented porch overlooks the river from its blufftop location. The walls of this house on a raised basement are lined with a row of thinly projecting pilasters that support a wide entablature. At the center of the roof is an octagonal belvedere.

ME349 **Captain Clark House**

1880, Cleveland and Jay (L. D. Cleveland). 206 Cherry St.

As with most late nineteenth-century revival styles, the American Queen Anne seemed to follow various directions, absorbing or emphasizing one feature or another. The Clark house is something of an urban version of the Queen Anne—similar to what one would have found at the time in Chicago and New York, and ultimately in London. These urban designs seem to keep the exuberance of the Queen Anne in hand through greater reliance on classical surfaces and detailing. In the Clark house, horizontal bands of varying widths layer the facades and are used to tie the headers and sills of the windows together. Though there are some curved details on the house, its main commitment is to the angular and rectilinear. There are a few places where the agitation of the Queen Anne style breaks through this general feeling of restraint. One of these is in the third-floor open porch of one of the bay towers; other relapses come about in some of the molded, turned, and sawed wood details. To the rear is a brick stable with a cupola, very much in keeping with the design of the house.

ME350 Johnson House

1857, 1867. 608 W. 2nd St.

From a distance this two-story house could easily be taken for a Colonial Revival house of around 1910. Its white painted clapboard walls have shuttered double-hung windows; the roof is a simple gable, and a pedimented entrance porch stands at the center of the street facade. A closer look reveals that the form of the house is late Federal; its entrance porch is Greek Revival, and its roof soffits and eaves with paired brackets are Italianate. At least a quarter of the present two-story front is the result of a remodeling of 1867. The house was restored and several later additions were removed in 1968.

ME351 Wilson House

c. 1843, 1884. 316 W. 4th St.

The 1840s form of this two-story brick house was mildly Italianate. The walls were treated in an unusual fashion. They were divided into arched bays by pilasters that were doubled at the top and then emerged into a single pilaster below. The 1884 remodeling added what is unquestionably the most assertive Italianate brackets and entablature to be found in the state. Every detail at this point is thick in dimension and elaborate in contour and cut-in detailing.

ME352 Baker House

1897, Joseph Hoopes. 811 Iowa Ave.

A commodious house, the Baker residence has all the delightful and refreshing atmosphere of a do-it-yourself design. Whoever put it all together was, to begin with, a wee bit behind in fashion, for he had recourse to the earlier French Second Empire and the spindly version of the Queen Anne. Confronting one toward the street is a two-and-a-half-story gable held in place by two bay towers; the one to the right is square and surmounted by a dormered mansard roof; the one to the left is octagonal with a segmented concave roof. Between the towers on the first floor and to the right are porches with elaborate but thinly delineated cast-iron railings. Within the central front gable are cut-out, spindled struts of inventive design.

ME353 Weed House (The Gables)

1853, Josiah Walton. 1124 Oakland Dr.

The Weed house is certainly Iowa's most widely known example of the Gothic Revival style.

ME353 Weed House (The Gables)

This fame is due not only to the quality of its design, but also to the importance of the owner-client and the architect. James Weed was one of those nineteenth-century horticulturists who followed in the footsteps of A. J. Downing, the pioneer American landscape architect. Weed came to Muscatine in 1839, and in 1842 he purchased some 400 acres. Here he established his famed nursery, the Iowa Pomological and Horticultural Garden. As with many mid-nineteenth-century figures, Weed's background and interests were broad, if nothing else. He had studied medicine at Yale University, and upon arriving in Muscatine he emerged as a dentist. From these avocations, he settled into horticulture. His nursery and gardens were the source for thousands of Iowa's fruit trees and other plants. At the end of the century, in 1899, he presented 54 blufftop acres of this establishment to the city for a public park (named Weed Park).

The architect of the Weed house, Josiah Walton, mirrored the typical evolution of a person trained as a carpenter, who developed later into an architect. He ended up designing a number of Muscatine's major buildings, including the Henry Waterman house, the Benjamin Hersey house, and the city's high school building. The Weed house closely reflects the direct influence of A. J. Downing, and of Downing's preference for the Gothic mode. The design of the house must certainly have been a close collaborative affair between the client and the architect builder. As a Gothic design should be, this house exhibits steeply pitched gables and dormers on all of its fa-

cades. All of the windows are pointed, not, it should be noted, with a pointed arch, but with an angular point. Within each of the windows, mullions divide the glass into diamond panes. Porches and angular bays project from the first floor. High on the gabled ends are small, delightful oriel windows. The patterns of the bargeboards illustrate Weed's horticultural enthusiasm, depicting leaves, berries, grapes, and various flower petals. All of these wooden parts, painted white, contrast sharply with the stone foundation and the red brick walls of the building. The mortar joints of the walls were tinted to match the color of the brick. Among the many innovations in the house are the porch windows which could be cranked up and down from pockets set within their foundations. The only appreciable changes to the exterior are the permanent closure of the first-floor porches. Recently an addition was built to the rear of the house, and a garage was added.

ME354 House

c. 1910. 407 Parkington Dr.

Here the do-it-yourself design entails several Craftsman images that have been brought together. The dwelling is essentially a Craftsman bungalow with the usual entrance porch and play of gable ends, supported by angular struts. But to the left, the scale changes and becomes miniaturized. This section of the house is of two stories, with the second floor cantilevered out on two sides and more or less worked into the eave sections of the main roof on the other two sides. As is characteristic of the Craftsman mode, the lower portions of the wall are in clapboard; above are alternating narrow and wide bands of shingles.

ME355 Weed Park

1899. Diagonal Rd., off Washington St.

The 54-acre park was given by the Weed family to the Muscatine Floral Society. Much of the planting was already in place since this was part of James Weed's horticultural grounds. The grounds were revamped by American Park Builders of Chicago, and the park now includes a lagoon, picnic areas, a small zoo, and a swimming pool building. Also to be found within the park is a brick-

and-wood hexagonal bandstand (c. 1915). The offices for the zoo are in a log cabin (c. 1835) moved from the nearby country into the park. The park also contains a small group of conical Indian mounds dating between c.e. 500 and 1000.

ME356 **Musser House** (now Laura Musser Art Gallery and Museum)

1908, Henry W. Zeidler. 1314 Mulberry Ave.

The local architect Henry W. Zeidler gave his client an up-to-date exercise in the Beaux-Arts mode. This "mansion" is a three-and-a-half-story structure in yellow pressed brick with stone trim. A broad porch runs across the front of the first-floor wing; the small windows on the third floor are situated just below the entablature, and a curved gable with pediment projects from the roof. To the right is a single-floor music room which was added in 1921.

ME357 **Phillips House**

1917. 2619 Mulberry Ave.

This house is a Prairie-school two-story box, covered by an extended hipped roof. The street facade presents a central entrance porch; above, there is a band of double-hung windows placed directly under the soffit. The walls are of stucco; the trim, painted wood.

ME358 **Saint Mathias Church**

1842. 211 W. 8th St.

Saint Mathias is a dollhouse-sized (20 feet by 30 feet) Greek Revival church. The angled pitch of the pediment is repeated in the gables of the small triangular window. Below this is a handsome entry with wide entablature and cornice supported by a pair of pilasters. The building was constructed at Prairie du Chien, Wisconsin, and then shipped to Muscatine by raft on the Mississippi River. Its original site was on the northwest corner of Second and Cedar streets. It was moved to its present site and restored in 1934.

ME359 **de Sinnette Octagon House**

1855. 2520 Park Ave. (US 61 and Iowa 38)

The de Sinnette house presents a large-sized version of Orson S. Fowler's octagonal houses. The walls of this house are of brick, with simple pilasters emphasized at each corner. The cupola is rather unusual in that each of its faces is a gable, with a seemingly flat roof behind which culminates in a central chimney. An extensive porch runs around much of the house. A few changes have occurred over the years: in 1912, a kitchen wing was added, and at some point in the house's history shed-roof dormers were placed on the roof.

ME360 **Barn**

c. 1860. 4 miles west of Muscatine city limits on Iowa 22

Set far back from the road among trees is this large three-and-a-half-story brick barn with a gable roof. Windows with segmental arches occur at the ground level; above are diamond-shaped brick screen windows that have been arranged to form a fascinating pattern on each of the building's facades. A tall, square wood cupola surmounts the center of the gable roof.

New Vienna

New Vienna was one of several communities of Austrian emigrés that were established in eastern Iowa.

ME361 Saint Boniface Roman Catholic Church

1884–1887

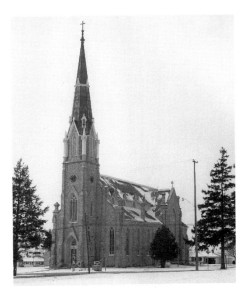

Because of its hilltop situation, the Roman Catholic church of Saint Boniface dominates the small town and surrounding countryside. The New Vienna church, like the one at nearby Dyersville, is French Gothic in inspiration, even though it too was built by German immigrants. Saint Boniface is entirely of stone, a white magnesia limestone obtained from a nearby quarry. Externally the side aisles appear to be separate from the higher nave section; small wall-dormer windows provide clerestory lighting for the nave. The single entrance tower with its narrow spire is 200 feet high. The simple interior, with its thin coupled columns, centers on a finely carved mahogany altar. In the adjoining cemetery is a playhouse-sized cruciform chapel (1900) crowned by an open six-sided tower at the crossing. The tower, its roof, and the roof of the chapel are sheathed in shimmering metal shingles.

ME361B Saint Boniface Roman Catholic Church, Cemetery Chapel

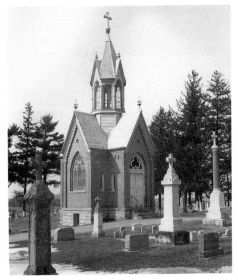

Nichols

The Muscatine architect Henry W. Zeidler provided a somewhat stylish late Queen Anne design for the 1897 Nichols Townsend house (at the northeast corner of High and Nichols streets). Its most telling design feature is its second-floor porch over the entrance. Here a pair of C-shaped lattice screens draws attention to the accompanying pencil-thin turned column that supposedly supports the roof.

On Grand Avenue, one block west of Main Street, is the brick and stone-trimmed Saint Mary's Church (1904). In plan the Gothic Revival church is the type with a central entrance tower. To each side of the tower are low quarter-curved wings with crenellated parapets. Bold, slightly projecting crenellations occur as well on the parapets at the top of the central tower.

Oxford Junction

The first "monument" to greet visitors when they enter Oxford Junction is the DX Service Station. At 215 First Avenue North is the Carter house (c. 1878). The style in this instance is Eastlake with a shed-roofed entrance porch, steep gabled roofs above, and extended outrigger wood struts supporting the gable ends.

ME362 **DX Service Station**

c. 1922. Northeast corner of Borady and First Ave. N.

This tiny service station with a gable roof is sited at an oblique angle to the street. Pilasters of a sort define its corners, and a round medallion is centered within the gable. The do-it-yourself design is classical, dignified, and domestic in scale. The present sign, pumps, and lighting are somewhat new and bring the whole ensemble up to date. (A near twin to the station is a now deserted one located just west of Letts, Iowa, on route G40.)

Petersburg

Just down the road (route C64) west of New Vienna is the small community of Petersburg. Like New Vienna it is dominated by an impressive stone Gothic Revival Roman Catholic church, Saints Peter and Paul. It was started in 1867–1868 as a church with a central entrance tower. In 1904 it was substantially enlarged. The central tower and spire were joined at the front by two additional towers, each placed at a 45-degree angle to the corners of the building.

These towers are lower in height than the central tower, and each contains an open eight-sided belfry. The interior of this church with nave and side aisles is elaborate in its decoration, which ranges from the sumptuous main altar and the stations of the cross, to ceiling paintings and richly delineated stained glass windows.

Postville

Postville is located at the southwest corner of Allamakee County. Its center four blocks were platted in 1850, and additional plats were laid out between 1864 and 1874. The town developed slowly until 1871 when the Burlington, Cedar Rapids, and Minnesota Railroad arrived. The town conveys a sense of openness with its wide residential lots set within plantings of trees and of well-kept flower and vegetable gardens.

ME363 **Cottage**

c. 1875. 104 Ogden St.

This one-and-a-half-story brick cottage displays a long front porch with an Eastlake flavor, while its south bay, with its metal crenellations and bracketed roof, appears Italianate.

Saint Donatus

Driving northwest from Bellevue on US 52, one traverses hilly country to which older highways such as 52 respond. Some of the hills are wooded, others are grass covered or have crops. Some 10 miles from Bellevue the road gently dips down into a river valley, and one will encounter a mixture of contemporary service stations alongside what certainly has the appearance of ancient stone buildings. This is the Luxembourgian community of Saint Donatus. A group of Luxembourgers settled in the area in the 1850s, and in the small town itself and in the outlying country they built a number of stone houses, barns, and other outbuildings.

Along the commercial strip of the highway is a group of two-story gable-roofed (with jerkin ends) stone houses, most of which date from the late 1840s on through the 1860s. Accompanying these are several stone barns, smoke-houses, and other outbuildings. The largest of these houses is the Gehlen house of 1848. Originally, the living quarters were on the second floor, and the ground floor was used to house animals.

At the center of town is a cross road that intersects with US 52. Take this road to the west approximately .3 miles. At this point one will come across a two-story stuccoed stone house. This is the Frank Stephen house, built in the middle to late 1850s. In plan it is of the central hall type, and externally it is essentially a very late continuation of the nineteenth-century Federal style.

ME364 Pieta Chapel (Chapel on the Mount)
1885

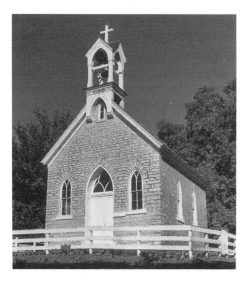

On the hill overlooking the town is the Pieta Chapel, a small stone Gothic Revival chapel with an entrance tower. Along the pathway winding up the hill to the church are the 14 stations of the cross, built in 1861, under the church's first leader, Father Michel Flamming. Across the valley on the sloping hill can be seen another church, the German Lutheran Church, constructed in 1918. Its format is that of a twin-towered and spired masonry Gothic church.

Salem

Salem, situated on the open prairie southwest of the Skunk River in Henry County, was the first Quaker community in Iowa, founded in 1835. In town half a block south of route J20 is the Henderson Lewelling house (1840–1845). This is a two-story stone house with a gable roof. The chimneys are in the end gable walls, and a porch runs across the first-floor front of the house. In style the house is late Federal, with a balanced composition of windows and doors.

East of Salem 2.2 miles on route J20, on the north side of the road, is a handsome two-story house of finely cut limestone (c. 1860). Its principal facade presents a central entrance with side lights and transom, balanced by one window to each side. The upper floor is similar, except that the central door is without side lights or transom. This door, one assumes, led to the roof of a porch that no longer exists. The roof of the house is hipped, with a small flat section at the top; the overhang of the roof is supported by paired brackets. The design represents the late Federal style taking on the proportions and some details of the Italianate.

Southeast of Salem is the True-Round Barn (1918) of Bernard J. Holtkamp, built from plans provided by the Permanent Building Society of Des Moines.

The diameter of the barn is 50 feet; its roof, with its central aerator, is of the double-pitch gambrel type. The walls of the barn are of terracotta brick. The upper, main floor of the barn is reached by an inclined earthen ramp. To reach the Holtkamp barn travel east on route J20 3.2 miles to US 218; turn right (south) on US 218; at 2.1 miles is a gravel road leading to the west; the barn will be visible at this point.

Strawberry Point

The community's name was chosen because of the wonderful abundance of native strawberries in the area. There are several nineteenth-century houses to be visited in Strawberry Point. An Eastlake-style house is located at 110 East Mission Street (c. 1875), and a small French Second Empire cottage (c. 1870) can be seen at 411 South Commercial Street. The Eastlake dwelling has a three-story tower with an iron crown railing still intact; a later Colonial Revival porch has been added on the first floor. Not to be outdone, the Second Empire cottage counters with its own small tower.

Four miles southwest of Strawberry Point is Backbone State Park, Iowa's first recreational park. The land for the park was acquired in 1918 and it was dedicated in 1922. This 1,780-acre park contains some excellent examples of rustic park architecture. Its large picnic shelter (c. 1930), with walls of rough stone and a log beamed roof, is almost identical to the one at Springbrook State Park, located near Guthrie Center. To reach Backbone State Park take Iowa 13 south from Strawberry Point; at .7 miles turn right (west) on Iowa 410; proceed 2.3 miles to the park.

ME365 Gigantic Strawberry

1967. West side of Commercial St., north of Spring St.

The architectural treasure of Strawberry Point is a gigantic brightly painted strawberry (12 feet by 15 feet) on a pole that has been placed before the city hall. The strawberry was erected by the city in 1967. This is one of the most widely published programmatic sculptures within the state.

Tipton

The community of Tipton enjoys what was considered to be the ideal location for a county seat, for it is perfectly situated at the geographic center of the Cedar County. The site was selected in 1840, and the town, including its courthouse square, was platted in the same year.

ME366 **Cedar County Courthouse**

1965–1968, Soenke and Wayland. Courthouse Square, northeast corner of Cedar and 2nd streets

The present courthouse replaced the earlier, much remodeled 1859 courthouse. It represents the effort frequently encountered after World War II to produce a design that was both traditional and modern. The Davenport firm of Soenke and Wayland devised a single low, horizontal two-story box whose facades make a slight nod toward Beaux-Arts Classicism. At the front the architects brought the center section out ever so slightly, emphasized the entrance by a frame with a composition of three small windows above, and then in the fashion of the 1920s and 1930s treated the upper and lower windows and their spandrels as narrow vertical bands. They also suggested that the building has a traditional horizontal base, and a termination above of a false cornice carried below the upper parapet.

ME367 **Free Public Library**

1903–1904, Mauran, Russell, and Garden. Cedar St., between 2nd and 3rd streets

This brick and stone-trimmed building is the type of design that would have been referred to as "Georgian" at the time it was built. The ends of the gables and of the entrance gable have parapets. The entrance is elaborately detailed with a stone arch over the door supported by engaged columns. The earth has been built up around the building to minimize the height of its raised basement. The library is situated within its own tree-planted park, and smaller shrubbery carries the greenery up to the base of the building.

ME368 **Miller House**

1898. 104 E. 7th St.

The two-story Queen Anne/Colonial Revival Miller house displays an especially impressive gable with a double volute over the entrance porch; the second-floor horizontal oval window is enclosed within a decorative panel with pediment.

ME369 **Britcher House**

1899. 208 W. 8th St.

The vertical form of this dwelling is Queen Anne, but all of its detailing is Colonial Revival. Especially captivating are the sawed balustrades of the entrance porch. The curved contour of a traditional balustrade has been rendered in one-inch boards, and the curved sawed profile has been turned at a right angle and projected outward.

ME370 **Spear House**

1889. 120 E. 9th St.

Even though the house has been re-sided, the ornamentation is strong enough to maintain the original Queen Anne character of the building's design. Especially assertive are the detailing of the third floor of the corner bay tower, the wide bargeboards of the gables, the tiny cut-in corner porch of the second floor, and finally the substantial entrance/veranda with columns.

ME371 **Reichert House**

1883, S. B. Reed. 508 E. 4th St.

This suburban house was designed for John C. Reichert by the New York architect S. B. Reed and represents one of the most impressive Eastlake-style houses still standing in Iowa. The two-and-a-half-story wood-sheathed house exhibits a classic Eastlake tower on its left corner. The tower's steeply pitched broken roof contains narrow hipped dormers on each side. Below the overhanging roof, supported by corner brackets, is the usual pattern of vertical boards with semicircular ends. The gable to the right has bargeboards and a double wheel pattern projected as open work between the bargeboards. The shed-roof entrance porch is carried around to the side and joins onto a light framework porte-cochère with its own steeply pitched hipped roof.

ME372 County Fairgrounds Pavilion

c. 1900. W. 7th St. extension, .7 miles beyond Cedar St.

A low wooden octagonal building is dwarfed and pressed into the ground by a tall cupola with windows.

ME373 Lustron House

c. 1951. 400 East St.

This gray-colored model of the metal Lustron house was built for Fred Roland. Some changes are evident in parts of the roof, and at the entry.

Toolesboro

As one would expect, the confluence of the Mississippi and Iowa rivers was a site of importance both before and after the European settlement of the area. At this location, the community of Toolesboro was platted, with the usual high expectations that it would quickly develop into a major city, but somehow this never came about. Today Toolesboro is still a small, pleasant river town.

Adjacent to the community is an extensive group of prehistoric Indian mounds. These low conical mounds (originally there were approximately 100 of them) are arranged to form a gentle crescent. They were constructed between 500 B.C.E. and 300 C.E. by the Hopewell people. A number of these mounds were excavated in the 1870s by the Davenport Academy of Science, and materials from these excavations may be seen at the Putnam Museum in Davenport (1717 West Twelfth Street). In 1963 the Iowa State Historical Society acquired 15.6 acres of this site, and in the early 1970s a visitors' center was built.

Wapello

Wapello, established on the west bank of the Iowa River, was platted in 1838 and became the county seat the following year.

ME374 Louisa County Courthouse

1928, Keffer, Jones and Thomas. Southeast corner of Franklin and Fourth streets

This two-story building of light tan brick and stone trim is a successful example of abstract Beaux-Arts Classicism. Its centerpiece is a slightly recessed portico composed of wide undecorated pilasters, accompanied by an entablature which is sparsely decorated with deep-set horizontal lines and the name of the building. On each side of the portico is a lower wing. Each wing contains a classical niche on the lower level, and above these is a

ME374 Louisa County Courthouse

single band of three windows with an eagle projecting from the continuous lintel.

ME375 **A. Garrett House**

c. 1850s. 336 N. Main St., southeast corner of N. Main and Mechanic streets

ME375 A. Garrett House

Each facade of this engaging one-and-a-half-story Gothic Revival cottage is gabled, and the gable eaves are decorated with a filigree-like bargeboard. On the right side of the house is a long angular bay covered by a concave roof. There is a large cut-out wood cartouche where the peak of this roof joins the house.

Waukon

The grid scheme of Waukon, with its central open courthouse square, was recorded in 1853. Andreas paints a picture of it that is not too different from what one encounters today: "The town is regularly laid out, with straight and broad streets, adorned plentifully with shade trees in the vicinity of the more retired residences and public buildings."[35] The fertility of the soil and the abundance of springs encouraged the establishment of two of the state's best-known nurseries, one run by D. W. Adams and the other by C. Barnard.

ME376 **First Allamakee County Courthouse** (now Allamakee County Historical Museum)

1860–1861, attrib. John W. Pratt. Southeast corner of Allamakee Ave. and 2nd Ave. N.E.

A good number of similar courthouses were built throughout eastern Iowa in the 1850s and early 1860s. The Allamakee Courthouse is one of the very few still surviving. The underlying form is based upon the rectangular block Greek Revival design, but this has been modified by a bracketed roof and a strong sense of verticality in the high pitch of the roof. This brick building, set on a limestone base, has the usual pilastered walls and two-tiered wooden tower over the entrance. Though some changes have been made on the interior, the courtroom, halls, and other spaces are close to their original design. Now a museum, the building is open to the public.

ME377 **Allamakee County Courthouse**

1939–1941, Charles Altfillisch. Northwest corner of Allamakee Ave. and 1st Ave. N.W.

The PWA Moderne style is here only a bland version of modernized classicism. There is a classical entrance, a kind of frontispiece, which projects slightly in front of the brick facade. In a fashion characteristic of vertical skyscrapers of the twenties and thirties, the windows and their spandrels are slightly recessed to create a patterned vertical effect. The Decorah architect Charles Altfillisch was a graduate of the University of Iowa and the Carnegie Institute of Technology. He designed a number of public buildings in Iowa.

ME378 **Town Theater**

c. 1939. 36–38 W. Main St.

Motion picture theaters of the mid-1930s and later were the commercial type that added a new note of liveliness and modernity to a downtown area, and this is certainly the case with this theater. The facade of the building is clothed in cut limestone, providing a neutral surface that functions as a backdrop for two striking elements: the marquee, with the neon sign reading "Town" raised above it, and a circular tower with banded neon and the name of the theater, also in neon. The tower and the marquee project out far enough so that they can be seen quite far down the street.

ME379 **Cottage**

c. 1860s. 403 W. Main St.

This one-and-a-half-story Gothic Revival cottage exhibits pointed windows in its gabled ends and dormer, and a light, lacy, sawed wood bargeboard around the gables. Projecting Gothic headers appear above the first-floor windows. The porch has been modified and expanded, but other than this everything seems in place for a mid-century midwestern Gothic cottage.

ME380 **Octagon House**

c. 1850s. 23 E. Main St.

This small octagon house is realized in ashlar block limestone. There are wide segmental openings within each wall. Some of these have been filled in with stone, others contain pairs of double-hung windows or doors. A wide entablature plus a bracketed roof suggest that the designer/builder had an Italianate image in mind. The small shed roof over the main entrance is probably not original.

ME381 **O. J. Hager House**

c. 1910, Spencer and Powers. 402 Allamakee Ave.

Robert J. Spencer, Jr., the designer of this house, was one of the most successful of Chicago's Prairie school architects. In 1914 William Gray Purcell wrote of the work of Spencer and Powers that "anything in the way of a building to which you can really attach a 'style' is really not architecture."[36] The designs of Spencer and Powers do not really fit comfortably within the Prairie school, though we associate them with it. The Hager house goes far and wide in its references, to Vienna, to England, and to Louis H. Sullivan, Frank Lloyd Wright, and Chicago, but it ends up being recognizable (as Purcell pointed out)

only as a product of Spencer's own sensibility. In the single brick-clad two-story volume, Spencer plays with symmetry and symmetrical fenestration, and with projecting bays. The recessed entrance porch has a pair of Sullivanesque columns, and the casement windows have a delicate design based upon the tulip. The tulip motif for the leaded and colored glass windows was suggested to the architect by Mrs. Hager.

ME382 **J. H. Hager House**

1913–1914, George W. Maher. 17 4th Ave. N.E.

Like Frank Lloyd Wright, who worked out innumerable variations on his scheme presented in a 1906 *Ladies Home Journal*, George W. Maher of Chicago developed his own personal version of the midwestern Prairie type similar in many ways to Wright's Winslow house (1893) in River Forest, Illinois. He took the midwestern stucco box, extended it, then covered it with a strongly articulated hipped roof; he then placed a second-story band of windows directly under the roof soffit; he almost always provided a segmented roof over the entrance. The J. H. Hager house is a variation on this theme. In Maher's hands these Prairie houses had the advantage of being reassuringly familiar and at the same time new and avant-garde.

ME383 **Barn and Silo**

c. 1910. 7 miles southeast of Waukon on Iowa 76

The red barn with gambrel roof, accompanied by a cylindrical silo and other outbuildings, mirrors what we expect to see in a midwestern farm. The barn is of board-and-batten, painted dark red (of course) and punctured by white framed windows. Alongside the barn is a concrete silo with a small projecting dormer and a roof of sheet metal.

ME384 Meyer's True-Round Barn

1912. 1.4 miles south of Waukon on route X12

The Meyer barn is a structure 56 feet in diameter with a frame of wood and a surface sheathed in horizontal wood siding. The ground level of the barn is stone, with the wood walls above. The roof is a double-pitched gambrel type with a metal aerator at the peak. Within is a central silo constructed of wood staves and lined inside with cement.

Welton

In the small village of Welton, in central Clinton County just off US 61 (which goes through the town), is the Welton Roman Catholic Church. It was built in 1910 and presents an early-1900s version of the Gothic Revival style: in this instance the building has a tower-entrance scheme based loosely upon French provincial examples. The building is of brick, with limestone used for the basement and for trim. Although not especially tall, the tower is particularly effective; high pointed gables help to form the transition from the square base to the octagon, and finally to the double-layered spire roof. The figural stained glass windows of the church are particularly impressive.

West Branch

Though West Branch is not far distant from Iowa City and the University of Iowa, it still conveys an idea of what Iowa was like in the late nineteenth century. The Herbert Hoover National Historic Site is nearby, and within the town of West Branch itself are several small-town vernacular buildings.

ME385 Herbert Hoover National Historic Site

dedicated 1965. Adjacent to Wapsinonoc Creek, on south side of West Branch

The Herbert Hoover National Historic Site is in a beautifully laid-out park adjacent to Wapsinonoc Creek, on the south side of the small community of West Branch. The park was dedicated in 1965, and in addition to the Hoover grave site (designed by Richard J. Wagner) it contains the Herbert Hoover Presidential Library and Museum, a visitors' center, and several historic buildings relating to the Hoover family. When one thinks in terms of the more recent presidential libraries, the building devoted to Hoover clearly represents a far different era.

Several concepts are expressed within the historic site. There is a play between the surrounding rural, small-town character and the perfection of an English garden expressed within the site; there is a suggested link between the "Colonial" architectural image of the 1857 Friends Meetinghouse and the Colonial Revival references in the Presidential Library and Museum building.

ME385.1 Birthplace Cottage

1871

This board-and-batten cottage contains two rooms and an ell. It was built by Herbert Hoover's father, Jesse Hoover, and his grandfather, Eli Hoover. The cottage stands on its original location.

ME385.2 Blacksmith Shop

1950, William J. Wagner

This shop is a reconstruction of the shed-roofed clapboard blacksmith shop operated by Hoover's father between 1871 and 1879.

ME385.3 Schoolhouse

1853

A simple, direct version of the Greek Revival style, the schoolhouse has an entrance on one of the gable ends. Built elsewhere, the one-room schoolhouse was moved several times before it was brought to its present location and restored in 1971.

ME385.4 Friends Meetinghouse

1857

This gable-roofed Greek Revival building with a wide undecorated entablature was moved to this location from a site several blocks away.

ME385.5 Herbert Hoover Presidential Library and Museum Building

1964; Eggers and Higgins; Wetherell, Harrison and Wagner

The New York firm of Otto R. Eggers and David Paul Higgins was engaged to design the library and museum. Both Eggers and Higgins had been longtime associates (since 1922) of John Russell Pope; and it was their firm that completed Pope's work in Washington, including the Jefferson Memorial and the National Gallery. The selection of the firm for the Hoover project was a logical one, not only because of its Washington connections but because of the many Colonial Revival buildings the architects had designed, both while they were with Pope and afterward. Their solution to the design for the combined Hoover library and museum was meant to be a modest one, a design that in scale and size would seem at home in a small

community. Their product was a single-story stone-sheathed building somewhat reminiscent of a post-World War II suburban dwelling, with just the needed light flavor of the Colonial Revival (and a slight hint of the then-popular California ranch house).

ME386 Opera Block

1895. East side of Downey St., just north of Main St.

The street facade of this two-story block is clothed in brick and pressed metal. More recently, wood siding has added a "rustic" quality to its second floor.

ME387 Store Building (now West Branch Heritage Museum)

1884. 109 W. Main St.

This is a classic example of the single-floor false-fronted wooden store building, a type encountered throughout the country. This building retains its storefront windows and the wood paneling below.

ME388 House

c. 1885. West side of Downey St., 2 blocks north of Main St.

The most commanding feature of this two-story early Queen Anne dwelling is a shingled panel between the first- and second-floor windows. Superimposed on the shingles, almost as a two-dimensional drawing, are classical volutes.

ME389 Gerlits House

c. 1905. Northwest corner of Main and Oliphant streets

In the design of this turn-of-the-century Colonial Revival house, a play has been carried out between the forms of the gambrel roofs and the arch. A large arch has been fitted within the third-floor end gables, and entrance to the wide porch is through an arched opening.

West Liberty

West Liberty contains one of Iowa's several libraries designed by the Chicago firm of Patton and Miller (located at the northeast corner of East Fourth Street and North Spencer Street). This brick-clad, tile-roofed Carnegie Library building was constructed for the sum of $7,500. As such it is relatively simple in overall design and detail. Its most interesting feature is the entrance doorway with side quoining and a lunette window separated from the door below by a Prairie-style band that terminates in squares. Above the door, the entrance gable has a parapet and contains a narrow window with cross-banded stone carried across its center.

Another of the community's public buildings is the Rock Island Depot (c. 1900), at the end of West Fourth and Elm streets. The brick station displays a playful pattern of varied roofs; the main block is covered by a cross-gabled roof and is accompanied by lower wings with hipped roofs. The roofs of these wings continue over the main block to provide a sheltered porch on the platform side of the building. The station is slightly, but not strongly, Romanesque in imagery .

Three miles west of West Liberty, on the north side of US 6, is a stagecoach stop (1842–1843). The building represents a characteristic "transplant" from the East Coast; according to tradition it was modeled after a house on Long Island. Its form is that of a clapboard-sheathed side-hall dwelling, two and a half stories high. It is a relatively plain structure, except for its handsome recessed entrance with side lights and transom. The original owner of the inn was Egbert T. Smith, who was its architect and builder.

A little closer to town (2.5 miles west on US 6) is the delightfully odd Walter I. Smith house (1911). The house itself is a conventional two-story, somewhat Colonial Revival box; but what "makes" the building are two tall conical roofs, one of which covers part of the right porch, the other, to the left, the porte-cochère. These roofs and some other parts of the house were salvaged from an earlier dwelling.

West Point

West Point was one of the early communities in Iowa, platted in 1840. Its situation some 8 miles northeast of the Mississippi River placed it in rolling countryside, with extensive forests to the south and open prairie to the north. With the abundance of limestone for building, a large number of structures both within the town and in the surrounding countryside were constructed of masonry. A drive in the rural areas around West Point will lead one to discover a number of these quite early stone farmhouses, and occasionally barns.

ME390 Saint Mary's Roman Catholic Church

1858, 1903. Southwest corner of 4th St. and Ave. C

The 1858 church was constructed under the direction of Father J. G. Reffe, who may also have been its designer. An extensive remodeling of 1903 was accomplished by Father W. Jacoby. The tall, narrow entrance tower implies the medieval, but the church really turns out to be English Baroque. Surmounting the brick portion of the tower is an octagon surrounded by four large consoles; above these are lunette dormers. The space over the crossing bursts forth with a high drum surrounded by columns. The culmination of all of this is a dome with eight lunette dormers.

ME391 Municipal Water Well No. 1

c. 1900. South end of 4th St.

A tiny gable-roofed "house" sprouts a canted tower from its ridge. One side of the tower, which is covered in sheet metal, has its own private small window.

ME392 Masonic Temple Building

c. 1875. Northwest corner 4th St. and Ave. D

The two-story brick block with a gable roof houses the Masonic Hall above and a retail store below. The storefront has three arched openings on one side and a fourth on the other side. The single entry on the side street still has its original door. The arched openings of windows and doors with their ac-

cented keystones nudge the building over into the Italianate style.

ME393 Cottage

c. 1860. Northwest corner of 5th St. and Ave. F

The general horizontality of this one-and-a-half-story brick cottage belongs to the Greek Revival or Federal style, but most of the emphasized detailing is Gothic. A small rectangular balcony with a metal railing projects from the second-floor pointed window in the gable and faces the street.

ME394 Danover House

c. 1878. 4 miles northwest of West Point on route W76

The Danover farmhouse is a relatively quiet two-story dwelling with a T-shaped plan. What takes it out of the ordinary with great force is one singular feature: the large first-floor angled bay window to the left of the entrance porch. The top of this bay has small individual gable ends mirroring each plane of the bay and fragment gables on the return of the bay into the wall. These gabled ends project out slightly and have bracketed supports; within they have corbeling at the roof edges. Projecting boldly above the edge of the gable ends is a cut-out pattern in wood, which hints at a row of connected finials. All these details are effectively played off against the plain brick walls of the house. In style, the basic form of the house is traditional Italianate, but the wood detailing of the bay and the entrance porch is Eastlake.

Wilton

The town of Wilton was platted in 1855, and very early it developed as the location of repair shops for the Chicago, Rock Island, and Pacific Railroad. From the 1920s on it was a major "gas stop" on US 6, between Davenport to the east and Iowa City to the west.

ME395 Wilton Feed and Produce
(originally a service station)

c. 1937. 304 E. 5th St.

This is a high point of the popular Moderne in Iowa: a feed and produce store clothed in

bright, shimmering red, blue, and white glazed brick and tile. The checkerboard pattern, a trademark of the Ralston Purina Company, was added later to the building's street facade. A large-scale checkerboard pattern runs across the entire upper section of the building, meeting at the center of the building a composition of vertical pilasters that curve into the projecting sign. The geometry and color of the design make the whole building (appropriately) a sign reaching out to its potential vehicle-oriented clientele.

ME396 Dartings Sinclair (now a Mobil Service Station)

c. 1925. Northeast corner of 5th and Maurer streets

This small service station suggests that it is a miniature, many-gabled dwelling. Each of its two small entrances reaches up into a steeply pitched gable, which is repeated a few feet back onto the roof. The walls of these second gables are shingled, as is the roof beyond.

ME397 Presbyterian Church

1900. W. 5th St., between Elm and Cedar streets

The steep roofs and, above all, the pointed windows and doors pull the viewer toward the Gothic, but the two hip-roofed towers (one lower, the other a higher, corner entrance tower) suggest the French Romanesque. The stone walls of the building are so finely cut and joined that they almost appear to be artificial concrete Art Stone.

ME398 Commercial Building

c. 1877. 129 W. 4th St.

Although the lower section of this two-story brick block is painted a bright tangerine color, it still retains its original storefront of cast iron and glass, its segmental arched windows on the second floor, and its wide overhanging bracketed cornice.

ME399 House

c. 1870. 519 N. Maurer St.

It is the pair of projecting wall-dormer windows on this Gothic Revival dwelling that catches the eye. At the center is a two-story gable section (which probably once had bargeboards on the gable ends); on each side, forming a balanced composition, are one-and-a-half-story wings with projecting wall dormers. On the ground level, two porches (the one on the left is original) complete the design.

Central (CE)

THIS PORTION OF THE STATE PROVIDES A NEARLY PERFECT picture of the variation in topography encountered in Iowa. The eastern sections reveal a mixture of wooded river valleys and hills broken by open grasslands; to the west, the undulating open prairie asserts itself, with only occasional wooded sections generally found adjacent to the rivers and streams. Once the railroad reached this region, and new and improved farm equipment was developed and made available, this section quickly became (and remains) one of the richest agricultural areas of the state, the nation, and the world. The location of the railroad lines, and in the twentieth century the system of roads and highways, determined in most cases where towns and cities were laid out. Because of the more open nature of the terrain, the north-south, east-west grid system of land division is increasingly apparent as one travels west.

Although there are a number of post-Civil War communities within central Iowa, most of the larger towns and cities were founded quite early, in the late 1840s and on through the 1850s. Several of the cities in the eastern part of this area—Cedar Rapids, Iowa City, and Washington—still contain excellent examples of pre-Civil War architecture. Des Moines, the state's largest city and its capital, is essentially both a late nineteenth-century Victorian town and a twentieth-century modern city.

Adel

Adel, the seat of Dallas County, was laid out in 1847 on the west bank of the North Raccoon River, and among the notable structures there is the Dallas County Courthouse. Another building to be visited in Adel is the Presbyterian

Central Iowa

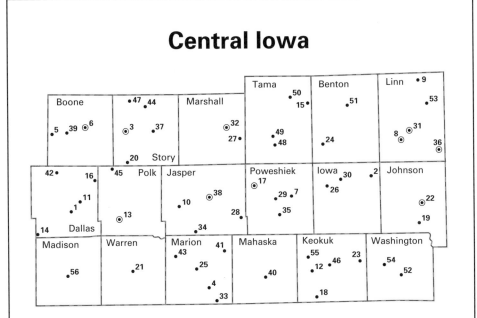

Boone	
•47 •44	Marshall
•5 •39 ⊙6	•3 •37 •32
	•27
•20 Story	

Tama •50 15• Benton •51 Linn •9 •53
8 ⊙31 36 ⊙

42• 16 •45 Polk Jasper •38 •10 •13 •34 28• Poweshiek ⊙17 •29 •7 •35 Iowa 30 •26 •2 Johnson ⊙22 •19

Madison Warren Marion 41• Mahaska Keokuk Washington
•56 •21 43• •25 4• •33 •40 55• 12• 46 23 •18 54• •52

1. Adel (Dallas Co.)
2. Amana Colonies (Iowa Co.)
3. Ames (Story Co.)*
4. Attica (Marion Co.)
5. Beaver (Boone Co.)
6. Boone (Boone Co.)*
7. Brooklyn (Poweshiek Co.)
8. Cedar Rapids (Linn Co.)*
9. Coggon (Linn Co.)
10. Colfax (Jasper Co.)
11. Dallas Center (Dallas Co.)
12. Delta (Keokuk Co.)
13. Des Moines (Polk Co.)*
14. Dexter (Dallas Co.)
15. Dysart (Tama Co.)
16. Granger (Dallas Co.)
17. Grinnell (Poweshiek Co.)*
18. Hedrick (Keokuk Co.)
19. Hills (Johnson Co.)
20. Huxley (Story Co.)
21. Indianola (Warren Co.)
22. Iowa City (Johnson Co.)*
23. Keota (Keokuk Co.)
24. Keystone (Benton Co.)
25. Knoxville (Marion Co.)
26. Ladora (Iowa Co.)
27. LeGrand (Marshall Co.)
28. Lynnville (Jasper Co.)

29. Malcom (Poweshiek Co.)
30. Marengo (Iowa Co.)
31. Marion (Linn Co.)*
32. Marshalltown (Marshall Co.)*
33. Marysville (Marion Co.)
34. Monroe (Jasper Co.)
35. Montezuma (Poweshiek Co.)
36. Mount Vernon (Linn Co.)*
37. Nevada (Story Co.)
38. Newton (Jasper Co.)*
39. Ogden (Boone Co.)
40. Oskaloosa (Mahaska Co.)
41. Pella (Marion Co.)
42. Perry (Dallas Co.)
43. Pleasantville (Marion Co.)
44. Roland (Story Co.)
45. Sheldahl (Polk Co.)
46. Sigourney (Keokuk Co.)
47. Story City (Story Co.)
48. Tama (Tama Co.)
49. Toledo (Tama Co.)
50. Traer (Tama Co.)
51. Vinton (Benton Co.)
52. Washington (Washington Co.)
53. Waubeek (Linn Co.)
54. West Chester (Washington Co.)
55. What Cheer (Keokuk Co.)
56. Winterset (Madison Co.)

A detailed map of site locations has
been provided for cities indicated
by ⊙ on the map and by * in the list
at left.

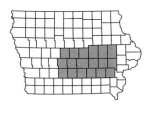

Church of 1868, located at 820 Prairie Street. In this gable-roofed brick structure, a Greek Revival format is blended with Gothic Revival details (a steeply
pitched roof and windows with pointed arches).

On North Twelfth Street, between Rapids and Court streets, is the Adel Primary School Building (c. 1915), which is no longer in use. The image in this
case is that of the Craftsman mode, with several references to buildings erected
in England by the British exponents of the Arts and Crafts movement. The
four-room school building has a raised basement, and its brick sheathing has
been brought up to the sills of the windows above. The upper sections of the
walls are covered in plaster. The center entrance wing has a parapeted gable
end, in front of which is a hooped hood supported by masonry consoles and
columns. On each side of these columns the brick walls turn a 90-degree angle,
and they then swoop out in a concave curve toward the street. The upper
sections of the large classroom windows have been filled in.

CE001 **Dallas County Courthouse**

1902, Proudfoot and Bird. Main St., between 7th and
8th streets

The present Dallas County Courthouse, built
in 1902, replaced a handsome pilastered Greek
Revival structure of 1852. The Des Moines
architectural firm of Proudfoot and Bird
modeled their new design after that of a
French chateau, specifically Azay-le-Rideau at
Indre-et-Loire. In decided contrast to the
Châteauesque image of the building, the central tower with its pilasters, clock faces, and
lantern is reminiscent of the Beaux-Arts style
of the early 1900s. The building is sheathed
in smooth Bedford limestone, and its roof is
of red tile. Within, many of the walls are
paneled in marble, accompanied by painted
fresco designs.

CE001 Dallas County Courthouse

Amana Colonies

Members of the Amana Society first came to America from southwestern Germany in 1842, settling initially on lands near Buffalo, New York. "After some
years . . . the elders of the community decided to look up a new location where
a large area of cheaper land could be obtained, further away from the unpleas-
ant influences of a rapidly growing city like Buffalo. . . ."[1] In 1855 they traveled west and purchased 18,000 acres of land above and below the Iowa River
for colonization. The community of Amana was established in 1855, followed by West Amana and South Amana in 1856, High Amana in 1857, East
Amana in 1860, Homestead in 1861, Middle Amana in 1862, and New South
Amana in 1883. (Several of these will be discussed following the entries for
Amana, below.) When established, all of the lands and property were held in

common, administered by thirteen elders. This communal approach continued until 1932, when a separation was made between religious and economic (land and production ownership) activities.

In addition to the pursuit of agriculture, the Amana people established a number of manufacturing activities, including gristmills, sawmills, cotton mills, woolen mills, a furniture factory, and several other enterprises. As was mentioned as early as 1875, there is a distinct quality about the towns, farmlands, and buildings of the Amana communities which sets them off from what one considers typical for Iowa. Andreas wrote, "Their towns are well built, the houses being mostly large, many of them being built of brick or stone."[2] Today the communities are oriented in many ways to visitors. At Amana is the Museum of Amana History and the Wool Mill Machine Shop Museum; at Homestead, there is the Amana Art Guild Center, and at South Amana is the Amana Society Historical Agriculture Collection. All of the initial buildings of the 1850s through the 1860s reflect what the colonist had first encountered in upstate New York: the late Federal and the Greek Revival modes. While a selection of buildings is listed below, it is the people themselves, together with their lands and buildings, that create the distinctive, much-admired atmosphere of the place.

AMANA

CE002 **Amana General Store**

1858. North side of Iowa 220, 2 blocks east of Iowa 149

The gable end of this one-and-a-half-story stone building faces the street. The proportions of the building, the pitch of its roof, the cornice with its eave returns, and the pattern of window and door fenestration are derived from the Greek Revival. The building was added to and remodeled in 1934.

CE003 **Haas House** (now Ox Yoke Inn)

c. 1855. South side of Iowa 220, 2 blocks east of Iowa 149

The simple, unadorned brick house has, to a degree, been engulfed by an offshoot of several wings. As in a good number of Amana buildings, the street front of the house is the gable end of the building. The proportions and details relate to the Greek Revival.

CE004 **Group Housing** (now The Kitchen Sink)

c. 1850s. Northeast side of Iowa 220 diagonal extension, southeast of town

Two separate Greek Revival stone housing units, each two stories tall, have been joined together by a two-story wood clapboard section. The first-floor section of this "connector" has been recessed to form a covered porch.

CE005 **Christian Metz House**

c. 1856. Center of town, north side of Iowa 220

The Metz house is an ashlar block one-and-a-half-story dwelling whose fenestration, proportions, and roof slope are indicative of the Greek Revival. Brick chimneys project above the gable ends, and there are transom lights over the deeply recessed doorways.

CE006 **Mill Complex**

c. 1868. Rebuilt after 1922. Southeast edge of town

This is a complex of two- and three-story mill buildings, mostly of brick, a few sheathed in clapboard. There are even some smaller buildings (c. 1900) in concrete block that was cast to imitate ashlar stone blocks.

CE007 **Drive-through Corncrib**

c. 1880s. Northeast section of town

This large corncrib building is a beautiful example of how abstract the vernacular tradition can be. The building is a straight-forward one-and-a-half-story gable-roofed structure, crowned by a cupolalike monitor with its gable roof set at a right angle to the ridge below. The walls of the building are composed of narrow horizontal boards, with venting air spaces between.

HOMESTEAD

On the north side of Main Street, at the west end of town, is the Smokehouse Tower, built around the 1860s. The gable end of this one-and-a-half-story brick building has been placed close to the street. In style the structure is mildly, nearly puritanically Greek Revival. Off the rear of the structure is a tall gable-roofed tower, surmounted by a small venting cupola. The tower was used for the smoking of meat. One block south of US 6, in the center of town, is the Amana Heim (c. 1859). This one-and-a-half-story dwelling is in brick, with brick chimneys breaking forth above the gabled ends of the roof. The windows have segmental tops, and on the front and rear the second-floor windows break into the wood entablature.

MIDDLE AMANA

The center of Middle Amana is the woolen mill picturesquely situated alongside a wide raceway. The 9-mile-long canal bringing water from the Iowa River was built in the 1860s. The complex of mill buildings encompasses structures built in both the nineteenth and twentieth centuries. The Amana School (1865) is within the southwest block of town, on the north side of Iowa 220. The 1865 section of the school is a two-story brick building, to which a later one-story addition has been made. Although the windows of the school have segmental arches, the general proportions and detailing are Greek Revival. At the northeast edge of town are several wood-sheathed combined barns and corncribs (c. 1870s). As designs, these seem as sensitively studied and composed as the houses and other

buildings within the town. The larger of these barns has a low-pitched gable roof broken by a central gabled monitor plus a series of tiny gabled dormers. The wall surfaces—which are closed or open (when used for the storage of corncobs)—along with their fenestration are as impressively delineated as the volumes themselves.

HIGH AMANA

Amidst the many brown sandstone and wood-sheathed houses and their gardens is a one-and-a-half-story stone building now occupied by the Amana Arts Guild. This Greek Revival building (1858), which has a right-angle ell with porch, is situated within the southwest block of town, north of Iowa 220. Within the same block and built in the same year is the stone Amana General Store (along with its later two-story wood addition). The dwelling located within the northeast block of town, across the street from the Amana Store, is typical of many of the larger stone houses within the colony. It too is a Greek Revival one-and-a-half-story building. Its street facade has paired windows on each side of the entrance door and three windows above.

SOUTH AMANA

Some of the colonies' farm buildings are of brick, such as this granary (c. 1875) located at the northwest corner of South Amana. Within its broad horizontal expanse of walls there is a central entrance with a segmental arch; on each side—quite small in relation to the wall—are double-hung windows. Above these are narrow attic windows, as one often finds in a one-and-a-half-story house. A later rural vernacular building is a wood barn (c. 1890) found at the north edge of town, east of Iowa 220. The barn features a vigorous composition consisting of a roof structure with a long gable roof from which project several shed-roof forms; one of these is a covered shelter running along the front of the building.

Ames

The college town of Ames was platted after the Civil War, in 1865. Its slightly rolling prairie site was situated between the Skunk River to the east and Squaw Creek to the west. In 1874 Ames was connected by rail to Des Moines; by 1900 it had become a crossroads for the Chicago and Northwestern Railway. The community's principal activities center around Iowa State University. This institution was established just west of Ames in 1859, and it was first designated as the State Agricultural College. As the authors of the 1938 WPA guide to Iowa pointed out, the area around the college emerged as one town, and then to the east was Ames itself.[3] More recently the newer residential sections north of Thirteenth Street have begun to merge the two rather distinct communities. The devotees of Fowler and the octagonal mode of building will be disappointed to find that Dr. Samuel J. Starr's octagon house of 1870, once located at 126 Sumner Street, is now gone.

CE008 **Boyd's Dairy Store**

c. 1965. Northwest corner Duff Ave. and Main St.

The tradition of roadside architecture is here carried on into the 1960s. The small white building boasts a band of signs advertising its wares—ice cream, milk, malts, shakes, and cones. To reinforce the image of these products, a large ice cream cone is poised over the entrance and a calm cow stands on top of the multiple-pole sign.

CE009 **House**

c. 1880. 720 N. Duff Ave.

This is an Eastlake version of the Italianate style. Each of the roof brackets has been extended below the entablature, and this treatment provides a series of segmental arches on the wall surface.

CE010 **Mcfarland Clinic**

1963, Crites and McConnell. N. Duff Ave.

The design concept here is pure Miesian: two-story frames are joined together as building blocks to form open and closed spaces. The vertical-support members are extended as legs so that the form hovers a few feet above the ground. As befitting a pristine exercise in geometry, it is set upon a well-landscaped site.

CE011 **House**

c. 1905. 502 N. Douglas Ave.

The design of this house was seemingly meant to be formidable and impressive. As with many similar houses, it is difficult to pin down stylistically. Overall, its massing and detailing are classical, but these features are used in a free fashion. The body of the building and its entrance porch are in brick; to the left side is a polygonal stair tower whose roof continues on into the main hipped roof. Hipped dormers add substance to the steeply pitched hipped roof.

CE012 **United States Post Office Building**

1935, Louis A. Simon. 525 Kellogg Ave.

A surprising composition for the mid-1930s, this is a rather pure example of a mid-1920s Beaux-Arts building. There is a slight emphasis on the plain, unadorned wall surfaces, but this is the only strong "modern" element present. The central portion of the building is treated as a pavilion by means of a two-story porch. Within is a small Federal Art Project mural whose subject is based upon the cultivation of corn.

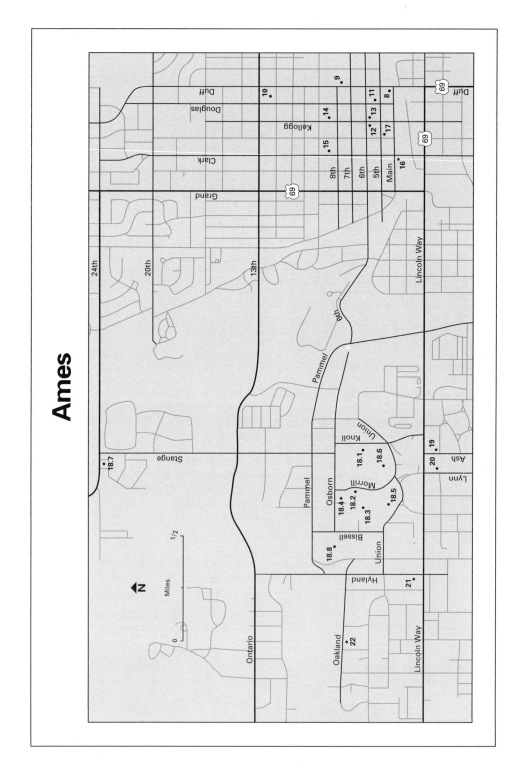

Ames

CE013 First Methodist Episcopal Church (now United Methodist)

1907. Southeast corner of 6th St. and Kellogg Ave.

A large church auditorium seemed to be the first concern of the architect of this building. Having established this, he then proceeded to enrich the design, inside and especially outside. He articulated the roof by projecting gables into its two street elevations. At the corner he placed a wide octagonal bay; and at the peak of the roof, a small octagonal tower displays large "Gothic" windows.

CE014 House

c. 1870. 804 Kellogg Ave.

This square box-shaped two-story Italianate house has been modified over the years, but it is still a strong composition within its large suburban lot. The windows have segmental arches of stone, and the brackets of the roof are arranged in close pairs.

CE015 Schwertley House

c. 1900. 1981–1983, Robert Setterburg. 818 Clark Ave.

The architect has, with sensitivity and humor, remodeled an early twentieth-century cottage and brought it into the Postmodern world. The porch with pediment and columns has the atmosphere of a primitive hut in a folly that one might come upon in an eighteenth-century English or French Picturesque garden. The columns' capitals are mirrored boxes and the metal standing-seam roof is bright blue.

CE016 Chicago and Northwestern Railway Passenger Station

1900, Frost and Granger. Off W. Main St. at Clark Ave.

One could characterize this station as domesticated Beaux-Arts; its brick-sheathed, ivy-covered walls are appropriate for the entrance to a university town. The firm of Frost and Granger designed many of the stations for the railway, including the Beaux-Arts station in Minneapolis. The Ames station is a single-story building. Two slightly projecting pavilions have gable ends that are treated in the form of a gentle curve.

CE017 Ames City Armory (now O'Neil's Dairy)

1905. 308 5th St.

Essentially this is a facade and nothing more. The center two-and-a-half-story portion has a parapeted gable roof and on the first floor an arched window. The street facade is of rusticated masonry. The whole adds up to a type of very late Richardsonian Romanesque design. The neon dairy sign to the left, with its stepped vertical form (late 1930s), was more up-to-date in its time than the building was in its.

CE018 Iowa State University

North and south of Lincoln Way near Beach Ave.

Funds for a State College of Agriculture were appropriated by the Iowa State Legislature in 1858, and the site on Squaw Creek was purchased the following year. In 1861 a model farmhouse was built, followed during 1864–1868 by the construction of a French Second Empire building designed by Charles A. Dunham. This structure (its wings were extended in 1872) was an imposing one, four stories high on a raised basement. Its end pavilion wings were treated as towers, one of which had a picturesque lantern with balcony. The building was added to by Josselyn and Taylor in 1892; it burned in 1900.

The plan of the college campus began to take shape in the late 1860s, and it has on occasion been credited to Frederick Law Olmsted.[4] The scheme was in fact developed by the college's president, A. S. Welch,[5] who based it on the English Picturesque Garden tradition as espoused in America by both A. J. Downing and Olmsted. The approach was that of creating a great park, dotted here and there by groves of trees and crossed by curvilinear roads; even the tracks of the small railway between the college and Ames proceeded in an undulating line.

Fortunately, this park has essentially remained intact, though of course many buildings have been added, especially in the surrounding area where agricultural lands have given way to sites for new buildings. In 1906

Frederick L. Olmsted, Jr., was consulted about its design, and he did prepare a report, but his involvement with the campus went no further. During 1915 and 1916 the Chicago landscape architect O. C. Simonds was engaged; his work on the campus was followed by that of several members of the college faculty, especially P. H. Elwood.

The post-World War II years produced an extensive program of new buildings, as was generally true for American colleges and universities across the land. These new structures have usually been built at the edge of the campus, creating a somewhat bland effect (here, nature assumes a poor secondary position); but, as noted before, the core of the campus is still an effective expression of the nineteenth century's version of the Picturesque Garden. An impressive element within the campus is the number of examples of sculptures from the 1930s by Christian Petersen, for many years an artist-in-residence at the university. In front of the Student Union is a fountain designed by Petersen, with figures representing the four seasons. Other outdoor works of his are to be found in front of MacKay Hall and between Oak and Elm halls. Among Petersen's most delightful works are the terracotta panels of the Dairy Industry Building, depicting four cows apparently drinking water from the wall fountain and pool. The Dairy Industry Building was designed by Proudfoot, Rawson and Souers in 1927–1928. Petersen's relief sculpture was added in 1934.

CE018.1 Model Farmhouse

1861, Milens Burt.

The farmhouse is a 14-room structure with a gable roof and walls of soft red brick (which were later stuccoed over). In style, the building is Italianate. The present entrance porch was added around 1895, and a number of other changes, particularly in the interior, were made over the years. The dwelling was restored between 1971 and 1976 in a general way, as it had been during the years 1861 through 1910. The house is now open to the public.

CE018.2 Morrill Hall

1890

This hall is a two-story exercise in the Richardsonian Romanesque. The building sits on a raised basement. The foundation and trim are of limestone, the upper walls of brick; shingles clothe the gable ends. There is a large bay tower at the left side of the building, and a small lantern pops up on the ridge of the roof.

CE018.3 Engineering Hall

1900, Proudfoot and Bird

Beaux-Arts Classicism, almost of the richness displayed at the 1893 World's Columbian Exposition, prevails here. The really inventive element of the design comes from the way in which the architects introduced the pedimented entrance, set within a two-story arch that breaks through the horizontal masonry of the raised basement story.

CE018.4 Alumni Hall

1904, Proudfoot and Bird. 1989–1990, Herbert Lewis Kruse Blunck

The Colonial Revival style appears here on a rather grand, pretentious (but likable) scale. The two-and-a-half-story brick structure with a gambrel roof boasts not one but three two-story porticoes; the entrance one is rectangular, while those on each gable end are semicircular. Arched windows appear within the many gabled dormers. At the center of the gambrel roof is a large dormer with broken pediment and a version of a Palladian window within. Even larger Palladian windows tied by masonry to an upper oval window pop out of each gable end. The interior is organized around a cruciform reception hall, with each arm defined by a set of columns. Though good sized, the feel of the building is domestic, not institutional.

In 1989–1990 Alumni Hall was substantially remodeled and in part restored. The north, east, and west facades were restored, while a new curved stairway bay was added to the south facade. The interior was remodeled with larger, more open spaces. The general detailing of the remodeling and additions mirrors the original Colonial Revival appearance of the building.

CE018.5 Parks Library

1926–1928, Proudfoot, Rawson and Souers

When built, the library was described as based on Italian Renaissance architecture of the early sixteenth century. The stone facade is delicately detailed, with the usual rusticated basement as the ground floor; above is a rendition of the Ionic order on pilasters, with a play of groupings of windows between the pilasters. Especially fine is the interior central glass-domed rotunda, together with its major stairways. On the walls of the stairhall is a group of murals painted by Grant Wood and his assistants in 1934; a second group was painted in 1937 for the lower lobby of the library. The eight murals in the stairhall have as their themes agriculture, engineering, and home economics; those in the lobby depict breaking the prairie.[6] In 1984 Charles Herbert and Associates added a modernist cut-into three-story addition to the older building. When this addition received a design award in 1986 it was described as an "appropriate but restrained facade." Everything is relative, and the new addition carries on the principle of anticontextualism; with that concept in mind, it carries it out very well.

CE018.6 Campanile

1922, Proudfoot, Bird and Rawson

Set in the center of the central campus is this 110-foot-high campanile. The historic precedent for its design was set in Venetian Gothic architecture. At the corner of its four-sided spire roof are Gothic pinnacles; below are three elongated Gothic-style openings. The entrances at its base are also Gothic, but as one finds especially in Italian examples, the Gothic has an Islamic tinge to it.

CE018.7 ISU Energy Research House

1977–1978, Ray O. Crites

This is an experimental dwelling meant to indicate how a modernist architecture could respond to energy needs. A two-story trombe wall (a masonry wall that absorbs solar heat) projects as a screen to one side of the house. The wood-sheathed house itself is a rectilinear box in which great care has been devoted to the fenestration and detailing of the walls. With the growth of trees and shrubs around the house, it no longer seems as insistently modern as when it was built. In truth, it fits in well with the nearby housing, which seems closely related to spec housing one might find in California.

CE018.8 ISU Design Center

1974–1978, Charles Herbert and Associates

Two narrow five-story boxes are connected by an intervening glass atrium. The roof of the atrium is in the form of a barrel vault, similar to many other glass-roofed buildings of the 1970s and 1980s. As is generally true of this firm's work, the building is carefully detailed, but in this instance its form and detail seem somewhat on the dry side.

CE019 Delta Gamma Sorority House

c. 1928. 117 Ash Ave.

This 1920s version of an English medieval manor house almost seems like a fragment of a castle. The height of the brick walls is accentuated by compositions of vertical windows. The steeply pitched roof is enriched by various forms of dormers, parapeted gables, and chimneys. The roof, strongly accentuated by multicolored slate, adds to the building's romantic charm, as does the red trim and cream infill.

CE020 Sigma Alpha Epsilon Fraternity House

1928–1929, Kimball, Cowgill, and Beatty. 140 Lynn Ave.

The source for this fraternity house is the French Norman style, resulting in another wonderfully romantic medieval exercise. The walls are of stone and brick, and as in the Delta Gamma house (CE019), the architect

CE020 Sigma Alpha Epsilon Fraternity House

seems to have projected the walls and steeply pitched hipped roof just as high as he could.

CE021 **Sigma Chi Fraternity House**

125 N. Hyland Ave.

The medieval English design of this brick building features second-floor sections in white plaster and half-timber. The character of this two-and-a-half-story fraternity house is less exuberant, more staid than the previous two examples.

CE022 **Dunagan House**

1940, Clark Souers and Amos B. Emory. 3424 Oakland Ave.

The Streamline Moderne Dunagan house has been described as a "poured concrete pill box," as in the contemporary French fortifications along the Rhine (the Maginot Line). The auto is the means of entering the house; the garage is on one side, and a curved cantilevered roof covers the adjacent front entrance.

Attica (and Marysville)

South of the small community of Attica is one of Iowa's remaining nineteenth-century covered bridges. This is the 60-foot single-span Hammond Bridge over North Cedar Creek. This 1870 bridge of the Howe truss type has a single long, gabled roof; the board-and-batten wood walls have been brought up to a point about 2 feet below where they would otherwise meet the roof. This intervening open space, which was protected from the weather by the overhang of the roof, provided much-needed ventilation and light to the interior of the bridge. To reach the bridge travel south from Attica on route G76 for 1.5 miles; where G76 turns directly to the west take the gravel road that proceeds to the southeast; North Cedar Creek and the bridge are about 1.75 miles further. If one wishes to approach the bridge from Marysville, to the south, take the gravel road at the northwest corner of town; at the first junction, .3 miles from town, take the left fork (to the west); it will then be 1.6 miles to the bridge and the creek.

Beaver

The town of Beaver is bypassed just to the south by the US 30. At the southwest corner of town, crossing over US 30, is a gravel county road; proceed south .5 miles on this road to the Doran Farm complex, located on both sides of the road. The 1896 farmhouse and the outbuildings present a perfect picture of a late nineteenth-century Iowa farm complex. The commodious house displays a veranda across the front; there is a polygonal porch on the second floor, with a strange steeply pitched gable placed within its roof. Heavy brackets support the roof overhang at each corner. The house is essentially a single large box, with a few bays and porches projecting from it. In style, some of its features point to the early Queen Anne, and some take one back to the post-Civil War Italianate. The adjoining wooden farm buildings are gable roofed; there is a large barn with a center monitor and a smaller barn that exhibits a basilica plan.

Boone

The city of Boone was laid out in 1864 on open prairie some 3 miles west of the Des Moines River. Between the river and Boone was the earlier community of Boonesboro. Boonesboro remained as the seat of Boone County until 1887 when it was absorbed into Boone. The most-visited building in the community is certainly the Mamie Doud Eisenhower Birthplace. This small Eastlake cottage, moved to 709 Carroll Street, was built in the middle to late 1880s. The house has been restored and furnished, and it is open to the public.

CE023 **Clyde Sparks House**

1917, E. V. Fitzgerald. 408 S. Story St.

Here one is confronted with Prairie-style monumentality of a highly inventive type. Brief horizontal roof slabs play off against a low-pitched gable, and giant overscaled and canted piers support the two balanced porches.

CE024 **Hanson House**

1926; Vorse, Kraetsch, and Kraetsch; Holm and Olson, landscape architects. 421 S. Marshall St.

A symmetrically composed brick-and-stucco bungalow, the Hanson house seems somewhat English, somewhat Prairie-esque and Craftsman. The brick terrace at the front overlooks the open park across the street. The Saint Paul, Minnesota, landscape architects Holm and Olson laid out the grounds around the house so that they seem like an extension of the adjacent park.

CE025 **First National Bank Building**

1916, Woodburn and Son. Southeast corner of 8th and Story streets

An office building entailing a narrow eight-story Beaux-Arts composition, the bank's most arresting feature is the row of second-floor windows with their highly stylized pilasters and cornices.

CE026 **Germania Block** (now Bilden's Sav-Mor Drug)

1904. 804–806 Story St.

This is by far the most handsome building in the downtown area. Its lively street facade consists of six Romanesque arches, and above, the entablature exhibits a strong primitive version of triglyphs. The rugged Mankato quartzite surface reinforces this sense of the primitive. The first floor has been remodeled, but the upper two floors and the pediment remain intact.

CE027 **Municipal Building**

1939, Dougher, Rich, and Woodburn. Northeast corner of 8th and Allen streets

The public emphasis of this PWA Moderne building is placed on its entrance pavilion situated on the narrow side of the structure. Within the entrance pavilion is a high vertical recess containing doors below, then a spandrel of polished stone, and finally a decorated metal-screened window above. There are V-shaped metal lamps on each side of the entrance, and a small round-cornered canopy projects out over the tall entrance recess.

CE028 **Service Station**

c. 1932, Connors and Sadle. Southeast corner of 11th and Story streets

Boone

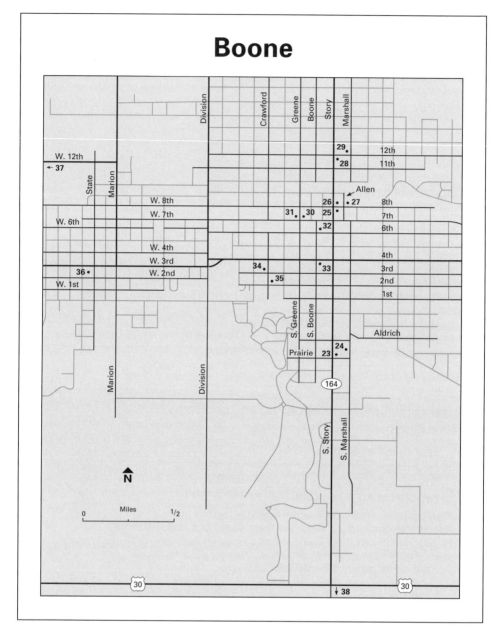

The metal roof with Mission tiles and the white stucco walls of this building evoke something in the way of a 1920s period revival image—Mediterranean, one assumes in this instance. The roof that shelters the pump area is steeply pitched and has a round window in the center of its gable end. The pair of stout piers supporting the roof project on through the tile surface, creating the feeling that the gable roof is hung onto the piers, rather than held up by them.

CE029 Sacred Heart Church

1891–1893, J. P. Eisentraut. Northwest corner of 12th and Marshall streets

This stone Romanesque Revival church has an English flavor. The five-story corner tower with its crenellations seems more military than religious. The church is provided with two entrances, one at the center and base of the gable end, the other at the base of the corner tower. These entrances are serviced by a single wide terrace and an L-shaped flow of stairs. The character of the building is chaste, but warm.

CE032 Taxi School Service Garage

CE030 Erickson Public Library

1900–1901, Liebbe, Nourse and Rasmussen. 1922, Frank Wetherell. Northeast corner 7th and Greene streets

Beaux-Arts Classicism appears here on the spare side, with a decided Italian character. Over the entrance is a loggia with balcony that is hemmed in on each side by wide, solid pilasters, each equipped with a bold cartouche. The entrance itself is contained within its own set of pilasters and heavy entablature. A dark reddish brown brick has been used for the base up to the first-floor window sills; above is a light tan brick.

CE031 First Presbyterian Church

1878–1879. Northwest corner of 7th and Greene streets

This brick Eastlake church has now been painted white. The roof of the corner tower starts with four wall gables and ascends to the small open belfry, topped by its own spire roof. The exterior decoration is in brick and is sharp, right angled, and crisp. The pointed Gothic Revival windows are narrow, almost what one encounters on the walls of a castle rather than a church.

CE032 Taxi School Service Garage

c. 1938. Northeast corner of 6th and Boone streets

The centerpiece of this Streamline Moderne garage is a composition in cast stone of three shafts that plunge up and over the parapet and are then contained by a horizontal curved form. The larger of the garage doors is contained within an L-shaped decorative pattern of variously colored brick.

CE033 Barkley House

c. 1895. 326 Boone St.

The porch, with its assertive turned wood columns, retains the atmosphere of the Queen Anne style while the house itself expresses the Colonial Revival. A large recessed arched opening dominates the third-floor gabled end facing the street.

CE034 Shelders House

1869–1871. 303 Crawford St.

What started out as a delightful one-and-a-half-story Gothic Revival cottage, with Italianate detailing, has acquired a Craftsman shed-roof dormer and an arched Colonial Revival entrance porch. All of these different elements end up working very well together.

CE035 House

1879. 204 Crawford St.

A simple two-story clapboard box exhibits a wonderful Eastlake porch. A row of five thin, turned wood columns supports a band of turned and sawed woodwork.

CE036 Boone County Courthouse

1916–1917, Norman T. Vorse. Northwest corner of 3rd and State streets

The Beaux-Arts courthouse has a pronounced rusticated stone base. Above the raised basement is a central two-story colonnade of eight columns. Behind the colonnade, a loggialike effect is created by two stories of windows and a repeat of lunettes.

The corners of the building are treated as end pavilions with stone walls articulated by horizontal coursing.

thin-membered X-frame steel bridge is 2,685 feet long and it is 185 feet high at its highest point above the river, making it one of the longest and highest of its type in the world.

CE037 **High Bridge** (Kate Shelley Bridge)

1901. West on 12th St.; 3.5 miles from Marion

This impressive double-track bridge spans the Des Moines River not far from Boone. The

CE038 **Ledges State Park**

1921, John R. Fitzsimmons, landscape architect. 6 miles south of Boone on Iowa 164

Pease Creek flows by this 1,200-acre state park. The park was planned by John R. Fitzsimmons, a graduate in landscape architecture from Harvard University. He laid out a picturesque series of roads and trails in an Olmsted-like fashion. He set aside a "wilderness" area, and also a secluded section which he labeled "The Sanctuary." During the later 1920s and on through the 1930s the park acquired a number of rustic constructions, one of the most handsome being a wide-arched stone bridge.

Brooklyn

From the 1920s on, Brooklyn was a stopping-off point on the principal highway between Iowa City and Des Moines (US 6 in the 1930s; Interstate 80 at present). The Standard Service Station (CE039) is a testament to that role.

Also in the community is the Beyers house (1875, now the Brooklyn Hotel), located at 154 Front Street. This building is a characteristic L-shaped Italianate house with a gable roof and a three-story tower placed within the ell. The arches of the windows are highly emphasized, as are the paired brackets supporting the eaves and gable ends of the building. Sometime around 1900 a Colonial Revival porch replaced the original porch; other later additions are present at the rear.

At the southeast corner of Green Street and North Orchard Street is a Prairie house (1917) that bears the name "Pine Crest." This two-story horizontal wood-sheathed house was designed by the Chicago architect Robert S. Smith for Kenneth McAra. Its general boxlike form, steeply pitched hipped roof, and other details remind one of the contemporary work in and around Chicago by the firm of Tallmadge and Watson. Small curved eye-window dormers occur in the roof, and their curve is repeated in the projecting bay window of the dining room. To the left side of the main section of the house is a two-story porch, with an enclosed sunroom on the ground floor and an open screened sleeping porch above.

CE039 **Standard Service Station and Oil Products**

1930s. Southeast corner of Jackson and Second streets

This white glazed-brick and terracotta service station is a 1930s monument to the automobile and the highway. Its principal sign, consisting of Moderne-style letters, projects into and above its cornice.

Cedar Rapids

The city was platted in 1841 on the northeast side of a wide bend of the Cedar River. The location was an advantageous one, for it was possible for steamboats to operate on the river up to this point, and the rapids meant that this was a logical place to produce water power. A few years after the city's founding, a dam was constructed and mills were built. The river remained as the principal transportation link to the Iowa River and thence to the Mississippi and beyond until 1858, when the first of the railroads reached the community. The initial grid plan laid out for the future city followed the northwest-southeast alignment of the river; on the southwest side of the river a second grid system (platted in 1855 as Kingston City) ran loosely parallel to the east bank of the Cedar River. Most of the later platted additions revert to the traditional north-south, east-west alignment; an exception is the single-family subdivision area east of Nineteenth Street, where the hilly terrain encouraged the layout of curvilinear streets within the English Picturesque Garden tradition.

Through the late nineteenth century, and much of the twentieth, the dominant industry for the city was the Quaker Oats Company, which was founded in 1873. Its production plant, north of A Avenue Southeast and west of Fourth Avenue Southeast, conveys an industrial landscape we could easily equate with those often depicted in the 1920s and 1930s paintings of Charles Sheeler. The first units built at a site on Third Street Northeast were two concrete structures that were five stories high. These were constructed in 1910. The centerpiece of the Quaker Oats plant is a modular 10-story factory building (1914, and later) which was joined to other buildings by high aerial bridges of steel, and these were connected to elevator storage buildings and to water tanks. Out of this complex of buildings rise a number of tall, slender smokestacks. Other "industries" expanded the economic base of the community, including meat-

Quaker Oats Company

packing and food-processing plants, box factories, financial institutions, and, more recently, high-tech instrument firms.

One of the unusual geographic features of the city's location was the existence of an island, May Island (now Municipal Island), situated just below the rapids in the middle of the river opposite the original 1849 plat. By the 1870s this low, wooded island was connected to the east and west banks by a pair of iron truss bridges, one for the railway and one for horsedrawn vehicles and pedestrians.

As with numerous other American cities and towns, the people who governed Cedar Rapids were deeply affected by the turn-of-the-century City Beautiful movement. They centered their attention on May Island (which was purchased by the city shortly after 1900) and the adjacent river frontage as a locale that could be revamped into public parks, boulevards, and a municipal civic center. In 1902 the city established the River Front Improvement Commission. Seven years later the community engaged the newspaper-writer-turned-planner Charles Mulford Robinson to prepare a report "on the civic affairs in the city of Cedar Rapids." A few years later the community commissioned Daniel Burnham and Company of Chicago, and Burnham's associate, Edward H. Bennett, to make "a survey and plan for the development of the River Island, and for the landscape and architectural treatment of the River Front. . . ."[7] Bennett's scheme proposed that the city hall be located on Municipal Island, with the remaining space of the island to be a formally landscaped park. Other public buildings were to be situated facing onto boulevards that were to run parallel to the walled river embankments. Parts of Bennett's scheme were carried out, including the Beaux-Arts Classical bridges and some of the masonry embankments, but the concept of the river being paralleled by tree-lined boulevards was never carried out; and instead of one public building being placed on Municipal Island, two were finally located there (City Hall and the Linn

County Courthouse), destroying in part the Beaux-Arts play between the necessary landscaped open park and the buildings.

In the later 1920s and the early 1930s, the city's planning commission engaged another of America's foremost planning firms, Harland Bartholomew and Associates of St. Louis, who responded with a series of planning reports on topics ranging from the question of "civic art" to the more pragmatic design considerations for the location of major streets and for the needs for public transportation and housing. The Bartholomew firm pressed for a realization of Bennett's earlier river boulevard scheme and went on to suggest that eventually this plan should be extended along the river far out to the east and west. Though many of the recommendations of Bennett and Bartholomew were not carried out, enough was realized to make Cedar Rapids an important example of America's approach to a Beaux-Arts civic center.

As with other American cities, the downtown area of Cedar Rapids experienced numerous economic problems in the years after 1945. Suburban shopping centers arose, causing the usual retail shift to the suburbs, and eventually a freeway (I-380) cut its way through the northern portions of the downtown.

Cedar Rapids, outer map

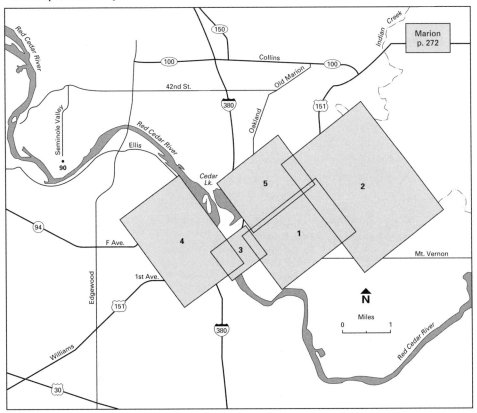

The community's response was a classic one for the time: to create a redevelopment authority to replan and rebuild the downtown. To a degree this activity of redevelopment has been successful. The older, 1920s Roosevelt Hotel has been renovated and restored, a new Stouffer's Hotel has been built, and new and revamped office and retail shopping structures have been injected into the downtown. What is lacking is the grand vision expressed in the Robinson, Bennett, and Bartholomew schemes, where the horticultural element of landscape design would pull all of these old and new parts together and finally would meaningfully relate the civic and business features of the downtown to the river.

Turning from the downtown, the visitor will certainly feel that the middle- and upper-middle-class suburban areas to the east and north constitute some of the most pleasant and successful to be found in the state. The low, hilly terrain, with its vegetation and general large individual lots, means that nature indeed predominates as it should within the suburban ideal.

Another planning plus for the community is the number of parks, many of which are of appreciable size. Especially worth a visit are Ellis Park, Shaver Park, and Van Vechten Park. Two nearby "regional" parks should also be experienced as excellent examples of park planning. These are Seminole Valley Park (off Seminole Valley Road and Forty-second Street) and Squaw Creek Regional Park (east on Twenty-ninth Street to route E44).

Historic preservation and restoration activities in Cedar Rapids have recently brought to light the Monroe School (1873), a school that primarily served the local Czech population. Located at the northwest corner of Third Street and Tenth Avenue Southeast, this Italianate brick building with the usual wide entablature, bracketed cornice, and tall roundheaded windows is presently hidden behind a number of later additions. Still visible above the nearly obscured entrance are the name and date of the school rendered in cast concrete. Current plans are to remove the later additions and then restore the original building, which will be used as a cultural center for conferences and exhibitions.

CEDAR RAPIDS, SOUTHEAST

CE040 Douglas House

1895. 800 2nd Ave. S.E.

The Douglas house is a free and easygoing yet authoritative version of the Colonial Revival of the 1890s. An extensive pattern of large windows, including wide side lights and transom windows around the entrance, conveys a feeling of open acceptance of the suburban landscape. The brick wall and its gatepost, together with the entrance porch with paired columns, are formal but not pretentious. The house is now occupied by Turner Mortuary East.

CE041 Immaculate Conception Roman Catholic Church

1914, Emmanuel L. Masqueray. Corner of 3rd Ave. and 10th St. S.E.

Masqueray, who designed many of the principal Roman Catholic churches in the Midwest in the teens, has so freely utilized historic sources that it is difficult to pin this building down to one historic precedent. Its round-arched windows and its gabled corbeling draw

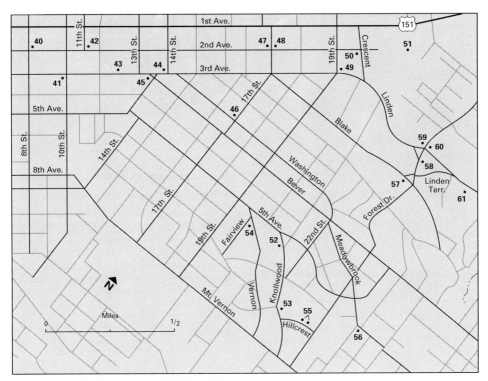

Inset 1, Cedar Rapids, Southeast (CE040–CE061)

it into the Romanesque; but its bracketed roof and peculiarly small-scaled tower are not so easy to assign. As with many public buildings in Cedar Rapids, substantial planting of trees would add greatly to the building and its relationship to the adjoining streets.

CE042 **Averill House**

c. 1885. 1120 2nd Ave. S.E.

A substantial two-and-a-half-story brick pile, the Averill house is accompanied by its own two-story brick stable. The obliquely placed corner bay tower is topped by a high hipped roof. The tower and the wall dormers suggest that the source is the French Second Empire style.

CE043 **House**

c. 1898, attrib. George F. Barber. 1228 3rd Ave. S.E.

Several variations of this design were published in George F. Barber's pattern books, as well as in his magazine, *American Homes.*

This is a remarkable composition with an irregularly contoured central fireplace and chimney mass, off which projects a brick arched entrance porch on one side, and on the other side a wonderful bulbous bay tower. Note such delights as the oval "Colonial" window plunging through the brick chimney, and the "witch's hat" roof topping the bay tower.

CE044 **Saint Paul's Methodist Episcopal Church**

1910–1914, Louis H. Sullivan. 1340 3rd Ave. S.E.

The history of the design of the church, and the resulting building, represented a major disappointment for Sullivan and ultimately for the congregation of the church. In 1910 a competition limited to twelve architects was held. The two designs that most attracted the attention of the church's building committee were those submitted by Louis H. Sullivan and by Purcell, Feick and Elmslie. The committee finally selected Sullivan's design, and he was commissioned to proceed with the

CE044 Saint Paul's Methodist Episcopal Church

working drawings and specifications. These were sent out for bids, all of which were far beyond the budget available. Sullivan then simplified his design in a second scheme, but again the bids for construction were considered to be too high. The church then engaged another architect to reduce the scheme further. This watered-down design ended up as a hollow utterance of what Sullivan had had in mind. At this point George Grant Elmslie of the firm of Purcell, Feick and Elmslie entered the fracas; refusing any professional fee, he reworked the drawings to bring the design back as close as possible to Sullivan's second scheme. Sullivan was incensed by the whole affair, but eventually forgave Elmslie for his intervention.

Sullivan's scheme consisted of three parts: a semicircular auditorium (reflecting in part the fashion for the nineteenth-century Akron plan); a long rectangular volume that housed classrooms and other public spaces, located next to the auditorium; and finally a high tower with hipped roof, to the rear. The planning concept was brilliant, but the stripped-down quality of the exterior and interior leads to a bland, rather unsuccessful design. If the building could have been carried out as planned, it would have had a place alongside William Steele's and Purcell and Elmslie's Woodbury County Courthouse as one of the great monuments of the midwestern Prairie movement.

CE045 Westminster Presbyterian Church

1904–1905, Charles Bolton. Corner of 3rd Ave. and 14th St. SE

Charles Bolton, an architect from Philadelphia, designed a number of churches in the

East and Midwest. In the case of the Cedar Rapids church he utilized late English Gothic themes in designing this auditorium building. At the street corner he created three angled gables, each with a large pointed window. A tower with a pinnacle stands midway between the auditorium and the Sunday school wing. All of the Gothic details have been reduced to simple basic shapes, and the ornament tends to be sharp and angular.

CE046 First Congregational Church

1919, Josselyn and Dodd. Northwest corner of Washington Ave. and 17th St. S.E.

The entrance of this Colonial Revival church with a steeple has a two-story gabled porch. The detailing, ranging from the stone quoining at the corners to the pedimented entrance and arched windows, has all been "correctly" and sensitively carried out.

CE047 House

c. 1910. 1644 2nd Ave. S.E.

A competent clapboard Colonial Revival design is raised two or three notches by its central dormer with balcony surmounted by a barrel-vaulted roof.

CE048 Newman House

1909, Brown Brothers. 1700 2nd Ave. S.E.

The two-story stucco-sheathed Craftsman box often tended to be crude in proportion and in detail. However, in this example, sophistication and finesse dominate. The shed-roofed living porch has delicate segmented openings, the walls between them covered with trellises. The brick chimney is delicately tapered as it climbs, and paired lunette windows in the attic lighten the surface of the wall. When published in the magazine *Concrete* in February 1910, it was noted that the interior was in the "Craftsman style" with the exception of the dining room, which was "Colonial."

CE049 Stark Bungalow

c. 1911, William J. Brown. North corner of 19th St. and Linden Dr. S.E.

This one-and-a-half-story Craftsman bungalow seems to play a game between assertiveness and reticence. Its stepped entrance walk-

CE049 Stark Bungalow

way leads diagonally from the street corner to an entrance porch with a segmented roof, cleverly placed at a 45-degree angle within the building's L-shaped plan. The formality of the low stone walls parallel to the public sidewalk is repeated in the parapeted stone terrace. In contrast the low, hovering gable and hipped roofs provide a scale associated with the modest California bungalow. Look carefully at the plastered surface of the upper walls, for here you will find stones of various colors worked into the surfaces.

CE050 **House**

c. 1910. 215 Crescent St. S.E.

The turn-of-the century Colonial Revival box is here brought to perfection. Everything seems just right: the thin porches with wooden columns and delicate wood balustrades; the central second-floor Palladian window, so delicately realized; and finally, the narrow curved roof dormers, gently sunk into the roof.

CE051 **Sinclair House** (Brucemore)

1884–1886, Josselyn and Taylor. 1908, Howard Van Doren Shaw. 2160 Linden Dr. S.E.

Unquestionably, Brucemore represents one of the great country estates of Iowa. It is indeed a mansion, impressively situated within extensively landscaped grounds. When built, the house was referred to as "French Renaissance," though we today would pigeonhole it with no difficulty as a classic example of the Queen Anne emerging out of the earlier Eastlake style. The exterior, other than the addition of a glass-enclosed loggia, remains pretty much as designed by the Cedar Rapids architectural firm of Josselyn and Taylor. In 1908 much of the interior was radically transformed according to the eighteenth-century French style. This interior design was attributed to the Chicago architect Howard Van Doren Shaw. After the house changed hands in 1906, the gardens and grounds were expanded from 11 to 45 acres. The sensitive and well-planned layout of the gardens indicates the design of a gifted landscape architect, whose identity remains unknown. Just off Crescent Street is the Colonial Revival garden house of 1911, which was probably designed by Howard Van Doren Shaw. The beautifully preserved, well-maintained house and gardens are open to the public.

CE052 **Ely House**

1909. 509 Knollwood Dr. S.E.

The gabled roof of this loose, well-carried-out version of the Colonial Revival extends out to cover a deep porch running across the entire front of the dwelling. Above, the long, narrow shed-roof dormer has a rhythmic pattern of three paired double-hung windows separated by two very small casement windows.

CE053 **Marshall House**

c. 1925. 532 Knollwood Dr. S.E.

The proportions and details of the two-story Colonial Revival-Georgian Revival Marshall house are realized with perfection. Note especially the entrance frontispiece with side lights and transom. The broad lawn with a sprinkling of trees provides the classic suburban setting.

CE054 **Collins House**

1922–1924, Harry Hunter. 514 Fairview Dr. S.E.

As early as the mid-1920s, clients and architects began to look directly at Iowa's Greek

Revival/Federal houses of the 1840s–1850s for sources of inspiration for their own regional versions of the Anglo-Colonial. The Marshall house (CE053) and the Collins house exemplify this interest. Both houses are of native sandstone, as were many of their mid-nineteenth-century prototypes; the gable roof and the balanced facade are other features characteristic of this adaptation. While these houses do indeed convey a sense of archaeological correctness, they reveal equally the decades within which they were built.

CE055 **The McKay Houses**

1919, Gordon McKay. 2302 and 2304 Hillcrest Dr. S.E.

These two graceful two-story brick-sheathed Colonial Revival houses visually complement one another. Each is distinct in details, the entrances, chimneys, and other features indicating how individual the Colonial Revival image could be.

CE056 **Lustron House**

c. 1950. 2567 Meadowbrook Dr. S.E.

This is the side-entrance model of the prefabricated metal Lustron house. It snuggles into its suburban setting in the same fashion as any spec or architect-designed dwelling. There are several other Lustron houses in Cedar Rapids. One can be seen at 3616 First Avenue.

CE057 **Farmer House**

1934–1935, Morehead Fredrickson, contractor. 2179 Blake Blvd. S.E.

In the 1930s the machine image of the Moderne house was frequently softened by delicate details associated with the early nineteenth-century English Regency and its American version, the Federal style. In this house a large ground-floor bay window and an indented columned porch add the needed traditional quality to an otherwise Moderne form.

CE058 **House**

c. 1920. 308 Forest Dr. S.E.

A two-story suburban stucco dwelling, this house poses as an English thatched-roof cottage. The feel of a thatched roof has been effectively realized with asphalt shingles, which are brought over the fascia of the eaves.

CE059 **Kesler House**

1942, Carl C. Kesler. 2168 Linden Dr. S.E.

At the end of a long lawn, framed by tall deciduous and coniferous trees, is this perfect version of a classic two-story New England Colonial Revival house. A handsome doorway with side lights and a fanlighted transom has been recessed into its masonry wall.

CE060 **Shaver House**

1909–1911. 2200 Linden Dr. S.E.

Set in a deep woods of leafy deciduous trees, far back from the road, is this Prairie-style house. A wide porch with a thinly detailed cantilevered roof dominates the front of the house. Above, a long band of casement windows has been placed directly under the roof soffit. The interior is light and airy with extensive glass areas. The walls and ceilings are articulated by rectangular geometric banding of wood strips. The windows reveal a treasure of leaded glass, suggesting pairs of elongated flowers. The grounds, landscaped within the English Picturesque Garden tradition, were design by the landscape architect Ossian Simonds.

CE061 Hamilton House

1929–1930, Ernest Kennedy. 2345 Linden Dr. S.E.

A large stucco, tile-roofed Mediterranean house is just barely visible at the turn of a long driveway leading up from the public road. A band of three arched windows surrounded by a stone frame dominates the projecting entrance wing of the house. Ernest

Kennedy, the designer of this well-carried-out period revival dwelling, was a well-known Minneapolis architect who designed houses for many of Minneapolis's first families, the Pillsburys, the Gales, and others.

CE062 Grant House

1946–1951, Frank Lloyd Wright. 3400 Adel St. S.E.

This post-World War II Usonian house for Douglas B. Grant is situated at the end of a small lane. The hill upon which it has been placed drops off steeply to the north and east, providing views of a countryside that is rapidly being suburbanized. The house is essentially a narrow two-story volume, with the north-facing two-story living room acting almost as a glassed prow of a ship. All that can be seen from the lane is the carport. One enters the house at the side; to the right is a long single flight of stairs leading down to the living/dining/kitchen area. The three bedrooms and a sitting room are on the upper level. A horizontal slab of concrete, 117 feet long, covers the whole of the house.

CE063 Robert Armstrong House

1932, Bruce McKay. 370 34th St. S.E.

The Robert Armstrong house has often been cited as an example of Iowa's own regional version of the Colonial Revival style. It was modeled after the Eugene Doe house (1860) in Waubek, a house that carried on the very late Federal tradition. The architect, Bruce

CE063 Robert Armstrong House

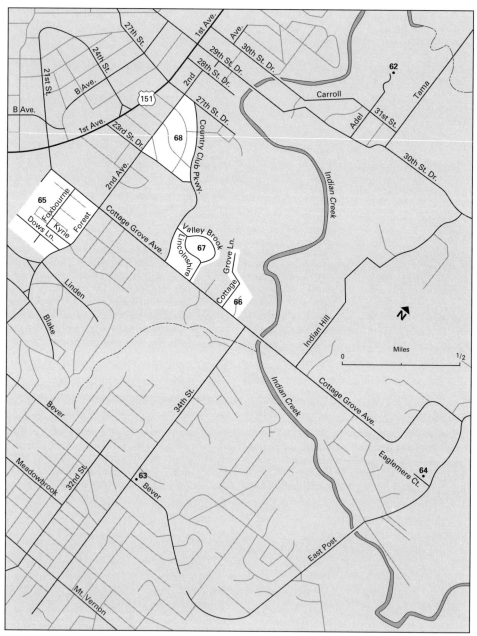

Inset 2, Cedar Rapids, Southeast (CE062–CE068)

McKay, wrote of his intent, "As to the house, a century from now, when the last of Iowa's old stone houses have crumbled to ruin, posterity will still have one authentic copy of the early Iowa houses."[8] Both the Doe and Armstrong houses are sheathed in stone, both have gable roofs, and both exhibit a balanced arrangement of double-hung windows. However, the Armstrong house reads as a characteristic 1930s version of the Colonial, horizontal, low to the ground, and accompanied by an exterior living porch, large windows on the ground floor, and wide bay windows. The painter Grant Wood is said to have "assisted" in the design of the house, though his specific contributions are not fully known.[9]

CE064 **Crites House No. 1**

1959, Crites and McConnell. 4340 Eaglemere Ct.

The architectural firm of Crites and McConnell emerged in the years after World War II as one of Iowa's principal exponents of the Miesian post-and-beam version of International-style Modernism. In a way, the houses the firm produced can be thought of as Midwestern counterparts of the post-and-beam houses that came to constitute the Case Study House program in Southern California, of John Entenza and his magazine *Arts and Architecture*. The Crites house consists of a delicate, thin steel frame which is lightly cantilevered out over a steep wooded hillside. The walls of the house, placed between the vertical steel posts, are of horizontal wood sheathing or of glass. Another, somewhat similar dwelling designed by Crites and

McConnell is the Shuttleworth house (1964) at 2403 Indian Hill Road Southeast. Other architects who carried on the Miesian mode in Cedar Rapids were Thomas Reilly (his Farris house of 1967 is at 2148 Glass Road Northeast), and the firm of Kohlmann-Eckman-Hukill (in the Hukill house of 1967 on Northwood Drive, south of Mount Vernon Road Southeast).

CE065 **Sutherland Square**

c. 1960s, later. Southwest of Forest Dr. and Cottage Grove Ave. S.E.

Sutherland Square is an upper-middle-class suburban district of the 1960s and later which maintains the quality of openness and landscape design of the early suburban districts. Some of the houses are low-spreading stone-and-brick versions of the California ranch house; others exhibit a modern image, reminiscent of the post-World War II houses of the Californian Richard J. Neutra.

CE066 **Cottage Grove Meadows**

post-1945. North side of Cottage Grove between 32nd and 34th streets S.E.

This is a post-World War II suburban district that openly conjures up the Colonial image. One enters between Colonial gateposts with metal lanterns; within the complex are Colonial Revival houses loosely placed on gentle sloping lots. The meandering street pattern has been carefully laid out to reflect the gentle hilly terrain.

CE067 **Valley Brook**

1950s and 1960s. Northeast of Cottage Grove Ave. and Commercial Country Club Pkwy. S.E.

As in the nearby Cottage Grove areas, the streets in Valley Brook wander around the hilly terrain. The planting is lush, and in this case the imagery of the houses is quite varied.

CE068 **Country Club District**

Bounded by S.E. 2nd Ave. and Country Club Pkwy., between 23rd and 27th streets S.E.

This is an excellent example of a pre-World War II subdivision, with curved streets, extensive planting, large individual lots, and no sidewalks to suggest that this is the country not the city. The single-family houses range in style from the Colonial to the English medieval half-timber.

CEDAR RAPIDS, DOWNTOWN

CE069 The Civic Center

In 1911 the Chicago planner and successor to Daniel Burnham, Edward H. Bennett, prepared a Beaux-Arts Classical scheme for downtown Cedar Rapids. In addition to proposing boulevards adjacent to the river, he suggested that a grouping of civic buildings be established centering on Municipal (formerly May) Island. Bennett's scheme formalized an approach to the riverfront improvement that had been initiated in 1902. The 1911 plan called for the construction of masonry embankments, boulevards with formal plantings of major trees, arched masonry bridges, and the location of the principal governmental buildings on the island, facing onto the river and the boulevard on the adjacent bank. By the beginning of the 1930s, four of the city's principal public buildings were located within this "civic center." Because of

the openness of space provided by the boulevard, river, and island, and the seven-story tower of the Veterans' Memorial and City Hall building, this complex of public buildings constitutes one of the few instances in America where a Beaux-Arts scheme has continued to dominate a downtown area.

CE069.1 Veterans' Memorial and City Hall

1927–1928, Henry Hornbostel and William Jay Brown. North side of 2nd Ave., Municipal Island

The idea of symbolizing government by playing off the theme of the skyscraper, associated with laissez-faire business, against the public image of the classical temple was introduced on the American architectural scene in the second decade of this century. Its earliest complete manifestation was the Oakland (California) City Hall (1911–1914) designed by the New Yorker Henry Hornbostel. In Iowa this theme underlay the Prairie-school design of William Steele and Purcell and Elmslie's Woodbury County Courthouse at Sioux City (1915–1917). And it was, of course, in the twenties that the most famed version was created—Bertram G. Goodhue's Nebraska State Capitol building at Lincoln (1922–1926).

Inset 3, Cedar Rapids, Downtown (CE069–CE082)

CE069.1 Veterans' Memorial and City Hall

Cedar Rapids engaged Hornbostel for its towered Veterans' Memorial and City Hall. Along with the Iowa architect William Jay Brown, he produced an intriguing variation on the theme, placing the tower at the front, as a frontispiece, with the lower three-story building serving as a backdrop. Equally inventive was their treatment of the termination of the building, where a solid masonry cenotaph surges up through and then above a small, delicately detailed classical temple. The building, which was designed to be theatrically floodlighted at night, contains a spectacular stained glass window, designed by Grant Wood early in his career.

CE069.2 **Linn County Courthouse**

1925–1926, Joseph W. Royer. South side of 3rd Ave., Municipal Island

Like its companion piece, the Veterans' Memorial and City Hall, the county courthouse was to have a low tower rising out of a classical temple base. The elimination of the tower in the final design produced an adequate Beaux-Arts background building, but not one which strongly enhances the uniqueness of its site on Municipal Island. The recent "modernist" five-story addition to the rear should, if possible, be ignored.

CE069.3 **United States Post Office, Federal Building, Courthouse**

1931–1933, James A. Wetmore. West corner of 2nd Ave. and 1st St. S.E.

This version of the Beaux-Arts tradition was carried out fairly well, yet the building is somewhat bland. The design, which came from the Washington, D.C., office of the Architect for the Treasury (under the direction of James A. Wetmore), is enlivened externally by its finely proportioned front of engaged Ionic columns and a pattern of recessed windows. Inside, the high point is a series of tempera murals depicting the theme of "Law and Culture." Located on the walls of the lobby and in the courtroom, they were produced in the mid-1930s as a part of the WPA Federal Arts Project. They were painted by Don Glassell, Everett Jeffrey, Harry Jones, and Robert Francis White.

CE069.4 **Central Fire Station** (now Science Station Museum)

1917. West corner of 5th Ave. and 1st St. S.E.

This fire station is a small, low-key classical exercise in brick. It is subtly invigorated by an odd pattern of segmental arched garage doors, not balanced (as is the rest of the composition), but with a rhythm of one large door, then a small one, followed by a large and then smaller opening.

CE070 **Cedar Rapids Ground Transportation Center**

1982–1983, Olson, Popa, Novak. Block bounded by 4th and 5th Aves., between 1st and 2nd streets S.E.

This meeting place for buses, private cars, and pedestrians is contained within a low, formal, modernist building dominated in a constructionist fashion by glass and metal. Its purpose, and particularly its public use, is difficult to discern from the street. Its anti-contextualism in relation to the older buildings around it and its lack of space for public landscaping means that it does not add much to the public sense of the civic center.

CE071 **James Jewelers Store**

c. 1937. 307 2nd St. S.E.

The lively sign visually dominates the jewelry store. Its neon-lighted lettering, its lighted clock, and its double band of incandescent lights invite a night viewing.

CE072 **Brenton Financial Center**

1970–1976, Charles Herbert Associates. West corner of E. 1st Ave. and 2nd St. NE

A smooth-skinned "modernist" building of Cor-Ten steel, the center is composed of two seemingly independent pieces of angular geometric sculpture. The principal entrance is pulled off the street by the sharp angle of one of the blocks; once inside, one is greeted by a glassed atrium.

CE073 **Merchants National Bank**

1925, Weary and Alford. West corner of 2nd Ave. and 3rd St. S.E.

This 12-story office and bank building was the city's most distinguished skyscraper of the twenties. The architects employed the traditional tripartite design in the building; there is a base articulated by three-story arcades, a neutral shaft of paired and single double-hung windows, and then a terminal attic composed of arched windows, decorative cartouches, and a strongly cantilevered roof. The most unusual feature here is the way in which the three-story base has been designed to be experienced almost as a separate podium upon which the rest of the building has been placed.

CE074 **World Theater**

1923, William Jay Brown. 314 2nd Ave. S.E.

A theater building here passes as an urban Italian palazzo. A great semicircular window above the marquee is played off against a suggestion of rustication. Above, an attic story is terminated by a bracketed shed roof. The present brow-shaped marquee, as well as the shop fronts to each side, are of a later date.

CE075 **Dragon Chinese Restaurant**

326 2nd Ave. S.E.

The presence of a Chinese restaurant is delightfully and effectively announced by a neon sign in the outline form of a pagoda, and at the entrance by the suggestion of a temple roof terminated by dragons. All of this has been "plopped" onto the corner of a nineteenth-century brick-and-stone commercial block.

CE076 **Central Branch YMCA**

1971, Crites and McConnell. North corner of 1st Ave. N. and 5th St. S.E.

The low, brick-sheathed walls of this complex, with its deeply cut-in windows, seems a fortress of sorts. The modish style of the brick box works best when placed within a landscape site. Here it tends to add a sense of bleakness to the landscape.

CE077 **Scottish Rite Temple**

1927. A Ave. between 6th and 7th streets N.E.

Although their order is Doric, the "primitive" and ponderous scale of the columns comes close to that of the proto-Doric encountered in Egyptian architecture. The main building is balanced by low dependencies, each with its own smaller pedimented portico.

CE078 **Paramount (Capitol) Theatre**

1928, Peacock and Frank. 183 3rd Ave. S.E.

The theater was restored in 1976 and is now used by the Cedar Rapids Symphony and other performing groups. Its 2,000-seat auditorium with balcony boxes conveys a subdued and restrained classicism, somewhat in the spirit of late eighteenth-century English Adamesque design. Much of the interior wall decoration was seemingly carved out, an illusion created using plaster cast in low and high relief. The luxurious lobby was, according to local tradition, inspired by the Hall of Mirrors at Versailles.

CE079 **Hotel Roosevelt**

1928, Edwin D. Krenn and Herbert B. Beidler. North corner of 1st Ave. and 3rd St. N.E.

The Roosevelt is a vertical 12-story brick-sheathed box; the division of the facade into three parts, base, shaft, and capital—a treatment based on classical architecture—has been articulated by a sparse use of Regency-inspired detailing and ornamentation. Medallions, garlanded panels, and finials projecting from the top of the parapet crown the building. Within, the public spaces, especially the two-story lobby, employ the then-popular Italian Renaissance details.

CE080 **Cedar Rapids Savings Bank Building** (now Guaranty Bank and Trust Company)

1895–1896, Josselyn and Taylor. North corner of 3rd Ave. and 3rd St. S.E.

The local firm of Josselyn and Taylor designed many buildings in downtown Cedar Rapids. There were once a number of Queen Anne and Richardsonian Romanesque buildings in the downtown, but now only a few remain. This bank building is a six-story rusticated stone Richardsonian Romanesque structure with a traditional bay tower at the corner. An open loggia occupies the top floor of the tower.

CE081 **Cedar Rapids Museum of Art**

1987–1989, Charles W. Moore, Centerbrook Architects and Planners (Glenn Arbonies). Northwest side of 3rd Ave., between 3rd and 4th streets S.E.

Here is Postmodernism at a glance, tinged with Moore's usual twists of humor.[10] Since every public building needs columns, he has provided a single row of them standing in front of the building. The three-layer entablature resting on the columns is broken here and there, as if to emphasize that this colonnade is a stage-set screen that has nothing to do with the building. The free-standing colonnade does succeed in establishing the building's civic presence overlooking Green Square Park. Behind this screen to the left are three connected pavilions, and a fourth which is a loading dock.

To the right is the glass "grand" entrance pavilion which poses between the new pavil-

CE081 Cedar Rapids Museum of Art

ions on the left and the remodeled Carnegie Library building on the right. In contrast to the others, the entrance pavilion has a tiered gable roof, and its placement to one side seems to hint that eventually the building will move over and replace the older building. Color, ranging from the black of the drum-like columns to shades of warm tan for the walls, is used to accentuate the elements of the building. Within, the entrance pavilion is carried up two floors to a glass roof, and a forest of tall, thin columns (should one call them of the "Byzantine order"?) greets the visitor. On exhibit one will find the works of a number of Midwest Prairie Regionalists of the 1930s, including Grant Wood, Thomas Hart Benton, and Marvin Cone.

CE082 **Masonic Library, Museum, and Auditorium**

1953–1955; Hansen and Waggoner; William L. Perkins. 813 1st Ave. S.E.

In the hands of architects trained within the Beaux-Arts tradition, the classical mode continued with some vigor after World War II. The Masonic Library building is a good case in point. The architects carried on the late-1930s WPA version of the classical tradition, but at the same time they abstracted it even further than had been the case in the 1920s and 1930s. The design of the Masonic Library is a series of boxes sheathed with white marble; the major emphasis is placed on the entrance pavilion. What greets the visitor is a windowless rectangular volume that projects out over the entrance. This volume is supported at each corner by "primitive" but sophisticated drum columns. Sculpture in low relief appears on the front face of this upper block, to the right near a block of lettering.

CEDAR RAPIDS, WEST SIDE

CE083 Peoples Savings Bank

1909–1911, Louis H. Sullivan. 101 3rd Ave. S.W.

This Prairie bank was the second that Sullivan designed and saw built in the Midwest. He took the format often used in Beaux-Arts Classical bank buildings—a two-story clerestory-lighted banking room flanked by low, one-story open office space. In contrast to his earlier bank at Owatonna, Minnesota, where he encompassed the two functions within a single volume, here in Cedar Rapids he created two highly separate volumes. In fact, they are so separate that they almost read as two independent buildings. The separateness of the high public room is accentuated by the four perpendicular chimneys and vents at its corners, a design device often

used by English Arts and Crafts architects, especially Charles F. A. Voysey.

Though Sullivan had a sympathetic client in the bank's vice president, F. H. Shaver, he was forced by cost considerations to reduce substantially the richness of his first scheme; this is especially apparent in the reduction of terracotta ornament. Thus, as the critic Montgomery Schuyler observed in a 1912 article, "the exterior is the envelope of the interior reduced to the simplest expression."[11] However, the interior when built still exhibited a wonderful array of Sullivan's ornament, accompanied by Allen E. Philbrick's murals on the theme of an allegory of seasonal changes expressed through scenes of agriculture, commerce, and industry.

Numerous changes have been made in the building over the years, especially with the exterior and interior alterations that took place in 1951 and 1966; gone are the four brick-pier streetlights that so tellingly reiterated (on a small scale) the four vertical chimney/vents of the bank building, and the richness of the interior is a ghost of its former self. In early 1990, Norwest Bank Iowa, which now owns the building, announced that extensive restoration would take place under the direction of Wilbert R. Hasbrouck of Chicago. The restoration, together with additions to the building, were completed in 1991.

CE084 Acme Building

1923–1924. South corner of 3rd Ave. S.W. and 2nd St. S.W.

An unpretentious single-story brick commercial building has acquired a high degree of sophistication through the articulation of its brick surfaces, and above all through the use of colorful glazed terracotta. The walls have been divided into panels by narrow brick pilasters. Below the parapet the designer has created horizontal, slightly recessed panels, their interiors composed of bricks laid in a herringbone pattern. Splayed across the facade, just above the pilasters, is a brightly colored terracotta cartouche. The lower portion of this cartouche acts as a delicate Ionic capitol for the pilaster; the upper design centers on an open seashell with a gold crown within it. The colors of the glazed terracotta are bright blue, gold, and white. It is worthwhile to compare this use of terracotta to that of Sullivan in the adjacent bank building.

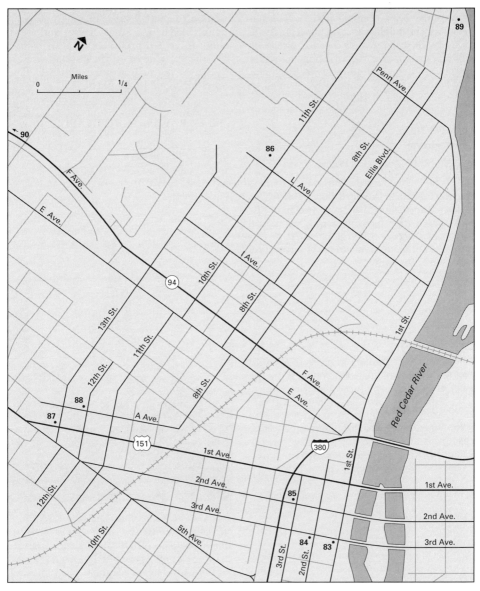

Inset 4, Cedar Rapids, West Side (CE083–CE090)

CE085 **Police Department Building**

1937–1938. 310 2nd Ave. S.W.

This is a PWA building, both in its funding and in style. The structure is two stories high, sheathed in light tan brick, with sandstone trim. A centrally placed entrance wing projects slightly from the building. The entry doors are deeply set within pilasters; above, the wall surface is filled with glass brick. In plan, the center of this H-shaped building contains a drive-through garage with storage to the rear for cars and motorcycles.

CE086 **Harrison School**

1929–1930, Harry E. Hunter. Northwest corner of 11th St. and L Ave. N.W.

A two-story brick building is clothed in elements of the English Gothic image that was often recalled for schools. Leaded glass windows appear above the principal entrance. Within the lobby are murals with the theme of "Transportation." These were painted by William Henning in 1934–1935.

CE087 House

c. 1898. 1304 W. 1st Ave. N.W.

The small gable over the entrance porch reflects in miniature the third-floor gable of this Queen Anne/Colonial Revival dwelling. The two-story corner bay tower with its conical roof contributes both to the irregular picturesqueness of the design and to the suggestion of Colonial formality.

CE088 House

1895. 202 12th St. N.W.

One suspects that the designer of this large brick house was thinking in terms of Richard Morris Hunt and his interpretation of the small chateaux of the Loire Valley in France. The bulkiness of its mass and of its three-story corner tower seem to have more to do with the earlier Richardsonian Romanesque than with the then-current vogue for the Châteauesque. The house has been converted to housing for the elderly.

CE089 "Ranger"

1982, William Jay Brown. 1895 Ellis Blvd. N.W.

An over-life-sized male figure, westernized by Levis and a Stetson hat, beckons one to enter Harper's Marine City. The cut-out fish on the wall behind the figure programmatically makes it all apparent.

CE090 Seminole Valley Farm Inc.

West on F Ave. N.W. to Edgewood Rd. N.W.; north on Edgewood, cross the Cedar River to 42nd St. N.E.; west on 42nd St. N.E. to Seminole Valley Rd.; south on Seminole Valley Rd. to Seminole Valley Park

This restored farm complex was typical of rural farmsteads of Iowa in the 1880s. In addition to the dwelling, there is a barn, a summer kitchen, a smokehouse, and other outbuildings. The grounds have been planted with the sorts of trees, shrubs, and flowers which were normally grown in the 1880s. The complex is open to the public.

CEDAR RAPIDS, NORTHEAST

CE091 Coe College

1926. Edward H. Bennett; Graham, Anderson, Probst, and White. 1st Ave. E between Coe Rd. and 13th St. N.E.

The college came into being in 1851 and officially assumed the name Coe College in 1881. The plan of the campus and its architecture is a mild variant of Jefferson's design for the University of Virginia. The dominant building is the Sinclaire Memorial Chapel (1950) which, like the nearby Stewart Memorial Library (1931), was referred to at the time as "modified Georgian Colonial." The designs of these two buildings illustrate the popularity within the Colonial Revival for the red brick, stone-trimmed early nineteenth-century buildings of New England. The interior of the library was remodeled in 1988, and on the second floor is the Grant Wood Gallery. Here one will find six large murals depicting the Iowa farm, plus a number of smaller works.

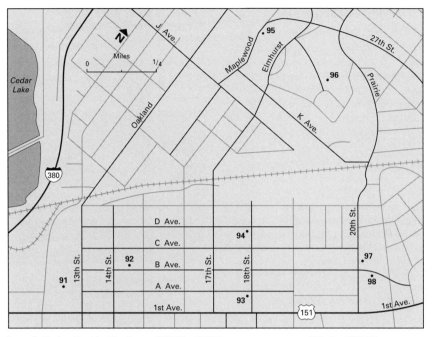

Inset 5, Cedar Rapids, Northeast (CE091–CE098; see outer map, p. 173, for CE099)

CE092 **Fire Station No. 3**

1925, Charles B. Zalesky. 1424 B Ave. N.E.

This fire station poses as a suburban single-family Tudor house. Its half-timbered second floor together with its low roof dormer help to pull it down in scale so that it contextually fits into the residential neighborhood.

CE093 **Bungalow Court**

1932. 117–123 18th St. N.E.

Here is a U-shaped court composed of stucco Spanish Colonial Revival bungalows complete with red tile roofs. Like the earlier bungalow and the later ranch house, the bungalow court was one of California's major exports during the decade of the teens and later. This one could really succeed if its landscaping could be enriched.

CE094 **House**

c. 1890. 1757 D Ave. N.E.

The verticality of this two-and-a-half-story Queen Anne dwelling is enhanced by its nar-row arched porch and the roof forms which seemingly tumble over and cover the side porte-cochère entrance. The small-scaled gable-roofed pavilion which projects forward boasts a playful false balcony.

CE095 **Cottage**

c. 1950. 1302 Maplewood Dr. N.E.

A tiny post-World War II Cape Cod Colonial cottage becomes stately by virtue of its grand entrance doorway surrounded by broad pilasters.

CE096 **A Folly**

c. 1920. On the grounds of Mount Mercy College, near northeast corner of 17th St. and K Ave. N.E.

The Ten Commandments are memorialized in a templelike pavilion composed of a tile-and-quartzite base from which rise primitive columns supporting a Romanesque-inspired sequence of arches. The composition culminates in a sphere coated in brilliant colors—red, blue, green, and shimmering gold. Nearby one will discover a second folly, an arched rock grotto.

CE097 **Franklin Junior High School**

1923. 20th St. N.E., between B and C Aves. N.E.

The architectural character of this two-story red brick school is entirely announced by its monumental entrance. For this, the architect turned to the late English Gothic, adding buttresses, canopied niches, paneled walls, and suggestions of finials. The building is similar in design to the Harrison School (CE086).

CE098 **Cottage**

c. 1898. 2015 B Ave. N.E.

A long, curved brick drive leads up to and past a one-and-a-half-story cottage. Its double gabled front dormer is Edwardian, while its corner tower with an open second-floor porch looks to the Colonial Revival.

CEDAR RAPIDS, ENVIRONS

Northeast of Cedar Rapids is the small community of Whittier, where the Friends Meetinghouse (CE099) is located. To reach Whittier, take Iowa 13 at the eastern end of Cedar

Rapids; proceed north 3 miles to route E34; then go east on E34 4.2 miles.

CE099 **Friends (Quaker) Meetinghouse**

1893, William Hoyle, builder. Northwest corner of route E34 and X20

Like the smaller Quaker Meetinghouse at West Branch, this one is essentially a very late Federal/Greek Revival building, a single-story clapboard structure covered by a gable roof, with a porch running down one side. It is said to be similar to other Quaker meetinghouses built earlier in Ohio.

Coggon

Three miles north of the Wapsipinicon River in Linn County is the town of Coggon. At the northeast corner of East Main and Second streets is the Zion Presbyterian Church (c. 1900). The design of this white clapboard church with a corner tower looks to the turn-of-the-century Colonial Revival. The four-unit window within the principal gable end has its own pediment. Its enclosing return at its base is broken by a single circular window. Rising from the square tower is an octagonal belfry with a tall bell-shaped dome. Down Main Street, at 202–204, is a well-preserved single-story commercial store building with a pressed-metal front (c. 1880). The design of the two storefronts appears unchanged, as is the simulated masonry of the upper facade which is rendered in pressed metal.

Colfax

Colfax, in western Jasper County, developed initially as a shipping point on the Chicago, Rock Island, and Pacific Railroad and as a developing center for the mining of coal. With the discovery of mineral spring water in the area in the mid-1870s, Colfax entrepreneurs began to export this new product. By the early 1900s, it was noted, "The town is made famous by its mineral springs and has become a great health resort, and its mineral waters are bottled and shipped to all parts of the country, and also in bulk."[12] At that time Colfax, by then known as "the Carlsbad of Iowa," boasted nine hotels, the largest of which and the only one now left was the 150-room Hotel Carlsbad.

CE100 Hotel Carlsbad (Family Life Center)
early 1900s. 1911, remodeling. Route F48, 1.8 miles
east of Colfax

Though referred to at the time and after as an example of the "Moorish design," the Hotel Carlsbad is in fact Iowa's most luxurious example of California's Mission Revival. From the beginning of the 1900s on through the mid-teens, the image of California's missions spread all across the country. Considered exotic (by Anglos) and associated with Califor-

nia as a place of perpetual play, the style came to be used often for recreation buildings, amusement parks, and resort hotels.

The architect who through remodeling gave the older Carlsbad Hotel building its Mission Revival appearance around 1911 was obviously aware of many California examples, particularly Arthur B. Benton's famous and widely illustrated hotel, the Mission Inn at Riverside. The design also reflects the state buildings constructed by California at the 1893 World's Columbian Exposition in Chicago and at the later expositions held at Buffalo and Saint Louis. The three-story stucco hotel with a red tile roof has a freestanding entrance screen almost identical to that of the Mission Inn in California. The paired towers, parapeted gable ends, and rows of arched windows are hallmarks of the style, whether in Iowa or California. At the beginning of the Great Depression in the 1930s the hotel was forced to close. It was later used as a hospital, and more recently as the Family Life Center, a church-related institution.

Dallas Center

The William H. Brenton house (1878), at the northeast corner of Kelloge and Walnut streets, was one of the many designs by the pioneer Des Moines architect William Foster. The house is of brick, with a limestone foundation. In the Brenton house Foster adopted the format of a late Italianate scheme and modified it with a sprinkling of Eastlake details. The Eastlake elements are most apparent in the front entrance porch which wraps around to the side of the house. Also Eastlake in design are the exaggerated U-shaped stone lintels of the windows. The central motif on these lintels is the sunburst, below each of which is a horizontal scalloped motif. The roofs of the porch and of the main house still retain their iron fencing.

Delta

Proceeding south from Delta one mile on Iowa 21, at the crossing of the North Branch of the Skunk River, one comes to the Delta covered bridge (1867). This single-span 76-foot-long bridge was initially built without cover. A housing with a gable roof was added the following year. The bridge was constructed by Joseph Merryfield and James Harlan using a Burr arch truss system, a form often used on nineteenth-century Pennsylvania bridges. In 1955 the bridge was restored, and it is now used only for foot traffic.

Des Moines

The first settlement at the confluence of the Des Moines and Raccoon rivers was the establishment of Fort Des Moines (see CE128) in 1843.[13] The fort consisted of two rows of log cabins, one group for the officers and another for the enlisted men. Other buildings and structures were added: a dock on the river, a commissary, and a hospital. With the opening of this section for settlement, a town was platted in 1846. The first frame building was erected in July 1846; the first brick building in 1848. The site for the future capital of the state was described in 1875 by Andreas as "picturesque, occupying chiefly the valley and slopes of the hills on both the east and west sides of the river, the hills swelling into a grand circle of bluffs, which sweep the horizon on nearly all sides."[14] The city's initial grid consisted of square blocks, oriented slightly off from the points of the compass.

In 1846, Des Moines won out as the designated seat for Polk County, and the first courthouse was built in 1848. The next, even more advantageous move for the community was the removal of the state capital from Iowa City to Des Moines. Agitation for such a move started in 1851, and the change of location took place in 1855. Construction of a new capitol building, located on a high hill looking out over the Des Moines River valley, began in 1871.

During its early years the new community relied on the Des Moines River for transportation, but the low water level during parts of the year made this mode of transport unreliable. The Des Moines Valley Railroad from Keokuk finally reached the city in the summer of 1866. Some ten years later, the city had emerged as a hub for six different railroads. As with other cities throughout the country, Des Moines inaugurated a narrow gauge horsedrawn street railroad in 1868; this was replaced by electric street railways which started service in 1888. At the end of the following decade, in 1898, an interurban electric railroad was initiated, reaching first to Colfax to the east. Later additions to the interurban rail line eventually connected with Perry and Rockwell City to the northwest.

As Des Moines expanded in the 1860s and later, the original grid was simply extended; eventually a sense of order returned, and the newer additions reverted to a traditional north-south, east-west grid system. By the mid-1870s Des Moines had acquired in South Park its first picturesque, curvilinear suburban street pattern. Within its grid system Des Moines provided for a number of open spaces. These included the four-block site for the state capitol building, a

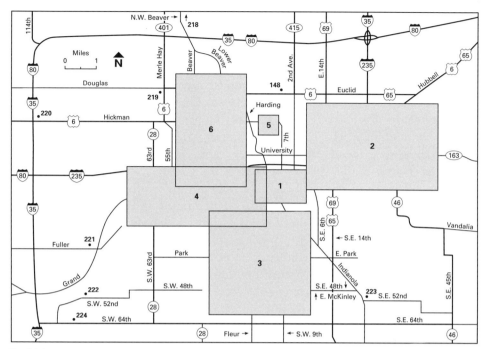

Des Moines, outer map

site for the county courthouse, and a two-block location for a public market. These were augmented by smaller park sites such as the Joseph B. Stewart Square (corner of Fourteenth Street and Grand Avenue) and by open spaces provided by several cemeteries. By 1898 the city possessed eight parks (in addition to its public squares and the park site for the state capitol). The largest of these was Waveland Park (190 acres), followed by Grandview Park (98.5 acres), and Greenwood Park (81 acres). Another extensive and partially wooded open space was the Iowa State Fair and Exposition Grounds. The 263-acre fairground site, located some distance east of the state capitol building, was acquired and became the state fairgrounds in 1886.

Iowa in general, and above all Des Moines, actively participated in the turn-of-the-century "City Beautiful" movement. The initial group behind such planning was the Civic Improvement Committee of the Des Moines Commercial Club. The activities of this group were expanded by an enlarged Town Planning Committee (incorporated in 1916). The eventual goal of the Town Planning Committee was to provide for riverfront improvement (including the creation of a civic center), for the expansion of the public grounds around the capitol, for open space and for sites for future state public buildings, for the development of a system of boulevards, and finally for the expansion of the city's park system (especially along side the city's two rivers). In 1900 the landscape architect Warren H. Manning proposed the creation of a set of riverside parks, to which would be connected a system of parklike boulevards. Charles Mulford Robinson prepared a study in 1901 that expanded on the concepts put forth by Manning.

In conjunction with these city studies and projects, the state commenced an expansion and improvement of the grounds surrounding the capitol building. The key participant in this planning activity was Emmanuel L. Masqueray, trained at the Ecole des Beaux-Arts and nationally known for his designs for churches and public buildings. His recommendations (1913) were to develop a strong cross-axial scheme (centered on the state capitol), the principal axis of which would reach west to the Des Moines River.

Several elements of these City Beautiful ideas were assuming reality by 1919. "Des Moines has a famous river front," wrote one of its Park Commissioners, Harry B. Frase, ". . . the banks of the river have now been thoroughly cleaned up and improved . . . and a number of public buildings have been erected fronting the river."[15] The design concept of the city's civic center was to utilize the river as the principal axis, and then let the streets and their elegant concrete bridges over the river become the secondary cross axes. Not only was this a highly innovative Beaux-Arts scheme, it was even more remarkable that by the mid-1920s it had in fact been pretty well carried out.

Within the 1920s philosophy that "the business of America is business," planning in that decade tended to have an aura of down-to-earth practicality. This was a period for Des Moines during which the recreational aspects of the city's parks were improved, a large-scale natatorium was built near the river, and civic leaders dealt with broader questions of zoning and streets. From 1926 through 1940, much of the planning for these activities came from the Saint Louis office of Bartholomew, Harland and Associates. During the depression of the 1930s, considerable improvements were made within the city's park system, and a number of new public buildings were constructed through the federal PWA program.

In August 1939, the editors of *Architectural Record* initiated a survey of responses to contemporary architecture. Taking Des Moines as first point of call, the *Record* commenced for its readers a survey of what the "lay" citizen considered to be noteworthy examples of recent architectural work in the cities of the United States. The range of imagery cited was remarkably broad, ranging from Proudfoot, Rawson and Souers's First Church of Christ Scientist, a modernized Gothic edifice; to the Moderne Bankers' Life Building by Tinsley, McBroom and Higgins; to the recently completed Streamline Moderne Central Fire Headquarters by Proudfoot, Rawson, Brooks, and Borg. As the *Record*'s later visits to other American cities indicated, the taste and response of the citizens of Des Moines perfectly mirrored the responses from other parts of the country.

Although much smaller in scale than any of America's major urban environments, Des Moines essentially reflected what was going on elsewhere in planning in the years after World War II. With the usual spread of housing and shopping to the suburbs, parts of the downtown began to be treated as urban renewal areas, and of course, an urban freeway (I-235) was plowed right through the community. The 1970s and 1980s witnessed the construction of a number of important public buildings, including an addition to the former post office building, a new convention center, and several buildings for the state of Iowa, including the Iowa Historical Society Museum building.

Downtown Des Moines was essentially a low-rise city at the end of the nineteenth century, but at that time it did possess several commercial buildings of six to eight stories. By 1918 these buildings had been joined by several real "skyscrapers," including the 11-story Hotel Fort Des Moines. With the general American love affair with the skyscraper during the twenties, Des Moines acquired several even higher buildings, among them the 19-story Equitable Insurance Company building (1924). From the 1960s to the present, Des Moines has been right "up and at 'em" in strengthening its downtown image as the locale of sophisticated buildings. The latest of these, currently the tallest building in the state, is the 44-story 801 Grand Building (1989–1990). Located at that address, this is a conservative Postmodern building sheathed in granite, glass, and copper. The architect, Gyo Obata of the Saint Louis firm of Hellmuth, Obata and Kassabaum, has provided Des Moines with a design that starts off at the ground with a classical-inspired gabled entrance, and ends at the top with a star-shaped pyramidal form.

The malady of skyways has also hit the city, and as is almost universally true elsewhere in the country, these have turned out to be aesthetically disappointing and have had a negative effect on the uses of the streetscape. On the positive side, there has been a near renaissance in the restoration of and sensitive additions to many of the older downtown commercial buildings in Des Moines.

In a fashion characteristic of American cities, strip villages have developed in recent years adjacent to the highways that now bypass Des Moines (I-80 and I-35). These villages at the major interchanges (and many of the minor ones) exhibit the usual assortment of hotels, motels, restaurants, stores, and office buildings. At the junction of I-80 and US 65 is Adventureland Amusement Park, which among other things presents several Disney-like themes: Main Street, River City, Last Frontier, and Iowa Farm. Adventureland opened to the public in 1975, and since then additions and changes have been made in the park.

If one delights in parks and in the middle-class and upper-middle-class ideal of low-density suburbia, then one can experience its realization along the western reaches of Grand Avenue and in the region to the south, below the Des Moines Waterworks Park, developed since World War II. Greenwood Park and the adjacent Ashworth Park are a pair of the most successful suburban parks in the country. These are supplemented by wonderful settings for public schools, some reminiscent of the settings of country houses. Design imagery in this suburban section of the city takes one from the late nineteenth century through the period revivals of the 1920s and 1930s—both in the dwellings themselves and with respect to landscape architecture. The most interesting post-World War II single-family housing exists in the southern section of the city. Further to the northern and western edges of Des Moines one will encounter extensive areas of postwar single-family housing, and of course the classic commercial strips, shopping centers, and highway-oriented architecture. Des Moines has its share of Lustron houses, two well-preserved examples of which (along with their garages, c. 1950) are located at 1609 and 1703 Beaver Avenue. The houses are side by side; the one at 1609 is gray and the one at 1703 is yellow.

DES MOINES, DOWNTOWN

CE101 Polk County Courthouse

1900–1906, Proudfoot and Bird. 500 Mulberry St.

The site for a courthouse west of the Des Moines River was purchased by Polk County in 1846. Because of the offset of the city's grid along Fifth Street, the courthouse site served as the termination of the eastern portion of Court Street. Two years after the site was acquired, the first courthouse was built—an unpretentious two-story building with a brick veneer. This plain, simple structure was

replaced by a far more opulent masonry building designed by Dyer H. Young. Construction of this second building started in 1858, but it was not occupied by the courts until 1866. In style this second courthouse was French Second Empire; it was surmounted by a tall, spirelike, segmented dome and lantern.

To accommodate the expanded needs of county government, the third and present courthouse was built in what was labeled as "a modified Renaissance style," i.e., Beaux-Arts Classical. In general the design of the building is sophisticated and correct; it has a multifloor central rotunda and a gray lime-

Inset 1, Des Moines, Downtown (CE101–CE138)

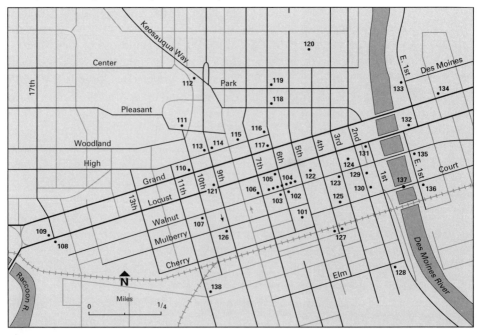

CE101 Polk County Courthouse

stone facade articulated by a rusticated base and rows of pilasters above. Externally, its most unusual feature is its 116-foot-high central tower with large clock faces and the wonderful array of 28 sculptured masks found in the keystones of the arched second-floor windows. Within, around the fourth level of the central rotunda, is an impressive group of murals. These are: *The Indian in His Natural State*, by Bert Phillips; *The Coming of the White Men*, by Douglas Volk; *The Departure of the Indians from Iowa*, by Charles A. Cumming; and *Presenting the Flag*, by Edward Simmons. In 1985 restoration of the building was carried out by Bussard/Divas and Sven Paulsen.

CE102 Des Moines National Bank (now Valley National Bank)

1931–1932, Proudfoot, Rawson, Souers, and Thomas. 520 Walnut St.

The Valley National Bank building is one of the really outstanding examples of the Art Deco style in the country. Externally and in-

ternally it strikes a wonderful balance between the assertive opulence of this late twenties Moderne style and a sense of classical sophistication and reticence. On the ground floor a band of highly polished black granite from Wisconsin is interrupted by the entrances and by repeated large glass openings. Above this is a file of wide, flat, fluted pilasters (without capitals) which rise through three floors of the building. The fifth floor is stepped back, and was meant to be the first level of a tower that was to have risen 16 stories. Because of the depression, the project was scaled back, and the tower was never built. The ground-floor entrance and lobby, and the second-level two-story banking room exhibit elaborately decorated ceilings and upper walls, as well as an extensive amount of ornamentation in metal. This building was cited in a 1939 survey as one of the outstanding recent designs within the city. In 1979 the building was extensively restored by Charles Herbert and Associates, and Sven Paulsen.

CE103 Fleming Building

1907, Daniel H. Burnham and Company. Southwest corner of Walnut Ave. and 6th St.

The 11-story Fleming Building is one of Burnham and Company's seemingly stock designs for an office and banking skyscraper. Similar examples were built by this firm all across the country. Direct historic references were usually kept to a minimum in designs such as this. What stylistic comments are made in proportions and details are mildly Beaux-Arts Classical. The Fleming Building was one of the earliest steel-frame structures to be built within the state.

CE104 The Kaleidoscope at the Hub; Hub Tower

1984–1986, Charles Herbert and Associates (The Kaleidoscope), Herbert Lewis Kruse Architects (Hub Tower). Walnut St., between 5th and 7th streets

At the base of this multiuse complex is the Kaleidoscope, a double-layered enclosed pedestrian shopping mall. This two-story section of the complex exhibits low, open towers with hipped roofs and other design elements that have become the hallmarks of the Postmodern vocabulary. The second level of the Kaleidoscope is connected to adjacent buildings by skywalks, which typically do little to encourage pedestrian use of the street. The Hub, a 25-story highrise, as often happens with skyscrapers of the late 1970s and 1980s, ends up being bulky rather than the soaring romantic structure Louis H. Sullivan had in mind. The fenestration of the upper floors of this glass and metal-sheathed building, together with its metal-detailed glass corners, easily fits in with what we usually think of as Postmodern. The architects have emphasized the vertical fenestration of the brick skin of the building in the fashion of the "Vertical Style" of many American skyscrapers of the 1920s. But there is not enough variety of depth in the facade of The Hub to make this work. The crown of the building is composed of a glass-and-metal gable end to the front of the building, behind which is the characteristic (for Postmodernism) central tower with its own hipped roof. The interior space housing the entrance and elevator lobby utilizes a 1980s version of the late-twenties Art Deco.

CE105 Equitable Life Assurance Company

1922–1924, Proudfoot, Bird and Rawson. 604 Locust St.

The ability of period revival architects of the teens and twenties to combine successfully, and with ease, past styles is well attested to in this 19-story skyscraper. The central decorative theme is unquestionably Gothic Revival, but the medieval detailing in granite and glazed terracotta is organized in a purely classical manner. From a distance, the character of the building is established by its rooftop lantern, with its elongated round-arched windows, its terracotta paneling, and its spirelike roof.

CE106 Younker Brothers Department Store

1899, Liebbe, Nourse and Rasmussen. 1981, 1983, Charles Herbert and Associates; Schafer Associates with Business Images, Inc. Northwest corner of 7th and Walnut streets

All that really remains of the original turn-of-the-century building is its external shell. As with many remodelings of the 1970s and 1980s, the new windows of this building have been brought out to the surface of the adja-

cent masonry, so that the old and new read as a paper-thin skin. The original exterior design was Beaux-Arts Classical, with the second through third floors treated as a large arcade. There is a thin cornice above the keystone of these large arches, and above are two additional floors articulated by large Chicago windows. The interior has been completely transformed and now reads as a modernist design of the 1980s.

CE107 Hotel Fort Des Moines

1918, Proudfoot, Bird and Rawson. Southwest corner of 10th and Walnut streets

The decade of the teens saw a rash of construction of hotel buildings throughout the United States. A good number of these hotels, as in the case of the Hotel Fort Des Moines, followed a set formula in their layout and architectural imagery. The architects usually employed a U-shaped plan, with the open end of the "U" facing the street. Generally the lower two floors of the "U" were filled in with stores and public spaces. The facades of these hotel buildings were divided horizontally into three parts in the traditional fashion, with ornamentation generally confined to the lower levels and to the top of the building just below the projecting cornice. The Hotel Fort Des Moines exhibits all of these characteristics, and they are carried out with knowledge and sensitivity.

CE108 Successful Farming / Meredith Publishing Company

1906, 1912, Proudfoot, Bird and Rawson. 1981–1982, remodeling, additions, Charles Herbert and Associates. 1716 Locust St.

The modest-sized three-story towered building (1906) now appears to be snuggled in, somewhat like a dollhouse, next to the glass-and-metal-skinned addition of the early 1980s. Though small, the strongly quoined six-story tower (1912) of the original building continues to draw one's attention from its larger neighbor. The imagery of the 1906 structure is loosely Italian, though it would be difficult to pin it down to a single historic period. The architectural impact of the Meredith Publishing Company lies not so much in its old and recent buildings, but in its publishing ventures, especially *Better Homes and Gardens*, begun in 1924, and *Metropolitan Home,* a more recent magazine. In addition to these publications, Meredith has provided a home plan service, published plan books, and sponsored the construction of exhibition model houses, a number of which were built in Des Moines as well as elsewhere in the country.

CE109 Valley National Bank (now an automobile dealership)

1978. Northwest corner of 17th and Locust streets

This single-story building of white painted brick almost seems to be posing as a Beverly Hills mansion. In style it is classical, with slight references to late eighteenth-century French architecture and to the English Regency tradition. A central entrance with classical pediment is balanced on each side by wide bowed English bays. Though small in size, the assertiveness of the bank's classical design, reinforced by its siting on an extensive green lawn, produces a building that dominates the corner.

CE110 Brenton National Bank, Grand Office

1966, John Stephens Rice. Northwest corner of 10th St. and Grand Ave.

Set back from the street and behind trees is this small drive-in bank. Its design is essentially that of a sculptured open cube space frame, which is close to domestic in its size and detailing. The modernist rectangular geometry of the building helps to relate it to other larger downtown buildings.

CE111 First Methodist Episcopal Church (now United Methodist Church)

1905–1908, Proudfoot and Bird. Pleasant St., end of 10th St.

Architects designing within the fold of the Beaux-Arts had a decided fondness for the Roman Pantheon of the second century as a source for a number of twentieth-century building types. This Proudfoot and Bird church, with its central auditorium, could hardly be seen as a replica of its Roman ancestor; still, the ancient building served as an inspiration. In the Des Moines church, the pedimented porch with Ionic columns is Greek

rather than Roman in its proportions and detailing. The building's siting perfectly expresses the Beaux-Arts ideal: a location at the terminus of a street (Tenth Street), near the slope of a hill which necessitates a pair of ramplike stairs leading up to a low terrace platform, upon which the church was placed.

CE112 Northwestern Bell Data Center

1976–1978, Charles Herbert and Associates. 900 Keosauqua Way

This is a piece of sharp-angled minimalist sculpture enlarged to carry out the function of a building. The center section of the building has been cut into, providing open parking visible on the ground level, and above, a connected band of angled bays on the second and third floors. The play between what appears as a "real" building within the cutout and the surrounding piece of minimalist sculpture is well carried out.

CE113 Northwestern Bell Telephone Company

1928, George B. Prinz. Northwest corner 9th and High streets

The Northwest Bell building is a Des Moines example of the popular late-1920s Art Deco "Vertical style" skyscraper. Each of its bays is defined by pilasters that continue above the roof parapet; within each of the bays is a minor, much thinner pilaster, and this also reaches upward, culminating in stone crowned finials. As is appropriate for the style, the upper reaches of the building step back. Brick was used not only for the skin of the building but also as the means of patterning for the repeated spandrels.

CE114 Saint Paul's Episcopal Church

1885, Foster and Liebbe. 815 High St.

The church was designed by one of Iowa's early architects, William Foster, who opened his practice in Des Moines in 1857. Foster gave this Gothic Revival church a strong Victorian appearance. The Gothic pointed windows are wide in relation to their height, and even the sanctuary and its various appendages are broad in conjunction with their height. One enters the building, not at the

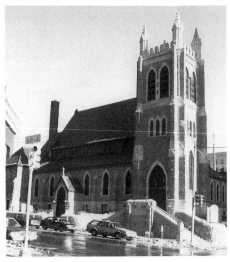

CE114 Saint Paul's Episcopal Church

base of its corner tower, but through a small vestibule with gable roof which projects from the right front of the building. In 1963–1965 an open spire of Cor-Ten steel was added to the crenellated tower, but this has been removed. A sympathetic wing with a dormered roof has been added, facing directly onto the sidewalk and street.

CE115 **Bankers Life Building**

1939–1940, Tinsley, Higgins, Lighter, and Lyons. 711 High St.

With the renewed building activity at the end of the 1930s, the earlier "Vertical style" in skyscrapers continued, generally following the precedent set by the design of buildings within Rockefeller Center in New York. The pronounced Gothic verticality of the 1920s was replaced by a classical and more restrained approach, an approach that often incorporated elements of either the High Art International style or the popular Streamline Moderne. The Bankers Life Building is a near-perfect summation of all of these late-thirties tendencies. Its plan is symmetrical and balanced; the traditional smooth stone sheathing (dark rainbow granite at its base and cream-colored limestone above) is played off against extensive openings of glass bricks, bronze window frames, and sheet rubber employed for wall covering. The building's ornamentation ranges from molded decorative

glass panels (pre-Columbian in feeling) designed by Lowell Houser and Glenn Chamberlain, depicting scenes from Iowa history, to a large low-relief panel above the auditorium entrance. Within, the decoration is at times traditional, as in the president's office and in the boardroom, while at other times it is Modern and Moderne in imagery, as in the auditorium and in the main-floor club room.

CE116 **Saint Ambrose Roman Catholic Cathedral**

1890–1891, James Eagon. 607 High St.

The Richardsonian Romanesque, conveying a strong kinship to historic churches in southern France, is the style of this cathedral. The parapeted gable front contains a band of four elongated round-arched windows separated by pairs of columns; below the great entrance arch is a slightly projecting gabled porch. The corner tower with its entrances terminates in a steeply pitched hipped roof. The sanctuary has a barrel-roofed ceiling that has been elaborately painted. The Richardsonian Romanesque theme in rusticated stone masonry was continued in the adjacent rectory built in 1927.

CE117 **Home Federal Savings and Loan** (now American Federal Savings)

1962, Ludwig Mies van der Rohe. 601 Grand Ave.

This is a post-World War II exercise in a steel-frame, glass-infill building, carried out by Mies van der Rohe, one of the pioneer modernists of the German Bauhaus of the 1920s. Though modest in size (it is only three stories high), the building could be endlessly extended upward and/or sideways to form either a skyscraper or a low horizontal building occupying a full block. The detailing is meticulous, as is always the case in Mies's best work, and the materials are "posh": granite and travertine marble. Mies's initial scheme for the building called for a roof suspended from a pair of lengthwise trusses, similar to several of his 1940s designs at the Illinois Institute of Technology in Chicago. This more elaborate and expensive treatment was abandoned for the simpler, more direct design of the present building.

CE118 American Republic Insurance Company

1965, Skidmore, Owings and Merrill (Gordon Bunshaft). Northeast corner of 6th St. and Keosauqua Way

Bunshaft perfectly translated into concrete, glass, and steel the client's ideal of creating a "clerical factory." A six-story set of concrete "bureau drawers" (open at the ends) is suspended over a walled compound. A vertical barred gate leads into a hygienic, pristine courtyard, self-consciously elegant in its white polished stone floors, concrete walls, and acres of plate glass. This conveys the idea that it naturally functions best with no humans about. Though a modest-sized project for SOM and Bunshaft, it beautifully sums up the impersonal corporate machine-image of the post-World War II decades. The one human note is the playful Alexander Calder stabile, *Spunk of the Monks.*

CE119 Scottish Rite Temple

1926–1927; Wetherell and Harrison; Keffer and Jones. Northeast corner of 6th St. and Park Ave.

The decades from 1910 through 1930 provided this fraternal order with the opportunity to expand the Beaux-Arts tradition across the whole of the country. The Des Moines Scottish Rite Temple, like many others, sits on its corner site as a distant, aloof piece of classical sculpture. It openly makes passersby aware of its presence, but it is secretive in hiding what goes on within. The base of the building is punctured by a single small door accompanied by small deep-set windows to each side. The principal facade exhibits a recessed porch with a screen of six Ionic columns two stories high.

CE120 Veterans Memorial Auditorium

1954, The Architectural Committee. 1983–1984, Brooks, Borg and Skiles. 833 5th Ave.

The Beaux-Arts tradition was in a continual state of change from 1900 through the 1950s. The tendency was to abstract volumes and surfaces, returning them in a sense to their primitive (but sophisticated) forms. The Des Moines Auditorium presents a long, low (and mildly Modern) face to the street. The dominant feature of the design is the gable front, banded horizontally with thin lines of stone placed within its brick wall. Another thin line of stone defines the roof edge, which is without an overhang. Everything is organized around an axis that seems to plunge into the center of the building or upward to the apex of the roof.

In 1983–1984, Brooks, Borg and Skiles added a new Modernist entrance to the building. They kept their new addition symmetrical and utilized the same Mankato stone and brick used in the original building. They also redesigned the double walkway and steps leading to the building, again carrying on the symmetry of the initial design. In 1989 the same architects provided a pair of skyway entrances running across the front of the building, connecting to their new entrance. As is too often the case, the new skyways will hardly enhance the older Beaux-Arts facade design—but one must wait and see the results before forming a final judgment.

CE121 Naylor House

1869, 1873, attrib. William Foster. 644 9th St.

Thomas Naylor, a dealer in flour and groceries, built (in 1869) the single-story, clapboard-sheathed two-room house that now serves as the rear wing to the later dwelling. In design this small building looks to the Gothic Revival for its imagery. A few years later, in 1873, in building the two-story brick house, Naylor and his architect turned to the Second Empire style (with several leftovers from the earlier Italianate mode). The small entrance porch has a cornice that curves around a central medallion. There is a larger porch on the side, and an angled bay in ashlar block stone with a small balustrade extends from the south side of the house. Still accompanying the house at the front is the original cast-iron post and woven wrought-iron fence. Within, the side-hall plan house is almost unadulterated; its staircase, doorways, many fireplaces, cornices, and decorated ceilings remain.

CE122 **Capitol Square**

1983–1984, Skidmore, Owings and Merrill. 400 Locust St.

Early-1980s Modernism, its insistent theme being strong horizontal layers, is here realized through bands of continuous horizontal windows and accompanying spandrels. This same theme is repeated in the interior eight-story atrium court. On the ground floor of the court is a small circular pool accompanied by six raised circular rings; within each of these is a small, forlorn, somewhat lost tree. It all adds up to SOM's usual design sophistication, with a strong sense of the hygienic.

CE123 **The Plaza**

1984–1985, Stageberg Partners. Southwest corner of 3rd and Walnut streets

The plaza is a mixed retail and housing complex that is essentially a modernist exercise, with a slight nod to Postmodernism in its alternately light and dark banded base, and above all in its blue gabled and hipped roof. Though there are taller buildings in the downtown, the steeply pitched gables and brilliant roof of this structure are visible miles away.

CE124 **Civic Center / Nollen Plaza**

1979, Charles Herbert and Associates. Northeast corner of 3rd and Walnut streets

This period piece is an example of academic 1960s Modernism carried out at the end of the 1970s. Granting the premise of late Modernism, this hardscape project of concrete surfaces has been carried out well. The 2,700-seat auditorium, a cut-into volume comprised of concrete panels, rests on the surface of the plaza like a not quite real model. Plantings of trees, pools, fountains, flagpoles, and even Claes Oldenburg's *Crusoe Umbrella* do not relieve the correct, cold atmosphere of the place.

CE125 **Kaplan Hat / Des Moines Saddlery**

1887. 307 Court Ave.

Brick commercial blocks trimmed in stone were characteristic of the late nineteenth century. Above the ground-level tall shop windows in this one are four horizontal bands within which are rows of roundheaded windows. The light-colored stone used for the horizontal floor banding is employed in the projecting semicircular headers of these windows. While the fifth floor of the building is a later addition, it sensitively carries on the theme of the original facade. There are several other late nineteenth-century commercial buildings still standing nearby (within the Court Avenue Historic Area). Among these are the F. M. Hubbell Building (1891) at 107

CE126 Fire Department Headquarters

Third Street, and the Seith Richards Building (1889) at 300–310 Court Avenue.

CE126 **Fire Department Headquarters**

1937–1938, Proudfoot, Rawson, Brooks, and Borg. 900 Mulberry St.

This full-fledged essay in the 1930s Streamline Moderne style was financed through the PWA program. The six firetruck bays facing south are divided from one another by a row of vertical curved pylons that rise from the ground to the top of the parapet of the wall. The street corner of the building is dramatically curved, and the windows on both floors are treated as continuous bands. To accentuate the machinelike curve and horizontality of the building, thin bands of recessed brick or stone are carried across the facade. Brick was used for the wall sheathing; the pylons, entrance panels, and other details are of stone, with some terracotta detailing. Surprisingly, this public building was one of those selected in 1939 by leaders in the community as an outstanding example of recent Des Moines architecture.

CE127 **Rock Island Railroad Depot**

c. 1905 (west); c. 1910 (east). 107 and 108 4th St.

The commanding feature of this railroad station is the open metalwork arch with its lower hipped roof which connects the two buildings and spans Fourth Street. The arch provides something of a ceremonial entrance into the city, and by connecting the two buildings creates the image of a large single structure. The brick building to the west, which is two stories high, is covered by a wide overhanging tile roof. Pronounced voussoirs define the row of second-floor arched windows. The single-floor building to the east, also of brick with a tile roof, is more modest in its fenestration. The composition of the two buildings and the arch have the flavor of a domesticated (close to a do-it-yourself) version of the Beaux-Arts Classical tradition.

CE128 **Barney Sakulin Log Cabin**

c. 1843–1846. Southeast corner of 2nd and Elm streets

In an open field, sitting all alone and somewhat forlorn, is this small split-log cabin—almost as if by the touch of a magic wand, one of John Lloyd Wright's toy Lincoln Log cabins had been enlarged to adult size. The cabin marks the site of Fort Des Moines number two, which was established in 1843. This rural log cabin, constructed in the mid-nineteenth century, was moved to this location and reconstructed under the direction of the Des Moines architect William J. Wagner. Though it is not original to the fort, the cabin suggests what some buildings of the fort must have looked like.

CE129 **United States Post Office Building (now Polk County Heritage Gallery)**

1908, James Knox Taylor. Southeast corner of 2nd Ave. and Walnut St.

The Beaux-Arts appears here at its best. Four corner pavilions contain among them a centerpiece composed of a repeated pattern of Corinthian pilasters. Between each pair of these pilasters is a large arched main-floor window, and above, hugging the lower line of the entablature, is a horizontal pattern of three windows. A light gray limestone has lent itself well to the fine carving of ornament and the tactile vertical tooling of the surfaces. The high vaulted lobby of the public space runs across the entire front of the building. The two entrances, their vestibules, and the public space were extensively restored in 1980, and the space is now used as the Polk County Heritage Gallery. The interior has been opened up to the Polk County Office Building (1979) to the rear so that one can walk through one building to the other.

CE130 **Polk County Office Building**

1979; Woodburn and O'Neill; Wagner, Marquard, Wetherell, and Ericsson. Northeast corner of 2nd and Court avenues

In 1975 the voters of Polk County approved the appropriation of funds to purchase the former post office building and to build a modest-sized annex to it. The project was to encompass some restoration of the old building and to remodel its rear section and add space for additional county offices. The architects sheathed the addition in a matching limestone, kept the general height and scale of the older building, and carried an abstracted version of the entablature/cornice of the older building around the new building. They provided for a symmetrical south facade with a central solid block, and a portico on each side. Instead of employing columns or piers, they utilized a pair of three free-standing fin-walls, which end up reading as both traditional and contemporary design features. The county office building in conjunction with the old post office building represents one of the most sensitive additions/adaptive reuses of the decade of the 1970s in Iowa.

CE131 Des Moines Public Library

1898–1903, Smith and Gutterson. Southeast corner of 2nd Ave. and Locust St.

An interest in developing the riverfront for public parks and buildings surfaced as early as 1897 with the purchase of land on the river's west bank. Though the building was designed and built before Warren H. Manning and Charles Mulford Robinson had drawn up their City Beautiful schemes, the Des Moines architects Oliver O. Smith and Frank Gutterson sited the building so that its long axis ran parallel to the river. At the building's principal entrance (which faces west) a double flight of exterior stairs leads up to a two-bay-wide entrance porch whose flat roof is supported by widely spaced Ionic columns. Above the entrance is a large semicircular window that provides light for the interior central stairway. The interior exhibits the architect's well-informed use of Beaux-Arts sequential spaces and of detailing. Most impressive is the multilevel reading room, with its wonderful circular metal stairs, and the murals, *Boys and Girls* and *A Social History of Iowa,* produced by Harry Donald Jones and others (1937–1941). The exterior of this two-story classical composition on a raised basement is sheathed and detailed in a Minnesota limestone which is now weathered to a warm, slightly salmon pink color. The design was supposedly patterned after the art museum in Nancy, France. In 1985 the building was remodeled and restored by Wagner, Marquardt, Ericsson; and Sven Paulsen.

CE132 Des Moines Municipal Building

1909–1910; Liebbe, Nourse and Rasmussen; Hallett and Rawson; Proudfoot and Bird; Wetherell and Gage. Northeast corner E. 1st and E. Locust streets

If one were to enlarge this Beaux-Arts civic building a few notches, it could be dropped into Washington, D.C., where it would perfectly match the numerous federal buildings constructed there during the first three decades of this century. The Des Moines building is impressively sited in an extensive park setting overlooking the Des Moines River from the east. It was the first civic building that directly reflected the Robinson plan for a civic center. The building, of Bedford limestone and Tennessee and Vermont marble, exhibits the time-honored classical composition of a rusticated base carrying a two-story central section with columns. Within, the principal public space on the second floor has a low hooped ceiling punctured by colored art glass skylights.

CE133 Argonne Armory

1934, Tinsley, McBroom and Higgins. E. 1st St., end of Des Moines St.

Although it is PWA Moderne, this armory's scheme is Beaux-Arts Classical, with a central projecting pavilion flanked by lower matching wings on each side. Columns and pilasters, cornices and entablatures have disappeared, leaving only a few direct indications of classical ornamentation—vertical fluting in the slightly recessed spandrels between the windows on the first and second floors, a suggestion of a balustrade at the top of the wall plane, and, of course, the usual spread-wing eagle within the central pavilion. Large bronze wall lamps project out from a pair of rectangular buttresses situated to each side of the entrance.

CE134 Conoco Service Station

1934. 201 E. Grand Ave.

The low-pitched bright-red tile roof and the white glazed terracotta block walls project a loosely Mediterranean image in this building. There are low angled buttresses at each corner, and the white glazed blocks are laid in a random fashion. A single service-bay exists to the side of the office, the windows are steel framed, and the building is topped by a chimney of domestic scale.

CE135 United States Courthouse

1928, James A. Wetmore. Southeast corner of E. 1st and E. Walnut streets

This courthouse is another later addition to the Beaux-Arts Classical civic center. As with the Municipal Building to the north, the United States Courthouse faces the river to the west, its main axis running parallel to the river. The four-story building on a raised basement is successful not in its overall design (its proportions are a bit on the ungainly side) but in its fine detailing, both within and without. Note especially the pair of bronze lanterns at the entrance, where a large drumlike light has been placed atop a classical urn.

CE136 Municipal Court and Public Safety Building

1920; Keffer and Jones; Kraetsch and Kraetsch; Sayer and Watrous. Southeast corner of E. 1st St. and E. Court Ave.

Although this three-story Bedford limestone building is shaped like a rectangular box, its detailing is far more three dimensional than the adjacent United States Courthouse. The building's Beaux-Arts design includes a series of central recessed porches with heavy Doric columns and a wide cornice that provides an effective, deeply shadow termination to the design. An unusual feature of the building is the way in which the second-floor windows have been placed within a projecting picture frame, the upper portions of which exhibit a winged medallion.

CE137 Court Avenue Bridge

1917, Norman T. Vorse. Court Ave. between 1st St. and E. 1st St.

Both Manning and Robinson, the turn-of-the-century planners, called for a series of broad-arched masonry bridges to cross the Des Moines River. These were to be tied together with embankments on each side of the river. The stone balustrades on top of the embankments were designed to match those on the bridges. The Court Avenue bridge is a graceful example of a Beaux-Arts composition. On the shore side, each of the low segmental arches springs from a projecting semicircular buttress; delicate voussoirs define each of the arches; and at the crown of the arches are shieldlike cartouches.

CE138 Pyramid Cement Company Storage Units

c. 1922. SW 11th St., 1.5 blocks south of Railroad Ave.

The image of concrete cylindrical silos has been one that has continually enticed the exponents of modern architecture, from Wright to LeCorbusier, as well as such American School painters as Charles Sheeler and Charles Demuth. This impressive array of 26 units was designed for the storage of cement, not grain. In the early 1920s, 6 units 33 feet high were constructed on the site. These were eventually joined by even higher units reaching up to 110 feet. Their construction is that of reinforced concrete using the slip-form method of building. Originally there was a cement manufacturing facility that accompanied the silos, but this is now gone. The silos are currently operated by the Iowa Concrete Company, headquartered in Davenport. The dry cement is manufactured at Buffalo, Iowa, and shipped to these storage silos for use in the Des Moines area.

DES MOINES, EAST SIDE

CE139 Iowa State Capitol

1871–1874, John C. Cochrane and Alfred H. Piquenard. E. 10th St. between E. Grand Ave. and E. Walnut St.

A competition was held for the projected state capitol building in 1869. Fourteen architects submitted designs, and from these, the design of Cochrane and Piquenard was

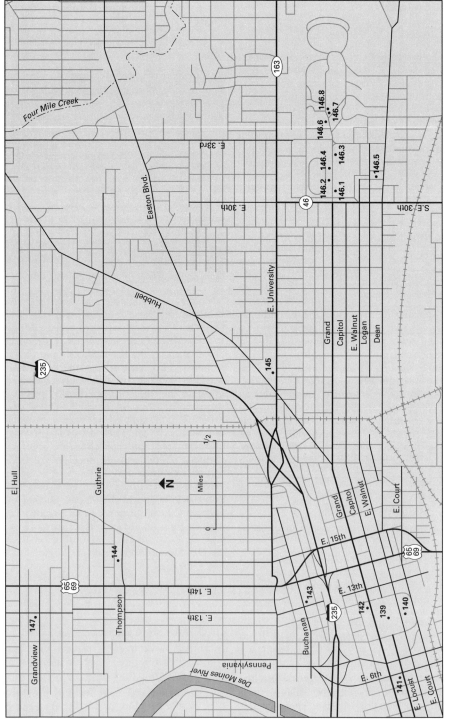

Inset 2, Des Moines, East Side (CE139–CE147)

206

CE139 Iowa State Capitol

selected. The Capitol Commission consulted Edward Clark, the Capitol Architect in Washington, D.C. He recommended that the best elevations were those provided by Piquenard but that the most satisfactory plans were by the Des Moines architect J. C. Farrand. The commission proceeded to appoint Cochrane and Piquenard as the architects for the Iowa State Capitol—and then gave the prize money to Farrand. Cochrane and Piquenard, who were then involved with supervising their winning design for the Illinois State Capitol, modified their Iowa plans and supervised the construction during its first years. With Piquenard's death in 1876, M. E. Bell, who had been in the Piquenard office, formed a partnership with the Des Moines architect W. F. Hackney, and they became the official architects for the Iowa State Capitol. Bell and Hackney modified the design for the drum and dome and also revised the interior. The interiors of the first floor and the legislative chambers were decorated by a consortium of artists that included Andreas Hansen, August Knorr, Fritz Melzer, E. S. Mirgoli, and several studios, those of Albert, Emeric, and McIvor; Noxon; and Toomey. After the turn of the century the interior decoration was brought to completion through the murals of Elmer Garnsey. Garnsey's work was joined by Edward Bashfield's *Westward,* a group of six mosaic panels over Frederick Dielman's grand staircase, and Kenyon Cox's series of eight lunette paintings within the rotunda.

The hilltop location of the capitol building is a splendid one. Ernest E. Clark, writing in 1895, noted, "It stands upon a commanding site, from which its golden dome can be seen for many miles. No Iowan who has a clean heart and wholesome State pride can catch a glimpse of that dome, when approaching the Capitol City, without a thrill of pleasure."[16] Piquenard's final scheme for the building was directly inspired by the architect's recollection of L.-T.-J. Visconti and M.-H. Lefuel's mid-nineteenth-century design for the new Louvre in Paris. Its most Louvre-like quality is found in the four almost independent corner pavilions, each with its own small-scaled drum and dome. The building's plan was a traditional one: a central block organized around a rotunda that terminates in a dome, and then a cross axis on the ground floor and the first floor that penetrates through the two matched wings. The legislative chambers and the impressive law library are located on the second floor.

Much more than Cochrane and Piquenard's design for the Illinois State Capitol at Springfield, the Iowa State Capitol is an impressive summation of how the late nineteenth century viewed the classical tradition. Its forms and detailing are rich, and this was equally mirrored in the varieties of marble (29) and the many woods used inside. Instead of being a white shimmering pile on a hilltop, the Iowa capitol is a varied, warm-colored building that fits, at least symbolically, what the twentieth-century critic Lewis Mumford labeled, "The Brown Decades." The exterior of the central dome of the capitol was first gilded in 1882, and was re-gilded in 1965. The building was extensively restored during 1983–1986 by Bussard Dikis, and improvements were made in the surrounding Capitol Mall (now some 165 acres) by Hansen Lind/ Meyer/Sasaki Dawson DeMay.

CE140 Soldiers and Sailors Monument

1889–1897, Harriet A. Ketcham. E. Walnut St. at E. 10th St.

A special state commission was appointed in 1888 to supervise a competition for a monument to honor Iowans who fought in the Civil War. Forty-eight submissions were received the following year, and from these the commission selected the design of Harriet A. Ketcham of Mount Pleasant, Iowa.[17] Her initial design was an equestrian figure placed upon an elaborately decorated sarcophagus. The sarcophagus was in turn set on a four-step

CE140 Soldiers and Sailors Monument

podium; within one of the niches of the sarcophagus was a seated female figure (symbolizing the state of Iowa), and standing on two of the corners were the figures of a soldier and a sailor. After winning the competition Ketcham revised her design by replacing her equestrian figure with a column surmounted by a wingless figure of Victory. Ketcham died before the state legislature appropriated funds for the monument in 1892. In 1894 the Danish-born sculptor Carl Rohl-Smith was commissioned to construct the piece based on Ketcham's revised design. Work started in September of 1894, and it was basically finished in 1897. As built, the sarcophagus came close to looking like a small classical temple; two additional figures joined the soldier and sailor at the base, the figure of Iowa became a partially nude maiden holding her breasts, and she was matched on the other side by a seated figure of an old woman (History) accompanied by a standing young child. At the four upper corners of the sarcophagus are equestrian figures. Functioning as a sort of entablature around the sarcophagus are rows of commemorative cast-bronze medallions. The figures are also cast in bronze; the rest of the monument, including its Corinthian column and capital, is in granite.

CE141 State of Iowa Historical Building

1985–1987, Brown and Healy. Northwest corner of E. Locust St. and E. 6th St.

The approach taken by the architects for this public building bears some points of resemblance to Kevin Roche's Oakland Museum of 1969. Roche's desire was to submerge his building under a landscaped city park; the architects of the Des Moines research and museum building pursued a somewhat similar approach. There are, as one would expect, a number of differences between the two buildings. The 1980s Iowa building is a much more aggressively high-tech modernist design in its desire to display an encyclopedic array of late Modernist images; and the landscape proposed in Des Moines will never push the building into the background.

CE142 State Historical Memorial and Arts Building

1898, 1904–1905, Smith and Gutterson. Northwest corner of E. 12th St. and E. Grand Ave.

As with many other late nineteenth-century Beaux-Arts designs, the architects of this building seem to have approached the classical ideal with the same abandonment entailed in their interpretation of the Queen Anne or Colonial Revival designs of the time. The visitor to the building is greeted by a two-story composition of a temple in antis, with a pair of wide pilasters flanked by two Roman Ionic columns. Above, the entablature and cornice are "correct," but from this point on, things become confused (and delightfully so). Above the cornice is a kind of attic, and on top of this a pediment. Farther back one can just barely see the central drum and dome. Within, one will discover a group of mural paintings that once decorated the ceiling of the Supreme Court Room within the Iowa State Capitol. These panels and medallions were designed by August Knorr of Des Moines and were executed in Germany by Fritz Melzer. They were installed in the Court Room in 1886, but were removed after a fire in the room in 1904.

CE143 East High School

1910, Proudfoot, Bird and Rawson. Southeast corner of Buchanan and 13th streets

The design centers on a gable-roofed temple front with Ionic columns, set on a high podium. This design was, according to the architects at the time, modeled after the north porch of the Erechtheum in Athens. The two bands of large classroom windows on each side of the temple front are contained between flat sections of the wall that give the appearance of being pilasters without in fact being pilasters. The continuous repeats of these windows and pilasters, plus the continuous entablature and cornice and the uniform use of a light gray limestone for surfaces and details, strongly tie the whole composition together. The siting of the building within a spacious tree-shaded lawn enhances its readability as a temple one might come across within a late eighteenth-century Picturesque English garden.

CE144 Thompson Avenue

c. 1910–1930. Thompson Ave., between E. 14th St. and Glenbrook Dr.

This is suburbia as it should be. A street meanders between two double rows of tall sycamores; the public walkways parallel to the street go between the trees and are separated from the street by a wide boulevard and from the adjacent houses by deep lawns. The houses are all modest in size, reflecting the Midwestern version of the Craftsman mode and the California bungalow. Many are single-story bungalows with entrance/living porches. Others are two-story dwellings that appear low to the ground because of their wide overhanging roofs and the banding of their walls; they have shingles above and painted clapboard below.

CE145 *Cow and Calf*

c. 1980. Northeast corner of E. University and Hubbell avenues

A sculptured mother cow and her calf are posed in front of an anonymous contemporary brick building. Though twice normal size, their scale seems purposely difficult to sense, with the neutral wall behind, reinforced by clipped shrubbery, and the finely mowed lawn upon which they stand.

CE146 Iowa State Fairgrounds

1886, later, William F. Hackney. E. Grand Ave. at E. 30th St.

The first Iowa State Fair was held at Fairfield in 1854. After being held at several different cities, it was transferred to Des Moines in 1879. A few of the original buildings constructed in 1886 remain, as do the pre-1886 Charles Thorton farmhouse and barn. The 1886 buildings were designed by the Des Moines architect William F. Hackney. The largest of these is the gable-roofed Agricultural Building/Pioneer Building. There is also a group of racehorse barns dating from 1896. The most interesting buildings are discussed in the next eight entries.

CE146.1 Patrol Headquarters Building

c. 1934. South side of Grand Concourse at 31st St.

This is a tiny Streamline Moderne box (flat-roofed and sheathed in stucco, of course), with vertical design elements that take one back to the Art Deco of the 1920s.

CE144 Thompson Avenue

CE146.2 **Conservation Building** (State Game and Fish Building)

1926, Proudfoot, Rawson and Souers. North side of Grand Concourse, east of 31st St.

In contrast to most of the buildings within the fairgrounds, this structure presents a 1920s version of a small mid-fifteenth century Italian Renaissance building. A three-arched loggia projects toward the street, and to each side are high double-arched windows with metal balconies. Do not miss the pair of wonderful sculptured swans poised on the corners of the roof.

CE146.3 **Varied Industries Building**

1911, Oliver O. Smith. South side of Grand Concourse, east of 31st St.

This is a classical composition with a strong Arts and Crafts flavor. A gabled pavilion in brick, defined by heavy corner pilasters, projects from the front of the building. Connected to this on both sides are glass walls set far back under a wide cantilevered roof.

CE146.4 **Grandstand**

1909, Oliver O. Smith. 1927, Keffer and Jones. North side of Grand Concourse, at 32nd St.

A Roman amphitheater has been translated in new materials—a thin fabric of steel and concrete—and then sheathed in brick with limestone trim. There are metal factory sash windows, and accompanying metal spandrels between each of the arches. A grand eagle in high relief is situated above the principal entrance.

CE146.5 **4–H Club Building**

1939–1942. Logan St., just east of Gate 9

A three-story WPA structure of poured concrete manages to reflect the Streamline Moderne style. The corners of the building are curved, and, as expected, contain glass brick. The centerpiece of the building's front facade is a central hexagonal window, with a thin vertical section dropping below it appearing like an abstracted keyhole. Around the first floor is a metal porch detailed like those on an ocean liner.

CE146.6 **Postal Telegraph Station**

1884. Heritage Village area, north side of E. Grand Ave. at Hoover Ave.

This telegraph station, one of several historic buildings moved to the site, is a miniaturized delight. The square structure with a steeply pitched hipped roof has acquired a strong architectural presence through an angled corner tower with a small segmented curved roof.

CE146.7 **"Iowa's First Church"**

1834. Heritage Village area, east corner of E. Grand Ave. at Hoover Ave.

This split-log church is a replica of the original church, which was located in Dubuque. The shingled roof has gabled ends sheathed in clapboard.

CE146.8 **Schoolhouse**

c. 1880s. Heritage Village area, east corner of Grand Ave. and Pioneer Ave.

The late nineteenth-century Lincoln Schoolhouse from southeast of Indianola was moved to the fairgrounds and restored (1965–1969). The clapboard structure has a single covered gable roof; the windows are double hung. The interior has been restored and furnished to represent a typical schoolhouse of the late nineteenth century.

Other buildings within the Historic Area include the pre-1886 Thornton house (an Eastlake-style dwelling) and its original barn; Pioneer Hall (1886, originally the Poultry Palace); and a replica of one of the log blockhouses built at Fort Madison.

CE147 **Old Main, Grandview College**

1895–1904, 1929. 1200 Grandview Ave.

Supposedly the inspiration for the design of Old Main at Grandview College was the Belmont Seminary (1890) in Bedford, Virginia. Northern European Baroque architecture of the seventeenth century was an architectural style frequently employed around the turn of the century for American colleges and universities. The Des Moines example illustrates how architects and clients in Iowa were keenly aware of current fashion. The most telling

CE147 Old Main, Grandview College

feature of Old Main is its roofscape, composed of curved gable ends and dormers. The walls of this two-and-a-half-story structure on a raised basement are of brick. Stone was used for quoining, as framing around windows and doors, and to bring added accent to the series of dramatic curved gable ends.

CE148 French Way Cleaners and Dyers

1916, Fred A. Harris. 413 Euclid Ave.

This exotic Prairie-school building has all the appearance of a bank building rather than a dry-cleaning establishment. Two brick piers break up the front, and they rise to form bases for a pair of stone figures of enthroned horn players. Balanced above and to the side of each player are large globe lights. To the sides and between the players are stone light standards in forms that almost look like fishes. The sculptural figures and light standards were produced by the local stone firm of Rowot.

DES MOINES, SOUTH SIDE

CE149 Clifton Heights United Presbyterian Church

1923–1924, F. A. Harris. 1931 S.W. 1st St.

Located on a rather small side-lot on a steep hill is one of Iowa's most unusual church buildings. F. A. Harris took the theme of the "Akron plan" centralized auditorium and placed it within a flat-roofed brick box. He provided light to the interior through factory-made steel window units, and he articulated the facades of the building utilizing the language of the Prairie style. The auditorium section has the feel of Frank Lloyd Wright's Unity Temple (1904) in Oak Park, Illinois, or of Purcell and Feick's Stewart Memorial Church (1909) in Minneapolis. In the Clifton Heights church, however, the four corners of the cruciform have been filled in, and the corners are defined as slightly projecting lower volumes. Harris employed the usual Prairie-style device of engaged piers with a suggestion of capitals in a band but without an entablature or cornice above. The terminal cornice of the building is composed of three outward-projecting bands of cast stone and bricks, with a final coping of cast stone. The exterior of the building suggests something between an industrial image and that of some sort of public building. Without the sign, one would never guess that it is a church.

CE150 Lincoln High School

1922–1923, Proudfoot, Bird and Rawson. Northwest corner of S.W. 9th St. and Loomis Ave.

Lincoln High is one of a series of public schools within the community that are highly successful, both in their wonderful landscaped siting and in the design of their buildings. Seen from a distance through groves of trees, the principal frontispiece of the Lincoln School conveys the romantic impression of a seventeenth-century English house. The three-arched entrance is set between two narrow turrets, each with a second-floor bay window. With the exception of small panels of brick on the first floor, this entrance piece is realized in stone, and it contrasts strongly with the long projecting brick wings on each side. These two-story wings contain a repeated pattern of wide, five-window units, each provid-

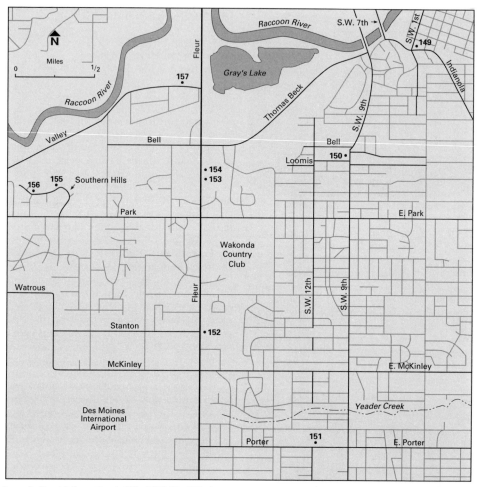

Inset 3, Des Moines, South Side (CE149–CE157)

ing an almost complete glass window wall for each of the classrooms. An industrial atmosphere is avoided by the architects' having treated each upper and lower pair of these windows as a slightly projecting bay. Stone trim was used around these windows, as spare ornamentation, and for occasional finials projecting from the roof parapet.

CE151 Des Moines Public Library, South Branch

1977, 1981, Charles Herbert and Associates. 1111 Porter Ave.

The South Branch Library reads as a public building only because of its location within a

CE151 Des Moines Public Library, South Branch

public park. The library is like something built with a child's Erector set, placed within stepped brick walls under a thin shed-roofed plane. The exterior is pleasant in a modest way; the interior, on the other hand, is almost Baroque in the way metal supports are used for its ceiling. With the natural light streaming in from above, one feels that one has entered a playful Modernist forest out of science fiction.

CE152 **Wakonda Branch, South Des Moines National Bank** (now Brenton Bank)

c. 1976, Charles Herbert and Associates. 4303 Fleur Dr.

A Modernist version of minimalism is conveyed by white ribbed metal-sheathed boxes arranged horizontally. Thin ribbon windows reinforce the horizontal aim of this design. Though a good example of Mies van der Rohe's tenet "less is more," its small size and careful spare detailing (there is almost none, except for the shape and placement of openings within the metal skin) make this suburban bank building a forceful example of Modernism in the decade of the 1970s.

CE153 **Rollins House**

1925, Boyd and Moore. 2801 Fleur Dr.

In the teens and twenties the English Tudor was one of the favored domestic images for buildings ranging from the smallest of "spec" cottages to large and grand suburban and country houses. The Rollins house represents the latter—a large house situated on a landscaped hilltop site. The theme of 1920s romanticism is beautifully carried out in this dwelling, with its angled volumes, many gables, and tall projecting chimneys. The materials used externally are equally varied: half-timbered gable ends rest on brick walls, wooden gabled dormers penetrate the weathered slate roof. As befits a country house of the twenties, the approach to it is by automobile, along a curved drive leading to the stone entrance with balcony. To the side is a large, partially enclosed auto court and a multicar garage. In the interior of the house, many of the walls are paneled; sixteenth-century designs were used for the plaster ceilings and leaded stained glass windows appear throughout.

CE154 **Butler House** (now Kragie, Newell Advertising Agency)

1935–1937 Kraetsch and Kraetsch. 2633 S. Fleur Dr.

When completed in 1937 the Butler house was described as "the world's most modern house,"[18] and there is little doubt that this house stands as one of the half dozen or so great monuments of the Streamline Moderne style of the 1930s. As presented in numerous magazine articles of the time, the Butler house was supposedly not the result of adherence to any style then in vogue, but ensued purely from useful technology and practical considerations. Its owner, the engineer Earl Butler, and his architect, George Kraetsch, used reinforced concrete for the structure of the house, and equipped it with metal-framed double glass windows. The latest in technology is employed within this "push-button" house, including air conditioning and extensive use of indirect electric lighting; and when family members would drive up to the three-car garage, they would merely "point their lights at an electric eye, wink them twice, thrice, or four times, and the first, second, or third door [would] rise, allowing [them] to drive in."[19] Within the 28-room house, a Le Corbusier-like ramp is used rather than a traditional staircase. There are floor-to-ceiling windows in a number of the rooms, and the third-floor sunroom commands a remarkable view of Des Moines and the surrounding countryside (which is now pretty well built up).

The weight and mass of concrete is openly acknowledged through the deep penetration of doors and windows. Curved and angled corners define the edges of the building; a ring of four cut-in bands is carried around the walls of the house, suggesting the location of the internal ceilings of the first and second floor. Because of its size and monumental character, the Butler house ended up reading more as a public building than as a private dwelling. The house was remodeled and added to in 1988–1989 for office use by Wells, Woodburn and O'Neil, Des Moines architects. To a marked degree the remodeling was really a restoration. A new auditorium was added, but this was carefully tucked into the hillside.

CE155 **Goldman House**

1961, Richard J. Neutra. 3417 Southern Hills Dr.

Set within a manicured upper-middle-class suburban site is this characteristic version of a rambling single-floor house by the California Modernist Richard J. Neutra. The horizontality of the design, reinforced by the thin, wide overhanging roof slab, is countered at the entrance by a vertical stone pylonlike wall. Windows on the street side are in narrow bands directly under the roof soffit. On the garden side of the house are extensive areas of floor-to-soffit fixed glass, and glass doors open onto terraces.

CE156 **Valone House**

1984–1985, Charles Herbert and Associates. 3605 Southern Hills Dr.

The module of the square, enlarged here and reduced there, comprises the faces of this dwelling. The entrance facade of the house is treated as a freestanding screen wall in front of which is a lower volume completely clothed in glass brick. The house refers back to the early days of European and American

CE156 Valone House

International style Modern and to the design-cultivated complexities and contradictions of Postmodernism of the 1970s and 1980s. An example of this is the thick masonrylike entrance frame, which seems to float out in front of the two-story glass brick entrance of the building.

CE157 **Des Moines Waterworks Headquarters**

1985, Shiffer, Frey, Baldwin. 2201 Valley Dr., west of Fleur Dr., West Des Moines Waterworks Park

The classical tradition has in this instance been reduced to several "pure" geometric shapes: rectangular volumes and slabs, triangles, and upright drums. An open metalwork gable balanced on two drums announces the entrance into the building. This building is Postmodern, but with the reserve one associates with the work of the 1930s, such as the designs of the Swedish architect Eric Gunnar Asplund and others.

CE157 Des Moines Waterworks Headquarters

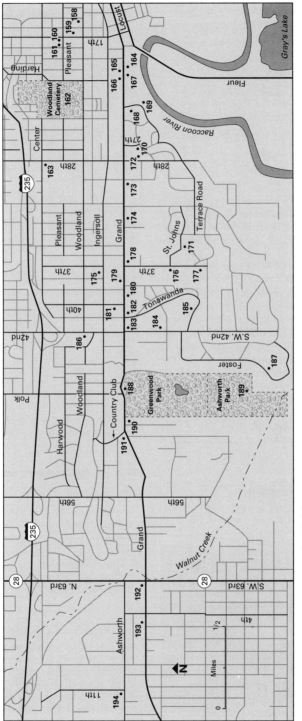

Inset 4, Des Moines, West Side (CE158–CE194)

DES MOINES, WEST SIDE

The Sherman Hill Historic District encompasses an area bound by 15th and 19th streets, between Woodland Avenue and Cottage Grove Avenue. Within this district are houses and apartment buildings dating from the 1880s through 1920.

CE158 Hoyt Sherman Place (Art Gallery / Auditorium)

1873–1877, 1907. 1922, addition, Vorse, Kraetsch and Kraetsch. 1501 Woodland Ave.

Since 1907 the Hoyt Sherman house has been the home of the Des Moines Women's Club. The style of the 1873–1877 house was Italianate, with a central three-story hipped roof tower, round-arched windows, a richly detailed entablature and bracketed cornice, and a number of wooden porches and verandas. The architect/historian William Wagner has speculated that the house may have been designed by William Foster, who designed many buildings in Des Moines. The house now sits to the side of a large art gallery added in 1907 and an auditorium built in 1922. The somewhat eighteenth-century image of the auditorium/art gallery seems to suggest that the house is a mere leftover. The porches and other elaborate stone-and-wood detailing of the house have been removed, and a stone surround, sympathetic to the auditorium/art gallery, provides entrance to the building.

CE159 Crowell Apartments

pre-1905, 1906, Proudfoot and Bird. 665–671 17th St.

According to the building permits for this project, there was as existing frame residence that disappeared within the present 12–unit apartment building. What appears to be a pair of independent buildings hides behind one of Iowa's most impressive facades. Each section of the building has a porch with two-story Ionic columns; above and behind the flat porch roofs arise elaborate scalloped gable ends. Between the building sections is a sumptuous double entrance door contained under a single broken entablature. Behind this wonderful frontispiece inspired by classical architecture are four good-sized apartments, one to a floor. The sense of dignity conveyed by the building is enhanced by the gray glazed brick and the similar colored cast-stone trim used to sheathe the walls.

CE160 Colonnade Apartments

1905, Proudfoot and Bird. 1705 Pleasant St.

A two-story portico with Ionic columns sits atop a brick entrance porch. The entrance itself has a curved lintel that seems to thrust itself into the floor of the upper portico. Individual balconies appear behind the columns on the third floor, enabling each apartment to have an outdoor porch. The first floor has been treated as a rusticated raised basement, and the entire classical composition is contained by a deep, wide wood cornice.

CE161 Lexington Apartments

1908–1909, Frank Weitz. 1721 Pleasant St.

The city's first tall high-rise apartment building (six stories tall) is comprised of a thin vertical brick slab from which protrude four rows of angled bays on each of the long facades. A stone pedimented entrance, stone banding, and a strong cornice add up to a mild classical image.

CE162 Woodland Cemetery

Northwest corner of Woodland and Harding roads

Woodland Cemetery was laid out in the mid-nineteenth century. A system of picturesque winding roads was established throughout its gently rolling tree-covered hills. The cemetery houses a full contingent of characteristic nineteenth- and twentieth-century monuments and mausoleums. None of these is extraordinary, but as a group in relationship to the landscape, they create a romantically picturesque image.

CE163 Smouse Opportunity Center (School)

1930–1931, Proudfoot, Rawson, Souers, and Thomas. Southwest corner of 28th and Center streets

This is another of the city's beautifully sited school buildings. The low two-story brick building terminates in a slightly projecting wing containing a wide two-story bay. The bay is detailed in limestone, and the same smooth stone is used around the groups of large classroom windows, as well as around the entrances. One enters the building on the east side through a narrow set of doors. Here one is greeted by a narrow interior court containing a fountain and glazed tile walls. The atmosphere of this high, enclosed courtyard comes close to what one experiences in European Expressionist architecture, or here in America in the then-current designs of Barry Byrne or Frank Lloyd Wright.

CE164 Technical High School (The Homestead)

c. 1910. 1912 Grand Ave.

With its main facade running parallel to Grand Avenue, the Homestead building presents a Beaux-Arts classical design modeled in this case after Greek examples. The entrance is a temple with two Ionic columns in antis pressed closely to the side walls. The remainder of the two-story front has widely spaced fluted Ionic columns between which are repeated Chicago windows. White glazed tile and brick have been employed for all of the exterior surfaces and details. The gleaming white surfaces of the building make it all seem fragile and a bit unreal. The siting of the school within a large area of lawns and parks indicates that it is one of the earlier examples of the suburban park-office complex.

CE165 Finkbine House

1896, attrib. William Foster. 1915 Grand Ave.

The design of this brick Queen Anne house depends upon the classical inspiration of the

Colonial Revival. Classical pediments, cornices detailed with dentils, and porches supported by Doric columns contrast with the general narrow verticality of the volumes and of the windows and doors.

CE166 Great Western Insurance Company

1928–1929, John Nomile and Amos B. Emory. 2015 Grand Ave.

A deeply set Roman coffered arch with an infill of metal-framed windows and doors leads into the central two-story space of this suburban insurance company building. On each side of the entrance, on the second level, is a pair of four-arched windows that open out onto masonry balconies. Contrasting with the solidity of this limestone-sheathed building were narrow metal lamps hung to each side of the entrance from long chains (they are no longer present).

CE167 Polk House (Herndon Hall)

1881–1883; T. A. Roberts; Foster and Liebbe. 2000 Grand Ave.

The architect of Herndon Hall must have been in close touch with the latest in fashion in the Northeast and in England, for he provided a Queen Anne design, a style that would have been up-to-date in those areas. Although picturesque, everything is kept under firm control. The brick-surfaced first floor of the house provides a solid base for the lighter wood-sheathed walls above. Even when the playful device of a window through a masonry chimney was introduced, it was treated coldly with its own picture-frame surround and pediment. The house has lost some of its detailing, including its porte-cochère, some of its porches, and its patterned slate roof, but it still commands its large site overlooking Grand Avenue. The house was restored in 1979 by Bloodgood Architects and is now used for offices.

CE168 Allen House (Terrace Hill; now the Governor's Mansion)

1867–1869; William W. Boyington; J. T. Elletson, landscape architect. 2300 Grand Ave.

Terrace Hill perfectly fits everyone's idea of a Victorian mansion such as one might en-

CE168 Allen House (Terrace Hill) (now the Governor's Mansion)

The entrance to the dwelling is at the base of its principal 90-foot-high tower. This leads into a vestibule, and then into a large reception hall. At the far end of the hall is a freestanding staircase that ascends to a landing from which a pair of returning stairways brings one to the second floor. Marble fireplaces, wood overmantels, paneled walls, round arches, and stenciled ceilings and walls are found throughout the first floor. During the years 1972 through 1983 the house was extensively restored under the direction of the architect William Wagner (Wagner, Marquardt, Wetherell, Ericsson). The house now serves as the Governor's Mansion; tours of the house are available.

CE169 **H. M. S. Byers House** (Saint Helen House)

1894. 2300 Terrace Rd.

counter in the paintings of Edward Hopper, or in one of the well-known *New Yorker* cartoons of Charles Addams.[20] Not one but two towers with mansard roofs look down on an assemblage of other mansard roofs, dormers, and chimneys. The verticality of the house is accentuated by its situation atop a high, steep hill. The English landscape architect J. T. Elletson cut down some of the existing trees, resculpted some of the land (there were 29 acres), and provided views of the house, accentuating its size and grandeur. The 20-room house, which cost some $250,000, was designed by the Chicago architect William W. Boyington. Boyington, who established his practice in Chicago in 1853, was a highly successful midwestern practitioner, perhaps best known today for his storybook castle, the 1867–1869 Water Tower and Pumping Station in Chicago. Boyington was well known in Des Moines for his designs for the (old) Arsenal Building and for the Central Presbyterian Church. The imagery he provided at Terrace Hill for his client, the wealthy Des Moines businessman Benjamin F. Allen, was one typical of the day: a combination of a late version of the Italian Villa style and the then-popular French Second Empire style. Richness of contrast was a central theme of such designs. The light-colored limestone quoining, window headers, and bracketed entablature/cornice contrast sharply with the building's red brick walls.

The hilly terrain to the south, west, and east of Terrace Hill is now a National Register Historic District (Terrace Road and Owl's Head Historic Districts). Within this district on a precipitous slope overlooking the Raccoon River and Water Works Park is one of the city's most original houses, Saint Helen House, built by the former Consular General of Switzerland and Italy, H. M. S. Byers. The main section of the house (there have been later additions) has an architectural character one associates with late nineteenth-century French summer houses. The flat roof of this two-story house is hidden behind a parapet. At the northeast corner, slightly projecting from the adjacent brick walls of the second story, is an open square tower with a steeply pitched hipped roof. The design of the street entrance is unusual: to the right of the door the wall steps in, like an abstracted buttress; brickwork projections define the pointed arches above the door and continue as horizontal banding to the left side, terminating in a T-shaped stone plaque bearing the name of the house in lettering that has an Art Nouveau flavor.

CE170 **Huttinglocker House**

1893–1895, George F. Barber and Company. 410 27th St.

George F. Barber and Company of Knoxville, Tennessee, were responsible for the design of many houses and other types of buildings throughout the Midwest, and especially in Iowa. Sometimes the designs came from the company's pattern books and mail-order plans, and on other occasions the firm was engaged to design individual dwellings, as was the case with the Huttinglocker house. Like most Queen Anne dwellings of the 1890s, this one is quite restrained (especially for Barber). The wide veranda projecting from the east and south sides of the house is, with its columns and gabled entrance, Colonial Revival. The solidity of the design is enhanced by the use of red stone and pressed brick for the first floor; the second and third floors rely much more on volumes and gables, rather than on any display of molded, sawed, or turned woodwork. Inside, there is a Colonial Revival fireplace in the parlor, and a richly decorated Queen Anne fireplace with scenes and designs in glazed brick in the entrance/stair hall.

CE171 **Helen Johnston House**

1938, Proudfoot, Rawson, Brooks, and Borg. 3420 Saint John Rd.

The 1930s Moderne here appears more angular than streamline. A V-shaped bay marked by horizontal lines protrudes out over the front entrance surrounded by glass brick. The white stucco two-story facade has few openings to the street, but it is opened up with large glass areas to the rear. When built for the Weitz Investment Company this house was advertised, using Le Corbusier's terms, as a thirties "machine for living."

CE172 **House**

1901, Liebbe, Nourse and Rasmussen. 331 SW 28th St.

The turn-of-the-century willingness to combine varied elements from more than one past style is well captured in this dwelling surfaced with brick and dark stained shingles. The gables with their sawed patterned bargeboards and the diamond-paned windows establish a loosely English medieval theme. And then there is the commanding presence of the entrance; projecting above a Colonial Revival entrance and side lights is a wide, open seashell with carved medallions at the spring of the arch. The entrance leads out onto a low-walled terrace, in a somewhat miniaturized Italianate style. The seashell entrance is certainly one of the high points of domestic architecture in Des Moines.

CE173 **Witmer House**

1905, Liebbe, Nourse and Rasmussen. 2900 Grand Ave.

There is generally a quality of ease and self-assuredness conveyed through the images of the turn-of-the-century Colonial Revival dwelling. These designs, such as that of the Witmer house, are generally conservative and traditional in imagery, but at the same time innovative in their planning and in their free and easy-going use of Colonial Revival detail. Across the front of the two-and-a-half-story Witmer house are four large engaged Ionic columns. Flanked by the center pair is a central gable that helps to contain the second-floor Palladian window. Below this is a wide, curved porch with small Ionic columns. On the east side, a large living porch projects from the house.

CE174 **Saint Joseph's Academy** (now College of Osteopathic Medicine)

1896, Hallett and Rawson. 3200 Grand Ave.

This is design characterized by a mild medievalism expressed through a row of buttresses and adjoining pointed-arched windows that help to center one's attention on a four-story tower. The tower has a Viennese Secessionist flavor about it—similar not only to European examples, but also to the contemporary work in Chicago of Howard Van Doren Shaw and of George W. Maher. There is strongly shadowed quoining on the tower, and each of the facades terminates in a segmental curved roof, above which is a small drum and dome.

CE175 **Ingersoll Theatre**

1939. 3711 Ingersoll Ave.

As usual, it is the Streamline Moderne marquee that advertises the presence of this late-thirties suburban theater. The angled marquee, with the letters of the theater's name projecting above, terminates in a layered semicircle covered with lights. The body of the theater is sheathed in light tan brick which displays a series of lined patterns running vertically and horizontally.

CE176 **Reynolds House**

1910. 180 S.W. 37th St.

At the end of a long driveway one can catch a glimpse of a brick and half-timber suburban house. Formal entrance is through a brick piered porte-cochère, while the service drive penetrates under the second floor to a rear auto court. A large living porch overlooks a formally laid out garden with changes of levels, balustraded walls, stairs, garden structures, and pergolas.

CE177 **Cowles House**

1909. 100 S.W. 37th St.

A central gabled pavilion whose corners are emphasized by brick quoins suggests the source as eighteenth-century Georgian, either En-

glish or American. A number of liberties have been taken with the historical source: French doors open onto the roof of the entrance porch, and to each side of the central pavilion are two-story wood-sheathed bays, classical in detailing, but medieval Tudor in feeling.

CE178 **First Church of Christ Scientist**

c. 1931; Brooks-Borg; Proudfoot, Rawson and Souers. 3750 Grand Ave.

Spurred on by the designs of Eliel Saarinen, Bertram G. Goodhue, and others, architects in America had an intense interest in how one might go about modernizing the medieval images of the Romanesque and the Gothic. The usual ingredients of this process consisted of great emphasis placed on plain, uninterrupted wall surfaces; in a reduction of the building's volume to basic geometric forms (cubes, rectangular volumes, etc.); a stress placed on the horizontal rather than the vertical; and a sparse use of ornament. When ornament was used it was abstracted and was meant to read as "modern." The First Church of Christ Scientist carries out these modernizing principles: the horizontal stone wall surfaces predominate; the tower is a low rectangular volume with an abstracted suggestion of a turret on one corner, and a tiny spire is placed well into the center of the tower roof. Instead of pointed arched windows, the ones here have an inverted V-shape, and the round-arched doors and windows are delineated as shapes cut into the wall surface. This church building and the nearby Central Presbyterian Church were voted in 1939 as the "most noteworthy examples" of recent architecture in Des Moines.

CE179 **Central Presbyterian Church**
(originally Second Presbyterian Church)

c. 1936, Souers and Spooner. 3829 Grand Ave.

Another exercise in modernized medieval re-vival architecture, this church bears open yet abstracted references to the European Gothic tradition. The smooth stone walls of the church are cut in a sharp, angular manner that de-cidedly enhances the modern feeling of the building. The buttressed front of the church contains broad pointed arches for the en-trance and for the large window above. This window in turn houses a double-arched win-dow that is more Romanesque than Gothic. The Gothic theme is repeated in the solid balustrade of the entrance terrace which is punctured by a row of small open pointed arches. The Central Presbyterian Church, along with the First Church of Christ Scien-tist, were the two religious buildings singled out for praise in the 1939 survey of "note-worthy" recent buildings in the city.

CE180 **The Barbican**

1979, Englebrecht, Rice and Griffin. 3920 Grand Ave.

A 42–unit condominium is accommodated here in a complex that includes an 11-story building. Though the buildings are of ex-posed concrete, the curved corners (with their curved corner windows) hark back to the Streamline Moderne of the 1930s. A bridge-like unit connects the high-rise and low-rise buildings at the third- and fourth-floor levels. A 60-car garage is part of the project.

CE181 **House**

c. 1915. 520 40th St.

This brick-sheathed Prairie house is covered by the usual wide overhanging hipped roof. The balanced facade with its central entrance takes one back to Frank Lloyd Wright's 1893 Winslow house in River Forest, Illinois, and also to many of the midwestern houses of George W. Maher. Vertical engaged piers define the center of the building, and from these is cantilevered a thin slab roof that provides shelter for the entrance door below. To the left side of the house is a two-story porch, living below and sleeping above.

CE182 **Wetherell Apartments**

1924, Frank Wetherell of Wetherell and Harrison. 4024 Grand Ave.

A picturesque 1920s apartment building ex-hibits a remarkable abstract geometry in its projecting and receding wall surfaces. The first three floors are sheathed in brick; above, the walls are in stucco, with brick used for detailing around some of the windows. The white stucco walls, tile roofs, and above all the Churrigueresque ornament at the top of the entrance tower make this a Spanish Co-lonial Revival composition, but certainly of an unusual sort.

CE183 **Francis House**

1893. 4140 Grand Ave.

This low-profile stone "mansion" boasts a front dominated by two circular three-story towers with conical roofs. While the house seems to be generally French Châteauesque in style, the detailing conveys the impression of clas-sical restraint. Beside the recessed entrance porch between the two towers, there is a pattern of two groups of stepped windows that mirror the principal staircases of the interior.

CE184 **Dewey House**

c. 1912. 305 S.W. 42nd St.

The Dewey house is another Prairie-style house, similar in scheme to the house at 520 40th Street (CE181). A thin slab roof covers the entrance, which is placed at the center of the building. A balanced composition of case-ment windows is created on each side of the entrance. A horizontal wood band connects all of the window sills on the second floor. The stucco walls are carried up and cover the soffits of the wide overhanging hipped roof.

CE185 **Weeks House** (Salisbury House)

1923–1928, William Whitney Rasmussen (Boyd and Moore). 4025 Tonawanda Dr.

When Salisbury House was published in the April 5, 1928, issue of *The American Architect,* it was noted that "the entire house represents a growth of development after the old En-

CE185 Weeks House (Salisbury House)

glish manor house." As with a number of the more famous period revival houses of the 1920s, the architects enhanced the sense of age and authenticity by employing some historic fragments and materials from England. "Most of the sixteenth-century tile," it was written, "came from Trafalgar Place, Lord Nelson's estate in Wiltshire. . . . Leadwork is both old and new; windows are glazed old crown glass and some inserts are early stained glass. . . . In one instance a doorway was removed from a house in England and transported to and erected in Salisbury House." The decision to model the house after the sixteenth-century King's House in Salisbury, England, was that of the clients, Carl and Edith Weeks. They had visited Salisbury in 1922 and had become enamored with the sense of history conveyed by the flint and limestone walls of that Tudor house.[21]

Although modeled after King's House (for example, the north entrance porch served as the direct prototype for the house in Des Moines), the Weeks house exhibits the siting and plan characteristic of a 1920s American country house. Entrance is made in the automobile on the north side of the house, the south and east sides being reserved for the terraces and formal gardens. To the west side was the motor service court, surrounded on three sides by various service buildings. The plan centers on a two-story great hall, with the principal common room and its projecting bay to the east. The hollow tile, brick, and reinforced concrete walls were sheathed externally in brick, limestone, and flint, and internally with limestone, wood paneling, and plaster. The owner, Carl Weeks, the manufacturer of Armand cosmetics, first engaged the local architectural firm of Byron Boyd and Herbert Moore; later he brought in the

New York architect William Whitney Rasmussen (Rasmussen and Wayland), who ended up doing the final design of the house. Salisbury House is now used for offices; however, its principal public rooms remain intact, and arrangements can be made to visit the house and its grounds.

CE186 Harwood House

1907–1908. 646 42nd St.

As with several other Prairie-style houses in Des Moines, the Harwood house displays a symmetrical two-story facade with a central entrance. The entrance of this dwelling is recessed within the block of the house; on each side a U-shaped pattern of trelliswork surrounds each of the first-floor windows. There is leaded glass within the casement windows. The shingles of the low hipped roof are doubled at three points to create a banded effect, a technique frequently used by the Chicago architect George W. Maher.

CE187 Weaver House

1938, Kraetsch and Kraetsch. 635 Foster Dr.

The thirties Moderne mode is expressed here in a rectilinear two-story box sheathed in steel sheet metal. Although there are consciously devised window patterning and lines throughout the dwelling, the design seems to convey out-and-out rational functionalism. The architects succeeded, however, in projecting a sense of domesticity by the scale of the openings and by the projection of a number of boxlike volumes off the first floor.

CE188 Des Moines Art Center; Greenwood Park and Ashworth Park

1942–1948, Eliel Saarinen (Saarinen and Swanson; John Brooks, Elmer Borg). 1965–1967, I. M. Pei and Partners. 1982–1984, Richard Meier Associates. Thomas Church, landscape architect. Greenwood Park (off Grand Ave. at Polk Blvd.)

Nationally, the Des Moines Art Center is undoubtedly the best-known building in the city. On three separate occasions, over a period of four decades, the museum trustees have engaged major architects to design and add to their building. Each of these episodes pointedly illustrates not only changes in architec-

CE188A Des Moines Art Center

CE188B Des Moines Art Center, west side

tural fashion, but attitudes toward nature, the art of architecture, and the art found in and around the building. The engaging of Eliel Saarinen for the initial building was a logical choice for the time. Saarinen's Cranbrook Museum and Library (1940–1943) at Bloomfield Hills, Michigan, was without question the best-known modern museum building in the country. And although not built, Eliel and Eero Saarinen's winning scheme for the Smithsonian Art Gallery in Washington, D.C., of 1939, received extensive press coverage. As with all of his work at Cranbrook, Eliel Saarinen (in conjunction with Thomas Church) produced for Des Moines a building that let the park and nature predominate. The one- and two-story building clad in dolomite stone was placed on the south slope of a hill, almost hidden from Grand Avenue. A gentle curved drive leads around the hilltop to a modest-sized parking area. The unity of the building with nature is immediately apparent at the entrance where one looks through an opposite glass wall to a pool court with a Carl

Milles sculpture, *Pegasus and Bellerophon*. This court in turn is related to Church's rose garden which meanders down the hill into the forested park. Within, the principal galleries form a "U" around the court and open onto it via windows and glass doors. An important element in Saarinen's scheme was the education wing where children as well as adults could actively participate in art. Saarinen wrote in 1949 of his intent for the building: "To build up an atmosphere of art creation about the whole Art Center, and to create a place of interest for all strata of the population, old and young—through the young."[22]

In 1968 the trustees again surveyed the museum scene and selected another well-known figure, I. M. Pei. Pei's firm added 18,000 square feet to the Saarinen building. That addition followed the International style's predilection for discarding the old for the new, i.e., anticontextualism. Pei created a Brutalist exposed concrete building with the pattern of the board forms revealed, somewhat reminiscent of the work of Louis I. Kahn.

The next phase of asserting the new was the 1982–1984 addition by Richard Meier. His product was what one has come to expect of his work—an assertiveness upscaled to open exhibitionism. Meier's wing, which poses as one of his modernist houses enlarged in scale, is plunked right on top of the hill, not only pushing the earlier Saarinen and Pei designs to the side but destroying the sense of this being a public park. If one grants Meier's borrowed modernist imagery and ideology, then the presence of this shimmering white design clearly visible from Grand Avenue is a success. Inside the building, both the Pei and the Meier additions are at best fitted awkwardly into the spaces provided by Saarinen.

CE189 Ashworth Park Pool and Bathhouse

1984, Bussard/Dikis Associates. Greenwood Park; Grand Ave. at 45th St.

The Postmodernist design of the pool and bathhouse suggests that the architects used as a source of reference the rectilinear geometry of early Modernist architecture of the 1920s and early 1930s. The playful lightness of touch conveys much the same atmosphere that one associates with early Swedish Modernism of

CE189 Ashworth Park Pool and Bathhouse

CE191 Temple B'nai Jeshurun

the 1930s. The main facade of the bathhouse, looking out onto the pool, consists of three receding volumes that center on a basket/ticket area defined by bright green. White, light blue, and terracotta red define the other wall surfaces. The module of the square or rectangle is repeated in colored glazed brick inserts and again in the windows.

While in Greenwood Park one should visit the various small-scaled rustic recreational and picnic structures, especially those of stone and wood constructed in the 1920s and 1930s.

CE190 Ogilvie House

1939. 4816 Grand Ave.

This example of the Streamline Moderne style is held in check by references to the interest in English Regency and American Federalist architecture that prevailed in the middle to late 1930s. The street facade of this two-story house conveys balance and symmetry. The entrance is placed within an elongated rectangular recess which also houses a window on the second floor. All of the front windows are of glass brick detailed so that their surfaces are parallel to the adjacent painted concrete-block walls. The service entrance together with the attached two-car garage projects from the right side of the dwelling.

CE191 Temple B'nai Jeshurun

1931, Dougher, Frevert and Ramsey. West corner of Grand Ave. and Country Club Rd.

A tight, compact design utilizing the Romanesque style has perhaps a touch of the round-arched forms associated with the early Christian architecture of Syria. A deep, high two-story loggia gives entrance to the tall, solid mass of the building. The side walls of

this mass exhibit three elongated arches that frame three windows. Finely worked stone was used for the details of the building as well as for sheathing the walls.

CE192 Midland Financial Savings and Loan Building

1971, Lynch, Payne, Chapeon, Bernabe, Inc. 401 Grand Ave., West Des Moines

The Midland building is assembled from two small stucco volumes, one of which is open at both ends to accommodate automobiles for a drive-in facility. The small scale of the building, placed as it is in a suburban setting, suggests much more the feeling of a house than a commercial building. The design itself is closely akin in many ways to the 1950 and 1960 Modernist houses designed by the California architect Richard J. Neutra.

CE193 House

c. 1939. 525 Grand Ave., West Des Moines

The traditional single-story bungalow is rendered here in the thirties Moderne style. Again, as is the case in the Modernist house on Foster Drive (CE187), this dwelling relies on a grouping of attached rectangular volumes, sheathed horizontally in wood. The usual hallmarks of the style are here: stucco walls, corner windows, and parapeted flat roofs.

CE194 Preferred Risk Insurance Company

1967, Brooks, Borg and Skiles. 1979–1980, addition. 1111 Ashworth Rd., West Des Moines

Strange, vastly overscaled pairs of extended concrete beams suggest that the architect may have been thinking in terms of modern Japanese architecture as it emerged after World War II. Between these pierced beams and their brick supports is a continuous band of glass for both floors of the building. To add to the visual richness of the design, each of the supporting piers has been placed on concrete supports penetrated by a single arch. The narrow sides of the building exhibit dramatic cantilevered balconies. The 1979–1980 addition to the structure essentially placed the new space underground, with an aboveground cafeteria connecting the new addition with the old. The building is located in a suburban setting; it is approached axially down a long driveway that ends in a turnaround.

DES MOINES, NORTHWEST

CE195 Mussetter House (Model House)

1933, Carl Johnson. 1116 Chautauqua Pkwy.

The depression of the 1930s encouraged the building of suburban model homes, with the hope that such dwellings would help to revive the building industry. This house, located on one of the curved streets within the suburban section adjoining Crocker Woods Park, was sponsored by the local newspaper, *The Des Moines Register and Tribune*. Its image was that of the popular English Tudor, realized in this instance in brick, stone, and half-timbering, accompanied by steel-frame casement windows. The essentials of a late twenties or early thirties suburban house are here: a well-worked-out central hall plan, a living room that opens out onto the rear garden terrace, and of course, the essential attached two-car garage.

CE196 Marcusen House

1939, Kraetsch and Kraetsch. 2027 Nash Dr.

Kraetsch and Kraetsch, who had designed the Moderne Butler house (CE154), here pro-

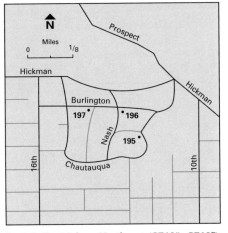

Inset 5, Des Moines, Northwest (CE195–CE197)

duced a smaller middle-class suburban model. The front entrance lies adjacent to the garage that projects from the flat-roofed two-story white stucco box. To the rear is an enclosed screen porch and large windows looking out onto the private garden.

CE197 Galinsky House

1941. 1410 Burlington Terrace

A plan type that came into its own after 1900 was that of a small or modest-sized single-floor bungalow with living room, dining room, and kitchen running down one side, and a bedroom, bath, and second bedroom opposite (with a number of variations). This narrow bungalow scheme responded very logically to the usual narrow suburban lot (40 to 60 feet wide) and to the needs of the inhabitants for distinct public and quiet private interior areas. Variations on this scheme continued into the 1950s. This example employs the Streamline Moderne style: stucco walls, flat roof, corner windows, and walls of curved glass brick.

CE198 Drake University

University Ave. and 26th St.

Drake University was established in 1881 on what was then the outskirts of the city. The rectilinear nature of its large three-block site has conditioned the layout of its landscape, street and walk patterns, and the location of its buildings, down to the present day. The

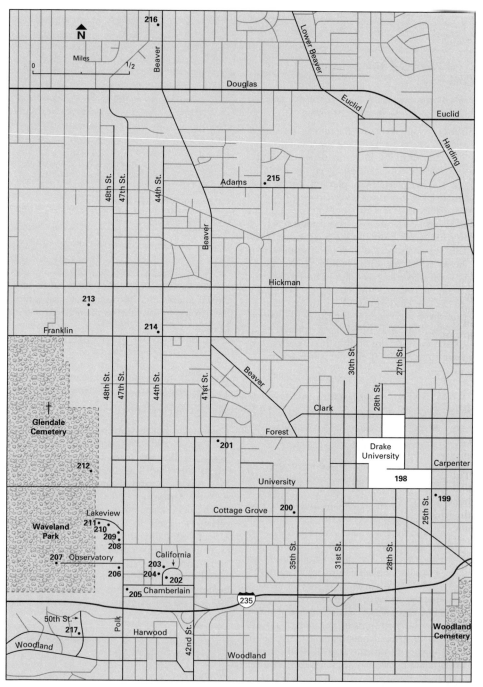

Inset 6, Des Moines, Northwest (CE198–CE218)

most extensive updating of its original grid plan occurred in 1959, with a new scheme drawn up by Sasaki, Walker and Associates (with Harry Weese). The design of its buildings and landscape today is primarily Modernist. The only older buildings that still strongly assert themselves are Old Main and Cowles Library. As the buildings discussed below indicate, the university sought out a number of the most famous architects of the time—Mies van der Rohe, Eero Saarinen, Edward Larabee Barnes, and Harry Weese—to bring the campus up-to-date.

CE198.1 Old Main

1882, C. B. Lakin

This fits everyone's idea of what a "Victorian" collegiate building should look like, with its tall open tower, narrow upward-thrusting walls and fenestration, and an overall goal of being picturesque. In style it is Queen Anne, with touches here and there of the Romanesque Revival. The realization of the Queen Anne in this brick and stone-trim building is in fact much closer to English examples (Richard Norman Shaw and Philip Webb) than the more typical highly fanciful American versions.

CE198.2 Cowles Library

1937

The two-story brick Colonial building of the late eighteenth century has been modernized. The second-floor reading rooms are lighted by large arched windows and by really grand-sized Palladian windows placed in the gable

ends. A small, rather under-scaled lantern/tower tops the center of the roof.

CE198.3 Harmon Fine Arts Center

1972, Harry Weese and Associates.

Patterns of doors and windows have been deeply cut into the attached two- and three-story brick boxes.

CE198.4 Cartwright Hall

1976, Edward L. Barnes

A two-story brick-sheathed volume here plays off an exaggerated largeness of scale on the upper level against a narrow horizontal scale for the ground floor. This building provides an excellent example of Barnes's sparse but sophisticated minimalist approach to design.

CE198.5 Meredith Hall

1965, Ludwig Mies van der Rohe

As is almost always the case with Mies's designs, this two-story steel frame and glass infill building is beautifully proportioned and handsomely detailed. It conveys a sense that two floors have been extracted from one of his skyscrapers and simply set on the ground.

CE198.6 Medbury Hall / Scott Chapel

1955, Eero Saarinen and Associates

Narrow brick end-walls contain lateral walls with metal-and-glass fenestration. The change in site level provided the architect with the

CE198.6 Drake University, Medbury Hall / Scott Chapel

CE198.7 Drake University, Ingham / Fitch Halls

opportunity to inject a metal bridge into the second floor of his building.

CE198.7 Ingham / Fitch Halls

1949, Eero Saarinen and Associates

Taking his cue from Walter Gropius's 1924 Bauhaus in Dessau, Germany, Saarinen introduced a glass skyway bridge over a street to connect his two metal and glass-sheathed rectangular boxes. The bridge consists of two thin slabs (roof and floor) with a fenestration of repeated metal-and-glass squares. The design of this bridge and the manner in which it is connected to the two buildings make it one of Iowa's most successful examples of a skyway.

CE198.8 Herriott / Carpenter / Crawford / Stainaker Residence Halls

1949–1957, Eero Saarinen and Associates

A repeated vertical band of windows moves across the facade of these four-story brick boxes. The neutrality (even dullness) of these facades is somewhat relieved by the thin metal "Erector set" balconies and the bridge over a sunken pathway.

CE198.9 Hubbell Dining Hall

1953, Eero Saarinen and Associates

The east facade of Hubbell Hall is probably Saarinen's most handsome elevation on campus. Here is fifties Modernism at its best. The

building is low, fitted partially into a hillside. Its surface is divided into rectangles of brick, plate glass, and plaster; a thin slab roof covers the entrance, penetrates the large glass area, and forms the base for the white plaster rectangle.

CE198.10 Olmsted Center

1974, Harry Weese and Associates

Large circular windows, angled corners, and angled cut-ins add to the complexity of this building. Its brick walls are in part lifted off the ground by rows of piers; on the roof a metal-and-glass monitor unit goes from one end to the other.

CE198.11 Goodwin / Kirk Residence Hall

1961, Harry Weese and Associates

Three stories of stacked bay windows set into brick walls are supported on the first floor by thin concrete piers. The buildings are joined by glass bridges which are not as successful as those realized on the campus by Saarinen.

CE198.12 Aliber Hall

1982, Bussard/Dikis Associates

This is a play on the Modernist brick cut-into box style. The third floor of the right section of the building is supported on circular columns; out of this space projects a semicircular mass. The theme of the semicircle is repeated inside by a glass brick wall in the student lounge area.

CE199 **Drake Diner**

1988, Savage and Ver Ploeg. 1111 25th St.

One of the nostalgic rediscoveries of the 1970s and 1980s was the Streamline Moderne diner of the 1930s. Diners were rediscovered first by writers and painters, and then starting in the late 1970s a number of clients and architects began to produce contemporary versions of them. The Drake diner is a wonderfully playful example of this contemporary version of the older form. And yet, as it should be, this more recent interpretation mirrors not only the 1930s, but the prevailing influence of Postmodernism. The hooped glass roof, the sheathing of gleaming, shiny metal, and even the checkerboard tile pattern are all ingredients of the late 1970s and 1980s.

CE200 **Elmwood United Presbyterian Church** (now Saint George Greek Orthodox Church)

1906, Proudfoot and Bird. Northwest corner 35th St. and Cottage Grove Ave.

The gabled front of a classical Greek temple of the Doric order sits atop a Roman podium. Tall doors lead into a simple volume behind. The enclosed pediment of the gable with its projected beam ends and the stout fluted Ionic columns are all strongly three dimensional.

CE201 **Culbertson House**

1943. 4020 Forest Ave.

A two-story, thirties, white stucco Moderne box, the Culbertson house has an entry contained within a single-floor angled volume thrust out from the center of the first floor. The double-hung windows, including those that wrap around the corners, have horizontal lights within them.

CE202 **Schenk House**

1928. 917 California Dr.

During the first two decades of this century the tendency among architects in America was to project the image of the English Tudor filtered through the Arts and Crafts movement. In this dwelling the design is dominated by two overlying gables, the lower of

CE202 Schenk House

which hovers over a wide veranda-style entrance porch. The half-timbering of these two gables is regularized into repeated rectangular and angled patterns. The various gables of the house as well as all of the second-story walls of plaster and half-timber rest on the solid brick walls of the first floor. Though this house is of good size, its emphasis on the horizontal and the scaling of its facades help it to appear as something domestic.

CE203 **House**

c. 1920. 928 California Dr.

A large brick-and-stone chimney, set beside the Gothic-style arched entrance, establishes the personality of this one-and-a-half-story English Tudor cottage. Though the house is modest in size, all of the brick, stone, and half-timbering details have been carefully carried out.

CE204 **House**

c. 1920. 916 California Dr.

As with the previous house, English Tudor detailing has been effectively realized in this one-and-a-half-story cottage. A steeply pitched half-timbered gable with bargeboards projects well above the adjacent hipped roof. The pointed arch of the central entrance doorway is repeated in the window of the door itself.

CE205 **Theodore Roosevelt High School**

1922, Proudfoot, Bird and Rawson. Southeast corner of Polk Blvd. and Chamberlain Dr.

Lincoln High School on the south side of Des Moines (CE150) was designed at the same

CE205 Theodore Roosevelt High School

time as this school, and the architects (the same firm in both cases) used English architecture of the seventeenth century as their source. The central pavilion of the Roosevelt school is three stories high, compared to the two-story section of the Lincoln school building; other than this, the schools are very much the same. The spacious grounds of the Roosevelt school building suggest, as is true for the Lincoln school, that what we are experiencing (at least from a distance) is an extensive English country house.

CE206 **Tifereth Israel Community Synagogue**

1929. 924 Polk Blvd.

The architect has obviously sought to create a form for the synagogue that would be different from that of a Christian church, and he has certainly succeeded. The principal facade of the building appears as a pylon with two low towers projecting above the roof cornice. A large arch embraces a three-part entrance, the center of which terminates in a circular window with semicircular windows to each side. The remainder of the building has a fortresslike quality, with the walls penetrated by patterns of arched windows.

CE207 **Drake University Municipal Observatory**

1920. Waveland Park (48th St. and Waverly Blvd.), end of Observatory Walk

Appropriately, the stone drum surmounted by the moving roof and telescope is the focus of this design. The drum intersects the lower central gable-roofed volume of the building; projecting behind and opposite the drum is

a parapeted flat-roofed volume. The detailing of the stone-clad building is classical, with a strong nod toward the Greek. On its hilltop location within the park, the building has the appearance of being a folly within a picturesque English garden.

CE208 **House**

1925. 1044 Polk Blvd.

The French Norman manor or farmhouse enjoyed wide popularity as a source for large and small suburban houses in the 1920s. One of its hallmarks was the circular drum tower with a steeply pitched spire-roof. Such towers, as in the case of this dwelling, were generally placed at the juncture of two wings, and the entrance often was situated at the base. Picturesque roofs, some almost reaching to the ground, frequently are a part of the style. Since the roof surface is highly visible, it was in most instances covered with slate or flat tile. The multicolor tile on this house, with its warm red hue, complements the color of the brick walls below.

CE209 **Gordon Wickes House** (Model House)

1937, Wetherell and Harrison. 4706 Lakeview Dr.

Numerous model houses were built throughout the 1930s, some sponsored by national and regional magazines, others by local newspapers, various building industries, and local groups of architects. The Wickes house, "America's Most Beautiful Modern Home," was sponsored by the Des Moines Architects Association. The "ideal suburban dwelling" designs depicted in the 1930s in the pages of the Meredith Corporation's *Better Homes and Gardens* (and in their pattern books) were generally Colonial Revival—the Cape Cod cottage was popular—but they occasionally indicated that a new day was on hand with Streamline Moderne designs, similar to that of the Wickes house. In its proportion, symmetry of fenestration, suggestion of fluted pilasters, and stone sheathing, the Wickes house conveys a sense that its design also has something to do with the then-fashionable English Regency and American Federal styles. Though it was a steel-frame dwelling, the Wickes house reads as a typical wood-stud building.

CE210 **Schindel House**

1939. 4716 Lakeview Dr.

English period revival picturesqueness is displayed here at its fullest. The roofs tumble down in a wide variety of quaint and delightful ways. Out of the roof springs an overscaled chimney and tucked-in dormers. The front door to the dwelling is inconspicuously placed to one side under a small shed roof; what greets the visitor (as it should) are the large paneled doors of the attached garage.

CE211 **Leachman House**

1922. 4822 Lakeview Dr.

In this romantic period revival English Tudor cottage there are abrupt changes in scale, and the visitor is presented with a stately entrance contained within an arched stone frame. Fragments of stone emerge here and there from the chimney and the first-floor walls; there is half-timbering above, with clapboards in the gable end.

CE212 **Glendale Abbey**

1912. Glendale Cemetery, 4909 University Ave.

Glendale Abbey is an example of the classical tradition, as one might find in an eighteenth-century English Picturesque garden. A pedimented temple front with exaggeratedly widely spaced columns faces the road and parking area. Behind this rises the rest of the stone-clad building, rather strangely surmounted by a low drum and equally low dome (they almost read as parts of a distant building). Everything about the design is simple and clean, with a decided nod toward the primitive.

CE213 **Allen Hazen Water Tower**

1930. Southwest corner of 48th St. and Hickman Rd.

Starting from the base and working upward, one finds that everything is correct and refined about the design. A circle of stone Tuscan columns surrounds an inner drum. The columns support a circular entablature and cornice; but at this point something peculiar happens, for above the cornice is a very large-

CE213 Allen Hazen Water Tower

scaled circular metal tank to hold water, and off of this sprouts an antenna. Technology and traditionalism are united.

CE214 **Zeller House**

1939, Proudfoot, Rawson, Brooks, and Borg. 1900 44th St.

Toward the end of the 1930s, Streamline Moderne designs became lighter, fragile, and more delicate (refined) in detail. Since this was also the moment when the Regency Revival was strong, it should not be surprising that many Streamline Moderne houses such as the Zeller house (originally a double house) share numerous points of similarity with Regency Revival examples. The Zeller house even has a slight terminating cornice, and its fenestration is symmetrical. To the side of the front entry door (with a pattern of four square windows) is a narrow band of glass brick which rises through the second floor. Behind this is the staircase leading to the second floor.

CE215 **Wood House**

1937. 3803 Adams Ave.

One can almost read the thin two-by-four stud wood frame of this white stucco two-story Streamline Moderne house as a cube. The stairway is to the left of the entrance and is lighted by a narrow, elongated corner window. Attached to the other side of the two-story box is a single-floor garage.

CE216 **Cunningham House**

1940. 3940 Beaver Rd.

A Streamline Moderne appliance has here been enlarged to become a dwelling. The corners are curved, a band of three inset lines flows into the second-floor windows, and corner windows occur throughout the house. The Marcusen house (CE196) declares its allegiance to the modern with reticence; the Cunningham house does it with a vengeance. The Cunningham house is almost a perfect match to a house built in Maumee, Ohio, designed by Stephen M. Jokel, of Toledo, Ohio. The Ohio house with plans was published in the April 1937 issue of *Better Homes and Gardens*.

CE217 **Casson House**

1939, Kraetsch and Kraetsch. 5003 Harwood Dr.

In the two-story Casson house the popular Streamline Moderne edges over and comes close to the High Art Modern style of those years. Banded steel casement windows are carried across the facades, and they are played off against the white stucco walls. In an advertisement by the Portland Cement Association in the February 1939 issue of *Better Homes and Gardens*, the homeowner is quoted as saying, "I prefer modern—and the cost must be low."

CE218 **Trier House**

1956–1958, Frank Lloyd Wright. 1967, Taliesin Associates Architects. 880 N.W. Beaver Dr.

The plan of the Usonian Trier house is closely modeled after the exhibition house (1953) built on the site of the Guggenheim Museum in New York.[23] The original scheme for the Trier dwelling was for a concrete-block house, but this was changed at the request of the clients to a house built of larger than normal red brick laid with the usual Wrightian horizontal mortar grooves accentuated. The living wing of the flat-roofed dwelling has ceilings that are 10 feet, 8 inches high, while the height of the bedroom wing sinks down to a cozy 6 feet, 8 inches. In plan there is the usual Usonian central core of workspace (kitchen) and utility; the combined living-dining room extends to one side, and a bedroom to the other. The entry and carport project off the north side of the dwelling. Much of the interior furniture was designed by Wright and built by the owner. In 1967 Taliesin Associates Architects added a north wing to the house.

CE218 Trier House

CE224 Fred W. Hubbell House, Helfred Farms

CE219 **Barn'rds Restaurant Building**

1983, Jack Schofield. 3605 Merle Hay Rd.

As this restaurant building indicates, programmatic roadside architecture is still being designed for the strip. The image here is that of a barn with gabled roof, accompanied by a high, eye-catching sign mounted appropriately on a silo. The design is playfully and lightly handled, and quite successful.

CE220 **Living History Farms**

organized 1967. 2600 111th St., Urbandale, near intersection of Hickman Rd. and I-35/80

The principal exhibitions at the Living History Farms are an Ioway Indian village of c. 1700; an 1850s pioneer farm; the 1870s town hall of Walnut Hill; the 1867 Flynn house and barn; a 1900 farm; and the Henry A. Wallace Crop Center. The Flynn house and outbuildings are original to the site; the other buildings are either historic structures that have been moved to the site (such as the nineteenth-century Horton log cabin), or are recent reproductions. Architecturally, the centerpiece of this outdoor museum is Martin Flynn's 1867 Italianate "mansion" and accompanying barn. The house is a post-Civil War version of the Italian Villa style. A central cupola looks down on a brick-clad dwelling with stone quoining and the usual bracketed

roof. Small pavilions with gable roofs are centered on three sides, and these are accompanied by porches and bays. The center is open to the public daily from May to October.

CE221 **Jordan House**

c. 1850s. 2251 Fuller Rd.

The designer of this substantial two-story country dwelling played with two images, the Italianate and the Gothic. Brackets support gable roofs whose pitch is more Gothic than Italianate. Entrance into the dwelling is through a wide set of double doors at the base of a projecting pavilion. Above the entrance is a flat roof (which one assumes originally must have had a balustrade). The flat roof serves as a balcony for a second-floor door accompanied by side lights, a transom, and a louvered pointed fan-device above.

CE222 **Walnut Woods State Park**

Grand Ave. west to I-35, south on I-35 to S.W. 64th Ave., east on S.W. 64th Ave. to S.W. 105th St., north on 105th St. to park

Within the 300-acre park are several examples of rustic architecture in wood and stone. The largest of these structures, a park shelter, looks nearly like a period revival (medieval) single-family dwelling of the late 1920s or early 1930s. Its front, looking out onto the parking area, gives the appearance of a completely enclosed house, but the shuttered windows to each side of the masonry chimney are simply openings for the partially enclosed shelter that lies behind.

CE223 Owens Covered Bridge

1887–1888. Ewing Park/Lake Easter Park, south on Indianola Rd. to S.E. 48th Ave.

The Owens bridge was built over the North River near the town of Carlisle (about 10 miles southeast of Des Moines). It was in continuous use from 1888 until 1940, when it was abandoned because of the construction of a new road, and a change in the location of the riverbed. In 1968 the bridge was moved and reconstructed in the park on an arm of Lake Easter. The bridge was built by Sam Gray, who employed a Howe truss structure. The 100-foot-long single-span bridge is covered by a low gable roof and its walls are sheathed in vertical planks.

CE224 Fred W. Hubbell House, Helfred Farms

1926–1928. 9265 S.W. Army Post Rd.

Within the state of Iowa there are only a handful of what can really be called country houses, i.e., country estates. One of these, still standing, is Helfred Farms. Writing in *Country Life,* Martha B. Darbyshire noted that "in 1928 Mr. and Mrs. Fred W. Hubbell closed their Des Moines town house, and with their two children took up their permanent residence in their English manor house at Helfred Farms."[24] On their 1,200-acre farm they had erected an impressive English Tudor dwelling, in brick, stone, and half-timber. A two-story brick-and-stone entrance hall with a crenellated parapet faces onto the motor court. On each side of the entrance there are one- and two-story slate-roofed sections of the house that seem to wander informally over the site. Surrounding the house are various outbuildings and informal gardens, and nearby is a large swimming pool. Further still from the house are numerous barns and other utilitarian farm buildings.

Dexter

Dexter's Community Meetinghouse (1917), located at 207 Dallas Street, appears as if it were a single-floor round barn set down within a town. Its walls are brick, and its roof is suspended from trusses covered over with roofing material. The building's image is pragmatic, its only ornamentation being three layers of brick that project out at the top of the walls to receive the roof. The building was, according to local records, designed by Maj. Matthew Leander.

Dysart

Within Dysart, at the southwest corner of Main and Wilson streets, is the Dysart State Bank (c. 1919). The design is Beaux-Arts Classical, the street facade centering on a Roman temple with columns in antis that works like a thin frontispiece in front of the two-story brick building. With the exception of the new storefront glass door, the remaining fenestration of the first and second floors appears original to the building. While in town, do look at the Queen Anne house (c. 1889) at 409 Sherman. At first glance the house appears plain and one is quickly aware that it has been partially remodeled, but the sawed work within the two street-front gables is quite vigorous, especially the ornament within the upper gable (which somehow ends up suggesting cogwheels).

Granger

Just northwest of the town of Granger is one of the earliest realizations of New Deal public-supported housing.[25] One element of Roosevelt's National Industrial Recovery Act of 1933 was the Federal Subsistence Homesteads Corporation. The task of this new federal corporation was to provide low-density single-family housing where the plot of land would be sufficient for families to grow at least part of their own food. Granger was selected as one of these homestead communities because of the economic plight of the coal miners of the area and because of the energetic activities of the local Catholic priest, Father Luigi Ligutti. In the spring of 1934 Granger was funded for 50 homesteads, each of which would have 3 to 5 acres of land. Construction of these four- to six-room houses started in the winter of 1935, and all 50 were completed by the end of the year. In 1942 the project became a cooperative. As with other Subsistence Homestead projects across the country, the image selected for these modest one-and-a-half-story dwellings was the Colonial, in this case the Colonial Cape Cod cottage which was then very popular. These little cottages exhibit a side-hall plan, and there is a pair of narrow gabled roof dormers within the front roof plane. Many of the original 50 houses have now been modified, some expanded to well over double their original size. New single-family housing has also been injected in the area, so that it has the feel of a partially planned suburban development. The Granger homesteads can best be reached by traveling due west out of Granger on route F31.

Within town, at the northwest corner of State and Sycamore streets, is a new building that is easy to miss, the Benton State Bank, designed in 1981–1982 by Charles Herbert and Associates. The reason the building is so easy to overlook is that it reminds one of a midwestern farmhouse sited among both lawn and trees. The lower floor with its clapboard sheathing and double-hung windows seems purposely ordinary. Its Postmodern character emerges in the large stepped window placed within its street-side dormer. Within, the architects have provided a play between a Modernist open space and detailing that hints at nineteenth-century design.

Grinnell

Grinnell was one of many Iowa communities "founded on the treeless prairie, in advance of civilization."[26] The choice of this site, midway between Iowa City and Des Moines, was carefully made by the New Englander Reverend J. B. Grinnell and his associates. The "treeless prairie" meant that farms could be easily established. Transportation was another consideration, for by the 1870s two major railroads passed through the community, one connecting Iowa City and Des Moines, the other a principal north-south route. The 1854 north-south, east-west plat contained the usual one-block public square; it also housed

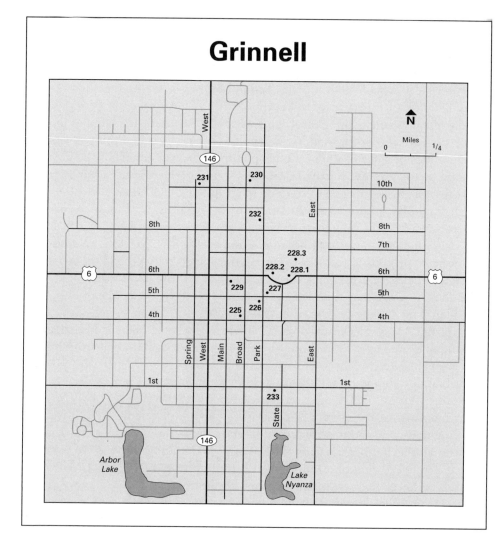

the grounds for Grinnell College, founded in 1853. Andreas's general view of the city, published in 1875, indicates how quickly and completely the site was planted with shade trees (in fact or in Andreas's mind), among which emerged commercial and public buildings. Most of these buildings, such as the Grinnell Bank Block, the public school, J. B. Grinnell's own house, and the buildings of Grinnell College, were masonry variations of the Italianate style.

Although Grinnell's economy has profited by its proximity to railroad transportation, it has from its beginning been a college town. The pleasant quality of the community essentially lies not in its buildings but in its public and private landscaping. At the southwest edge of the city, off Iowa 146, is the 37-acre Arbor Lake County Park. The artificial lake, planned to store water for the community, was designed by Isham Randolph, the consulting engineer for the Panama Canal. Around this developed, from 1902 on, a variety of recreational features, including a bandstand, bathhouse, clubhouse, and other buildings.

CE225 Merchants National Bank (now Poweshiek National Bank)

1913–1915, Louis H. Sullivan, Parker N. Berry. 833 4th Ave.

Together with the earlier bank at Owatonna, Minnesota, the bank at Grinnell is one of Sullivan's most admired buildings. That admiration has tended, perhaps rightly so, to be concentrated on the spectacular entrance to the bank. Here the viewer is confronted with exuberant and in many ways almost unbelievable exercises in terracotta ornament. A sumptuous, quite three-dimensional cartouche seemingly hovers in front of and separate from the plain brick wall that lies behind it. The cartouche has its own tenuous base, composed of paper-thin walls adjacent to the brick and then a pair of facet-surfaced columns. To give some stability to this base, short plinths are projected to each side. On top of these plinths are winged lions holding tablets. Though the design elements of the cartouche include Sullivan's usual rectangles, circles, and oak leaves, the general effect is remarkably similar to what one encounters within the Spanish Churrigueresque tradition. If one considers that this was the moment that Bertram G. Goodhue was designing and constructing the Churrigueresque Panama California International Exposition at San Diego, then Sullivan's design firmly

mirrors its time. Some of the designs for the ornament of the bank were drawn by Parker N. Berry, Sullivan's draftsman at this point.

The bank exhibits a traditional plan: a central two-story public space lighted by high windows (including the circular one contained within the cartouche) plus a skylight. Internally the round window is quite secondary to the extensive leaded stained glass side window and the central skylight. Surrounding this space are a variety of workspaces, including a consultation room, a "women's room," and a vault. The interior walls are of brick and plaster, and their decoration is realized in terracotta, sawed wood, and stained glass. Though the color and textures internally are warm and tactile, as in the Craftsman movement, there is an appropriate, almost Beaux-Arts elegance in detailing and in the use of materials, such as grained black marble for the counters.

Externally we are presented with a simple brick box dominated at its entrance by the terracotta cartouche and a pair of low horizontal windows. One of these windows is wrapped around and joined by the side window. This rectangular window is articulated by a row of nine thin columns. The only other ornamentation in the building is the row of terracotta at the top of the parapet which, like the cartouche, has a highly Churrigueresque quality. As Robert C. McLean, editor of *The Western Architect,* observed in February 1916: "The art of Louis Sullivan above all exemplifies the real value of academic tuition. A graduate of the École des Beaux-Arts; a consequent grounding in its practice and tradition in its outward form, no trace of the academic form is observable in the outward expression of his work" (p. 13).

As with other Sullivan banks, changes have been made over the years. The 1976 alteration was designed by Stewart-Robison-Laffan. Their addition took out the vault and opened up the original public area to the rear for additional space. Street "beautification" has also taken place, including an unbelievable decision to place a planter right in front of the entrance to the bank. In a few more years the vegetation will all but hide the building.

CE226 **Grinnell Methodist Church**

1895. Southwest corner of 5th Ave. and Park St.

The plan of the church is that of a wide central auditorium that projects out and is lighted by windows in the gable wings. Between the wings are towers, the one on the left rising to a dormered spire. The stone masonry has been laid as ashlar blocks, with alternating wide and thin horizontal rows. The voussoirs of the arches, though on the same plane as the adjacent walls, have been emphasized, as have the various projecting table moldings. In style the church is loosely Romanesque Revival, but a somewhat miniaturized version of the Romanesque, as one often encounters in Episcopal churches.

CE227 **Grinnell House**

c. 1860. 1002 Park St.

This is a near-perfect example of a one-and-a-half-story Greek Revival cottage. The gable end facing the street exhibits the usual returns of the eaves at the base of the gable, and there is a suggestion of pilasters at each corner. The entrance has its own pair of simple pilasters, an entablature, and side lights. The building is sheathed in clapboard; the windows are twelve-lighted double hung, and their framing lintel boards project slightly to the sides.

CE228 **Grinnell College**

founded 1853. 6th Ave. and State St.

Grinnell College was founded in 1853, and the first buildings on the campus were in the Italianate mode. Other structures were added in the late nineteenth and twentieth centuries. Of these, mention should be made of Goodnell Hall, a mildly Romanesque Revival building designed by Stephen C. Earle in 1884. Another pre-1900 structure is Mears Hall, built in 1888, whose design reflects the then current Queen Anne with a touch of the Colonial Revival. Among the older remaining buildings are Mears Cottage, a brick dormitory for women, built in 1888 (designed by Charles D. Marvin of New York, with an addition of 1904 by Hallett and Rawson), and the original Carnegie Library building (now Carnegie Hall) of 1905 (designed by Hallet and Rawson, remodeled in 1959 by Skid-

more, Owings and Merrill of Chicago). The Boston firm of Brainard, Leeds and Russell designed several buildings on campus, including Herrick Chapel (1907). The most important campus buildings to visit are those of the post-World War II years.

CE228.1 **Burling Library**

1959, Skidmore, Owings and Merrill. 1982–1983, renovation, Weese, Seegers, Hickley, and Weese.

CE228.2 **Fine Arts Center / Roberts Theater**

1961, Skidmore, Owings and Merrill.

CE228.3 **The Forum, the College Union**

1971, Skidmore, Owings and Merrill.

All three of these buildings are tasteful, well detailed, and well scaled (for the site) Modern buildings, as one would expect from this architectural firm. The SOM buildings play off brick walls against detailing (and structure) in steel, glass, and concrete. The Forum is of exposed concrete, countered by projecting groups of bays with metal and glass walls and roofs.

CE229 **Auto Showroom** (now a retail store)

c. 1930. East side of Main St., between 5th and 6th avenues

A well-proportioned single-floor brick commercial building has been enlivened by small cartouches of winged automobile tires placed above each of its piers. The decorative device of half of a tire and wheel has, in the fashion of the Art Deco, been effectively integrated with the surrounding wings and with the flat capital of the piers below. This is all very subtle programmatic architecture, but effective.

CE230 **Ricker House**

1911, Walter Burley Griffin. 1510 Broad St.

The richness of the Prairie school, and specifically of Griffin's work, is well illustrated by the design of this house. Though it shares many features found in the work of Frank Lloyd Wright, it is highly dissimilar to his designs in its plan and massing. The main two-story gable-roofed section is stretched out to the sides by a veranda to the right and a partially enclosed breezeway and garage to the left (the garage itself was added somewhat later and was designed by Barry Byrne). One enters the house by the front terrace and thence into a central hall. The living space on the first floor is remarkably open, yet demarcated enough to suggest different uses. The large glass areas and the glass doors leading to the veranda effectively let nature and light enter through the patterned glass screens. On the second floor each corner of the building is opened up with a balcony that could be used as a sleeping porch. The suburban nature of the house, as fact and symbol, and its reliance on the automobile is emphatically stated by the importance placed on the garage and auto court as one of the principal entrances to the house.

CE231 **Lustron House**

c. 1949. 601 10th Ave.

This is one of the Lustron Company's side-entry plans. As is usual, this prefabricated porcelainized metal-paneled dwelling is in excellent condition.

CE232 **Shifflet House**

1919, Morton B. Cleveland. 1329 Park St.

Waterloo architect Morton B. Cleveland has produced a two-story midwestern stucco box with mild Prairie-style overtones. He used wood detailing to join many of the windows together, both horizontally and vertically, and placed the second-floor windows directly under the soffit of the overhanging hipped roof.

CE233 **Chicago, Rock Island, and Pacific Railroad Station**

1892–1893. South of 1st St. between State and Park streets

This small brick-and-stone building focuses attention on a two-story bay tower surmounted by a conical roof. The building's stone base is carried up to the window sills, and stone is used as a banding throughout the building. As to style, the building is a combination of Queen Anne and Richardsonian Romanesque.

Hedrick

The Dick L. Doak house, at 508 Young Street (between Iowa 149 and Fifth Street) was designed and built by its owner during the years 1956–1976. The house conveys the generally wild mood one associates with the work of Bruce Goff. The walls of the house are sheathed in weathered wood, some of which has been laid at a 45-degree angle. It is the roof, however, that catches one's eye, for it seemingly undulates (though in an angular fashion) over the building beneath it. It almost seems independent of the house, and this is especially apparent in the porte-cochère, where the roof's eaves angle sharply upward. The dwelling's design is on the idiosyncratic side, but at the same time it appears highly rational.

Hills

The Joseph Miller True-Round Barn, designed and built during 1918–1920 by John Schrader, is found just west of the small village of Hills. The walls of the barn are sheathed in board-and-batten and its double-pitched gambrel roof has wood shingles. A metal aerator is at the peak of the roof. Because of the slope of the land, a lower level opening out on ground level has been provided. Within the barn, at its center, is a terracotta tile silo. The diameter of the barn is 60 feet; that of the silo, 10 feet. The barn can be reached by traveling .3 miles north of Hills on the frontage road parallel to the east side of US 218; turn left (west) on F62, proceed 4.2 miles.

Huxley

Twenty miles north of Des Moines, just to the west of Interstate 35, is the small community of Huxley. North of Huxley are two houses by Ray Crites. One of these is Crites's own house (1976); the other, to the west, is the Bellizzi house.

CE234 Bellizzi House

1975, Ray Crites. Timberline Lane, north of Huxley, just west of I-35 on a gravel road

The style of the Bellizzi house and of Crites's own house contrasts with this architect's characteristic early work. Each house is enclosed primarily by wood-sheathed walls (rather than by glass), and their forms are more vertical and picturesque. The houses both blend into and contrast with their wooded hillside location. The wood walls read as thin sheets of cardboard that beautifully enclose each grouping of volumes.

Indianola

The site of Indianola was selected in 1849 as the future seat of Warren County; it is located in the center of the new county, between the Middle and South rivers. The town was platted and first settled in 1850. A single unusual feature of its grid layout was the central courthouse square, which was originally laid out as an octagon rather than the usual square block. In 1860, the Indianola Seminary was founded, and this school later emerged as Simpson College.

CE235 Warren County Courthouse

1938–1939, Karl Keffer and Earl E. Jones. Courthouse Square, corner of S. Burton and E. Salem streets

The second Warren County Courthouse, designed by Charles A. Dunham and constructed between 1866 and 1868, was a particularly strong example of the Italianate and French Second Empire styles. The front elevation of this brick and stone-trimmed building was composed of two square towers with high mansard roofs, between which was a three-story pediment with a group of three elongated round-arched windows. The accentuated verticality of the composition, especially that of the central gabled section and its fenestration, came close to suggesting that the building housed a religious institution, not a civil one. Regrettably the building was not well maintained over the years, and because of serious structural problems it was demolished in 1938.

The third county courthouse was funded by a bond issue, plus funds provided by the PWA. The new building is a traditional example of thirties PWA Moderne. The visitor is greeted by a central pavilion articulated by six fluted pilasters, each rendered as a flat surface and without any base or capital. The wings on each side are of brick, with central panels of light-colored Bedford limestone.

CE236 Municipal Building

c. 1922. Northwest corner of S. Buxton St. and W. 1st Ave.

A single-story public building with a gable roof, built in the Georgian Revival style, has been carried right out to the edge of the sidewalk. The central entrance exhibits a ped-imented roof supported two pilasters, and between them is a semicircular arched opening containing the door. The two groups of three windows to each side of the entrance have panels above them containing classical swags. At each end of the building the walls have been projected out a few inches, hinting that they are end pavilions. Within the one on the right is a garage, while the one on the left displays a Palladian window. This well-scaled brick and stone-trim building is covered with a tile roof.

CE237 Simpson College

1860, later. N. Burton St. and W. Clinton Ave.

What greets the visitor today at Simpson College are two sets of conflicting images of the twentieth century. One was formulated in the teens and twenties to express a unified version of the brick English Collegiate Gothic style; countering this, the second produced a group of noncontextual modernist buildings, mostly in the 1960s and on through the 1980s. The majority of the buildings are organized around a central mall space, and the design of the landscape has been well carried out.

CE237.1 Kresge Hall

c. 1920

This hall is a good example of a two-and-a-half-story brick collegiate building, rendered in brick with stone trim around windows and doors. The steeply pitched roof is broken by tall chimneys and small, flat-roofed dormers.

CE237.2 Hillman Hall

1919

The three-story central section of this brick and stone-trimmed building has crenellated parapets, Gothic arched windows and entrance, and a large bay window projecting from the second floor. The wings to the side have buttressed walls, parapeted gable ends, and strikingly steeply pitched roofs.

CE237.3 Robertson Music Center

1982–1983, Brooks, Borg and Skiles

Though modernist in image, this brick building seems to have been designed to sit modestly next to the older adjacent chapel. A sunken courtyard joins the music center to the chapel.

CE237.4 A. H. and Theo Blank Performing Arts Center

1966–1971, Charles Herbert and Associates

An exposed concrete box has been placed within a sunken area, almost creating the atmosphere of a prewar military installation. The building is approached either over concrete bridges or via a sunken ramp.

CE238 Grange House

1934, Oren Thomas. 1108 N. B St.

When the Grange house was published in the August 1935 issue of *The Architectural Forum*, its qualities of "individuality," "beauty in de-

sign," and "livability" were lauded. In imagery the house is somewhat midway between the Art Deco of the 1920s and the Streamline Moderne of the thirties. The walls of the house are of concrete block, the floors and roof of reinforced concrete. The single small bedroom on the second floor opened onto a roof terrace. The house has been extensively remodeled in recent years.

CE239 House

c. 1898. 309 E. Salem St.

A late Queen Anne dwelling with a classic round bay tower has been pushed over into the Colonial Revival style by the large two-story pedimented porch. The porch has a layer of corner Ionic columns, and between these columns is a group of pencil-thin Ionic columns. The closed pediment above displays a single oval window.

Iowa City

Iowa City was created as a fiat governmental center, similar to the way in which towns were established to house county seats throughout the state.[27] Early in 1839, the territorial governor and the legislature authorized the creation of a commission to "locate the seat of government of the Territory of Iowa."[28] The city's name was selected at this time, and the governor, Robert Lucas, instructed the commission to place the proposed site for the territorial capitol within Johnson County, which was then on the western frontier of Iowa. The commissioners settled on a picturesque location on the Iowa River, at a point where the river was "a clear, limpid stream" and where the land on the western bank climbed up some 50 feet "to the level of a smooth prairie, which approaches the bank of the river at this place, and then sweeps off westward in beautiful undulations."[29]

The site for the future capitol building was selected on the eastern bluff overlooking the Iowa River valley. The site was surveyed in July 1839, with Leander Judson drawing up a grid plat for the city. Befitting a place that was to be the capital for the state, Judson made a number of modifications in the usual repetitious grid scheme. On the bluff, he laid out a 12-acre square for the capitol building; one block east of this he proposed a city park defined on its north and south edges by sites for future churches. Eight blocks farther to the east was a full square block for the governor's house. The town's principal street was to be Iowa Avenue, which was to be 120 feet wide. Four other public open spaces were also provided: a college green, a market square south of Iowa Avenue, and two additional market squares north of the avenue. Two half-

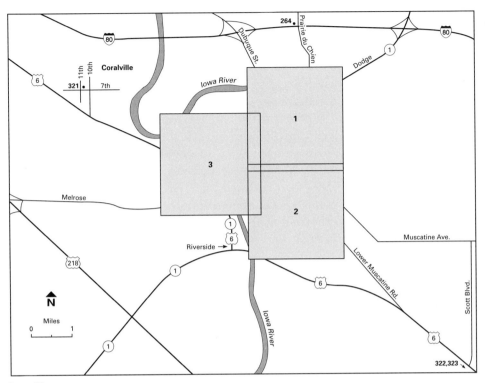

Iowa City, outer map

block sites were reserved for additional churches. Finally, in a move that was quite unusual for most nineteenth-century American cities, a public "promenade" was designated along a section of the east bank of the river. By the mid-1870s, much of this original generous public open space still remained intact. The capitol grounds (as well as the old capitol building) had become the site of the University of Iowa in 1857, and with the expansion of the city to the south, a block was set aside for the county courthouse.

In the early years, high hope was held for the utilization of the Iowa River for transportation. Construction of locks was started downstream by the federal government, but this project was finally abandoned as being far too costly.

The 1850s witnessed both losses and additions to the community. On the plus side was the arrival of the railroad in 1856; on the negative side was the loss of the state capitol to Des Moines. The economic and physical growth of the community from the 1850s on until the present day has been a moderate one. By the early 1900s, when its population was around 8,000, it was "the Iowa State University in its midst [which gave] it great prominence and the hundreds of students who flock[ed] there add[ed] life to the town."[30]

The preeminence of the university within the community increased appreciably in the 1920s, until indeed Iowa City became a college town in every sense of the term. In its growth the university eventually spilled over onto the west bank of the river, which now houses many of its largest buildings. The low, somewhat swampy land on the river's west bank was reclaimed in the late 1930s for a "Fine Arts Campus" for the university. During the years 1964 through 1978, extensive urban renewal and expansion of the university took place east of the river. Also, the university's presence is expressed in the impressive number of wonderful period revival sorority and fraternity houses, which so effectively sum up the decades from 1900 through 1930. As was par for the course for post-World War II urban renewal, an appreciable number of significant historic neighborhoods and buildings have disappeared. In the 1970s and 1980s the downtown acquired an urban enclosed mall (Old Capitol Center), a multi-storied parking structure and adjacent hotel, and streets were closed to provide for new buildings and pedestrian malls. As one would expect with the presence of the university and offices of the Iowa State Historical Society, Iowa City has in recent years been active in the field of historic preservation. Both in the downtown, and in the outlying areas, a good number of important buildings from the nineteenth and early twentieth centuries have been restored and modified for new uses.

In recent years the university has emerged as the community's avant-garde patron for contemporary architecture. This is very much apparent in such buildings as Walter Netsch's (SOM) Bowen Science Building (1970–1972); his Hardin Library for the Health Sciences (1972–1974); Gunnar Birkerts's 1985–1986 Boyd Law Building; The CRS/Durrant Group's Carver-Hawkeye Arena (1980–1982); and in the commissioning in 1988 of the Los Angeles architect Frank O. Gehry to design the Laser Science and Engineering Center.

For a variety of reasons, including a history of decades of slow growth, Iowa City has avoided many of the planning and architectural errors and devastation usually inflicted on American cities over the past four decades. Notwithstanding the usual strip development (which could be anywhere) along US 6, "the Coralville Strip" northwest of the city, and more recently along I-80 and US 218, the community still reads strongly as a university town that was founded and began its growth in the middle to late nineteenth century.

IOWA CITY, TOWN CENTER, NORTH

CE240 First Presbyterian Church

1856–1865. Northwest corner of Market and Clinton streets

The designer of the First Presbyterian Church looked to the northern Italian Romanesque for his precedent, and he loosely transposed this tradition into the mid-nineteenth century. The brick and stone-trimmed church features an English central entrance scheme, with a crenellated tower and paneled side walls. The windows and the smaller doors are all arched, and here and there the architect provided Romanesque corbel tables. The principal entrance at the base of the tower has a low, broad, pointed arch, and its stone lintel is articulated by another corbel table. The spired tower of the original church was destroyed in a storm in 1877, and it was rebuilt with its present crenellated parapet.

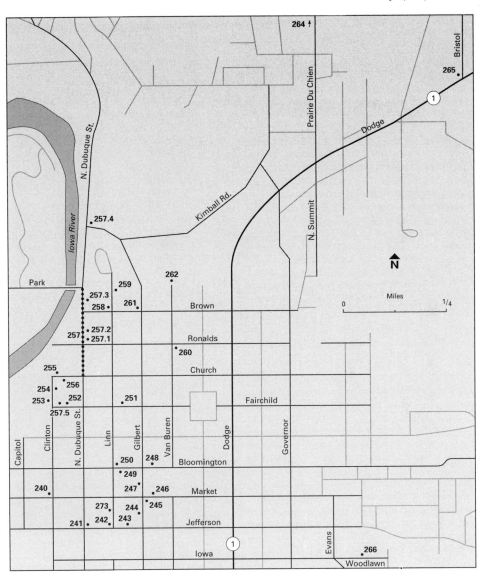

Inset 1, Iowa City, Town Center, North (CE240–CE266)

CE241 **First United Methodist Church**

1906, Sheetz and Gesberg. Northeast corner of Jefferson and Dubuque streets

If one were to change this church's windows and detailing to the Romanesque, it could easily pass as a Richardsonian Romanesque design. Its massing, with its one large and one small corner towers, its strong ashlar block stone walls, and the specific pattern of its windows are all logical for the late nineteenth-century versions of the Romanesque. But its entrance with three gable roofs, its single rose window above, and its windows with pointed arches are all meant to be experienced as Gothic. The tower, its crenellation rising at each of its corners, its corner-angled gargoyles, and its almost classical entablature and cornice certainly matches no known historic style. The building was restored in 1990, and short buttresses were added to the east and west sides of the building.

CE242 Saint Mary's Roman Catholic Church

1869, attrib. Father Emonds. Northwest corner of Jefferson and Linn streets

As with the nearby First Presbyterian Church, the format of this church is nineteenth-century Gothic Revival, but its arched windows and doors and other details are Romanesque. The tower entrance, with its low-pitched gable roof, has two sets of windows, side by side, held in place by two corner pilasters that rise to the cornice. Rather delicate buttresses and a corbel table occur on the two side walls of the sanctuary. The Gothic buttresses were added in 1912.

CE243 Hutchinson House

1883. 318 E. Jefferson St.

Robert Hutchinson and his son Frank P. Hutchinson were local stone contractors who built and most likely designed their own house. Their good-sized two-story masonry house was a little old fashioned in its references at this late date to the Italianate in its bracketed roof, the front porch with paired columns, and the segmental arched windows. But they brought the design up-to-date with a wide porch across the front, and through the central two-story bay that houses the entrance with side lights and high transom on the first floor, and a group of four elongated windows on the second floor. The first-floor windows for all of the principal rooms are carried to the floor, and all of the windows exhibit strongly projecting stone lintels.

CE244 Rohret House

1850. 115 N. Gilbert St.

The Rohret house represents a Greek Revival type frequently built in Iowa in the decades of the 1840s and 1850s. The two-story house exhibits a simple, direct plan; there is a central hall with staircase on both floors and then one room on each side of the two halls. There are stone lintels over the windows and doors; a row of dentils flows along under the soffit of the gable roof and a transom light is car-

ried above the front door. In 1910 this brick house was moved a short distance to make way for another dwelling. At that time a porch with piers and balustrade was added to the front of the house.

CE245 Baker-Alberhasky Grocery Store

1883. 401 E. Market St.

This is a well-preserved two-story corner commercial building of the 1880s. On the ground floor, up a few steps from the street, is a retail store whose fenestration of glass and wood is well preserved. The space above served as a meeting hall. As is frequently the case with commercial blocks located on a corner, the corner is emphasized by a wall at a 45-degree angle to the two adjacent facades, and the bracketed cornice supports a low, curved gable end.

CE246 Nickering House

1854, Finkbine and Loveless, contractors. 410 E. Market St.

A frequently encountered house type of the mid-nineteenth century was the one-and-a-half-story Greek Revival dwelling with a central hall. In this example the upper row of five half-windows is directly under the roof soffit. To the rear, the roof is carried down to the first floor, producing the effect of a miniaturized New England saltbox. The builders of this yellow sandstone dwelling were likely its designers as well.

CE247 Wentz House

1847. 219 N. Gilbert St.

A substantial two-story Greek Revival house realized in stone, the Wentz house has a wide

CE247 Wentz House

then dwellings such as this were well behind the latest fashion.

entablature/cornice displaying a row of dentils; its entrance, with its pair of narrow side lights and transom, is deeply recessed into the wall. Each of the two side walls has a symmetrical pattern of windows, and to each side of the ridge of the gable roof are small chimneys. The central-hall plan has the usual staircase and pairs of rooms on each side of the hall on the first and second floors. The lean-to at the rear was probably original to the house.

CE248 Stach House

1924. 412 E. Bloomington St.

The popularity of the California bungalow continued on through the mid-1920s, as this one-and-a-half-story dwelling attests. The elements of the style are all here: a low structure that hugs the ground; shingle walls; broad overhanging gable and roof ends with exposed rafter ends; brackets to support the roof overhang on the gabled ends; and the rafter tails carried out beyond the roof's edge. If one thinks of the twenties as the moment for the historic imagery of the period revival,

CE249 Graf House

1872. 319 E. Bloomington St.

Though modest in size, the Graf house attracts one's attention immediately because of the strong three-dimensional quality of its ornamentation. The gable end of this Italianate house faces the street and has a wide entablature/cornice accompanied by pairs of thick brackets. The sides of the entablature curve at the eave ends to receive the roof return. In the center, connected to the entablature, is an overscaled oval window with an extended horizontal sill. A piered entrance porch runs across the ground floor; on the second floor, the window over the door has been doubled in size to match the double door and transom below. Conrad Graf, who had the house built, was a partner in the Shultze and Graf Brewery.

CE250 Slezak Hall (now Pagliai's Pizza)

1875. 302–304 E. Bloomington St.

This commercial building is composed of two parts: a second-floor meeting hall with store space below facing onto East Bloomington Street, and a three-story hotel block, set slightly back, that looks out on North Linn Street. Both sections have round-arched windows and bracketed entablature/cornices. Surmounting the cornice of the meeting-hall section is a false curved gable front. On the basis of present information it is difficult to know whether the hotel or the meeting hall and store section may have been built first.

CE251 **Rumple House**

1908. 314 E. Fairchild St.

A popular house type within the Colonial Revival of the 1890s through the 1900s was one that used the gambrel roof. Generally, as in the case of the Rumple house, the gabled end faces the street. To dramatize even more the effect of the gabled end, it was often projected as a volume out and over the floor below. In the Rumple house this is accomplished by having an angled bay to one side, and then an open porch on the other side. The architect made the gambrel roof more complex here by carrying a cornice across the roof at the point where the two slopes meet, and then projecting this cornice as a return onto the gable front. In plan, modest examples such as this have an entry porch, entry, and stairway to one side, and then the living room and dining room ranged down the other side.

CE252 **Jackson / Swisher (Keyser) House**

1877, Louis H. Jackson. 120 E. Fairchild St.

Steeply pitched roofs and elaborate bargeboard gable ends were hallmarks of the Eastlake style in America. Louis H. Jackson, the builder, placed almost all of his emphasis on the many gabled ends of the Swisher house. For extra measure he added a gable at 45 degrees to the house extending out above the entrance porch. The wide bargeboards have sawed cut-out patterns of alternating circles and crosses, terminating at the eave end in a circle (with its own center cut-out circle). The angled gable over the entrance porch is supported by thin angled struts that meet at the

corner. Other classic Eastlake features are the tall chimneys and the sharp angular headers above the second-floor windows.

CE253 **Dey House** (now University Institute for Public Affairs)

1857. 507 N. Clinton St.

The Dey house is a two-story Italianate house in clapboard with end gables. The house is extended one more bay to the south, as if this portion were to have had a tower. The front entrance porch exhibits elegant pairs of columns mounted on a high base, and at the entrance itself the porch is pulled forward. The windows for the principal rooms on the first floor are carried down to the floor level. To the left side of the house are two false shuttered windows, one above the other. A flat deck surrounded by a cast-iron railing surmounts the ridge of the low-pitched roof.

CE254 **Tri Delta Sorority House**

1920. 522 N. Clinton

A delicately detailed two-story semicircular porch, together with its balustraded roof, declares the stability and good taste of our forebears of the Federal era. Roof dormers, as well as wall dormers, quoining, and fanlights, help to reinforce the vividness of the Colonial Revival. This large two-and-a-half-story brick and clapboard sorority house may be a remodeling of a smaller, older house.

CE255 **President's House, University of Iowa**

1908, Proudfoot and Bird. 102 E. Church St.

An appropriate dwelling for the president of a state university was, of course, a Colonial Georgian mansion, almost always equipped, as is the case here, with a two-story entrance porch. The porch of the president's house, with Ionic columns and heavy balustrade, used in conjunction with the overscaled pedimented entrance, declares that this is as much a public building as a dwelling. Chimneys rise from the end gable walls, and three large dormers puncture the front roof plane. Wood and glass porches (two stories on the left) balance the central two-story brick block.

CE256 **Baldwin House**

1926, Mark Anthony. 111 E. Church St.

The Cedar Rapids architect Mark Anthony was a strong and gifted proponent of the period revivals of the 1920s. For the Baldwin house he turned to the English Tudor, stone sheathed below, half-timber above. The roof rises two stories from the first floor, and, together with the steeply pitched gables, it dominates the design. Roof forms are used to tie the composition together, as one can experience at the entrance, where the left slope of its roof (with its eaves almost reaching the ground) joins onto the high half-timbered gable above.

CE257 **"Fraternity Row"** (and other fraternities and sororities)

c. 1920–1930. N. Dubuque St., between E. Church St. and Park Rd.

The high wooded hill overlooking the Iowa River was the site for a number of the university fraternity houses built in the decade of the twenties. With the exception of William L. Steele's Kappa Sigma (now Pi Kappa Alpha) house, all represent one or another of the historic types associated with the period revival of these years. All of the houses were conceived as large-scale suburban or country houses. The heavily wooded location of many of these buildings makes them, on the whole, difficult to see when the foliage is out during the summer months. Several of them can be seen better from the west, across the river on North Riverside Drive.

In addition to the group of fraternity houses on North Dubuque, there are several others scattered about the northeast and northwest sections of the city, especially west of the river, in and around Ellis and Ridgeland avenues, north of River Street.

CE257.1 **Sigma Phi Epsilon**

1929–1930. 702 N. Dubuque St.

The English Tudor house in stone and half-timber; a pair of two-story stone-sheathed crenellated bays appears on each side of the front of the building.

CE257.2 **Pi Kappa Alpha** (now Phi Kappa Sigma)

1931. 716 N. Dubuque St.

A picturesque gathering of steeply pitched gables, chimneys, and irregular massing characterizes this exposition of the English Tudor Revival style. Half-timbering is employed in the second-story wing that projects out over the large porch on the west side of the building.

CE257.3 **Beta Theta Pi**

1929. 816 N. Dubuque St.

A two-and-a-half-story large but compact English Tudor Revival block, this house has a commons room with a large one-and-a-half-story bay clothed in diamond-paned windows from which one can look out over the river.

CE257.4 **Kappa Sigma** (now Pi Kappa Alpha)

1926, William L. Steele. 1032 N. Dubuque St.

Steele's later designs in the Prairie style, like those of George Grant Elmslie during the same years, retain only a few elements that one can directly associate with the style. Rows of vertical pilasters occur on the west side of this brick building, and a horizontal band of three lines is carried through the rows of windows on the first and second floors. Except for elements such as these, the design of this elongated three-story gabled block seems to convey a sense of rationalism and directness.

CE257.5 **Alpha Xi Delta Sorority**

1929. 114 E. Fairchild St.

The English Georgian style here is rendered in brick, with a recessed center section containing a wide segmental arched entrance. The steeply pitched hipped roof (which in this case is really related to the French Norman Revival) displays dormers with hipped roofs, and tall end chimneys.

CE258 **Ford House**

1908. 228 E. Brown St.

California's Mission Revival was one of the exotic modes that spread across the country

CE258 Ford House

CE261 **Slezak / Hubbard House**

1892, O. H. Carpenter. 328 E. Brown St.

The Romanesque, Queen Anne, and Colonial Revival styles are all imaginatively brought together here, but in such a manner as to read as a "normal" brick house of the 1890s. The two-story corner bay, instead of having a tower, stops at the roofline and is surmounted by a Colonial Revival balustrade. Arched openings pierce the third-floor gable ends, but below, the columned entrance porch is pure Colonial Revival. The house still retains its one-and-a-half-story carriage house to the rear.

during the first two decades of this century. Examples of this style were presented in the pages of *The Craftsman* magazine, and in many pattern books. The plan of these houses, especially the two-story version as we see in the Ford house, was essentially a rectangular box that could easily be adapted to create any number of images. The Ford house is sheathed in stucco and has a tile roof, parapeted scalloped gable ends, and deep round quatrefoil windows. Records indicate that the house was apparently built for Arthur H. Ford, a professor of engineering at the University of Iowa.

CE259 **House**

1916. 818 N. Linn St.

A two-story Midwestern cube house veers from the normal with its elaboration of decorated rafter tails which extend beyond the eaves and are sawed in a step pattern. The windows are carefully grouped, and their arrangement, plus the general horizontality of the cube together with its broad front porch, conveys a Prairie-esque quality.

CE260 **Welch House**

c. 1858. Southeast corner of N. Van Buren and E. Ronalds streets

This early small side-hall cottage has a pair of parapeted gable ends with chimneys. This brick dwelling is set on a rather high stone basement, and stone has been employed for the flat window and door lintels. The house has recently been restored.

CE262 **Vogt House**

1889. 800 N. Van Buren St.

There is a do-it-yourself design quality in the porch with its extended turreted pavilion; it seems to exist in a different world from the roofscape, which has the appearance of a professional, subdued design. The two-story brick-sheathed volume of the house acts as a neutral ground upon which the roof and the porch can act.

CE263 **Payne House**

1883. 513 Summit St.

The sharp and brittle angularity of the Eastlake style has in this dwelling nearly given way to the Queen Anne, but not quite. The center section of the house seems ready for an Eastlake tower; instead it is crowned on the third floor by a open porch covered with a gable roof. The entrance porch, which seems too small, swings around the side of the house and becomes a real veranda. A 45-degree cut-in angled corner occurs on the second floor, looking out onto the triangular porch supported at the corner by a single column.

CE264 **Johnson House**

1857. 2155 Prairie du Chien Rd.

The first floor of this dwelling, with its thin piered posts and connecting segmental arches, is correct Italianate, as is the front door with side lights and transom and the heavily articulated cornice. But it is impossible to determine what the designer had in mind for the second floor. It is treated as a shingled mansard roof, but the roof at the front is carried up to a low gable that is equipped with a small window. The three front dormers are pedimented and wide, not at all typical of the French Second Empire or the Italianate. The mansard roof ends up at one moment reading as a roof, and at another, as a shingled wall.

CE265 Dyer House

1973, Bruce Abrahamson. 1309 Bristol Dr.

The Minneapolis architect effectively created a minimalist two-story cut-into box. The main floor mounted over the garage has a pair of side-by-side porches deeply cut into the volume of the house. A high clerestory arises behind, its end walls forming a single plane with the house below. The wide garage door, which is painted to match the white color of the wood-sheathed house, has as its decoration a single row of four projecting aluminum "can" lights, while the front door to the side is painted a contrasting color and is deeply set into the wall.

CE266 Kenyon House

1895, George Kenyon, builder. 1036 Woodlawn Ave.

This house, constructed by the builder George Kenyon for his own use, looks to the late Queen Anne style, with a glance at the Colonial Revival, to suggest a country house, not a suburban dwelling. The extensive wooded site at the end of this dead-end street provides the illusion that the house is in wooded countryside. The house lies low to the ground, and this horizontal quality is reinforced by a long front porch. Above, on the second floor,

the corner bay tower opens up into another porch, and the adjacent window on the front gable end contains a pretend porch, above which is yet another miniature porch off of the attic window.

Woodlawn Avenue, which in part is treated as a divided boulevard ending in a cul-de-sac, was outside of the city's original 1839 plat. It was laid out in the late 1880s, and in 1889 it appears in records as S. M. Clark's subdivision. In addition to the Kenyon house, there are several other late-1880s houses on the street. Among these are the houses at 1011 Woodlawn (1888), 1025 Woodlawn (1891), and 1047 Woodlawn (1888). Woodlawn Avenue is now a historic district within the city.

IOWA CITY, TOWN CENTER, SOUTH

The center of the downtown commercial center bounded by Burlington, Washington, Clinton, and Linn streets has been closed off to automobiles, and pedestrian malls have been created from the various streets. Within this superblock and adjacent to it, a number of older buildings have been restored or revamped (see next seven entries). Other noteworthy buildings are also located in the southern part of the town center.

CE267 College Street Block, 1878

Inset 2, Iowa City, Town Center, South (CE267–CE295)

CE267 College Street Block

1878, Chauncy F. Lovelace

Stylistically this is the usual mixture encountered in commercial buildings of the 1880s—the Italianate, the Eastlake, and the Queen Anne. The ironwork was by the Iowa City firm of Maresh and Holubar. The building was restored in 1979 by the architectural firm of Hansen Lind Meyer.

CE268 Franklin Printing House Building

1856. 115 S. Dubuque St.

This is a three-story brick block that is mildly Italianate in style. The lintels and the columns are of cast iron.

CE269 Bacon Building

1858. 111 S. Dubuque St.

The Bacon Building is also Italianate in brick, similar to the Franklin Printing House Building.

CE270 Shepherd Building

1882. 118 S. Dubuque St.

The French Second Empire-style Shepherd Building was restored in 1984 by Richard Kune and Hawkeye Construction.

CE271 Brossart Building

c. 1853. 16 S. Clinton St.

The building started out as a three-story

structure with a parapeted chimney. The Italianate cornice with the small gable above was probably added in the 1880s.

CE272 Sanxay Hardware Store
(Whetstone's Drug Store Building)

c. 1850, 1870, 1882. 32 S. Clinton St.

A building was situated on the corner by 1850; in 1856 a three-story addition was built behind it, at 108 Washington Street. In 1870 the corner building was enlarged to three stories, and in style it became Italianate. Whetstone's Drug Store came in 1880, and the 1856 building was provided with a matching cornice.

CE273 Brewery Square: Holz and Geiger Brewery Building, Economy Advertising Building

1856. 1867 addition, brewery. 1926, advertising building. 127–131 N. Linn St.

The exteriors of these two commercial buildings were restored by the firm of KNV Architects in 1987 to serve as a location for restaurants, shops, and offices. The corner structure, that of the Holz and Geiger Brewery, is a brick Italianate building, with round-arched windows, a bracketed hipped roof, and at one time a small cupola. The 1920s Economy Advertising Building is a straightforward two-story brick building with horizontal factory sash windows. Its only ornamentation is its name in cast stone, surrounded by a raised brick frame set within a raised portion of the parapet.

CE274 Carnegie Public Library (former)

1903–1904, Liebbe, Nourse and Rasmussen. Southeast corner College and S. Linn streets

In 1902 the Carnegie Foundation made a grant to Iowa City for a new public library. The Des Moines firm of Liebbe, Nourse and Rasmussen provided a Beaux-Arts design that looked back to the classical Greek temple with columns in antis. To bring emphasis to the temple, the architects pulled it forward from the bulk of the building and then added a high paneled attic. The walls of the stone building were left smooth and plain and serve as a background for the ornament around the windows and for the pronounced quoining. The workable plan is a typical one for smaller libraries: a central rotunda, with the delivery counter opposite the entrance; a bookstack bay behind; and then a general reading room to one side and a children's room to the other. Both the children's room and the general reading room have fireplaces. Within the raised basement are offices, a meeting room, and storage space. In the post-World War II years a new, unsympathetic wing was added to the rear of the building, and in recent years the building has been used for private offices.

CE275 Trinity Episcopal Church

1871, Richard M. Upjohn. Northwest corner of S. Gilbert and College streets

Samuel N. Watson, in his *History of Trinity Parish*, asserts that "on January 16th, 1871, the plan of the Church was selected, being a modification of one of [Richard] Upjohn's plans for Gothic Churches."[31] Whether the design of this Gothic Revival board-and-batten church was derived from a pattern book or from stock plans of the New York architect Richard M. Upjohn is not clear. It is similar to several of his designs he published in *Upjohn's Rural Architecture* (1852); it also could have been taken from Upjohn's designs published in George E. Woodward's *Rural Church Architecture* (c. 1868–1875). A steeply pitched roof covers the rectangular volume of Trinity Church, and two small wings (one of which was formerly the entrance) protrude from the building. A small pedimented screen-wall tower (this was originally a bell tower) projects from the ridge of the roof at the front. There have been a number of changes made in the building over the years, including a new entrance on the south gabled end.

CE276 Iowa City Press-Citizen Building

1937, Fisk and Ruth; Kruse and Klein. 319 E. Washington St.

Throughout the country, newspaper companies often clothed their buildings in architectural forms that suggested that they were really an element of government (or equal to it). The setback of this PWA Moderne building and the wide steps leading up to the entrance enhance its image as a public building. The *Press-Citizen* building has a raised center pavilion, with the body of the brick sections to each side containing narrow panels filled with glass brick. The windows to the side and rear are all of glass brick, placed close to the face of the brick walls. At the rear a truck ramp leads down to the basement delivery room.

CE277 Johnson County Courthouse

1899–1900, Rush, Bowman and Company. Southwest corner of S. Clinton and Court streets

Iowa City was designated as the location for the Johnson County seat in 1840. The first of the three courthouses in Iowa City was erected during the years 1842–1848. It was a two-story stone building, mildly Greek Revival in its design (built by James Tremble). In 1856, this many-chimneyed building burned to the ground, and it was replaced by a vigorous, unusual Gothic Revival building in 1859. The third and present courthouse built in Iowa City, designed by the Grand Rapids, Michigan, firm of Rush, Bowman and Company, was started in 1899 and finished one year later. The style selected was that of the Richardsonian Romanesque, somewhat calmed by references to the Ecole des Beaux-Arts. The large Richardsonian arched entrance is contained on each side by matching bay tow-

ers, while the rows of large, tall windows do open battle with the heavy rusticated masonry of the building. The courthouse's most picturesque element is its tall central tower, projecting turrets at each corner, and tall wall dormers that project into the steeply pitched hipped roof.

CE278 Clark House

1840, 1867. 319 S. Linn St.

The essential scheme of this two-story side-hall brick house is derived from the Federal/Greek Revival tradition; but its vertical proportions and its details are Italianate. A narrow porch runs across the first floor of the house; the entrance to the side has side lights and a transom. The roof of the house, with its returns on the gables, has paired brackets on both the eave and gable ends.

CE279 Bradley House

1881. 335 S. Clinton St.

A substantial example of the post-Civil War Italianate, this house is very late in fashion. The wide gable end facing the street boasts a round window within the gable. The cornice has the usual paired brackets and end returns on all of the gables. The roundheaded windows have been filled in at the top, and sometime after 1900 a heavy classical porch was added across the first-floor face of the house.

CE280 Musser House

1890. 715 College St.

Though the Musser house is large, it conveys an easygoing nonpretentious atmosphere. A wide porch encircles the corner bay tower, which on its third floor becomes a loggia. One immediately is aware of the thin balloon-frame construction of the building because of its surface of horizontal alternating bands of shingles and clapboard. In addition the clapboard bands are articulated by narrow, thin, vertical wood members.

CE281 Carson House

1875. 906 E. College St.

The Carson house presents a three-story French Second Empire design, with a central hall and a single low tower. Within the front porch, which runs across the front of the house, is a wonderfully overscaled arched entrance. The entrance, with its wide surround of stone, counters the domestic scale of the porch. This sense of grandness is carried over to the surrounds for the three front windows. Those to the side have concave frames surmounted by broad convex lintels. The center window seems to place its energy in its elaborate lintel complete with its own cornice.

CE282 **Lindsay House**

1893, attrib. George F. Barber. 935 E. College St.

The George F. Barber Company of Knoxville, Tennessee, published not only pattern books but also a magazine entitled *American Homes.* Both the numerous editions of Barber's *New Model Dwellings* and his magazine offered stock plans that could be purchased for a small sum. One design element that Barber seemed to be fond of was a heavy masonry chimney that extends from the corner along the front wall to encompass a large semicircular window. In addition to this feature, which is displayed in the Lindsay house, there are a number of typical delightful Barber touches in this exuberant Queen Anne design. At the entrance corner is a small extension of the porch which forms an open turreted pavilion; above, another porch, cut into the volume of the house, is set forward of a three-story octagonal tower. While the house has been remodeled and added to as apartments, it still has not lost its original liveliness as a "Victorian" design.

CE283 **Cornog House**

1922. 1155 E. Court St.

A Prairie-style house, one would assume, should match the horizontality of the land in its design, but as the Cornog house indicates, that is not always the case. Here one has a cubelike box, seemingly more vertical than horizontal. A thin, low-pitched hipped roof with extended eaves covers the stucco-sheathed box below. A band of wood starts at the soffit, goes down the wall, and then proceeds well under the first-floor windows; it then turns another 90-degree angle and returns to the roof soffit. An entrance porch with a nearly flat roof projects from the front of the house.

CE284 **Oakes (Grant Wood) House**

1858. 1142 E. Court St.

Nicholas Oakes, who had this house built, was a manufacturer of brick and tile, and his brick and tile yards were located just down the street to the south. His house has the format of a late Federal/Greek Revival design, but it was brought up-to-date with Italianate details: segmental arched windows and a bracketed gable roof. The house was purchased in 1936 by the painter Grant Wood, and he lived in the house until his death in 1942. Wood "restored" the house during his occupancy—which meant in part that he "Colonialized" it, to a degree. The brick walls of the two-story house are now contrasted with white painted wood trim, green shutters, and a requisite white picket fence.

CE285 Bloom House

1908, J. J. Hotz. 116 S. Dodge St.

When completed, the Bloom house was described as "purely Mission style, much like those residences so common in California"; but the design is in fact a variation of the Prairie school mode popularized by George W. Maher. A single two-story stucco sheathed wood-frame volume is covered by the usual broad hipped roof with a four-foot overhang. The entrance is on the side; facing the street is a pair of porches cut into the two-story volume. Below is a large living porch; above is a sleeping porch. The windows are of leaded glass, and within one will discover Craftsman detailing and art glass chandeliers.

CE286 Summit Apartments

1915, Parker N. Berry. 228 S. Summit St.

Parker N. Berry succeeded George Grant Elmslie in the Chicago office of Louis H. Sullivan in the years after 1909. Before opening his own office in 1917, Berry designed a few buildings on his own while working for Sullivan, one of which was the Summit Apartment building. A gifted designer in the Prairie mode, Berry died in 1918 at the age of thirty. The Summit Apartments were commissioned by Dr. Frank C. Titzell, who wished them to be as up-to-date and modern as possible. Berry provided a design in many ways identical to what could be found in and around Chicago. The plan was U-shaped, with the entrance within the "U." The four floors of 14 apartments of five rooms each were all well lighted by wide windows. Within they contained such amenities as Murphy beds and a built-in vacuum cleaner system. The most distinguishing feature of the exterior is the stuccoing of the walls, and the suggestion of pairs of engaged piers at ground level.

CE287 Reece House

1883. 415 S. Summit Ave.

As with several other houses in the city, the designer of this dwelling settled on the older Italianate style, but he slightly modernized it to bring it up into the 1880s. The center projecting pavilion has a wide, low-pitched roof, a form that seems almost to be Colonial Revival rather than Italianate. Thin horizontal windows have been injected within the entablature, and instead of brackets, the roof soffit is articulated by thick projecting rafter tails. Though there are paired wood piers on the porch running across the front of the house, the porch seems more in the Queen Anne style than the Italianate.

CE288 "The World's Smallest Grotto"

1946–1976, John Korbes. 520 S. Governor St.

Iowa City's contribution to America's folk follies was constructed over a period of some 30 years by a retired motel-keeper, John Korbes. The builder/designer started off with a tiny chapel, to which he later added a small-scale windmill, a "museum," a wishing well, a cross, and a podium upon which cement animals are corralled. He introduced electric lighting, often in unexpected locations, and fountains here and there. The surfaces of all of these concrete constructions were enriched with an unbelievable array of colorful objects, ranging from pieces of broken pottery to seashells and plastic objects of the 1950s and 1960s. As is so frequently the case with folk follies, "The World's Smallest Grotto" seems to be designed for the moment, not as an object meant to last decades or more. Korbes's grotto is slowly disintegrating, but this ruinlike quality only adds to its melancholy charm.

CE289 **Close House**

1874. 538 S. Gilbert St.

The Close "mansion" is Iowa City's largest remaining Italianate house. C. D. Close, who owned a linseed-oil mill to the west of the house, engaged the builder August Hazelhorst to construct this three-and-a-half-story brick dwelling. The style selected was the late Italianate, realized in this design with all of the richness one associates with this image during the post-Civil War years. A wide cornice/entablature with brackets and large scale band of dentils caps the house. Below, the windows have heavy projecting curved lintels of stone. On the first floor is a small make-believe canopied balcony with a miniature balustrade. On the other side of the entrance porch is a wide bay with its own bracketed cornice. Large round windows originally occupied each of the third-floor gable ends. Within, the central stair hall is open all the way to the cupola. The house has recently been extensively and carefully restored, and is now used for offices.

CE290 **Burkley House** (Ardenia)

c. 1926. 925 E. Kirkwood Ave.

Though decidedly large in scale, and perhaps conceived as a serious work of architecture, Ardenia should still be considered as another of Iowa's folk follies. The hotel owner, Albert Burkley, took a mildly Italianate house of 1855 and enclosed it within the towering brick walls of a medieval castle. Thin towers together with adjacent crenellated parapets look down on brick walls articulated by narrow windows and various diamond-shaped and rectangular inlaid patterns. At the south side of the building Burkley decided for some reason to go off in a different direction, and he added a wing that is in the respectable Colonial Revival style, not medieval. Currently, the heavy overgrown vegetation around the building enhances the house, for the structure appears from a distance as a medieval ruin.

CE291 **Crum House**

1866–1867. 1110 E. Kirkwood

This high "Victorian" Italianate house seems to pose as a country house. It is a large cube

CE291 Crum House

with a rear two-story dependency, and it displays a roofscape of chimneys as well as a central widow's walk with a balustrade. The heavy brackets of the roof are accentuated by drop finials. A large scale tripartite round-headed window appears on the front, directly over the lower, equally broad arched entrance door; and exaggerated quoins define the edges of the building. The house was built for a prosperous Iowa City meatpacker.

CE292 **Lucas House** (Plum Grove)

1844. 1030 Carroll St., south of Kirkwood Ave.

Robert Lucas was the first territorial governor of Iowa. He modeled his 1844 house, built on some 80 acres south of Iowa City, on his earlier house, Friendly Grove, in Ohio, where he had served two terms as governor. Plum Grove, a 30-by-30-foot two-story gable-roofed brick house, is a classic example of the Federal architectural tradition continuing with almost no change right down to the middle of the nineteenth century. The gabled end of the building forms its front, and the entrance is off to one side. Other than the slight returns of the roof eaves, a round window within the gable end, and a transom light over the entrance door, the front is plain and undecorated. Within the house and its one-story wing to the rear are seven rooms: four on the first floor, three above. Each of these rooms has its own fireplace. Restoration of the house began in 1940, and was completed in 1946. The furnished house is now open to the public.

CE293 Lustron Houses

1949–1951

There are six Lustron houses in Iowa City, and one in Coralville (CE321). All of them were built between 1949 and 1952. The Iowa City examples are: the Bartley house (1950), a gray model with an attached garage at 1815 East Court Street; the Witterman house (1950), another gray model, at 627 Third Avenue; the Graham house (1951), at 705 Clark Street, a green version; the Spriestersbach house (1951), a gray house at 709 Clark Street; the McGuire house (1949), a house with a yellow exterior, at 805 Melrose Avenue; and the Mickey house (1950), another gray Lustron house at 29 Prospect Place.

CE294 Parker House

1939, Howard F. Moffitt. 1302 Ginter Ave.

The designer/builder Howard F. Moffitt is best known for his romantically charming medieval houses. In the Parker house he looked to California's Monterey Revival—a style that was popular throughout the country in the 1930s. As with examples of this style in California and elsewhere (in Florida and Louisiana it was referred to as "Caribbean Georgian"), Moffitt has both Colonialized and Modernized the original nineteenth-century California style. Moffitt's fondness for miniaturizing is present even here, for the Parker dwelling is not at all as large as it seems from a distance. This house, like most of those of Moffitt, was built as a spec house, and George F. Parker was the first owner.

CE295 Moffitt Houses

c. 1931–1949, Howard F. Moffitt

Howard F. Moffitt entered into the contracting and real-estate business in the early 1930s. His interest and obvious delight was to build tiny single-family houses as wonderful little Hansel and Gretel cottages. The enlarged dollhouse forms of Moffitt's cottages represent a building type that came to the fore across the country in the decades of the 1920s and on into the depression years of the 1930s. The largest contingent of these fairy-tale dwellings is found in California, especially in and around Carmel and Berkeley. Moffitt's versions of this type can easily hold their own with examples from California and elsewhere. In the decades after World War II these dollhouselike Moffitt cottages were much out of fashion, but now they are much admired and sought after.

These cottages are scattered around Iowa City, apparently wherever Moffitt could locate and purchase property, and were built on speculation. In and around Friendly Avenue and Pickard Street there are so many of his houses that the neighborhood has become known as "Moffitt Hollow." The storybook quality of these designs was created not only by their small size, but in the way Moffitt played with roofs, bringing them almost down to the ground, and interrupting them with wall dormers and bays. He had a fondness for playing off normally scaled elements—a door, a bay, a large chimney—against the small scale of the building and the other details. Although all of these houses are charming, they are nonetheless functionally designed, with attached garages, good internal circulation, and main living spaces that often open out onto garden terraces.

These houses can be found at the following addresses (their dates are given in parenthe-

CE295A Spec house, 1941

CE295B Stoltz House

ses; otherwise unidentifiable houses are labeled as "spec houses"): spec house (1941), 1322 Muscatine Avenue; spec house (1942), 1324 Muscatine Avenue; spec house (1940), 1326 Muscatine Avenue; spec house (1940), 1328 Muscatine Avenue; spec house (1939), 1330 Muscatine Avenue; Stoltz house (1943), 1215 Pickard Street; Pontius house (1941), 1217 Pickard Street; spec house (1934), 1213 Yewell Street; spec house (1937), 1215 Yewell Street; spec house (1937), 1217 Yewell Street; Miller house (1940), 1326 Yewell Street; Anderson house (1943), 1202 Friendly Avenue; Weatherly house (1940), 1217 Friendly Avenue; Engle house (1941), 1218 Friendly Avenue; Gray house (1932), 837 Kirkwood Avenue; spec house (1938), 431 Rundell Street.

IOWA CITY, UNIVERSITY OF IOWA

The University of Iowa was founded in 1847. Ten years later, when the state capital was moved to Des Moines, the 1840 capitol build-

ing and its plat of land were given to the university. By the mid-1870s the university campus had acquired several additional buildings; the two largest (in the Italianate mode) were situated to each side of the Old Capitol building. At the end of the 1890s, with the impact of the World's Columbian Exposition of 1893 before them, university officials turned to the Ecole des Beaux-Arts for a new, up-to-date image. In 1898 the Des Moines firm of Proudfoot and Bird won a limited competition for Schaeffer Hall, which was to be one of four Beaux-Arts buildings to be arranged around the Old Capitol building.

Between 1902 and 1924, four buildings—Schaeffer Hall (1902), McBride Hall (1908), MacLean Hall (1912), and Jessup Hall (1924), all by Proudfoot and Bird, or Proudfoot, Bird and Rawson after 1910—were sited in a balanced composition with the Old Capitol building as the centerpiece. An impressive series of terraces with balustrades and stairs leading down toward the river was added in 1922 at the time of the restoration of the Old Capitol building. This "acropolis," referred to as the Pentacrest, was conceived of as the symbolic center of the new campus. The Beaux-Arts imagery was effectively carried over into the three-arched concrete bridge (1916; rebuilt, 1988) to carry Iowa Avenue over the river, thus connecting the east and west campuses of the university. Slowly the university expanded north and south along the river, east into the town center, and to the west bank of the river. Up through the 1920s almost all of the buildings were designed in a version of the Beaux-Arts style by Proudfoot and Bird (and their successor firms). The one notable exception was the University Hospital building (1929), which was designed in the "English Gothic style."

In the early 1930s a 30-acre strip of land along the west bank of the river was reclaimed, and this became the site for three buildings (a music building, a dramatic arts building, and a museum and arts building) which were to make up a fine-arts campus.

As with almost all of America's state universities, the University of Iowa experienced a rapid growth in acreage and in the number of new buildings after World War II. With the triumph of Modernism, the older Beaux-Arts image—both in campus planning and in architectural design—was dropped. It was replaced by aggressive noncontextualism, coupled with the image of utilitarian practicality.

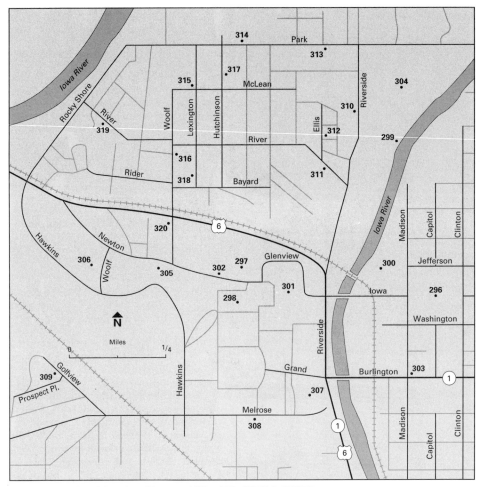

Inset 3, Iowa City, University of Iowa and West Side (CE296–CE320)

This utilitarian quality was reflected not only in the buildings but in the general lack of vision pertaining to open spaces and landscape architecture.

A critic once commented that if one wishes to see the worst architecture within a city or on a university campus, then one should immediately look for a post-World War II hospital and/or medical school. The University of Iowa's medical school provides no exception to this adage.

The most recent years have signaled an appreciable shift in the attitude of the university toward its own environment, and in its relationship to its host city. Historic preservation and restoration (with the crowning achievement of the restoration of the Old

Capital building in mind), a new concern for planning and landscape architecture, and an increased desire to engage prominent local and national architects to design the new buildings (the most recent instance being the 1988 engagement of Frank O. Gehry to design the Laser Science and Engineering Center) have characterized the university's approach during the 1970s and 1980s. Construction on the Gehry building, supposedly modeled after a collection of farm buildings, began in the fall of 1990.

CE296 Old State Capitol Building

1840–1842, John F. Rague. Capitol St., between Washington and Jefferson streets

The Iowa State Capitol building of 1840–1842 and the Illinois State Capitol of 1837–1841 in Springfield were two of America's major monuments of the Greek Revival. In his 1944 volume *Greek Revival Architecture in America,* Talbot Hamlin called the Iowa capitol building "a simple but excellently designed building."[32] Both capitols were designed by a fascinating figure, John Francis Rague.[33] This architect had been trained in New York in the office of Minard Lefever before leaving for the Midwest in the early 1830s. After trying his hand at a number of activities, Rague turned to architectural practice when he was selected to design and supervise the Illinois State Capitol building. In Iowa, Rague obtained the commission to design and build the new capitol building from the Capitol Site Commission, and he went to Iowa City in 1839 to begin work.

It has been asserted over the years (history as myth, history as fact) that Rague almost immediately ran into problems with one of the commissioners, Chauncy Swan, who is said to have had his own ideas for the design of the new building. It has been conjectured that what Swan may have had in mind was depicted in the 1839 site plan for Iowa City (though in fact this drawing of a building may have been devised by the printer of the map). The building portrayed on the map was a rectangular structure, lined on the front with a row of Corinthian columns (whether freestanding or engaged is not clear); an open two-tiered lantern occupied the center of a flat roof; and on each side were two low pointed domes, which one assumes would have covered the two legislative chambers. This design was indeed amateurish in many

ways, but nonetheless it was intriguing to see such a proposed return to an eighteenth-century image. The design depicted can be looked upon either as an image considerably behind the time in fashion, or as an almost futuristic anticipation of the coming revival of Colonial architecture.

The question of who was responsible for this little elevation drawing, and whether it was ever taken seriously, has been debated for many years. Did it represent what Swan felt should be the design, or was it simply a diminutive "ornament" added to the 1839 map by its Saint Louis publisher?[34] Added to this "mystery" is the possible participation of Father Samuel Charles Mazzuchelli (another historical conjecture), who was in Dubuque when Rague received the commission.

It was Rague's design that was built, but before it was finished the architect had resigned and left Iowa City, and the final construction of the building was left in Chauncy Swan's hands.

Since Rague's plans have not survived, it is difficult to understand fully what changes were made by Swan in furthering the construction of the building. The substitution of a lantern tower for a column-wrapped drum and dome was possibly his idea, as was perhaps the elimination of the traditional triglyphs within the entablature. The lantern tower, a paramount element in buildings rendered in the 1839 map, was a remembrance of similar towers found on eighteenth-century Colonial buildings, such as Independence Hall in Philadelphia. As mentioned above, the inclusion of it here in the 1840s can be seen not only as a stylistic retrogression, but also as an anticipation of the Colonial Revival which was to come into being several decades later, in the late 1870s.

The plan of the Iowa State Capitol was a traditional one with offices and a room for the Supreme Court on the ground level; above, the two legislative chambers were separated by a domed central hall. Within the hall, between four Corinthian columns, is a dramatic freestanding spiral staircase. The interior of the capitol building, especially if compared to that at Springfield, is plain, even puritanical, due one suspects to the fact that with the move of the legislature to Des Moines the building was never finished.

The Iowa capitol building was constructed of a warm, somewhat yellowish local limestone; the Doric columns on the east and west porticoes are of painted wood; and the interior walls are covered with a lime plaster. Compared to the Illinois building, that at Iowa City is not as "correct" or sophisticated; but its smaller size, its hilltop location, and its "incorrect" proportions bring a charm and delight to it, which is not conveyed in Rague's earlier building at Springfield.

After its initial use for the territorial legislature and then the state legislature, the building was given to the University of Iowa. The university has utilized the building since that time. While a number of internal changes were made in the building by the university, the exterior has remained basically intact. During the years 1921–1923 the west portico was finally added to the building. But it was in the 1970s that an extensive restoration of the capitol building was begun under the direction of Margaret N. Keyes.[35] The goal of the restoration, in the manner of the nineteenth-century French restorer and scholar Eugene Viollet-le-Duc, was to bring the building back to a specific moment in time, in this instance to the mid-1840s when it was used as the state capitol. This restoration was successfully carried out, and the furnished building was reopened to the public in 1976.

CE297 University Psychopathic Hospital

1920–1921, Proudfoot, Bird and Rawson. Newton Rd.

Medicine and the medieval architectural image were closely associated in the teens and on through the 1920s. This complex of low buildings (one to two and a half stories) has the feeling of a Tudor Revival university dormitory rather than a hospital. The brick and sandstone-trim building seems to meander informally over its site. The late medieval details—pointed arched openings; tall, narrow chimneys; step roofs with dormers—together with its well-landscaped site, pose a fine example of the early-1920s Tudor Revival.

CE298 University Hospital

1928, Proudfoot, Bird and Rawson. later additions. Newton Rd.

The architects of the university hospital selected the English Gothic for their theme, and expressed it in a 145-foot-high stone and brick tower. With the visual chaos of post-World War II additions to the hospital complex, the tower and what is left of the lower wings are quite difficult to find, let alone to see. But they are there, perhaps best observed from atop the hospital parking structure number 1.

CE299 Lagoon Boat and Shelter House

1938. East of N. Riverside Dr., between the music and theater buildings

A thirties rustic WPA recreation pavilion is given the image of a suburban house. The rough stone building has low earth-hugging roofs, a deep stone porch, and an oversized chimney. As is usual for recreational park architecture of the 1920s and 1930s, this example is beautifully proportioned and carefully detailed.

CE300 Danforth Chapel

1952, George Horner. West end of Jefferson St., west of Madison St.

This small brick chapel was based on a mid-nineteenth-century example, described in the dedication brochure (January 11, 1953) as "an exact replica of Saint John's Methodist Episcopal Church, Johnson County, 1874." While some of the detailing is Gothic—pointed windows and the thin tower and roof—the flavor is that of the late Colonial Revival; it has the best of both worlds.

CE301 Bowen Science Building

1970–1972, Skidmore, Owings and Merrill (Chicago office, Walter Netsch). Newton Rd.

This building and two others designed by Walter Netsch on the University of Iowa campus are supposedly an application of a design concept that was in fashion in the late 1960s and early 1970s. This was labeled "Field Theory," which entailed, as Netsch commented, "an ordering device, a way of looking at things."[36] This way of looking at things was to impose a geometric pattern, an "environmental module," on the building. In the Bowen Science Building Netsch played a fascinating game with superimposing rotating squares against octagonal shapes. The horizontal and vertical columns and their accompanying lintels are openly revealed, and brick-framed, deeply set windows and doors are used as infills.

CE302 Harding Library for the Health Sciences

1972–1973, Skidmore, Owings and Merrill (Chicago office, Walter Netsch). Newton Rd.

The architect's fascination with geometry becomes even more complex in this building, with angled and vertical triangles soaring off in one direction or another.

CE303 Lindquist Center (Educational Research Building)

1972, Skidmore, Owings and Merrill (Chicago office, Walter Netsch). Northeast corner of Madison and Burlington streets

This is a calmer version of the Field Theory, still composed of squares and octagons. Angled bays project from the walls, and are attached to the surface of the walls by identical brick surfaces and by thin horizontal bands of glass. The third floor is dramatically suspended two floors above the entry, and it is supported by a row of tall concrete tubular columns.

CE304 Hancher Auditorium

1972, Charles Herbert and Associates. N. Riverside Dr., south of Park Rd.

Located on reclaimed river land, Hancher Auditorium is the center of the Fine Arts campus. In addition to the auditorium, two other components of the complex are Clapp Recital Hall and the Music Building. The overscaled design in concrete with a cantilevered glass prow sums up what was conceived of as Modern at the end of the 1960s, and on into the early 1970s.

CE305 Dental Science Building

1972–1973, Smith, Hinchman and Grylls. Newton Rd.

Two exposed concrete masses are joined by a connector of light glass and metal. Entrance is gained via a steel bridge set above a slanted apron and stairs leading to the lowest level.

In the fashion of Louis I. Kahn's work of the 1950s and 1960s, the venting occurs within concrete vertical projecting roof modules (frequently treated as cantilevered bays).

CE306 Carver-Hawkeye Arena

1980–1982, CRS/The Durrant Group. Woolf Ave. near Hawkins Dr.

From a distance, and as one approaches this arena, one is aware of a low steel truss system supporting the roof. A curved, cantilevered metal band defines the edge of the roof; below this is another band, in this case of glass bricks. Most of the actual arena is sunk into the ground within a natural ravine. The curved, undulating walls of glass brick are arranged to lead one to various entrances. Within, one comes upon an oval arena with a clearspan of 300 by 340 feet. One can gain some idea of the size of this space in knowing that there are 13,200 fixed seats, and another 2,000 movable seats can be added. It all works best at night, with the glass block walls seeming to meander around the perimeter, and the low roof suspended above.

CE307 Boyd Law Building

1985–1986, Gunnar Birkerts and Associates. Grand Ave., north of S. Riverside Dr.

Here is another example of the University of Iowa's homage to the purity of geometry—in this case the circular drum. Birkerts is quoted as saying that he selected this self-contained form as an expression of "perfection, clarity, integrity, and geometric purity";[37] all of this, of course, has a ring of the late eighteenth-century French architect and theorist Etienne-

CE307B University of Iowa, Boyd Law Building

Louis Boullee, or of Le Corbusier in his *Towards a New Architecture* (1922). Birkerts has taken the five-level cylinder and then proceeded to cut into it in various ways. As is usually the case when one designs a circular building, the architect ends up trying to fit rectangular spaces within curved spaces, with, as one would expect, mixed results. Much of the building is sheathed in silver-colored aluminum, including a centerpiece of a small dome that tops the building. The rationale cited for the dome is that it mirrors the Old Capitol building's dome across the river. Much of the law building seems to be a well-detailed high-tech design of the 1980s; other spaces and exterior forms have the quality of science fiction about them.

IOWA CITY, WEST SIDE

CE308 **Pratt House**

1885. 503 Melrose Ave.

This brick Italianate house with a wide gable roof was built like a number of others in Iowa City, but much too late. Paired brackets support the gable and eave overhang of the low-pitched roof. The voussoirs and the keystone of the arched windows are accentuated in light-colored stone. Sometime in the early 1900s a substantial Colonial Revival porch with Ionic columns was added to the house. Other additions have also been made, but it all holds together very well.

CE309 **Koser House**

1929. 305 Golfview Ave.

Projecting out from the surrounding foliage is a pair of steeply pitched gables that almost droop down to the ground. Between them is a segmental arched entrance with a center

arched door flanked by small arched side windows. Though the dwelling is reasonable in size, it conveys a near-perfect picture of an enlarged fairy-tale cottage. Stylistically, it is medieval—more English than anything else.

CE310 **Theta Xi** (now Alpha Epsilon Pi) Fraternity House

1928–1929, Charles Altfillisch. 339 N. Riverside Dr.

A romantic 1920s period revival cottage serves as a fraternity house. Its small tower with a conical roof, its steeply pitched hipped roof and thin towering chimneys refer to the French Norman tradition as it was interpreted in this decade. Sunlight catches the wall surface of the segmental arched porch, leaving the deep interior of the porch almost black; above, the roof displays both cut-in recessed dormers and small semicircular eye dormers.

CE311 **Alpha Sigma Phi (now Phi Beta Pi) Fraternity House**

1929, 109 River St.

The Italian Mediterranean style of the twenties is displayed in a composition made up of a three-story building with projecting arched walls at each end. The building has a hipped roof.

CE312 **Delta Upsilon Fraternity House**

1929. 320 Ellis Ave.

The American eighteenth-century Georgian style is revived here in stone. A dignified two-story porch with a flat roof bearing a balustrade runs across the entire front of the building. There is another balustrade on the top of the main roof, set between pairs of chimneys that project above the end-wall gables.

CE313 **Hutchinson House**

1843, 1927. 119 Park Rd.

The limestone blocks used for the walls of this one-and-a-half-story mid-nineteenth-century stone cottage were supposedly rejects from the state capitol building then under construction. The house was built by Robert Hutchinson, a carpenter and its probable designer. A balanced arrangement of paired windows focuses on a central door with its transom light. The house was "Colonialized" by the addition of three gabled wall dormers on its street facade during an extensive re-modeling carried out in 1927 by the architect Mark Anthony for Professor E. P. Kuhl of the University of Iowa. Besides adding the dormers, Anthony raised the roof, added a second floor, and made many changes to the interior. At a distance, the house has all the appearance of a typical Colonial Revival dwelling of the late 1920s or early 1930s.

CE314 Patton House

1937–1938, Henry L. Fisk. 524 Park Rd.

Often, as in the case of this suburban house, architects in the twenties and thirties looked to the French Norman farmhouse for precedent and then loosened it up and spread its forms over the site. The center of this composition is an almost square central block covered by a steeply pitched hipped roof. Projecting from it in various directions are a round tower and a series of low one-story wings. Facing the public road there is a double garage with a gable roof, alongside of which is a low-walled entrance courtyard. The building is sheathed in stone, brick, and unpainted clapboard.

CE315 Smith House

1935, J. Bradley Rust. 708 McLean St.

The small, more formal French country house (generally referred to as French Provincial) came into popularity in America at the end of the 1930s. Its balanced, classical composition related it to the English Regency as well as to the American Colonial Revival. In this brick two-story dwelling the Iowa City architect J. Bradley Rust let the wall dormers break

CE315 Smith House

into the roof with segmented curved roofs. He centered attention on the front entrance with its double doors, accompanied above by wide French doors leading onto a small balcony with a metal balustrade. The brick walls have been painted with a light wash to enhance the appearance of age.

CE316 Tester House

1931, Tinsley, McBroom and Higgins. 228 Woolf Ave.

The illusion of age created in the design of period revival houses of the 1920s and 1930s fascinated both architects and clients during these years. Here in a classic English Colonial Revival house, the building and its detailing have been rendered in brick, the brick has then been painted, and finally parts of the paint have been weathered off. Unusual details of this two-story house are the use of brick around the entrance, the quoining at the corners, the large stair window above the entrance, and the round windows in the gable ends.

CE317 Koelbel House

1941, J. Bradley Rust. 416 Hutchinson Ave.

The Streamline Moderne forms of the Koelbel house are clothed in clapboard and red brick. The curved bay of the living room is of brick, which connects to the brick chimney. Other essential ingredients of the style are present: flat roofs; corner windows; curved, thin slab roofs; and a horizontal band carried around the building, separating the first and second floors. The house is currently painted appropriately in shades of dark and light green, with white trim.

CE318 Davis House

1930, Henry L. Fisk. 215 Lexington Ave.

The architect provided a one-and-a-half-story brick-sheathed Tudor cottage for his client. A single steeply pitched gable with half-timbering and brick infill faces the street. The roof of this gable changes pitch on the left side, assuming a gentle curve. Various types of dormers with hipped or flat roofs project from the main roof of the dwelling. Though of reasonable size, the house reads as a small, modest cottage.

CE319 Birch House

1966–1969, Crites and McConnell. 1005 River St.

After turning a bend in the suburban road, one comes across this modernist house of the late 1960s. A two-story wooden box hovers over its hillside site, supported by linear walls of concrete block. On a lower level is a porch/deck; below this is the carport. The street front displays dramatic projecting balconies, held in on each side by thin, concrete-block walls. Another Crites and McConnell house in Iowa City is the Kitzman House (1965), located at 12 Longview Knolls. This house has been placed on concrete piers, is sheathed in grooved plywood, and has a two-story screened deck.

CE320 Woolf Avenue Court Apartments

1939. 25–31 Woolf Ave., off N. Newton Rd.

Five white stucco boxes housing ten units constitute this Streamline Moderne residential court. Each of the boxes contains two dwelling-units, each of which is of two floors. The principal windows are metal casement corner windows, and a thin projecting slab serves as a roof over the two entrances below. Two insistent horizontal bands wrap around the building. The higher of these occurs around the top of the parapet; the second band composed of four lines has been placed between the first- and second-floor windows. The apartments were acquired in 1964 by the University of Iowa, and are now used for faculty and staff housing.

CE321 Lustron House

c. 1950. 708 11th Ave., Coralville

This gray Lustron house was built for John Drew. There are in addition to this one, six other Lustron houses in Iowa City (CE293).

CE322 A "Long" Barn

c. 1875. Take US 6, southeast of Iowa City; turn left (east) one block southeast of Scott Blvd. intersection; travel .7 miles, barn is on south side of road

This is a long board-and-batten basilica-plan barn. There is a gable over its entrance at the center of one of the side aisles. A degree of elegance is added by a window with pediment (accompanied on each side by rectangular louvered vents) placed within each of the high "nave" gables.

CE323 Secrest Round Barn

1883, George Frank Longerbeam. US 6, southeast of Iowa City; turn left (east) one block southeast of Scott Blvd. intersection, travel 5 miles; turn right (south), travel 1 mile; turn left (east), .8 miles; barn is within grove of trees on north side of road, west of small community of Downey

This octagonal barn, 80 feet in diameter, is of the basement type. The barn is covered by a gracefully shaped bell-form roof, and at its crown is a small venting cupola with its own miniature bell-shaped roof. At the time the barn was built, the editors of a local newspaper commented that "it will be the largest building of its kind in the county," containing "stable room for thirty-two horses and sixteen cows, room for two hundred tons of hay, and furnished with all the modern improvements."[38]

Keota

At the western edge of Keota, turn off of Iowa 77 onto route W15; travel 1 mile north on W15, then west .5 miles on the gravel road. There one will discover a large Colonial Revival dwelling of 1917–1918, the S. Omar Singmaster house, center of the extensive Singmaster Farm. The two-story house mixes late Queen Anne and Craftsman details with its basic Colonial image. The symmetry of the entrance front is broken by the projection of a second-floor bay to one side; the low-gabled roof dormers have a Colonial flavor, but the band of two windows within each dormer is Craftsman in spirit.

Keystone

The tiny town of Keystone possesses a really fine building in the Bank of Keystone (c. 1910), located on Main Street between Railroad and First streets. The designer of this little building would seem to have been aware of the Beaux-Arts revival of English and American Georgian architecture that took place at the turn of the century (in this country it is encountered most frequently in and around Philadelphia). The Keystone Bank building presents facades that are almost like rectangular pieces of cardboard upon which lines have been drawn and into which openings have been cut. The left side has two windows contained within a "pasted-on" gable supported by a pair of pilasters. To the right, the entrance has a small circular window above the door. This is outlined by the suggestion of a curved pediment; an overly large keystone projects from the top of the circular window through the suggested pediment. Everything is really very sophisticated and well handled.

Knoxville

In 1845 appointed commissioners selected the centrally located site of Knoxville for the future seat of Marion County. The usual grid was platted and the sale of lots was held later that year and again in 1846. The railroad was late in reaching the community, but by the end of the century the Chicago, Burlington, and Quincy railroad ran through, and a spur line from the east provided a connection with the Rock Island and Pacific Railroad. The land around Knoxville is agriculturally rich, and for a time, coal mining was important to the economy of the county.

CE324 **Marion County Courthouse**

1896, Mifflin E. Bell. Courthouse Square, northeast corner of Robinson and 2nd streets

The first courthouse was a wood frame two-story building erected during 1846–1848. The second Marion County Courthouse was designed by D. H. Young and was built in 1858. That courthouse was one of Iowa's outstanding examples of the Greek Revival mode. All of the walls of that two-story brick building were articulated with wide pilasters reaching from the ground to the entablature. The recessed entrance exhibited small pilasters and Doric columns. At the center of the gable roof was an open square tower. By 1895 this second courthouse was considered to be structurally unsafe, and the following year it was replaced by the present building.

The architect Mifflin E. Bell of Chicago selected the popular Richardsonian Romanesque for the third courthouse. The structure is three stories tall, plus an attic. The central tower, with arched openings for the bells and the heavy round corner buttress of its base, is a particularly strong example of the style. The architectural treatment of the body of the building and its roof carries one over just a bit into the French Châteauesque style. Some restoration of the building took place in 1968.

CE325 United States Post Office Building

1939, Louis A. Simon and Neal Melick. 201 E. Marion St.

A rectangular block is here relieved by a face of flat, wide pilasters, and by a central arch housing a well-detailed Colonial Revival entrance. The white cornice effectively holds the building in place, and it is matched by the horizontal band of Kasota stone just above the basement windows. Other details like the small eagle perched above the entrance and the single-stem metal lights by the exterior stairs help to relieve the basic somberness of the design.

CE326 House

c. 1878. 713 Robinson St.

Three gables of this richly detailed wooden Eastlake-style dwelling look out upon the street. The stepped roof of the main gables and the three gables to the front have cut-out patterned bargeboards. Do not miss the V-shaped bay window at the right side of the house, with its raised and recessed panels, its decorated "skirt" flowing from its eaves, and

the pair of tall finials. The present porch is the result of a Craftsman remodeling, c. 1910.

CE327 First Methodist Episcopal Church (now United Methodist Church)

1895–1896. Northwest corner of S. 4th and E. Montgomery streets

The architect of this impressive church building would seem to have started out taking Henry Hobson Richardson and his version of the Romanesque quite seriously. There are features about the gable end and its low and high flanking towers that have some points of similarity to Richardson's Brattle Square Church (1870–1872) in Boston. But having paid this homage, the architect turned to the Gothic Revival tradition of the late nineteenth century for his corner entry tower and its spired roof. Although the medievalism encompassed in this church runs from the Romanesque to the Gothic, the building does end up seemingly of one piece—a remarkable feat.

CE328 Marion County Park

West edge of Knoxville

Next to the Marion County Historical Society building (1969) are several historic buildings and structures that have been brought to the site. Among these are the Pleasant Ridge Schoolhouse of 1874; the late nineteenth-century Valley Church building; the Chicago, Burlington, and Quincy Railroad Station from Donnely; the reconstruction of a nineteenth-century log cabin from a location near Pleasantville; and the Marysville Covered Bridge. The Marysville bridge was originally built 3.5 miles north of Dallas in 1891. In 1926 the bridge was taken apart and reconstructed over South Cedar Creek, south of Marysville. In 1968 it was dismantled and divided in two, with one 40-foot section going to Marion County Park, the other to the park at Pella. The Town truss wood bridge is covered by a single gable roof.

Ladora

Just north of Big Bear Creek and 5 miles south of the Iowa River is the small railroad town of Ladora. In addition to housing a number of grain elevators, it also contains a picture-postcard example of architecture of the Beaux-Arts

Classical tradition in the late teens and early 1920s. This is the Ladora Savings Bank building on the north side of Main Street, designed c. 1921 by C. B. Zalesby. He provided the bank with a temple form in antis and an entrance defined by a pair of fluted Roman Doric columns. These columns support a wide entablature with guttae and a suggestion of triglyphs. Above this is a substantial false cornice. Adding dignity and authority to the building is the slight hint that it is on an elevated podium with a flight of stone stairs leading up to the entrance. The building is of brick with limestone for its extensive trim, including the large horizontal name plate of the building projecting above the surrounding parapet walls. Since the building is freestanding, with a raised lawn on three sides, the architect has carried his entablature and cornice around three sides of the building.

LeGrand

Two and a half miles east of LeGrand on US 30 (the Lincoln Highway), at the southwest corner of its junction with route T74, is a romantic, deserted farmhouse. This two-story clapboard dwelling is a near-perfect example of the continuous employment of the Federal/Greek image on into the 1860s. The house exhibits a classic sidelighted door, with a projecting entablature/cornice above; the fenestration on the front and on the ends is perfectly balanced. There are chimneys within the two end gables of the house, and to the rear is a two-story wing.

Lynnville

The Skunk River provided water power for a number of the early mills of the 1840s and 1850s. The Wagaman Mill (Lynnville Mill) was the first mill in Jasper County, and it is one of the few still standing. It is situated on the south side of the North Skunk River (north end of East Street, across the North Skunk River). The original mill building was a structure with a steeply pitched gable roof and was two-and-a-half stories high. The entrance facade of this clapboard-sheathed building contains a symmetrical layout of windows and doors; the wide entrance door has narrow windows to each side, and above is an elongated double-hung window. Over the years a tower with a gable roof, a service area with a shed roof, and other additions have been made to the building. In 1868 the mill was converted to hydraulic turbines, and it was remodeled again in 1918–1919. Originally it ground flour and later feed grain; finally, it generated electric power.

Malcom

In addition to having a really fine, well-preserved group of two-story nineteenth-century commercial blocks on its main street (US 63), the town possesses a dwelling with one of the most extravagant oriel bays to be found in the state. This is on the clapboard and wood-trimmed P. P. Raymond house of 1874, located opposite the northeast corner of the town square (off US 63). The Raymond house is a three-story French Second Empire dwelling that exhibits some Eastlake detailing. There are a number of two-story bays on the house, but the great bay is one that dramatically projects out from the corner of the two-story wing. The bay is supported by a curved corbeling, and is surmounted by its own abbreviated mansard roof.

Marengo

The site for the future seat of Iowa County was selected in 1845. The town site was then surveyed and lots were put on sale in October of the following year. The location of the town plat was in a section of open prairie just south of the Iowa River, east of its confluence with Big Bear Creek. Andreas noted in 1875, "The Town is built around a public square, three hundred feet on each side, which is enclosed with a good fence, and set with a variety of shade trees, including numerous evergreens."[39] Some twelve years after its founding, in 1857, the Rock Island and Pacific Railroad arrived at Marengo. The town's first great period of growth was in the years immediately after the end of the Civil War when 150 dwellings were built between 1865 and 1866. In the 1920s Marengo became a stopping point on the east west US 6. With the construction of Interstate 80, 8 miles south, the town is now off the normal travel route.

CE329 Iowa County Courthouse

1892–1893, Foster and Liebbe. Southwest corner of Court Ave. and Hilton St.

Three successive county courthouses were located off the public square. The first of these, a one-room log building, was built in 1847. It was replaced by a permanent stone building in 1850. This in turn was supplanted by a brick structure in 1861–1862. The present and fourth courthouse was sited upon the square that Andreas had mentioned in 1875. This Romanesque Revival building is sheathed in hard Beria stone and it is dominated by a 137-foot-high entrance tower. The upper portion of the tower consists of a high two-story octagonal lantern with finials projecting above each corner of the parapet. A four-sided spire with a steep roof crowns the tower. The designers of the building, the Des Moines firm of Foster and Liebbe, provided the usual balanced composition of slightly projecting pavilions on each side of the tower. The lateral aspect of each of these pavilions is in turn broken by a slightly projecting gable bay.

While there are a few trees on the public square today, it bears little resemblance to the forested park commented on by Andreas.

CE330 People's Savings Bank Building

c. 1917. Northwest corner of Court Ave, and Hilton St.

A corner bank building appears as a Greek temple with columns in antis. Two Ionic columns are placed close to the adjacent projecting walls, which are articulated with deep-set horizontal joints. The brightness of its light-colored limestone sheathing, together with its size and height, conveys a sense of the importance of this institution for the community.

CE331 Lustron House

c. 1950. Northwest corner of Court Ave. and Randolph St.

This model Lustron house has a side entry.

CE332 **Marengo Cemetery**

1875, later. Corner of US 6 and Iowa 82

In addition to a nineteenth-century monument to Civil War soldiers, the cemetery contains a large Egyptian-style mausoleum. The center of this building has been projected forward to form a pylonlike entrance. Within this pylon gate are two columns in antis; above, sculptured in stone, is the usual winged motif.

CE333 **Pioneer Heritage Museum**

Southwest corner of Marion St. and Wallace Ave.

The historic buildings within the park include: the 1856 Henrich Meyer one-room log cabin; the Rock Island Depot of 1861 from the nearby town of Victor; and the Gritter Schoolhouse (c. 1875), which was located near Millersburg, south of Marengo.

CE334 **Plagmann True-Round Barn**

1912. South of Marengo on route V66, 5 miles; turn left (east) on gravel road

The size of this barn, some 100 feet in diameter, makes it one of the largest hollow-tile barns in the state. Terracotta hollow tile was looked upon in the years 1900 through the early 1920s as one of the new modern materials of the century. Generally in utilitarian buildings such as this barn, the tile was left unstuccoed both internally and externally. The roof is composed of two different slopes, and at the center is a small metal venting cupola. The structure is built around a central silo 16 feet in diameter. The stalls are at ground level, with a basement below and a hayloft above.

Marion

Marion has been, to a considerable extent, absorbed within the urban area of Cedar Rapids, its larger neighbor to the southwest. Located on Indian Creek, Marion started out both as the county seat in 1839 and as the site for water-powered mills; later it served as a division point for several railways. Andreas in his 1875 *Illustrated Historic Atlas of the State of Iowa* suggests a picture of the city which still holds true today, calling it "beautifully located in what appears to be an archipelago of groves, or forest-bound prairie, interspersed with fine residences, stores, churches."[40] Many of the dwellings still remain, but such major buildings as the stone Linn County Courthouse (1855) and the tall cupola-topped masonry schoolhouse (1869) are now gone.

CE335 **House**

c. 1872. Northwest corner of 6th Ave. and 10th St.

This one-and-a-half-story brick dwelling delightfully eludes any easy style designation. Though it boasts a mansard roof, it is certainly not French; the narrow windows within the wall dormers with their brackets and spindly columns are neither French nor Eastlake.

And the inventive entablatures (more like a piece of furniture than an architectural detail) over the first-floor windows also cannot be pinned down stylistically. The ample grounds and plantings surrounded by a low stone wall and iron fence create an idealistic picture of an early 1870s "Victorian" residence. This house is similar in design to the one at 1325 Eighth Avenue. These two houses

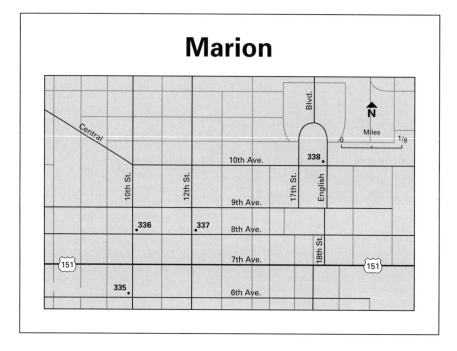

Marion

must certainly have been influenced by one another, or perhaps designed by the same individual.

CE336 **Victory Christian Church**

c. 1905. Northeast corner of 8th Ave. and 10th St.

A low, broad octagonal drum and roof emerge from the low brick-and-stone body of the building. A small, almost dollhouselike open belfry tower marks one of the entrances. The red brick walls contrast beautifully with the bright green shingled roof.

CE337 **First Presbyterian Church**

1884. Northeast corner of 8th Ave. and 12th St.

The corner tower has been placed at a 45-degree angle, facing the junction of the two streets. Pointed windows with tracery, plus the high pitch of the gables and roofs, establish the design as Gothic Revival. The tall roof of the tower has been divided into two parts by a suggestion of an attic with vent dormers. An unsympathetic post-World War II modernist addition has been built to the rear.

CE338 **House**

c. 1888. 1024 18th St.

A bold composition of a second-floor horse-shoe bay supported by a single slender column marks this classic Queen Anne Revival house. As with many other late nineteenth- and twentieth-century houses in Marion, this house is well set back from the street, with extensive surrounding lawns and gardens.

Marshalltown

"Marshalltown is situated on a handsome piece of ground near the Iowa River, some four miles east and a trifle north of the exact center of the county," according to Huebinger.[41] The site of the city on the rolling prairie between

Marshalltown

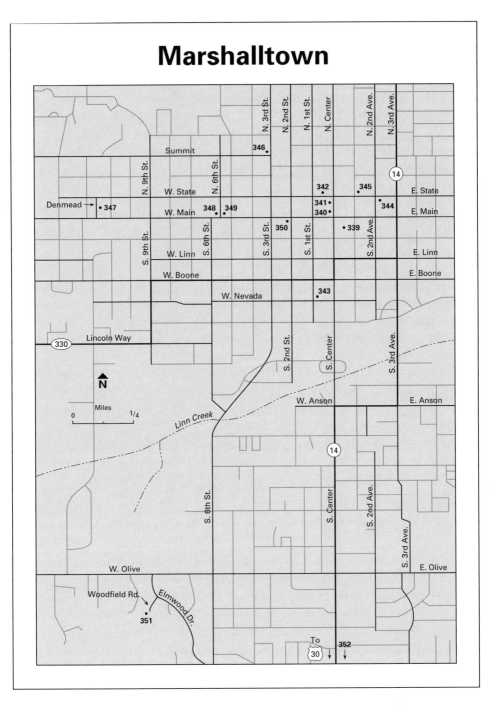

the Iowa River to the north and Linn Creek to the south was platted in 1853. After several years of the usual battle as to which town would finally house the county seat, Marshalltown was selected in 1859. With the arrival in 1863 of the Chicago and Northwestern Railroad, the community increasingly became not only a distribution center for the region, but an important railroad and manufacturing center.

In the late nineteenth century the city won the statewide battle to became the site of the Iowa Soldier's Home. The city became the hub for three railroad systems (including the location of a large repair shop for the Minneapolis and Saint Louis Railroad), and by 1900 it had developed one of the state's most extensive electric streetcar systems (in operation from 1892 to 1928).

Following the lead of Elbert Hubbard and his popular *Little Journeys* series of the 1900s (which included such titles as *Little Journeys to the Homes of Great Business Men* and *Little Journeys to the Homes of Great Teachers,* published by the Roycrofters at the Roycroft Shop, East Aurora, New York), Marshalltown created its own "Little Journey to Marshalltown," advertising itself in the mid-teens as a "City of Progress." A 1916 publication of the Marshalltown Club reported that "the moral tone and social betterment of the city are steadily progressing," and that "twenty-two churches and nine schools . . . bear further testimony to a spirit of social progress."[42]

The twenties and thirties brought increased manufacturing and also US 30, the famed Lincoln Highway. Even in the depression years of the thirties there were some 56 factories still in business in the city. The development of the industrial section adjacent to the railroad and Linn Creek meant that the northern boundary along the south bank of the Iowa River was not despoiled, as was so often the case with riverfronts in Iowa and throughout the country. Thus, much of the area around the Iowa River was developed for parklike uses, including the grounds of the Iowa Veterans Home, Riverside Cemetery, and Riverside Park. (Note that there is a Memorial Log Cabin within Riverside Park, at the end of North Third Avenue. It was built in 1936–1937 to honor early pioneers.)

Generally, the nineteenth-century parts of Marshalltown have the flavor of the mid-1870s and later, due in part to an extensive fire in 1872 that destroyed many of its business and factory buildings, as well as a number of houses. The section just west of the downtown still contains a number of historic buildings. People interested in post-World War II suburbia should travel south on Center Street to West and East Olive Street, and then begin their wanderings to the south. The "best" area is to the west, around Elmwood Country Club. In the postwar years the city has gained one monument and lost another. The usual suburban ranch houses built within the community were joined by a side-entrance Lustron house (c. 1950) at 901 Fourth Street North. However, Marshalltown lost the Coffee Pot Cafe (1933), a tavern and restaurant with curb service. This two-story stucco building in the form of a giant coffee pot was demolished in the 1970s.

CE339 **Marshall County Courthouse**

1884–1886, John C. Cochrane. Southeast corner of E. Main St. and Center St. S.

Since its completion, the 175-foot-high tower of this early Beaux-Arts building has dominated the community. The 1884–1886 courthouse building was the third one to be built within the county. The first was a small wood structure built in 1851 in Marietta. When the county offices were moved to Marshalltown, a second, two-story brick courthouse was built, in 1857–1858. John C. Cochrane, who designed the third building, was responsible not only for the initial plans for the Illinois State Capitol (1867–1883), but for a number of courthouses in Illinois and Indiana. Stylistically the Marshall County Courthouse was an advanced design for the mid-1880s, anticipating the surge of interest in the Beaux-Arts Classical tradition which developed in the 1890s. The scheme of the building is that of a central rotunda that reaches upward to a dome contained within the base of a central tower. The high tower is open on its lower level, above which are four clock faces and then a segmented dome and tall, thin lantern. During the 1950s and 1960s various proposals were made to replace the existing courthouse with a new building, but these proposals were rejected by county voters. In 1974 funds were voted by the residents of Marshall County to restore and update the building, a project carried out by the Des Moines firm of Wagner, Marquart and Wetherell.

CE340 **Municipal Building**

1920–1921, H. E. Reimer. West side of Center St. N., between W. Main and State streets

A marginal amount of open greenery at the sides, together with a narrow planting area at the front, helps to convey the impression that this is a public building. The local architect H. E. Reimer provided a more or less Georgian image; the building is sheathed in stone on the first floor, with brick above. A center pavilion is pulled away slightly from the rest of the building, and this is surmounted by a gable. Two pairs of closely grouped columns support the entablature over the entrance. The five windows on the street facade are all three-unit Chicago windows; the three on the second floor are grandly encompassed within decorated stone frames.

CE341 **Carnegie Public Library**

1902–1903, Patton and Miller. Southwest corner Center St. N. and State St. W.

The community received a grant of $30,000 from the Carnegie Foundation in 1901. The Chicago firm of Patton and Miller, who seemed to have captured commissions for so many of the Midwest library buildings, was engaged to design the new building. The scheme was that of an L-shaped building with entrance provided within a columned corner octagon. Opposite the entrance was the bookstack area, which spread out like a fan between the two wings of the building. A central octagonal reception desk sat within a circular space, with a children's reading room on the left, and a general reading room and study on the right. On the second level was a museum room, a lecture room, and additional space for expansion within the fanlike bookstack space. The exterior of the stone-clad building, with its engaged Corinthian columns, corner quoining, and roof balustrade is pure turn-of-the-century Beaux-Arts classicism.

CE342 **Northwestern Bell Telephone Company Building**

c. 1976, Charles Herbert and Associates. North side of State St. W., between Center St. N. and 1st St. N.

A pristine two-story rectangular box clad in dark brick contains a band of glass that extends from end to end on the second floor. Below, there is an entrance within a cut-in space, defined to each side by tubular columns. A similar play between glass brought right to the surface of the surrounding brick walls and a cut-in entrance occurs on the building's east facade. The row of trees bordering the sidewalk along the south front helps to relate the building to the older streetscape, but still this elegant design seems to have little to do with the downtown of a small city.

CE343 **Marshall Lumber Company Building**

1964, John H. Howe. 312 S. 1st St.

The Minneapolis architect John H. Howe, who had been a member of Frank Lloyd Wright's Taliesin Fellowship, designed this building in a mode that carries on the vocabulary of his teacher. Concrete blocks of different colors, together with horizontal roofs and pergolas, have been arranged in a composition of interlocking horizontal and vertical planes. In the center is a small entrance court, made more private by a pergola that extends across its street side.

CE344 Binford House

c. 1870s. 110 2nd Ave. N.

The entrance and the three windows on the street facade of this two-story brick house display curved lintels that sorrowfully droop down each side. The south side of the house has a composition of a single-story porch, then a two-story wing with a large angled bay, and, further toward the back, a porch that repeats the one in front. A pattern of large and small brackets supports the overhang of the low hipped roof. It all adds up to a solid-looking post-Civil War version of the Italianate style.

CE345 Sower House

1860. 201 State St. E.

The Sower house is a one-and-a-half-story brick Downing-like cottage with a long wrap-around porch. The segmental arches of the porch as well as the bargeboards of the gable ends are realized in lacelike sawed work. At the front of the cottage where the two wings meet, the designer injected on the second floor a wooden wall dormer equipped with a single large window.

CE346 Bungalow

c. 1915. 401 3rd St. N.

Heavy stucco-covered piers support groups of three stubby posts at the end of the entrance porch and on the enclosed porch to the side. These seemingly thick concrete-like walls rise upward from the base of the building, forming the posts and balustrades for the porches and their entrance stairs. The ends of the roof ridges have been turned up slightly to suggest that elements of the design came from Japan.

CE347 Cottage

c. 1928. East side of Denmead Blvd., south of State St. W.

Though this dwelling seems to put on the pretense of being a French Norman cottage, it is in fact a good-sized suburban house. Even more than usual in period revival houses of the 1920s, the designer of this house has obviously enjoyed playing a game of scale. A miniaturized tower sits between the two wings; its upper windows are "correctly" proportioned, but then below, the front door returns us to normal scale (or perhaps the world of the giant). The brick and half-timber front gable has a balconied door, suggesting that the space within is between the first floor and the second floor. While the wing to the right of the entrance is small and low to the ground, it too is part of the game of scale, its small size countered with a large three-tier chimney.

CE348 William Fort House

1890. 607 Main St.

If one knows what one is about, and then proceeds to break most of the rules, it is possible to create wondrous designs, and the design of this house is such an example. The sharply pitched roofs of this two-and-a-half-story house, together with the narrow dormers with hipped roofs, suggest the French Châteauesque, while much of its detailing comes from the Colonial Revival. The "wild" elements of the design are found in the right-hand roof of the front gable, which sweeps down to the roof of the entrance porch; in the composition of the stubby Ionic Columns, with their high decorated impost blocks; and even in a heart-shaped window (and this is only the beginning of its assortment of architectural oddities). This house is certainly one of Iowa's domestic monuments.

CE349 **House**

c. 1870. 503 Main St. W.

It is the square three-story corner tower that helps to set this house far above the usual combination of Italianate/French Second Empire designs created in the years after the Civil War. The cornice of the small tower is broken in its center by a small curved wall dormer; above this on all four sides of the tiny mansard roof are narrow overscaled dormer windows. A Colonial Revival porch with a rounded end has been added to the house (c. 1900).

CE350 **First Methodist Episcopal Church**

1894. Southwest corner of Main St. W. and 2nd St. S.

Instead of the usual version of the Richardsonian Romanesque church, with a central or corner tower, this one has the appearance of a medieval monastic building. Because of the church's elevation above the street, two flights of stairs and their balustrades lead up to the entrance platform. To the right is a large rose window contained within a round arch; to the left is the entrance, which goes into a two-story wing with a central gable roof. Each of the gables has a three-arched pattern of smooth stone voussoirs that contrast with the rougher surface of the adjoining stone walls.

CE351 **Sunday House**

1955, Frank Lloyd Wright. Southwest end of Woodfield Rd.

This is one of Wright's late Usonian houses. The walls are of a beautiful warm red brick, and the exposed wood-framed windows, roof soffits, and fascias are darkly stained. The L-shape plan features the usual high-ceilinged living room, countered by the lower spaces for bedrooms and other rooms. The volumes and surfaces of the house are composed in a strong, almost nondomestic manner. In 1969–1970, John H. Howe extended the house, transforming it into a T-shaped building.

CE352 **Dobbin True-Round Barn**

1919, Gordon-Van Tine Company. On US 30, proceed west of Marshalltown 12.25 miles; take route S62 south 1.2 miles; then turn right (west) and travel 1 mile

The Dobbin barn was obtained as a pre-cut building from the Des Moines firm. It was listed in the company's catalogue as "Barrel Barn No. 214." The diameter of the vertically wood-sided barn is 60 feet; within, at the center, is a terracotta silo 12 feet in diameter. The roof is of the double-pitch gambrel type, with a large cupola on top. The cupola has louvered windows, and a wide overhanging cone-shaped roof.

Monroe

CE353 **Kling House**

c. 1860s. 416 North Monroe Street.

One of Iowa's few remaining octagonal dwellings, the Kling house is located in Monroe. In style, this brick (now stuccoed) octagon is Italianate. Small brackets support an almost flat projection of the roof, which further back turns into a narrow mansard roof. The windows have segmental arches, and the small entrance porch (which originally had a balustrade) exhibits a pair of piers supporting segmented headers above the windows. On one side, on the first floor, is an Italianate splayed bay with its own small bracketed roof.

Montezuma

The small community of Montezuma was platted as the seat for Poweshiek County in 1848. The present courthouse was started in 1857 and was completed the following year. As originally built, the courthouse was Greek Revival in design. Thin, wide pilasters surround the building on all sides, and support an entablature with triglyphs. At the gabled entrance front, a three-story square tower supports an octagonal domed lantern. In 1890 a two-story wing was added to the rear, and in 1934 the brick building was raised to provide additional space in the basement (an act which obviously did not help the design of the building). Though compromised by these later changes, the Poweshiek County Courthouse, described by Andreas in 1875 as "handsome and commodious," remains one of the oldest courthouses still in use in the state. It is located within the public square, south of Main Street between Third and Fourth streets.

To the east of the courthouse, on the southeast corner of Main Street and Fourth Street, is the three-story New Carroll House Hotel (1892). The design of this brick building is essentially simplified Italianate. Its two unusual features are its setback angled corner, and the wooden porch which has been carried around the corner.

Mount Vernon

Mount Vernon presents a classic picture of a midwestern college town. The buildings of Cornell College, especially the 1876 King Memorial Chapel, dominate the community. The small commercial downtown exists as a minor backdrop, and the built-up area around the campus is pure suburbia. The layout of the town is unusual; the original plat of 1847 is northeast-southwest by northwest-southeast, and while Main Street (or First Street) follows this grid, it meanders off almost as a farm road at both ends. Running through the southern section of the community is US 30, the famous Lincoln Highway of the teens and 1920s.

CE354 Office

c. 1920. Southwest corner of 1st St. W. and 2nd Ave. S.

This building is distinguished by four-story Ionic columns (all delightfully wrong in their proportions) set on high stone bases; above, a gentle roof is covered with tile. The image is that of a classicized bungalow. The present front porch has the look of having been devised as a drive-through for a gasoline service station.

CE355 House

c. 1850. 601 1st Ave. S.

A Greek Revival dwelling, this house has two stories and a gable roof. The wide entrance has a low pediment supported by wood pilasters. The entrance door has side lights and a horizontal transom.

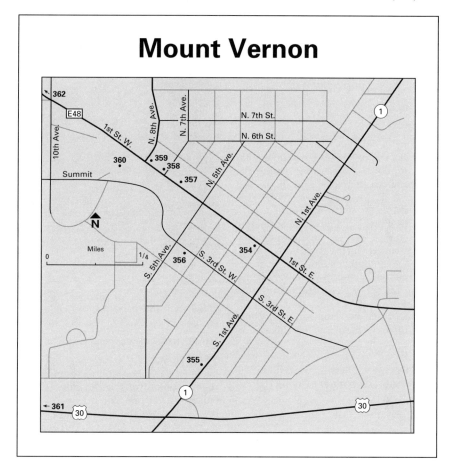

Mount Vernon

CE356 Cottage

c. 1855; 402 3rd St. W.

The gable front of this small Greek Revival cottage faces toward the street. The entrance is particularly handsome, with thin Tuscan columns separating the side lights from the door; above, the shaft of a column has been used as a header separating the top of the door from the very narrow transom above. This whole composition is set into the brick wall with a low-pitched pediment above.

CE357 "Rood House"

c. 1883, attrib. Marsden Keyes. North side of 1st St. (Main St.), between 6th and 7th avenues N.

This Eastlake composition includes an angled bay tower to the side. The walls are articulated with diagonal and crisscross boarding

suggesting medieval timbering. The cut-out and routed designs of the entrance porch are typically Eastlake. The house was designed by the Mount Vernon carpenter/builder/architect Marsden Keyes. It is now used as a dormitory by Cornell College.

CE358 House

c. 1887. 701 1st St. W.

This presents a somewhat later version of the Eastlake mode than the house discussed above. The elaborated cross-bracings on the gable ends are particularly dramatic.

CE359 Platner House

c. 1890, attrib. Marsden Keyes. 725 1st St. W.

Keyes turned to the Queen Anne image for this house, though his interpretation of it was a little on the old-fashioned side. A singular feature of the design is the three-story corner tower with its steeply pitched gable roof; it ends up reading as part of the house, not as a tower.

CE360 Cornell College

1853. W. 1st St.

The principal buildings of the 110-acre Cornell College campus are situated in a commanding position on a hill overlooking the whole town. Both the oldest and the newest buildings are set well back from West First Street, so that one's impression is of a park within which a few buildings have seemingly been scattered. The most important structures are discussed in the next four entries. However, other buildings on the campus should be noted. These are the President's House, the former William Hamilton house (1850); College Hall (1857); and Old Seminary (1853). They are Italianate in feeling. More difficult to pin down is South Hall (1873).

CE360.1 Carnegie Library (now William Harmon Norton Geological Center)

1904–1905, Barlett and King. Cornell College campus, off W. 1st St.

This Beaux-Arts design centers attention on the entrance, set between two wide piers from which springs a central arch. Above the door is a porch with classical pediment embraced at the side by two dolphins.

CE360.2 King Memorial Chapel

1876–1882, Charles Chapman. Cornell College campus, off W. 1st St.

What starts out as a traditionally conceived stone Gothic Revival design ends with a pencil-thin French Second Empire tower. The windows contain brilliantly colored designs in glass.

CE360.3 Bowman Hall

1885, Charles Chapman. Cornell College campus, off W. 1st St.

The hilltop location accentuates the Victorian verticality of this brick three-story building. A mansard roof caps and accentuates its Second Empire design.

CE360.2 King Memorial Chapel

CE360.4 Collins House (now Faculty House)

1889. Cornell College campus, off W. 1st St.

The architect of this turn-of-the-century Colonial Revival house put the emphasis on the repeated motif of the Palladian window: an eminent-sized one dominates the entrances below, while to the side, smaller ones occur on the first floor. All in all, this is a vigorous and original design.

CE361 Palisades Kepler State Park

1922, later. 4 miles west of Mount Vernon on US 30

This 603-acre park is situated within hilly forest land overlooking the Cedar River. The roads and trails and the open glades for picnicking and recreational activities have been planned in an Olmstedian "naturalistic" fashion. As one enters the park one comes upon a pair of rustic stone posts and wood gates (c. 1934); further on is the ranger's office and house (c. 1934), mildly Colonial Revival in character. Architecturally, the jewel of the park is the Stone Lodge (1934). The image tends to the rural Colonial.

CE362 Abbe Creek School (Museum)

1858. 2 miles northwest of Mount Vernon on route E48

The small 20 feet by 26 feet schoolhouse is credited with being the oldest brick schoolhouse still standing in the state. The building is the usual rectangular volume covered by a low-pitched gable roof. The interior has been restored and refurnished as in the period of the 1860s and 1870s. The school building is now a museum open to the public.

Nevada

Nevada "is pleasantly located on the Chicago Northwest Railway, 318 miles from Chicago. It is surrounded by a rich, gentle prairie, near the head of a grove which borders West Indian Creek," noted Andreas in 1875.[43] The site had been selected by the county commissioners as a central location for the county courthouse.

CE363 Story County Courthouse

1967–1968, Stenson and Warm. Courthouse Square

The first masonry courthouse was built during 1875–1877 and was designed by the Des Moines architect William Foster. This was a three-story building with mansard roof, in the French Second Empire style. In 1967–1968 the older building was replaced by an insistent modernist design by Stenson and Warm. The new building is wedge-shaped and is composed of two wings articulated by narrow vertical solid volumes, with windows between. The balance and symmetry of the design bring the modern ever so slightly into the classical tradition.

CE364 Briggs Block

c. 1882. Northwest corner of 6th St. and K Ave.

At the street corner of this two-story red brick and white-trim commercial block, attached to the second floor, is a projecting bay tower with a spired roof—a grouping so thin and narrow that it suggests an enlarged pencil. The ground floor storefronts have been remodeled, but the second floor remains as built, its lower band connecting the window sills and the upper band connecting the headers of paired windows. The original chimneys almost seem to peer from above the wide cornice.

CE365 Farmers Bank Building

c. 1916. West side of 6th St., south of K Ave.

The two-story portion of this limestone-sheathed bank building is relatively conventional, including its updating of glass brick inserted within the lower windows. The entrance to the right, which is only a single story high, is articulated by horizontal stones and by pronounced voussoirs above. Although it is part of the adjoining two-story section of the bank, this little entrance comes close to appearing as a completely separate, miniaturized building.

CE366 Central Presbyterian Church

1925–1926. Southwest corner of 5th St. and J Ave.

A Presbyterian church is cast as a Roman Doric temple: there is a pedimented porch with Ionic columns, steps, podium, and all. The use of brick for the walls tends to push the building slightly into the Greek Revival phase of the 1920s Colonial Revival. The plan of the building is in the form of an "H," with the upper two floors set upon a high raised basement.

CE367 Log Cabin

1854. 807 2nd St.

The tiny gable-roofed cabin is of split logs, with board-and-batten gable ends, double-hung small-lighted windows, and a stone chimney. The cabin and its surrounds are labeled "Native Prairie c. 1854."

CE368 House

c. 1875. 1204 H Ave.

While this red brick Italianate dwelling is an excellent example of this style in the 1870s, it is the brick outbuildings that attract one's attention. One of the two-story stable/barns has a low central roof monitor, outlined on all four sides by small windows. The outbuildings, like the house, have hipped roofs with eaves supported by pairs of small, delicate brackets.

CE369 Edwards-Swayze House

1876. 1110 9th St.

A drive leads past the small entrance porch that exhibits open spindlework above the thin columns. The windows on the first and second floors have wide, thick, slightly curved lintels, and the roofscape features dormers, tall chimneys, and spire tower roofs. It all adds up to a classic early Queen Anne design. The interior still possesses much of its original woodwork and wall covering, including an embossed ceiling and papered wainscot.

CE370 Bungalow

c. 1912. 1204 9th St.

A long, low gable roof with wide overhanging eaves and gable ends covers this stucco and brick-trimmed Craftsman bungalow. The front porch, its roof supported by pyramidal piers, continues out to the left side and becomes a pergola. The central gabled dormer facing the street has the familiar break where the center portion is sunk some feet back. Accompanying the house and reflecting its style is a garage to the rear.

CE371 Soper's Mill Bridge

1876, Zenus King and Peter M. Frees. Proceed north of Nevada on route S14, 5 miles; turn west on route E23; pass under I-35; the bridge is .75 mile farther west

This riveted bowstring iron-truss bridge, a single-span structure measuring 90 feet, was produced by the King Iron Bridge and Manufacturing Company of Cleveland, Ohio. The bridge spans the Skunk River on the principal early route between Nevada and Fort Dodge.

Newton

This community, first named Newton Center, was platted in 1846 as the seat of the newly formed Jasper County. Some twelve years later a handsome two-story brick Greek Revival courthouse was built. On two sides this building had porticoes with Ionic columns, and there was an octagonal open-domed lantern on the roof. This 1858 building was eventually replaced by the present Beaux-Arts courthouse (1909–1911). During the nineteenth century, Newton's economy was based on the city's position as a distribution point on the Chicago, Rock Island, and Pacific Railroad (the railroad arriving in 1867), a producer of farm equipment, and a center for the milling of lumber.

In the twentieth century the city has been dominated by one company, Maytag, the manufacturer of automatic washing machines and kitchen appliances. F. L. Maytag endowed the community with many buildings, and the Maytag Dairy Farm was operated as an ideal Iowa farm. (To reach the Maytag Dairy Farm go north on East Eighth Street, past Nineteenth Street.) If one has an interest in the historical development of household technology, then the Maytag exhibit at the Jasper County Historical Museum (1700 South Fifteenth Avenue West) should be visited.

Newton

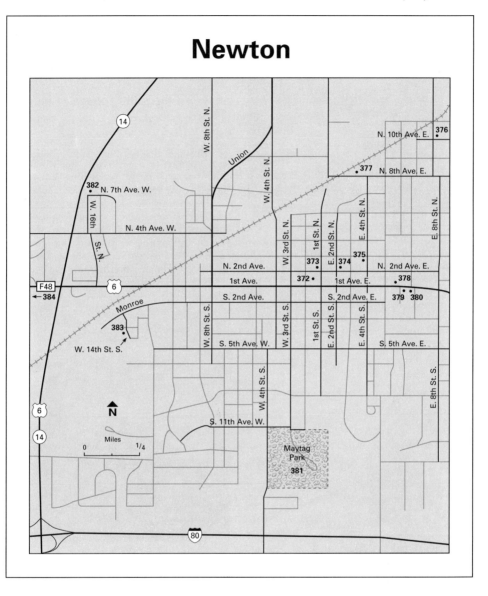

CE372 Jasper County Courthouse

1909–1911, Proudfoot and Bird. Northwest corner of 1st Ave. and 1st St.

Rising from the center of the community's public square is this two-story Beaux-Arts Classical essay. Architects from the Des Moines firm of Proudfoot and Bird were correct and observant in creating this lively version of the classical tradition. The building is composed of six cubes; each of the facades has Ionic columns, and the entrance is located in the raised basement. At the center of the composition is a 56-foot-high drum and dome. The walls are of gray Bedford limestone with emphasis placed on the horizontal joints of the stone. Inside, corridors proceeding from each of the four sides of the building converge on a central rotunda. The second level of the rotunda is surrounded by eight Doric

CE372 Jasper County Courthouse

columns; above, on the third level, is a circle of eight Corinthian columns. In the four arches of the pendentives of the rotunda are paintings by Edgar Cameron of Chicago that illustrate events in the history of the county. Above these is a vaulted ceiling of colored art glass. The building has been renovated and the frescoes and stenciled designs have been restored.

CE373 First National Bank Building

1919, A. H. Andrews Co. Northwest corner N. 2nd Ave. W. and 1st St. N.

This bank building appears in the full guise of a Greek Doric temple, at least on two of its sides. The general tendency of Beaux-Arts classicism was to look to Rome or Renaissance Italy; here we encounter a well-done version of a Greek temple with columns in antis, its only omission being a stylobate base. The upper portions of the temple design are larger and more boldly articulated than the walls and columns below. The entablature with its

triglyphs and the pediment with its elaborately sculpted tympanum are of grand scale and seem (in a charming fashion) to push the lower part of the temple into the ground.

CE374 First Methodist Episcopal Church

1914. Northeast corner of N. 2nd Ave. E. and E. 2nd St. N.

Another of the community's Beaux-Arts designs appears in a Methodist church. It is a cruciform scheme centered on a low drum and a green dome. The entrance is a temple front with four Doric columns in antis. The large segmented curved window opposite the entrance arm carefully breaks through its lower cornice, and its keystone just touches the base of the tympanum above. Like the nearby courthouse, the building is sheathed in Bedford limestone.

CE375 Saint Stephen's Episcopal Church

1871–1874. 223 E. 4th St. N.

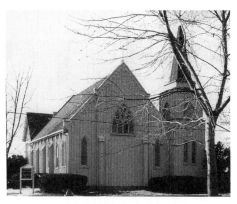

This Gothic Revival small-scaled church is covered in vertical board-and-batten. The low tower with its spire and the low-pitched roof over the nave seem almost like twentieth-century versions of Gothic features. The gable wall adjacent to the corner entrance tower exhibits a pair of buttresses that help to give some traditional weight and substance to the building. The sanctuary within has a hammer beam ceiling.

CE376 Service Station

1919. Northeast corner of E. 8th St. N. and N. 10th Ave. E.

Here is a classic example of a brick-pier service station. The pump area is covered by a flat roof supported by two thick brick piers. The station and its large rear garage area are sheathed in patterned brick with a suggestion of pilasters carried up above the roof parapet. The front corners of the building have been cut at a 45-degree angle; the windows are large double-hung units with small lights above and single sheets of glass below. The service station is currently not in use.

CE377 **Arthur House**

1866–1867. 322 N. 8th Ave. E.

A Gothic Revival one-and-a-half-story brick cottage has been transformed into a major structure by the inclusion of a romantic circular tower with a high concave spired roof. The upper windows of the tower, which are arched, narrow, and quite long, add to its illusion of height and size. Some additions and changes have occurred, including a wide Colonial Revival porch (c. 1900) placed across the front of the building.

CE378 **House**

c. 1910. 524 1st Ave. E.

A well-proportioned turn-of-the-century Colonial Revival box, with a porch with Ionic columns, becomes something out of the ordinary through its single front roof dormer. The dormer sits on a thin, extended wide base and centers on a circular "bullet" window that is mirrored in the arch of the dormer's roof. The visual attraction of this dormer is so strong that it fully dominates the street facade of the house.

CE379 **Radio Station KCOB**

c. 1938. 611 1st Ave. E.

The Anglo-Colonial Revival popular in the east was the "in" image during the depression years of the 1930s. One of the stimulants of that revival was the restoration/rebuilding of Colonial Williamsburg. The architect of this two-story house (now a radio station) looked directly to Williamsburg for his inspiration. His specific source was the late eighteenth-century James Semple house, but he took a number of liberties with that source, broad-

ening the horizontal proportions of the center section and its entrance porch, and placing the house directly on the ground, with no visible foundation. These and other changes have brought the building up to date, conveying a fairly modern image.

CE380 **Bergman House**

1909, Proudfoot and Bird. 629 1st Ave. E.

This house was designed and built at the same time that Proudfoot and Bird were working on the county courthouse. We have a case of California's Mission Style being exported to Iowa, with white stucco walls, red tile roof, parapeted gables, and pergolas. As in many California examples, this is essentially a large Mission Revival bungalow, augmented by a small second-floor pavilion. The tour de force of this dwelling is a single immense stucco column whose top spreads out to receive the beams of the pergola.

CE381 **Fred Maytag Park**

W. 3rd St. S. at S. 11th Ave. W.

This park, originally set aside as the county fairgrounds, was revamped in 1935. In the southeast corner of the park is located the 1848 Reese log cabin, which was moved from its rural site in nearby Palo Alto township. This small one-room cabin has a shed-roofed front porch and a large masonry chimney at its right gable end. The most eye-catching element in the park is the Streamline Moderne band shell of 1937. This semicircular shell is similar to many others constructed throughout the country, including, of course, the well-known Hollywood Bowl in Los Angeles. The Maytag Park band shell is unusual in that a different radius has been used for the exterior form from that of the inner bowl.

CE382 **Denniston House**

1959–1961, John Howe. 1506 N. 7th Ave. W

The Minneapolis architect John Howe was one of the very few Wright-inspired architects of the post-World War II years who was able to expand successfully on the "master's" visual language. The single-floor Denniston house is closely held to its site by a low-pitched gable roof. The walls of brick, wood, and glass underneath carry on their own horizontal theme. A central masonry corner containing the fireplace, utility room, and kitchen serves as a center between the open living, dining, and family rooms on one side and the long bedroom wing on the other.

CE383 **Vernon House**

1965, Jerome C. Cerny. 300 W. 14th St. S.

The Chicago architect Jerome C. Cerny, along with David Adler, was one of the country's most sophisticated exponents of traditional architectural imagery. Cerny's general preference was for the American Colonial (Georgian and Federal) and the French Norman or Provincial. The Vernon house represents one of his post-World War II French farmhouse types. Though of reasonable size, this one-and-a-half-story dwelling was seemingly maneuvered by the architect around courts and terraces so that one experiences only a fragment at a time. The second floor is snuggled down beneath low gables, roofs, and wall dormers so that the house really appears as a single-floor dwelling. What is evident in a house such as this is that the architect, knowing his precedent well, has been able to transform it into something that is modern and at the same time highly personal. This is apparent in the overall composition of the Vernon house and in the way in which wood detailing has been carefully injected into the painted brick walls.

CE384 **House**

c. 1880; 2 miles west of Newton on route F48 (old US 6)

An ordinary Queen Anne dwelling becomes quite extraordinary through its system of bay windows and the sheathing of its walls and roof. On the facade toward the road is a pair of two-story bay units, standing side by side. These are roofed with three gables each. Since the sides of the dormers are angled, these gables meet the center gable at a peculiar position. Above these odd roof junctures of the bay is an additional large end-gable that tries to hold everything together. The main roof of the house is sheathed with large metal shingles laid at a 45-degree angle. Below, the walls are covered with a pattern of curved fishscale shingles.

Ogden

On Ogden's main street, Walnut, are two Streamline Moderne service stations of the late 1930s. Claussen's Texaco (c. 1936) at Fifth and Walnut streets has a raised center section, balanced on each side by low service wings. Curved corners and horizontal banding appear on the street facade of this stucco building. Down the street, at Sixth and Walnut, is a Standard Service Station (c. 1957) composed of a single horizontal box with rounded corners and the usual banding.

CE385 **Ogden Grain Company Storage Units**
c. 1900

Agriculture in an industrial image is presented by the Ogden Grain Company (c. 1900 and later). Behind a large "Pillsbury Co." sign is a group of older buildings sheathed in corrugated metal, and these have been joined by newer cylindrical storage units.

Oskaloosa

The site of Oskaloosa was selected as the seat of Mahaska County in 1844. It was situated on an open prairie between the Des Moines and the Skunk rivers. Two colleges were eventually located within the community, William Penn College and John Fletcher College. At present the two colleges are Oskaloosa Christian School and Vennard College.

CE386 **Mahaska County Courthouse**

1881–1885, H. C. Koch and Company. Southeast corner of High Ave. E. and S. 1st St.

One assumes that the architect H. C. Koch of Milwaukee was most likely thinking in terms of the Romanesque in his design for this three-story brick and stone-trim building. But the insistent narrow horizontal banding of the structure reflects the mid-century Ruskinian Gothic. There are large-scale lunette windows in the many fourth-floor gables. The projecting tower with its round-arched entrance at its base is the center of the composition. The top of the tower was lowered in 1934 and was replaced by a design somewhat reminiscent of some of the early work of Eliel Saarinen.

CE387 Oskaloosa Bandstand

1912, Frank E. Wetherell. City Park, Market St. S. at High Ave. E.

The octagonal bandstand is reminiscent of the nineteenth century in the exotic filigree of its metalwork, but at the same time its detailing with references to the classical and Arts and Crafts tradition brings it well within the present century. Small curved metal balconies project from every other side, and a curved metal staircase leads up from the ground to the platform. The solid balustrade contains tile designed by Charles L. Barnhouse.

CE388 Old Post Office Building

c. 1912. Northeast corner of N. Market St. and A Ave. E.

A civic, governmental presence is strongly asserted by this stone-sheathed building designed within the Beaux-Arts Classical tradition. Deeply grooved drums make up the pair of engaged columns that define the entrance and support an open pediment. To bring even more emphasis to the entrance, deeply grooved voussoirs define the arch above the entrance door. On each side is a pair of pedimented windows, above which are rectangular panels suggesting low attic windows.

CE389 Rock Island Passenger Railroad Station

c. 1890. S.W. Rock Island Ave. and 2nd St. S.

When built, and during much of the years following, this station looked out onto a small park planted with trees. By the early 1980s the park was overgrown, and the building was fast becoming a picturesque ruin. The station itself is essentially undecorated, and relies on its plain brick walls and variously gabled roofs (supported by struts) to establish its character. The usual control room projects from the body of the station on the platform side, and a good-sized lunette window has been placed in its gable end.

CE390 Smith-Johnson House

1853. 713 High Ave. E.

The format of this two-story brick dwelling with a side hall is that of the Italianate style. Except for the entrance porch detailed in wood, the building relies on its simple undecorated brick walls to convey an almost puritanical frontier presence. Two unusual features of its design are the wide entablature and cornice carried out entirely in brick, and, to the side, the tripartite roundheaded window, which seems more Queen Anne than Italianate.

CE391 Alsop House

1948–1951, Frank Lloyd Wright. 1907 A St.

A version of Frank Lloyd Wright's post-World War II Usonian houses, this one has a low gable roof and a characteristic wide, cantilevered flat roof that shelters both the entrance and the open carport. The small kitchen/workspace forms the central module of the house, with the entrance, living, and dining space off to the right; to the left, a long gallery leads to the three bedrooms. The walls of the dwelling are of finely laid brick; the fenestration is cypress, and the roof is a contrasting red color. Much of the furniture—freestanding as well as built in—was designed for the house.

CE392 Lamberson House

1948–1951, Frank Lloyd Wright. 511 N. Park Ave.

Even more than the nearby Alsop House, the Lamberson dwelling mirrors the horizontality of the prairie and its hilltop location. Dramatic low-pitched roofs sail out of the central brick core of the building, their extensive overhangs producing deeply shadowed patterns below. The design of the house is based on equilateral triangles set on four-foot modules. Again as in Alsop House, the brick-encased kitchen forms the core of the design, with public living space on one side, and private sleeping space on the other side.

CE393 Cottage

c. 1880. 1246 C Ave. E.

All of the elaboration one might associate with a large, grand house has here been min-

CE392 Lamberson House

iaturized. A dramatic, finely detailed wooden bay porch projects from the center of the street elevation. Above the entrance is a wide gable end containing a tripartite window. This is balanced on each side by projecting wall dormers. Wide bargeboards are present on each gable end, and paneling and fishscale shingles are used on the upper walls of the house.

CE394 William Penn College (Oskaloosa Christian School)

1917–1920s, Dwight Perkins and others. US 63, north end of town at Trueblood Ave.

CE394.1 Women's Building

1917, Dwight Perkins

While there are some Prairie-style details present in this two-story building (such as the row of engaged piers to the side surmounted by a small flat roof), its design reads as a refined version of the Craftsman mode.

CE394.2 Natural Science / Arts and Letters Building

1917, Dwight Perkins

The sense of kinship of the designs here reminds one of the several schools and industrial buildings constructed around Chicago in the teens. The composition is classical Beaux-Arts; there is a dominant central three-story entrance pavilion, and then a balanced pavilion on each side. There is Prairie-style detailing within each of the pavilions. Each

exhibits a central motif of engaged piers terminating in a flat projecting roof.

CE394.3 Spencer Memorial Chapel

1922

In contrast to the buildings designed by Perkins, the Spencer Memorial Chapel is eighteenth-century Colonial Georgian in style, constructed of red brick with white detailing. A porch with Ionic columns provides entrance, and there is an open, low tower midway back on the roof ridge.

CE395 Nelson Pioneer Farm

1852–1853, house. 1856, barn. Glendale Rd., northeast of US 63

This mid-nineteenth-century farm complex, plus other buildings which have been moved to the site, is operated by the Mahaska County Historical Society, and is open to the public. The 1852–1853 Nelson farmhouse is a late example of the Federal style. The building is of brick, and it is covered by a simple gable roof. The house boasts a porch across the entire front, within which is an entrance doorway with side lights and transom. The barn is a modest building with a gable roof, and sheathed in board-and-batten. Accompanying these buildings is the Nelson log cabin (1867), and a later summer kitchen, meat house, and windmill. Other buildings brought to the site are an "old country store," a one-room schoolhouse, an early voting house, a scale house, a post office, and the Coal Creek Friends Meetinghouse.

Pella

The town of Pella was established in 1847 by a group of Dutch settlers led by Peter Scholte. As with neighboring Oskaloosa to the southeast, Pella was laid out on the open prairie between the Des Moines and Skunk rivers. With its many simple brick buildings and its wonderful beds of flowers, Pella does indeed strongly convey the atmosphere of a Dutch town. Today, within the architectural profession, Pella is known for its windows, doors, and other building products produced by the local Rolscreen Company.

In recent years Pella has become even more Dutch than it ever was. The classic image of the Dutch windmill has cropped up everywhere, sometimes as a 3-foot miniature in a garden and on other occasions as a full-scale creation. In the middle of the town's Central Park is a windmill that houses the tourist information kiosk.

Over the years a number of historic Pella buildings have been either completely rebuilt or restored. Proposed for restoration in 1989 was the Opera House, built in 1900 and designed by Stanley DeGoyer. The three-story facade of the building is unusual in its pattern of vertical arched windows, and especially in the introduction of a row of large round windows between the second and third floors.

CE396 Scholte House

1848, later. 734 Washington St.

There have been so many additions to the house of the founder of Pella that it is difficult to discern what it was like when first built. It would seem to have been a narrow two-story structure of wood, covered by a single gable roof. The front now provides an array of open and enclosed porches, the largest of which is on the second floor. West of the Scholte house is the two-story Walters (Holland) house of 1856. The structure is now painted white with bright blue trim. It has been used as a historical museum, and it is presently a restaurant.

CE397 Wyatt Earp (van Spanckeron) House

1849. 507 Franklin St.

The Wyatt Earp house, the lawman's boyhood home, is composed of a pair of two-story brick houses with gable roofs. The side-by-side houses are quite plain; the brick walls (now painted white) are broken by rows of double-hung small-light windows. The Earp house is now part of Pella's adjoining Historical Village Museum. Among the buildings either moved to the site or recently built are a mid-nineteenth-century split-log cabin, the gambrel-roofed Beason Blommers Grist Mill, and a replica of Pella's first church, built by Peter Scholte. One of the reconstructed buildings within the Historic Village is the 1848 Roelofsz (Vierson) house. This is a rather plain two-story brick dwelling, with wings to each side. It was reconstructed in 1975–1976.

CE398 Baarda House and Shrine

1954. Iowa 163, at the western city limits

Here one encounters a wondrous house and shrine dedicated to "God's victory over evil." The house and shrine are really one, and they are pure folk follies of the mid-1950s. The configuration of the house is that of a two-story box with a shed roof, from which project all sorts of wood ornament, fin walls, porches, and even an attached garage. At the street corner of the house is a thin Gothic Revival arched niche, which effectively introduces the onlooker to the underlying religious theme of the house and shrine.

CE399 Marion County State Bank

c. 1970. Southeast corner of Main and Independence streets

An auto-oriented bank building is here clad as a windmill, or perhaps one should say that a windmill has been placed upon the top of a bank building. The detailing of the building itself—including large-scale roof brackets, diamond-paned windows, and wood paneling—carries on the general theme of historic nineteenth-century architecture.

CE400 Cottage

c. 1875. Northwest corner of Main and Huber streets

Though briefly in fashion, the Eastlake mode could and did lend itself to a variety of inventive interpretations. This is one of them. The principal gables boast a variety of surfaces—fishscale shingles, horizontal insert panels covered with small boards laid at a 45-degree angle, quarter sunburst motifs, and more. Within the gable facing the street is a wonderful projecting porch on the second floor. Thin posts join the deck to the roof above, and the triangle of the roof centers on an arch articulated by patterns of turned and sawed wood. Finally, between two of the large gables is a miniature gable thrust out at a 45-degree angle, mirroring the angled wall below. The upper sashes of the double-hung windows display a surround of squares of brightly colored glass.

CE401 Calvary Wayside Chapel

c. 1950. Iowa 163, .5 mile south of the city limits

A clapboard-sheathed and shuttered Colonial Revival church has been rendered at the scale of a small child's playhouse. The only element that is full size is the narrow 6'8"-high entrance door in the base of the tower.

CE402 Voorhees House

1871. Iowa 163, 4 miles south of the city limits

The John Voorhees house was illustrated on page 232 of Andreas's 1875 *Atlas*. It was depicted as a large Italianate dwelling with French Second Empire overtones. It was placed upon a gentle rise, which helped to increase its vertical dominance of the site. Its most assertive feature was its steeply pitched roof similar to a mansard roof (bearing the date 1871 on one side, and the initials J.V. on the north side, both realized in slate shingles) with a broad bracketed cornice and an entablature emblazoned with medallionlike oval windows. In form the house is T-shaped, with a two-and-a-half-story main section and a one-and-a-half-story service wing to the rear. The entrance porch, supported by decorative wood piers, was carried across the front of the house and extended to meet the wall of one of its wings. Except for its pronounced quoining and a little stone detailing, the house is of brick.

CE403 Smith House

1869. 4.5 miles south of the city limits

The John Smith house presented the classic image of a large (14-room) mid-nineteenth-century Italianate villa—an imposing square volume surmounted by a wide cupola. The secondary windows on the upper floor have segmented tops; the center of each facade was emphasized by either a round-arched window, or, on the principal facade, by three joined arched windows. The corners of the building were defined by paneled engaged piers, and a balustraded porch ran across the entrance front. The roofs of both the main block and of the cupola were bracketed, and a row of six arched windows adorned each side of the cupola. A recent remodeling has eliminated much of the house's elaborated detailing.

Perry

Near the center of the town, at the northeast corner of Third and Linda streets, is Saint Patrick's Roman Catholic Church (1901). The side walls of this stone-sheathed church with a gable roof are low, with the roof eaves brought close to the ground, so that each of the principal windows occurs within a small wall dormer. A small corner entrance tower adds to the dollhouse scale of this Gothic Revival church.

At 1716 Willis Avenue is an Eastlake-style dwelling (c. 1885) with a pair of two-story bays brought out at a 45-degree angle from the adjoining walls. A later Colonial Revival porch has been added to the house. Further down Willis Avenue, at 1908, is a 1920s period revival English cottage (c. 1926). Its pointed-arched entrance is in stone, which contrasts with the brick first-floor walls and the stucco and half-timbering above.

Pleasantville

Just off Iowa 5 as it passes through Pleasantville, at the corner of Breckenridge and East Monroe streets, is the elementary school building (1922) designed by Frank E. Wetherell (of Wetherell and Harrison). At the turn of the century, several architects of the English Arts and Crafts movement began to incorporate elements of the eighteenth-century Georgian style into their work. Examples of this work were widely published and by the teens were well known to American architects. The elementary school at Pleasantville is an American expression of the view that an architect could play with classical (Georgian) details and at the same time pursue his commitment to the Arts and Crafts. In this brick building, two low wings flank a central section articulated by a loggia-like row of large roundheaded windows. Wide overhanging tile roofs hold the composition in place, and a wide variety of terracotta ornamentation depicting books, lamps of knowledge, and cornucopias (some in bright glazed colors) enlivens the faces of the building. Much of the ornament conveys a Prairie-style atmosphere, both in its location on the building, and in its design.

On Breckenridge Street itself, at the corner of North State Street and West Broadway, is another important school building. This is the Pleasantville High School (1940–1942), designed by Oren Thomas of Des Moines. This two-story brick-and-concrete building is a handsome classical example of the PWA Streamline Moderne. There is a horizontal concrete band at the base, and another curves around the middle of the building. The corners of the building are curved, and the bands of steel-frame windows are carried around these curved corners. Patterns of square wall-grilles have been placed at various points within the brick-sheathed walls. A reasonably successful addition was made to the building in 1972, designed by Frevert-Ramsey, Architects-Engineers.

Roland

Those who are enamored of the Streamline Moderne of the late 1930s should proceed to Roland, at the outskirts of town on the northeast (off route R77). A part of the complex of buildings of the Great Lakes Pipe Line Company is Pump Station No. 65 (c. 1937). A checklist of the features of the Streamline

Moderne style will quickly reveal that all of the essentials are here in this two-story brick building. These include a curved corner with glass brick, a long narrow band window on the second floor that is carried around the corner, a porthole window, and an entrance dealt with so as to suggest a vertical pavilion, with a parapet higher than the surrounding roof.

Sheldahl

The First Evangelical Lutheran Church (now Sheldahl Norwegian Lutheran Church) of 1883 is the perfect prototype of a prairie building that might be used as a grange hall, a schoolhouse, or, as in this instance, a church. Without a sign indicating use, this building could be any one of these building types. Its form is that of a single-floor rectangular box topped by a gable roof. The walls are clapboard and the roof is covered with shingles; the windows are double hung, with four lights per sash, and their proportions tend to the vertical. One end-gable contains the entry door and a small open belfry crowns the roof. The building itself overlaps the foundation so that one feels as if it could be easily lifted up and placed on another site (which of course happens to buildings all the time). The church is located in the northeast section of town, two blocks east of route R38.

Sigourney

The community was named for the Connecticut poet and writer Lydia Huntley Sigourney. The site for the town was selected as the future county seat in 1844 for the usual reason that it was near the geographic center of the county.

CE404 **Keokuk County Courthouse**

1909–1910, Wetherell and Gage. South of Washington St., between Main and Jefferson streets

After the usual conflict as to where the courthouse should be located, a single-floor log building measuring 20 by 24 feet was built in Sigourney in 1845. This was replaced in 1857 by a two-story brick courthouse with a high central lantern. In 1909–1910 the 1857 building was in turn supplanted by a sophisticated version of the Beaux-Arts Classical tradition. This third Sigourney courthouse was designed by the architectural firm of Wetherell and Gage of Oskaloosa. The building's principal entrance is located between two projecting pavilions. The doorway itself projects through the rusticated base of the structure; above the doorway is a pair of Ionic columns rising two stories high. A small-scaled central tower supports a lantern whose four sides are dominated by four clock faces. The courthouse is located south of Washington Street, between Main and Jefferson streets.

CE405 **Woodin House**

1872. 118 W. Marion St.

The architectural high point in Sigourney is the Woodin house. Even though it is only one-and-a-half stories tall, it presents one of the boldest renditions of the Italianate/French Second Empire design within the state. The projecting brackets surrounding each of the dormer windows convey a crisp angular quality one associates with the designs of the Philadelphia architect Frank Furness. As these brackets proceed through the roof eave they become consoles that support the projecting gable roofs over each of the second-floor windows. The only appreciable change that has been made to the exterior of the house is the substitution of a turn-of-the-century Colonial Revival porch for the original Italianate design.

CE406 **House**

c. 1850s. Iowa 92, west edge of town

At the west edge of Sigourney is a handsomely sited two-story brick Italianate box of a house. The central arched entrance is balanced on each side by arched casement windows that descend to the floor. The second floor, above the entrance, has a tall double-arched window with double-arched windows to each side. The house is framed by an open lawn that is pressed in on each side by evergreen trees.

CE407 **Flander Farm**

c. 1900. East of Sigourney on Iowa 92, milepost 216

Proceeding east of Sigourney on Iowa 92 one comes upon the Flander Farm complex (c. 1900). Here there are two classic midwestern barn types side by side. One of these is a wooden structure with a steeply pitched gable roof, accompanied by a low shed-roofed appendage; the other, to the left, is a barn with a gambrel roof, topped at the ridge by a monitor with a gable roof, and spreading out over the ground with shelters topped by low-pitched shed roofs.

Story City

Story City, located north of Ames and just west of Interstate 35, was platted in 1850.

CE408 **Franson House**

1914. 319 Grant St.

This is a vigorous assertion of the Craftsman aesthetic. The one-and-a-half-story house has a light, floating roof that extends far out over the walls and is supported by brackets. Below, the concern of the designers seems to have been to reduce surfaces and volumes to basic rectilinear shapes. The lower walls are of brick carried up to the plate line of the second floor. The entrance/living porch, which extends across the entire face of the house, has a hipped roof supported by large square wood piers. On the two long sides of the house, the second-floor windows peer out of wall dormers covered by paper-thin roofs. The upper walls and the projecting bays exhibit a geometric pattern of half-timbering squares set into the stucco walls. In 1979 a single-floor addition was added to the house.

CE409 **Senti House**

c. 1755. Take Timberline Drive north off Broad Street in Story City; proceed 1 mile north, then west for a short distance

While there may be reused fragments of older European houses present in several examples throughout the state, the Senti dwelling can probably lay claim to being the oldest complete house in Iowa. The house was built c. 1755 in the small Connecticut town of Portland. It was purchased by the Senti family, shipped to Iowa, and then reconstructed.[44] This Colonial dwelling is a characteristic example of a mid-eighteenth-century New England house. It is two stories high, with a steeply pitched gable roof, and has a slight suggestion of a second-story overhang at the front of the house and also around on the sides. The wide entrance door has a simple, wide entablature/cornice, below which is a narrow transom window. A good-sized chimney projects from the center of the roof ridge. The exterior is sheathed in clapboard which has been left in a natural weathered condition. The owners have added a new one-and-a-half-story wing with a gambrel roof, and a garage to the rear, both of which have the feeling of being original to the house. The setting for the house within a grove of trees in the open farmland enhances the rustic quality of the building.

CE410 **Standard Service Station** (later a DX Station)

1917. Northeast corner of Pennsylvania Ave. and Washington St.

Here, placed at an angle to the street, is a double-pier brick service station with the building and the pump area sheltered by a single low-pitched gable roof. The surrounding trees increase the suburban atmosphere of the station.

Toledo (and Tama)

The present twin cities of Toledo and Tama were, until the end of the nineteenth century, separated from one another by a mile or more of open farmland. By the early 1900s the two communities had blended into one another, although they did retain their separate identities. Toledo was selected in 1854 as the site for the county seat, while Tama was platted to the south in 1862 in anticipation of the arrival of the railroad. By the 1890s the joint cities of Toledo and Tama were served by both the Chicago and Northwestern Railroad and the Chicago, Milwaukee, and Saint Paul Railroad. An electric suburban railroad went into operation between the two cities in 1894. With the construction of paved highways in the years 1910 through the 1920s, Toledo and Tama were traversed by the Lincoln Highway (US 30). One of the most interesting early public projects of the city of Tama was the formation of the Tama Hydraulic Company in 1874. This company constructed a dam across the Iowa River, creating a large lake that could be used to provide water to the community as well as to generate power.

CE411 **Tama County Courthouse**

1865–1867, 1892. 1892 remodeling, W. R. Parsons and Son. Courthouse Square, northwest corner of High and Broadway streets, Toledo

When Toledo was platted, a large public square measuring 312 feet by 312 feet was provided at the center of the town. The county's business was first conducted in a two-story wooden building (built in 1854), but a permanent masonry structure was constructed in 1866–1867. In style this was an Italianate building, two stories high, of brick with a metal roof. Andreas wrote of it, "The whole building is a model of neatness and taste, both in architectural design and beauty of finish."[45] In 1892 the Illinois architects W. R. Parsons and Son appreciably enlarged and updated the older courthouse. In their hands a new Richardsonian Romanesque building emerged. Entrance to the building was through a large typical Richardsonian arch, and a five-story tower with four clock faces hovered over the building. When the architects were finished almost no vestige of the original building remained.

CE412 **Commercial Block**

c. 1870. Northeast corner of High and Broadway streets, Toledo

As with numerous mid-century Italianate buildings, the strong visual character of this three-story brick structure is created by its cornice and the pronounced lintel hoods over the roundheaded windows. Paired arched windows are found on the first floor, and the entrances were articulated by hooded lintels with semicircular transom windows below. Some changes have been made at the first-floor level, but the upper facade appears to be untouched.

CE413 Commercial Blocks

c. 1870s-1890s. South side of High St., east of Broadway, Toledo

Here one can experience an entire nineteenth-century downtown streetscape, composed of brick buildings of one and two stories. In style they range from the late Italianate to the Queen Anne. Their upper-floor facades, entablatures, and cornices generally remain intact, while most of the storefronts on the street level have continually been brought up to date (including using the usual "Wild West" image of a "rustic" wood-shake mansard roof).

CE414 House

c. 1885. 302 Church St., Toledo

A good-sized two-story Queen Anne dwelling is here hidden behind a luxurious two-story porch. The term "gingerbread ornament," so often applied to woodwork of this sort, is certainly an apt description of the ornamentation of this porch. A lacy pattern of molded, sawed, and turned woodwork bursts forth in this design, forming a remarkable transition from the exterior world to the interior of the house.

CE415 House

c. 1905. 1412 State St., Tama

The primitiveness of the eighteenth-century Colonial style was here infused into a commanding design that was not reticent about reflecting the affluence of the upper middle class as America entered the "new" century. The house sits in the center of a wide lawn, some distance from the street. It states its case through a stately two-story temple front; but at the same time, through its extensive front veranda, it bespeaks a life of ease. The house is appropriately painted (at this writing) yellow for the clapboard and white for the trim.

CE416 Toledo Public Library

1942; Russell J. Prescott; Gilbert T. Steger, WPA engineer. 206 E. High St.

The Toledo library building appears like a PWA Moderne county courthouse reduced almost to dollhouse size. The top of the central entrance wing rises slightly above the rest of the building. Two decorated bands, one at the edge of the parapet, the other below it, articulate the facade of this exposed reinforced concrete building. The pairs of front windows on each side of the entrance are contained within slightly recessed panels. A curved roof canopy covers the entrance, and large-scale metal wall lamps are placed on each side of the door. A few external changes have occurred: there is a new entrance doorway, and a ramp, rather than steps, leading to the entrance.

CE417 Lincoln Highway Bridge

1915. US 30, E. 5th St.

The Lincoln Highway, a completely paved route from coast to coast, was proposed in 1912 by Carl G. Fisher, the automotive industrialist. He was joined by several others, including Henry B. Joy, president of the Packard Motor Company. Acknowledging the intense public interest in Lincoln at the time, they attached his name to the proposed transcontinental highway.[46] Because of Iowa's system of local taxation to pay for roads, the state's section of this proposed highway was slow to be realized. The Tama bridge is one of the few remaining monuments of this highway system. The bridge itself is a simple reinforced concrete slab; it is the bridge's railing that pulls it out of the ordinary. The city of Tama paid extra, and had the railings cast with the words "Lincoln Highway" forming the balustrades.

Traer

Traer and much of Tama County were initially settled in the middle to late 1850s. The site selected for the town was in a small grove of trees adjacent to Wolf Creek. In contrast, the surrounding lands were open prairie, and were quickly adapted to agriculture. In the railroad expansion after the Civil War, Traer first became a terminus for a branch of the Burlington Chicago Railroad, and later other railroads were brought to the community.

CE418 Carnegie Public Library

1914–1915, J. G. Ralston. South side of 2nd St., west of US 63

In June 1914 the community of Traer received a $10,000 grant from the Carnegie Foundation for the town library. By the end of July the architect J. G. Ralston of Waterloo was drafting his initial sketches for the building. The scheme provided was a conventional one: a structure on a raised basement, with steps leading up to a central entrance and reading rooms on either side. The architect's frontispiece for the building entailed a shallow pediment and accompanying entablature supported by two pairs of pilasters placed on each side of the entrance. The scale of this Beaux-Arts building is something between that of a public building and a larger domestic design.

CE419 Traer Winding Stairs

1894. 534 2nd St. (north side of 2nd St., west of US 63)

Projecting from the second floor of the Star Clipper Building is an iron bridge that extends out over the sidewalk; near the street the bridge is connected to an iron spiral staircase. The lightness of the iron members of the bridge and the stairs makes them almost disappear within the downtown landscape. The stairs were provided so that one could go directly to the newspaper office on the second floor. Nearby, at 423 Second Street, is the Brooks and Moore building, an Italianate business block. This 1873 building displays an exuberantly detailed entablature and cornice, and windows with projecting keystones and hoods.

CE420 House

c. 1875. Southeast corner of 5th and Walnut streets

A boxlike two-story late Italianate dwelling has been made more commanding by the addition of a fancifully detailed wraparound porch. The entablature of the flat-roofed porch exhibits a pattern of small brackets; between the wood piers, below the entablature, is a cutout pattern that curves upward, then bends downward at the center. The house is sheathed in clapboard and has segmental arched windows; there is a grouping of pairs of brackets under the main roof.

CE421 House

1890. Northeast corner of 6th and Walnut streets

Porches are the theme in this large suburban Queen Anne dwelling. The entrance porch and connecting wide veranda start off with arches rendered in light sawed and turned wood; gradually a new motif of spindles and segmental arches is introduced. This latter motif then continues around the corner. The second-floor porch over the entrance has much heavier columns, and its segmental arches are now solid.

Vinton

Vinton became the county seat the same year it was platted on the south bank of the Cedar River, in 1849. To the east the landscape was wooded, while to the west it was open prairie dotted every now and then with groves of trees. A conventional grid was laid out, only slightly modified by one square set aside for the courthouse, another for a schoolhouse; somewhat later a cemetery was established at the eastern section of the town. In 1864 a 40-acre site at the southwest edge of town was obtained for the Iowa College for the Blind (now the Braille and Sight Saving School).

CE422 **Benton County Courthouse**

1905, Bell and Detweiler. 4th St., between 1st and 2nd avenues

The first courthouse for Benton County was a two-story wood structure that burned down in 1853, although it was eventually rebuilt. This was followed by a building in a fascinating version of the Greek Revival style (1856). This two-story brick building had an almost flat roof, with a tall, narrow cupola at the center. Bold projecting pediments over the windows and doors were supported on each side by brackets. This second courthouse was demolished in 1905 and replaced by the present building.

The full impact of the classical images associated with the Ecole des Beaux-Arts was slowly felt in the designs of most midwestern county courthouses. There was a tendency among architects, even after 1900, to retain the surface busyness and the picturesque qualities associated with the late nineteenth-century French Second Empire style. Such is

certainly the case with the Benton County Courthouse. The verticality of the building is accentuated by the high (112 feet high) double-tiered and domed central tower. However, instead of using contrasting surface materials, as so often seen in late nineteenth-century buildings, Bell and Detweiler uniformly sheathed the Benton County Courthouse (including its details) in a light-colored Buckeye sandstone.

CE423 **Bank Building** (now American Legion Building)

1916. 1st Ave., near northwest corner with 5th St. E.

The bank as a dominant "public" institution within a community is given here the pedimented facade of an Ionic temple. It is set off from its two-story neighbors on each side by being pulled back on each side and by the use of limestone for the entire facade. Its current occupation by the American Legion is entirely in keeping with its public presence.

CE424 **United States Post Office Building**

1922, James A. Wetmore. 516 1st Ave.

This post office is another of the many instances where the Colonial Revival was used for smaller public buildings. The phase of the Colonial expressed here is the Federal style. The facade exhibits five slightly recessed arched openings with windows and doors placed within them. Above the pedimented entrance is a stone balustrade running around the entire roof.

CE425 Horridge House

c. 1870s. 612 1st Ave.

The gables and the eaves of this two-story brick house exhibit a playful lacy pattern of sawed bargeboards, and this single feature more than anything else pushes the design into the Gothic Revival camp. The building's entrance is unusual, consisting of two thick columns supporting consoles, which in turn hold up a cantilevered flat roof. One assumes that this strong feature of the present building was added later, perhaps after 1900.

CE426 House

c. 1882. 913 2nd Ave.

The design of this substantial two-story dwelling was balanced between the late Eastlake and the Queen Anne. The design fulfills the Victorian ideal of being varied and picturesque. It is composed of narrow vertical volumes, each covered by a steeply pitched gable roof. Tall paneled chimneys add verticality to the building, as do all of the window units. Panel-work occurs above many of the windows, and in a number of instances the horizontal paneling forms bands across the facade. Ornamentation carried out in sawed or turned work abounds on the porches of the first and second floors.

CE427 House

1869. Southwest corner of 2nd Ave.

A richly bracketed two-story brick Italianate house has been sited on a slope rising from the street. Its plan is cruciform; the entrance is within the gabled wing facing the street, behind which is a long two-story service wing.

The recessed double-door entry has side lights and a curved transom.

CE428 Prairie Creek Christian Church

c. late 1870s, later. Iowa 150 north and east of Vinton, 3 miles

The church was established in 1858, but the present building was constructed some 20 years later. Projecting in one direction from the central octagon is an entrance wing with a hipped roof and a tower; a large rear wing, also with a hipped roof, issues forth in the other direction with its own tower and chimney. The building is sheathed in clapboard, and the only hint at style is the open lantern of the entrance tower. The detailing at this point is Eastlake. It all adds up to what we usually think of as Carpenter's Gothic at its best.

CE429 McQuilkin True-Round Barn

1918, attrib. Johnson Brothers Clay Works. West and north of Vinton on US 218, 13 miles; left (west) on route D65, 4 miles to gravel road, turn right (north) 1 mile

In this section of Benton County there are several True-Round Barns, which were probably built by the Johnson Brothers Clay Works of Fort Dodge. These barns are characterized by the use of a smaller terracotta tile brick on the lower level and then larger tiles above. The McQuilkin Barn is 60 feet in diameter, and at the center, also in hollow tile, is a silo 14 feet in diameter. The roof is cone shaped and has a dramatic gable dormer projecting above the ground-floor entrance. Two other nearby True-Round Barns can be seen by traveling north 2.4 miles on route V37 to route D56 (a gravel road); turn right (east); in about a mile, one 1914 barn can be seen; 3.5 miles further is a 1910 barn.

Washington

The site for the future town of Washington was established near the center of Washington County by the appointed commissioners in 1838; and in 1839 it was platted as the seat for the county courthouse. Its site on the open prairie just east of the Crooked River placed it at the center of agricultural production in this region. In 1858 the Mississippi and Missouri Railroad reached the community, and by 1900 Washington was a hub for six railroads.

CE430 Washington County Courthouse

1885–1887, William Foster and Henry F. Liebbe. Northwest corner of W. Main St. and Ave. B

The county's first permanent courthouse was built in 1845–1847 and was designed by its builder, Alex Lee. It was a two-story Greek Revival building with a low central tower and an open lantern. It was torn down in 1869 because it was viewed as unsafe. A new courthouse was designed by the Des Moines firm of Foster and Liebbe; construction commenced in 1885 and it was completed in 1887. Its design is certainly one of the most exuberant and successful Richardsonian Romanesque courthouses within the state. A wonderful tiered corner tower dominates the design. This brick-and-stone tower, which is 181 feet high, contains four clock faces, each 8 feet in diameter, with a spire above. The architects dramatically contrasted the light-colored stone trim against the dark red Muscatine brick, creating a visual battle between the suggested solidity of masonry and the linear quality of the stone. Above the two principal entrances are two 8-foot-high cast-metal sculptures: over the south entrance is Justice, over the west entrance, the Goddess of Liberty. (Regrettably, neither of these principal entries at the base of the tower now functions as an entrance into the building.)

CE431 Milwaukee Railroad Passenger Station

c. 1892. N. Iowa St. at 5th St.

A broadly extended curved roof is poised like a hat over the building below. At the center of the building, facing the passenger and loading platform, is an angled control bay that extends through the roof to form a low bay tower. The walls under the roof overhang are divided into two bands: the lower one of vertical wood, the upper part of narrow clapboard. The building is placed in what was a well-tended park, and the large trees with their extended branches echo the station's dramatic roof.

CE432 Washington City Hall

1881, William Foster. Southeast corner of E. Washington St. and S. 2nd Ave.

A two-and-a-half-story Italianate house functions as a city hall. The house was built as a private dwelling for the Blair family; it became City Hall in 1926. A tall tower capped by a mansard roof rises between two wings of the structure. Verticality is the visual theme of this building, stated in the ornamental volutes and the wall planes that define them, through the narrow vertical windows and doors, and in other external and internal detailing.

CE433 Keck House

c. 1850. 504 W. Washington St.

This dwelling was probably designed by its owner/builder, Joseph Keck, who later became an important figure in finance within Washington County. The late version of the Italianate style is here combined with a French Second Empire mansard roof. The character of the design is strongly asserted in the pronounced array of angular wall dormers that are thrust through the eave line of the roof. The entrance facade exhibits a central curved roof dormer, balanced on each side by dormers with sharply pitched gable roofs. The porch, instead of being linear and delicate as it would have been treated in the earlier phase of the Italianate, is here thick and substantial. With the exception of a few missing details—such as the projecting finial and ornament of its central curved dormer and its metal iron fence by the public sidewalk—the building is much the same as it was when built.

CE434 Young Log Cabin

1840. Sunset Park; W. Adams St. between G and H avenues

The Alexander Young two-story log cabin was originally located on a 320-acre farm situated 4.5 miles northwest of Washington. The Daughters of the American Revolution moved it to Sunset Park and restored it in 1912. The walls of the cabin are of split logs and the windows are double hung. A large stone fireplace and chimney dominated one of the building's gable ends. Next to the Young log cabin is a single-room log cabin (1840), also of split logs. This was moved from a farm northwest of Washington in 1974.

CE435 House

c. 1882. 703 W. Monroe St.

The design of this splendid, playful dwelling merges the late Eastlake into the Queen Anne. Two delicate, spindly porches greet the visitor. The porch on the left has a horseshoe arch; that on the right presents a small circular pavilion with its own spired roof. Small dormers and porches with shed roofs occur on the second floor, and the gabled roof ends exhibit wide, elaborate bargeboards.

CE436 Conger House

1847, 1868, 1906. 903 E. Washington St.

The southeast wing of this building was the original house. Jonathan Clark Conger, who had bought the house in 1848, transformed it in 1868 into a two-story Italianate house with a gable roof. Below the gable end facing the street is a wide veranda. In 1906 the brick walls were stuccoed, a new Colonial Revival porch was added to the side, and other "modernization" took place. The dwelling is now owned by the Washington County Historical Society and is open to the public.

Waubeek

The small Linn County town of Waubeek lies up the Wapsipinicon River some 9 miles northwest of Stone City (see Anamosa, p. 39). Being this close to available good stone, builders erected several interesting limestone structures within the community, including the Gothic Revival general store building (CE437).

Another Gothic Revival structure built in 1868 is the one-and-a-half-story Stone Stable, located to the southeast of the Mercantile Building. The Stone Stable was erected as a commercial enterprise (a stock farm) by Frederick Braun and Ignatius Beek. The walls of this building are of random ashlar limestone, the roof is steeply pitched, and there is a central gable with bargeboards.

The best-known building in Waubeek is the 1860 Pitzer-Bowdish-Doe house, situated at the west end of town (south side of Marion Street, at the west end). This house was built for Joseph Pitzer by the Pennsylvanian stonemason Bennefield Wertman. The house was purchased from Pitzer in 1863 by John Bowdish, and later was acquired by Eugene Doe. The two-story stone house with a gable roof is a classic example of the late Federal style, with a central entrance, large balanced double-hung windows on each side, and a row of double-hung windows on the second floor. This house was used as a historic source for the 1932 Colonial Revival Robert Armstrong house in Cedar Rapids (designed by Bruce McKay).

CE437 **Frederick Braun and Ignatius Beek Mercantile Building**

1868. East side of Main Street, between Marion and Union streets, (corner of Whittier Road and Boy Scout Road)

At the edge of Waubeek's own limestone quarry is situated this mercantile building. It is a two-and-a-half-story structure with a gable roof, constructed of finely cut and laid limestone blocks. Its roof is steeply pitched and its windows are roundheaded; these and other details place it in the mid-century Italianate style.

West Chester

The 1867 Gracehill Moravian Church is situated southwest of West Chester. (Drive west of town on Iowa 92, turn south on county road 114; proceed 5 miles to the small community of Grace Hill.) This church is one of seven or more built by the Moravian Church in Iowa. The wood clapboard church conveys the impression that it is of the Greek Revival style, even though there are no explicit Greek details. The format of the church is that of two volumes with gable roofs, brought together at their gables ends. The steeply pitched roof is surmounted at the entrance by a two-tiered series of gabled boxes, and these in turn are topped by a small spire. Adjacent to the church is the cemetery, which was also laid out in 1867.

Returning to West Chester, take route W38 which leads to the southeast edge of town; proceed 3.25 miles to the Isaac Kleese Farm Complex. Here one will discover a group of rural buildings that provide a nearly perfect picture of an Iowa farm of the late nineteenth century. The modest one-and-a-half-story farmhouse was built in 1872, and most of the other buildings (with the exception of the principal barn, which was built in 1893) were constructed at just about the same time. In approaching the complex one first encounters a trimmed hedge fence of Osage orange, behind which is the remains of the orchard. Beyond the end of the hedge is the farm road. To the left of this is the house, behind which is located the smokehouse, a chicken house, the privy, a wood shed, a granary, then a blacksmith shop. On the right side of the farm road is the well and windmill, the corncrib, and beyond these the hog house and the 1893 barn. All of the buildings have simple gable or shed roofs and are sheathed in vertical or horizontal wood.

What Cheer

The town was established in 1865, and within a few years coal mining began in the surrounding region. After the depletion of the coal, attention was turned to the extensive deposits of a fine white clay that lent itself to the production of ceramic products.

Within the center of town are two interesting brick buildings. At 201 Barnes (Iowa 21) is the restored What Cheer Opera House (1892). It is mildly Richardsonian Romanesque in style; a central large arch is carried up into its second floor and then there is a third-floor fenestration of arched windows. The building houses an 800-seat auditorium with a horseshoe balcony. Further south on Barnes from the Opera House is the two-story masonry Baines Block (1887). The building retains intact the vertical showcases for the retail stores. The metal entablature/cornice has a small shed roof of metal tiles, and a central gable with the building's name and date.

At the corner of Barnes and South streets is a 1942 WPA gymnasium building. This reinforced concrete building is composed of two rectangular volumes, the one to the right somewhat higher than the major section of the building. A center row of seven large vertical steel-frame windows is held in place by vertical windows of glass brick, one on each side. Thin horizontal grooves run across the surface of the building; between these one can see the imprint of the wood panels used in forming the concrete.

Winterset

The site selected in 1849 for Winterset was in the "exact" center of Madison County. The rolling hills of the surrounding landscape meander down into the wooded valleys of the Middle River to the south and Cedar Creek to the north and east. The original grid of the community consists of a rectangle of forty blocks centering on the usual courthouse square. The historic fame of Winterset today rests on its many nearby covered bridges, its courthouse (1876–1878), and its many limestone houses.

CE438 Madison County Courthouse

1876–1878, Alfred H. Piquenard. Northwest corner of Court St. and 1st St.

Andreas described the courthouse, then under construction, as "magnificent." "The building," he went on to note, "is in the form of a Greek cross, one hundred feet each way, with four fronts exactly alike. The building is constructed of cut stone [limestone], taken from the excellent quarries near the place, and is surmounted by a grand octagonal dome."[47] The architect of the courthouse, Alfred H. Piquenard of Saint Louis and Chicago, along with his partner, John C. Cochrane, entered a number of competitions for midwestern governmental buildings. Their most widely known public building was the Illinois State Capitol at Springfield (1871–1874). For the courthouse at Winterset, Piquenard provided an Italianate scheme with single-story entrance piazzas repeated on all four facades of the building. He then topped his composition with a faceted roof upon which was placed a high vertical octagonal drum and dome. The architect's design was partially restrained by the need to utilize the foundation of the earlier courthouse (designed in 1868 by G. P. Randall), which had burned in 1875.

CE439 Group of Three Commercial Blocks

c. 1880s. Northwest corner of Court St. and 2nd Ave.

All three of these two-story brick buildings have dramatic overscaled window headers, entablatures, and cornices. The corner block could be loosely labeled Italianate, with its slight references to pilasters and quoined corners. The smaller commercial building to the right, with its central pedimented cornice and round-arched windows, is medieval, looking toward the Romanesque Revival.

CE440 United States Post Office Building

1934, Louis A. Simon. Southwest corner of 2nd Ave. and Jefferson St.

In this variation of the PWA Moderne, the pilasters are of the same brick as the surrounding walls, and it is their vertical grooves which read most intensely. Stylized capitals surmount each of the pilasters, and they in turn are dropped down from a narrow horizontal terracotta band.

CE441 House

c. 1860s. 320 Jefferson St. W.

An expansive hood with sawed wood ends covers the first-floor windows of this two-story brick late Italianate house. The wood brackets of the roof and the sawed work of the gable ends are equally elaborate. The flat-roofed section between the two wings seems ready to receive a tower.

CE442 House

c. 1895. 602 Court St. W.

The Queen Anne form of the house is restrained by the Colonial Revival details. The delight of this two-story dwelling is its location within extensive landscaped grounds, and then the way it spills out into this space through a wide veranda and second-floor porch, both of which boast spired roofs.

CE443 Guiberson House

c. 1865. 302 4th Ave. S.

The two-story Guiberson house, with its low-pitched gable roof and end-wall chimney, reflects the continuation of the Greek Revival mode through much of the 1860s. As with a number of the limestone houses in and around Winterset, these dwellings may have been built by the local stonemason Caleb Clark. There are several other mid-nineteenth-century limestone houses on Fourth Avenue. These include the Kelso house (1866), at the southwest corner of Fourth Avenue South and Summit Street, and the Tiddrick house (c. 1856 and later), at the northwest corner of Fourth Avenue South and Washington Street. Caleb Clark's own small stone single-story cottage (1854) is situated at the south end of Eighth Avenue South.

CE444 Twelve-sided Barn

c. 1910. 1100 Summit St. W.

This unusual 12-sided single-story barn was given walls of concrete. The roof is supported by steel beams and wood framing. A wide low monitor surmounts the center of the roof.

CE445 Sawyer House

1934–1936, R. S. Lanse. 420 Court St. E.

The client for this house had visited the 1933–1934 World's Fair in Chicago, where he saw the model houses and was converted to the cause of modernism. He engaged the Boone architect R. S. Lanse to carry out his version of the modern. The end product was a mildly Streamline Moderne house consisting of a second-floor stucco box hung over a stone-sheathed first floor. The symbolic importance of the automobile is announced by the stone-clad attached garage adjacent to the entrance. Metal casement windows wrap around the corners; within, round mirrors and a step-down living room enhanced the modern theme.

CE446 City Park

South end of 9th St. S.

At the south edge of the park is what appears to be a medieval ruin, the Clark Tower (1926 and later). An external staircase leads up to the observation porch of this crenellated stone tower. This monument was built as a memorial to Ruth and Caleb Clark by their descendants. In another section of the park is the single-floor split-log Bennett cabin, built in 1852 and restored in 1917. In August 1970 the Cutler-Donahue covered bridge was moved and installed within City Park. The bridge had been built in 1870 by Eli Cox at a site on the North River, some 18 miles from Winter-

set. The roadway is covered by a shingled gable roof; presently the side walls are painted barn red, and the two gabled roadway entrances are in white.

CE447 Pearson Barn

c. 1900. Iowa 92, .5 miles east of US 169

This large 70 foot by 80 foot grade barn with a gabled roof has a spectacular interior that rises to a height of 72 feet, its roof carried on a forest of braced-beam trusses. Close to the barn is a tiny one-and-a-half-story stone farmhouse that dates from 1862.

CE448 Bevington House and Stone Barn

1856. 805 S. 2nd Ave.

A mid-1850s farm complex was composed here of a two-story frame dwelling with a few light Gothic Revival touches, and a rough limestone barn.

CE449 Round Barn

c. 1920s? South of Winterset on route P71 to intersection with county road G50; turn left; proceed east 4 miles on G50 to intersection with gravel road; follow gravel road 2 miles south

The walls of this single-story round barn with a conical roof are of vertical concrete staves held together by horizontally placed iron bands. This method of construction, as Soike has pointed out,[48] was more generally used for silos.

CE450 James Bush Barn

1875. 10.5 miles west of Winterset on Iowa 92; take gravel road south 1.3 miles

This grade barn with stone walls and gable roof was built as part of the James Bush stock farm. The gabled side elevation is most impressive, with two arched openings that each serve a different level of the barn. Nearby, the farmhouse is a small cottage constructed of overscaled large blocks of stone.

CE451 Covered Bridges in Madison County

1870, later

Originally Madison County had 16 covered bridges; of these, 7 now remain, including the Cutler-Donahue bridge which was moved to Winterset City Park. On the second full weekend in October the county holds a Covered Bridge Festival.

CE451.1 Cedar Creek (Casper) Covered Bridge

1883, H. P. Jones, builder. Proceed on gravel road leaving from the northeast corner of Winterset; travel on this gravel road toward the east side of Winterset City Reservoir, 1.8 miles.

This is a single-span flat-roofed bridge of the Towne lattice type of structure. The Cedar Creek bridge was built by H. P. Jones over the North River. In 1920 the bridge was moved to its present location over Cedar Creek. The Towne latticework bridge structure was invented by the Connecticut architect/engineer Ethiel Towne. He patented this design in 1820, and examples of this type of bridge structure were built throughout the country in the middle to late nineteenth century.

CE451.2 McBride (Burger) Covered Bridge

1870–1871, J. P. Clark, builder. Proceed north from Winterset on Hwy. 169 to county road G4R; east on G4R for 7.3 miles to gravel road; north on gravel road 1.2 miles to bridge.

The builder, J. P. Clark, provided the county with a single-span, flat-roofed bridge over the North River. The upper sections of the entrances cant outward to provide additional protection for the wood plank roadway.

CE451.3 Imes (King) Covered Bridge

1870, J. P. Clark, builder. Proceed south 1 mile from Winterset on county road P71 to county road G50; east on G50 6 miles to town of Saint Charles; north on R35 for 1.3 miles to bridge.

In this bridge with a gable roof, its builder, J. P. Clark, again employed the Towne lattice truss together with queen posts. The bridge has been moved twice from its original location at Wilkins Ford on the Middle River. In 1887 it was transported to the Imes Crossing of Clanton Creek; in 1977 it was moved to its present location on the eastern edge of Saint Charles.

CE451.4 Holliwell Covered Bridge

1880, H. P. Jones and G. K. Foster, builders. South from Winterset .3 miles on gravel road that leaves from southeast corner of city; then east and southeast on gravel road to bridge.

This bridge was constructed, without covering, over the Middle River in 1854–1855. In 1880 it was moved to Sulgrove on the North River, and when it was re-erected the roof was added. The Holliwell bridge, with its 110-foot single span, is one of Iowa's most picturesque covered bridges. The builders employed the Towne arch and arched queen posts in constructing this flat-roofed bridge.

CE451.5 Roseman (Oak Grove) Covered Bridge

1883, H. P. Jones, builder. Proceed west on Hwy. 92 from Winterset 8 miles; south on county road P53 for 1.8 miles; east on G47 for 2.8 miles; north .6 miles on gravel road to bridge.

The 113-foot single-span Roseman Bridge spans the Middle River. H. P. Jones, its builder, used the Towne lattice with queen posts for the construction of this flat-roofed bridge.

CE451.6 Hogback Covered Bridge

1884, H. P. Jones, builder. Proceed north from Winterset on Hwy. 169 for 1.5 miles; west on gravel road 1.4 miles; north on gravel road 1.2 miles to bridge over North River.

Another H. P. Jones flat-roofed design utilizing the Towne truss, this was the last of the remaining bridges to be built.

In addition to bridges, while one is touring around the county one should take note of the many stone farmhouses and barns. A good concentration of these buildings can be found on route G50 as it proceeds east from Winterset to the small town of Saint Charles. Almost all of these structures date from the late 1850s through the 1860s.

South (SO)

THE NARROW BAND OF THE SOUTHERN AREA OF IOWA, WHICH runs parallel to the state of Missouri, exhibits a much flatter terrain than one finds to the north. The four eastern counties—Jefferson, Van Buren, Wapello, and Davis—present a landscape, town patterns, and architecture closely related to those found along the Mississippi River. The Des Moines River, which traverses the eastern part of this section of Iowa, was navigable by smaller steamboats, at least during the spring of each year, but the rest of the region had to await the advent of the railroads and highways for its principal transportation linkage.

Within the cities of Keosauqua and Ottumwa on the lower Des Moines River there are a number of excellent examples of pre-1860s buildings; and in the small, bypassed community of Bentonsport one is easily carried back into the 1850s. To the west, Osceola and Red Oak convey the flavor of the late nineteenth-century Victorian period or that of the early decades of this century. Other attractions of this region are the landscape and architectural designs of the numerous state parks, several of which were developed adjacent to dams and their extensive reservoirs.

Albia

The county commissioners had the town laid out as the county seat in 1845. The grid system was composed of square blocks, with one of the center blocks reserved for the future county courthouse. By the 1870s Albia was the crossroads of several railroads, and coal mining was well under way. Extensive restorations and renovations of buildings have taken place within the community since the mid-1980s, especially in the commercial structures surrounding the courthouse square.

South Iowa

Montgomery	Adams	Union	Clarke	Lucas	Monroe	Wapello 17	Jefferson
•27 •30 •32	•11	•13	⊙24	•9	•1	25⊙ 14	•15

Page	Taylor 21	Ringgold	Decatur 18	Wayne	Appanoose	Davis	
•29 10•	•2		•22 •20	•12	•8	•5 31•	•28 •4 26 •23 Van 3 Buren 19 •6 •7 16•

1. Albia (Monroe Co.)	17. Farson (Wapello Co.)
2. Bedford (Taylor Co.)	18. Garden Grove (Decatur Co.)
3. Bentonsport (Van Buren Co.)	19. Keosauqua (Van Buren Co.)
4. Birmingham (Van Buren Co.)	20. Lamoni (Decatur Co.)
5. Bloomfield (Davis Co.)	21. Lenox (Taylor Co.)
6. Bonaparte (Van Buren Co.)	22. Leon (Decatur Co.)
7. Cantril (Van Buren Co.)	23. Mount Zion (Van Buren Co.)
8. Centerville (Appanoose Co.)	24. Osceola (Clarke Co.)*
9. Chariton (Lucas Co.)	25. Ottumwa (Wapello Co.)*
10. Clarinda (Page Co.)	26. Pittsburg (Van Buren Co.)
11. Corning (Adams Co.)	27. Red Oak (Montgomery Co.)
12. Corydon (Wayne Co.)	28. Selma (Van Buren Co.)
13. Creston (Union Co.)	29. Shenandoah (Page Co.)
14. Eldon (Wapello Co.)	30. Stanton (Montgomery Co.)
15. Fairfield (Jefferson Co.)	31. Troy (Davis Co.)
16. Farmington (Van Buren Co.)	32. Villisca (Montgomery Co.)

A detailed map of site locations has been provided for cities indicated by ⊙ on the map and by * in the list at left.

SO001 Monroe County Courthouse

1902–1903, O. O. Smith. Courthouse Square, corner of Main and Benton streets

The present courthouse is the third one to occupy the square. Though the design is loosely Beaux-Arts Classical, the building's vertical proportions and rusticated stone sheathing refer back to the Richardsonian Romanesque. The cruciform scheme of the design terminates in a double-layered central clock tower. The principal entrance facade is emphasized by a slightly recessed porch within which is a pair of Ionic columns. The square itself, which was densely wooded in the nineteenth century, is now open, and walkways lead from every side and every corner into the building, forming a geometric scheme.

SO002 Skean's Block

1889. Benton Ave., facing onto Courthouse Square

The visual drawing card for this two-story brick commercial block is the patterning of the headers of the second-floor windows, and then above, the elaboration of its entablature, cornice, and false pediment. Each of the stone headers of the second-floor windows is angled and terminates in a bold keystone; these headers are joined to form a wavy line across the facade. In the late 1980s the entablature and cornice were painted in bright contrasting colors.

SO003 Dutch Service Company Building

1926–1927. US 34, east side of town, alongside the railroad tracks

Here one will discover the remains of one of Harry Gholson's Dutch Mill service stations, which used to dot the highways of southern Iowa. The three-story mill structure, once complete with windmill blades, originally housed the facilities for the service station, as well as a small restaurant. There was a roofed service area in front. Eventually the mill was accompanied by 12 tourist cottages.[1] The former station has now been sheathed in aluminum siding and converted into a residence.

SO004 Saint Patrick's Roman Catholic Church, Georgetown

1860. 8 miles west of Albia on US 34

Saint Patrick's is a church with a gable roof and is sheathed in somber cut gray stone. It is situated within the small community of Georgetown. The sanctuary is Gothic Revival in image, but the accompanying tower seems more Italian Romanesque than Gothic. The corner and the wall buttresses are rendered in square-cut stone, whereas the masonry walls were constructed on a more random pattern. The siting in the open, cultivated rolling prairie is romantic and compelling.

Bedford

The town was settled and became the seat of Taylor County in 1852. The site selected was located on the east bank of a small river with an unusual name, East One Hundred and Two River. The town's grid was organized around a larger than usual two-square-block public square which in turn surrounds the county courthouse.

SO005 Taylor County Courthouse

1892–1893, F. M. Ellis. Northeast corner of Jefferson and Court streets

The architect F. M. Ellis of Omaha, Nebraska, was active during the 1880s and 1890s in designing county courthouses in Nebraska, Iowa, and Minnesota. The Taylor County Courthouse is of brick with stone trim and rises three stories on a raised basement. Its principal facade has a projecting porch centered on a large Richardsonian Romanesque arch. To each side of this porch are narrow turrets with conical roofs. While the body of the building is pure Richardsonian Romanesque, its central high tower with segmented dome looks to the French Second Empire mode.

SO006 Public Library

1916–1917, Wetherell and Gage. Northwest corner of Jefferson and Court streets

A grant of $10,000 was made to Bedford by the Carnegie Foundation in 1907, but the library building was not constructed until ten years later. Frank E. Wetherell (sometimes listed as Wetherell and Gage, at other times as Wetherell and Harrison) designed a number of Carnegie libraries in Iowa from the early 1900s through the teens. The design of this parapeted building with a gable seems to look back to Dutch and Flemish architecture of the seventeenth century. The stucco walls are contained by the brick base, corner quoining, horizontal brick bands, and windows surrounded by brick frames. The centrally placed entrance pavilion displays a classically framed door, and above this is a small pedimented stone frame within which is the name of the building.

SO007 First Presbyterian Church (now United Christian Presbyterian Church)

1893. Southwest corner of Court and Pearl streets

This low brick church with stone details has the character of a late nineteenth-century English Victorian village or country church. The windows with their stone lintels are either square headed or display a wide pointed arch. Above the first floor, the entrance tower is shingled and four corner finials embrace the tall spire.

SO008 First Methodist Episcopal Church

1889. Northwest corner of Court and Pearl streets

This church and the Presbyterian church across the street form a small-scale urban composition. Their small size and low scale are really suburban, and they provide appropriate backdrops to the distant county courthouse and its tower. The Methodist Episcopal church is Romanesque Revival; if it were covered in shingles rather than brick one would probably label it as an example of the Shingle style. The entrance tower of this church was placed toward the center of one side, and there is a deep entrance porch within its base. A post-World War II flat-roofed "modernist" addition has been added unsympathetically to one side of the building.

SO009 Service Station

c. 1928. Northwest corner of Madison (Iowa 148) and Main streets

California's Mission Revival style was employed at a very late moment in time for the office of this small service station. Arched windows and doors seem to peer through white stucco walls. Scalloped gable ends project above the roof's edge.

SO010 **Bedford House** (Hotel Garland)

1857, 1877, 1910. 306 Main St.

Though this building has been augmented and remodeled a number of times, its exterior street facade still expresses the plain version of the mid-century Italianate style. The upper groups of windows on this three-story brick building have wide stone lintels within

which a segmental curve was cut for each window unit. The 400 block of this street presents a classic picture of an Iowa small-town Main Street, an image conveyed by a number of well-preserved late nineteenth-century one- and two-story business blocks as well as by a fine example of a Beaux-Arts bank building (the Bedford National Bank, c. 1912).

SO011 **House**

c. 1889. 907 Central

The house itself is rather severe and plain, hinting at the late Queen Anne/Colonial Revival. But then there is the wraparound entrance veranda, a wonderfully exuberant, spindly creation of the Eastlake style with thin posts and turned lathe work, held together by an array of sawed wood details. The porch stylistically should have been built in the late 1870s, and the house some ten years later. Nonetheless, it all holds together very well.

Bentonsport

The town of Bentonsport was platted on the north bank of the lower Des Moines River in 1839. In 1840 a dam and accompanying locks were built, helping to assure the town's importance for river navigation. River transportation was supplemented in 1857 by the arrival of the railroad. By the time of the Civil War, Bentonsport and the community of Vernon across the river had developed a number of industries, including gristmills, a paper mill, a pottery works, and, in Vernon, a woolen mill. Along with several other towns on the lower Des Moines River, Bentonsport did not prosper very much in the late nineteenth century. Today it relies primarily on visitors who wish to see "Iowa's liveliest ghost town."[2] In 1972 the two communities were designated a historic district on the National Register of Historic Places. In addition to the buildings listed below, note the remains of the mid-nineteenth-century locks and dam, and also the 1882 iron bridge joining the two communities.

SO012 **United States Post Office Building**

1852. North side of Front St., east-southeast of the river bridge

Now a public building, this single-story board-and-batten Gothic cottage was originally built as a residence. The bargeboard gable ends and roof eaves are countered by double-hung windows and a Federal-style entrance with a

transom. Set back from the street and surrounded by ample trees and lawn, the building does not at all seem to be a public building.

SO013 **Mason House**

1846. North side of Front St., east-southeast of the river bridge

This two-story brick structure (originally called Ashland House) was built as a 21-room inn, a use that has continued to the present day. The building reads as a large Federal-style dwelling such as one might encounter anywhere in the northeastern United States. Its broad gable end faces the street; two entrances are provided on the ground level; and in the gable end a central window is balanced on each side by quarter-circle windows. As with the small post office building to the east, the hotel is set in ample grounds.

SO014 Herman Greef House

1863. West side of Bridge St., north of Front St.

The gabled end of this two-story Federal-style house faces the street. The small entrance porch and the bay on the south side of the house are Italianate in design, and their wooden fabric and detailing contrast with the unadorned brick walls of the dwelling.

SO015 Julius Greef House

1867. 2nd St., 2 blocks west of Bridge St., just north of the railroad tracks

The general verticality of its design, plus its bracketed roof, places the Greef house within the late Italianate mode. The pair of pointed arches of the entrance porch have a Gothic ring, while the corner two-story bay on the right of the entrance seems to anticipate the Eastlake and Queen Anne styles of the 1870s and later.

SO016 Hancock House

c. 1850s. West side of 1st St., 1 block north of the river and the railroad tracks

The basic format of the Hancock house is that of a two-story Federal-style dwelling: a central entrance with side lights and transom, balanced by double-hung windows on each side. The composition of the entrance has been carried up to the second floor where there is a wide window balanced by side lights. Other stylistic touches are present in this central-hall plan dwelling. The gable ends, with lunette windows, are enclosed in the fashion of the Greek Revival; a wider than usual cornice/entablature is carried on paired brackets, as in the Italianate style. The house was one of the first that was recorded in Iowa

(1934) by the Historic American Building Survey (HABS).

SO017 Bentonsport Academy Building

1851. Walnut St., west of 2nd St.

One of the ideals of the newly developed communities of Iowa (as was true throughout the country) was not only to develop a school system as quickly as possible, but also to encourage and sponsor an academy or college. Bentonsport's Academy building is a simple two-story brick structure covered by a steeply pitched gable roof. The flavor of the building is Italianate in its vertical proportions, but all of the windows and the entrance with transom are late Federal. A belfry, no longer in existence, added much to the building's public presence.

SO018 Presbyterian Church

1854–1855. North side of Walnut St., corner of 2nd St.

The proportions and roof pitch of the church are Greek Revival, although all of its detailing, including its tower and spire, is Gothic Revival. Thin buttresses project from the walls and corners of the building, and those on the corners have finials. Windows and doors have pointed arches and there is a small round window (containing three circles) over the entrance doorway.

SO019 Vernon School Building

1867–1868, Riley Cass. Cross the iron bridge (now closed to automobile traffic) into Vernon, proceed south on Bridge St. to first cross street, then proceed west; the schoolhouse lies on the north side of the street

The 80-foot tower of the schoolhouse rises over a rather pure and correct version of the mid-century Italianate style. The two-story brick building is cruciform in plan. The roof brackets are paired, and a wide arched doorway leads into the building. As is frequently encountered in the Italianate, windows and other details are late Federal.

SO020 James A. Brown House

1853. West end of Walnut St.

The Brown house is situated on a knoll overlooking the river valley. The design format is late Federal: brick, two stories with a gable roof. The recessed entrance with its side lights and transom exhibits a small, rather delicate pediment. There is a pair of chimneys within each of the gable ends.

SO021 **Paine House**

1851. Proceed east on Front St. as road turns and crosses railroad tracks; the house is located about .25 miles from this point

Though the roof is steeply pitched, the side-hall scheme and the detailing of this one-and-a-half-story clapboard cottage are late Federal. Extremely narrow side lights at the entrance are played off against a wide tran-

som. Centered above the first-floor entrance is a door, indicating that a porch was planned for the second floor.

SO022 **Bentonsport Bridge**

1882. South of Front Street, over the Des Moines River

The Bentonsport bridge spans the Des Moines River on four limestone piers. The iron bridge itself is a variation on the Pratt truss bridge, a type invented in 1844 by Caleb Pratt and built extensively throughout the Midwest. The open, lacy design is enhanced by the open horizontal girders and the crisscross bridge railing. The bridge is now open only to foot traffic.

Birmingham

Within this small crossroads village, on the east side of Iowa 1, is a two-story Queen Anne dwelling (c. 1885). Though its T-shaped form is relatively plain for this style, the house is set off from the usual by its patterned surfaces. The center of the street-front gable has a center panel of narrow clapboard; at its apex is a triangular sunburst pattern, a pattern repeated within two triangles at the eave end of the gabled roof. On both the first- and second-floor walls there is a chevron pattern, and there is a variation of this motif in a band tucked under the roof eaves. Since the exterior surfaces of the house are all painted white, the delicate patterns are only sketched by the thin lines of cast shadows.

Bloomfield

Bloomfield was platted and designated as the seat of Davis County in 1844. Its location at the geographic center of the county fulfilled the ideal of a county seat's being equidistant from all locales. In Bloomfield's situation on "dry rolling prairie with plenty of timber within convenient distance," as noted by Andreas, in its grid plan with a central public square for the post office, and in its preservation of late nineteenth-century architecture, the community beautifully characterizes the image one usually entertains of Iowa.

SO023 **Davis County Courthouse**

1877–1878, Thomas J. Tolan and Son. Courthouse Square, corner of Washington (US 63) and Franklin streets

When Bloomfield was selected as the county seat, a two-story structure of hewn logs was built. It continued to be used as a courthouse

up through 1851, when it was sold and moved to a rural location to be used as a farm residence. Temporary quarters for court business were then secured in several commercial buildings until the present courthouse was finally designed and built under the supervision of its architects, Thomas J. Tolan and Son of Fort Wayne, Indiana. This was an-

SO023 Davis County Courthouse

other of the several Midwestern firms actively involved in the design of county courthouses in Indiana, Ohio, Illinois, and Iowa. Among courthouses built across the country, Bloomfield's is unquestionably one of the most impressive ever realized in the French Second Empire style. There are many other courthouses in this style that are much larger and more opulent, but very few equal the sense of competence and delight conveyed by this cruciform building. Upward-thrusting verticality is the theme of its design. The detailing of the building, its quoining, and the window pediments are sharp and angular, playing off the plain stone walls. The high central tower with its spirelike truncated roof contains four semicircular dormers, each exhibiting a large clock face. The courthouse was restored in 1978, and is now the center of the Bloomfield Historic District. The courthouse is listed on the National Register of Historic Places.

SO024 Traverse Block

1893. Southwest corner of Madison and Franklin streets

The two-story brick Traverse Block matches the courthouse in its strong, assertive character. One could describe its style as Queen Anne, based more on its overall character than on the specifics of its detailing. The building has been restored, so the rhythm of its ground-floor shop windows and intervening piers can be clearly seen. The second floor displays a corner cut off at a 45-degree angle, a pair of bays, then a grouping of pilasters, all in metal. Above, there is a projecting cornice in the same material; it centers on a projecting panel bearing the building's date. At the corner is a small false-front pediment.

SO025 Findley House

c. 1860s. 302 Franklin St.

As seen from the street, the Findley house presents a classic two-story facade with a central entrance, as well as a balanced composition of windows on each side of the door. However, all of the detailing is late Italianate: a bracketed entablature and cornice for the gabled roof, roundheaded windows, and an entrance porch with splayed sides that is topped by a small balustrade. To the rear is a two-story wing (the whole building has a T-shaped plan) with a two-story arched porch on one side.

SO026 House

1872, 1904. 402 N. Madison

One of the easiest methods of changing the image of an older house into a more stylish mode was by revamping the entrance facade with the addition of a new porch. In this instance a grand two-story porch was added to a late Italianate wood-sheathed dwelling. While the designer of the new porch wished it to be read as Colonial Revival, he was very sensitive in carrying out the detailing. The cornice of the porch with its paired brackets matches that of the original house, and the usual columns are wood piers, somewhat Italianate in feeling.

SO027 Russell Octagon House

1856. Proceed west of Bloomfield on Iowa 2 to the small community of West Grove; travel south on gravel road, 1.5 miles; turn right (west) on intersecting gravel road and drive 2 miles; the house is on the north side of the road

Each year one wonders if the important Russell octagon will be with us much longer; it has been unoccupied for many years, and it is close to being a ruin rather than an old building. The Russell octagon was modeled directly on the William Howland octagon illustrated in Orson S. Fowler's 1849–1854 volume, *Home for All; or The Gravel Wall and Octagonal Mode of Building*, the bible of mid-nineteenth-century octagonal dwellings. As in the Howland house, a traditional rectangular plan has been imposed on an octagonal form. The first floor of the Russell octagon is almost an exact copy of the Howland house; the second floor, distinguished by its peculiar corners and interior projections, is even odder than that of its model. The Russell dwelling was built of a soft, low-fired brick, rather poorly laid. This and other structural defects plus years of neglect have led to the slow disintegration of the building. The house was partially recorded by the Historic American Building Survey in 1976.

SO028 Terrence True-Round Barn

1911, Gordon-Van Tine Company. Take Iowa 2 west of Bloomfield 10.3 miles; turn left (south) on gravel road, proceed 1.1 miles

According to Soike, this barn is the first known example of the work of the Davenport firm of Gordon-Van Tine.[3] This firm provided the plans and the precut material needed to construct the barn. The Tarrence barn has a diameter of 50 feet and is covered by a conical roof with its central cupola still in place. As with other barns by this firm, the walls are covered by vertical siding.

Bonaparte

The original scheme in this area was to pose two towns across from one another on the Des Moines River. Napoleon was to be on the south bank and Bonaparte on the north, but only Bonaparte was realized. A gristmill and dam were built on the river during the years 1839–1841, and Bonaparte was the site of one of the sets of locks built to make the lower Des Moines River navigable by steamboats.

On the northeast corner of Main and First streets is a mildly Prairie-style two-story brick building housing a bank on the ground floor and a Masonic Lodge above. Farther down Main Street are several excellent two- and three-story commercial blocks with metal facades. The most exuberant of these is the Cresap and Stadler Opera House (1894). The Bonaparte School, designed by H. W. Underhill in 1915, was built on the hill overlooking the town (at 807 Washington Street). A conventional two-story brick schoolhouse was made unconventional by the inclusion of two slightly projecting towers surmounted by broad-eaved hipped roofs on brackets. The detailing is sparse, but what there is adheres to the Prairie mode.

Hillcrest, the William Meek house, occupies a site on the north side of Fifth Street, between West and Main streets. In the 1890s a good-sized two-story brick Italianate house (1865–1869) was dramatically remodeled into the then-fashionable Queen Anne style. A three-story tower with a conical roof was added at one corner; a wide porch with Tuscan columns was taken across the front and terminated in a projecting spire-roofed pavilion. At the same time a new steeply pitched roof was added and overscaled gabled dormers were introduced. One can still discern the original Italianate structure at the sides and rear, but it has been completely swallowed up in the new front of the house.

Cantril

A little more than 2 miles east of Cantril, on Iowa 2, is a large brick Italianate house (c. 1860) that was restored in the late 1980s. The windows are arched and there is the usual overhanging hipped roof with brackets. The vertical height of the walls is impressive, as is the height of the rooms on both floors.

SO029 **Wickfield Farm True-Round Show Barn** (Silvers Show Barn)

1917–1919, Alva Hunt. 2 miles east of Cantril on Iowa 2, on the south side of the highway

One of the most exotic of Iowa's round barns is the Wickfield Farm True-Round Show Barn, built and designed by Alva Hunt. An unusual feature of the barn is its two layers of pedimented dormers that seemingly puncture its double-pitched roof here and there. The walls of the building, which is 50 feet in diameter, are terracotta hole tile, and the roof has wood shingles and a large metal ventilator at the peak. The barn was used by its original owner, Frank Silvers, as a sales pavilion for his Hampshire hog farm. The second floor is sectioned off into rooms that work around a central hall. The third floor was designed as a card room and parlor.

Centerville

"The site of the town," Andreas noted in 1875, "is located upon high ground, very near the center of the county, as its name indicates."[4] When Centerville was platted in 1846–1847, an octagonal courthouse square was provided near the center of the town. Within the county, agriculture was augmented by coal mining and limestone quarrying, activities that have essentially ceased.

SO030 **Appanoose County Courthouse**

1903–1904, Smith and Gage. Courthouse Square, corner of Main and Jackson streets

The first structure to house the functions of the county was a one-and-a-half-story cabin measuring 24 by 20 feet. This was replaced by a brick two-story structure with a cupola, built between 1860 and 1864. This building was partially destroyed by fireworks during the Fourth of July celebration in 1881. The architects of the present courthouse gave the community a somewhat old-fashioned design that reflected the late Richardsonian Romanesque. The two-story structure on a raised basement terminates in a low, double-tiered tower containing four clock faces. The central arched entrance is embraced by two bay towers. Rusticated Bedford limestone has been used to sheath the building; its roofs are covered in tile. On the courthouse grounds is a stone obelisk surmounted by a classical urn, a monument set up in 1869 to commemorate soldiers who died in the Civil War.

SO031 First Presbyterian Church

1892. Northwest corner of Maple and Main streets

Though the plan of this Romanesque Revival church with a corner tower is conventional, its detailing is not. The wood-shingled gable ends wrap around and hang over the brick body of the building. The theme of wood-shingled triangles at the apex of the gable and at the eave ends is repeated by paired bracketed triangles placed at the sides of the two entrances located at the base of the tower. The tall tower with its corner shingled columns contains pairs of vertical bands composed of an elongated, narrow arched window together with a row of small circular openings. The whole adds up to an original and vigorous design.

SO032 House

c. 1885. Northeast corner Maple and 12th St.

The designer of this two-and-a-half-story Queen Anne dwelling seems to have first established a simple rectangular volume for his building and then enriched it with projections into the body of the structure, outward projections of bays and porches, and then a constant embellishment of its surfaces. The triumph of the house is the curved floral pattern realized in an appliqué of sawed wood within its principal gable end.

SO033 Service Station

c. 1935. Southeast corner Maple and Drake streets

This former service station building is a version of the Spanish Colonial Revival, presented in white glazed brick and boasting a bright blue tile roof that seems to form mansard-like awnings over various openings. The gable above the office curves upward like an element in the Mission Revival style. Originally a lighted sign was placed within the center round window of the gable.

SO034 Vermillion House

1870, Dunham and Jordan. End of Valley Dr.

This two-story side-hall Italianate house sits far back from the road within an extensive lawn and grove of trees. The front facade of the house remains basically as designed, with a small piered entrance porch and paired brackets under the eaves. Nearby are a number of farm buildings, several of which date to the nineteenth century.

Chariton

Chariton is situated on the divide between the watersheds for the Mississippi River to the east and the Missouri River to the west. The town was platted in 1849 as the location for the Lucas County Courthouse. The only interruptions to the grid were the block set aside for the courthouse and the site for the public school three blocks away. By the late 1860s the Burlington and Missouri River Railroad had traversed the county, and a spur line had been built extending south from Chariton. The railroad's construction of a large two-story (somewhat Italianate) brick building combining a depot, eatery, and hotel was unusual for Iowa at that time.

SO035 **Lucas County Courthouse**

1892–1894, Foster and Liebbe. Courthouse Square, northeast corner Main St. and Court Ave.

In 1850 the county erected its first courthouse, a hewn-log one-and-a-half-story structure with an outside stairway providing entry to the upper floor. This temporary wood structure was replaced in 1858 by a two-story brick building that was 60 feet square. At the center of the roof of this building was a two-tiered tower crowned by a small dome. In style the building combined Greek Revival and Italianate features.

During 1892–1894 a new courthouse was built by the Des Moines architectural firm of Foster and Liebbe. The design of this two-story stone building is Richardsonian Romanesque. An entrance tower appears at the center of the principal facade of the square building and there are slightly projecting pedimented pavilions on the other three elevations. The assertiveness of the tower was diminished in 1954 by the removal of its high spired roof and four corner finials.

SO036 **Chariton City Hall**

1931, William L. Perkins. West side of Main St., south of Court Ave.

This long, low, parapeted two-story brick building establishes its mildly Colonial Georgian imagery through a few details. The windows are small paned and double hung and are accompanied below the parapet by stone panels bearing classical swags. The entrance pavilion is the building's strongest feature. Engaged two-story piers enclose a central stone panel that contains the entrance doorway, a single window above, and decorative swags between the piers. The general flavor of the building's design is Colonial Georgian brought up to date by subtle references to the Art Deco Moderne.

SO037 **United States Post Office Building**

1917, James A. Wetmore. Northeast corner of Grand St. and Linden Ave.

The image of America's eighteenth-century Colonial Georgian style is carried out here as beautifully as one will find in any public building of the teens. A pedimented porch with four Tuscan columns dominates the front; within the porch, the building's facade bears a composition of windows and upper panels to each side of the high entrance doorway with its lunette window. Each side of the building displays a central white panel articulated by pilasters, niches, and arches. The building's balustrade forms a strong horizontal termination to its design; here, panels of balustrades are placed between a lower false cornice and a white band of stone that forms the cap for the parapet.

SO038 **Masonic Temple**

1936, William L. Perkins. Northeast corner of Grand St. and Armory Ave.

This building is a simple rectangular box that has the appearance of being partially hidden in the ground. Its architectural treatment is reserved for the carefully studied placement of windows (there are very few), the angled parapet, and the detailing of the entrance with its recessed door, the suggestion of corbeling, and the richness added by the pair of bronze wall lamps. Everything about this limestone-sheathed building is sparse, but quite refined.

SO039 **First Presbyterian Church**

1908. Northeast corner of 8th St. and Beaden Ave.

In this instance, the "rational" desire for a square auditorium has lead to the design of a single boxlike form. Each of the facades has a false cornice that centers on a false pediment. The principal windows are round arched with wood mullions forming interior arches and circles. To bring a more decidedly architectural character to the building, its designer placed a pedimented temple with columns in antis at a 45-degree angle to the cross-street corner of the structure. Viewed from an angle, this pediment repeats the pattern of the two false pediments on the adjoining walls.

SO040 **Payne Cottage** (Dual Gables)

1889. 702 Auburn Ave.

This unusual Y-plan cottage has a wall at a 45-degree angle between the branches of the "Y," forming the entrance and porch. There

SO040 Payne Cottage (Dual Gables)

is an Eastlake band of sawed crosses just below the roof's eaves, and some walls have been treated with a herringbone pattern. Horizontal bands of paneling have been carried across the walls below and above the windows. A single dormer with a gable roof, placed at a 45-degree angle, looks out over the entrance porch.

SO041 Smythe House

1927–1928, William L. Perkins. 320 N. Grand St.

The theme of the one-and-a-half-story Smythe house is that of the English medieval cottage. An oversized wide oriel window looks out from the gable end, and a tall chimney climbs the side of the dwelling. A non-medieval feature of the design is the pair of arched windows on the lower floor of the front gable. It all adds up to an excellent example of the period revival of the 1920s.

SO042 First Methodist Episcopal Church

1899. Northeast corner of Main St. and Roland Ave.

This Methodist church is an example of the Gothic Revival in stone, with a corner entrance tower. The Gothic arches of the entrance rest on a decorated horizontal band of finely carved stone, and the arches in turn are supported by inset columns. The eaves of the tower's spire roof are interrupted by wall gables that contain stone pointed arches that extend up from the lower louvers.

SO043 Stephens-Carpenter House (now Museum of the Lucas County Historical Society)

1907–1908. 123 17th St.

A. J. Stephens, who built this house for his own family, was a successful building contractor in Chariton. The principal front of this Colonial Revival house presents the classic, often repeated scheme of cross porches; there is a two-story porch with columns, and a single-floor porch running parallel to the building and underneath the high porch. The fenestration of the long sides of the house and its rear seems to have been based on utilitarian considerations, not style. The walls of the house are of ashlar block masonry, and their solidity contrasts with the lightness of the wood bays, porches, and other features. Next door to the house is a schoolhouse (1889) that was moved to the site.

Clarinda

Clarinda, the seat of Page County, was established in the early 1850s in the valley of the West Nodaway River. In the center of the public square, defined by Main, Washington, Fifteenth, and Sixteenth streets, is the Page County Courthouse (1885–1887). The Des Moines firm of Foster and Liebbe devised a design in brick with limestone trim which partakes of both the earlier Italianate and the Romanesque Revival. Some of the tall, narrow windows have V-shaped headers, others are round arched. A low, square platform projects from the center of the roof—seemingly waiting for a tower. Within, the several halls center on a small rotunda.

The single-story Lincoln School (1921), at the southwest corner of Nineteenth Street North and Lincoln Street, was designed in the classical yet domestic vein. The entrance consists of a hooped roof supported by a projecting set of Tuscan columns. The segmental curve of the entrance roof is repeated by a pair of louvered roof vents. The windows on each side of the entrance have been treated as a horizontal band, glass below and wood panels above.

Two houses on Lincoln Street should be noted. At 321 is the Hepburn house (1867), home of the longtime congressman William Peters Hepburn. His house is a simple, somewhat Italianate dwelling with a corner tower boasting a French mansard roof with small curved roof dormers. Very different is a stucco and tile roofed Spanish Colonial Revival bungalow at 323 Lincoln. The bungalow has been lifted above the ground on a raised basement, with a garage tucked into one side.

On the northern outskirts of town, on the west side of Twelfth Street, is the Iowa Hospital for the Insane (now the State Mental Health Institute), a large building on a raised basement (1884–1899). For this structure the architects Foster and Liebbe updated somewhat the earlier Eastlake mode. Horizontal stone banding connects the sides and lintels of the windows, and this banding contrasts dramatically with the general verticality of the three-and-a-half-story design. The more than five-story central tower with its gabled clock dormer conjures up the nearly perfect image of a "Victorian" building.

Corning

Corning, the county seat of Adams County, was one of a chain of towns established along the East Nodaway River in the mid-1850s. Its growth was rapid during the years just before the Civil War; after the war the coming of the railroad brought a second period of intense development. The town's grid is unusual, with a narrow north-south strip of blocks constituting the business and public center of the community. One of these blocks was set aside as a central park which was to house the county courthouse.

SO044 Commercial Blocks

c. 1895. Southwest corner of 8th St. and Davis Ave.

At the corner is the Weidner Block (1895), a two-story Queen Anne building with a second-floor bay tower at the street corner. Though somewhat remodeled, the ground floor storefronts are still intact. Next door to the Weidner block is another late nineteenth-century block with two bay towers. Its face suggests the French Châteauesque style, with a few references to the Richardsonian Romanesque.

SO045 United States Post Office Building

1938, Louis A. Simon. Northeast corner of 7th and Nodaway streets

The strongest design feature of this single-floor brick building is its small central cupola modeled after eighteenth-century Colonial examples. Within the post office is a WPA mural, *Band Concert*, painted by Marion Gilmore.

SO046 Saint Patrick's Roman Catholic Church

1930. Southeast corner of 6th St. and Grove Ave.

Saint Patrick's is a brick basilica whose tower is almost a freestanding campanile. The details of the church, with its round-arched windows and domed tower, are derived from Italian Renaissance examples, more provincial than anything else.

SO047 **House**

c. 1890. Southwest corner of 6th St. and Grove Ave.

A small tower with a convex spire roof rises over the entrance of this one-and-a-half-story cottage. The second-floor window within the gable is contained by a wooden patterned moon gate. In style, the late Queen Anne is here simplified by references to the American Colonial.

SO048 **House**

c. 1860. 906 6th St.

This is a finely detailed example of the Italianate; there are elaborately carved lintels over the windows, and thin piers support the various porches. Instead of resting on the usual brackets, the entablature below the overhanging second-floor roof is paneled. The walls are clapboard and all of the detailing is in wood.

SO049 **House**

c. 1916. Northwest corner of 9th St. and Loomis Ave.

This two-story stucco Craftsman house has an entrance-porch roof supported by heavy projecting brackets. The entrance door and its two side windows are slightly recessed between two Tuscan columns. The general horizontality of the design reflects the then-current influence of the Prairie school architects.

SO050 **Frank House** (now Happy Hollow Country Club)

c. 1873. .25 miles east on US 34, 2 blocks north

The builder of this dwelling, George Frank, purchased 120 acres for his projected estate, something quite unusual for Iowa in the 1870s and 1880s. Forty acres were laid out in the manner of a Picturesque English park, and included an artificial lake (with a boathouse), curved roads, and other amenities. The two-story brick walls of this two-and-a-half-story Eastlake dwelling support a number of steeply pitched gables. These gables exhibit a wide fascia cut into a series of curved forms. The fascia of the adjoining roof edges is carried on small brackets across the front of each gable. Numerous changes have been made on the first floor, including the elimination of the wood porte-cochère with its upstairs open porch, but the building still reveals its strong Eastlake character.

SO051 **Sixteen-sided Barn**

1917, Sprague, builder. 13 miles west of Corning on US 34, 5.5 miles north on US 71

This barn is 60 feet in diameter and is covered by a gambrel roof with a center cupola vent. The walls are of board-and-batten.

SO052 **True-Round Barn**

1912. US 71, 8.5 miles north of US 34; route H20, 5.5 miles

The diameter of this board-and-batten round barn is 60 feet. At the center within is a wood stave silo. The roof is a double-pitched gambrel form with a single small gabled roof dormer.

Corydon

Corydon, the seat of Wayne County, was founded in 1851. Within Dotts Park, off Iowa 2, is the Miles Log Cabin (1853). The logs of this cabin were first brought to Walden Park (c. 1927) where the building was restored by the Daughters of the American Revolution. In 1969 the cabin was moved to Dotts Park and was rebuilt the next year. The little cabin perfectly fits one's preconceived idea of how a prairie log cabin would look; the walls are of split logs and the shingle roof is very low in pitch.

At 312 South West Street is the Tedford house (1887), a handsome dwelling built far behind what was then the latest fashion in architecture. The brick body of the house, with its roof on paired brackets, is Italianate; but its splendid, richly decorated porch and the low gable dormers on the roof are pure Eastlake. Such a combination of styles was the rage in the 1870s, but by the 1880s it was out of fashion.

Creston

The town was established in 1869 as a division point by the Burlington and Missouri River Railway Company, and by the mid-1870s a roundhouse, machine shops, and railyards had been constructed. Eventually the county seat was transferred from Afton to Creston, and in 1890 a French Second Empire/Eastlake courthouse was built. This building was replaced in 1951 by the present bland modernist courthouse. Creston was the site for two of Iowa's exotic exposition palaces, the Bluegrass palaces of 1889 and 1890.[5] Both were exotic, fanciful, storybook designs which were sheathed in bluegrass. The second of these palaces at Creston was 285 feet long, 132 feet wide, and its principal tower (covered by an impossible combination of a dome and a spire) was 120 feet high.

SO053 Chicago, Burlington, and Quincy Depot

1898–1899. Northeast corner of Adams and Maple streets

The Creston station was one of the larger railroad stations built in Iowa. Its steeply pitched hipped roof and large gabled dormers suggest the French Châteauesque tradition which was so popular late in the nineteenth century. This brick-and-stone-trimmed two-and-a-half-story building has now been restored and has presently assumed a new life as the Creston City Hall.

SO054 United States Post Office Building

1901, James Knox Taylor. Northwest corner of Maple and Pine streets

A three-story Georgian-style box, this post office building has a heavily articulated cornice. A two-story porch with Ionic columns is set into the box.

SO055 Jefferson School

1937. Northeast corner of Summit and Cherry streets

Here in this school are the elements of the PWA Moderne: horizontal windows, curved walls, and horizontal banding, all handled in a somewhat formal fashion. The detailing of the brick walls of this two-story building carried on into the 1930s many features usually associated with the Art Deco of the late twenties.

SO056 House

c. 1860. 711 Adams St.

A solid Italianate house of low silhouette, this dwelling has masonry walls that are now painted white, but the U-shaped stone lintels above the windows have been left untouched. The entrance to this house is to the right; on the left side is a two-story angled bay. A masonry piered porch and enclosure have been added to the first-floor front of the house.

SO057 House

c. 1878. Southwest corner of Sumner and Montgomery streets

This residence is in the Eastlake style fashionable after the Civil War. The low line of the eave is broken by wall gables sheathed in vertical boards; the walls below are of clapboard. The windows and doors have U-shaped Gothic lintels, many of which are decorated with applied jigsaw ornament. The principal porch exhibits a string of wide, slightly cusped arches.

SO058 Bill's Service Station

c. 1925. US 34 (New York Ave.) at Lincoln St.

One of the "musts" for devotees of roadside architecture, this station consists of a large horizontal steel drum placed on low concrete walls. A second large drum placed on edge projects above the building as a tower to announce the presence of the station. In front, the service bay has a flat roof surmounted in the center by a hooped roof composed of a third metal drum.

SO059 First National Bank of Shannon City

c. 1920. Take route P27 south 5 miles, then travel east on route H45 4.5 miles; take improved road south to Shannon City

In the small town of Shannon City, southeast of Creston, there is a well-preserved example of a small-town bank building. The low, one-story box is sheathed in brick, with the cornice, entablature, and base of the building constructed of Indiana limestone. The flat pilasters, together with the entablature/cornice, establish the building as an example of down-to-earth, rational classicism.

SO060 Nine-sided Barn

c. 1910. Proceed south of Shannon City on US 169 for 8 miles; turn west on route J25, travel 2.1 miles; the barn is on south side of the road

The plan of this unusual barn is similar to one published in *Wallace's Farmer* in the January 16, 1903, issue. This design was republished in 1907 and 1910 in the same magazine. The high attached sheds on either side of the barn obscure its nine-sided design, and its center interior configuration of six sides is not immediately apparent. The barn is sheathed in a combination of board-and-batten and vertical siding.

Eldon

SO061 Jacques House

1881, W. H. Jacques, builder. 1905, addition. Corner of Barton and Gothic streets. To find these streets take Iowa 16 to the southeast side of town; opposite the fairgrounds, take the gravel road north, then proceed across the railroad tracks where one can then see the dwelling

The small Des Moines River village of Eldon harbors probably the most widely known house in Iowa. This is the Jacques house, the small cottage Grant Wood used as a background for his well-known, often reproduced painting of 1930, *American Gothic* (now in the collection of the Art Institute of Chicago). The painter came across this dwelling when driving through Eldon, and he photographed it at the time. He used this photograph together with his sister Nan and his dentist, Dr. B. H. McKeeby, as models for the painting.

The board-and-batten one-and-a-half-story cottage is indeed what one would label as Gothic Revival. Its higher than normal gable roof encloses a single large pointed window, the same gable and arched window that assert themselves in the center of Wood's painting. It is interesting to note that the painter reduced the width of the window in order to accentuate the building's Gothic verticality. The L-shaped porch that wraps itself around the front and part of the left side of the cottage exhibits thin, turned-wood columns that we would usually associate not with the Gothic Revival, but rather with the Eastlake style. (Such combinations are, of course, quite common in American domestic architecture of the late 1860s through the 1880s.)

The construction of the cottage was finished in December 1881, and it received a coat of paint the following year. The small west wing was added in 1905. The cottage was built by W. H. Jacques, who owned the property at that time.

Fairfield

Fairfield was first settled in 1839, and from that date to the present it has been the seat of Jefferson County. Fairfield has been a university town since the founding of Parsons College in 1875 (the college is now Maharishi International University). The traditional grid of square blocks with a central courthouse square was platted 2 miles northeast of the Cedar River.

SO062 Jefferson County Courthouse

1891–1893, H. C. Koch and Company. Briggs St. between Main and Court streets

A courthouse was built in 1839, at the time Fairfield was established as the county seat. By tradition this structure has been considered to be the first wood-frame building in the state. This first courthouse was replaced by a stone-and-brick building that was finished in 1851. The Milwaukee architect H. C. Koch, who designed a number of courthouses in Iowa, Wisconsin, and Kansas, provided an up-to-date version of the Richardsonian Romanesque. The architect countered the verticality of his design by providing a light-colored sandstone base that is carried through the first floor of the building; above this the walls are sheathed in dark red Saint Louis pressed brick. The design originally centered on a corner clock tower which was 142 feet high, but the top of the tower was removed in 1948.

SO063 McElhinney House

c. 1850. 300 N. Court St.

The McElhinney house perfectly fits the general picture of a two-story clapboard house-type found throughout much of the country in the years 1830 through 1850. Its front boasts a two-story balconied porch, behind which (on both floors) are central recessed doorways with side lights and transoms. The design is late Federal in style, accompanied by a few Greek Revival details.

SO064 Jefferson County Public Library

1892–1893. Northwest corner of E. Washington Ave. and S. Court St.

In 1892 the community received a substantial grant of $30,000 from the Carnegie Foundation to help with the construction of a public library building. The design produced is that of a flat-roofed and parapeted two-story masonry block, somewhat Richardsonian Romanesque in character. As in the courthouse, a light-colored sandstone was used for the raised basement, and the body of the building above is of dark red brick. The fact that the courthouse and the library were both built at the same time suggests that both may have been designed by the same architect.

SO065 **Clarke House**

1915–1916, Barry Byrne. 500 S. Main St.

When the Clarke house was described in *Western Architect* in April 1924, it was noted that this design had a "tendency to break with the manner of the past, although even here there is still much that is reminiscent of the work of Wright." While the Clarke house is indeed a Prairie-style house, it is a highly personal interpretation. Its plan, with an entrance at one end, an attached garage at the other, and the open living/dining room space between, is not a classic Prairie-style design. Neither is the interior; its light-colored walls and furniture share much with the Scottish designer Charles Rennie Mackintosh and the Viennese architect Josef Hoffmann. Equally individualistic is the external color scheme, described in *Western Architect* as "brick of dark golden color, woodwork black with white sash; roof green, and balcony blue." The Chicago artist Alfonso Ianelli collaborated with Byrne in this design. The beautifully laid-out garden surrounding the house was designed by Arthur Seifried.

SO066 **Beck House**

1896. 401 E. Burlington St.

This classic Queen Anne dwelling is sited on a large corner lot. The house is oriented to the street corner through a three-story corner bay tower. The tower has the appropriate round windows on the third floor, and there is a steeply pitched roof with a segmented dome. A wide veranda wraps around the base of the bay tower, and the veranda in turn matches the tower with its own projecting round pavilion with a conical roof. The house is rich in wood details, ornament, windows of various shapes, and porches cut into the sec-

ond floor. To the right of the entrance is a moon-gate pattern with a rectangular window. A large two-story stable-barn accompanies the house to the rear.

SO067 **House**

c. 1915. 407 W. Merrill Hill Ave.

A somewhat elongated Prairie-style stucco box, this house has the usual overhanging wide hipped roof. The roof in this instance has paired brackets at each corner. The walls of the house are divided into two horizontal zones by a band at the walls' midpoint. On the lower level are suggestions of corner pilasters holding up this cornice band. The projecting entrance has a roof reminiscent of those in Maher's work, with flat sections to each side and a segmented roof section in the middle.

SO068 **Bonnifield Log Cabin**

1838. Old Settlers' Park (Waterworks Park)

Rhodam Bonnifield arrived in Jefferson County in 1837, and the following year Iowa was created as a territory. In 1838 he built this one-and-a-half-story log cabin on a site some 8 miles southeast of Fairfield. In 1906 the cabin was moved to its present location in Old Settlers' Park. The cabin was a large one for its time. It measured 16 by 28 feet, had a low second story, and featured a front porch with a shed roof. The walls are of hewn logs, and the roof was originally covered by rived and shaved walnut shingles (now by modern wood shingles). A large masonry chimney of native stone was situated at the left gable end.

SO066 Beck House

Farmington

The community was platted on the northeast bank of the Des Moines River in 1839. By the late 1850s, Farmington had begun to emerge as a manufacturing center because of its location on the river and the existence of nearby coal deposits; later it was a railroad center. The Lewis Berg Wagon Works (SO069) is also located there.

Just southwest of the city limits of Farmington, off of Iowa 81, is Indian Lake Park. Within the park are several examples of rustic wood-and-stone park architecture. One of these structures is an enclosed picnic shelter constructed of native limestone with a shingle roof. Wood rafter tails project beyond the roof edges, on the gable ends and out from the eaves. Each gabled end of the building contains a large segmental arched window. Two large stone chimneys service the pair of stone fireplaces.

SO069 Lewis Berg Wagon Works

1867–1868. 131 South 2nd St.

This two-story limestone building houses one of Farmington's industries, the Lewis Berg Wagon Works. It exhibits iron window lintels and a metal entablature/cornice. The imagery of the building is mildly Italianate.

Farson

SO070 Baldwin House

1920, G. M. Kernes. North of Farson on route V41 1 mile; drive left (west) on the gravel road .8 mile

Generally throughout Iowa, dwellings of the Prairie school tended to be built by individuals living and working within the towns and cities. In the case of the C. B. Baldwin house, designed by G. M. Kernes and built in 1920, the Prairie image was used for a farm dwelling. But the Baldwin house is no ordinary farmhouse in size and appointments, or in image. The architect of this good-sized two-story house looked to the more formal and monumental Prairie style associated with the work of George W. Maher of Chicago. Like much of Maher's work, or Frank Lloyd Wright's Winslow house (1893) in River Forest, Illinois, the Baldwin house is a large rectangular volume covered by a steeply pitched hipped roof covered with red tile and equipped with extended overhanging eaves. Dark red-

SO070 Baldwin House

brown brick is carried up the walls to the sills of the banded second-floor casement windows; then a lighter-colored brick fills in between the windows and is terminated by a thin horizontal band of cast stone. At the center of the entrance front is a porch supported by a pair of brick piers, and a similar living porch projects from the left side of the house.

Garden Grove

Garden Grove was one of the early Mormon settlements in Iowa. In their journey west the Mormons settled the site in 1848 and remained until 1851. Andreas provides a picture of the location, remarking that "it is on a fine, rolling prairie, adjacent to a splendid grove of timber, on the Weldon Fork of Grand River."[6] It was not until 1867 that the plat of the town was officially recorded. By the beginning of the 1870s Garden Grove had become a station on the Leon Branch of the Chicago, Burlington, and Quincy Railroad. In 1904 its population was 651, but in 1987 it was only 297.

SO071 **Robey's Service Station**

c. 1924. South side of Iowa 204, west side of town, across from the park and its bandstand

A single gabled roof contains the station and the service pump area. The two front wooden posts are tapered toward the top and rest on high brick piers. The single-light double-hung windows are far out of scale with the building. Like a miniature, a small, sturdy chimney pops up from the center of the roof.

SO072 **J. J. McClung House**

1908, Charles F. Church. North side of Iowa 204, center of town, across from City Hall

The self-taught architect Charles F. Church of Lamoni provided his client with a Colonial Revival image, one frequently utilized for an upper-middle-class dwelling. The two-story entrance porch has pairs of Corinthian columns at each corner. The tympanum of the pediment above contains a delicate lunette window. Within the porch there is a bracket-supported balcony over the sidelighted entrance. On each side of the central pediment on the roof there are pedimented dormers with diamond-paned windows.

SO073 Stearns House

1883. South side of Iowa 204, eastern edge of town

The domed roof of this commodious Queen Anne-style house is shaped like a gigantic bell that seems to float in space. A somewhat Châteauesque French dormer (very small in scale) projects from the roof, and next to the bay tower is a chimney. The placement of all the windows is quite controlled; they are arranged within pairs of horizontal bands. The roof ridge still retains its lacy metal cresting.

Keosauqua

The town of Keosauqua was platted in 1837 and 1839 by the Van Buren Company. The site selected lay on the north bank of the Des Moines River within a broad oxbow. In 1846 construction was started on the Des Moines River Improvement Project—a scheme using a series of dams, locks, and canals to make the river navigable. Three sets of locks were built, making it possible to travel as far as Keosauqua, but the larger scheme was never carried out. The town's grid was laid out parallel to the river, and a courthouse square was provided three blocks from the riverfront.

SO074 Van Buren County Courthouse

1841–1843. 904 4th St.

The plainness of this Greek Revival building did not appeal to Andreas when he wrote of it in 1875, "The courthouse is not a building of any particular architectural beauty, and does not present a very imposing appearance."[7] The brick building about which he had reservations is the oldest county courthouse in Iowa. It is a simple rectangular structure with narrow enclosed pedimented gable ends; its fenestration consists of two rows of undecorated windows. The only purely decorative details are the wide banded entablature and the lunette windows within each of the gable ends. Inside the building a large courtroom occupies much of the second floor. The courthouse remains essentially unaltered, with the exception of the loss of its low square tower and the shutters that flanked each of the windows. The courthouse was built by Edwin Manning, a founder of the town; its design was supposedly drawn up by the first members of the County Commission.

SO075 Pearson House

c. 1845. Northeast corner of Dodge St. and County Rd.

The first floor of this late Federal-style house is of stone, while the second floor is of brick. There is a pair of wall chimneys in each of the gable ends of the building. The house was rebuilt after being damaged by a tornado in 1968; the present four-light double-hung windows are not original. The house was probably designed by its owner, Franklin Pearson, who was a master mason.

SO075 Pearson House

SO076 **Hotel Manning**

1854. Corner River and Van Buren streets

Edwin Manning, the contractor for the Van Buren County Courthouse, built this structure for himself. It originally consisted of his own general store together with a bank. In 1894 he added a second floor and remodeled the building into a hotel. The first two floors

of the building open onto a two-story porch; above, a series of small gabled dormers puncture the roof. The wide porch dominates the building, and its detailing has elements of the Eastlake style.

SO077 **Christian Church**

c. 1892. Corner E. 2nd St. and Main St. (Iowa 1)

The Romanesque Revival style has in this case been realized in wood, and the scale is almost domestic. Entrance to the church is gained through a porch and doorway at the base of the small open lantern tower. The front gable end contains a large arched window composed of a full circle above accompanied on each side by half-lunettes, and, below, by a row of narrow rectangular windows. Although it was constructed of wood, the open lantern tower has been designed to suggest its masonry antecedents.

SO078 **Lacey-Keosauqua State Park**

1919. Off Iowa 1, adjoining Keosauqua

The original 1,200-plus acres (the park now has 1,653 acres) were acquired in 1919, and the park was dedicated the following year. Within the park, a quarter of a mile from Ely's Ford, are six prehistoric Indian mounds, one of which is C-shaped. The park has several recreational buildings that are of interest. Of these, the two most impressive are the open stone pavilion (c. 1928) and the bathhouse (c. 1936), the latter a successful Colonial Revival design in stone, clapboard, and board-and-batten.

Lamoni

In 1870 the Reorganized Church of Jesus Christ of Latter-day Saints purchased 3,330 acres of land in Decatur County, Iowa. At the end of that decade, in 1879, they platted the town of Lamoni, located on the main route of the Chicago and Burlington Railroad.[8] From 1881 through 1906 Lamoni was the home of Joseph Smith III, president of the Reorganized Church. In 1895 the church established Graceland College, which was expanded in the twentieth century to a four-year college. The 70-acre campus is beautifully laid out on gently rolling wooded hills. What we see today in the design of the college grounds is largely the work of the landscape architect Kenneth F. Jones which was carried out in the late 1920s and early 1930s. His essential goal was to create a feeling that the landscape was not something introduced to the place, but was natural to it.

SO079 Eugene E. Colosson Physical Education Facility, Reorganized Church of Jesus Christ of Latter-day Saints

c. 1950. W. 4th St. at Clark St.

The design of this facility (which contains five playing courts) entails elements directly associated with several of the late churches of Eero Saarinen, together with features of the late 1930s Streamline Moderne. The straightforward rectangular brick tower, with its pattern of large square openings, was a form often used in modern churches built in both Europe and America. The horizontal bands of metal corner windows on the body of the building take one right back to the Streamline Moderne.

SO080 Smith House (Liberty Hall)

SO080 Smith House (Liberty Hall)

1881. 1300 W. Main St., .5 mile west of city limits

This house, built for Joseph Smith III, appears to be a good-sized two-story farmhouse that has been embellished in a reserved fashion with Eastlake ornamentation. The entrance porch displays sawed brackets at the top of each of its wood posts, and below is a sawed-work balustrade. The only other external decorations are the paneling at the base of the bay windows and the U-shaped wood molding carried over the windows and extended partway down each side. The 14-room house was restored in 1975, and it is now open to the public.

Lenox

Situated in an open field at the corner of Van Buren Street East and Oak Street North in Lenox is a substantial two-story brick dwelling (c. 1870) which does not fit comfortably into any of the normal stylistic categories of the mid-nineteenth century. Essentially the house mirrors the late Italianate mode in the heavy stone lintels over the windows and doors and in the wide overhanging hipped roof with paired brackets as supports. But the roof is high and double pitched, and there is a dominant gabled dormer at the front. Both the dormer and the main roof boast a narrow monitor decorated with cut-out sawed work and small brackets.

Nearer the center of town, at the northeast corner of Main and Michigan streets, is a Queen Anne house (c. 1890), now the Larkin-Bender Funeral Home. A round bay tower at the corner rises one full floor above the two-story body of the house. Matching the tower in plan and projecting from the ground floor is a semicircular veranda.

Four-and-a-half miles south of Lenox along Iowa 49 is one of Iowa's famed round barns, the Cameron True-Round Barn (c. 1899), possibly the earliest round barn still standing in the state. The barn measures 100 feet in diameter; its walls are sheathed in board-and-batten and the roof is topped by a monitor section with walls punctured by louvered vents.

Leon

The county commission originally selected a site 4 miles west of Leon for the county seat, but in 1883 it was moved to Leon. This section of Decatur County was described as "high, gentle and rolling prairie, through which runs the main road from Fort Des Moines to Independence, Mo."[9] Andreas's bird's-eye view of the community illustrates how commercial businesses grew up around the courthouse square, how a branch of the Chicago, Burlington, and Quincy Railroad entered the town from the northwest, and how the forest along the banks of the Little River formed almost a windbreak to the west. By 1900, the Chicago, Burlington, and Quincy had been extended south and a second railroad, the Des Moines and Kansas City, also went through the community. By virtue of the post-World War II episode of freeway building within the state, Leon now lies 5 miles west of the north-south route of Interstate 35.

SO081 Decatur County Courthouse

1907–1908, Smith, Wetherell and Gage. Courthouse Square, 1 block east of Iowa 69

The tale of the earlier courthouses for Decatur County is a saga of damage and destruction by windstorms, fire, and dynamiting by would-be burglars. The county's third courthouse, built in 1875, was a two-story brick Italianate structure, with pavilions on each facade articulated by segmental curved roofs. At the center of the cruciform-plan building was a central open cupola surmounted by a small dome and augmented by high finials at each corner. Because of the damage caused to the building's foundation by the dynamiting of 1877, and also because of a lack of careful repair, the building was finally torn down and replaced by the present building in 1907.

The present courthouse is based upon the Edwardian classical brick-and-stone buildings being erected in England at that time. The design could loosely be termed Georgian Revival, with a touch of the English Arts and Crafts. Its strongest features are the circular eye dormer windows, the central tower with its four clock faces, and the small drum and dome.

SO082 Commercial Block

c. 1885. North side of Courthouse Square

This two-story brick commercial block exhibits a playful corner bay tower. The building's most distinctive element is a shallow porch with an accompanying roof that is cantilevered out over the storefront below. The storefronts remain basically intact, but those at each end have been appreciably remodeled.

SO083 Octagonal Barn

1905. 2 miles north of city limits, on east side of road

A large cupola with windows and vents tops this eight-sided barn. The roofs of both the barn itself and the cupola are quite steeply pitched. The walls of this barn are board-and-batten painted white.

Mount Zion

Five miles north of Keosauqua on Iowa 1 is the crossroads community of Mount Zion. At the north edge of the community, a half mile south of the junction of Iowa 1 and Iowa 16, is the Barker House (c. 1875). The vertical volumes of this two-story Italianate dwelling with a gable roof are strongly edged with quoining. The brick of the quoining and of the adjoining walls is dramatically played off against the small touch of dark stone used at the springing and crown of the segmental arches over each of the windows and doors. The over-hanging roof displays a rich pattern of large and small brackets; below, the entrance porch still contains its original piers and brackets.

Three-quarters of a mile south of the junction of Iowa 1 and Iowa 16 is the Mount Zion Presbyterian Church (1903). The pointed arches of the church windows suggest the Gothic Revival, while the general simplicity of the build-ing's design would seem to entail a Craftsman ethic. The corner tower with its open belfry and conical roof has been turned at a 45-degree angle in order to command both the highway and the crossroad.

Osceola

As with a number of other Iowa communities, Osceola was founded as the county seat. The town was laid out in 1851, in the center of Clarke County, and situated in a high, rolling prairie. Though the Clarke County Courthouse (1884) is now gone (replaced by a modernist building in 1955–1956), the east side of Main Street facing the courthouse square still possesses a number of nineteenth-century commercial buildings.

SO084 United States Post Office Building

1935, Louis A. Simon and Neal Melick. 104 Fillmore St., near southwest corner with Washington St.

The Georgian Colonial image is here pared down to the bone. Instead of projecting the center portion of the building out from the rest of the building, the architects left the facade completely flat and suggested a pavil-ion by slightly lifting the center parapet. Two unusual features of the building are the slightly pointed arch of the entrance—with a striking pattern of stone surrounding the doorway—and the horizontal band below the parapet which contains a repeated pattern of cornu-copias. Inside, the visitor will discover Byron Ben Boyd's WPA mural *Arrival of the First Train*. Note not only the train but also the revered log cabin depicted in the painting.

SO085 Lyric Theater

c. 1940. West side of Fillmore St., north of Jefferson St.

The Lyric is a late-thirties Moderne theater with a composition in dark brown brick that encompasses the center of the building above the extended marquee. There are three good-sized windows with textured brickwork in this central composition. The metal-and-glass marquee seems original to the building.

SO086 House

c. 1870. 222 S. Fillmore St.

A classic two-story brick Italianate cube has emerged from the ordinary through the lux-urious wood console brackets that support the small flat roof over the side entrance

Osceola

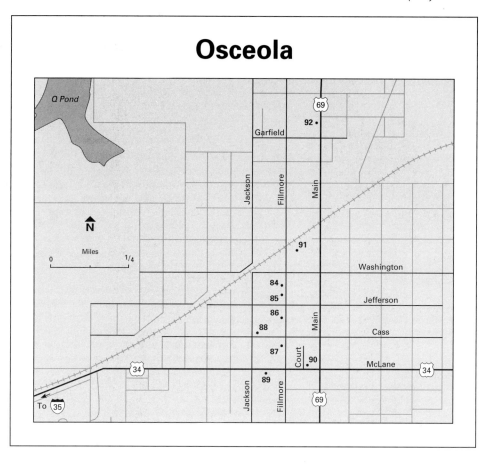

door. These seem almost like two carved supports for a Victorian sideboard. In striking contrast, the curved wood lintels over the windows are refined and quite delicate.

position. The house is quite coloristic, with red brick walls below, dark stained wood siding above, blue trim, and an orange tile roof.

SO087 Bungalow

c. 1916. 310 S. Fillmore St.

The roof plunges over a wide porch that is carried across the front of this one-and-a-half-story bungalow. The ends of the porch are supported by overscaled wide brick piers. At the center of the porch is a gabled roof with an unusual U-shaped dormer (the center section of which has been set far back into the roof). The sides and rear walls of the dwelling reveal a rich irregular pattern of windows and doors (seemingly casually arranged, but in fact well composed); the front itself, however, presents a symmetrical com-

SO088 George H. Cowles House

c. 1867. Northeast corner of Jackson and Cass streets

This remarkably well preserved Italianate dwelling is situated within ample grounds. Penetrating the bracketed roof with a wide overhang is a typical Eastlake-style gable with the usual exposed cross-bracing, a finial projecting from the roof peak, and even metal cresting at the side. On the ground floor the heavy solidity of the large projecting bay is played off against the delicacy of the thin porch columns and the iron fencing on the roof. The thickness of the projecting stone carved lintels creates the impression that the

SO088 George H. Cowles House

windows have been cut deeply into the fabric of the building.

SO089 **Banta House**

1902–1904, George F. Barber. 222 W. McLane St.

Barber's various designs in the Queen Anne style are never retiring; they convey the feeling that the architect wished to encompass as much as he could in each one. In the Banta house there are a few hints at the early Colonial Revival, such as the roundheaded stair-hall window on the left side of the building; but beyond such details everything is pure Queen Anne. The porches on the first and second floors of this house are alive with lacy patterns of turned work that join with molded members to form wonderful curved openings. The house appears to be a variation on Barber's Design No. 58 B, which is illustrated

in his *New Model Dwellings and How to Build Them* of 1895–1896. (Design No. 58 B is listed as the "Residence of Church Howe, Esq., Auburn, Neb.") The Banta house is the reverse of the illustrated plan but otherwise incorporates only a few changes.

SO090 **House**

c. 1917. Northeast corner of McLane and Court streets

What at first glance appears to be a Colonial Revival house with a hipped roof is in fact only the central portion of the residence. Behind it on each side are wings with gambrel roofs. From the street the building comes close to reading as three separate dwellings, or perhaps two separate houses with gambrel roofs that at some later date were joined together by the projecting hip-roofed section. As with a good number of the Colonial Revival houses of the teens, this one incorporates some Craftsman details, especially in the groupings of the casement window units. Still, it was meant to be experienced as a Colonial dwelling. Its small entry porch has wood Tuscan columns, and the doorway exhibits Colonial-style side lights.

SO091 **Circle D Ag Elevators**

c. 1905. Alley north of Washington St., east of Fillmore St.

The two-and-a-half-story central building with a gable roof is sheathed in corrugated steel and it is surrounded by prefabricated drums with conical roofs. The roof of the central building is surmounted by a small one-and-a-half-story monitor. This group of utilitarian buildings brings agriculture and the image of the machine close together, not as high art but as a form of folk architecture (which could supply an appropriate image for a painter, or for that manner, a contemporary architect).

SO092 **House**

c. 1892. 600 N. Main St.

An earth-hugging Queen Anne/Colonial Revival cottage centers on an octagonal tower which penetrates a semicircular porch. The porch exhibits thin Ionic columns, and the tower is covered by a spired roof with upturned eaves in the fashion of a witch's hat.

Ottumwa

The city was laid out on the north bank of the lower Des Moines River in 1843 by the Appanoose Rapids and Milling Company. In the following year Ottumwa became the seat of Wapello County. Up through the 1870s the community was essentially confined to the low, hilly area north of the river. The city expanded to the flatlands across the river to the south with the arrival of the meat-packing industry at the end of the 1870s. The largest of these facilities eventually became the extensive John Morrell and Company plant (founded in 1878).

The existence of vast deposits of bituminous coal led to the development of a coal industry. The glowing and optimistic view of what this industry might do for the region's economy was beautifully summed up in the 1890 Coal Palace.[10] This fairyland exposition building was one of a series erected in Iowa in the late 1880s and early 1890s—others being the Corn Palace at Sioux City, the Bluegrass Palace at Creston, and the Flax Palace at Forest City. Other, more modest structures were built at Mason City and Algona. Still others, such as an Onion Palace at Davenport, were projected, but not built.

With the success of the earlier Corn Palace at Sioux City before them, the citizens of Ottumwa decided to advertise their own major industry, coal. They engaged the Sioux City architect Charles P. Brown, who was then planning the second corn palace, to design their extravaganza. Brown produced quite a different building from that at Sioux City. The new one was described as being "erected in an architectural style that is a compromise between the Gothic and the Byzantine."[11] In size the structure measured 230 by 130 feet, and its central tower was 200 feet high. The walls of the building were sheathed in uncut blocks of coal, and the crenellated walls projected skyward with spired roofs and bulbous domes with lanterns. Beneath the building, in wonderful Disneyland fashion, was a replica of a coal mine—viewed by visitors within a car which descended and ran through the mine. The palace was used for a second season in 1891, and it was later torn down.

SO093 Wapello County Courthouse

1892–1893, Foster and Liebbe. Northwest corner of 4th and Court streets

The construction of courthouse buildings in Ottumwa followed the usual course within the state: the initial use of a log cabin, then construction of a two-story frame building, next the building of a brick courthouse (in 1855, in this case), and eventually the erection of the present building (1892–1893). In plan the building is basically a square, with pavilions projecting slightly on each side. A square corner tower originally dominated the building, but with the removal of this tower and its clock faces in 1950 the statue of Chief Wapello on the apex of the front gable became the most eye-catching feature of structure. The building is sheathed in rough-cut sandstone blocks, the heaviness of its masonry enhanced by the apron treatment of stone at its base.

SO094 Ottumwa Municipal Building

1912, James Knox Taylor. Southeast corner of 4th and Court streets

Ottumwa

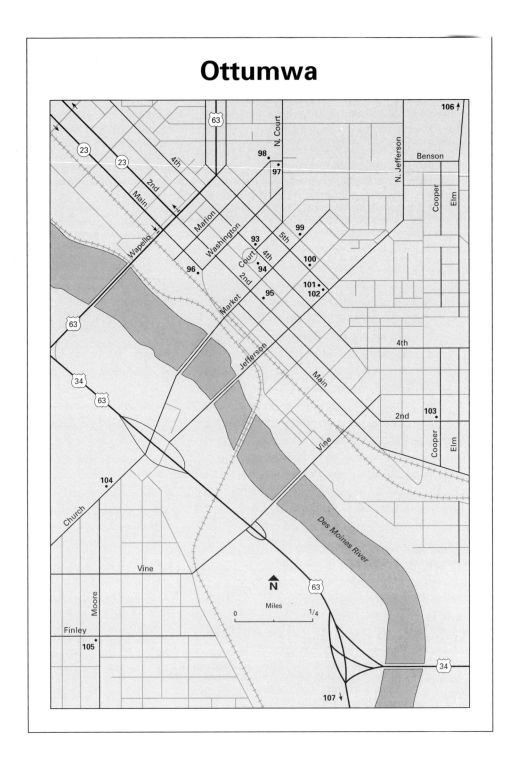

This building was designed in the office of the Architect of the Treasury, James Knox Taylor, as a post office and federal building. Taylor's office provided Ottumwa with one of the state's finest and most sophisticated versions of the Beaux-Arts Classical style. The three-story building exhibits a rusticated first floor, a second floor defined by thin pilasters, and a third floor as an attic. All of the windows and doors on the first floor are arched, suggesting an enclosed loggia; the rectangular windows of the second floor are accompanied by pediments set within arched openings; the square windows on the third floor are simply set deeply into the wall. The most impressive facade of the building is at the rear, where the building works itself into the hillside via a T-shaped staircase.

SO095 Ottumwa Daily Courier Building

c. 1916. 200 block of E. 2nd St.

The pair of great columns set within the front recess of the building, plus the templelike entrance and other details, declare the design to be Egyptian. The building's brick front suggests a pylon; the detailing is carried out in vibrant yellow, blue, and green glazed terracotta (including the relief sculpture of a globe of the world at the apex of the building). The post-World War II modernization of the facade, including the grillwork and the horizontal slab roofs, do not enhance the original design.

SO096 Ottumwa Union Depot, Chicago, Burlington, and Quincy Railroad

1887–1889, Burnham and Root. 1951, Holabird and Root, and Burgee. Main St., south end of Washington St.

The Chicago firm of Burnham and Root designed a number of small to large passenger stations in Missouri, Kansas, Illinois, and Iowa. In Iowa their major stations were the ones at Des Moines, Keokuk, and Burlington, and the other one was at Ottumwa. It is almost impossible to conceive that under this post-World War II modernist shell are parts of Burnham and Root's Romanesque Revival building. A tall chimney now soars into the sky, replacing their open tower, and a flat roof now exists as a replacement for their gabled and dormered tile roof. The station

as it now exists conveys a mild modernist image, similar to but in certain ways more conservative than the station at Burlington. Like that station, this one is sheathed in light-colored limestone, and the windows and the intervening wall surfaces are treated as horizontal bands. A thin cantilevered roof tops the building, and the principal glassed entrance to the building also has its own thin slab roof. This building, which houses the usual station functions as well as the divisional offices of the Chicago, Burlington, and Quincy Railroad, was one of the last stations to be built in Iowa.

SO097 Johnson House

c. 1882, Edward Clark. 531 N. Court St.

With the removal of the tall, truncated roof of the three-story tower (its upper windows treated as wall dormers), the lowering of its projecting chimney, and the removal of its original porches, the house is no longer a strong interpretation of the French Second Empire style. As one often encounters in houses of the 1870s and early 1880s, other fashionable modes entered into its design. The corner staircase bay tower and the gables that projected through the eaves of the roof are really Eastlake. The present Colonial Revival porch at the front (c. 1900) replaced a small piered entrance porch. There is a change of level to the side and rear of the site, exposing a basement treated in stone, with brick used for the body of the building above.

SO098 Bungalow

c. 1910. 359 N. Marion St.

A turn-of-the-century Colonial Revival bungalow of strong character, this house has a deep porch with Tuscan columns and a balustrade running across the entire front. Within the porch, the entrance doorway is emphasized by two overscaled oval windows, one on each side. At the center of the low pitched roof is a dormer with a hooped center portion, accompanied on each side by lower shed-roofed sections.

SO099 Foster House

c. 1915. 405 N. Market

The popular Tudor Revival style was utilized for this substantial upper-middle-class house.

(The building is now used as the school district headquarters.) The half-timbering in a number of the gables contrasts with the solidity of the brick walls. A large living porch with low segmental arches projects off the front of the house. Much of the wood detailing, in both the interior and exterior, is decorated. Some of the more lavish decoration can be seen in the bargeboards of the gable ends with their alternating pattern of floral motifs and shields.

SO100 House

c. 1910. 227 E. 5th St.

This is another of Ottumwa's Tudor Revival dwellings. In this instance the architect has enriched his design by references to the classical tradition, and to the Craftsman style which was then the rage. Although this design was probably meant to be responded to as English Tudor, its plan, the general horizontality, and the low pitch of the roofs are purely Craftsman. The deep entrance-cum-living-porch, which is really treated as a separate open pavilion, exhibits two "primitive" classical columns; above this porch on the second floor is a wide splayed bay window, with dentils and a classical cornice.

SO101 House

c. 1900. 334 E. 5th St.

The two-story gable end of this Colonial Revival house faces the street. However, instead of having a central entrance as its dominant point, the design focuses on a brick chimney that makes its way up through the wall and gable. At the first-floor level, the chimney is behind the projecting living porch (with its small, delicate, broken curved pediment); on the second level the brickwork disappears behind a projecting gable and its consoles and entablature; finally, at the apex of the gable, the chimney is hidden behind a small projecting and bracketed gable. The remainder of the substantial clapboard dwelling is treated simply and directly.

SO102 House

c. 1870. 328 E. 5th St.

In the design of this two-story clapboard dwelling, the rich roof eaves with their wide entablature and brackets are joined with pronounced gables; these refer to the Eastlake style popular after the Civil War. Within these gables are pointed Gothic windows that contrast sharply with the surrounding complexity of brackets supporting the overhang of the roof. Sawed Eastlake details appear also in the supporting entablature of the small entrance porch, and within the projecting bay at the south side of the house.

SO103 Sacred Heart School Building

1959, Barry Byrne. 119 Cooper Ave.

Like all of Byrne's post-World War II churches and schools, this one does not directly reveal his earlier involvement with the Prairie mode, or with Expressionism in the late 1920s and 1930s. In his design for the Sacred Heart School, Byrne seems to have used the traditional elements of architecture, then abstracted them, and finally arranged them in a loose fashion into a single composition. The gable roof is here but its ridge is off-center; there are buttresses, but they end up being extensions of the lateral walls; some of the roof edges are essentially flush with the wall surfaces below, others are extended. Though much is indeed going on within this composition, it ends up being calm and reticent.

SO104 Rowe Drug Store

c. 1936. 531 Church St.

Remodeling as repackaging was a popular affair in the depression years of the 1930s. Such a remodeling should suggest that the

SO106 Foster House

establishment within is highly up-to-date, and this should be accomplished as inexpensively as possible. The owners of the Rowe Drug Store simply used Vitrolite, glass, metal, and neon to revamp their store's older image. The style employed here is Streamline Moderne, and the signage transforms the whole front into a singular billboard. Lighting, especially the neon, makes the front highly visible at night; during the day the building's presence is maintained by the brilliant color of the Vitrolite—midnight blue played off against a strong cream background.

SO105 **Cottage**

c. 1875. 101 S. Moore St.

Often times, as in the case of this small cottage, elaboration of detailing occurs regardless of the size of a building. Each end of the narrow front porch of this cottage turns 45 degrees, and the gabled ends of these projections provide the entrances to the house. The entablature and capitals of the porch columns are decorated with sawed and spindle work. Even the bargeboard of the house's main gable is decorated with thin raised paneling and rosettes.

SO106 **Foster House**

1933, Tinsley, McBroom and Higgins. 1560 N. Elm St.

As was the case with other architects who

practiced in the 1930s and before, the architects used a number of different points of historic references in their designs. In the thirties and on into the post-World War II years, they tended to employ one of three images: the American Colonial, the French Provincial, and on occasion, the French Norman. The Foster house is one of the largest and most impressive of their post-1945 designs in the latter mode. This large suburban house is sheathed in brick that has been whitewashed to give an aged effect. Beside the entrance is a round tower with spire roof which houses the principal staircase. The steeply pitched gable roofs are picturesquely varied, and the skyline of the house is broken by a number of tall chimneys. Small hipped and round dormers break from the roof surface, and below, on the second floor, there is occasional half-timbering. In the realm of the late period revival, the Foster house is one of America's classics.

SO107 **Baptist Church at Mars Hill**

completed in 1857. Proceed 10 miles south of Ottumwa on US 63; turn east on J15 toward Floris; proceed 2.5 miles; travel left (north) on gravel road 1.1 miles; then turn left and go west .5 miles; drive north (right) .7 miles; turn right and proceed . 2 miles, then left, to the north, for .8 miles

The Mars Hill Baptist Church is one of the few remaining nineteenth-century log churches in Iowa. In addition to this distinction, the gable-roofed structure is the largest remaining log cabin in the state (measuring 26 by 28 feet, with walls 10 feet high). The walls utilize split logs, some stretching the entire 28 feet in length. The church building is situated within a grove of trees; adjacent to it is the graveyard and then patches of open fields.

Pittsburg

SO108 Jo Strong General Store

1889. South side of route J40

A classic example of a single-story false-front store building is located on Pittsburg's main street. This clapboard building houses the Jo Strong General Store of 1889. The shed-roofed section to the side also has its own lower false front. A porch with a metal shed roof goes along the front of the building, and the fenestration of the show windows and entrance seems original to the building. Just north on route J40, on the same side of the road, is the Phil Strong House (c. 1850s). This two-story Greek Revival dwelling has brick walls, gable-end wall chimneys, and a dentil cornice of brick. Of course, the present porch, of Eastlake design, is a later addition.

Red Oak

The town was originally called Red Oak Junction, so named in anticipation of the community's being at the junction of north-south and east-west railroads (which eventually it was). The first buildings were erected on the site at the end of the 1850s, and it became the seat of Montgomery County in 1865. Its location at the confluence of the Nishnabotna River and Red Oak Creek meant that adequate water power was available for the operation of mills.

SO109 Montgomery County Courthouse

1890–1891, H. C. Koch and Company. Northwest corner of 2nd and Coolbaugh streets

The Milwaukee architect of the Montgomery Courthouse, Henry C. Koch (a Fellow of the American Institute of Architects), designed courthouses in Kansas, Iowa, and Wisconsin. His 1890–1891 building replaced a modest 1857 two-story wooden building that had been moved in 1866 to Red Oak from Frankfort, the first county seat. Koch provided the county

SO109 Montgomery County Courthouse

with the then-fashionable Richardsonian Romanesque image, but his design strongly conveyed a High Victorian atmosphere. This was due to the verticality of the design and to the emphatic division of the building into two layers: the raised basement and the ground floor sheathed in light tan Missouri limestone, and then the area above in red pressed brick and terracotta. The seven-story clock tower at one corner is balanced at the other corner by a bay tower capped by a Queen Anne roof with a segmented dome. The roofscape is sprinkled with vertical projections: a central pencil-thin cupola, small towers, a tall ribbed chimney, and numerous finials. The Montgomery County Courthouse is one of Iowa's principal contributions to the design of the nineteenth-century American courthouses.

SO110 Carnegie Public Library

1909, Patton and Miller. Northeast corner of 2nd and Washington streets

For this library building the architects turned to the stylistic features of the contemporary American Arts and Crafts (Craftsman) movement. The lower portion of the walls is brick, and brick piers extend upward as pinnacles above the roof eaves. The upper section of the building, including its central gable, is of stucco and half-timbering, and the stepped gable roof is covered with flat terracotta tile. The gabled end on the right has been sympathetically extended, doubling the building in size.

SO111 Commercial Blocks

c. 1890–1910. Coolbaugh between 3rd and 5th streets

Most of these brick blocks along Coolbaugh Street are two stories high, and a good number of them still exhibit something approaching their original ground-floor shop fronts. Two contrasting types of second-floor bay windows can be seen in a pair of Flemish gabled bays of a building (c. 1895) located on Coolbaugh between Fourth and Fifth (now housing Bon Ton Cleaners), and in a nearby c. 1910 building (Brown's) with references to the English Gothic on Coolbaugh near the corner of Fourth Street.

SO112 Church of Christ

1912. Northwest corner of 7th and Coolbaugh streets

The plan of this church with a central auditorium is that of a Greek cross with a central octagonal drum and low dome. The space between the arms has been filled in, and one corner has been cut at a 45-degree angle so as to command the street corner. This angled facade has a double-columned porch inspired by the classical style. Overall, the design represents a warm, domesticated version of the Beaux-Arts tradition.

SO113 Reifel House

c. 1896. 711 Coolbaugh St.

This commodious two-and-a-half-story Queen Anne dwelling was much modified by the simplicity and details of the Colonial Revival. The principal front gable centers on a Palladian open porch; the extensive first-floor veranda has paired narrow Tuscan columns, and its roof is gabled. The general horizontality of the first two floors is countered by the upward thrust of the steeply pitched roof with its many gables.

SO114 Howard House

c. 1889. 909 Coolbaugh St.

Though much remodeled, the corner bay tower that terminates in a porch with an open Moorish dome establishes this dwelling as one of rare character. The tall paneled brick chimney is also noteworthy.

SO115 **Hinchman House**

c. 1890. 610 8th St.

Another residence that mixes the Queen Anne and the Colonial Revival, the Hinchman house boasts two towers: the one on the right is octagonal in form, and that on the left is square. The wide lintels of the veranda bear open and applied sawed wood designs, as do the fascias of the third-floor roof gables.

SO116 **Hebard House**

1874. 700 8th St.

This high, square, Italianate dwelling was built by Col. Alfred Hebard, the founder of Red Oak. There are narrow curved corner windows between the heavy paired brackets within the entablature. Quoining appears at the corners of the brick walls, and U-shaped stone lintels were used above all of the major windows and doors.

SO117 **House**

c. 1875. 601 Reed St.

An interestingly remodeled brick Italianate house, this building was given low-pitched wall dormers that have been thrust up from the wide entablature through the edge of the roof. Between the dormers is a narrow curved corner window similar to those on the nearby Hebard house. A veranda with wide arches and pilasters is carried across the front of the house.

SO118 **Cottage**

c. 1889. Northwest corner of 3rd and Joy streets

Delicate open and applied details of sawed and turned wood characterize this one-and-a-half-story cottage. There are two superimposed layers of sawed work in the lower of the two front gables, their motif suggesting abstracted apples.

SO119 **Powell-Anderson House**

c. 1903. 1118 Boundary St.

The upper reaches of Boundary Street contain several good-sized dwellings represent-

ing the Colonial Revival tradition. There is the Deemer house of 1896 at 1112 Boundary, and the 1897 Osborne house at 1020 Boundary. Then there is the Powell-Anderson house at 1118 Boundary, which conveys a Central European version of the classical tradition as it existed at the turn of the century. Its front is dominated by a two-story porch supported at each corner by pairs of stout, primitive piers. Tucked in behind this porch is a single-story porch which runs underneath it. There is a highly decorated gable in the central section of the lower porch's roof directly over (but behind) the two-story porch.

SO120 **Park Shelter**

1908. Northeast corner of Oak and 8th streets, Chautauqua Park

The segmented circular roof together with the central clerestory and its roof seem to float delicately over the landscape, for the thin steel columns supporting the roof (which is 160 feet in diameter) are almost invisible from a distance. The pavilion was built for gatherings of the Red Oak Chautauqua Association.

SO121 **Stennett House and Barn**

1869. Proceed north from Red Oak 4 miles on Iowa 48; at route H20 travel east about 2 miles to tiny community of Stennett; house and barn are at east edge of town, off a gravel road

Town founder Wayne Stennett built this two-story limestone house in a late version of the much earlier Federal style. The front entrance door and accompanying side lights look out onto a small porch whose roof is supported by pairs of narrow piers at each corner. The symmetry of the front facade is matched by a balanced placement of windows on each of the side elevations. A two-story stone utility wing, also with a porch, extends from the back of the dwelling. Within the main block of the house, two brick chimneys project through the low hipped roof. Across the gravel road is the original one-and-a-half-story stone barn with an exposed basement; later wooden additions have been attached to the structure.

Selma

At the eastern side of the village of Selma, on the north side of Iowa 16, is the Hinkle log cabin, built by Thomas Benjamin Saylor in 1835 and then sold to Capt. Abraham Hinkle in 1868. As the cabin now stands one should refer to it as a log house, for it is a two-story building of some length. It appears to have been built in at least three stages. The center part has a central door with one small window on each side, and on the second floor there is another set of windows over the lower ones. The wings, on the other hand, have pairs of 12–light double-hung windows. The building was put together with wooden pegs rather than nails. The cabin was moved to its present site, restored and furnished by the Van Buren County Historical Society, and is open to the public.

Shenandoah

The town was laid out in 1870 by the Chicago, Burlington, and Quincy Railroad. The plan is unusual in that one of the principal streets, Clarinda Avenue, is at a 45-degree angle to the grid, and this avenue is attached to a segment of a circle, South Crescent Street. The theme of the circle is repeated in the northeast section of town in the layout of the cemetery. The civic center of the community lies at the intersection of Clarinda Avenue, Church Street, and Thomas Street. Here one will come upon City Hall, the First Baptist Church, the First Christian Church, the First United Methodist Church, Saint Mary's Roman Catholic Church, and a Civil War memorial column.

SO122 Bank Building

1905. W. Sheridan Ave. between Elm and Blossom streets

A strong Beaux-Arts design here dominates the street. The ground floor has two entrances: one with a dramatic pediment leads to the bank, another to the stair leading to the offices on the second floor. Between these two entrances is a recessed bay window. The second floor has a large arched window flanked by engaged Ionic columns.

SO123 Fourplex Housing

c. 1905. 307–309 Clarinda Ave. W.

It seems that it is often the case in architecture that a singular feature ends up setting off a building from the ordinary. In this instance it is a double exterior stairway placed at the center of a two-story porch which "makes" this building. The first run of the pair of stairs leads to a central landing, and then another run leads up to the second-floor porch. The columned porch itself is a simple Colonial Revival design; the building behind is a rectangular brick box.

SO124 House

c. 1860s. 109 Clarinda Ave. E.

This is an exemplary instance of the late Italianate, which is beginning to take on some of the linear "sticklike" qualities one associates with the Eastlake mode of the 1870s. The segmental arches of the porch are here thin lines of wood, the posts are thin sticks, and the balustrades of the porch railing are narrow and delicate. The two-story house is of wood; in plan it is a side-hall type, but it is the front porch wrapping around one side which creates the appealing character of the dwelling.

SO125 **House**

c. 1910. 404 Center St.

In this instance the Craftsman style has been carried out with great sophistication. This two-story brick dwelling has a Prairie-style entrance with a segmented roof that is reminiscent of George W. Maher's work. The theme of the roof is repeated in the three dormers set in the flat tile roof. The large living porch to the side also returns to the theme of the segmental arch in all of its openings. A single band of light-colored cast stone continues on top of the porch parapet and then goes onto the walls of the house, connecting the sills of the second-floor windows. The wood shutters are quite interesting; they are of thick, heavy timber with thin vertical slots arranged in two rows.

SO126 **House**

c. 1895. 604 West St.

A low-spreading entrance porch with pairs of piers at both corners and an open gable roof with returns at the eave ends declare this large two-story clapboard house an avowed example of the turn-of-the-century Colonial Revival. But it is not the street facade that really establishes the personality of this house; rather the extra-broad bay tower to the left continually draws one's attention. While the concept of a tower such as this (including its pointed domelike roof) is Queen Anne, much of its ornament—recessed panels and bands of small medallions joined by wreaths—represents motifs one associates with the Colonial Revival of the time.

SO127 **House**

c. 1895. 709 Church St.

If this one-and-a-half-story dwelling were sheathed in stained shingles instead of white painted clapboard, it would probably fall into what historians from the late 1940s onward have often labeled the Shingle style. The principal gables of this cruciform-plan house reveal a lower band of windows lighting the second floor; above, the cantilevered upper gable contains a miniature Palladian window. On the first floor a great porch, its roof supported by pairs of columns, wraps around the forward section of the house.

SO128 **Cottage**

c. 1880. 705 Church St.

The designer of this moderate-sized cottage with a hipped roof would seem to have played with a number of styles that were either just going out of vogue or just arriving around 1880. The roof supported on paired brackets, the posts and detailing of the side porch, and the treatment of the window headers look back to the Italianate. What entices one to examine the cottage more closely is the small entrance porch thrust into the corner of the building, and then the adjacent, quite unusual keyhole window. These two features transport one from the Eastlake into the then-developing Queen Anne.

SO129 **Henry Field Seed and Nursery Company**

c. 1924. Sycamore St., between Valley and Palm avenues, northeast of town off Iowa 48

An older three-story brick building has been imaginatively wrapped with a stucco-and-tile Mission Revival "stage set" of one and two stories. On ground level a deep-arched "corridor" marches around two sides of the building. Above, four narrow pavilions topped with curved gables spring from the tile roof. The nursery company was established in 1892; obviously by the 1920s it was felt that the exotic California Mission style somehow fit the horticultural activities of the firm.

SO130 **Braymen Barn**

c. 1914. Proceed east on Iowa 2 for 3 miles; travel south on route M32 for 2.2 miles; go left (east) on J40 1 mile, then right (south) .25 miles on the dirt road

This low 16-sided barn has a frame and walls built entirely of wood. Within, there is a single large post in the center, and then a circle of posts. The roof is sheathed in metal, and a small-sized metal aerator sits on the crown of the roof.

SO131 **Saint Patrick's Roman Catholic Church**

1915. 7 miles north of Shenandoah on US 59, travel west on Iowa 184 2 miles to the small community of Imogene

Saint Patrick's is a free interpretation of the rural English Gothic church developed via the English Arts and Crafts movement. The ridge line of the front gable reads as a fine line with no indication of the roof behind. The numerous buttresses act as vertical lines on the front and sides of the church and upon the walls of the corner crenellated tower. The projecting pediments and arches of the triple-doored entrance form a single light-colored stone band set in front of the building. The interior of this seemingly puritanical brick shell is quite elaborate, boasting surfaces and detailing in Carrara marble.

SO132 **Chautauqua Pavilion**

1897. City Park, Riverton; travel south of Shenandoah on US 59, then west on route J46 to Riverton

This open Chautauqua pavilion was placed in a clearing in a broad wooded park. The

SO132 Chautauqua Pavilion

building is dominated by a steeply pitched, segmented shingled roof that seems to hover above the supporting thin wood columns to the wood lintel beams above. About two-thirds of the way up the slope, the broad roof exhibits a slight inward bend that adds to its charming hatlike quality.

Stanton

The town of Stanton, which was settled by Swedes, turns out to be the birthplace of the actress Virginia Christine, who played "Mrs. Olson" in the television commercials for Folger's Coffee; thus the town's high water tower is in the form of a gigantic Swedish coffee pot (built in 1971). A plaque at the base of the tower (the "World's Largest Swedish Coffee Pot") provides you with all the vital information: height of tower, 125 feet; capacity of water-tank pot, 640,000 cups.

At the end of Center Street, situated on a hill, is the 1939–1940 Mamrelund Lutheran Church, designed by Harvey Peterson of Omaha, Nebraska. The church with central entrance tower presents a sophisticated picture of an abstracted version of the traditional Gothic church. The walls of the church are sheathed in smooth, finely cut and joined limestone; the decorative aspects have either been eliminated or reduced to their simplest form.

The combined city hall and library (1912) located on the east side of Broad Street south of Thorn Street entails a lively essay in pre-World War I Beaux-Arts Classicism. Placed directly on the street with no landscaped space around it, the building strongly announces its public presence. The center section of the street facade is recessed between two fluted Doric columns. In a central position is a lushly articulated door frame with bold consoles supporting a projecting roof. All of the detailing has been carried out in cream-colored terracotta that contrasts sharply with the red brick walls. The community's present city hall and public library building was originally built for the Stanton Bank.

Troy

The crossroads village of Troy, in east-central Davis County, houses one of the few remaining private educational buildings from the 1850s, Troy Academy (SO133).

One mile due south of Troy on a gravel road is the Springtown Inn. Local histories date the building as early as 1832; others have indicated that it may have been built after 1846. The form of the inn is that of a one-and-a-half-story saltbox. The walls are sheathed in clapboard; the foundation is limestone. The inn has the appearance of having been constructed in two stages, with two identical salt boxes placed end to end. The proportions of the building, its roof pitch, and the detailing of the windows and doors are what one would associate with the late Greek Revival.

SO133 **Troy Academy**
1853, founded. Off route J40

This wood frame building was constructed in 1853, joining two of the popular images of the mid-nineteenth century, the Greek Revival and the Gothic. The main section of the building is Greek Revival in its proportions and fenestration. Its pediments are enclosed, and there is a suggestion of paneled pilasters at each corner. The front consists of a narrow gabled wing, which centers on a thin, high, Gothic window. A shed roof section is attached to each side of this Gothic entrance, giving the building an informal appearance. Perhaps in an effort to tie all of this together, the architect placed a Greek-style double-layered tower above the higher pitched Gothic roof.

Villisca

The community was established in 1857 on a site between the West and Middle forks of the Nodaway River. Like nearby Stanton and Red Oak, Villisca became a station stop on the east-west Burlington Northern Railroad line.

The Villisca National Bank (c. 1917) at the southwest corner of Third Avenue and Fourth Street is a narrow two-story block, mildly classical in its image. Three pilasters grace the front of the building; in the entablature above are three classical wreaths, and the projecting cornice is supported by a tight row of brackets. The detailing is rendered in smooth limestone, sharply contrasted against the red brick of the walls. At the south end of the downtown, west of Third Avenue is the Burlington Northern Railroad Station (c. 1912). Its plaster-and-brick walls and flat tile roofs seemingly look to central European Arts and Crafts architecture of the years after 1900. Brick is employed for the base of the building and for random quoining, and heavy wood struts support the extended eaves at the gable ends.

In the residential section of town is a fine, spindly two-story Queen Anne dwelling (c. 1885). This house at the northeast corner of Third Avenue and High Street displays a moon-gate pattern in wood, within which is a single rectangular window. Above this composition, on the second floor, is a tripartite window with two quarter-circles and a lunette in wood above its central window. The linear quality of the design is emphasized by the sawed bargeboards and by the pattern of turned open work of the porch and corner window.

North (NO)

THE NORTHERN SECTION OF THE STATE WAS GENERALLY THE last to be settled. The landscape of the area is essentially that of the classic, slightly undulating open prairie with very little in the way of groves of native trees. The trees and shrubs that do exist tend to reinforce the strong right-angle geometry of the roads—land divisions—or mark the location of farm complexes. While a number of small rivers and streams penetrate the area, their run-off and degree of flow limited their use for water power. An exception is found in the eastern part of this section, especially along the Cedar and Wapsipinicon rivers, where water power was fully developed.

Architecturally this region is very rich. There are elegant examples of nineteenth-century public, commercial, and domestic buildings in communities such as Decorah and Independence. After 1900, Mason City emerged as one of America's centers for Prairie architecture and landscape architecture. Throughout the region one will discover smaller communities with picturesque late-nineteenth- and early twentieth-century high-spired churches of stone and brick, and towns with quiet tree-lined residential streets along which bungalows and classic Prairie-style houses were built between 1900 and 1920. Also common to the region are the sculptural banks of tall concrete grain elevators alongside the railroads, and their more recent counterparts, high-tech metal silos and agricultural processing facilities.

Ackley

The small railroad town of Ackley, on the northern boundary of Hardin County, houses two dwellings influenced by the Arts and Crafts movement. At 321 Hardin Street is a good-sized Craftsman bungalow built around 1915 for Dr. I. L.

North Iowa

Dickinson · 71 · 5 · 22 — Emmet · Kossuth · 42 · 73 · Winnebago · 27 · 24 · 47 · 41 Worth · 53 · Mitchell · 65 · 56 · Howard · 44 · 26 · 16 · 45 · Winneshiek · 18 · 70 · 57

Clay · 69 — Palo Alto · 21 — Hancock · 7 · 30 · 14 · 48 · 75 · 61 — Floyd · 10 — Chickasaw · 11 · 39 · 51 · 50 · 28 · 25 · 8 · 66 · 15 · 82

Buena Vista · 43 · 60 · 72 — Humboldt · 37 · 17 — Wright · 6 · 31 · 12 · 35 — Cerro Gordo · 32 · 67 — 33 · 13 · 3 · 68 · 58 — Butler — 59 Bremer · 77 — Fayette · 4 · 55 · 23 · 81 · 2 · 80 · 9

Sac · 64 · 54 — Pocahontas — Calhoun · 46 — Webster · 29 · 19 — Hamilton · 78 — Franklin · 40 · 1 — Hardin · 20 · 36 · 52 · 74 — Grundy · 79 · 34 · 49 · 62 — Blackhawk · 9 · 76 — Buchanan · 38 · 61

1. Ackley (Franklin Co.)
2. Algona (Kossuth Co.)
3. Allison (Butler Co.)
4. Arlington (Fayette Co.)
5. Arnold's Park (Dickinson Co.)
6. Belmond (Wright Co.)
7. Britt (Hancock Co.)
8. Castalia (Winneshiek Co.)
9. Cedar Falls (Blackhawk Co.)*
10. Charles City (Floyd Co.)
11. Chickasaw (Chickasaw Co.)
12. Clarion (Wright Co.)
13. Clarksville (Butler Co.)
14. Clear Lake (Cerro Gordo Co.)
15. Clermont (Fayette Co.)
16. Cresco (Howard Co.)
17. Dakota City (Humbolt Co.)
18. Decorah (Winneshiek Co.)*
19. Duncombe (Webster Co.)
20. Eldora (Hardin Co.)
21. Emmetsburg (Palo Alto Co.)
22. Estherville (Emmet Co.)
23. Fayette (Fayette Co.)
24. Fertile (Worth Co.)
25. Festina (Winneshiek Co.)
26. Florenceville (Howard Co.)
27. Forest City (Winnebago Co.)
28. Fort Atkinson (Winneshiek Co.)

29. Fort Dodge (Webster Co.)*
30. Garner (Hancock Co.)
31. Goldfield (Wright Co.)
32. Goodell (Hancock Co.)
33. Greene (Butler Co.)
34. Grundy Center (Grundy Co.)
35. Hampton (Franklin Co.)
36. Hubbard (Hardin Co.)
37. Humboldt (Humbolt Co.)
38. Independence (Buchanan Co.)*
39. Ionia (Chickasaw Co.)
40. Iowa Falls (Hardin Co.)
41. Lake Mills (Winnebago Co.)
42. Lakota (Kossuth Co.)
43. Laurens (Pocahontas Co.)
44. Lime Springs (Howard Co.)
45. Lourdes (Howard Co.)
46. Lytton (Calhoun Co.)
47. Manly (Worth Co.)
48. Mason City (Cerro Gordo Co.)*
49. Morrison (Grundy Co.)
50. Nashua (Chickasaw Co.)
51. New Hampton (Chickasaw Co.)
52. New Providence (Hardin Co.)
53. Northwood (Worth Co.)
54. Odebolt (Sac Co.)
55. Oelwein (Fayette Co.)

56. Osage (Mitchell Co.)
57. Ossian (Winneshiek Co.)
58. Parkersburg (Butler Co.)
59. Plainfield (Bremer Co.)
60. Pocahontas (Pocahontas Co.)
61. Quasqueton (Buchanan Co.)
62. Reinbeck (Grundy Co.)
63. Rock Falls (Cerro Gordo Co.)
64. Sac City (Sac Co.)
65. Saint Ansgar (Mitchell Co.)
66. Saint Lucas (Fayette Co.)
67. Sheffield (Franklin Co.)
68. Shell Rock (Butler Co.)
69. Spencer (Clay Co.)
70. Spillville (Winneshiek Co.)
71. Spirit Lake (Dickinson Co.)
72. Storm Lake (Buena Vista Co.)
73. Titonka (Kossuth Co.)
74. Union (Hardin Co.)
75. Ventura (Cerro Gordo Co.)
76. Waterloo (Blackhawk Co.)*
77. Waverly (Bremer Co.)
78. Webster City (Hamilton Co.)
79. Wellsburg (Grundy Co.)
80. Wesley (Kossuth Co.)
81. West Bend (Palo Alto Co.)
82. West Union (Fayette Co.)

A detailed map of site locations has been provided for cities indicated by ⊙ on the map and by * in the list above.

349

Potter. The dwelling and its extensive terrace, pergola, and living porch are set on a raised brick basement. Underneath the porch, terrace, and pergola, the wall of the raised basement is broken by a rhythmic pattern of low, arched openings. Brick walls are carried up to the first-floor window sills, and narrow clapboarding above continues up to meet the stuccoed gable ends. The broad overhanging roof of the gable ends is supported by groups of three open-angled brackets.

One block to the north, at 903 Main Street, is the Fred E. Trainer house (1915). This Prairie school dwelling designed by the Chicago architect Henry K. Holsman is similar in spirit to the work of George W. Maher and Spencer and Powers. The street facade of the house is essentially symmetrical, with windows on each side of the entrance and nearly identical porches at each end. A single steeply pitched hipped roof, broken by dormers with hipped roofs, covers both the main volume and the two porches. Brick veneer covers the walls up to the second-floor window sills, then plaster forms a horizontal band between the top of the brick walls and the roof soffits above. A pair of simple columns supports the open-truss gabled roof of the entrance porch. All of the roofs are covered with red tile. At the rear of the dwelling is a one-and-a-half-story building containing a garage and workroom; it is designed to match the forms of the walls and roof of the main house.

Algona

Algona, the seat of Kossuth County, was platted south of the east fork of the Des Moines River in 1856. This first plat provided for a public square (at State and Hall Streets), a courthouse, and a public park at Nebraska and Blackford streets. The delightful Kossuth County Courthouse (1872), Italianate in style, was torn down in 1955 and replaced by a bland modernist building. Other losses from the nineteenth century are the French Second Empire Algona House Hotel, the Italianate Russell house, and the mill that stood on the south side of the river, north of Thorington Street.

NO001 **Land and Loan Office** (The Adams Building)

1913, Louis H. Sullivan. Northwest corner of E. State and Moore streets

The Adams Building is one of the smallest of Sullivan's late designs for midwestern financial institutions. Sullivan took a rectangular brick box and cut deeply into it for the usual side window and for the entrance on the narrow front of the building. The horizontality of the side window wall was enhanced by the architect's trademark projecting brick sill, terminated on each end by terracotta squares. Within the opening are eight piers with terracotta capitals. The windows were divided above by units of opaque colored glass and below by pairs of opening casement windows. The most unusual feature of the design (now regrettably changed) was the entrance. Two screens of brick projected from each side, creating what Sullivan labeled a "loggia"; the actual entrance vestibule was to the side. Other subtleties of the design included the basketweave pattern of brick and terracotta squares indicating the entablature

NO001 Land and Loan Office (The Adams Building).

and the slight but effectively pulled-out foundation of the building.

NO002 Methodist Episcopal Church (now First United Methodist Church)

1898. Northeast corner of E. Nebraska and Moore streets

This is a successful interpretation of the Richardsonian Romanesque accomplished in red sandstone. The corners of the entrance tower continue above the roof eaves, forming small round finials. The bands and eaves of the tower's tile roof terminate at each end in a concentric circle motif, similar in concept to the way Sullivan treated the horizontal window sill of the nearby Adams Building. The composition of the church's west street facade is especially well arranged with a low roofed arcade contained at one side by the square entrance tower and at the other by a lower round tower with a conical roof.

NO003 House

c. 1870. 503 N. Thorington St.

The highly individual features of this one-and-a-half-story Gothic cottage are the tripartite window in the center of the gable and the two delightfully overscaled first-floor dormers and their windows to the side. The first-floor bays are paneled, and the windows on each of these three sides are large double-hung units.

NO004 House

c. 1928. 602 N. Thorington St.

A one-and-a-half-story living room projects from a corner of the main body of the house at a 45-degree angle. The roof of the living room wing is carried so low to the ground that the windows are treated as wall dormers. The lower portion of the house is sheathed in red brick, and the upper section is half-timbered. Situated on the entrance terrace is a wood bench reminiscent of the designs of the turn-of-the-century English Arts and Crafts architect Charles F. A. Voysey.

NO005 Cottage

c. 1926. End of N. Dodge St. at E. Elm St.

This mid-1920s period revival English cottage is faced with brick below and half-timbering above in the gables. The asphalt roofing has been rolled over the eaves to help create the impression of a thatched roof. The driveway and entrance walk are side by side, and beyond the house is a gabled two-car garage.

NO006 House

c. 1917. 706 N. Thorington St.

The two-story Craftsman brick-sheathed dwelling serves as a quiet, retiring backdrop to a theatrical two-story stucco porch. On the first floor the glassed-in porch has primitive stubby columns in rough-cast stucco; on the second floor (and continuing up into the gable) is an intricate pattern of half-timbering worked around the horizontal groups of casement windows. The asphalt shingles have been wrapped around both the roof eaves and the gables.

NO007 Ferstl Grain Terminal

c. 1965. E. State St., east of Phillips St.

A high-tech "composition" of cylindrical metal grain elevators is topped by a series of thin, linear catwalks, rails, tubes, and platforms.

Allison

Within the small community of Allison, which is located almost in the center of Butler County, is the Richardsonian Romanesque Farmers Savings Bank (1902). The designer of this stylistically late building pulled a narrow arched entrance out from the building and brought attention to it by creating an alternating pattern of light stone and dark brick voussoirs and then supporting the large arch on a pair of stubby columns. To the left of the door is a large arched window providing a view into the public banking area. On the second floor, four windows are grouped together within a stone frame that rests on a stone band extending across the entire facade. The bank is located at the southwest corner of Main and Fourth streets.

Farther up Main Street is the present Butler County Courthouse (1974–1975), designed by the Marshalltown architects Cervetti-Weber and Associates. This modernist brick courthouse consists of a series of rather severe interlocking blocks. It does retain a vestige of the Classical tradition in its central piered portico. Behind the present courthouse is the site of what was once a delightful and successful version of an Italianate courthouse. All that remains of this 1879 building (it was torn down in 1975) is its round, many-windowed cupola which now sits on top of a small building ("The Butler Hall of Fame") within the courthouse grounds.

Eight miles east of Allison on Iowa 3 is the even smaller community of Dumont. Just east of the corner of Main and Second streets is the Roder house of 1925, designed by the Waterloo architect Howard B. Burr. In this house, which is in fact a double double house, Burr investigated the then-fashionable Dutch Colonial style, giving the dwelling a gambrel roof and large dormers with shed roofs. A pair of columned porches with arched ceilings and small gable roofs brings attention to each of the separate entrances.

Arlington

At the southwest corner of Main and Upper streets is the building that housed the First State Bank (1915), now a retail store. While most of the warm-tan terracotta displays classical motifs, the design of this small building (almost domestic in size) is not classical in feeling. The design focuses on vertical rectangles and on gabled and projecting piered parapets. Narrow bands of terracotta surround the large front and side windows and the corner entrance cut into the building; in some cases the bands simply create rectangular panels within the brick walls. The two front ends of the building are treated almost as pavilions surmounted by gabled pediments and piers. Since the building is completely free standing, all four walls are formally treated.

Two miles east of Arlington, on the north side of the gravel road that leaves the southeast corner of town, is a 12-sided barn centering on a tall silo composed of terracotta blocks. The wood-framed and wood-sheathed barn was built in 1906. The barn itself has a diameter of 60 feet, with the silo measuring 14 feet in diameter. Soike speculates that the current silo may have replaced an earlier one.[1] There are only three known examples of this barn type within the state of Iowa.

Arnold's Park

Lakes of any size are rare in Iowa; here, three of them—Spirit Lake, West Okoboji Lake, and East Okoboji Lake—adjoin one another. Arnold's Park offers all that one would expect in a resort town: an amusement park (with a great roller coaster), park, restaurants, shops, and motels. The main historic attraction of the place is the Gardner log cabin (1856, restored in 1975), located on Monument Street, a quarter mile west of the roller coaster. Next to the cabin is a granite obelisk erected in 1893 to commemorate the "Spirit Lake Massacre."

Belmond

The auditorium and gymnasium (1941–1942) building, located at the corner of Fifth Avenue Northeast and Fourth Street Northeast, beautifully illustrates how abstract the PWA Moderne could be at the end of the 1930s. The two flanking walls of this building, which was constructed of exposed reinforced concrete, reveal a pattern of four window pilasters between which, on the upper part of the building, are windows of glass brick. At each end are ornamental features in the form of cast-concrete shields, with a band of vertical indented lines projecting above and below the shields. Below the horizontal upper band of glass brick windows is a series of indented horizontal bands.

At 507 Second Street Northeast is a c. 1916 Prairie style dwelling. This brick-clad two-story box has a side-entrance plan, with a bay window projecting out from the living room and a living porch extending to the side. The living room bay is held in place by the usual pair of piers, topped by horizontal banded capitals. The hipped roof is covered with red Mission terracotta tile.

Britt

This community in central Hancock County was traversed by two railroads, so quite early it acquired two adjacent groups of tall concrete grain elevators that are visible some distance from the town. Within town is the Lewis Larson house (1896), now operated as the Hancock County Museum. The good-sized dwelling, designed and built by John Victoria, represents the late nineteenth-century combination of the Queen Anne and the Colonial Revival styles. The silhouette of the dwelling is lively and picturesque, with bays and a small round tower to the left and a larger octagonal tower to the right. The building is richly detailed with a spindled porch, different patterns of shingle and clapboard, and windows with stained glass. The Larson house is located at 266 Second Avenue Southeast. Another design of John Victoria, built some ten years earlier, is the Stubbins house (NO008).

Britt boasts an energetic version of the Prairie style, the C. W. Erwin house at 278 First Avenue Southwest. The house was designed by J. H. Jeffers of Mason City, and was built in 1918–1919. As in a good number of Iowa's Prairie houses, the designer of the Erwin house employed brick for the walls and tile for the hipped roof, which helps to convey a sense of traditional mass and stability. The corners of the two-story house are treated as piers carried up to a thin line of cast stone which circles around the house (and also links the window sills of the second floor). To the right, a single-story wing containing the entrance projects from the house, matched on the other side by a living porch.

In traveling through Britt, do stop at the now-deserted service station (c. 1922) in the northeast section of town, at the corner of Diagonal and Fourth Avenue Northeast. The service station building is a small structure that conveys the impression that its gable roof is supported by four corner piers. There are large circular openings/signs in each of the gable ends. At what would appear to be a later moment, a pergola/canopy was added over the pump area.

NO008 Stubbins House

1886, John Victoria. 248 1st Ave.

The Stubbins house expresses the Eastlake mode with a few touches of the Queen Anne. Its sawed-work entrance porch is one of the finest examples of the Eastlake style within the state. The corner oriel window on the right of the entrance balances the angled bay on the other side of the entrance porch.

Castalia

In the center of the small town of Castalia, on the south side of US 52, is the former Castalia Savings Bank building (c. 1892). This tiny building, now used as the post office, is one of the gems of Richardsonian Romanesque architecture in Iowa. Its facade—just 20 feet wide—is strikingly divided into horizontal bands, the bottom one in light-colored limestone. This same limestone, which contrasts sharply with the brick of the building, is also used for the capitals and impost blocks of the pair of columns at the entrance, for the capital of the single pilaster which is carried around the corner, and for the flat cornice of the parapeted roof. The entrance with its great arch is brought out from the front of the building and has its own bracketed roof. The short, stubby columns of the entrance are of polished granite. The vigor of this small building reminds one of the work of Frank Furness of Philadelphia.

Cedar Falls

As with so many communities in Iowa, the site for Cedar Falls was selected because of the potential of water power, in this instance the dramatic 14-foot-high falls of the Cedar River. An initial platting of the site took place in 1851, but the north-south, east-west grid of streets south of the river, which actually established the town pattern, was made in 1853. When first settled, this section of the river contained extensive stands of trees, but by the 1870s most of this "native" forest had vanished. Very quickly a number of mills were built to take advantage of the water power of the river. These included a number of flour mills, a woolen mill, a starch factory, and a factory that made wooden pumps. South of this river-oriented manufacturing district was the downtown, site of a good number of two- and three-story masonry buildings. The residential area developed to the south and to the west. Here were eventually located three of the city's early parks. Later residential development occurred still further to the south, and from the 1920s onward it moved to the east.

The railroad reached Cedar Falls in 1861, and by 1875 the community was served by two lines, the Illinois Central and the Burlington, Cedar Rapids, and Minnesota. Separate depots were built for each of the railroads, and the later stations still exist (see NO012; NO015). The community was selected for the Iowa State Soldiers' Orphans Home in 1865. Permanent buildings were erected for the home in 1869. These consisted of a large combined school and residence three-story masonry structure on a raised basement, a chapel, and other buildings. The home was located on a 40-acre site which is now encompassed within the University of Northern Iowa. All of the principal buildings of the former home are now gone.

Though parks had been established within Cedar Falls early in its development, it was in the teens through the forties that the city acquired its major

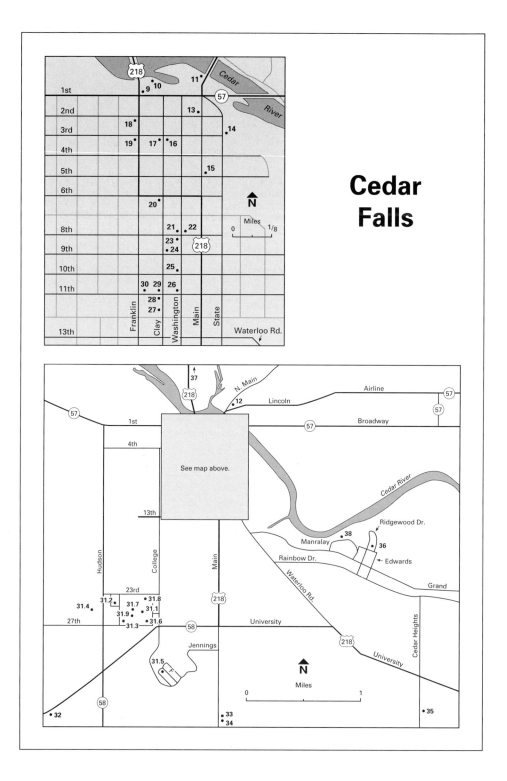

Cedar
Falls

parks. Four of these (Pfeiffer Springs Park, Washington Park and Golf Course, Look Out Park, and George Wyth Memorial Park) were located on the river itself. On the northwest outskirts of the city, at the north end of Ellen Street and South Park Road, is Riverview Park, established in 1916 as the Iowa Conference Center of the Evangelical Church. The double gates, some remaining conference buildings, and a number of private riverside cabins create a strong sense of an informal, somewhat rustic 1920s resort community.

The former milling district along the river has lost most of its buildings; the only remaining mill building (NO011) is now a restaurant. There are still a few early commercial buildings to be found in the downtown. The most important of these is the four-story Burr Hotel (now Black Hawk Hotel) at 115 Main Street. This was built as a hostelry in the late 1870s in the French Empire Style, with mansard roof, central roof pavilion, and projecting iron balconies. Much of the more exuberant exterior detail has now been removed (including the balconies), and the interior has been extensively remodeled.

One can still visually read Cedar Falls as a separate community, yet it is slowly being encompassed within the continual expansion of the Waterloo metropolitan area directly to the east. George Wyth Memorial Park now serves as a boundary between the two cities, and the Waterloo Airport situated in the far northwestern section of Waterloo serves both communities.

NO009 **Cedar Falls Ice House** (now Ice House Museum)

1921–1922. Northeast corner of 1st and Franklin streets

The ice house was built with walls of hollow terracotta tile, a material often used in the Midwest for silos and barns. The building has a circular form (100 feet in diameter), and the 30-foot-high walls are capped by a wood roof and a small, centrally placed venting lantern. The present roof is recent and does not completely follow the original roof's double slope. The building was designed to store ice cut in the winter months from the nearby Cedar River for summer use. From 1938 to 1975 the building was used for boat storage, but now it has been converted into a museum displaying historic ice-cutting equipment.

NO010 **Dam and Spillway on the Cedar River**

1938–1940, C. H. Streeter, engineer. North of 1st St., opposite Clay St.

A small-scaled but still quite impressive engineering project of the late depression years, this complex includes four rotating steel spill-way gates that open between graceful concrete abutments; these abutments are in turn connected at the top by a concrete walkway.

NO011 **Cedar Falls Starch Company Mill** (John Forrest Oatmeal Mill)

1862, 1875. 115 W. Mill St.

This utilitarian three-story brick mill was built in three stages over a period of 10 years. The unadorned brickwork walls are punctured by a few small double-hung windows. From the 1860s on through the early 1900s, the building was used for milling and other operations. After 1910 its space and power were employed in the production of brooms. By the late nineteenth century there were a number of mill structures at Cedar Falls that took advantage of river power; today this mill is the only one surviving. The building has recently been converted to a restaurant (The Old Broom Factory Restaurant).

NO012 **Illinois Central Railroad Depot**

c. 1900. West side of river, between N. Main and Lincoln St.

An unusual gambrel roof caps this brick one-and-a-half-story station. There is a suggestion of brick pilasters along the platform face of the building, and these together with the gable over the stationmaster's office suggest that this small building is one of the public entries into the city.

NO013 **Regent Theater** (originally Cotton Theater)

1909–1910. 103 Main St.

The Regent started out as a legitimate theater, with a large stage house, dressing rooms, and an auditorium that could accommodate 1,034 theatergoers. It was converted into a motion picture theater in the late teens, and the present Moderne neon and incandescent marquee and front were added around 1939. Next door is another 1930s remodel, Wong's Cafe, which with its curved window and glass brick beautifully sums up the commercial streamline Moderne of that decade. Both the cafe and the theater facades are sheathed in Vitrolite.

NO014 **Dannervirke Building** (now Veterinary Hospital)

pre-1882. 321 State St.

This one-and-a-half-story nineteenth-century stone house was, at a much later date, made medieval and English by an addition to the side in stucco and half-timber and by a pair of wall dormers that have half-timbering in their gable ends. For many years (1882–1932) the building housed the local Danish-language newspaper, *Dannervirke*. Its stone and half-timber architectural image well suits its original use.

NO015 **Rock Island Railroad Depot**

c. 1890. Northeast corner of 5th and Main streets

A picturesque building composed of a stone base carried up to the window sills, with brick walls above, the depot was built on a domestic scale. Dramatically extended brackets and struts support the cantilevered roof; below the wide roof soffit is a pattern of round, segmental arched, and square-topped windows.

NO016 **Knapp / Townsend House** (now Cedar Falls Woman's Club)

1867. 224 W. 3rd St.

Certainly one of the most refined of the wood-sheathed Italianate houses in Iowa, this two-story house has a T-shaped plan that encompasses a dependency to the rear. The gabled ends of the dwelling are articulated by a pattern of brackets of a similar scale. There are traditional round windows in the gables; the remaining windows have lintels that are segmented curves. Extensive porches, now glassed in, appear at the front and to the side.

NO017 **Barnum Bryant-Dempster House**

1861. 303 Clay St.

A classic two-story brick Italianate villa, this residence has the hallmarks of the style, including widely projecting eaves with brackets and a central belvedere on the roof. There is a porch with fluted columns to the front, and windows with small lights. The porch is a later but sympathetic addition. The house is open to the public under the auspices of the Cedar Falls Historical Society.

NO018 **Fox House**

1863. 402 W. 2nd St.

The brick Italianate house on a corner lot still dominates this section of the street, though it has been considerably remodeled over the years. The present entrance porch is only a fragment of one that encompassed the entire front and then wrapped around to the side of the house. Also now missing is the bracketed central belvedere on the roof; inside the house there was a grand circular front staircase, now gone.

NO019 **Wyth House**

c. 1907, 1925; 303 Franklin St.

The simple, voluminous, two-story box, usually covered by a hipped roof, emerged throughout the country in the 1890s as a pragmatic type for the middle-class house, whether in suburbia or on the farm. In some cases these box houses might refer to the Queen Anne style; in others, to the Colonial

Revival. The Wyth house has touches of the Mediterranean Revival as well as hints of Dutch or Flemish architecture, especially in the parapeted roof dormer. This house was originally built for F. W. Paulger around 1907. It was purchased and extensively remodeled by George and Alice Wyth in 1925. They sheathed the dwelling in brick and introduced an early midwestern version of the Art Deco through remodeling and furnishings. The house is now a museum and is open by appointment through the Cedar Falls Historical Society.

NO020 **Sartori Cottage**

late 1860s. 603 Clay St.

A charming combination of the Gothic and the Italianate have been brought together in this brick one-and-a-half-story cottage. Below the delicate sawed bargeboards of the gabled roof are elaborate cast-iron window lintels composed of a single arched form within which there are two smaller segmental arches. Inside are an impressive curved stair in the entrance hallway and a marble fireplace in the living room.

NO021 **First Methodist Episcopal Church** (now Methodist Church)

1894. Northwest corner of 8th and Washington streets

The Richardsonian Romanesque has been highly abbreviated in this light-colored rusticated stone church. Externally the building's design revolves around its high, impressive corner tower. At the base of the tower are a pedimented entrance and small stair tower. The tower's high stone spire has a small tower at each corner; these are carried up and terminate in their own separate roofs.

NO022 **Saint Patrick's Roman Catholic Church**

1915, E. L. Masqueray. Northeast corner of 8th and Washington streets

The Romanesque here returns to imperial Rome. The principal facade is centered on a triumphal arch within which is a circle of brick. On each side of this building are rows of large stained glass windows. The tower has a shining metal segmented dome.

NO023 **DuGane House**

c. 1895. 815 Washington St.

This building could be described aptly as a commodious Queen Anne house whose style is beginning to embrace (ever so slightly) the Colonial Revival. The corner bay tower with its tall "witch's hat" roof turns into a porch on the second floor.

NO024 **Trinity United Methodist Church**

1915. Northeast corner of 9th and Clay streets

A church with a utilitarian rectangular brick auditorium, Trinity has an attached frontispiece comprised of a classical pedimented temple with four columns in the Tuscan order. The low, squarish tower above the entrance seems to be waiting for a lantern spire and roof.

NO025 **House**

c. 1927. 919 Washington St.

This is a Tudor Revival house in half-timber, stucco, and stone. The roof of the living room wing has been brought down so close to the ground (almost to the scale of a dollhouse) that the windows at the eave side have been treated as wall dormers. The main front entrance is through a deep porch set between two projecting stone walls.

NO026 **Townsend House**

1878–1884. 1017 Washington St.

The design of the Townsend house playfully combines a delicate version of the Italianate with a reference to Eastlake details. The entrance tower, its steeply pitched hipped roof broken by a single gable and four small dormers, is a classic example of the Eastlake style. The interior, with detailed woodwork and 11-foot-high ceilings, is still intact. Externally the only missing item is the iron railing that stood atop the roof.

NO027 **House**

c. 1899. 1117 Clay St.

The Richardsonian Romanesque is here interpreted through a wood frame sheathed in shingles. There is a thin, full arch that forms an entrance into the broad front porch. A second small-arched opening has been placed in the central third-floor gable, and mirrors the entrance below. There is a strong hint of classicism conveyed by the Colonial Revival elements evident in the design of this house.

NO028 Cottage

c. 1926. 1103 Clay St.

A 1920s version of the English Cotswold cottage is here dominated by its roof forms, including a suggestion of a thatched roof. One approaches this period revival house from the street by a narrow stone pathway that winds its way in through clipped shrubbery.

NO029 Cottage

1867. 1021 Clay St.

This one-and-a-half-story T-plan Gothic Revival brick cottage has lost its original pair of porches, but the gable ends and wall dormers still exhibit delicately sawed bargeboards.

NO030 Jamerson House

1915. 1020 Franklin St.

The Jamerson house is a larger than normal, midwestern version of the stucco, brick, and wood-trim Craftsman bungalow. The horizontal band of the front windows is compositionally contained between the projecting flower box below and an unusual horizontal flat roof above which joins the eave ends of the front gable. The house's gable roof is dramatically extended out and supported by projecting beams. A quality reminiscent of Japanese architecture is apparent in the way the eaves are drawn beyond the rafters of the dormer roof.

NO031 University of Northern Iowa

23rd and College streets

The University of Northern Iowa was founded in 1876 as the Iowa State Normal School. In 1909 it became the Iowa State Teachers College, and in 1967 it acquired its present name. With the exception of the much-remodeled president's cottage of 1890 (now the Ethnic Minorities Cultural and Educational Center), the major early buildings have disappeared.

Of the older structures only the 100-foot-high Campanile (1926), in the "Italian Renaissance Style," and the Beaux-Arts Seerley Hall convey a strong sense of continuity with the past. The older as well as the recent landscape design for the university has been well carried out, and with the maturing of the vegetation the varied and disparate architectural images and the scattering of sculpture and fountains may eventually coalesce into some sort of unified entity. The character of the campus as a whole is dominated by recent "modern" buildings, such as NO031.1 through NO031.5. More worthy of an architectural visit are several of the pre-World War II buildings, NO031.6 through NO031.9.

NO031.1 Maucker Student Union

1969, Hunter, Rice and Engelbrecht; Brooks, Borg and Skiles; 1969

NO031.2 Education Center

1970–1972, Thorson, Brom, Broshar, Synder

NO031.3 Strayer-Wood Theater

1977–1978

NO31.4 UNI-Dome

1975–1976

NO31.5 UNI Married Student Housing

Engelbrecht/Rice. Located below 3600 block of College St.

With the exception of the housing, most of these buildings of the late sixties and seventies read as aggressively and self-consciously modern in a popular sense. The exception is the Maucker Student Union (1969), a structure essentially sunk into a gentle slope of the hill. Its small-scale forms work well with the older buildings, but its design and siting cry out for the hands of a landscape architect. The Married Student Housing translates a similar grid of angular volumes into wood.

NO31.6 Seerley Hall (Library)

1908

Beaux-Arts Classicism with an Italian Renaissance character was well carried out here.

The building is composed of a rusticated first floor, second and third floors enclosed by an arcade behind Ionic columns, and a fourth-floor attic under a broad overhanging tile roof. Within the main reading room are murals painted by William de Leftwich Dodge in 1920 depicting the phases of civilization.

NO031.7 The Campanile

1926

In the teens and twenties, architects often referred to Italian late medieval or early Renaissance churches as sources for educational buildings. These designs were usually realized in brick with stone or cast-stone trim, as in this campanile. Though more than a decade apart, Seerley Hall and the Campanile indicate what stylistic unity was being developed during the first three decades of the century.

NO031.8 Barlett Hall

1933

Described as "Georgian Colonial" in brick, Barlett Hall refers directly to England as much as to eighteenth-century Anglo-American architecture.

NO031.9 Baker Hall for Men

1936

Of lukewarm quality, this hall is still a fine example of mid-depression Moderne.

NO032 Fields Barn

1875. 1.5 miles west of Hudson Road on University Ave.

This three-story limestone barn with double cross-gable has venting cupolas of miniature scale. Though barns of this form are occasionally encountered in the Midwest, this one is by far one of the most handsome in its proportions and in its carefully designed fenestration. Within the barn is a square masonry silo. This stone barn is all that remains of a 3,000-acre farm established in 1873 by two English brothers, William and Charles Fields. Their stock-breeding farm once boasted houses for the two brothers and their families, a private chapel, a schoolhouse, a carriage house, and two other large stone barns.

NO033 True-Round Grade Barn

c. 1905. 4500 S. Main St.

The wood walls of this large circular barn (approximately 83 feet in diameter) have been placed on top of a poured concrete band that lies just below the beautifully disposed row of square windows. The structure is topped by a double-pitched conical roof. Changes in exterior ground level make it possible to enter the barn on two levels.

NO034 Rownd True-Round Barn

1911. 5100 S. Main St.

The walls of this true-round barn (66 feet in diameter) are of rusticated concrete block. The concrete blocks used in the construction of the walls were molded on the farm itself. The conical wood roof is hipped into two planes, and the whole composition is terminated by a circular metal ventilator. Nearby, at 4119 South Main Street, is the Samuel Rownd house, built in the 1860s. This one-and-a-half-story house continues the early Greek Revival tradition, modified by Italianate details. The Rownd farm complex of house and outbuildings was illustrated in Andreas's 1875 volume (p. 83).

NO035 Unitarian-Universalist Church

1966, Crites and McConnell. 3912 Cedar Heights Dr.

This small church building comes close to being a nonbuilding in the best sense of the term. Its thin, vertical forms appear as segments of a complex piece of sculpture that has been erected in the landscape. The fact that the building encloses space is not apparent.

NO036 Young House

1980, Gregory Nook. 1713 E. Ridgewood Dr.

A woodsy dwelling with a gable roof has been sensitively introduced into the gentle slope of the hillside. Solar panels and a clerestory dot the roof, and there are extensive screened porches below.

NO037 True-Round Barn

1915–1916. 4 miles north on US 218, .5 miles west on gravel road

This two-level true-round barn (60 feet in diameter) has walls of hollow terracotta tile. The round dome of the interior central silo rises above the gambrel roof. An unusual feature is a water tank that occupies the upper section of the central silo.

NO038 Litchfield House (Mandalay)

1922. 1603 Mandalay Dr.

A 56-room 1920s "mansion," the Litchfield house included a gallery for target shooting, a gymnasium, a billiard room, and a bowling alley. The architectural image is a bit difficult to pin down; probably what was intended was a recollection of the Central European Baroque, though at a casual glance it almost looks Mission Revival. The building's site, overlooking the river to the north with parkland beyond, is a splendid one. The house is now enshrouded in unkempt vegetation, and it has suffered from conversions to various uses and more recently from a fire.

Charles City

The open prairieland of Floyd County is interrupted by three water systems that run northwest by southeast, the largest of which is the Cedar River to the east.[2] In 1853 the town of Saint Charles was platted on both sides of the Cedar. The grid in this case mirrored the river's course, its streets running northwest-southeast and southwest-northeast. The city became the county seat in 1854. Bonds were issued in the late 1850s, which resulted in two railroads reaching the community: the Milwaukee and Saint Paul Railway and the Cedar Falls and Minnesota Railway. By the early 1900s the city nursery business, renowned for fruit trees and ornamental trees, had developed into an important industry. Architecturally, one of the significant products of the county has been limestone quarried for use in local buildings as well as those found outside of the area.[3]

From the late 1960s on, the inner core of the city underwent many changes. Some of these were due to a tornado that laid waste a large section of the town in 1968. Other "natural maladies" have been the Dutch elm disease that defoliated much of the town's elm trees, and the destruction of buildings by fire, the most recent resulting in the loss of the 1863 Union House hotel. Finally, urban renewal has lent a hand in the removal of a number of older buildings and the substitution of new ones. Notwithstanding these substantial changes, the town still possesses a good stock of buildings, especially from the years after 1900.

Two utilitarian "monuments" within the center of the city should be noted. One is the brick and tile-roofed Anderson Service Station (c. 1924) at 1005 Gilbert Street. The service bay of the station presents an arched opening toward the street, and its extended hipped roof is supported by brackets. The other monument is the Clark Street foot bridge (1906) over the Cedar River. The bridge is a light, delicate suspension bridge with a span of 270 feet. The engineer for the bridge was O. B. Zimmerman.

NO039 Floyd County Courthouse

1940–1941, Hansen and Waggoner. Corner of N. Main and Kelly streets

The first of Floyd County's courthouses was a two-story Greek Revival building with a gable roof that was constructed during the years 1857 through 1861. This first courthouse, distinguished by its square tower, dome, and spire over the entrance gable, was designed by the architect Theodore Mix. The building was destroyed by fire in 1881, and it was replaced in 1881–1882 by a larger building in the Italianate style. The second courthouse was torn down in 1939 and it was replaced by the present structure.

The architects Hansen and Waggoner of Mason City supplied a sparse, puritanical version of the 1930s PWA style. A central pavilion projects slightly from the front facade of the building, and at its base is the building's main public entrance. The windows of the four floors are grouped in recessed vertical bands. The surface of the structure is of tan brick, while Bedford limestone and polished red granite were used for the raised basement and for external and internal trim.

NO040 Charles Theatre

1935–1936, Wetherell and Harrison. N. Main St., south of Blunt St.

The Moderne style—in the form of its early Art Deco image—continued to be used through much of the 1930s. On occasion it was updated by architects who employed ma-terials and colors associated with the Moderne's second phase, the Streamline Moderne. This is the case with the Charles Theatre, which is nothing more than a facade treatment—but what a treatment. The background of the building is shimmering glazed black tile. Against this background is a series of vertical designs and patterns in brilliant gold, blues, and rust-colored glazed terracotta. The high point of the design is the facade's central panel over the marquee. This is composed in the fashion of an ascending group of organ pipes. This theater is unquestionably one of the major Art Deco monuments in the state.

NO041 Gilbert House

c. 1863. 307 N. Jackson St.

This solid-appearing two-story Greek Revival house exhibits a T-shaped plan. The gable section facing the street to the right has a small lunette window in the attic, and the entrance to the left of the porch exhibits a door with side lights and a transom. The building is sheathed in large ashlar blocks of light-colored limestone. The present piered entrance porch was added sometime after 1900.

NO042 Fitzgerald House

1903. 305 N. Jackson St.

High on the gambrel roof of this Colonial Revival dwelling is a set of three dormers with dramatic roofs. The wide center one exhibits a segmental curved roof with flat ends; the gable roofs of the two to the sides project out far beyond the face of the dormers. Below is the common composition of a central two-story porch with a single-floor porch crossing underneath it. The lower porch has a cut-limestone base carried up to form the balustrade.

NO043 (Old) Carnegie Public Library

1903–1904, Patton and Miller. 301 N. Jackson St.

One of some 13 public libraries in Iowa designed by this Chicago architectural firm, the

Charles City library has a design format typical of many small libraries throughout the country: a central entrance leading to the librarian's desk area, with reading or stack rooms off to each side. Patton and Miller always sought to give an individual personality to each of their buildings. They accomplished this goal with the Charles City library by using limestone for the raised basement and by carrying this up to form the walls of the projecting entrance pavilion. They treated the brick and stone-capped gable ends of the building with stone finials, and terminated the entrance gable at its ridge with a segmental curved parapet.

NO044 **Fox House**

1935. 301 Riverside Dr.

The Fox house is a period revival English Tudor home with a somewhat modern flavor conveyed by the building's general horizontality, and by the regularization of the geometric pattern of the second-floor half-timbering. The recessed front door has a V-shaped header instead of a Gothic arch. This nod to the Moderne helps to prepare one for the Moderne Art Deco living room within. The client for this house, Ray Fox, had visited the Chicago World's Fair of 1933 and felt that he could have the best of two worlds: traditionalism, which on the house's exterior presented him and his family to the public; and modernism, reserved for the interior as a setting for his own experiences.

NO045 **Smith House**

1914, attrib. Morton B. Cleveland. 103 Blunt St.

The midwestern Prairie box, with its wide, overhanging hipped roof, is here enlarged to form a substantial upper-middle-class suburban dwelling. The horizontal banding of the design is carried out by its brick-clad base, by a horizontal band of windows and front screen porch, by a low hipped roof carried out over the first-floor windows, and finally by the second-floor stucco band with its horizontal banks of windows. The exterior remains essentially unaltered except for the addition of a carport to the right of the house.

NO046 **Willeke House**

c. 1918. 104 Blunt St.

A strong Prairie-style design, the Willeke house is quite similar to many of the Chicago suburban dwellings of the firm of Tallmadge and Watson. The theme of the gable is asserted in the street facade of the house and then is repeated below in the first-floor living porch. The surface of the lower walls of the house are clothed in horizontal boards up to the first-floor window sills; above this are stucco surfaces divided into panels by linear patterns of boards. The header of the central attic window is V-shaped, and it mirrors the slope of the roof.

NO047 **Blake House**

c. 1913, Morton B. Cleveland. 106 Blunt St.

This house presents a variation on Frank Lloyd Wright's 1906 Prairie box to be constructed of concrete, published in the *Ladies Home Journal*. The Waterloo architect Morton B. Cleveland provided a number of Prairie-style designs within Charles City. Taking the Wright design as a cue, he placed the entrance to the side, provided a central bay with hipped roof that projects toward the street, and enriched the surface with vertical banding accompanied by inserted tiles. This latter decorative motif at the corners of the two-story stucco-sheathed walls suggests abstracted pilasters.

NO048 **Salisbury House**

1940, Morton B. Cleveland. 205 Blunt St.

By the 1920s Morton B. Cleveland had comfortably moved into the design realm of the period revival. In the 1930s many of his designs, as is the case here in the Salisbury house, expressed the popular Colonial Revival. The details of the house, especially the central gabled front with its pilaster supports and delicate, curved entrance porch, looked back to the American Federal style as well as to the English Regency mode.

NO049 **Waterbury House**

1900–1901. 501 Spriggs St.

The design of the Waterbury house would appear to be from the same hand as the

Colonial Revival Fitzgerald house at 305 North Jackson Street (NO042). Though not identical, the three roof dormers of the Waterbury house assert themselves in a fashion almost like that of the dormers on the Fitzgerald dwelling. The Waterbury house has walls of brick, a single-floor porch across the entire front, and an angled bay on the second floor directly above the entrance.

NO050 Junior High School Building

1932, Jacobson and Jacobson. 500 Grand St.

The centerpiece of this Art Deco, pre-PWA public building is its two-story entrance with limestone details. Wide, layered, but only slightly projecting pilasters appear on each side of the doors. A pair of bronze "Roman" lanterns and their stands flank the entrance steps. The remainder of the two-story building is simply articulated by wide groups of windows providing natural light for the classrooms and other spaces.

NO051 Dodd House

1910, Purcell, Feick and Elmslie. 310 3rd Ave.

This modest-sized Prairie house was designed for A. B. C. Dodd, a relative of William Gray Purcell. The working drawings for the house were prepared under Purcell's direction by Marian A. Parker, a designer/draftsperson in the PF&E Minneapolis office. The design shows Purcell's fondness for wide, cantilevered gable roofs that almost form a hat for the building. In plan, the entrance is to the side, with a living room and an enclosed living porch projecting out toward the street. A central fireplace serves as a screen between the living room and the dining room to the rear. At the entrance a T-shaped design was worked out: the door in the center, a square panel containing an electric light to the left, and a rectangular panel containing a window to the right. The architects also provided the landscape design for the property which entailed an axial walk down the right side of the house, leading through a geometric layout of vegetable gardens.

NO052 Cottage

c. 1875. 1103 Clark St.

This one-and-a-half-story Gothic cottage with a central gable has been "modernized" by sawed and turned Eastlake ornament. The principal roof is a steeply pitched hipped form, instead of being a gable. The pattern of the large window within the central street gable consists of a pair of V-header units, topped by a single diamond-shaped window.

NO053 Miller House

1946–1951, Frank Lloyd Wright. 1107 Court St.

Wright's design for the Alvin C. Miller house marks a high point of abstraction for his post-World War II Usonian houses. The building is also one of the most handsomely detailed and constructed of the Usonian dwellings. It exhibits a delicate composition of stone walls and hovering, layered flat roof planes. Facing the street is a carport; along one side of the carport and house, covered by the extended roof, is the walkway leading to the entrance. The entry is in the center of the T-shaped plan: off to the right is a study; opposite the entry door is the fireplace wall, the combined living and dining room, and a workspace-kitchen; to the left is a gallery and bedroom wing. The floor-to-ceiling glass walls and French doors of the living-dining room and the study look out over the rear garden and the Cedar River.

NO054 Salisbury Laboratories, Research, and Administrative Buildings

1969, Perkins and Will. West on Iowa 14

The center of this design is the landscaped courtyard around which the low buildings have been grouped. A wide variety of plant material (all identified for the viewer) grows within the courtyard, which also contains paved

NO055 Strawn / Cook Barn

terraces, banks of low steps, fountains, and a pool. The buildings are simple modular structures which seem self-effacing in relation to the landscape design. The buildings are of concrete, with extensive infills of glass.

NO055 **Strawn / Cook House and Barn**

Late 1850s. East side of US 218, 2 miles south of Charles City

This end-gable two-story Greek Revival house built of ashlar blocks of limestone has an elegantly detailed entrance. Under a small roof with pairs of end brackets is an entry door with diamond-paned side lights; above, the transom window is divided into three parts, and these too have diamond-paned glass. To the side of the two-story section of the house is a one-and-a-half-story wing with a recessed porch. The square shape of the cupola-topped barn is a form infrequently encountered in Iowa. The "feel" of the stone barn and its rear wing is Greek Revival. There is a suggestion of corner quoining, and the double-hung windows are arranged in a symmetrical fashion on all of the facades of the building.

Chickasaw (near Ionia)

NO056 **Chickasaw Octagon House**

1871–1874. Court Street

The small town of Chickasaw contains one of Iowa's few remaining octagonal houses. The handsome walls of this dwelling are of smooth-faced cut limestone laid

up in a somewhat irregular manner. Instead of a central cupola, a chimney protrudes from the center of the roof. The lower windows are elongated units; those on the second floor are smaller and some of them are grouped in pairs. The present entrance porch with gable roof is not original to the house.

Clarion

This is one of several towns in Iowa that was specifically established to be a county seat. The site was selected because of its central location within the county. A courthouse was built, and the platting of the town site took place in 1865. The community grew slowly over the years, finally assuming the urban form one associates with smaller midwestern communities. There is a small business and civic center, then tree-lined residential streets, and finally an "industrial" area of grain elevators and other businesses associated with the railway.

NO057 **Wright County Courthouse**

1891, William R. Parsons and Son. Northeast corner of Main St. and Central Ave.

The Des Moines firm selected to design this building produced other courthouses in Illinois, Missouri, and Iowa. The architect selected the appropriate image of that moment, the Richardsonian Romanesque, but the design seems to waver between public monumentality and domesticity. The situation of the building on courthouse square, and features such as the seven-story corner tower, effectively proclaim its public nature. In contrast, the long, low-pitched gable filled in with semicircular windows, and the scale and placement of the other windows and the door are what one would expect to encounter in a large private residence. In 1974 the building was extensively remodeled and it regrettably lost some of its most telling elements, though its essential external character remains intact.

NO058 **United States Post Office Building**

1939, Louis A. Simon and Neal Melick. 1st St. N.E. between Central and 1st Ave. N.E.

Here is a 1930s version of the Colonial Revival, with red brick walls and a small cupola. The base, pilasters, and entablature are all here, but they have been "modernized," i.e., simplified to thin, almost two-dimensional suggestions of those elements. In its park setting the building successfully states its public use.

NO058 United States Post Office Building

NO059 **Clarion Theater**

1937. 1st Ave. N.E. between Main St. and 1st Ave. N.E.

The street-level wall surface of this Moderne theater building and its angled marquee are bright red in color. The present marquee ends in a small drum, embracing a second drum. The remainder of the building is in a neutral buff-colored brick. An exciting pattern of shadows is created in the center of the second story where the walls play back and forth in a sharp angles.

NO060 **Clarion Meat Lockers**

c. 1960. Main St. at 2nd Ave. S.E.

Adjacent to the impressive industrial image of the Cargill Feed Plant is a small single-story building with a hoop-shaped metal roof. Above the entrance canopy stands a sculpture of a steer, signaling the building's use as a place to store frozen meat. The wall behind the animal has been painted with a scene of an Iowa farm, red barn and all.

NO061 **Clarion Municipal Pool**

1941. Southwest corner of 2nd Ave. N.E. and 6th St. N.E.

The Clarion public swimming pool was a WPA project at the end of the 1930s. The buildings are of reinforced concrete that has been painted a light bluish white. Running around the sides of the buildings is a reserved, rather elegant pattern of pilasters defined by thin vertical flutes; between the pilasters are windows, filled in and open. The windows are simple rectangular cutouts in the wall surface. Above the opening is a narrow horizontal panel of rectangular layered planes; this same motif, a little larger in size, is repeated below the window sills.

Clarksville

The platting of Clarksville's grid took place in 1853. It was advantageously sited on the Shellrock River which provided the usual much-needed water power. By the mid-1870s the community was traversed by two railroads. There are several nineteenth-century commercial buildings and houses still standing in town. Of these, one of the most interesting is the two-story house with a French mansard roof (c. 1875), at 514 South Main Street. As is often the case with houses exhibiting this type of roof, the detailing of this house is in fact late Italianate. Both the entrance porch across the front and the one at the side still exhibit the small-scaled cast-iron roof railing.

Clear Lake

Within the town itself and around the lake are numerous private cabins as well as groups of tourist cabins; those still standing generally date from the 1930s.

NO062 **Baago's Cabins**

1930s. North Shore Dr. and W. 7th Ave.

This is a typical gable-roofed auto court with two rows of cabins facing one another.

NO063 **Baago's Cottages**

early 1930s. 1204–1212 W. 7th Ave.

These five dollhouse-sized cottages combine both the Colonial and medieval cottage images. The design tour-de-force of these buildings lies in their entrances, where a curved roof goes down close to the ground, and

NO063 Cottage, c. 1931

within which is not only the entrance door but a small niche with a vaulted ceiling.

NO064 Andersen House

1941, Ernest Andersen. 901 North Shore Dr.

Here we find that modernity reached the lakeshore in the Streamline Moderne Andersen dwelling. The curved entrance is especially well worked out, with a horizontal glass block window placed above the entrance. The architect, builder, and owner of the house was Ernest Andersen. In 1987–1988 the house was extensively enlarged in a Postmodernist manner, all very well carried out.

NO065 Stillman House

1917, Einar Broaten. 400 N. 3rd St.

Within the town of Clear Lake itself is this two-story Prairie-style dwelling designed by a Prairie architect from Mason City, Einar Broaten. The tall, rectangular, boxlike form of the house was brought down to mirror more closely the horizontality of the prairie by a projecting stucco banding carried below the sills of the second-floor windows; by a spreading low-pitched gable roof over the entrance; by an attached garage wing to one side (note the original garage door); and by an exterior porch which extends out from the other side. While the Stillman house is not as idiosyncratic as several of Broaten's houses in Mason City, it does represent a peculiar gathering together of Prairie stylistic elements.

NO066 Reinhardt Andersen House

c. 1947, Reinhardt Andersen. 900 5th Ave. S.

Reinhardt Andersen, the son of Ernest Andersen, carried on the Streamline Moderne tradition into the post-World War II years in

NO066 Reinhardt Andersen House

his own single-story house. Two deepset bands have been carried around the middle of the house in the stucco walls. There are several rounded corners with windows and glass brick; glass brick is employed for the side lights of the entrance door, and of course there are the mandatory metal corner windows.

NO067 House

c. 1890. 315 4th Ave. N.

There are a few architectural remnants from the nineteenth century in Clear Lake, the best known of which is this dwelling. The scheme of this two-and-a-half-story house is Queen Anne. The front entrance porch with an angled corner entrance is light and lacy in feeling, and the roofscape of the dwelling is typically irregular and picturesque. As is often found in the 1890s, the house also displays some Colonial Revival details, in the Palladian window, the cornice detailing, and the regularity of the large rectangular double-hung windows (they are much wider than one normally finds within the Queen Anne style). The house still retains its fence-cresting atop the porch roof and its high metal finials at the peak of the main roof.

NO068 Clear Lake State Park

1938. South of Clear Lake

Going out to the south along the lake one will come across the 114-acre Clear Lake State Park. The principal shelter in the park presents itself as a medieval period revival dwelling (1938). The walls are of thick, rough limestone and the gable ends are of stained clapboard. The whole is covered with a low-

NO068 Clear Lake State Park, Park Shelter

pitched shingled roof, which presses everything down to the ground. A large bay window looks out from the end of one wing.

NO069 **Outing Club**

1895 and later. South Shore Dr.

On South Shore Drive is located the Outing Club, an old summer colony for the affluent. The main building is within the Shingle style, a long, meandering two-story structure where one is primarily aware of the extensive continuation of wide porches.

NO070 **Hormel Cottage**

1922. Dodge's Point

At Dodge's Point is a 1922 summer lakeshore dwelling that is decidedly Prairie style in design. The building suggests that two Prairie houses with hipped roofs have been placed on top of one another, and then this two-layered affair has been placed on a high rusticated basement. The windows, doors, and the corners of the basement are presented in stone; the intervening wall surface is in stucco. This is the type of design that could have come from the hands of Einar Broaten.

Clermont

The community was platted in 1849 on a sharp bend of the Turkey River. In 1851 a dam and a sawmill were built, and five years later this mill was joined by the large brick city mill (1854–1856). The town is situated on both sides of the river, with bluffs rising to the east. On the edge of the east bluff, William Larrabee built his house, which poses as a castle overlooking its village.

NO071 **Clermont State Bank Building** (now Clermont Museum)

c. 1895. Northwest corner of Mill and Clay streets

By elevating the building several steps above the street level on a raised basement, the architect of this small two-story brick-and-stone structure declared that it is a bank, not a retail store. This quality is further reinforced by the large front window with a gently curved lunette above. The Richardsonian Romanesque style is primarily conveyed in the first-floor front, which almost seems to have

been placed like a stage set in front of a simple brick building. A touch of refinement comes from the three stubby polished granite columns holding up the arches of the entrance and front window.

NO072 **Clermont House Hotel**

1853 and later. Northwest corner of Union and Larrabee streets

A tall cupola surmounts the hipped roof of this two-story brick Italianate building. What appears to be a later addition contains an unusual two-story balconied porch supported by four wood piers that spring from the ground and rise to the roof's entablature.

NO073 **House**

c. 1860. Southwest corner Larrabee and Thompson streets

This brick Italianate villa has a three-story central tower and an elaborate pattern of paired brackets supporting the roof. The small scale of the tower (it cannot be over 8 feet square) comes close to bringing the house into the realm of a dollhouse.

NO074 **House**

c. 1860. Southeast corner of Thompson and Mill streets

The commanding feature of this brick Italianate house is the entrance doorway where the brackets, piers, and consoles have been united in one vertical, undulating form.

NO075 **Clermont Presbyterian Church**

1858. Southeast corner of Larrabee and McGregor streets

This church is pure, classic Greek Revival; thin brick pilasters project from the wall surfaces, and a fascinating horizontal row of diamond-shaped patterns runs across the entablature. The tower with its tall, thin spire

NO075 Clermont Presbyterian Church

and four corner finials could be read as either classical or Gothic.

NO076 **Church of the Saviour Episcopal Church**

c. 1867. Southwest corner of Thompson and Mill streets

Episcopal church buildings tend to be small and elegantly designed, and this is no exception. The body of the church is rough gray stone; the trim is a finely cut yellow-tan limestone. The round-arched windows and the bracketed roof make it Italianate in style. The three-story corner entrance tower is currently missing its spired roof.

NO077 **William Larrabee House** (Montauk)

1874, Edward Townsend Mix. 1 mile east of Clermont on US 18

Montauk is certainly one of the most widely known and photographed of Iowa's houses. This well-deserved fame is due to the renown of its owner, William Larrabee, who was twice governor of the state; to its impressive location on a wooded hill overlooking the Turkey River and Clermont; and to the quality of its design. In style the two-story red brick dwelling is Italianate, and it has the usual characteristics of that mode: arched and circular or elliptical windows, bracketed eaves, and wide entablatures. In plan it has a ten-foot-wide central hall extending from front to back of

NO077 William Larrabee House (Montauk)

the house; the symmetry of the plan was made picturesque by the off-center placement of several porches. The design was old-fashioned for the time, although the architect, Edward Thompson Mix of Milwaukee, tended to be quite conscious of the latest

fashion in design. However, the Italianate style was employed in many sections of the Midwest and West after 1865, and often, as in the Larrabee house, with great aesthetic success. The heavily planted grounds of the estate and a curved drive lined by statues of Civil War heroes permitted occasional views of the house as one mounted the hill. The house and grounds are open to the public much of the year.

NO078 **Prairie Agra Enterprises**

c. 1970. US 18, 4 miles north of Clermont

A high-tech image was brought to the Iowa prairie to match the high-tech design and capabilities of the farm machinery. The result is a utilitarian composition of metal cylinders, boxes, and lacy patterns of tubes and chutes.

Cresco

In 1875, Andreas characterized Cresco in a fashion that is still apt today: "This flourishing new city is surrounded by far-stretching and rich prairies, the beauty of which is only exceeded by their high value as a rich productive district."[4] This richness was augmented by the town's location on one of the main lines of the Milwaukee Railroad, at a junction of that railroad with the Davenport and Saint Paul Railroad. The original plat for the city was established in 1866 and ran parallel and at right angles to the railroad. A large public square was set aside and in the late 1870s the county courthouse was situated here.

NO079 **Howard County Courthouse**

1879–1880, B. D. Everingham and Company (architects and contractors). N. Elm St. at Park Pl.

The Howard County Courthouse is essentially Italianate in design, with heavily arched windows; broad, overhanging eaves with entablatures and brackets; and the usual round windows within the gable ends. Its cruciform plan centers on a central cupolalike tower. The tower stylistically moves away from the Italianate, though the resulting image is difficult to pin down precisely. At the corners are attached heavy columnar forms which continue up and become finials projecting above the roof; each facade ends in a semi-circular roof which in turn projects into the spirelike roof. In the mid-1960s, additions and extensive internal remodeling took place,

none of which was sympathetic or contextual in nature.

NO080 **Berg Block**

1890. Northeast corner of N. Elm St. and N. Park Pl.

Though much of the ground floor of this two-story Queen Anne block has been remodeled, what establishes the building's hold on the street is the smallish bay tower at the street corner. There is a curved plate-glass window between two narrow double-hung windows; above is a tall, somewhat Islamic dome covered in metal.

NO081 **United States Post Office Building**

1935, Louis A. Simon and Neal Melick. 128 2nd Ave. N.

This brick building's design is lightly PWA Moderne, conveyed most effectively by a row of fluted brick pilasters. Inside, in the public lobby, is the mural *Iowa Farming* by Richard Haines, painted shortly after the building was completed.

NO082 Log Cabin

1853. Beadle Park, northwest corner Iowa 9 and N. Elm St.

Charmingly awkward proportions mark this log cabin; it's almost as high as it is square. The logs were squared, and the gable ends were covered with clapboard. The shake shingle roof is recent, of course.

NO083 Church Building

c. 1880. 3rd Ave. between N. Elm St. and 2nd St. E.

The design of this former church moves from the angularity and brutalness of the Eastlake style to the Queen Anne. The building is composed of steeply pitched gables, wood patterned walls, and a pilastered main entrance. The windows seem to be arched, but the arched pattern is actually within the wood surface. The triangles of the gables are repeated as a theme throughout the building.

NO084 First Congregational Church

c. 1895. Northwest corner of 3rd Ave. E. and 2nd St. E.

A late version of the Romanesque, this church was constructed in brick with slight touches of light-colored limestone trim. The three-tiered entrance tower is crenellated, and entrance into the tower is gained through a short loggia with a gable roof.

NO085 Church Building

c. 1905. North side of 3rd Ave. E. between N. Elm St. and 2nd St. E.

This Craftsman church combines shingles, board-and-batten, plaster, and half-timber. The single wall at one side of the main gable rises and becomes the wall of the gabled tower. In its own turn, the wall of the tower extends down into the shingled surface with a large-scale open X-frame of the belfry. The en-

trance, as if in a dwelling, is through a porch hidden to the side.

NO086 First Baptist Church

1882. Northeast corner of N. Elm St. and 3rd Ave. E.

Everything seems "normal" about this medieval-inspired design except for the overscaled tower with its crenellations and extended miniature corner turrets. The tower is delicately supported on the ground level by a single post at the corner, which in turn supports the spring of the two segmental arches. This tower and the small bay window next to it indicate either a casualness of approach to design or great erudition on the part of the architect. The wood-sheathed building has been covered in stucco.

NO087 First Methodist Episcopal Church (now United Methodist Church)

c. 1910. Northwest corner of N. Elm St. and 3rd Ave. W.

A vigorous and highly inventive interpretation of the Gothic, this church has plain dark-brick walls that have been carefully designed with great care taken in their proportions and in the placement of windows.

NO088 House (now a funeral home)

c. 1928. Southwest corner of N. Elm St. and 6th Ave. W.

The English Tudor phase of the period revival of the twenties has been employed in this residence. The telling feature of the design is the entrance. The narrow half-timbered section above has been brought down over and around the door, which in turn is set into a masonry wall. The scale of the door in comparison to the tall stairhall window above gives one the feeling that one is entering a medieval building through a postern gate.

NO089 House

c. 1870s. 601 N. Elm St.

A diminutive one-and-a-half-story cottage has been designed to suggest something of a delightful pretense in size. The small central bay containing the front door continues upward to form a gable with a bay. The windows of this bay have been narrowed, changing the scale entirely. The corners of the house have been cut by walls at a 45-degree angle; within each wall there is just enough room for a window. A shingled shed roof and canopies reminiscent of elements of the Eastlake style cover the windows on the first floor.

NO090 House

c. 1910. 212 6th St. E.

This is a turn-of-the-century Colonial Revival house which on one side of its round tower with conical roof poses as a one-and-a-half-story cottage; on the other it becomes more majestic, rising two stories and boasting a large-scale porte-cochère. The lower level is dominated by columned porches and the porte-cochère.

Dakota City

Within the town of Dakota City, the Humboldt County Courthouse (NO091) is especially noteworthy for its PWA Moderne style. Three-and-a-half miles south of Dakota City (on route P56) is the Old Mill Farm, the site of a mill and dam on the East Fork of the Des Moines River and the location a two-story brick Italianate house. The house, which still remains, was built in 1878 by Corydon Brown. Its almost flat roof is supported by paired brackets, and there are segmented stone headers over the openings. The restored house is owned by the Humboldt County Historical Society.

NO091 Humboldt County Courthouse

1938–1939, Dougher, Rich and Woodburn

The present Humboldt County Courthouse is a classic example of the PWA Moderne. The facades of this three-story box on a raised basement are vertically banded by recessed panels composed of the usual metal windows and recessed spandrels. Iron "Roman" light stands in the form of tripods originally flanked the entrance. The brick used for the exterior wall is gray in color; the trim is in gray Bedford stone. This building replaced an earlier (1893) Italianate courthouse which was torn down when the new building was completed.

Decorah

With its abundance of springs and timbered hills, the site of Decorah had been the location of Indian occupation. In 1857 it was noted that a number of mounds "had been leveled [in 1854] to prepare the site for the erection of the Winneshiek House, then building."[5] Europeans entered onto the site for settlement in 1849, and it was platted in 1853. The basis for the settlers' selection of the site matches that of many early Iowa communities; primarily there was the presence of water to provide power for milling operations. The first primitive log mill was built in 1849 by William Painter, and a few years later he constructed the larger store and wool mill, which still exists. By 1875 there were ten of these mills in existence, supplemented by several that utilized steam power.

The community was missed at first by the principal lines of the railroad, but in 1869 it was connected to the Milwaukee and Saint Paul line by a spur coming from Conover in the southwest. Later, a spur of the Rock Island Line reached Decorah from the southeast. The town's principal assets were its milling and shipping activities (via the railroad), its selection as a county seat (1851), and its location as the home of Luther College (1861), founded by Norwegians.

The grid imposed on the town site was the traditional one with a north-south, east-west pattern. A square block was set aside for the courthouse, and eventually sites were provided for the public schools. Because of the floodplain of the river, the far northern section of town remained open, but eventually dikes were built along sections of the riverbanks. To the north and west across the Upper Iowa River, a new grid section was laid out south of Luther College. The one distinguishing feature of this second grid was the provision of a circle (with a small park within) at the junction of Iowa and Center streets. The scale of Decorah together with its surrounding wooded hills conveys an image of a village in a forest. The city has enhanced this rural quality through the development of Palisade Park north of the river (take College Drive to Quarry Street, then go northeast to Ice Cave Road).

NO092 **Winneshiek County Courthouse**

1903–1905, Kinney and Detweiler. South side of Main St. between Court and Winnebago streets

The presence of the courthouse in Decorah is underscored by its being sited in an open city block that slopes steeply to the south. The building was designed by the Minneapolis firm of Kinney and Detweiler, who came close to cornering the market on courthouse design in Minnesota and northern Iowa in the two decades after 1900. Their designs were general Beaux-Arts, as is the case with the Winneshiek County Courthouse. The building settles into its site on a dark-red sandstone base and terminates above in an elaborate square open tower with four pediments boasting clock faces. Surmounting all of this is a tall circular drum covered by a domed roof and lantern. The principal axial entrance from the south is lined by cast-iron light standards; the walk itself is broken by three sets of wide stairs. As is so often encountered on the grounds of Iowa courthouses, a miniature Statue of Liberty is mounted high on its own stone base.

NO093 **United States Post Office Building** (now Decorah Public Library)

1910, James Knox Taylor. Southeast corner of Main and Winnebago streets

Decorah

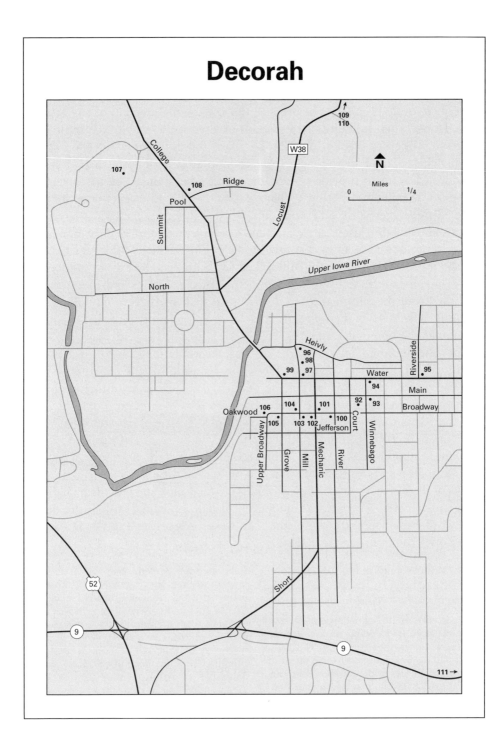

A Tuscan temple front with four columns opens to the north on Main Street, and a bank of high arched windows and a central door faces east on Winnebago Street. Both entrances have been left intact with their stairs, platform, and accompanying cast-iron light standards in place. The stone surface of the building has been kept smooth, and the openings are articulated by a thin, cut-in line designating the frame. The Decorah Post Office illustrates how many individual designs John Knox Taylor and his staff were able to devise within the Beaux-Arts Classical tradition. The recycling of the building into a library is a successful example of adaptive reuse.

NO094 Bank Block

1897. Southeast corner of Water and Winnebago streets

A classicized late Richardsonian Romanesque design in brick, the block displays a stone wainscoting that progresses across the two faces to the rounded corner. At this point the stone dips into the wall recess and moves upward to support a wide stone lintel. A single polished quarter-column dominates the entrance. Above, the rounded bay tower continues up above the second floor where it ends in a suggestion of medieval crenellation and a conical roof sheathed in metal shingles. Across Main Street facing directly onto Winnebago Street is the former Saint Cloud Hotel Building (c. 1878). Though the building has been remodeled on the street level, the third-floor central bay and the wonderful metal entablature, cornice, and gable above are what we all think of when we speak of Victorian architecture.

NO095 Milwaukee Railroad Station (now a medical office)

c. 1880. Northeast corner of E. Water St. and Riverside Ave.

This former railroad station poses as a picturesque shingled house. The bay of the stationmaster's office punches through the roof to form a low, square tower. Other portions of the sweeping roof have gabled ends and dormers with low-pitched shed roofs. The tracks and the metal turntable (this was the end of the line) have been removed. At the east end of the small railroad park is the former Rock Island Station, now used as a residence.

NO096 City Stone Mill (Painter-Bernatz Mill)

1851–1853. Southeast corner of N. Mill and Heivly streets

A classic four-story mill building, this structure has two lower floors of limestone rubble construction and two wood-frame upper floors sheathed in drop siding. The mill continued to utilize water power up through 1947. The building has been restored to its 1900–1914 period of use, and it is a part of the Vesterheim Norwegian-American Museum.

NO097 Arlington House (now Vesterheim Norwegian-American Museum)

1876. 520 W. Water St.

The three-story Arlington house was built in 1876 as a luxury hotel, but because the railroad station was built blocks away it did not prove economically successful. In the early

1880s it became a dormitory for students at the Decorah Institute, and then it was remodeled into the publication house of the Norwegian Lutheran Synod. It is now a museum open to the public. The building is of brick with stone detailing. Metal balconies project from portions of the second and third floors, and the building terminates in an elaborate wide overhanging bracketed cornice. The design of the cornice, the roundheaded windows, and the balconies loosely place its design within the Italianate.

Between the museum and the City Stone Mill is located one of America's earliest outdoor museums (modeled after earlier Swedish examples). This open-air museum consists of a group of buildings that were brought to the site and then reconstructed. There is a c. 1850 log blacksmith's shop (from Houston, Minnesota); the nineteenth-century Egge-Kern log cabin; a Lutheran schoolhouse of 1879; and a small wood building (some 200 years old) which came from Vang, Valdres Province, Norway.

NO098 Norris-Miller House (now part of Norwegian-American Museum)

1856. 520 W. Water St.

This small, one-and-a-half-story dwelling with a steeply pitched roof is of stovewood construction. The walls are built of short pieces of split oak, laid up in an ash-and-lime mortar. This mode of construction was employed throughout portions of Canada and the United States; some examples were built as late as the 1900s. When properly sheathed with shingles, clapboard, or ship lap, such structures have as long a life as any other form of wood structure. It is not known how many structures with stovewood walls were built in Iowa. Counting the number of examples recorded in neighboring Wisconsin, it seems likely that there may have been a substantial number of houses and barns constructed using this mode of wood structure. The Norris-Miller house may well be the only one still standing in Iowa.

NO099 Curtin House

c. 1900. 614 W. Water St.

A two-story turn-of-the-century Colonial Revival box, the Curtin house successfully plays the game between classical symmetry and the irregularity of the picturesque Queen Anne. The porch with its columned, pedimented entrances is countered by off-center bay windows and a third-floor gable with a barely suggested small circular balcony. Light classical garlands decorate the entablature of the porch, and the broadly overhanging roofs are supported by narrow brackets.

NO100 Ellsworth-Porter House

1867. 401 W. Broadway

A tall, thin central tower dominates this good-sized brick Italian villa. A later Queen Anne porch with an open round tower pavilion has been added, but the unique glory of the whole composition are the gardens and the stone-encrusted wall facing the street. The wall, which surrounds three sides of the garden, was built by the "collector-naturalist-artist" Adelbert Field Porter. An avid collector of almost everything, Porter encrusted the wall with agate, jasper, rose quartz, onyx, amethyst, petrified wood, and crystal. One will discover small pools, waterfalls, and hidden gardens enclosed by the walls and plantings. The house is now owned by the Winneshiek County Historical Society. It is open on weekends during the summer months.

NO101 Logan Octagon House

c. 1854–1855. 408 W. Broadway

This is one of the state's all too few remaining octagonal houses, a form popularized in 1848 and later by Orson Fowler in his book, *A Home for All, or the Gravel Wall and Octagonal Mode of Building.* The builder of this house took to heart not only the ideal form of the octagon, but also Fowler's recommendation for "gravel wall" construction. Decorah's octagon has walls of "grout," composed of a mixture of lime mortar, straw, and gravel that was poured and packed into wood forms. Though remodeled over the years, this octagon is still a textbook example of what Fowler was proselytizing: the use of an ideal form (the octagon) and a new material, the gravel wall, which was superior to wood in upkeep and longevity.

NO102 Baker (Grier-Green) House

1862, later. 503 W. Broadway

The Baker house is a one-and-a-half-story Gothic Revival cottage that still exhibits its delicately sawed bargeboards on the gable ends and its metal roof finials and ridge comb. At a later date, probably in the 1870s, two new porches were added in the Eastlake style. The delicate detailing of the porches fits in well with the earlier Gothic Revival features.

NO103 Boden-Steiner House

1860. 509 W. Broadway

A classical porch with Ionic columns gives entrance to a side-hall Italianate house in brick. The wide entablature is especially pronounced, and is accompanied by a broadly extended hipped roof supported by paired narrow brackets.

NO104 First Lutheran Church

1876. 607 W. Broadway

This Gothic Revival church on a raised basement has an appropriately abbreviated and buttressed central entrance tower with the usual tall spire roof. The locally produced brick of the walls is strongly contrasted with the light-colored stone trim. Within is a vivid altar painting by Hebjorn (1895).

NO105 Moss House

1898–1901. 302 Grove St.

This late Queen Anne dwelling responds to its corner site with a circular extension of the large first-floor porch. That extension is capped with a conical roof. The theme of the circle is repeated at the same corner with a three-story bay tower. The more extreme picturesque qualities of the Queen Anne style are held in check by classical Colonial Revival details.

NO106 Paine House

1867. 301 Upper Broadway

When one looks up Broadway to the west, one's vista is stopped by the Paine house, a large two-story brick and stone-trim Gothic Revival dwelling (now painted white). On the street side two step gables continue the wall plane up into the attic. There are elaborate pointed-arched headers over all of the principal windows, and both the street and garden porches have piers with typical cut-out designs. The garden elevation is more varied than the front. Here one will discover the asymmetrical composition of the main mass of the house: on the ground floor is a bay window with small semicircular lunettes, while on the second floor the windows have been appreciably enlarged and now appear monumental in scale.

NO107 Luther College

Founded 1861, moved to Decorah 1862. College Dr., north off North St.

In 1875, Luther College was housed in a building described as "an imposing structure in the Norman-Gothic style of architecture."[6] This building (built in 1865 and completed in 1874) was destroyed by fire in 1889. Its successor also burned, in 1942, and was replaced in 1951. The campus today is dominated by post-World War II Modernist buildings. Architecturally the most enticing structure now on campus is the Pioneer Memorial, located at the college entrance north of the junction of Leif Eriksson Drive and Ohio Street. It is a stone outdoor chapel with a pulpit modeled after a hollowed-out tree trunk.

The dominant quality at Luther College is not the architecture, however, but the landscape, a beautiful site overlooking the upper Iowa River to the west which was revamped in 1910 by the Chicago landscape architect Jens Jensen. Of his approach to design in the Midwest prairie, Jensen wrote, "As I look over the field of my endeavor, it seems to me that each locality had within it the possibility of certain definite expressions, or motives."[7] Jensen developed the feeling of a natural prairie park interspersed with native oaks and supplemented by evergreens and maples. He was emphatic that the blufftop view of the river valley below be maintained, and it has been.

NO108 Decorah Municipal Swimming Pool

1937–1938. Pool St. south of College Rd.

During the depression years of the 1930s the WPA (or the PWA) funded and built a number of municipal pools across the country. Several were built in Iowa, but most of these have either been modified or demolished (such as the splendid one at Dubuque). The swimming-pool building at Decorah presents a sophisticated version of the Streamline Moderne style, realized in reinforced concrete. The long, horizontal entrance pavilion with its pattern of three entrance doors has curved ends. Just below the dark horizontal band of the parapet is a thin horizontal vent opening into which the name of the pool has been inserted in letters using the Broadway typeface. The higher center block of the building has sets of five glass-brick windows, one set to the front and one to the rear.

NO109 Ashmore Farm Group (now part of Luther College)

1867, later. Northeast side of College Dr. and Ridge Rd.

These stone, brick, and wood barns and other buildings were a part of a large farm established in 1867 by retired English Army officer Capt. A. J. Ashmore. The long barn, with its stone first floor and dormered gable roof, exhibits the formality of a classically designed dwelling.

NO110 Locust School

1854. Take route W38 north of Decorah for about 10 miles to route A26; the school is located at the northeast corner of the junction

This is one of Iowa's earliest one-room schoolhouses. It is classical (almost Greek Revival) in its composition of limestone walls covered by a simple gable roof.

NO111 Washington Prairie Methodist Church

1863–1868. Travel 4 miles east of Decorah on Iowa 9, then south on route W42 for 2.5 miles

The style of this small stone church with pediments and entablature/cornice is Greek Revival. The entrance on the gable end is round arched, while the windows on the sides of the building are pointed Gothic. The church was restored in the early 1970s, and one can arrange to visit it through the Norwegian-American Museum in Decorah.

NO112 Harcourt-Horn House

1869. Drive north of Decorah on US 52, then northwest 8 miles on route W20 (Pole Line Rd.); take first gravel road to the right (east); cross Upper Iowa River; 300 yards beyond bridge turn right (south) on gravel road, then take first lane to right

The persistent traveler is rewarded with a view of this substantial two-story brick dwelling; in style it is Italianate. The house was built by Elizabeth and Henry Harcourt Horn, members of an English colony that sought to establish itself in the countryside around Decorah. The situation of the house within the landscape, its more formal qualities, and its details suggest a country house rather than a farmhouse.

Duncombe

Between Webster City and Fort Dodge is the small community of Duncombe, the center of a region containing extensive gypsum deposits. The town was laid out in 1869 by the Iowa Falls and Sioux City Railroad Company, and within a short time a number of mining companies were involved in the extraction of gypsum. At the northeast corner of the town's Main Street and Cedar Street is a former bank building (c. 1900). This one-story structure has walls of stone ashlar block arranged between more finely cut stone pilasters. An arched corner entrance centers on a low Ionic column. As one proceeds west on US 20 from Duncombe a small high-tech industrial complex comes into view. It is composed of tanks, towers, and piping. The complex is a Carbon Dioxide Plant run by COOP (c. 1980).

Eldora

Both the platting of Eldora and the establishment of surrounding Hardin County occurred in 1853. The site for the new community was an open section of rolling prairie west of the Iowa River. A square of 24 blocks was laid out; two blocks were set aside at the center, one for a park, the other as the location for the projected county courthouse.

NO113 Hardin County Courthouse

1891–1892, T. Dudley Allen. Southeast corner Iowa 175 and Iowa 215

Though the principal public entrance to the present, and third, Hardin County Courthouse is correct Richardsonian Romanesque, the building as a whole is something else. Perhaps the closest historical precedent would be the brick and stone-trimmed buildings of Holland and Flanders of the 15th and 16th centuries. The most striking aspect of the design is the manner in which the architect surrounded the windows with a strongly contrasting stone and then treated the windows as a series of bands by tying their headers and sills together. Other contrasting, coloristic effects are the checkerboard pattern surrounding the great entrance arch, the many bands on the upper parts of the building and its tower, and the raised foundation of limestone ashlar block. On the third level of the five-story entrance tower is a large niche which accommodates a sculptural group of three figures. The good size of the building, together with its high tower and the raised elevation of its site, means that the courthouse can be seen for miles around.

In 1969–1970 the courthouse was restored and remodeled by Donald McKeown, and in 1971 a "Pioneer Plaza" was created around the building.

NO114 House

c. 1880. Southwest corner of Edgington (Iowa 175) and 12th St.

Domestic architects in the decades of the 1870s and 1880s delighted in enriching whatever they might touch. Here the visitor comes across a one and-a-half-story brick cottage, modest in size but rich in form and detail. The cottage seems to have started out as an exercise in the Eastlake style which centered attention on a tower with a low-pitched gable roof. Then, the designer of the cottage obviously felt the need to update the image and introduce features of the Queen Anne, which he beautifully expressed in the pavilion with conical roof which is an extension of the front porch. Though the porch is now devoid of its columns and ornamentation, the rest of the house makes up for this lack.

NO115 First Congregational Church

1893, Charles A. Dunham. Southeast corner of 12th Ave. and 12th St.

What is seemingly a large-scaled Richardsonian Romanesque building has been magically miniaturized into this small church of ashlar block masonry. Entrance to the church is through a little circular tower at one corner; at the other corner is the principal tower, which is open from its second level up to the belfry. Within the main gable front, thin buttresses frame a composition of three arched windows, and above is an arrangement of circular and arched false windows.

NO116 Iowa Industrial School for Boys
(Iowa School for Boys)

1872–1873, later. West side of Eldora, off Iowa 175

The initial building constructed in the early 1870s was a two-story Italianate structure with a gable roof. By the mid-1870s this was joined by a number of other buildings, including three which, with their mansard roofs, were French Second Empire in style. Today the most interesting building is the gymnasium (c. 1910), a brick building with gable ends and a bit of the Mission style.

NO117 Pine Lake State Park

1921. Northeast of Eldora on Iowa 118

In 1921 the citizens of Eldora, joined by the Iowa State Park Commission, purchased 236 acres of land adjoining the eastern section of the city. This was formally dedicated as Eldora Pine Creek State Park in 1926. Pine Creek itself was dammed in 1922, and eventually a series of lakes was formed within the park. Additional lands were acquired, and the park now consists of 572 acres. Within the park is a group of prehistoric conical Indian mounds and a number of rustic park structures. The first of these structures were a bathhouse and a shelter constructed of the local red sandstone. A number of other structures were added in the 1930s and later.

Emmetsburg

At the northeast corner of Main and Lake streets is a classic example of what is often spoken of as "Carpenter's Gothic." This Episcopal church (c. 1880) has the usual narrow corner entrance tower with a high spire; the body of the clapboard-sided church is covered by a steeply pitched gable roof. An Eastlake-like open wood pattern adorns the principal gable end, and all the windows terminate in pointed arches. A two-story Queen Anne dwelling (c. 1890) at 801 Lake Street is edged out of the ordinary by the rich display of turned and sawed wood detailing of a small, almost miniature third-floor dormer balcony, and also by the gabled entrance of the front porch. Emmetsburg still possesses its Palo Alto County Courthouse (1880), but what was once a sumptuous Second Empire building has now been so stripped and remodeled that only the shell remains.

Estherville

The site selected in 1857 for the town was within a wooded section of the West Fork of the Des Moines River. The principal commercial buildings of the community are grouped around the courthouse square.

NO118 Emmet County Courthouse

1954–1958, James A. Dougher. 6th St. and 1st Ave. N.

In the post-World War II years an effort was made to modify the then-popular International style by retaining at least a few references to the earlier Beaux-Arts Classical tradition. One design device, exemplified in the Emmet County Courthouse, was to attach loosely a repetitive pilastered porch to what otherwise was a neutral Modern box. Other suggestions of the classical tradition included symmetry, coupled with an entrance that was balanced and formally laid out. The 1954–1958 courthouse replaced an 1884 building, which was designed by Foster and Liebbe in a blend of the French Second Empire and Eastlake styles.

NO119 United States Post Office Building

1910, James Knox Taylor. Northeast corner of 6th St. and 1st Ave. N.

A portico with six columns announces the entrance to a single-story Beaux-Arts building sheathed in smooth limestone. Everything seems "correct" about this building. It's perhaps a little on the dry side, but still public and dignified.

NO120 Estherville High School Building

1929. 6th St. N. between 3rd and 4th Aves. N.

This school building is a bold, abstracted exercise in the Gothic, a la Bertram G. Goodhue's work of the teens and early twenties. The massiveness of masonry is emphasized, especially in the central entrance block, and then repeated within the two end pavilions. Stylized Gothic ornamentation appears throughout the two-story building, its richest outlay being around the principal entrance doorway.

NO121 First Federal Savings and Loan Building

1978–1979, Ralph Rapson. Southwest corner of 6th St. and 1st Ave. N.

A highly serious modern design, this building is almost Constructivist in concept. A lightly articulated wood and glass-sheathed box is posed over a lower indented volume of brick and glass. Diagonal turnbuckles ride across portions of the upper glass wall. The building is assertive and dignified; at the same time its scale is contextual with the adjoining buildings.

NO122 Estherville City Hall (now Iowa Lakes Community College)

1930. Northwest corner of 1st Ave. S. and 7th St.

An Art Deco design is here saved from utter dullness by its limestone two-story entrance centerpiece. Above the entrance doors is a large, tripartite metal-framed window held in place on each side by wide, heavy pilasters.

NO123 First Presbyterian Church

c. 1892. Northwest corner 8th St. and 1st Ave. S.

The central gable presents a grouping of three arched entrances on the ground level; above is a tripartite window composed of a large central arched unit and smaller ones to each side. The central gable is contained by a pair of towers on either side. The larger of the towers, on the right, is square in form;

NO121 First Federal Savings and Loan Building

that on the left is octagonal. The style of the church is Richardsonian Romanesque, with a light-colored limestone base and trim accompanied by red brick walls above.

NO124 A. C. Brown House

1904. 1421 1st Ave. S.

The architect of this house held the irregularity of a picturesque design in check by carefully tying all of the volumes together, and then by emphasizing the horizontal through broad overhanging eaves, projecting

gable ends, bands of horizontal shingles, and an extensive array of wraparound porches. A visitor to the dwelling ascends a broad curved stairway that is oriented toward the dominant wide corner bay tower.

NO125 Fort Defiance

1862–1863. 2 miles southwest of Estherville on route A22

This frontier fort with wood stockade was in use for only 15 months. Parts of the palisaded stockade wall and a blockhouse have been reconstructed.

Fayette

NO126 Alexander Dickman Hall

1855. Southeast corner of Washington and Clark streets

A year before Fayette was platted in 1856, construction began on the three-story Alexander Dickman Hall, the center of the newly projected Upper Iowa University. Andreas described the structure as an imposing edifice, and it still is today. The format of the building's design is late Federal to which some Italianate details have been added. The principal elevation is one continuous stone wall with a gable center. Above the arched entrance, on the second and third floors, are Palladian windows. The cornice around the building has brackets to support the overhanging roof. The tall domed cupola has round-arched windows and louvered openings.

Fertile

At the south end of Main Street in Fertile is situated the Rhodes Mill (1868). The mill is located on the Winnebago River, which has been dammed to form a large mill pond. The mill was constructed as a flour mill, and it is still in use today for grinding food products. In design, the three-story building has a ridge monitor with low one-floor shed roof sections that visually hold the building to its site.

Festina

Southeast of the town of Festina is what is referred to as "the smallest cathedral in the world," another of Iowa's folk follies. The church is 14 feet wide and 20 feet long, with a 5-foot-square entrance tower. The walls of the church are of limestone rubble and the wood-frame tower is sheathed in drop siding. The windows in the building and the louvered openings of the tower are round arched. The sanctuary within has a wood barrel-vaulted ceiling. The church was built in 1885 by a former French soldier, Johann Gaertner (1793–1887), and was dedicated by him to his safe return from Napoleon's winter retreat from Moscow. The present belfry was added in 1888, and the small altar and the stained glass windows were put in place in 1903. The church can be reached be proceeding west from the junction of Iowa 150 and route B32 in Festina. At the western edge of town this street becomes a gravel road; travel 1 mile to the first gravel road to left (south) and drive 1.5 miles on this gravel road; one will find the church off to the east.

Florenceville

Between Cresco and the Minnesota border town of Granger are the few buildings constituting the crossroads community of Florenceville. On the northern outskirts of Florenceville, just below the Minnesota border, one comes across the Granger Methodist Church of c. 1866. The walkway leading to the front entrance of the church proceeds through a narrow row of trees; beyond the church one is strongly aware of the open prairie. This church comes close to summing up the ideal of a mid-century Greek Revival building. Below the enclosed gable is a wide entrance doorway with transom light and an entablature above; to the side are two double-hung windows. Above the front gable is a low, tiered square tower with four segmental arched vent openings. The only non-Greek elements in the design are the segmental arched windows, which reflect the Italianate mode. The church can be reached by traveling 8 miles north of Cresco on route V58; or it can be approached by traveling to Granger, Minnesota, and then proceeding south on route 15, then east on route 30.

Forest City

The community is situated just south of Lime Creek. To the east there are extensively forested lands; to the west the landscape opens up onto a slightly undulating open prairie. The original plat of 18 blocks, laid out in 1856, left three blocks open for public use, one for the hoped-for courthouse, one for a school, and one for a public park. The first courthouse was built in 1861, and it was replaced by the present building in 1896. Though more modest than its counterparts at Sioux City, Ottumwa, and Creston, Forest City's Flax Palace of 1892 was another of those wondrous fairy-tale exposition palaces that Iowa contributed to the national architecture scene in the late nineteenth century.[8] Architecturally (if one has a good imagination), the Flax Palace projects the solidity of Richardson's Romanesque, sheathed in flax, of course.

Forest City's primary influence on American architecture and culture comes through the thousands of Winnebago motor homes that have been produced by Winnebago Industries, Inc., since 1958. One encounters motor homes with the famous "Flying W" trademark (adopted in 1961) across the entire country as they provide mobile housing for thousands of Americans. The firm also produces travel trailers and camper coaches for pickups. The changing design of these mobile-home products has its own history, closely reflecting new technological considerations, the availability and cost of gasoline, the need for heating and cooling, and other factors.

NO127 **Winnebago County Courthouse**

1896–1897, Kinney and Orth. Between 6th and Clark streets, south of J St.

This two-story courthouse of red brick with stone trim was built on a raised basement. In style it is Richardsonian Romanesque and has a five-story tower. Among the usual pattern of vines and leaves carved in the upper stone banding is the head of a Winnebago Indian. Kinney and Orth of Minneapolis produced a number of turn-of-the-century midwestern courthouses. An axial walkway leading to the main arched entrance is interrupted by a pool within which stands the statue of a Civil War soldier. Some changes have been made to the building (including filling in some windows with glass brick), but essentially the building remains as designed.

NO128 **United States Post Office Building**

1940, Louis A. Simon and Neal Melick. Northwest corner of L and N. Clark streets

In the thirties the style of this building would have been called "Modern Regency." A horizontal brick box has been placed on a low gray stone foundation. The windows and entrance are all enclosed within a U-shaped frame; the entablature and cornice have been kept flush with the brick surface of the building. Two tall Regency lamps stand on each side of the entrance platform. Within is a WPA mural by Orr C. Fisher (1942). All in all, this building is a sophisticated composition that fits well in the community's tree-lined streets.

NO129 **Charles Thompson House**

1895. 516 N. Clark St.

The corner porch designed as a semicircular pavilion acknowledges the corner lot location of this Queen Anne dwelling. To balance the porch, a tower has been placed on the other side. The classical columns (Ionic) and the design of the balustrade railing of the porch refer to the Colonial Revival. Two other houses in town should be noted. These are another Queen Anne house at 345 North Clark Street (with elaborate turned work), and "The Mansion," the headquarters of the Winnebago Historical Society, located at the southwest corner of Clark and M streets. "The Mansion" excellently presents the Colonial Revival of the turn of the century.

NO130 **Pilot Knob State Park**

1922, acquired. Drive east of Forest City on US 69, then east on Iowa 9 to route R72

This wooded park of over 300 acres alongside Lime Creek was acquired by the state in 1922.

NO130 Pilot Knob State Park, Observation Tower

Its name is derived from a 300-foot-high hill where one can obtain a magnificent view of the surrounding prairieland. The romantic gem of the park is the 40-foot-high rough stone tower on top of the hill. As one approaches this tower, built by the Civilian Conservation Corps in 1934, it appears to be the remains of a medieval castle. Note the stone-and-wood outdoor amphitheater and the rustic, almost vernacular, medieval-style two-story service building (originally designed for horses and automobiles). The park itself is beautifully designed with a system of roads and paths that wind around the undulating wooded hills.

Fort Atkinson

Fort Atkinson State Park includes a number of buildings, including Fort Atkinson (NO131). Two blocks northwest of the fort is the romantic stone ruin of the Lutheran Chapel of Saint James German (c. 1857). In the town itself is the Gothic Revival 1873 Roman Catholic church of Saint John Nepomucene. This church is an appealing Gothic Revival composition of smooth stone walls and large pointed windows interspersed with buttresses, accompanied by a wood gable roof, tower, and spire. The interior of the church is a single aisleless nave covered with a barrel vault. In 1886 a sanctuary and two sacristies were added; over ten years later, in 1899, a wing was added on the left. A new side entrance was introduced in 1949.

At the northern limits of Fort Atkinson State Park on the Turkey River is the Wiest Mill (1857). The river has at this point been dammed to form a long mill pond. Reflected in it is the four-story mill building. Its lowest level is of stone, with wood above; it is topped by a gable roof.

NO131 **Fort Atkinson**

1840–1842

Fort Atkinson was built using local limestone. The original group of buildings consisted of two stone and two log buildings for officers and enlisted men. Other structures included cannon bastions at the east and southeast corners, a powder magazine, the quartermaster's storehouse, a store, and the guardhouse. The fort was abandoned by the military in 1849 and the land was sold in 1855; the state acquired the site in 1921. In 1940–1941 excavations and restoration were begun; the stockade was rebuilt in 1958, and other portions of the fort were rebuilt four years later. As with most western military architecture, these stone buildings are simple in form, the

NO131 Fort Atkinson

general stylistic reference being mildly Greek Revival. The fort is open to the public with hours and days varying according to the time of year.

Fort Dodge

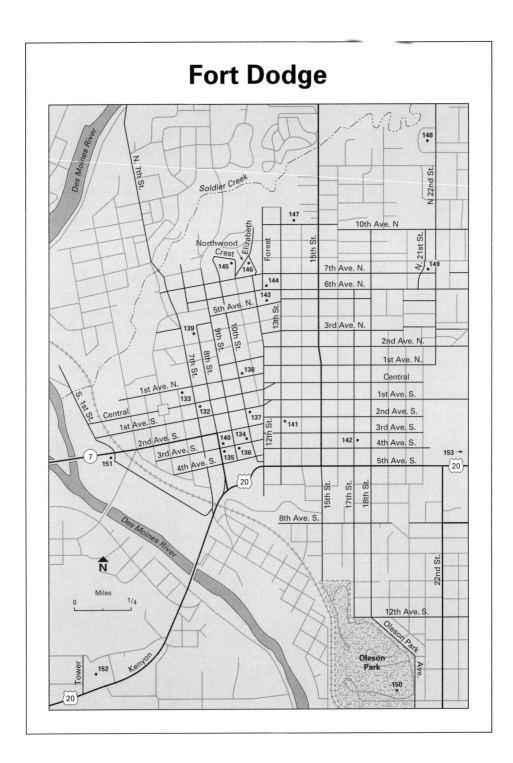

N

Miles

0   1/4

Fort Dodge

The military established a stockaded post at this site in 1850. The post was abandoned in 1853, and the following year the city of Fort Dodge was platted. This first plat was laid out on a grid that ran somewhat parallel to the east bank of the Des Moines River. Though a public square was provided, interrupting Central Avenue at Fourth Street, the site selected for the county courthouse was simply a corner lot at Central Avenue and Seventh Street. Later additions at the east and west brought the grid back to the cardinal points of the compass. Much later, curvilinear residential streets responding to the contours of the land were laid out both north and south of Soldier Creek. Over the years the community developed a system of parks parallel to both sides of the river. Other extensive parks (Crawford to the north and Olsen to the south) have provided additional green belts and recreational areas.

While the city's location on the upper Des Moines River did not allow river transport (because of the shallowness of the river), it did provide much-needed water power, and the surrounding land—a mixture of forests and open prairies—was rich agriculturally. Very early the city became an important rail-line stop for the Illinois Central and also served as a terminus for the Des Moines and Fort Dodge Railway. In addition to its economy based on transportation, the city took advantage of the extensive nearby deposits of gypsum and clay for the manufacture of tile and brick.

Architecturally, the city has lost a number of its most interesting nineteenth-century buildings, including its continually remodeled courthouse of 1859–1861 (by A. V. Lambert, an architect from Fort Dodge). After the turn of the century the city emerged as a center for midwestern Craftsman and Prairie architecture. The Prairie-style form that most interested the architects and clients in Fort Dodge was that classical, somewhat Viennese version so closely associated with the Chicago architect George W. Maher.[9]

NO132 **Webster County Courthouse**

1901–1902, A. V. Lambert. Southeast corner of 7th St. and Central Ave.

In contrast to most Iowa courthouses, the Webster County Courthouse stands directly on a downtown corner and has no open space around it. The architect took this into account in a classic Beaux-Arts manner by using horizontally lined rusticated walls penetrated by the entrances on the ground floor, and by providing a recessed central colonnade on the second level. He reserved his finest design efforts for the clock tower, which, with its shingled base, seemingly grows out of the roof. Each of the four clock faces is framed and pedimented, and the small dome of the tower is broken on each face by low, open-curved dormers.

NO133 **Public Library**

1901–1902, H. C. Koch and Company. 605 1st Ave. N.

This very correct Beaux-Arts exercise is *so* correct that it is on the dry side, but it was still carried out well. The principal facade of this Carnegie library exhibits a Roman Doric pedimented entrance. The architect has given all the principal windows rectangular false porticoes articulated by Ionic columns.

NO134 Blanden Memorial Art Gallery

1931–1932, E. O. Damon, Jr. Northwest corner of 3rd Ave. S. and 10th St.

The Fort Dodge architect E. O. Damon, responding to the taste of the time, utilized the mid-fifteenth-century Italian Renaissance mode as his point of departure. This was in deference to his patron, Charles Blanden, who had indicated to his architect his fondness for the Butler Institute of American Art at Youngstown, Ohio. A groin-vaulted three-arched loggia is flanked by blank walls. Each of these walls contains a niche with a seashell half dome. The tripartite division of the entrance facade is reinforced by Ionic pilasters that support a wide, carefully divided entablature and cornice. The building is idyllically situated within a park, which enhances its public character; the surrounding trees and shrubs bring out its small scale and intimate details.

NO135 Rich House

1880. 819 3rd Ave. S.

Generally when the Queen Anne was carried out in brick it tended to be subdued. Any exuberance, such as one experiences in the Rich house, comes out in the wood detailing of the porches, balconies, and gable ends. An unusual feature of the Rich house is its square entrance tower; its roof, with its round window dormers, is French Second Empire in style. On the exterior the house remains as built, except for the removal or lowering of a number of the chimneys.

NO136 Roberts House

1888. 919 3rd Ave. S.

The Roberts house illustrates how closely in tune a client and an architect in Iowa could be with the rapidly changing world of architectural fashion. This house has some vestiges of the Queen Anne in elevation and plan, but basically it is Colonial Revival. Present are such elements as overscaled round and lunette windows, Palladian windows, and porches with Tuscan columns and balustrades. The front and side porches are connected by a balustraded terrace; within, there is a central living hall with an open staircase.

NO137 Episcopal Church

c. 1890s. Southeast corner 1st Ave. and 10th St.

As sometimes happens with Episcopal churches, this building of randomly laid stone conveys a charming dollhouse scale. At the corner is a low tower with two arched openings giving entrance to an open porch; above, the stone walls have been carried upward, forming four piers that in turn form a tower with horizontal vents and a hipped roof. Above the low shed roofs that cover the side arches are the shingled walls of the clerestory with its own arched windows.

NO138 First Methodist Church

1914. Northeast corner of 1st Ave. N. and 10th St.

The inspiration for this church was the Pantheon, with a side look at the work of the sixteenth-century Italian architect Palladio. Added to this classical inheritance is an attached campanile-like tower that is surmounted by pedimented openings on all four faces and an octagonal drum and dome.

NO139 Corpus Christi Roman Catholic Church

1882, Fridolin Heer. 416 N. 8th St.

The Dubuque architect provided the community with a perfect example of what we think of as Victorian Gothic. The light-colored stone detailing contrasts sharply with the surrounding brick walls. Various forms of windows—arched, segmental arched, and circular—were used throughout the building. The verticality of the tower, with its insistence on climbing higher and higher, is realized through its layered corner buttresses, projecting pinnacles, and the pencil-point spire that springs from four steeply pitched gables.

Nearby is another Roman Catholic church,

Sacred Heart Church designed by William L. Steele in 1921. Here one can see how a Prairie architect handled the traditional Romanesque. The church is located at the southeast corner of South First Street and Second Avenue South.

NO140 Swain-Vincent House

1871. 824 3rd Ave. S.

Narrow pairs of roundheaded windows peer out of thick brick walls, and small semicircular dormers appear within the concave mansard roof of this two-and-a-half-story French Second Empire house. The house, including its third-floor ballroom, has been restored, and the building is used for public events.

NO141 Butler House

1903, Nourse and Rasmussen. 327 S. 12th St.

Like the Corey house of 1914 (NO144), this house is derived from the Chicago work of George W. Maher. The solidity of the classical has been updated by references to what was going on at the turn of the century in Vienna. The rectangular block of the house is covered by an extended hipped roof supported by a wide entablature. The walls are of smooth Roman brick, which aids in making the building read as horizontal. On the first floor is a wide porch supported by heavy brick piers with highly stylized capitals.

NO142 Joyce House

1915. 417 N. 17th St.

This house erected by Matthew M. Joyce, who later became a federal judge in Minneapolis,

NO142 Joyce House

is similar to several of the Prairie-style houses erected in the Chicago suburbs by Tallmadge and Watson. The two-story gabled facade facing the street displays a vertical patterning of wood that ties all the windows together. The scale of this one facade comes close to what one would associate with a church or library building. The remainder of the house is less assertive, although equally inventive. The entrance is at the right side of the dwelling, under a shed roof. To the right is a projecting two-story wing and a first floor porch.

Other mildly Prairie-style houses in the vicinity are the Thomas house (1912, 1200 Tenth Avenue North); the Thatcher house (1916, 1201 Tenth Avenue North); the Carter house (1915, 510 South Twelfth Street); and the Laufersweiler house (c. 1916, 775 Northwest Avenue).

NO143 Healy House

1903. 1218 5th Ave. N.

The Healy house is a Colonial Revival updating of a Queen Anne dwelling. The three-story bay tower with conical roof drops down onto a curved porch that joins the pedimented entrance porch. On the left side a two-story angled bay continues up into the shingled gambrel roof gable. Above the bay is one of several Palladian windows.

NO144 Corey House

1914. 1238 6th Ave. N.

This Prairie-style house refers to the classical sense of solidity and monumentality associated with the work of the Chicago architect George W. Maher. The entrance terrace has raised corner plinths with concrete plant containers on top. Above the projecting entrance is a recessed section.

NO145 **Armstrong House**

1919. 775 Crest Ave.

Another of the community's Prairie-style houses that looked to the Chicago work of George W. Maher, the Armstrong house is more delicate in scale and in detail than the Butler house of 1903 or the Corey house of 1914 (NO144), although it is as large. Windows occur as broad horizontal groups in the Armstrong house; the gable roofs have exaggerated overhangs, and the entrance has that Maheresque touch, a segmented curved roof over the entrance. Below are three small windows set behind two engaged columns. A low dormer with a center arched section is centrally placed within the tile roof. The hipped roof extends far out over the brick walls below.

NO146 **Damon House**

1916, E. O. Damon. 710 Northwood Ave.

The architect of the Blanden Art Gallery chose the American Colonial for the style of his own brick-clad house. As with many architects of Colonial Revival houses of the years 1910–1920, Damon introduced a number of compatible but archaeologically incorrect features. These included the segmental arched roof for the entrance porch, pairs of long casement windows on the ground floor, and the composition of two double-hung windows placed together above the entrance porch.

NO147 **Chase House**

1926. 1933, playroom wing. 1320 10th St. N.

The Chase house is a picturesque Tudor Revival home with stucco and half-timber walls, a stone chimney, and parapet walls for the terrace. The two-story playroom wing to the right has a beamed cathedral ceiling and a small balcony. The two principal windows of this wing are divided into three units and are filled with diamond-patterned leaded glass.

NO148 **Brady House**

1935. 1631 N. 22nd St.

In the 1930s variations on the English Regency were frequently used for suburban houses and even for medical offices and stores. The designer of the Brady house has arranged its principal windows into repeated groups of four casements and transom windows. A gentle segmented parapet projects above the eaves of the low-pitched hipped roof. On the garden side of the house is a veranda with wide arches.

NO149 **Trauerman House**

1925. 725 N. 21st St.

The client for this Spanish Colonial Revival house was the owner of a furniture store, and thus one assumes he was very much aware of the fad for the Hispanic in the mid-1920s. The home's entrance has been placed in a rectangular block which suggests a low tower. To the right of this is a recessed loggia containing a pair of Moorish twisted columns. To the other side of the entrance, the front wall swoops down and becomes a garden wall with a small gate.

NO150 **Band Shell**

c. 1936. Olsen Park, south end of 17th St.

Moderne-style bandstands of this type were built in a number of communities in Iowa during the depression years of the 1930s. One inspiration was certainly the nationally publicized Hollywood Bowl in California. Another, perhaps unconscious source was the image of radio speakers, which in the late 1920s and early 1930s were often separated from their receivers. The Fort Dodge bandstand exhibits metal gates at each side of the podium; in their exaggerated, twisted form the gates seem to be of hemp rope rather than iron.

NO151 **Sacred Heart Roman Catholic Church**

1921, William L. Steele. Southeast corner of S. 13th St. and 2nd Ave. S.

The Sacred Heart Church was designed some five years after the Woodbury County Courthouse in Sioux City. As was generally true with all of the exponents of the Prairie school, Steele turned to the use of historic imagery after World War I. In the case of this church, the southern European Romanesque was Steele's prime point of reference, but he did not abandon a number of Prairie stylistic elements that he had utilized in the teens. The series of setbacks on the upper reaches of the corner tower have far more to do with Bertram G. Goodhue's then-current work than with the European Romanesque. So too the repeated patterns of elongated arches supported by elongated pilasters, and especially the service section of the church at the rear, look back to the earlier Prairie school designs of Frank Lloyd Wright, Walter Burley Griffin, and Purcell and Elmslie. A similar Prairie-style abstraction of the Romanesque is found inside the church.

NO152 **Fort Dodge Historical Museum, Fort, and Stockade**

1850. Kenyon Rd (US 20) and Museum Rd.

The fort was constructed in 1850 and was abandoned three years later. What we experience today is a replica built between 1962 and 1964. The fort was rectangular in form, with two sides composed of buildings and two of a vertical log stockade. At one corner was a single blockhouse with a cantilevered second floor.

NO153 **Restaurant Building**

c. 1955. 3418 5th Ave. (US 20, east side of town)

Here is an adventuresome roadside building that captures much of the spirit of the decade after World War II. The roadside frontage of the building, which was once a restaurant, consists of two elongated boxes, one on top of the other. The lower box is sheathed in cast fake stone, except for the entrance area in the center. This has a covering of shiplap (now weathered). The upper box has dramatic walls that cant outward at the top. The center of the upper box continues the same shiplap as below, and the rest of the upper canted box is also covered with shiplap. The pair of windows on each side of the entrance door within the lower box are in the shape of elongated triangles with one apex cut off. Finally, the real substance of the enclosed space, which lies hidden behind these two stacked boxes, is a metal Quonset hut. Now deserted and constrained behind a fence, the building makes an effective and romantic highway ruin.

NO154 **Dolliver Memorial State Park**

1921, acquired; 1925, dedicated. Take US 169 south of Fort Dodge, 7.3 miles, then turn left (east) on Iowa 50 and travel 3 miles; turn left (north) on route D33 and drive .7 miles

Dolliver Memorial State Park, located on the west bank of the Des Moines River, is a park to be visited not only for its natural beauty but also for its rustic park architecture. The entrance kiosk to the park is a delightful circular building in stone. Its conical segmented roof sits like a light summer hat upon the thick masonry walls below. The interior, which measures 15.6 feet in diameter, is a single space dominated by a large fireplace. The kiosk is connected to the stone gateposts that define the entrance to the park. A similar entrance kiosk was built in the late 1920s at Lacey-Keosauqua State Park near Keosauqua.

Garner

Situated within a landscaped square south of US 18 within Garner is the Hancock County Courthouse of 1899. F. W. Kenney of Minneapolis provided the county with a simplified, somewhat abstracted version of the Richardsonian Romanesque. Though the three-arched recessed entry porch, the round-arched windows, and the pair of towers are correct for the style, the building as a whole has a classical reserve about it. Present within the facades of the building are pilasters, classical cornices, and pediments. The raised basement of the building is of limestone; above, the walls are of brick with a limited amount of stone trim. Now missing from the building is the upper portion of its principal tower.

NO155 **Vrba House**

1918, Einar O. Broaten. 590 Allen Ave.

Mason City architect Einar O. Broaten provided the community with a classic Prairie-style box, the John Vrba House. Again, as is so frequently the case, the theme is Frank Lloyd Wright's 1906 *Ladies Home Journal* house: a single rectangular volume covered by a low-pitched hipped roof with a wide overhang. The front is symmetrically organized with a long bank of casements, a planter box on the first floor, and then a group of three casement units above. The entrance porch (enclosed) projects from the left side of the dwelling. Instead of providing the usual brick surface below and stucco above, Broaten has used a dark brick up to the sills of the second-floor windows and a light tan brick above. A thin band of concrete accentuates and separates the two bands of brick.

Goldfield

Within the town of Goldfield is the site of an idealized log cabin (NO156). Farther out from the downtown is a Lustron house (c. 1949), at 203 Washington Street. This is an unusual one in that it is equipped with a breezeway and garage, all manufactured by Lustron.

NO156 **Boy Scout Log Cabin**

1926. 1976, restored. Northeast corner of Main and Wright streets

NO156 Boy Scout Log Cabin

In Goldfield is a building that matches one's idea of what a perfect log cabin should be. The Boy Scouts constructed the building, and it's almost as good as making one yourself with Lincoln Logs. This cabin has an appropriately crude chimney and fireplace on one gable wall, a door that reaches up and is tucked in under the eaves, and two wood barrels at each corner.

Goodell

Goodell, in southeast Hancock County, contains the remains of a Prairie school bank building (c. 1915). This small brick structure, now converted into a garage, has a composition of end pavilions whose presence is established by vertical paneling of different colors of brick accentuated by lines of creamy white glazed brick. In fact, the two street elevations read as fascinating linear patterns of horizontal and vertical rectangles. Above the entrance the pediment forms a small, low gable, and below this is a small pattern of ornament in cast stone. The building has a number of points of similarity to small banks designed by a Sioux City firm, The Lytle Company. It is located at the northwest corner of Broadway and First streets.

Greene

The Burlington, Cedar Rapids, and Minnesota Railroad constructed a line through Floyd County in the late 1860s, essentially following the course of the Shell Rock River. In 1871 the town of Greene was laid out by the railroad, with sections of the town on both sides of the river.

Near the intersection of North High and West Traer streets is the Church of the Brethren (1873), designed by William Buchman. The church building is a two-story structure with walls of local limestone. The proportions of the building and the slope of the gable roof are almost Greek Revival, but the narrow, elongated windows move the style slightly toward the medieval. The unusual feature of the church is that its sanctuary is on the second floor, with a fully exposed ground floor below. Its entrance is a tall, vertical composition of a door with a window above, and above this a lunette window (now closed in).

Grundy Center

Grundy Center, just south of Blackhawk Creek, was first settled in 1855. In the following year the county was organized and Grundy Center became the county seat. The terrain in this section was described by Andreas as "high rolling prairie,"[10] and it has long been noted that Grundy center is "surrounded by wonderfully rich farming country."[11] In the late nineteenth century it was connected to the Rock Island and Pacific Railroad.

NO157 **Grundy County Courthouse**

1891–1893, Kramer and Zoll. G Ave., between 7th and 8th streets

Though the county government set up shop in Grundy Center in the mid-1850s, it was not until 1870 that a courthouse building was constructed. This wood-frame building was one of the most unusual in Iowa, for it was in essence an enlarged octagonal house, with central cupola and all. The style of this octagonal courthouse was that of the Greek Revival, with the exception of the Italianate cupola.

NO157 Grundy County Courthouse

NO158 Central Block

The second and current courthouse was designed by the Fremont, Nebraska, architectural firm of W. Lewis Kramer and E. E. Zoll. The designers gave the county the latest stylistic image of the time for public buildings, the Richardsonian Romanesque. The principal entrance facade bears the classic hallmark of a Richardsonian design: a wide and deep arched entrance, with a tower on one side and a three-story wing with gable roof on the other. The tower, which is taller than one usually finds, exhibits four clock faces within its upper walls. Across from the courthouse are a number of well-preserved nineteenth-century commercial blocks. Two of the most interesting of these are the Central Block (1879) and the Geer Block (1880). These ma-

sonry buildings exhibit decorated metal window lintels and elaborate roof cornices.

NO158 Commercial Block (now Red Umbrella)

c. 1890. Northeast corner of G Ave. and 7th St.

This is a commercial building that exhibits the typical projecting corner round bay, in this instance sheathed in metal; but it is the surface fenestration of this two-story brick block that attracts one's attention. Carefully placed horizontal bands of stone tie the arched and square-topped windows together, and within the side facade the lower band of stone penetrates through the lower windows.

NO159 Grundy Community Center

1983, Charles Herbert and Associates. F Ave., between 7th and 8th streets

A segment of a circular screen has been placed in front of this single-story building made of concrete block. The design concept is classical, almost Palladian, but the fenestration and details are pure modernist. A slice has been cut out of the center of the curved screen wall, and through this cut one can catch a glimpse of a gabled end placed over a continuous glass area.

NO160 Willoughby House

1915, Howard B. Burr. 1002 G Ave.

A Prairie dwelling designed in the manner of George W. Maher, the Willoughby house is a box with a horizontal emphasis, covered by a low-pitched hipped roof with a wide overhang; there is a projecting center entrance with an upwardly curving roof supported by consoles. A living porch projects from the left side, and on the main roof of the house is a segmental arched dormer (matching the form of the curved roof above the entrance). Surprisingly this central dormer facing the street has been placed slightly off the centerline.

NO161 Wilson House

1916, Mortimer B. Cleveland. 802 I Ave.

An impressive sweeping gable roof dominates this Prairie-style dwelling. The gable end is treated in a vertical pattern of half-timbering.

A podium brick terrace together with the brick sheathing of the first floor ties the house firmly to its site. An extra-large tripartite window provides almost a picture window for the living room, which runs across the front of the house. To the left, the slope of the main roof is carried on to cover an enclosed living/dining porch.

NO162 Herbert Quick School

c. 1860–1865. City Park, northeast corner of G Ave. and 14th St.

A perfect picture of the typical one-room rural schoolhouse, this clapboard-sheathed building with a gable roof was moved from Colfax Township to its present location in 1933. The Iowa author Herbert Quick (author of *Vandemark's Folly* and *The Invisible Woman*) received his early education within this schoolhouse.

NO163 Bailey House

1916, Howard B. Burr. 805 7th St.

It would appear that the architect of this Prairie-style house with a gable roof had looked very closely at Louis H. Sullivan and George Grant Elmslie's earlier (1907–1908) design for the Bradley house at Madison, Wisconsin, and also at several of Walter Burley Griffin's designs for suburban Chicago houses. The gable ends of the roof project like the prow of a ship, and this form is repeated below in the roof over the entry. The lower walls of the house are sheathed in brick, and brick

piers rise to intimate that they support the broadly overhanging main roof. The second-floor window within the front gable has a V-shaped crown that follows the slope of the roof fascia and soffit above.

NO164 House

1002 7th St.

This is the quintessence of what we all think of when someone mentions a Queen Anne house. The expansive two-story dwelling and its wraparound first-floor porch are organized around a three-story octagonal bay tower with a spired roof. The delicate sawed and turned work of the porch and the appliqué of decorative wood on the wall surface suggest that the building is the most fragile of objects. Its current exterior color scheme of red, white, and blue enhances this feeling of lightness.

NO165 Briggs House

1916, Howard B. Burr. 1009 6th St.

The design of this Prairie house is so close to Walter Burley Griffin's Comstock house, no. 2 (1912), in Evanston, Illinois, that it would be easy to assume that he did this house as well. This house has a roof form similar to that of the Bailey house on Seventh Street (NO163): there is a central gable which flattens out at the eave ends, and a V-header window within the second-floor gable end. The roof of the entrance porch perfectly matches the main roof of the house.

Hampton

The town's 48-block grid, with one central block reserved for a park and an adjacent one for the site of a county courthouse, was laid out in 1856. At the end of the 1860s the north-south line of the Iowa Central Railroad had reached the community, and by the end of the century the east-west Chicago and Great Western Railroad traversed the town.

NO166 Franklin County Courthouse

1890–1891, T. Dudley Allen. Northeast corner of Central and Federal streets

A single-floor wood-frame building was the first structure built for county use (1857).

This modest building was replaced in 1866 by a two-story stone building in the Greek Revival mode. In 1889 the second county courthouse was condemned and torn down. For the third courthouse, the Minneapolis architect T. Dudley Allen supplied a rather

NO166 Franklin County Courthouse

personal version of the Richardsonian Romanesque. The two-story building on a raised basement was built of brick with stone trim. It seemingly sits quietly as a backdrop for two features of the design. First, the limestone entrance, with a beautiful deep Richardsonian arch set within it, is quite distinct, and gives the impression that it has been placed separately in front of the building. The second important feature of the design is the tall (133 feet) domed tower whose details are rendered in a light color (in stone and in painted wood and metal); it is played off

against the dark red brick walls of the building below. The tower appears as a discrete structure unrelated to the rest of the building.

Remodeling in 1975–1976 replaced the original wood-framed windows with metal-framed single-piece windows set almost flush with the surface of the building. As always, this type of modernization tends to compromise the quality of the masonry of the building. The strength of the courthouse design together with its own ample square and the adjacent public park creates a real civic center for the community.

NO167 Soldiers' Memorial Hall

1889–1890. Northeast corner of Central and Federal streets

Four wings with gable roofs project from the sides of a tiny octagon to form this memorial. The Gothic Revival pointed windows help to convey the impression that this is a small chapel. Atop the roof of the central octagon is a small platform supporting a statue of a Civil War soldier.

NO168 United States Post Office Building

1931, Louis A. Simon and George Van Nerta. Northeast corner of Federal and 1st streets

NO168 United States Post Office Building

A single-story rectangular brick box has been transformed into a piece of architecture by careful and thoughtful handling of the facades. The center of the street front has been pulled forward just a bit, and within this entrance wing the architects have arranged three long arches with elongated recessed panels on each side. The two flanking arches contain well-proportioned and detailed Palladian windows. The foundation of the building has been treated as a stone-sheathed band, and its horizontality is repeated in a second, quite thin band that runs around the building some 30 inches below the top of the parapet. As to imagery, the architects were, of course, thinking of eighteenth-century American Colonial architecture.

NO169 **Park School**

1938. East end of 1st Ave. at 5th St.

The Park School is characteristic of a number of small, late-1930s schools built in Iowa. In style, it is Streamline Moderne; its single story exhibits the usual horizontal band of windows and a horizontal cornice of concrete. The architect drew attention to the off-center entrance by pulling its volume slightly in front of the surrounding walls, by raising its parapet slightly higher, and by projecting an eyebrow out above the door. Windows with grilles are placed on each side off the doorway, within the yellow brick walls of the building.

NO170 **Harriman House**

c. 1863. 26 10th St. N.W.

This dwelling has been much added to and remodeled; it seems to have started life as an Italianate design, which was then taken over by Eastlake and Queen Anne influences. The main block of the house centers on a square bay on the first floor, with an open roofed porch above. To the left, the entrance porch cantilevers out of its gable and enriches it with fancy sawed bargeboards.

NO171 **Kohl House**

c. 1920, attributed to Einar O. Broaten. 122 4th St. S.E. (US 65)

This Prairie school two-story box has a porch that projects toward the street. The porch is covered by a low-pitched gable roof. The brick walls of the house have been carried up to the sills of the second-floor windows, and there is stucco above. Leaded glass casement windows with a simple geometric pattern are present in both the house and the enclosed porch.

NO172 **Breeds Lake State Park**

1938. Travel west of Hampton on Iowa 3 to Iowa 134, then north to the park

The 330-acre state park is oriented around a manmade lake formed by a 170-foot-long dam across Spring Creek. The lake was first formed in 1857 when a dam and gristmill were constructed by William Breed. The mill and the dam were demolished in 1916. The site was later acquired by the state for a park and was opened to the public in 1938. Just before that time, in 1936–1937, the Civilian Conservation Corps had built a new dam and spillway, re-creating the lake. The sloping 40-foot-high spillway was constructed of blocks of multicolored stones.

Hubbard

At 319 South Michigan Street, is a good-sized Craftsman house (c. 1912). The hipped gable end of this two-story dwelling faces the street; within this gable is a two-story porch with brick piers brought all the way up to the lintel on the second floor. The body of the building is brick, but plaster has been used for the lower sections of the second-floor porch and for the gable ends. Within the first-floor porch, the entrance vestibule has been pulled forward, and there are two high windows on each of the sides.

NO173 **Public School Gymnasium**

1940, Thorwald Thorson. South Illinois, between East Chestnut and East Elm streets

This community was among many in Iowa to receive funding for school projects during the depression of the 1930s. At the end of this period, Thorwald Thorson designed a public school gymnasium of exposed concrete with a hooped roof. He had the end facade follow the hoop of the roof, and then he repeated this form through a series of lines that formed open Vs terminating in a central vertical panel. The lettering style and the graphic layout of this vertical panel are splendid. Thorson placed the date "1940" at the top, and below, in letters interspersed with rows of dots and dashes, he laid out a quotation from Goethe: "One cannot always be a hero, but one can always be a man."

Humboldt

Three miles below Humboldt, the Des Moines River divides into two branches. On the east fork of the river is Dakota City, the location of the Humboldt County Courthouse. Just west of Dakota City is Humboldt, situated on the west fork of the river. The community of Humboldt was laid out in 1863 in conjunction with the establishment of Humboldt College (1869–1926). In addition to the large site for the college at its north end, the town grid plan contained a central four-block park, a skating park, plus other blocks set aside for other parks, schools, and a cemetery. The main building of Humboldt College (no longer standing) was in the form of an elaborate Italian villa with raised basement.

In John Brown Park is a stone mosaic fountain, the Fay Hessian Fountain. This fountain was built in 1916 by Father Paul M. Dobberstein, the designer of the Grotto of the Redemption in West Bend. The bowl-like form of the fountain is composed of thousands of stones gathered from all over the world. Above this rise marble statues of local young women. At the southeast corner of Taft Street and Avenue N is the Congregational Church (c. 1903). This limestone ashlar block church was inspired by medieval English churches. At the base of its corner crenellated tower is a handsome wooden entrance porch with delicate patterned sawed work in its gable.

At the north edge of town, on the west side of US 169 and overlooking the Des Moines River, is a Streamline Moderne house, the Bellows house of 1937–1938, at 6 Thirteenth Street North. The dominant feature of the cream-colored brick residence is its two-story curved wing and the abstract layered design of the overlapping planes of its chimney.

Independence

The city is located on a handsome site at a point where the Wapsipinicon River cuts through rolling hills, many of which were covered with oaks. The north-south, east-west grid was laid out in 1847, first on the east side of the river and

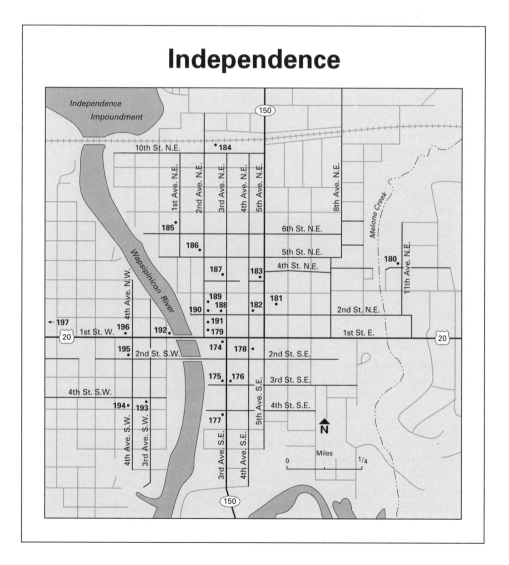

later on the west side. In the early 1850s a dam and mill were constructed across the river. The Illinois Central Railroad reached the community in 1859, and later the Burlington, Cedar Rapids, and Minnesota Railroad arrived. The courthouse site and its adjacent park were planned to be away from the commercial downtown. The earliest residential areas developed south and north of First Street East; later it extended across the river south of First Street West.

NO174 Security State Bank

1983, Daryl Anderson. Southwest corner of 1st St. E. and 3rd Ave. S.E. (US 150)

The architect has opened up the corner into a small plaza, but at the same time he has maintained a sense of enclosure and of the two streets coming together. At the corner, appearing almost as a ruin, is a sloped form sheathed in gray granite; this is connected to the L-shaped building by pergolalike horizontal beams sheathed in matte-finished aluminum panels. The fenestration of the glass area of the inner "L" of the building is almost domestic in scale.

NO175 House

c. 1895. Northwest corner of 3rd St. S.E. and 3rd Ave. S.E.

The Queen Anne format is here taken almost fully into the turn-of-the-century Colonial Revival. The porch has an entrance with a wide classical pediment, behind which seems to be situated the living porch with its segmental arched openings.

NO176 Mason Funeral Home

c. 1875. Northeast corner of 3rd St. S.E. and 3rd Ave. S.E.

This building, originally a private home, was initially designed in the Eastlake mode, but later (c. 1900) a Colonial Revival porch was added. The combination of these two elements worked out quite successfully. In the post-World War I years an unsympathetic box was added to the side, but the house is strong enough in design to maintain its earlier character.

NO177 Cottage

c. 1872 and later. Southwest corner of 4th St. S.E. and 3rd Ave. S.E.

This is one of those small-scaled domestic designs that are the result of an additive process, but the changes have been so well handled it is difficult to single out any one. It would seem that it all started with a little one-and-a-half-story, board-and-batten Gothic Revival cottage. Along the way the building acquired a stout wood and masonry Craftsman porch (c. 1910).

NO178 Church Building (now the Legion Hall)

c. 1860. East side of 4th Ave. S.E. between 1st St. E. and 2nd St. S.E.

The proportions and fenestration of this church building are characteristic of the Greek Revival. The wide double-banded entablature is especially impressive, as is the way the tower joins the gabled eaves. The spire is now missing and only a few of the tall windows remain.

NO179 House

c. 1875. 600 1st St. E.

Particularly dramatic on this two-story Italianate dwelling are the widely projecting gable ends with their returns. They are supported by jigsaw-cut brackets and at the corners by wood arches that become the cornice brackets.

NO180 Christian Seeland House and Brewery

1873. 1010 4th St. N.E.

This house is one of Iowa's most handsome examples of the symmetrical Italianate mode. To the right and left of the double front door are narrow French doors; on the sides, similar narrow openings house double-hung windows. Stone voussoirs have been introduced at the springing and keystone of each of the segmental arches covering the windows and doors. Now missing from the design is the ground-floor porch which went across the entrance front and then swung around the sides, and also a reasonably large-scaled cupola with finials and weather vane. The brewery, which bordered Melon Creek, is now in ruins.

NO181 Buchanan County Courthouse

1939, Dougher, Rich and Woodburn. 5th Ave. N.E. (Iowa 150) between 2nd and 3rd streets N.E.

As Andreas mentioned in 1875, the siting of the courthouse in Independence is particularly successful: "They [the courthouse buildings] are situated on the highest tract of land in the neighborhood, and command a fine view of the city of Independence, the Valley of the Wapsipinicon, and the surrounding Country."[12] The courthouse is a PWA Moderne structure set on a terraced platform within its own landscaped block. The three-story block with a center raised basement is held in place by one-story wings on each side. The tan brick and accompanying stone trim has retained its light color. On the courthouse lawn is a 1950 bronze miniature reproduction of the Statue of Liberty.

NO182 Saint John's Roman Catholic Church

1911. Northeast corner of 2nd St. N.E. and 4th Ave. N.E.

This red brick church trimmed in cast stone was loosely modeled after fifteenth-century French examples. The format includes twin towers, one on each side of the gabled front.

NO183 House

c. 1938. 408 3rd St. N.E.

A thirties Moderne dwelling sheathed in warm yellow brick with red brick trim, this building presents a series of two-story interlocking blocks, resplendent with the usual glass brick, corner windows, curved entrance wall, and obligatory porthole window.

NO184 Illinois Central Railroad Station

c. 1888. 10th St. N.E.

Though modest in size, this brick railway station on a stone base conveys a public scale.

The architect accomplished this by carrying the walls quite high before they meet the roof eaves, by using brick parapeted gables, and finally by creating a dignified procession of rectangular windows. The long platform is covered by an iron roof and passes in front of the train side of the station. On one side, the covered platform is joined to the separate baggage building.

NO185 Cottage

c. 1875. 613 1st Ave. N.E.

The porch facing the street is not the entrance to this cottage but a narrow veranda; the actual entrance is through a small porch to the side. Equally unusual is the manner in which the designer has taken the Eastlake style and modified it by numerous references to the Italianate. The roof, with a central flat section, hovers down over the house like a snug hat. It is occasionally lifted by gables and low wall dormers to provide light and space for the second floor.

NO186 House

c. 1889. 507 2nd Ave. N.E.

This Queen Anne house is distinguished by a pattern of vertical, horizontal, and curved half-timbering which flows like a double pencil line across the facade. Adding to the vigor of the facade is an overscaled lunette window in the attic gable end and a small but deep second-floor porch over the entrance.

NO187 House

c. 1887. Northwest corner of 4th St. N.E. and 3rd Ave. N.E.

A classic Queen Anne dwelling was given a delicate spindled entrance porch, angled corner bay tower, and an accompanying stable/barn to the rear.

NO188 Independence Free Public Library (Munson Building)

1893–1895. 210 2nd St. N.E.

French Châteauesque in style, the library's dominant theme is the entrance tower that rises to three stories plus an attic. The tower houses the staircase, which is reflected on the side by the ascending group of narrow arched windows. The fenestration on the west side consists of large second-floor openings carried up to the base of the entablature and interspersed with small arched windows. Above the entrance is a sculpture of a woman reading, surrounded on each side by intertwined foliage.

NO189 Saint James Episcopal Church

1863, 1873. East side of 2nd Ave. N.E., north of 2nd St. N.E.

Here is the usual format for an Episcopal church: a Gothic church miniaturized nearly to the scale of a dollhouse. This dollhouse quality is enhanced by the springing of the belfry and spire of the tower at a very low point and by the introduction of a small-scaled fireplace and chimney on the front facade. On the side is a row of small, low buttresses between which are pointed windows with painted glass.

NO190 United States Post Office Building

1934, Louis A. Simon. Northeast corner of 2nd St. and 2nd Ave. N.E.

Not a very inspired design, this post office is essentially a brick box which, through a few details—a keystone above the windows, and a lunette—hints at an eighteenth-century Georgian precedent. Inside, however, is a great 1930s WPA mural, *Postman in the Snow,* by Robert Taylor.

NO191 Malek Theater

c. 1941. East side of 2nd Ave. N.E. between 1st St. E. and 2nd St. N.E.

A curved glass bay projects from a picture frame of tan, white, and black vitrolite; the marquee below sports a horizontal pattern of blue and white. All these bright surfaces spring from a respectable box sheathed in cut limestone.

NO192 Wapsipinicon (Wapsie) Mill

1867. 1st St. W. on Wapsipinicon River

This is certainly one of Iowa's most impressive remaining mills. Parts of the present stone foundation derive from an 1854 mill. The building is of brick above the stone first level; above this is a second, smaller gabled section which runs the entire length of the building, and on top of that is a monitor unit. The 1854 mill was built to process wool; the 1867 mill to process feed. From 1915 to 1940 the mill generated electricity. With its location on the river and its accompanying dam, the Wapsipinicon Mill is a major monument in downtown Independence.

NO193 Toman House

1872, attrib. George Josselyn. Southwest corner of 4th St. S.W. and 3rd Ave. S.W.

A meandering Eastlake house is topped by a roof punctured by shed-roofed wall dormers, gables, and very tall chimneys. Yet the building seems to hug the ground because of its low-eaved roof and the horizontal band of fishscale shingles that runs along the facade, connecting the headers of the first-floor windows.

NO194 Cottage

c. 1870. 407 4th Ave. S.W.

A charming little board-and-batten cottage, this dwelling is somewhat Eastlake in feeling. It was moved to this site in 1900.

NO195 House

c. 1940. 115 4th Ave. N.W.

The two-story New England Colonial box is here brought up to date with Moderne curved walls leading into the entrance. These curved walls are in turn surrounded by an abstract rectangular pattern that mimics stone, rendered in wood.

NO196 Cobb House

1915–1916. 410 1st St. W.

An enclosed porch projects to the street and the entrance is to the side in this one-and-a-half-story Prairie house. The ends of the gable roof project in a "Japanese" fashion; a sloped header window is situated in the gable, and wall dormers gently lift upward to provide windows for the second level.

NO196 Cobb House

NO198 Iowa State Hospital for the Insane

NO197 **Rush Park Show Barn**

1889–1890. Southeast corner of 1st St. W. and 19th Ave.

The great attraction for Independence in the years 1889–1892 was the Rush Park Race Track. In its heyday, the park was connected to the city by its own electric railway, one of the earliest in Iowa. The barn is all that remains of this enterprise, but the quality of its design gives some indication of how impressive the whole park must have been. This large horse barn is pure Queen Anne, with an appropriate Queen Anne domed cupola, eyebrow dormers in the roof, shingle-pattern gable ends, and a deep porch with paired columns.

NO198 **Iowa State Hospital for the Insane**
(now Mental Health Institute)

1872–1873, later; S. V. Shipman; Josselyn and Taylor. West on 20th Ave. S.W. to 1st St. W.

The main building is impressively sited on a low rise of ground, and one approaches it and gains views of the building via a long, winding road. This main building (now named the Reynolds Building) presents a version of the French Second Empire style; there is a four-story central pavilion with a mansard roof, and flanking three-story wings terminated by projecting pavilions that also have mansard roofs. The building's front measures over 762 feet in length. The walls are sheathed in a smoothly cut and fitted light-colored limestone, and the building's base is of "native granite, worked from immense boulders."[13]

Iowa Falls

In 1904, the editors of the *Atlas of the State of Iowa* wrote of the site of Iowa Falls, "The Iowa River, close at hand, with bold and rocky bluffs, cut perpendicularly down in places, deep and shady glens, with native timber and smooth prairie land not far distant, combine to make up a most picturesque and romantic spot."[14] The city was laid out in 1855, and by 1857 it had acquired a three-story stone mill and a good-sized hotel.

NO199 **Ellsworth Building / Metropolitan Theater Building**

1889, c. 1915. South side of Washington, between Oaks and Stevens streets

The general impression conveyed by this three-story theater/office/retail-store building is that it is a Beaux-Arts version of an eighteenth-century English Georgian building. On the ground level a wide and grand Richardsonian arch with Sullivanesque overtones provides entrance to the theater. The second and third floors exhibit an almost Adamesque detailing of Ionic columns, quoining, windows with elaborate lintels, round windows, and an elaborate classical entablature and cornice.

NO200 **Iowa Falls State Bank**

c. 1920. Southwest corner of Washington and Stevens streets

A thin slice of a building, this bank is able to assert its presence by the boldness of its Beaux-Arts Classical design and by its wealth of ornamentation. The narrow front (less than 25 feet wide) is conceived of as a temple, dominated by a pair of fluted Corinthian columns in antis. For the side elevation the architect grouped the upper and lower windows into five panels that rest on a limestone base. Brick pilasters between these window panels rise to a false cornice; above this, the solid brick parapet has been interrupted by bands of Roman balustrades. The bank has expanded to the right into a glass-and-metal anticontextual box.

NO201 **United States Post Office Building**

1913, Oscar Weneroth. Northeast corner of Main and Estes streets

This is another episode within the downtown of the use of the eighteenth-century English Georgian precedent. A handsome temple front with four Doric columns faces out to the street and beyond to Estes Park. Within the portico one is greeted by a row of three wall arches, the center one containing the entrance to the building. Graceful sculptural garlands appear over these arches and then are repeated within the tympanum of the pedimented temple front.

NO202 **Saint Matthews-by-the-Bridge Episcopal Church**

c. 1912. Southwest corner of Oak (US 65) and the railroad

Episcopal churches in small communities are usually diminutive, but this one is really delightfully tiny. The sanctuary is housed within a narrow gabled structure perched on the very top of the river bank. An appendage projects slightly toward the street, its shed roof interrupted by two small gable roofs. The larger of these is the entrance, and its gable is carried up as a parapet, with a cross mounted at its apex. The door itself is sheltered by a projecting hood, similar to those often employed by the turn-of-the-century English architect Charles F. A. Voysey. The walls of the building are sheathed in brown stucco, the wood trim is painted red, and the shingle roof is green. As a design, the church is related to the English and the American Arts and Crafts movements.

NO203 **Round Barn**

1916. US 65/20, 2.5 miles north of Iowa Falls, on north side of highway

The idea of suspending the roof of a building by cables hung from a central mast resulted in a structural form that has cropped up (often accompanied by pretentious manifestoes) within the history of modern architecture from the 1920s to the present. Here in this barn and silo, such a structure is presented with directness and great simplicity. A silo drum, topped by a spired roof, is situated in the center of a single-story circular barn. Cables extend from the silo and support the barn roof, so that no interior columns are needed. The walls of this barn and its silo are of hollow terracotta tile; the roof of the barn itself is flat, covered with rolled asphalt roofing. There are three other similar barns within the state, but this is the only one with a flat roof and walls of terracotta tile.

Lake Mills

In downtown Lake Mills there is a handsome two-story Richardsonian Roman-esque commercial building (c. 1890) with a pair of polished granite columns that greet you at its entrance (south side of West Main Street, between Washington and Mill avenues). At the northeast corner of West Main and Mill Avenue is a commercial brick building with red sandstone trim. It exhibits a square corner tower with a metal roof; in style it is Queen Anne coupled with the earlier Italianate. Also on West Main between Washington and Mill avenues is a classic mid-1930s Moderne-style theater, the Mills Theater. The lettering on the marquee is especially effective. Going away from the downtown on Lincoln Avenue (northwest corner of Lincoln and Third avenues) one finds a two-story Queen Anne house (c. 1895) whose wood detailing is closer to the classicism of the Colonial Revival. Southeast of Lake Mills is Rice Lake State Park (drive south on route R74 to route A34, travel east to park entrance). The park contains wood and stone shelters and buildings, a number of which date from the 1930s.

Lakota

Lakota owns one of Iowa's key monuments of the Streamline Moderne of the 1930s. This is its city hall (1940), designed by Thorwald Thorson, a Forest City architect who produced a number of buildings sponsored by the WPA and PWA during that decade. The Lakota City Hall could easily be read as simply a good-sized single-family residence in the Streamline mode. Its front, with a circular bay enclosed by glass brick to the side; its central entrance sheltered by a thin, cantilevered roof; and its fenestration could easily match other houses built throughout the country. The architect has hinted at its more public nature by including a simplified row of dentils and horizontal and vertical grooved patterns. The sides of the building are a little less domestic than the front, but they still appear part of a dwelling. This quality is enhanced by the ample wooded grounds within which the building is situated. The city hall is to be found at the northeast corner of Third and Smith streets.

Laurens

The Des Moines architectural firm of Wetherell and Gage in 1909–1910 provided the community of Laurens with a new Carnegie Public Library. For the design, the architects turned not to the Beaux-Arts Classical but to the informal and homelike Craftsman mode. The resulting stucco building seems to pose as a dwelling, enlarged and made a bit more formal. The entrance wing with its central gable has a suggestion of half-timbering above the door; to each side there is a slight hint of wide pilasters, their capitals composed of a popular motif of the time, four inlaid tiles forming a square. The roof of the building has the feeling of a saltbox, with the rear pitch being longer and more gentle. There are diamond-paned windows within the front bays, and to the side, a Palladian window appears nearly medieval because of its slightly pointed arch. A fireplace originally dominated the interior space of the main floor. The library is located at 263 North Third Street.

Lime Springs

The Lidke Mill (1857, 1917) is located 1 mile north of downtown on Willard Street. The stone mill building and its dam were constructed in 1857 on the Upper Iowa River. The mill was initially planned as a sawmill; late in 1860 it was converted to process flour. The mill burned in 1894, and it was rebuilt to produce cattle feed. The dam was also rebuilt. An electric dynamo was added in 1915; this and the other machinery are still in place. As it exists today the building is a two-story brick structure with a gable roof. There are many small round windows on the second floor and the gable ends. Later modifications and additions included several metal-roofed canopies and entrances.

Another ode to technology in Lime Springs is the A and K Elevator No. 3 (c. 1970), located on the south end of town, off Iowa 157. It is pure high-tech, composed of Butler cylindrical storage units above which appears a fascinating composition of metal tubes, stairs, catwalks, and supports.

Lourdes

Just off US 63 as it passes through Lourdes one will easily see the tall spire of the Roman Catholic Church of the Immaculate Conception (1901). The design of the church is that of a Gothic church loosely derived from small medieval French examples. It has an entrance tower and a steeply pitched gable roof. The rusticated limestone base of the church supports the brick walls, which are accentuated by stone detailing. The quality of the geometric and pictorial designs of the many stained glass windows is impressive.

Lytton

The two-story brick Farmers State Bank building (1915–1916) at Lytton illustrates very clearly how close in many ways the imagery of the Beaux-Arts Classical tradition was to that of the Prairie style. The two street elevations of this building display a row of brick piers between which are placed the windows on both floors. In a traditional fashion the ends of the building are extended to bring a needed sense of solidity to the building. Each of the piers has a symbolic capital in the form of a stone square, and there is a raised rectangular brick panel in each of the spandrels between the windows on the first and second floors. Below the first-floor windows, presented in stone and then in brick, is a series of four shadow lines which work around the building. At each corner of the building and below the simple rectangular false cornice are additional stone squares. None of the stone bears ornamentation; it is as if a Prairie-style bank had been stripped of its ornament. The bank is located at the northwest corner of Main and First streets.

NO204 **Rainbow Bridge**
1914, James B. Marsh, engineer. 16 miles south-southeast of Lytton and south of the community of Lake City

The triple-arched, 525-foot, concrete arched Rainbow Bridge spans the Raccoon River. This bridge, a type in which the roadbed is suspended from arches, is considered to be one of the finest of the Rainbow Bridges in Iowa. The structure was designed by the engineer James B. Marsh, and it was built by the Marsh Rainbow Bridge Company. A similar bridge (the Rock Valley Bridge, 1918), designed by the same engineer, is located 2.9 miles east of Marshalltown, just off US 30. It can be reached from Lytton by traveling east on US 20 to route N41, then south on N41 to Lake City; at the southwest corner of Lake City proceed south on N37 for 2.5 miles.

Manly

Ten miles north of Mason City on US 65 is the small community of Manly, situated within an open and fertile prairie. On Elmore Street, west of Broadway, is the two-story First State Bank building (c. 1915). The designer of this narrow, elegantly detailed building utilized a Beaux-Arts Classical vocabulary of fluted Ionic columns, entablatures, and pedimented lintels. What helps to carry it off is the material of the facade, glistening white glazed terracotta and glazed brick.

While in town proceed to the southeast corner of Harris and Blanche streets where you can see a wonderful historical sequence of grain elevators (c. 1930–

1970); also one can contrast the town's older water tank, supported on four metal legs, to its newer water tower, a globe placed on a single gobletlike stem.

Mason City

By the mid-1870s, Mason City had emerged as the principal city of north central Iowa. The site for the city was selected, as Andreas noted in 1875, for its "advantage of timber, building stone and good water," and the town has also been "favored with excellent railroad facilities." [15] There is nothing remarkable about Mason City's original plat of 1854. The north-south, east-west grid was set out a short distance from the confluence of Lime Creek and Willow Creek. Subsequent additions to the grid in the nineteenth century continued the same basic alignment. The first mill was erected in 1854 on Lime Creek, and others followed shortly. The city's importance as a rail center began in 1869 with the completion of the McGregor and Mississippi Railroad line (now part of the Milwaukee Railroad). Other lines were added in the 1879s, 1880s, and as late as 1909.

The abundance of fine clay for brick and tile encouraged the establishment of several major industries. These were joined by enterprises that used the nearby lime deposit for the manufacture of cement. Other important elements of the economy, historically and now, are food processing, meat packing, and transportation and distribution.

Architecturally, little remains of the early decades after the city was founded. [16] The stone Canon house of 1866 off route 1 represents a late example of a simple one-and-a-half-story Greek Revival house. In the downtown area there are the remains (usually at the second or third floors only) of commercial blocks of the years 1880 through 1900. The Parker Opera House (1883) at 21 North Federal announces its links to the Italianate style quite strongly in its upper two stories. A number of the residential streets of the city still contain many examples of the Queen Anne and Colonial Revival. One of the most interesting of these houses is the Colonial Revival Patton house of 1902 (at 623 North Adams Avenue). The designer of the house seems to have started with the theme of a single two-story volumetric box and then with seeming delight added porches, bays, and wall dormers.

The City Beautiful movement with its characteristic reliance on the Beaux-Arts Classical is exhibited in several public buildings from the turn of the century and later. These include the (former) Mason City Carnegie Library of 1903–1904 (Patton and Miller, 208 East State Street), the former Post Office Building of 1907 (James Knox Taylor, now the city hall, 19 South Delaware Avenue), and an imaginative pergola entrance to the Public Comfort Station in the city's original Central Park of 1855 (Hansen and Waggoner, 1925, 2 North Federal Street).

What has put Mason City on the national scene is its active participation in

Mason City

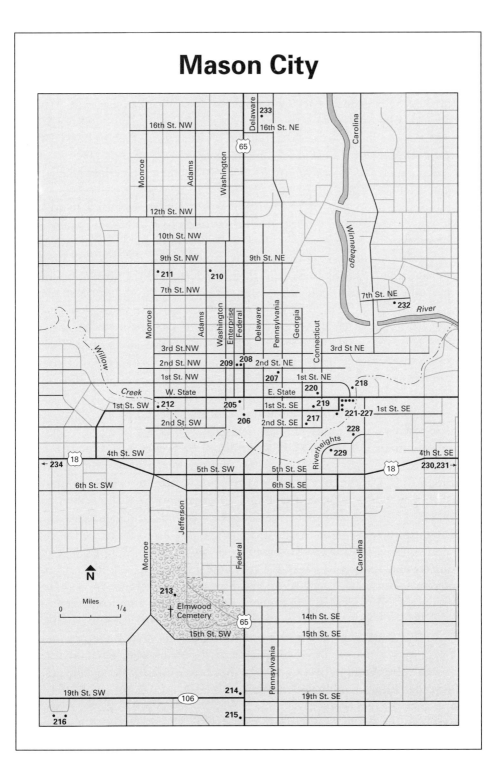

16th St. NW
Delaware
233
16th St. NE
Carolina
65
Monroe
Adams
Washington
Winnebago
12th St. NW
10th St. NW
9th St. NW
9th St. NE
•211
•210
7th St. NW
7th St. NE
•232
River
Monroe
Adams
Washington
Enterprise
Federal
Delaware
Pennsylvania
Georgia
Connecticut
3rd St.NW
3rd St NE
2nd St. NW
209 208
2nd St. NE
Willow
1st St. NW
207
1st St. NE
218
Creek
W. State
E. State
220
1st St. SW
•212
205
1st St. SE
219
221-227
1st St. SE
206
2nd St. SE
217
2nd St. SW
228
•229
Riverheights
4th St. SW
4th St. SE
234
18
5th St. SW
5th St. SE
18
230,231
6th St. SW
6th St. SE
Jefferson
N
Monroe
Federal
Carolina
213
Elmwood
Cemetery
Miles
0   1/4
65
14th St. SE
15th St. SW
15th St. SE
Pennsylvania
19th St. SW
214
19th St. SE
106
215
216

411

the development of Prairie architecture and planning. Frank Lloyd Wright was brought to the community in 1907–1909 to design the City Bank and its accompanying Park Inn (NO205). In 1911, Walter Burley Griffin and Marion Mahoney Griffin entered the scene and planned the idyllic suburban community of Rock Crest-Rock Glen. Previous to this, Wright's associate William Drummond, who had seen to the completion of Wright's bank and hotel, had designed a house in the area. Others of the Prairie group, such as Barry Byrne, realized buildings, or, like Purcell and Elmslie, proposed them. These architects were joined by an intriguing local Prairie school practitioner, Einar O. Broaten.

As always seems to be the case with a situation such as this, a handful of individuals were responsible for introducing the Prairie mode into Mason City and for sponsoring the Rock Crest-Rock Glen development. All of these people were involved in business or the practice of law in the community. They included two lawyers, James Blythe and J. E. Markley, and the development contractor, Joshua Melson. Griffin himself characterized the potential of the site and the approach that should be taken to it: "Rock Crest and Rock Glen occupy two sides of a valley which Willow Creek has carved out of the rocks within three blocks of the central square. . . . The endless fascinating possibilities for domestic architecture with the unexpected variations of view, soil and ruggedness, luxuriance, prominence and seclusion, need only the due attitude of appreciation to work themselves out." [17]

The approach that Griffin took to the suburban design of the valley was in principle identical to the one he had used earlier in laying out Trier Center in Winnetka, Illinois (1911–1912). This consisted of grouping dwellings close to the street, leaving a parklike open space in the center, a space which would be a common for all of the inhabitants of the place. Griffin took full advantage of all of this to produce his own version of a Picturesque English garden, almost a twentieth-century version of one of Capability Brown's mid-eighteenth-century English gardens.

Architecturally, Griffin felt this was a real opportunity—the presence of the tile and cement industry in Mason City could further his introduction of the use of reinforced concrete, both in structure and in aesthetic appeal. He was also enamored of the visual prominence of outcrops of limestone in the area, and this "natural" material entered into all of his designs. Griffin's departure for Australia, where he had won the design competition for the new capital, Canberra, meant that many of his projected dwellings were either never carried out or were modified when built. Griffin brought in Barry Byrne, another of the young Prairie architects, who left his mark through several of the Rock Crest and Rock Glen houses.

In addition to the Prairie houses around Rock Crest and Rock Glen, there are a remarkable number of houses in town which can be related to the style. These include, of course, Wright's 1908 Stockman house (NO218); the Yelland house of 1912–1914, attributed to William Drummond; plus a good number of houses (spec and otherwise) probably designed by the local architects Einar O. Broaten and J. H. Jeffers. If indeed Broaten designed such houses as the Critelli house (1909, NO210) and several other tentatively attributed to him, then the architect should be placed within the front ranks of the Prairie movement.

MASON CITY, DOWNTOWN AND WEST SIDE

NO205 City National Bank / Park Inn
(now Eddie Quinn's / Sylvan Learning Center and the Mason City Fountain Center)

1909–1910, Frank Lloyd Wright. 4 S. Federal Ave./15 W. State St.

The presentation of this bank in the pages of the December 1911 issue of *The Western Architect* characterized it as "an honest pioneer in a field where wasteful pretense and borrowed finery are used to characterize and give distinction to enterprises which are themselves simple and dignified, if treated honestly on their merits." The project was a complex one: to provide and advertise the function of a bank; to create rentable office space; and finally to create retail store space and an inn. Wright's answer to this set of requirements was to create two forms that appear quite independent of one another.

The corner bank building consisted of a solid brick box on the lower level with a much abbreviated volume above held in place by a cantilevered flat roof slab. This upper rectangular form, where the bank's clerestory win-. dows and upper windows are contained between the piers, is directly related to Sullivan's various skyscraper schemes, particularly the Guaranty Building in Buffalo. The hotel/re-

tail store building with its central cantilevered balcony and recessed sections on the second and third floors reads quite effectively as an enlarged domestic structure. Drawings of this complex were published in Wright's famed 1910 Wasmuth portfolio (Berlin), and the design of the hotel building especially had a marked influence on many European architects. In 1926 the building was drastically remodeled; it now stands ready for restoration to its original form. One of R. W. Bock's interior sculptures that originally stood in the main banking room can be seen in the reference room of the Mason City Public Library.

NO206 South Bridge Mall
1983–1985, The Architectural Alliance. S. Federal Ave. at 1st St.

The 1950s and 1960s witnessed the creation of a number of downtown malls across the country. With only a handful of exceptions, these malls were an economic and visual disaster. In the late seventies and eighties a new approach came to the fore: to inject a suburban mall anchored by a department store into an existing downtown grid system. This is what we have in the South Bridge Mall. A block of Federal Avenue (with Frank Lloyd Wright's bank on the corner) has been closed and made into a pedestrian mall. The enclosed shopping center has been built to the south, and behind this is the parking area. From the south the complex appears highly nonurban—it looks like a good, characteristic suburban mall. But the closing of one block of Federal Avenue and its termination with the gable-roofed shopping center is visually not very successful. The street has been divided so that a runway (for fire trucks and delivery) goes down one side; on the other are uncomfortable benches (visually and actually) and a parsimonious planting of trees. Two rows of sharp, rectangular streetlights do not help to tie it all together. To the south the parking lot is one vast surface plane, devoid of any internal planting. On the other hand, the shopping-center building with a glassed gable end and a central glass tower—which projects a rural image in its reference to the architecture of barns—is quite successful.

NO207 **Waltrip Radio Chapel** (now KIMT TV3)

1938, 1954. 122 N. Pennsylvania Ave.

This white stucco Streamline Moderne building has an interesting history. It started out as the radio station of evangelist Reverend Burrough A. Waltrip; then in 1940 it became a Baptist church. In 1954 it returned to radio (with the addition of television) as station KGLO. The marquee has been remodeled. The various satellite dishes on the roof and on the grounds do not add much to the aesthetics of the building.

NO208 **Kirk Modern Apartments**

1903, attrib. J. H. Felt. 206 N. Federal Ave.

A three-story brick apartment building here pays homage to the bay window. The six broad, angular bays and the corner bay tower are sheathed in copper divided into a pattern of square panels. While the two principal entrances reveal Richardsonian Romanesque elements, the building, with its metal balconies, conveys a general turn-of-the-century classical flavor.

NO209 **Suzy-Q Cafe**

c. 1960. Northeast corner of N.W. 2nd St. and N. Enterprise Alley

This is a delightful small restaurant building reminiscent of a diner. The walls are treated in alternating dark and light strips; beside the entrance is a small pylon with curtain signs on two faces and a clock on the narrow facing that looks out to the street.

NO210 **Critelli House**

1909, attrib. Einar O. Broaten. 811 N. Adams Ave.

The architect has taken the theme of the cruciform Prairie house and has manipulated it into a solid, sculptural form reminiscent of some of the pre-1909 Chicago suburban de-

NO210 Critelli House

NO210 Fred Lippert House

signs of Walter Burley Griffin. The arrangement of heavy piers, light wood members, and small openings is awkward, but this very quality creates a remarkable interpretation of the Prairie mode. Another nearby version of the Prairie box which is attributed to Broaten is the Fred Lippert house (1914) at 521 North Washington Avenue. An exact copy of this house was built around 1916 at West Bend.

NO211 **Lawrence House**

1930, Nick Netzel (builder and designer). 1217 N. Monroe Ave.

A charming Spanish Colonial Revival bungalow, this residence features an arched opening leading into the entrance porch, with a tiny walled terrace to the side. The roof is parapeted except for a tinge of tile over the entrance. The rough, tactile stucco walls are of a finish labeled "Spanish Lac" in trade journals. Mason City has several other Spanish Colonial or Mediterranean Revival houses. There are two small bungalows also designed by local contractor Nick Netzel, one at 904

Tenth Street Northeast (1938) and one at 415 Fourteenth Street Northwest (1940). The earlier Wiley house of 1917 at 24 South Vermont Avenue represents a transition between the Mission and the Spanish Colonial Revival styles.

NO212 **White Eagle Service Station** (now Home Video)

1930. 418 S.W. 1st St.

The ideal image for a service station in the 1920s was either the Colonial or the medieval revival style. This former service station announces its French Norman medieval heritage in its steeply pitched, sweeping roofs, and above all in its street-front gable with its pattern of half-timbering.

NO213 **Melson Mausoleum**

1915, Barry Byrne. Elmwood Cemetery, S. Federal Ave. and S.W. 14th St.

The Melson mausoleum brings the design principles of the Prairie architect into clear focus, with no disruption of mundane functional living requirements. Two low masonry slabs hug the center slab, which is slightly higher. Between them is a piece of finely polished granite with the family name on it. This slab sits on a thin, horizontal stone base which projects out and locks into the adjoining slabs. It is all very simple, but visually very impressive.

NO214 **Service Station**

c. 1925. Northwest corner of S. Federal Ave. and S.W. 19th St.

A tiny English cottage with a steeply pitched roof houses the office and small store of this service station. The design includes an entrance gable, a segmental arched door, and the needed rooftop chimney.

NO215 **Engine House No. 2**

1939, Hansen and Waggoner. 2020 S. Federal Ave.

A thirties Moderne building, this engine house is more Art Deco than Streamline Moderne. The local Mason City architects articulated the hose-drying tower with layered panels and central vertical piers. Especially impressive is the lettering over the fire truck en-

trance; it has been realized in wide letters actually indented into the brick surface.

NO216 **Odd Fellows Home / Orphan Home**

1901, 1906, 1912, Liebbe, Nourse and Rasmussen. 1037 S.W. 19th St.

The architectural theme of these two brick buildings with stone bases is English Georgian. The Odd Fellows home was built in 1901–1902; it burned in 1905 and was rebuilt the following year. Its grand feature is a two-story pedimented porch enclosed between two wings. The 1912 Orphans Home has a large pedimented entrance piece, and each of its encompassing end wings terminates in two-story porches with Ionic columns; the porches are elevated on raised basements.

MASON CITY, EAST SIDE

NO217 **First Methodist Church** (now United Methodist Church)

1951. Northeast corner of S. Georgia Ave. and S.E. 2nd St.

A post–World War II version of a Georgian church was brought up to date here by references to the 1930s Art Deco Moderne. The building's most decidedly Moderne feature is its tower composed of a square base surmounted by vertical and horizontal layered drums.

NO218 **Stockman House**

1908, Frank Lloyd Wright. 311 S.E. 1st St. (house was moved in 1988 to corner of 1st St. N.E. and E. State St.)

Here is the classic two-story Prairie house with a central block covered by a low-pitched hipped roof; on each side are single-floor wings. On the left is an enclosed living porch and on the right the entrance. The fenestration of the three principal facades is symmetrical, with the major emphasis on the horizontal. This scheme was often used by Wright and other Prairie architects during the years 1906 and later. Wright popularized this classic Prairie scheme in the pages of the April 1906 issue of the *Ladies Home Journal*. In the scheme, "a fireproof house for $5,000" was to be of concrete. Most houses of this type, including the Stockman dwelling, were of conventional wood frame and were generally sheathed in cement stucco.

NO219 **Franke House**

1916. 320 1st St. S.E.

The open block plan of the Prairie school was applied here: living room across the front, dining room and kitchen to the rear. Like the nearby Stockman house, the entrance is on one side and a living porch is on the other. As the Prairie style developed in the mid-teens, there was a tendency to conceive of the building as a series of rectangular volumes devoid of gable roofs with overhanging hipped ends. The Franke house exhibits this approach, except for the living porch where it seems casually to revert to the traditional wide overhanging hipped roof.

NO220 **Harper House**

1919. 16 N. Connecticut Ave.

A Prairie-style/Craftsman bungalow was realized here in brick with a tile roof. While the one-and-a-half-story bungalow conveys modesty in size, the house is in fact of good size and even includes a porte-cochère adjacent to the entrance porch. A fascinating design feature is the manner in which the windows in the front gable are made to follow the pitch of the entrance porch roof.

NO221 **Blythe House**

1913–1914, Walter Burley Griffin. 431 1st St. S.E., Rock Crest-Rock Glen

This was the second of two houses designed by Griffin for James Blythe, one of the partners responsible for the development of Rock Crest-Rock Glen. As befitting a city in which one of the major industries was the manufacture of cement, the Blythe house was constructed of reinforced concrete. The plan was a variation on the open two-story block plan so often used by Wright and others. But as with most of Griffin's designs, the scheme was made much more complex, with a narrow entrance/vestibule where one can look over a wall; interior partial openings between the living room and dining room; and a curious veranda that seemingly wishes to be both an enclosed porch and an open terrace.

The house was not built entirely as Griffin's original sketches indicate. The lower portion of the building is clad in stone, because of the slope of the terrain (not at all acknowledged in the sketches), and a podium was provided, but neither of these elements was present in the original design. Also changed was the drive-through garage (again, one suspects, because of the slope of the land). A number of exterior features were eliminated, including corner roof urns, pylons above the corners of the main roof, and a series of pergolalike beam ends projecting out over the cornice. The roof fascia has been kept close to the wall surface so that the rectangular volumetric form reads strongly.

NO222 **Page House**

1912, Walter Burley Griffin. 21 Rock Glen

This was the first of Griffin's realized designs for Rock Crest-Rock Glen. It is another exercise in the classic Prairie school open block plan. As in earlier work in the suburbs of

Chicago, Griffin here employed a low-pitched cross-gable roof with extensive overhangs at the gable ends. A drive-through garage (added later) was located directly on the street; at the rear, to accommodate the slope of the land, he placed the house on an ashlar block stone foundation punctured in the center by a deeply cut arched window.

NO223 **MacNider House**

1959, Curtis Besinger. 15 Rock Glen

The architect of this 1950s Usonian house had been a member of Frank Lloyd Wright's Taliesin Fellowship. He employed concrete block for the walls, and he covered and held the composition to the ground by a broadly overhanging gable roof.

NO224 **Blythe-Rule House**

1912–1913, Walter Burley Griffin. 11 Rock Glen

A two-story Prairie box, the Blythe-Rule house is beautifully realized and wonderfully sited. Griffin provided ground-pressing piers at each of the first-floor corners of the block; above these on the second floor there is a bank of corner casement windows that help to create a contrasting light feeling on the second floor. The roof extends far out over the second floor and is composed of a flat section around the perimeter and a low-pitched section in the center which terminates in the low, massive chimney block.

NO225 **Franke House**

1917, Barry Byrne. 507 E. State St.

In this instance the Prairie school mode has been modified so that the walls read as sur-

faces delicately punctuated by windows placed close to the surface. The Franke house illustrates how a number of the younger Prairie architects were looking directly to Europe for inspiration; for example, this house shares many features found in the pre-World War II work of the Viennese architect Josef Hoffmann, such as his 1908 exhibition for the Vienna Art School.

NO226 **Gilmore House**

1915, Barry Byrne. 511 E. State St.

A mixture of Viennese Secessionist architecture and the Prairie school has not quite been brought off in this Byrne design. The treatment of the gables, almost as applied triangles, and the feeling that the accompanying entablature has been merely applied signal a relationship to architecture in Central Europe, but the window grouping and the stone base refer to Griffin's nearby work.

NO227 **Schneider House**

1915, Walter Burley Griffin/Barry Byrne. 525 State St.

The Prairie school design of this house is similar to that of the 1912 Page house (NO222), but it seems less resolved in its detailing, due perhaps to the fact that it was partially redesigned by Byrne when he took over the commission. The house's two most unusual features are its entrance bridge from the public sidewalk and street, and the cantilevered sleeping porch which Byrne added to the house in the 1920s.

NO228 **Melson House**

1912–1914, Walter Burley Griffin. 56 River Heights Dr.

The Melson house can be considered one of the half dozen most significant houses of the Prairie movement, and it is certainly Griffin's most impressive realized domestic design. The house was designed for J. G. Melson, one of the developers of Rock Crest-Rock Glen. The site is unquestionably the most theatrical of any of the houses, for the house is situated right on the edge of a limestone outcropping overlooking the valley. Marion Mahoney Griffin fully captured the spirit of the house in her rendering published in the August 1913 issue of *The Western Architect*. Here the

NO228 Melson House

stone-clad house slowly but dramatically grows out of the natural limestone ledges, becoming more apparently man made near the top. Griffin penetrated the horizontal parapet with groups of immense, overscaled voussoir keystones over each group of windows. The heavy stone and pronounced masonry detailing convey an almost Baroque quality, such as one might encounter in Italian gardens of the late seventeenth or early eighteenth century.

A comparison of the Melson house with Frank Lloyd Wright's famed Kaufmann house at Bear Run, Pennsylvania (1936), effectively illustrates two radically different approaches to nature and the organic. Wright's scheme, with no reticence whatsoever, asserts itself and utterly dominates the scene; it heightens the sense of the organic by its strong contrast. In opposition, Griffin comments on nature in a more subtle fashion, by exaggerating that which is natural.

The plan of the house is actually a variation on the Prairie-style open block plan. As with his other designs at Rock Crest–Rock Glen, Griffin has dealt imaginatively with the automobile. A double drive-through garage intervenes between the street and the house. Directly behind the garage is an entrance corner; the front entrance is on one side and the service entrance on the other.

NO229 Yelland House

1912–1914, attrib. William Drummond. 37 River Heights

William Drummond, who had worked for Wright in the Oak Park studio, was sent to supervise the construction of Wright's City National Bank and Park Inn. This Prairie-style open-block-plan house has all the earmarks of Drummond's work in and around Chicago. Generally his designs, in contrast to Griffin's, have an almost Japanese lightness about them. One can really sense the thin wood balloon or platform frame, lightly sheathed in wood or stucco. And Drummond often had a tendency, as one can see in the Yelland house, to accentuate this delicate quality by applying patterns of small boards to his stucco walls. In plan the Yelland house provides a living porch on the front, with its entrance on the right side.

NO230 Krieger's Garden Center

c. 1970. US 18 (S.E. 4th St.), 2 miles east of Federal Ave.

A nursery garden center asserts its presence to the highway by means of a good-sized sign depicting a watering can.

NO231 MacNider House (Indian Head; now Gerard of Iowa School)

1929, Waddy B. Wood. US 18 (S.E. 4th St.), 3.5 miles east of Federal Ave.

The main block of this two-and-a-half-story house with chimneyed end walls is loosely based upon mid-eighteenth-century American Georgian architecture, especially the type found in and around Philadelphia. Though sheathed in stone, the building is in fact of reinforced concrete, befitting its owner, the president and general manager of the Northwestern States Portland Cement Company.

NO232 Egloff House

1939, E. Richard Cone. 655 N.E. 7th St.

The Saint Paul, Minnesota, architect E. Richard Cone provided his client with the latest image in this Streamline Moderne dwelling. Into the white painted brick walls of the two-story house he has placed a variety of window shapes, ranging from portholes to elongated stepped windows that mirror the internal circular staircase. A feature seldom encountered in Moderne designs is the sloped, exposed-steel roof used over a portion of the house.

Another Mason City example of this 1930s Moderne style (more Art Deco than Streamline Moderne) is the Sundell House (1911) at 40 Oak Drive, designed by Frank Pierce.

NO233 **Calvary Methodist Episcopal Church** (now North Side Multipurpose Center)

1913, E.R. Bogardus. 1615 N. Delaware Ave.

California's Mission Revival was surprisingly popular in the Midwest for churches, schools, and recreation buildings. This small example has a pair of scalloped, parapeted gable ends, arched windows, and stuccoed walls. It was constructed as a church for workers at the nearby meat-packing plant. Another example of the Mission Revival is the Gildner house

(1914) at 217 Fifth Street Northwest, designed by J. W. Trafzer.

NO234 **Drive-in Theater**

c. 1950. US 18, west of the city limits

The structure that intervenes between the highway and the interior of the theater, including the drive-through entrance, is loosely Colonial Revival, i.e., it has gabled roofs and dormers, and clapboard siding. But what greets those who purchase tickets is a ticket booth in a pure Streamline Moderne style. The front of the booth is a semicircle; the lower section of it, continuing around to the side walls, is covered in glass brick, with clear glass above. The roof of the booth is composed of layers of semicircles that descend to the top of the booth.

Morrison

Route 175 traverses the small town of Morrison. On the north side of the highway is a small clapboard-sheathed church (c. 1890) topped by a roof with hipped gable ends. The belfry of the square tower—almost a separate campanile—is housed within the church's steep roof, with four openings provided by shed-roof dormers. The T-shaped patterns of windows at the principal gable end are gathered together and contained within a single gabled panel.

Across the highway is a former public school building on a raised basement (c. 1905), now housing the Grundy County Museum. The schoolhouse—built of brick with stone trim—conveys the impression of a domesticated version of the Beaux-Arts style, except for the wide-arched entrance which takes one back to H. H. Richardson and his version of the Romanesque. Next door to the schoolhouse is the restored Peck log cabin (1853), which has been moved from a rural site to this location.

Nashua

A mile west of the Cedar River town of Nashua (on Iowa 346) is one of Iowa's most popular monuments, the Little Brown Church in the Vale. The church became known through the popular hymn "The Church in the Wildwood," written by William S. Pitts in the late 1850s after he visited the site of the church in 1857. The church itself was supposedly built on the very spot described by Pitts. It was designed by the Rev. J. K. Nutting and built during the years 1860–1864. The church building is a simple clapboard structure with an entrance tower at one end. Pointed arched windows and doors suggest that the building design was derived from the Gothic tradition. The church was located in the now nonexistent community of Bradford, a settlement has been reconstituted recently as the Bradford Pioneer Village, located down the street. The village consists of a number of historic and reconstructed buildings, including a railroad depot, a country schoolhouse, and a three-room cottage. Perhaps the best summation of the church and the village is the wonderful little model of the church, which stands in the parking lot.

Returning to Nashua, if one travels 2 miles west on route B60 one will come to the Brooks Round Barn (c. 1914). This barn with a double-pitched gambrel roof has walls of terracotta tile. Inside, at the center, is a silo that rises to the roof. The building measures 60 feet in diameter, and the silo is 16 feet across. In addition to the large doors, there are 21 windows.

Proceeding this time 5 miles south of Nashua on US 218, one will find an octagonal wooden barn dating from 1887. The building has a cone-shaped roof, and at one time it was probably surmounted by either a cupola or a windmill.

New Hampton

The town of New Hampton was platted in 1857 on the open prairie between the Little Turkey River to the east and the Wapsipinicon River to the west. In 1879 the town was connected to the Chicago, Milwaukee, and Saint Paul Railroad. The original town plat placed the courthouse square one block north of Main Street, and by the 1870s this public square had developed as a distinct civic center with two of the principal churches facing onto the open square. There are a number of surviving late nineteenth-century business blocks on G Avenue. The most vigorous of these is the two-story brick Central Block of 1879, located at 173–175 G Avenue. Though it has been remodeled, the Central Block retains a strong cornice, and stone-arched windows on the second floor.

NO235 **Chickasaw County Courthouse**

1929, Ralston and Ralston. Southeast corner of Court St. E. and N. Chestnut Ave.

The present Beaux-Arts courthouse (1929) replaced a lively Italianate/French Second Empire building (1881). The newer building is of Bedford limestone. Its three-story mass was designed in a traditional, classical fashion, with the ground floor as a basement and the upper two floors articulated by wide pilasters. The principal entrance is emphasized by a low entrance porch and a clock face projecting above the parapet.

NO236 **House**

c. 1889. 122 N. Chestnut Ave.

This two-story Queen Anne dwelling is set apart by a richly decorated porch of turned woodwork, together with gable ends surfaced in relief sculpture.

NO237 **House**

c. 1895. 215 N. Chestnut Ave.

A Queen Anne design establishes its character through volumes rather than a richness of details. The Colonial Revival details and the substantial stone foundation provide substance and a degree of classical sensibility to the two-story clapboard dwelling.

NO238 **Saint Joseph's Roman Catholic Church**

c. 1901. West side of Broadway between Court and Hale streets

The sharp contrast between the thin lines of the limestone trim and the brickwork of the walls comes close to conveying a sense of a drawing rather than an actual building. The references to the European High Gothic are loosely and inventively interpreted.

NO239 **House**

c. 1875. Southeast corner of E. Prospect and N. Water streets

The Gothic and the Italianate styles have been brought together in the design of this two-and-a-half-story house. The angled two-story bay window and the pedimented window are strongly Italianate, while the steeply pitched roof and wall dormers point to the Gothic. The specific manner in which all of these

features have been brought together is highly unusual.

NO240 **Cottage**

c. 1880. Southeast corner of E. Hampton St. and S. Locust Ave.

The designer of the little one-and-a-half-story cottage was obviously determined to get in as many references as possible, and he certainly succeeded. Though essentially Queen Anne in style, the composition is enriched with both Italianate and Eastlake details. The small gable over the entrance of the front porch is surfaced in a floral pattern, and this lush decoration continues down into the thin columns and the sawed and turned work of the porch. The windows and bays on the ground floor are all overscaled.

New Providence

The community's city hall (1928) is located right on Iowa 299 as it passes north-south through town. Under most circumstances the tiny city hall would not be recognized as a public building except for its name being cut into a limestone panel above the entrance door. The only decorative notes on this enlarged red brick building are the smaller bricks at each corner, the raised parapet above the sign panel, and the panel's definition by two squares of stone below the corners of the sign, with quarter-round pieces of stone used as a transition to the higher parapet. The building is situated on a corner lot, with space left around it. This is certainly an example of civic modesty, if nothing else.

Also within town is an early-1900s single-story dwelling in the Colonial Revival mode. While the dwelling is only on one level, it asserts its presence with a four-piered porch surmounted by a steeply pitched gable roof. Within this enclosed pediment is a single large-scale round window. The house is located at the northeast corner of Grape Avenue and Quincy Street.

At the northern outskirts of town on Iowa 299 is the community's auditorium and gymnasium. It was built in 1936 and was designed by Keffer and Jones. The brick-clad building consists of a circular drum covered by a low-pitched conical roof. It has a rectangular entrance pavilion that is equipped with two slightly projecting bays with some vertical decoration in brick. In style the building is PWA Moderne pared down quite a bit.

Northwood

Northwood, situated on the east bank of the Shell Rock River, had its economic future assured when it became the county seat of Worth County in 1863, and when the Central Railroad of Iowa was completed through the town. The town was laid out in 1857 and again in 1858, and it was described as being "regularly laid out, with wide handsome streets."[18]

NO241 (Former) Worth County Courthouse

1880. Southwest corner of Central and 10th streets

With buildings such as this, one can only wish that more counties had found it possible to retain their older courthouses and put them to new uses. The 1880 Worth County Courthouse was an enlarged two-story Italianate "house" on a raised basement. It was, for an 1880s courthouse, a rather plain, inexpensive building that cost $4,811. For that small sum the residents of the county obtained a dignified brick building whose major visual emphasis is concentrated on the solid lunettes (with their stone keystones) over the windows. Behind the courthouse (now used by the Worth County Historical Society) is the one-room wood Swensrude schoolhouse (c. 1860s) in the Greek Revival mode. The schoolhouse was moved to this location from a rural site northeast of Northwood.

NO242 Worth County Courthouse

1893, Henry R. P. Hamilton. Northeast corner of Central and 10th streets

The courthouse is mildly Richardsonian Romanesque, though the main tower, with a steeply pitched roof and elongated wall dormers, falls within the Châteauesque mode. The courthouse—built of red brick, with sandstone foundations and trim—was designed by the Cleveland architect H. R. P. Hamilton, who specialized in public buildings. The courthouse was remodeled in 1938 and in the process its centerpiece—the upper portions of its Châteauesque tower—was removed. The building also acquired at that time a few hints of the thirties Moderne, including, of course, glass brick.

NO243 House

1874. 907 1st Ave. S.

The Eastlake style in Iowa often tended to produce some of the state's most interesting examples of "Victorian" architecture. This house is one of them. The roof is composed of several low-pitched gables, each emblazoned with intricate sawed wood openwork.

The entrance porch, with stairs at a 45-degree angle to the corner, is one of the most intriguing designs found in Iowa.

NO244 Worth County State Bank

1906. North side of Central between 8th and 9th streets

Another of Northwood's significant contributions to American architecture forms the Beaux-Arts answer to the Prairie architects and their midwestern banks. The architect of this building has created a single two-story arched window held firmly in place by deep, horizontal, joined masonry piers on each side. Above, the entablature and cornice curve upward, mirroring the window arch below. Though the window has been filled in with glass brick, it still functions well.

NO245 Bob Helgeland Jeweler Clock Sign

c. 1925. South side of Central, between 8th and 9th streets

A narrowly faceted iron pole supports an enlarged pocket watch of the 1920s. The sign portion is attached above and below. It was manufactured by George Cutler and Company of South Bend, Indiana.

NO246 Commercial Building, c. 1900

NO246 **Commercial Building**

c. 1900; 611 Central

A high hipped roof has been dramatically placed on a simple two-story clapboard box; the hooped curve of the roof is mirrored below in the overscaled lunette window. The door on the second floor indicates that a porch or balcony is now missing.

NO247 **Log Cabin** (Worth County Historical Society)

c. 1860s. South side of Central, between 4th and 5th streets

This small building made of squared logs with corners treated as tenon joints conveys the "pioneer" image typical of the homes of nineteenth-century Iowa settlers.

Odebolt

On entering Odebolt from the east on Iowa 175 one is confronted by the roadside "ruin" of a late 1920s service station. Its steeply pitched roof with a central gable dormer is loosely medieval, though the double-hung windows relate to the Colonial Revival. On the opposite corner is a wonderful row of four corncribs with gable roofs (c. 1915), each with its own venting cupola.

West of Main Street on Second Street is the two-story brick and stone-trimmed Masonic Hall (c. 1889). A large-scaled arched opening announces the entrance to the hall and stairs leading up to the Masonic quarters on the second floor. Countering this entrance to the Masonic Hall is an assertive corner entrance to the ground-floor bank. The other storefronts of the building have been filled in with wood, yet the structure retains much of its original character; however, much of the facade has recently been covered with corrugated metal.

A little farther along on Second Street, in the 500 block, is the domestically scaled American Legion Hall (c. 1910), a single-story building with a garden pergola of projecting beams. The pergola has been enclosed and a wide river-boulder fireplace and chimney has been added.

Finally, at 314 Lincoln Street is a Prairie house reminiscent of George Maher's work. This house was designed for A. C. Petersmeyer in 1917 by the Des Moines firm of Liebbe, Nourse and Rasmussen. The low-pitched hipped roof has been projected out over the brick walls below. The proportions of the house, the balanced symmetry, and the shape of the windows hark back to Frank Lloyd Wright's Winslow house of 1893 in River Forest, Illinois.

NO248 **First National Bank (Odebolt State Bank)**

1914, Graham, Burnham and Company. Northeast corner of Main and Second streets

Within the small downtown is the First National Bank, which was designed by Graham, Burnham and Company of Chicago. Its design is that of a Doric temple; there is a row of six columns on the gable end and there are engaged pilasters along each flank. There is a severe, puritanical quality about the design, which seems to look back to early Greek Revival bank buildings of the 1820s and 1830s.

Oelwein

Within Orville Christophel Park, at the northwest corner of First Avenue and First Street Southwest, is the Burch Log Cabin (1852). This split-log, one-and-a-half-story cabin was moved to the park in 1941. In the downtown at 110 North Frederick Street is a Streamline Moderne Standard Oil Company Service Station built around 1939 and still very much in use. The community's United States Post Office Building at the southwest corner of First Street Northeast and First Avenue Northeast was designed by the Washington, D.C., office of James A. Wetmore and was built in 1931. This brick-sheathed box was meant to be read as Colonial Revival; the specific historical language used was that of the American Federal style coupled with the English Regency.

Osage

Osage was platted in 1853 on a low rise of the prairie, a little over a mile from the Cedar River. The extensive grid of the town was broken by a four-block public square, and, to the north, by Huldship Park, composed of another four-block segment. In the center of the town's grid, provision was made for a one-block square to encompass the county courthouse; a second block to the east was set aside as a "College Square." The tracks of the Illinois Central Railroad, along with the passenger station and yards, cut across the north-south, east-west grid at its southwest corner.

NO249 **Mitchell County Courthouse**

1856–1858. Southeast corner of 5th and State streets

With its location in a residential section of the town, the courthouse conveys the impression that it is a suburban college building. The design of the courthouse with a pedimented portico with four columns is in the Greek Revival mode. Added to this theme are a number of jarring, discordant notes: columns with mushroom capitals that are almost (but not quite) Egyptian in flavor; vertical segmented windows that one would associate with the Italianate; and a domed tower with pointed windows. The building has all of the qualities of a do-it-yourself vernacular design carried out with great enthusiasm.

NO250 **The Press Building**

c. 1870. South side of Main St. between 5th and 6th streets

In this two-story commercial building the designer compressed a richness of details into its relatively narrow streetfront. There are accentuated verticals composed of masonry and metal piers on the street level; above, two segmental arched windows crowd toward the central arched window from each side; finally the entablature and cornice exhibit dentils, different groups of supporting brackets, and then a segmental arch that projects above the parapet (covered by a centrally placed finial). Though somewhat remodeled and painted—

Colonialized—the building remains as an eye-catching assertion on Main Street.

NO251 **Commercial Building**

c. 1895. South side of Main St. near 7th and Chestnut streets

The street level has been "modernized" on this two-story building, yet its strong character is established by the open loggia on the second floor, a visual device seldom found in midwestern commercial buildings.

NO252 **Municipal Light Plant**

1941, Hubbard Engineering Company. Southeast corner of 7th and Chestnut streets

This Moderne structure in light tan brick incorporates glass-block openings and an entrance with doors bearing half circles of glass. The signage is unusual and successful, consisting of a band of polished granite blocks with modernized, delicately carved uppercase Roman letters.

NO253 **Cottage**

c. 1875, and later. 803 Pleasant St.

The nineteenth-century designer mixed the Gothic and Eastlake together, accompanied by a nod or two to the Italianate. Then in the twentieth century a new roof covered by large side-lap asphalt shingles was added, and the porch and bays were then clothed in stone (or concrete cast in imitation of stone?). Remodelings such as this can often destroy a building, but not in this case; each change has helped.

NO254 **Husting House**

1916, Howard B. Burr. 926 Pleasant St.

A two-story Prairie-style residence, the Husting house boasts a Maher-like segmental arched entrance, insistent horizontal banding, and a commodious screened porch projecting to one side. The entrance is particularly grand—it has wide steps and encompassing parapeted walls. The home's owner, V. A. Husting, ran a tobacco and cigar store in Osage; the house was built by the Smith Lumberyard in Osage. The architect, Howard B. Burr of Waterloo, designed three Prairie-style houses in Osage.

NO255 **House**

c. 1895. 820 Main St.

The Queen Anne is here reined in by the discipline of Colonial Revival classicism. The glassed-in second-floor porch above the entrance presents a semicircular opening to the front and windows with pointed arches to the side.

NO256 **First Baptist Church**

c. 1878. Southeast corner of 7th and Mechanic streets

This is a good instance of what is popularly thought of as Victorian "Carpenter's Gothic"; it is also an excellent illustration of how a design can be made up of separate parts seemingly casual in their assemblage. Around the upper section of the walls of the Akron-plan sanctuary is a pattern of stunted Gothic arched windows; in some instances all the windows in the group are of the same size, in others the central window is higher. Glass bricks have been used to fill in the windows in the raised basement, and surprisingly this is a plus for the building.

NO257 **House**

c. 1882. 633 Mechanic St.

One can certainly use the term "abstracted" here in reference to the designer's approach to this turn-of-the-century Colonial Revival building. Particularly thoughtful is the manner in which the clapboard skin of the corner bay tower simply becomes the surface for the adjoining gabled wing. At the side a two-story bay has been reduced to a simple segmental curve, the windows and door detailing flowing easily across it.

NO258 **House**

c. 1875. 628 Walnut St.

A sizable red brick Italianate villa is set within extensive suburban grounds that include a large barn and stables. A wide cupola enriched by groups of double-hung windows surmounts the roof of the main section of the house. The one-and-a-half-story service wing to the rear exhibits wall dormers with gable roofs that break through the wide entablature and projecting cornice of the roof.

NO259 **Gardner House**

1919, Howard B. Burr. 518 7th St.

Another of Osage's Prairie-style houses, this one is based on Frank Lloyd Wright's *Ladies Home Journal* Prairie-style box of 1906, with its porch projecting to the front. It is sheathed in narrow clapboard up to the sills of the second-floor windows, then plastered above and onto the wide soffit of the hipped roof.

NO260 **Carden House**

1919, Howard B. Burr. 420 Walnut St.

Burr would seem to have looked to the Chicago work of both Tallmadge and Watson as well as George W. Maher for the design of this house. The somewhat monumental entrance is contained in a wing to one side; a narrow glass-enclosed porch projects to the street. A typical Maher-like curved dormer looks out from the low-pitched hipped roof. The lower portion of the house is sheathed in narrow clapboard, and there is stucco between the second-floor windows.

NO261 **Cedar Valley Seminary** (now Mitchell County Historical Society)

1863. Southwest corner of Mechanic and 6th streets

This two-story brick Italianate building was to have been the first of a series of college buildings to be erected on the campus. Verticality was the theme in the design of the building; its surface is composed of projecting and recessed narrow vertical panels; the windows, especially those of the second level, are detailed as extremely thin, vertical rectangles.

NO262 **House**

c. 1889. 427 Mechanic St.

A one-and-a-half-story brick structure serves as a secure base for a wild array of wood porches and bays. At the entrance, a two-story bay projects right through the entrance porch; to the side of the porch area is a pair of diamond-shaped windows. As to style, the wood detailing of this house is Queen Anne.

NO263 **House**

c. 1931. 217 5th St.

The outstanding attraction of this well-executed English Tudor period revival house is the birdhouse in the garden, which turns out to be an exact miniature reproduction of the house. The dwelling is essentially a simple box made highly varied and picturesque by a steeply pitched roof and surfaces of brick, stucco, and half-timbering.

NO264 **House**

c. 1868. 333 Chase St.

An Italian villa in brick, this dwelling has a wide entablature that houses narrow attic windows. A cupola graces the rooftop, and the entrance doorway is deeply sunk into the body of the building.

NO265 **House**

c. 1872. 119 N. 4th St.

The three-story tower of this brick Italianate villa is crowned by a high mansard roof. The light-colored stone quoining adds a high degree of richness to the surfaces of the building.

Ossian

As one enters the town from the northwest on US 52 one will encounter a log cabin placed in a small park. This was brought to the park in 1976. The cabin is a one-and-a-half-story building with a shed-roof lean-to on one side. The logs for the walls have been squared up; the windows are six lighted and double hung. Continuing on Main Street, just before Lydia Street, one finds the former Ossian Opera House of 1893. The building is unusual in its design; it's more the type of structure one would expect to find in a parklike setting. The two-story gabled portion is flanked by a shed-roof section and an entrance loggia to the street front. It is sheathed in clapboard, and shingles are employed in the gable end.

Situated at the northwest corner of Brook and West Avenue is a one-and-a-half-story Eastlake cottage in brick. The gable ends continue T-shaped braces, and under the eaves is a wide entablature covered with sawed work, almost Gothic Revival in flavor. A new brick porch has replaced the original one at the front.

Parkersburg

Parkersburg was established in 1865 by the Dubuque and Sioux City Railroad Company. The site selected was a locale of hilly terrain, just south of the South Branch of Beaver Creek.

NO266 **Bank Building**

c. 1890. 222 3rd St.

A well-composed two-story Richardsonian Romanesque block, this former bank building has lower walls of rusticated quartzite, but brick and quartzite trim was used on the second floor. The commanding feature of the building is the horizontal band of short, thick columns that intervene between each of the three arched openings. This band of engaged columns is reinforced by an upper band of the capitals and by the slightly recessed headers of the two windows and the entrance. The building has a raised basement. The original stone balustraded stairs to the first-floor entrance are still in place.

NO267 **Parkersburg State Bank Building**

c. 1917. Northwest corner of 3rd and Coats streets

Beaux-Arts Classicism is here cast in a lighter mood than usual. The lower floor of this limestone building exhibits a pair of picture-framed large windows on each side of the center entrance. On the second floor, the three windows with transoms are separated from one another by a pair of thin, delicate engaged columns. The entablature bears the building's name in the center, and on each side is a pattern of classical swags.

NO268 **House**

c. 1890s. 202 Railroad St.

Here one encounters a one-and-a-half-story dwelling with a mansard roof and a tall central cupola. But the design is certainly not French Second Empire, nor is it Queen Anne or Colonial Revival. The proportions of the house, the row of strange gabled dormers

gazing out from the mansard roof, and the porch columns placed on raised stone piers have all the hallmarks of a grand do-it-yourself project.

NO269 **Wolf House** (now Parkersburg Historical Home)

1895. 401 5th St.

It is the tall, thin, three-story bay tower with a high conical roof, combined with the large-scaled arched entrance porch, which immediately captures one's attention in the design of this house. The local banker, C. C. Wolf, who had the house built, chose a designer who employed a Richardsonian Romanesque vocabulary, but the house seems like a series of large-scale building fragments that have not quite been put together. This fragmented quality is juxtaposed at various points with counterefforts to unify the design, as in the elongated corbel table that has been carried out under the eaves of the house and then continued and wrapped around the bay tower. With the large scale of the entrance on one side of the street facade, one expects that the house will also branch out on the other side, but it doesn't. The house has been restored by the Parkersburg Historical Society, and is open to the public.

Plainfield

Two miles north of Plainfield to the west of US 218 is an early example of an octagonal barn (1887). This barn has walls of horizontal shiplap boards and a roof that is shingled. Soike speculates that there was probably either a cupola or a windmill at the apex of the roof.[19] The interior is divided into the usual two levels, the upper floor used to store hay. A large door gives entrance to the main level; above is a door leading to the hayloft.

Pocahontas

In the design for the Pocahontas County Courthouse (1920–1923), the Des Moines firm of Proudfoot, Bird and Rawson produced one of its many Beaux-Arts schemes. The three-story block sheathed in light-colored Bedford limestone exhibits the traditional rusticated ground floor; above, the remaining two floors are encompassed within recessed panels of Doric columns. Everything about the design is well proportioned, "correct," and dignified. The courthouse is situated within a well-landscaped park (Courthouse Square) at the north end of Main Street.

Between Third and Fourth on Main Street is the Streamline Moderne Rialto Theater (1938), designed by Wetherell and Harrison. Its wedge-shaped marquee ends in a group of tumbling curved bands, and a similar pattern of bands climbs up the center of the theater building itself.

NO270 Giant Statue of the Princess Pocahontas

1958. Nielsen's Souvenirs, on Iowa 3, just east of the city limits

The architectural glory of Pocahontas is to be found on Iowa 3 just east of the city limits. This is Nielsen's Souvenirs (1958). A 25-foot statue of the maiden Pocahontas beseeches us to come into her nearby tipi to purchase souvenirs of the place. This is unquestionably one of Iowa's major monuments of programmatic architecture.

This steel and wood frame sculpture, sheathed in concrete, was created for local businessman Frank W. Shaw. It was designed by W. C. Ballard, who also designed the sculptural figures of the giant muskie and Paul Bunyon's sweetheart in Minnesota.

NO271 Walter House (Cedar Rock)

Quasqueton

NO271 **Walter House** (Cedar Rock)

1945–1950, Frank Lloyd Wright. 1945–1948, guest-house/boathouse. North on route W35, 1.2 miles from its junction with Iowa 282, on the north edge of Quasqueton.

Situated close to the small community of Quasqueton is Cedar Rock, the Lowell Walter house designed by Frank Lloyd Wright. The complex consists of the house itself (1945–1950) and the guesthouse/boathouse (1945–1948) located on the east shore of the Wapsipinicon River. As with a number of Wright's post-World War II houses, the scheme of the Walter house is based on his late 1930s Usonian house: there is a central module—con-taining the living, dining, and kitchen cor-ner—and then a long corridored wing containing, as in a railroad car, a line of bedrooms. Entrance to the house is off the carport and auto court, via a long sheltered walkway parallel to the bedroom gallery. The central module of the Walter house is the square garden room with walls of glass that provide a view of the river below. The other walls of the house are of red brick; the roof, a thin slab of concrete, was planned to be covered in black earth and peat moss. Almost all of the furniture was designed by Wright. The house is now owned by the Iowa Conservation Commission and is open to the public.

Reinbeck

In March 1916 the community of Reinbeck in southern Grundy County received a modest grant of $6,000 from the Carnegie Corporation to construct a new public library building. A site was obtained, additional funds were acquired, and the community engaged the Waterloo architect Howard B. Burr to design the building. In the following year the building was completed and open to the public. The scheme that the architect provided was modestly in the Prairie style: a raised basement supporting a single-story volume covered by a broadly overhanging hipped roof. Burr treated the main floor almost as a park or garden pavilion, similar in many ways to park pavilions then being designed in and around Chicago and elsewhere in the Midwest. All of the windows on the main floor are wide-arched units emphasized by slightly projecting brick voussoirs. The entrance too is arched, and a Maher-like arched hood projects over the glass lunette and door below. The wall surfaces were treated in the usual fashion of a Prairie building: brick below brought up to the main floor window sills and then stucco above. The Reinbeck Carnegie Public Library building is situated at 201 Blackhawk Street. Burr also designed a nearby Prairie-style house at 302 Blackhawk. This was built for George B. Saul in 1919.

Rock Falls

This tiny community is located northeast of Mason City on route B20. The terrain at this point is hilly and wooded, and the Shell Rock River runs by the town. At the northwest corner of Glover and Jackson streets is the 1867 Old Stone Church (now United Methodist Church). In style the church is a rectangular Greek Revival building with a gable roof. It is now enshrouded romantically in vines, but one can see through at places to the rough stone walls beneath. The tower of the church is of a more recent vintage, as is the brick addition to the rear.

Sac City

The town of Sac City was laid out in 1855 on the west bank of the Raccoon River, just above its juncture with Cedar Creek. The plan of the town is unusual for the Midwest. The center of the community is a large public square which is entered on the east or west by Main Street (US 20). The northern portion of this large public square is occupied by the Sac County Courthouse; to the south is City Hall and General Sherman Hall. The courthouse was designed by J. M. Russell, who had planned a similar courthouse at Storm Lake the year before (since destroyed). The Sac City building is a two-and-a-half-story brick and stone-trimmed building on a raised basement; it makes a minimal nod to the Richardsonian Romanesque. One enters the building through a stone-framed Richardsonian arched opening; each facade projects toward a central bay which rises to steeply pitched stone gables. The central tower that visually unified the design was removed in 1900.

On the west side of the river is a large public park containing the obligatory relocated log cabin (c. 1870) and an extensive six-sided park pavilion (c. 1900), open on the sides and rising in the center to a clerestory section.

NO272 **Carlson House**

1875. 612 Main St.

The architectural high point of the town is the Carlson house, designed in the Second Empire style (1875), located at 612 Main Street. This dwelling is certainly one of the most sumptuous Second Empire houses in Iowa. Above the dormered mansard roof of this two-and-a-half-story house rises a fanciful tower whose shingled

NO272 Carlson House

roof is so steep that it is almost vertical. Wide, projecting, heavy gabled lintels occur over the windows, and the roof of the L-shaped porch bursts forth with rows of finials.

Saint Ansgar

On entering town from the northwest on Iowa 105, one will encounter the First Lutheran Church (1864) on the west side of Main Street at Second Street. The general proportions of this stone church with a gable roof hark back to the Greek Revival, though its pointed windows and other details are Gothic. The form of the church includes a lower projecting gable section to the front, then the higher body of the church, and finally an octagonal belfry and spire placed upon a square tower base. In the public park north of Third Street, between George and Washington streets, is a hemispherical bandstand (c. 1938) similar to others constructed in Iowa through PWA funding.

At the northeast corner of West Fourth and Mitchel streets is the Ansgar State Bank. The first section of the bank was built in 1891. This was a two-story Richardsonian exercise in brick and red sandstone. In 1970 the architect Edward Novak added a substantial single-floor addition. The new work mirrored the sandstone Romanesque arches of the original building, and on the top of the parapet Novak placed an iron railing with a repeat of the arches.

Finally, on the north side of Fourth Street, east of School Street, is the Bridle Theater (c. 1937). The touch of design genius of this thirties Moderne building shows up in the pair of mobile, tinselly palm trees on the top edge of the marquee.

Off South Main Street in a southwesterly direction is the Saint Ansgar Mill. The two-story wood-sheathed mill building was constructed in 1861. The initial power source was a water wheel, but this was later replaced by a water turbine. The accompanying concrete dam across the Cedar River was built in 1915.

Saint Lucas

In a good medieval manner, the Roman Catholic Church of Saint Luke's (1914) forms the visual centerpiece of this small community. The imagery of the church is Gothic, but it is mixed in its borrowing, in this case from both French and German sources. In design the church has a nave and side aisles; its gabled front is contained between twin towers. The sharp contrast between the light-colored limestone trim and the red brick gives it somewhat the feeling of the Gothic Revival of the nineteenth rather than twentieth century. The interior remains intact, including the handsome Bavarian stained glass windows and the original main and side altars.

Sheffield

Hidden away in the small community of Sheffield is a classic example of a Prairie school dwelling, the Storck house designed by Einar O. Broaten around 1920. The house is located on the northwest corner of Sherman and Seventh streets. Its design is based upon Frank Lloyd Wright's *Ladies Home Journal* house of 1906. Its entrance is on the right, and there is a projecting living porch on the left. The lower parts of the house are sheathed in brick, with stucco above. The composition, especially that of the street facade, is highly abstract, consisting of two pierlike volumes between which is laid a geometric patterning of windows and rectangles of stucco outlined in brick. On the second floor, pairs of pilasters and consoles placed at each of the corners suggest that they are supporting the broadly overhanging roof.

Shell Rock

On the east side of the Shell River as it flows through the community of Shell Rock is the Shell Rock Grain and Milling Company building (1858). The two-and-a-half-story mill building sits on a high rock foundation looking directly over the river. The upper story, quite typical of mill buildings, has a high central monitor that runs from one end wall to the other. Wooden pegs rather than nails or bolts were utilized in much of the original structure (there are a number of later additions). In recent years the mill has used electricity rather than water power. The mill is situated beside the river just off route C45 and Iowa 3.

Spencer

The site selected in 1869 for Spencer was an unforested section north of the Little Sioux River. The city has long served as the southern gateway to Iowa's Great Lakes area to the north and northeast. Though the usual highway commercial strip has developed along US 18, the town itself seems remarkably self-contained. Much of the downtown of the community was rebuilt after a fire that took place on July 4, 1931.

NO273 **Clay County Courthouse**

1900–1901, Kinney and Detweiler. North side of 4th St. between 2nd Ave. W. and 3rd Ave. W.

The Minneapolis architects Kinney and Detweiler provided Clay County with a highly inventive interpretation of the usual Beaux-Arts Classical scheme. The red brick and sandstone walls give a human scale and warmth to the building. This quality is reinforced by the open square tower surmounted by a small-scale drum and dome. In contrast, the two-story entrance portico with its large polished Corinthian columns seems formal and distant.

NO274 **Gateway, Clay County Fairgrounds**

c. 1916. West of corner of 4th Ave. W. and W. 16th St.

California's turn-of-the-century Mission Revival style was employed off and on in the Midwest, especially for recreation and exhibition buildings. The designer of the entrance building at the county fairgrounds has simplified the style, but his composition of a three-arched loggia balanced on each side by towers with hipped roofs was a familiar scheme within the style. Even the wood gateposts have repeated the theme of a miniaturized hipped roof.

NO275 **Steffen House, "The House of Tomorrow"**

c. 1939. Southeast corner of 15th St. and Grand Ave.

This is a determined, well-carried-out episode of the thirties Streamline Moderne. The entrance is within the lower level of a small two-story cylinder. A horizontal band of metal-framed windows moves around the wide living room bay. On the second floor, two cylinders embrace an open porch leading onto the terrace of the roof of the living room. Corner windows and portholes break through the white brick walls.

NO276 **Higgens House**

c. 1908. Northwest corner of 12th St. and Grand Ave.

A wide, two-story portico supported by four stout Ionic columns makes it plain that this Colonial Revival "mansion" housed one of the community's leading figures. Within the portico is a narrow second-floor balcony, and on each side are matching pergolalike porches, one of which contains the porte-cochère. The roof forms dormers that depart from the Colonial into the then-current Craftsman mode.

NO277 **House**

c. 1890 and later. 1105 Grand Ave.

The low-pitched hipped roof and the stair bay on the side imply that a traditional side-hall Queen Anne dwelling was remodeled by someone affected by the Craftsman and Prairie styles, c. 1912. The mingling of these two styles has surprisingly resulted in a design that holds together very well.

NO278 **Clay County National Bank Building**

c. 1931. 407 Grand Ave.

The central portion of this two-story commercial block contains the bank itself; on each side are ground-level retail stores with offices above. The presence of the bank is made known because its tiered parapet projects above the rest of the building. The limestone sheathing of the bank, along with its ornamentation, adds to the formal quality. The Art Deco basis of the design is made emphatic by the ornamental patterns realized in the metalwork of the windows and spandrels and within the limestone surrounds.

NO279 **Medlar Studio Building**

c. 1931. 10–12 W. 4th St.

A two-story commercial building is realized here in white glazed terracotta, accompanied by a red tile roof. The overall design might well be labeled "Free Classical"; the ornamentation was certainly affected by motifs derived from George W. Maher and other exponents of the Prairie school.

NO280 **Grand Diner**

c. 1940. 208 Grand Ave.

The rectangular box of this diner takes on the Streamline Moderne in a curved projecting wall and, as one would expect, in the curved sign over the entrance door. The col-

ors of the building—cherry red and forest green—enliven it all.

NO281 **Oneota Park**

c. 1937. North side of US 18, at the eastern city limits

Within the park is a recreation building in the form of a log cabin some fifty feet long. The logs of the walls are beautifully matched, as if someone had purchased a set of John Lloyd Wright's Lincoln Logs and had magically transformed the toy into a real building.

Spillville

The small Czech community of Spillville is situated on the Turkey River southwest of Decorah. The terrain at this point begins to form the soft, rolling prairie that we associate with central Iowa. On the river itself are the remains of Joseph Spielman's 1849 mill and dam. In the center of town on Main Street is a two-story former commercial building, the Wenzil Taylor Building (c. 1860s). This two-story brick-fronted, stone-sided building is Italianate, with small arched windows and entrance door, a suggestion of cornice quoining in brick, and brackets below the projecting brick cornice. The building served as a summer residence in 1893 for the Czech composer Antonin Dvorak. Since 1947 the building has housed the House of Clocks. The core of this collection is comprised of clocks produced locally by the Bily brothers, Frank and Joseph. These clocks in themselves are wonderful miniaturized fantasies of architecture, and they have as much to say about architectural images as some actual buildings. The building housing the House of Clocks is open to the public.

NO282 Saint Wenceslaus Roman Catholic Church

NO282 Saint Wenceslaus Roman Catholic Church

1860–1870

The touchstone of Spillville's architecture is Saint Wenceslaus Roman Catholic Church, said by tradition to have been modeled after Saint Barbara's Church in Kutna-Hora, Czechoslovakia. The stone church building of cruciform plan lies low on a hilltop site. Set in the chevet of the church is a small-scaled chapel in the form of a classical temple.

Though the church's windows are pointed, the general detailing and proportions are classical. The interior consists of an aisleless nave, and the 1876 pipe organ still sits on the balcony. On the grounds of the church is a gateway of stone piers and iron which commemorates the jubilee of the church in 1910. In the adjoining cemetery are a number of cast-iron grave markers produced by a local craftsman, Charles Anders, between 1880 and 1920.

Spirit Lake

When Dickinson County was organized in 1857, Spirit Lake became the county seat. The site of the town is a peninsula of land between Spirit Lake to the north and the two branches of Okoboji River to the south. Though visited by tourists because of nearby lakes, the town is not a typical resort-oriented community because of the presence of the county courthouse and the community's connection to the Chicago and Northwestern Railroad.

NO283 Dickinson County Courthouse

1890–1891, Truman D. Allen. Southeast corner of Iowa 9 and Hill St.

Truman D. Allen, who had offices in Cleveland and in Minneapolis, was among several architects who designed a number of county courthouses in the Midwest. His design for the Dickinson County Courthouse appears more as a small-town school building than a courthouse. The stylistic references are mildly Richardsonian Romanesque. A square, three-story corner tower is the only really strong feature in the design of this brick and sandstone-detailed building. The first courthouse at Spirit Lake was a simple but handsome Greek Revival building of brick. This was designed by Harvey Abbott in 1859; it was not completed until 1868.

NO284 A. M. Johnson Building

1894. 1724 Hill St.

The large-scale arched windows of the upper floor of this brick commercial block convey a slight hint of the Romanesque. Three squat columns on the street level separate the entrances from the adjoining glass area, and they support a lintel formed by a single I-beam embellished with small rosettes. Recent "stylistic" improvements have provided awnings of rustic shake shingles.

NO285 Coca-Cola Bottling Plant

1948. Northeast corner of Iowa 9 and Jackson St.

The designer of this building has carried the PWA Moderne of the 1930s over into the early post-World War II years. The top of the parapet of this two-story building carries an undulating zigzag pattern, and the spandrel on the right of the entrance encompasses the name "Coca-Cola" within two stylized plant forms. The entrance motif is two stories high, and the walls on each side step inward to the door below and the window above.

NO286 Public Library Building

1911–1912, E. L. Barber. 1801 Hill Ave.

This plan is traditional for a small-town Carnegie library: there is a raised basement supporting a single-floor structure. Its roof form, windows, entrance, and other details suggest the medieval English Tudor style.

NO287 House

c. 1875. 1411 Hill St.

This is a French Second Empire dwelling with sharp, somewhat brittle details. It was extensively revamped in the Colonial Revival image of the early 1900s. A two-story porch with a gable roof supported by three Tuscan columns at each corner now presents the house to the street. Within the porch, the front entrance (c. 1900) acquired side lights and a transom.

NO288 Knight Templars of Iowa Lodge

1918. Templar Park, north of the town of Spirit Lake, off Iowa 276

The architect of this building looked to the Mission Revival. On each corner of the three- and four-story main block are open towers with hipped roofs. The broad overhanging roofs are tiled. Arched openings and deep wall reveals further establish the building's Mission image.

NO289 Foster House

1962–1963, Jerome Cerney. West of Spirit Lake on Iowa 9, past junction with US 71, county road to Okoboji Lake; take road to left .5 miles; turn right, proceed .2 miles north

For an informal house on the lake, Cerney turned to the time-honored Colonial Revival style, one he had frequently used with great distinction in the 1930s.[20] His theme for the Foster house was a type referred to in the

NO289 Foster House

thirties as the "Colonial farmhouse." The farmhouse in this instance is based upon the one-and-a-half-story houses built in the eighteenth century from Virginia to New England. Though the house was referred to as "Colonial Williamsburg architecture," that is only one of its several sources. Certainly the main section of the house, with a porch across its entire front and a group of narrow gabled dormers, does remind one of examples from Tidewater Virginia. Cerney modified his historic prototypes in many ways, including the introduction of large windows and floor-to-ceiling bays. Houses similar to the Foster house were designed by Cerney and his older Chicago colleague, David Adler, for many suburban locations in and around Chicago. As with all of his houses, this one reveals Cerney's concern for sympathetic siting and "correct" detailing.

Storm Lake

Though sections of Buena Vista County were settled in the late 1850s, the county's principal city, Storm Lake, was not established until 1870. The grid of streets was laid out just north of the lake of the same name. A meandering curving road, Lake Shore Drive, follows along the perimeter of the lake. Two parks, Willow Park and Elm Park, intervene between Lake Shore Drive and the lake. On East Lake Shore Drive is the restored Dahl log cabin (1871). This cabin of squared logs was moved from a rural site near Rembrandt.

NO290 Row of Commercial Buildings

c. 1890–1910. Main St. between 4th and 5th streets

The upper floors of these contiguous stone-and-brick business blocks remain basically unaltered. Each of the small buildings establishes its own personality through its individual pattern of windows and pilasters, and above all through its entablatures and cornices. Though the later continuous metal roof and canopy over the public sidewalk may be functional, they don't aesthetically help the buildings themselves.

NO291 Abner Bell's

c. 1928. 5th St., between Erie and Cayuga streets

The presence of the building is asserted through a raised rooftop lantern with a double row of bracket supports and a tile roof. Other accents are the tile sheet roof over the street windows and the entrance arch with its tile-filled lunette and columns to the side. If pressed, one supposes, the building's designer might have said that its image is Mediterranean.

NO292 United States Post Office Building
(now School Administration Building)

1935, Louis A. Simon. Lake St., north of 3rd St.

This small-town building is one of the Post Office Department's representative designs. In the 1930s the style of governmental buildings such as this one at Storm Lake was referred to as Regency; in a loose sense it was part of the rage for the Colonial Revival during the depression years of the 1930s. The two projecting side wings help to concentrate one's attention on the central pavilion, which has a stepped recessed door and windows and a mansard roof set back from the parapet.

NO293 Harker House

c. 1870s. Southwest corner of Lake and 3rd streets

Hidden behind a forest of conifers is one of Iowa's most enticing examples of the French Second Empire style. Though modest in size, everything is here, and all the details are beautifully and sophisticatedly handled. At the front, gabled dormers break through the roof's entablature and cornice; below is a small bracketed angled roof bay with a porch to the side. There are stone lintels over the windows and doors; in the front facade these projecting lintels are carried down the sides of the window frames. On the side elevations of the house the lintels have circular crowns, and on each side the design is terminated with additional circles.

NO294 Storm Lake Cemetery Gates

c. 1915. Northeast section of Storm Lake, north of Iowa 7

The cemetery has been provided with a wall and entrance that reflect the interest in California's Mission Revival that took place after the turn of the century. This revival was often closely associated with the Craftsman movement, and that influence is reflected in this design. The low, enclosing walls and the high, arched walls flanking the entrance are of rough stone. The arched openings are covered by tile roofs; at the center is a shingled gable roof with beams and struts exposed. What looks like an older cemetery sign has been placed above the eaveline of the entrance roof.

Titonka

There are many variations on how a service station building with a cut-into corner might be designed. The one at the northeast corner of North Main Street and First Avenue in Titonka has a much wider than usual cut. Four piers are needed to accommodate the two lengths of this cut. The walls and piers of the station (now the K. H. Co-Op Oil Company) are in dark red-brown brick with an overlay of patterns carried out in light tan brick. To bring emphasis to the corner, the architect designed the parapet as an ascending step pattern with the highest point at the street corner. The building was probably built in the late 1920s.

A "silo home," designed in 1983 by Arthur Peterson for himself, is located .5 miles east and .5 miles south of Titonka on route P66. It is a commercially produced round concrete silo banded with metal and topped in this case by a balconied octagonal penthouse. An entrance projects off one side of the silo; the silo interior is divided vertically into four levels: a utility room on the ground level, a gameroom above it, a kitchen on the third level, and a bedroom on the fourth. At the very top is the living-room penthouse. The various levels are connected by a central steel spiral staircase. It all adds up to a romantic combination of the high-tech style and vernacular traditionalism.

Union

NO295 **Union Town Hall**

1941, Thorwald Thorson. Southeast corner of Center and Third streets

Near the center of the little community of Union is the community's town hall and fire station. This small single-floor building of reinforced concrete was a WPA project of

1941, designed by Thorwald Thorson. It may well be the smallest WPA city hall in Iowa, but it still manages to convey the fact that it is a public building. The Moderne lettering cast into the building announces its specific purpose, and below the entrance canopy and above the door is the date of the building; a

NO295 Union Town Hall

pattern of three stars appears above the canopy. All of the entrances, including the large one for the fire truck, are covered by thin projecting slab roofs. The entrance door has side wings that are fluted, and similar fluting also appears beside the horizontal windows. At the top of the parapet a narrow band of projecting and receding rectangles provides a termination for the walls of the building.

Ventura

NO296 School Auditorium and Gymnasium

1941, Thorwald Thorson. Southeast corner of Main and Park streets

The PWA Moderne school auditorium and gymnasium is one of the more elaborate ones to be constructed in Iowa at the end of the depression. As with several other WPA buildings designed by Thorwald Thorson in the thirties, here he utilized exposed reinforced concrete. The hooped roof of the auditorium/gym is reflected in the semicircular ends of the building. The architect repeated this curve in decorative indented lines that spring from the tops of the corner pilasters and center on a vertical plane bearing a cast concrete relief sculpture of the head of a Viking. The lower walls of the building have been accentuated by indented horizontal lines, contrasted by vertical lines in the entrance wing. The side walls of the building have a repeated pattern of pilasters and intervening curved buttresses that taper in at the bottom. The upper northwest corner of the building bursts forth with a cast concrete high-relief figure of a basketball player.

NO296 School Auditorium and Gymnasium

Waterloo

In 1854 the owners of the land on both sides of the Cedar River at this point decided to join together to plat the new community of Waterloo. The grid in this case was established parallel to and perpendicular to the general southeasterly direction of the Cedar River. (As is almost always the case, much of the later platted additions to the city utilized a north-south, east-west grid.) Though no rapids or falls existed at this point of the river, the flow was sufficient to provide power for milling operations. A log-and-brush dam was initially built across the river, and in 1856 the first flour mill was established. The first bridge across the river, a wooden one, was built in 1859, and the first iron bridge was erected in 1871. In the early seventies, Waterloo instead of nearby Cedar Falls emerged as the key railroad point in this section of the state. The Illinois Central built its shops at Waterloo in 1870, and the roundhouse of this complex of buildings still exists.

By the early 1900s Waterloo had assumed the character of a typical small midwestern industrial city. The John Deere and Company works at 400 Westfield Avenue (which had absorbed the earlier Waterloo Gasoline Engine Company) is the city's largest industry, supplemented by others such as the Rath Meat Packing Plant.

Each of the two parts of the city divided by the river started out with a square-block public park: Lincoln Park for the east, and Washington Park for the section west of the river. As the city expanded, extensive additions were made to the park system. The largest of these are Gates Park, Exchange Park, and Cedar River Park to the east, and Hope Martin Memorial Park and Byrnes Park to the west.

Having developed on both sides of the river, Waterloo did not end up with one single public or business downtown. There has been a tendency to divide equally the major public buildings, and even in the early years of this century not one but two Carnegie libraries were built. The succeeding Black Hawk County courthouses were placed east of the river. The 1857 Greek Revival courthouse with portico and lantern was torn down in 1902 and replaced with a grand "French Renaissance" Beaux-Arts building. This in turn hit the dust in 1964, replaced with the current, rather bleak version of a corporate International-style building.

The normal wear and tear as well as post-World War II urban renewal have pretty well obliterated Waterloo's early past. The sawmills and flour mills situated in and around the Fourth Street bridge are gone, as are the principal Chautauqua buildings (from 1893 to 1906) that were located in Exchange Park.

The most fascinating residential neighborhood of the city is Highland Park, situated between Washington and Cedar, North Second and North Fifth streets. This area was platted in 1900 and again in 1907 in a grid following the course of the river. From the early 1900s on through the early 1930s, it was the upper-middle-class suburban enclave. A good number of the houses were designed by Waterloo's most famous architect, Mortimer B. Cleveland.

The general ins and outs of suburban development went back and forth across the river. At the beginning, the most prestigious area was the hill in and around Washington Park; then in the late nineteenth century attention seems to have shifted to the east side of the river. This focus was replaced west of the river by Highland Park starting around 1907; finally the post-World War II development has followed West Fourth Street, Kimball, Ridgeview, and Ains-

Waterloo

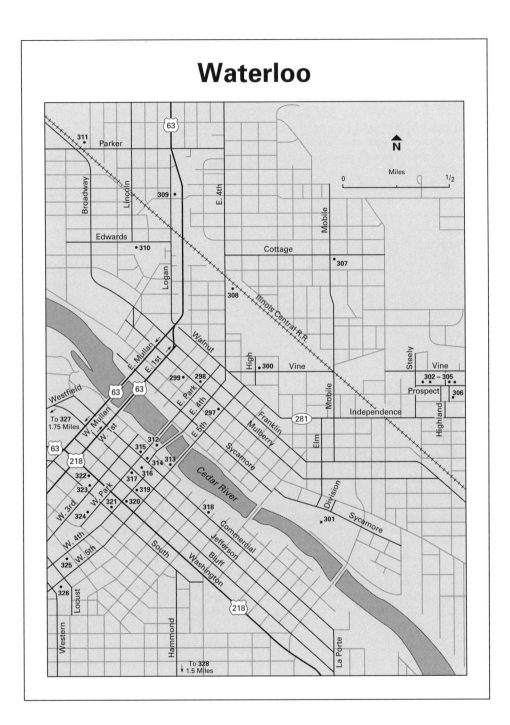

borough avenues to the southwest. In this area one will discover wonderful suburban planning: Graceland Boulevard (a real boulevard), plus numerous bent or curved streets accompanied by single-family detached dwellings, often with appreciable setbacks from the street (such as along Sheridan Road).

NO297 Carnegie Public Library

1902–1906, John G. Ralston. Corner of 5th and Mulberry streets

Ralston made a modest-sized Carnegie Library grand by emphasizing its central raised section with two pairs of closely spaced Ionic columns placed on a low, abbreviated podium. Above is a classical pediment with a lunette window, all reminiscent of buildings at the World's Columbian Exposition of 1893, held in Chicago. The sense of enhanced scale is heightened by having the entrance stairs narrow and then break into the podium upon which the columns rest. Another hint of stateliness is the suggestion of a balcony above the columned entrance.

NO298 Elks Lodge

1924. Corner of Park Ave. and Mulberry St.

In this 1920s example the Beaux-Arts tradition refers to Northern Italian Renaissance architecture of the early sixteenth century. The narrow entrance pavilion is composed of an arched opening and pilasters below, with an attic story delicately delineated with curvilinear plant motifs in relief, small paired pilasters, and a central circular window. Behind the heavy vegetation at each side of the entrance are two wings articulated by a pattern of tall arched windows. As with many 1920s public buildings in the Italian mode, the design has been carried out in brick with detailing in stone.

NO299 Saint Joseph's Roman Catholic Church

1900, Murphy and Ralston. 320 Mulberry St.

Saint Joseph's was described as "French Gothic" when it was built, though the basic format is nineteenth-century medieval. The corner tower is crowned by a high roof with narrow facets. The warm-orange brick walls create smoothly flowing surfaces, suggesting an early twentieth-century building rather than a traditional medieval design of masonry. This same weightless quality is equally apparent within. The real gem of this church complex is the children's chapel. This dollhouse of a Gothic chapel seats six and has its own miniature pipe organ.

NO300 East Waterloo High School

c. 1923. Northeast corner of High and Vine streets

A lively exterior stairway encompassed within a stone balustrade terminating in inverted consoles leads up to an academically correct portico on a raised basement, with arches below and Ionic columns above. An unusual aspect of the design is the row of overscaled vent grilles in the attic story. Within the building are murals of the 1930s by Herman O. Myre. Their subject is the early history of Iowa.

NO301 Rath Meat Packing Plant

1927–1937. Sycamore St., end of Division and Elm streets

The Rath Meat Packing Plant was built on this site in 1891, though most of the present buildings date from the years 1927–1937. The lowness of the complex of two-story-plus brick buildings is countered by the vertical thrust of the tall industrial chimneys. The complex does not openly convey any intentional design concept; instead it makes its aesthetic case through its signage and the pragmatic design of its utilitarian buildings.

NO302 Ortner House

c. 1915, Mortimer B. Cleveland. 131 Prospect Ave.

The Prairie mode seemingly derived from Viennese Secessionism of the early 1900s was utilized in the Ortner house. Here, a lightly placed, dramatically projected hipped roof lies gently atop a stucco box whose facade is busily articulated by a geometric pattern of windows and half-timbering. The central

NO302 Ortner House

theme of the arched and hooded entrance porch is adroitly repeated in small scale in the windowframe above. The narrowness of the boxlike form of the house is accentuated even more by its being raised high off the ground, creating the need for a long, narrow flight of stairs leading to the front door. The entrance in turn is protected by two stone lions placed on the balustrades. The Ortner house is unquestionably one of the most idiosyncratic—and strongest—domestic designs one will encounter in Iowa.

NO303 House

c. 1923, Howard B. Burr. 145 Prospect Ave.

This is the California bungalow as seen through the eyes of a Prairie architect. As with the Ortner house just down the street (NO302), this house has a Viennese Secessionist quality of design that we often associate with the Chicago architect George W. Maher. As one often finds in Maher's work, solid, classically inspired brick piers sit beside the entrance, and another group supports the adjacent porte-cochère roof. The heaviness of the stone base of the house is countered by the lightness of its roof, which is punctured by delicate, small-scaled gabled dormers. The primacy of the car in suburbia is evident in the combined driveway and front walk which leads to the porte-cochère, symbolically and actually the entrance into the house.

Two other post-World War I Prairie school bungalows that should be seen in Waterloo are the Toenies house (1925) at 1911 South Street, and the Down house (1925) at 803 Williston Avenue. These and several other

houses indicate that the fashion for the Prairie mode continued well into the mid-1920s.

NO304 Lichty House

1909, Mortimer B. Cleveland. 205 Prospect Ave.

Here Cleveland created a substantial brick Georgian Colonial Revival house. The three dormers with arched windows in the roof are characteristic of interpretations of the Georgian at the time. More unusual is the steeply pitched gambrel roof. The central splayed entry porch flanked by two wooden dependencies adds appreciable dignity and grandeur to the design.

NO305 Cleveland House

c. 1912, Mortimer B. Cleveland. 215 Prospect Ave.

For his own house Mortimer Cleveland produced a two-story box sheathed in red brick that is in a style that probably began somewhere between the American and English Georgian; however, he somehow seems to have ended up with a house that conveys a sense of the Italian. A high, extended glass bay (almost Queen Anne in feeling) adjoins the entrance and its terrace. To reach the front door one must traverse the width of a low terrace.

NO306 House

c. 1910, attrib. Mortimer B. Cleveland. 202 Highland Rd.

Cleveland's imagery here is the then-popular two-story Craftsman dwelling; the foundation was constructed of river boulders, and above is a surface clad in narrow clapboard sheathing, with a shingled surface above that. The tour de force of the house is its remarkable boulder chimney, split into two parts on the second floor to make way for a small window and then rejoined by an arch at the top. This dwelling is one of the outstanding examples of the Craftsman mode in the United States.

NO307 Grant Elementary School

1914, Mortimer B. Cleveland. Southeast corner of Mobile and Cottage streets

A sparse composition of plain brick volumes, this is a design that the Modernist of the

1940s and 1950s would have pointed to with pride as a "pioneer" example of great things to come. The columned entrance and simple stone decoration of the entrance pavilion would probably have been seen as just a touch backward, though today we might feel that these elements are the building's principal assets. The recently added bright, shining metal windows, as is so often the case, drastically mar the original design.

NO308 Illinois Central Railroad Shops

1870, after. 1006 E. 4th St.

A semicircular single-story roundhouse containing 14 stalls was created in brick. The external walls are divided by pilasters into repeated bays, each of which is filled with a band of high windows.

NO309 Dunsmore House

c. 1866. 902 Logan Ave.

This one-and-a-half-story stone house, somewhat Greek Revival in character, may have been built (and perhaps designed) by Thomas Chadwick, a stonemason who came to Iowa from England. The house was remodeled in 1913 and acquired a wing to the rear.

NO310 Longfellow School

1940, Mortimer B. Cleveland. South end of Lincoln St. at Edwards St.

In this instance, Cleveland looked to the PWA Moderne for inspiration. The principal Moderne ingredients are present: metal windows that read horizontally, corner windows, the absolutely imperative glass bricks, window sills tied together by horizontal bands. On the whole, it is all well carried out.

NO311 Litchfield Manufacturing Company Building

1903. Northeast corner of Parker and Broadway streets

This is a design to warm the heart of an advocate of Postmodernism. It features an informal series of stepped gable fronts that seem to wander casually up and down the building's immensely long street facade. The facade is constructed of brick together with

natural and artificial stone. The building is naturally lighted with some 600 windows filled with light-diffusing ribbed glass. The provision of natural light and ventilation plus other amenities was in part meant to produce a building for the "comfort, health, and pleasure of the employees."[21] The company manufactured metal products ranging from manure spreaders to power feed grinders.

NO312 YMCA Building

1930–1931, Mortimer B. Cleveland, W. E. Thompson. 154 W. 4th St.

Labeled "Modern" in style when built, this design by Cleveland would be designated today as late-twenties Art Deco. The entrance motif is suggestive of a two-dimensional Moderne perfume bottle with accentuated vertical lines that grow in intensity as they reach the top. While the building is generally reticent in overall design, the handling of the brick, limestone, and polished stone make this a vigorous example of the popular Moderne.

NO313 Black Hawk County Memorial Hall

1915–1916, attrib. Mortimer B. Cleveland. 104 W. 5th St.

This war memorial building was constructed by the GAR to honor those who participated in the Civil War. This single-story brick-clad building on a raised basement stylistically leans somewhat toward the Georgian Colonial. Design elements such as the dormer windows point to what was then occurring in Chicago in the work of George W. Maher and others. The building is situated within a small, pleasant park, which in addition to this building houses a classical fountain and pool and a miniature Statue of Liberty.

NO314 Waterloo Courier Building

c. 1925 and later, attrib. Mortimer B. Cleveland. Corner of 4th and Commercial streets

Originally English Georgian, this newspaper building has now been substantially remodeled on the ground floor, and additions have been made to it. The building currently looks out over an asphalt parking lot, picturesquely punctuated by parking meters.

NO315 United States Post Office Building
(now Public Library)

1937, Louis A. Simon and Neal Melick. Corner of Park Ave. and Commercial St.

In style this building is PWA Moderne in one of its severe guises. The architects have set a two-story volume upon a rusticated Kasota stone base. The building's central portico piers are close to the surface and continue the adjoining wall plane. A similar emphasis on flat surfaces occurs in the attic above the portico where the classical vocabulary has been reduced to the simplest of geometric forms. In the building's recent conversion to a library, new metal windows have been placed so that they project slightly beyond the adjoining stone walls, destroying to a considerable degree the classical intent of the original design. Within the building and still intact are two 1940 murals, *Exposition* and *Holiday* by Edgar Britton, who was in his younger years a student of Grant Wood. These murals were part of the WPA arts project carried out during the depression.

NO316 Conway Civic Center

1974–1975, Thorson-Brom-Breshar-Snyder. Block bound by Park Ave., Commercial, Jefferson, and 4th streets

Brick-sheathed volumes are covered here by a seemingly independent metal-truss roof; the design seems in many ways to be a small-scale version of the earlier McCormick Place (1970) in Chicago designed by C. F. Murphy Associates. The saving quality of the Conway Civic Center is its modest size and its setback from the street, which has allowed some planting of trees. Accompanying the building is that hallmark of midwestern modernity, a metal-and-glass skyway that bridges the street.

NO317 Service Station

c. 1928. 500 Jefferson St.

Though it boasts a tile roof, the building's small tower together with details such as corner piers projecting above the roof encourage us to respond to the design as Art Deco. Though not large, the building manages with ease to hold its own, and in fact ends up dominating the corner.

NO318 Row House

c. 1905. 919–929 Commercial St.

Six connected town houses have been grouped together as medieval castles in triplicate. The crenellated parapets, corbeled cornices, low-arched openings, and rough block masonry walls should have no problem withstanding a mythical siege.

NO319 Chicago, Rock Island, and Pacific Railroad Depot

c. 1890. corner of 4th and Bluff streets

The depot's abbreviated Richardsonian Romanesque design centers on a stocky central tower. Brick walls with stone trim have been set on a slightly projecting rusticated masonry base. Overscaled lunette windows in the second floor of the central tower provided light for the principal passenger waiting area below. This station, like so many others around the country, is presently unused, but one hopes it will be restored for some sort of adaptive reuse.

NO320 People's Bank Building

1980, Flinn-Saite-Andersen. 419 W. 4th St.

Here one encounters historicism of a classical sort, coupled with the fashionable barrel-vaulted glass roof found in so many projects of the late 1970s and 1980s. The building's broken stepped design scales it well for its corner site, even though the proportions and detailing seem almost purposely awkward.

NO321 Carnegie Public Library

1902–1906, John G. Ralston. Corner of 4th and South streets

A Beaux-Arts Classical design is held in check by a restrained hand (probably that of budget). Unusual in this design is the successful introduction of the library's main entrance into the raised basement under the portico. Given the prominence of the raised ground level around the building, some planting of trees and shrubbery would help.

NO322 **Snowden House** (now Waterloo Women's Club)

c. 1875. 306 Washington St.

On a hilltop eminence far back from the street sits this splendid brick Italianate house. The scheme is that of the two-story central-gable form with walls that display wonderfully inventive entablatures over the principal windows. A porch covering the entire front of the house helps to tie the building to the site. Under the broadly overhanging gable and roof eaves is a wide paneled entablature which is enhanced by numerous rows of dentils and the large roof brackets.

NO323 **Russell House**

1858–1863. 520 W. 3rd St.

The Russell house shares the same site and block of the street as the Snowden dwelling (NO322). It presents a classic, beautiful picture of an Italian villa, a style that was very popular in this country from the 1840s through the 1860s. The cubelike form of the Russell house is surmounted by the usual wide entablature and bracketed roof, which in turn is crowned by a central cupola. The well-preserved interior of this house is furnished with furniture of the middle to late nineteenth century. The house is maintained as a museum and is open to the public.

NO324 **Duplex**

c. 1910, attrib. Mortimer B. Cleveland. 624–626 W. Park Ave.

The complex composition of the central roof dormer of this double house strongly suggests Cleveland's hand. Almost as assertive as the central roof dormer—and equally successful—are the rough stone piers of the enclosed porches. The two-story brick-clad volume with widely projecting eaves of a hipped roof conjures the Midwest Prairie image.

NO325 **First United Brethren Church** (now Graves United Methodist Church)

1911, attrib. Mortimer B. Cleveland. 905 W. 4th St.

This church building is a single classical block accompanied by a pedimented entrance. The

strong hint of the rustic, which is especially apparent in the piers of the entrance portico and in the wide pilasters of the adjoining walls, has an almost eighteenth-century sense of a return to the primitive temple.

NO326 **West Junior-Senior High School Building** (now West Intermediate School)

1922, William Ittner. W. 5th Ave. between Locust and Western streets

A good, solid example of the classic midwestern school building of the years 1910 through the 1920s, this structure has red brick walls trimmed in Indiana limestone and punctured by banks of wide windows. The detailing of the central four-story pavilion would seem to indicate that we are to think of the Queen Anne period of English architecture, a period that recalls an inventive play between classicism and the late medieval. When built, this building was described as "a masterpiece in modern school planning." As is par for the course in so many recent remodelings in Iowa, new metal windows have been insensitively applied to the building.

At Sixth and Locust streets, behind the building, is a small brick and stone-trimmed ticket booth for Wallace Stadium. This delightful little building has all the appearance of a pavilion one might encounter in an eighteenth-century English garden.

NO327 **National Dairy Cattle Congress Buildings**

1912 and later. Rainbow Dr., end of Westfield Ave.

Waterloo is the site of the annual National Cattle Congress. The city's 8,200-seat Hippodrome is the building that dominates this site, yet the most handsome structures are the exposed hollow-tile stables with stepped gabled roofs and circular metal vents along the roof ridges.

NO328 **Banco Mortgage Company Service Center**

1980, The Durrant Group. Northeast corner of Hammond Ave. and Flammang Dr.

The office complex exists in a business "park" atmosphere; one could label the style late

Corporate International Style Modern, realized through horizontal banded volumes which in part overlook and are mirrored in an adjacent artificial lake. The only giveaway of its date comes in the occurrence of a low glass-and-metal barrel vault, which creates the usual high circulation atrium.

Waverly

The early settlers of Waverly "at once saw [that] the advantage of the site—good solid rock bottom, good banks, and ample fall of the river—constituted a particularly eligible locality for the building of a town."[22] The town was surveyed and laid out on the east bank of the river in 1853, and at the same time a log dam and sawmill were constructed. In the following year a grist mill was built, and in 1856 a bridge was constructed across the river. At the year of its founding Waverly was selected as the seat for Bremer County, and the first courthouse was built in 1854. The Cedar Falls and Minnesota Railroad reached the community in 1864, and by early 1900 Waverly had emerged as a hub for several north-south and east-west railroads. As with most Iowa communities, Waverly was active in church building in the late 1860s, and an institution of higher learning, Wartburg Teachers' Seminary, was established in 1878. The major change in recent years has been the construction of a new shopping center at the west end of the town.

NO329 Bremer County Courthouse

1936–1937, Mortimer B. Cleveland. Courthouse Square, northeast corner of Bremer Ave. E. and Court St.

The county went through the usual series of earlier courthouses before the present one, its third, was built in the mid-1930s. The first courthouse was a small wood structure built in 1854; this was replaced by a brick-and-stone building constructed in 1857–1858. This second, domed courthouse exhibited characteristics of the Greek Revival style, with a few nods here and there to the Italianate. It remained in use (with the addition of buildings to house public records) until it was torn down in 1937. A combination of PWA money and county bond funds was used to build the present building. In style it is PWA Moderne, with walls of brick contrasted against an almost white limestone trim. The fenestration seems to lie on the surface and consists of vertical bands of windows and sandstone panels slightly recessed between brick pilasters that terminate without capitals below the parapet.

NO330 First National Bank Building

c. 1895. 98 Bremer Ave. E.

The building has the flavor of being a late nineteenth-century two-story commercial block that has, almost as an afterthought, been brought up to date with a Beaux-Arts Classical banking floor. This lower level displays two walls of arched windows set between pilasters. The entrance, on the narrow facade, has a segmented curved lintel with a lunette window above it. The second level has tall paired windows simply set within the brick walls. The roofscape boasts a vestigial angled corner tower, and a second tower (quite low, like the other tower) over the side entrance of the building.

NO331 First National Bank Building

c. 1917. 100 Bremer Ave. E.

This two-story bank building, across the street from the older First National Bank building, has the appearance of a Beaux-Arts Classical design that has evolved under the direction of a Prairie architect. A much wider than usual entablature forms a horizontal plane supported at each corner by wide pilasters. A false gable is provided atop the parapet, articulated by the geometry of three elongated triangles. The recessed entrance and window area above have been "modernized" with aluminum frames, doors, and large sheets of glass.

NO332 United States Post Office Building

1936, Louis A. Simon and Neal Melick. 124 2nd St. S.E.

This is a Colonial Revival post office building in brick with stone and wood trim. The composition is a traditional one: a building with a central-gable roof and a slightly recessed facade formed by a triple arcade, then a flat-roofed wing on each side. The entrance bursts forth with a full-fledged Colonial broken pediment over the entrance. Within the building is a WPA mural (1938), *A Letter from Home in 1856*, by Mildred W. Pelzer.

NO333 Waverly House

1856. 402 Bremer Ave. W.

A three-story building with a gable roof was constructed as the first hotel and stage stop in Waverly. It is Greek Revival in design, with paired windows on each side of the central entrance. The building is now maintained as the county museum by the Bremer County Historical Society, and it is open to the public.

NO334 Old Main, Wartburg Teachers' Seminary (now Wartburg College)

1880. Bremer Ave. W. at US 218

Wartburg College was founded in 1878, and its first building was constructed two years

later. The three-story brick Old Main is an Italianate design that has been somewhat updated with references to the Eastlake. Instead of a bracketed, broadly overhanging hipped roof, it has a classical entablature and cornice with dentils. There is a deeply recessed entrance door with a high curved transom behind a small entry porch with four Italianate piers. Other than the changes in the entrance door and steps, and the addition of a metal fire escape, the exterior of the building remains basically intact.

NO335 Hemingway House

1938, Mortimer B. Cleveland. 500 1st St. S.E.

One of the "types" that were part of the Colonial Revival style in the 1920s and 1930s was the "rural farmhouse." Often, as one finds in the Hemingway house, the format of a medieval picturesque English cottage has been simplified and clothed in Colonial Revival details. The Hemingway house is sided with white clapboard; there are small-paned double-hung windows, shutters, and an entrance with side lights. It reads as an easy-going, confident design set within a broad suburban landscape.

NO336 Long House

1871. 12th St. N.W., north of the railroad tracks

The Long house is a two-story brick Italianate residence with a one-and-a-half-story ell to the side. The house has two formal entries, one at the center of the facade facing the public road, the other (the one most often used) fronting onto the driveway leading into the farm. Missing from the house today is the entry porch that faced the public road, and the cupola which, with its steeply pitched gables, was Eastlake in design. All in all, this is a late example of the Italianate style.

Webster City

Webster City was described in 1904 as being "laid out on a smooth plateau with a variety of scenery including prairie, timber, and river bluffs."[23] The city's grid was platted in the early 1850s within a meandering bend of the Boone River. Two adjacent blocks were set aside as city parks, and in 1857 another block was established for the county courthouse. Coal deposits south of the city were looked upon as a major source of income, but these were never developed to their potential.

NO337 **Wilson Brewster Memorial Park**

Southeast corner of Superior and Ohio streets

Relocated within the park is the restored former Webster City Railroad Station (c. 1895) and two split-log cabins dating from 1850 and 1856, respectively.

NO338 **Co-op Feed Mill**

1950 and later. Corner of 3rd and Seneca streets

This complex of prefabricated metal buildings is accompanied by high, cylindrical storage elevators. Even the signage and the electrical poles seem to have been composed as part of the design.

NO339 **First Federal Savings and the First State Bank**

c. 1980. Northeast and northwest corner of 2nd and Seneca streets

Each of these brick bank buildings facing one another across Seneca Street is situated within its own small park. The style used—loosely—was the Colonial Revival. The First Federal Savings building is flat roofed with a pronounced cornice. The First State Bank building has a gable roof with a small lantern.

NO340 **Webster Theater**

c. 1938. South side of 2nd between Willson and Des Moines streets

The angled metal-and-plastic marquee is terminated by a curved, layered neon sign announcing the theater's name. The marquee and the entrance/ticket area below represent a remodeling of an earlier building.

NO341 **Elks Building**

1906. North side of 2nd between Des Moines and Prospect streets

Below the elaborate corbeling of the building's cornice, on the second floor, is a band of vertical windows that have been filled in with glass brick. Though the large windows on each side of the entrance have been replaced with metal-framed units, their leaded glass lunettes remain.

NO342 **United States Post Office Building**

c. 1916. Southwest corner of 1st and Willson streets

Though modest in size, this is still a grand version of a Beaux-Arts building. A 45-degree cut has been made at the corner facing the juncture of the two streets, and this angled facade contains the entrance. Above the entrance is a stone lunette which projects into the roof area. Small, circular dormers line the low mansard roof. The building is sheathed in finely cut limestone carefully detailed with the usual array of classical details.

NO343 **House**

c. 1870 and later. 819 Prospect St.

This two-story brick house would appear to have been originally an Italianate dwelling to which was added a two-story entrance porch. Four Ionic columns support a gabled roof whose pitch levels out at the eave ends. The gable is filled in with a triangular glass window. The second floor of the porch (originally an open balcony) is now filled in.

NO344 **Masonic Temple**

1926. West side of Des Moines St. between Division and Bank streets

A severe but impressive three-story brick building has been realized within the Prairie school idiom. Two pavilions protrude slightly from the ends of the building. A set of two thin piers, placed in the center of each of these pavilions, rises to the cornice where there is a suggestion of a gable. A light-colored smooth stone band provides a base for the building, and another band is repeated at the top of the structure.

NO345 **House**

c. 1938. 1215 Des Moines St.

This is a perfect declaration of thirties' modernity: a Streamline Moderne box with an attached garage facing toward the street. The walls are pristine white stucco (with the appearance of concrete), the windows of metal; glass-brick windows appear around the entrance.

NO346 Kendall Young Public Library

1904–1905, Patton and Miller. 1201 Willson St.

Like the post office building downtown, this version of the Beaux-Arts style is rich in details. A classical pedimented porch with angled sides provides the entrance to this single-story structure on a raised basement. The corners of the main block are cut and angled, and their surfaces are treated by a horizontal banding of stone, somewhat suggestive of quoining. Though the walls are of brick, the amount of stone ornamentation so predomi-

NO346 Kendall Young Public Library

nates that the brick appears as an infill. The building's location on a small knoll, together with its steeply pitched hipped roof covered in tile, enhances its presence within the surrounding residential district.

Wellsburg

The town of Wellsburg (originally spelled Wellsburgh) was laid out in 1884 by George W. Wells. Its north-south, east-west grid was platted south of the tracks of the Burlington, Cedar Rapids, and Northern Railroad. A depot, grain elevators, stockyards, and corncribs were built parallel to the north side of the railroad. There was a modest amount of building activity in the community of the 1880s and 1890s, but changes and growth have been slow in the twentieth century.

NO347 Neessen House

1916–1918, Howard B. Burr. Corner of 4th and Washington streets

In addition to several large Queen Anne dwellings (such as the Koolman house of 1894

at 305 West Fourth Street), the architectural centerpiece of the town is the Neessen house, another of the many Prairie-style designs of the Waterloo architect Howard Burr. This good-sized dwelling looks to the more formal aspects of the Prairie mode that one associates with George Maher, Spencer and Powers, and others. The form of the house is that of a series of two-story volumes covered by low hipped roofs. The volumes project from a central mass and make the transition to the ground via low, single-story porches. Horizontality is emphasized by bands of Bedford limestone that run under the various groupings of windows. The interior features a white porcelainized brick fireplace, and woodwork with inlays of ebony and holly wood. The interior, including much of the furniture, was designed and selected by Kiewiet and Company, a Waterloo interior decorator.

Wesley

The community of Wesley lies just south of US 81, west of Iowa 17, within Kossuth County. At 403 East Street is a handsome turn-of-the-century version of the Gothic, Saint Joseph's Roman Catholic Church, built in 1901. The church is a wood version of the central-entrance-tower type, its side aisles covered by low-pitched shed roofs. Steeply pitched gable ends serve as independent frontispieces for each of the side aisles. The tower is particularly effective; each of its layers is defined by thin, steeply pitched gables that climb upward into the tall spire roof. Tall, narrow, pointed windows and thin buttresses (all in wood) add substance to the Gothic image. The use of a thin wood frame, together with the clapboard sheathing and details in wood, gives a strong, crisp, linear quality to the building—almost as if its facades still resided on the drafting board.

West Bend

NO348 **Grotto of the Redemption**

1912–1954, Father Paul M. Dobberstein. North Broadway, between 2nd and 3rd streets

NO348 Grotto of the Redempetion (view of the arched entrance)

The Grotto of the Redemption is Iowa's answer to England's numerous picturesque gardens of the eighteenth century. This block-long folly was begun in 1912 by Father Paul M. Dobberstein. He continued to add to it over the years until his death in 1954. It was then taken up by Father L. H. Greving. This wonderful folk folly is organized around 9 grottoes and the 14 stations of the cross. Stones and shells from all over the world have been utilized in the construction of the grotto, and a detailed and integrated series of biblical stories is revealed in the various grottoes. While the atmosphere of a succession of cave-like grottoes prevails within, externally the grotto looks like a medieval castle much worn by the effects of age. A circular tower surmounted by a cross projects above what appears to be the castle's keep. Accompanying the grotto is the church of Saints Peter and Paul. The landscaped garden spreads out to a small artificial lake.

NO349 **House**

c. 1916, Einar O. Broaten. Southeast corner of 4th St. S. and 1st Ave. E.

NO349 House, c. 1916

The scheme of this two-story house is that of the square Prairie box, in this case an exact copy of the Lippert house (1914) designed in Mason City by Broaten.

NO350 Harvestores

NO350 **Six Harvestores**

1976–1978. 9 miles north of West Bend on Iowa 15 at its junction with route B40 (just west of the community of Whittemore)

These six Harvestore high-tech silos are made of glass fused to steel, three tall and three short; all six fly the American flag.

West Union

The town was initially platted in 1849 and was resurveyed in 1850. The plat was organized around Rush Hill, which was set aside as a "public square" in anticipation of receiving the county courthouse. The lots around the square were arranged for business buildings, and over the years the square has been the governmental and business center of the community. In 1872 the tracks of the Burlington, Cedar Rapids, and Minnesota Railroad were constructed to West Union. They passed the south edge of the town, so the depot did not impinge on the town's center. The same situation occurred with the principal highways built from the 1920s on. They too skirted the public square, thus leaving the downtown uninterrupted by any of the major modes of transportation.

NO351 **Fayette County Courthouse**

1923–1924, John G. Ralston. Courthouse Square, bound by Vine, Main, Walnut, and Elm streets

The first courthouse (Italianate in design), its wonderful tall, square cupola surmounted by a segmented dome, was built in 1856–1857 and was destroyed by fire in 1872. The second courthouse, Italian Renaissance in style, followed in 1874. This burned in 1922. The

Waterloo architect John G. Ralston in 1923–1924 provided the city and county with a traditional well-detailed Beaux-Arts building in gray Bedford limestone and granite. At its dedication, it was described as rising "majestically from a base of granite, the whole scheme of architecture being classical and grand."[24]

Its two-story composition includes engaged piers and columns on a raised base; on the roof parapets there are four clock faces, one to a side. Though the building itself is low in profile, it does effectively dominate the downtown due to its hilltop location and the large size (400 feet by 400 feet) of its open site. Within, the building has a central rotunda surmounted by a colorful stained glass dome.

NO352 First Baptist Church

1867. Northwest corner of N. Vine and W. Adams streets

This is certainly a late use of the Greek Revival style for a church. The brick building was designed as a classical peripteral temple with pilasters (rather than columns) carried around the building. A simple triangle occupies the tympanum, and above is a two-tier tower and spire. The church was damaged by fire in 1910 and some changes were subsequently made, including the addition of the present small entrance porch.

NO353 United States Post Office Building

1940, Louis A. Simon and Neal Melick. Southwest corner of N. Vine and W. Maple streets

One of the numerous post offices built throughout the United States in the Great Depression, this one illustrates the Federal phase of the American Colonial, realized in brick with stone trim.

NO354 House

c. 1927. 108 W. Maple St.

This picture-perfect image of a small period revival house of the twenties contains references to the rural medieval, with just a touch of the Colonial Revival. The eaves of the steeply pitched roof sweep over to encompass the attached garage on one side and a gate on the other.

NO355 House

c. 1870. 206 W. Plum St.

The two-story wood-sheathed Italianate house has its entrance on one side with a large bay facing out to the street. The hipped roof is broken by wall gables filled in with triangular windows. Another two-story Italianate dwelling of approximately the same period can be seen at 109 West Maple Street.

NO356 Evans House

1886. 409 W. Vine St.

The designer of the Evans house took the Queen Anne theme and effectively reduced it nearly to the proportions of a children's playhouse. The small circular tower sheathed in board-and-batten is almost French Châteauesque, and the front projecting second-floor balcony is enriched by spindle-backed seats on each side. Everything else about the design is miniaturized—the tucked-in front entrance, the small gabled window dormers, and finally the little pencil-point brick chimney.

NO357 Fayette County Fairgrounds

End of S. Vine St.

The historic "village" element of the fairgrounds contains two 12-sided barns and several other historic structures, including the obligatory group of log cabins.

NO358 Grimes Octagonal Barn

c. 1880. Proceed to southeast section of West Union, take paved road to Echo Valley County Park (east); travel past park entrance on gravel road approximately .75 mile

Built by a local carpenter, Joe Buller from West Union, this barn's cone-shaped roof is of the self-supporting type. An unusual feature is the tall gabled hay dormer which projects away from the roof. The structure is wood framed, sheathed in horizontal shiplap siding.

NO359 **True-Round Barn**

c. 1910. West side of West Union on US 18; 3 miles to route W25, 6 miles south on route W25

According to Soike, this barn was built by the Johnson Brothers Clay Works of Fort Dodge, Iowa.[25] The walls are of terracotta tile. The conical roof contains a hay dormer with a low-pitched gable at the top of the roof.

NO360 **Nus Barn**

1906. South of West Union: take Iowa 150 south 13 miles, route IS4 east 3 miles, route C2W east 3.5 miles, passing route W51

A conical silo projects from the center of the 12-sided barn. The present terracotta tile silo probably replaced an earlier wooden one.

Missouri River— West (MW)

WITHIN THIS REGION, TWO OF IOWA'S LARGEST CITIES—
Council Bluffs and Sioux City—were platted as early as the 1850s.
The wide Missouri River provided the initial steamboat transportation in the area, but by the mid-1860s the great transcontinental railroads
had penetrated the region. Both Council Bluffs (along with Omaha, Nebraska,
across the Missouri) and Sioux City developed into and have remained major
regional shipping points for agricultural products and cattle. Transport by water
and rail gave way by the mid-1920s to shipping via trucks using the new concrete highways. The location of Council Bluffs and Sioux City adjacent to the
river meant that their commercial/industrial areas developed on the river flats,
while their residential districts eventually spread over the bluffs and high hills
overlooking the river valley or its secondary rivers and streams.

Surprisingly for an area this far to the west, there are a number of well-
preserved buildings in the late Federal and Greek Revival styles to be found in
Council Bluffs as well as in a good number of smaller towns and out in the
countryside. Sioux City was once the state's prime center for large-scaled stone
Richardsonian Romanesque and Queen Anne dwellings of the 1880s and 1890s.
Many of these are gone, but a few splendid examples remain. As in other
sections of the state, public buildings, banks, and dwellings in the Prairie style
are found in large and small towns, the center being Sioux City, with its famed
Woodbury County Courthouse.

Alton

Though now appearing somewhat forlorn, the Chicago and Northwest Railroad Station at Alton presents a sophisticated image—c. 1915—that one often

Missouri River - West

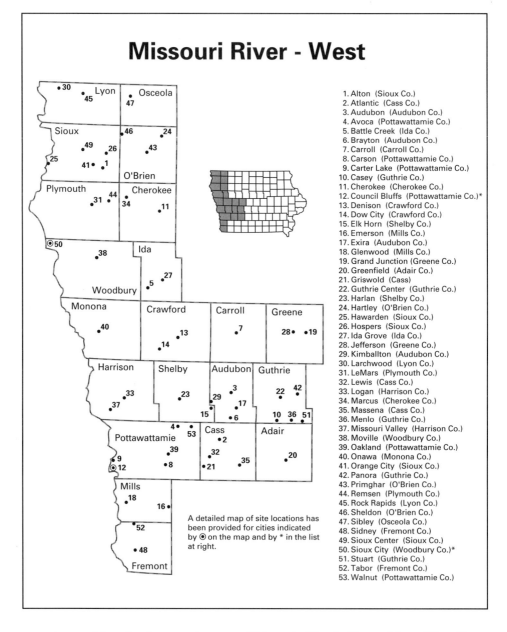

1. Alton (Sioux Co.)
2. Atlantic (Cass Co.)
3. Audubon (Audubon Co.)
4. Avoca (Pottawattamie Co.)
5. Battle Creek (Ida Co.)
6. Brayton (Audubon Co.)
7. Carroll (Carroll Co.)
8. Carson (Pottawattamie Co.)
9. Carter Lake (Pottawattamie Co.)
10. Casey (Guthrie Co.)
11. Cherokee (Cherokee Co.)
12. Council Bluffs (Pottawattamie Co.)*
13. Denison (Crawford Co.)
14. Dow City (Crawford Co.)
15. Elk Horn (Shelby Co.)
16. Emerson (Mills Co.)
17. Exira (Audubon Co.)
18. Glenwood (Mills Co.)
19. Grand Junction (Greene Co.)
20. Greenfield (Adair Co.)
21. Griswold (Cass)
22. Guthrie Center (Guthrie Co.)
23. Harlan (Shelby Co.)
24. Hartley (O'Brien Co.)
25. Hawarden (Sioux Co.)
26. Hospers (Sioux Co.)
27. Ida Grove (Ida Co.)
28. Jefferson (Greene Co.)
29. Kimballton (Audubon Co.)
30. Larchwood (Lyon Co.)
31. LeMars (Plymouth Co.)
32. Lewis (Cass Co.)
33. Logan (Harrison Co.)
34. Marcus (Cherokee Co.)
35. Massena (Cass Co.)
36. Menlo (Guthrie Co.)
37. Missouri Valley (Harrison Co.)
38. Moville (Woodbury Co.)
39. Oakland (Pottawattamie Co.)
40. Onawa (Monona Co.)
41. Orange City (Sioux Co.)
42. Panora (Guthrie Co.)
43. Primghar (O'Brien Co.)
44. Remsen (Plymouth Co.)
45. Rock Rapids (Lyon Co.)
46. Sheldon (O'Brien Co.)
47. Sibley (Osceola Co.)
48. Sidney (Fremont Co.)
49. Sioux Center (Sioux Co.)
50. Sioux City (Woodbury Co.)*
51. Stuart (Guthrie Co.)
52. Tabor (Fremont Co.)
53. Walnut (Pottawattamie Co.)

A detailed map of site locations has been provided for cities indicated by ⊙ on the map and by * in the list at right.

associates with suburban stations on Chicago's North Shore Line. The Alton station joins the image of the English cottage with the Craftsman aesthetic. On the first floor there are long bands of windows right beneath the soffit of the broad overhanging roofs. The second-floor gable ends are half-timbered, with stucco infills. The station is located at the east end of Twelfth Street. A few blocks away, on Sixth Avenue between Tenth and Eleventh streets, is a small, delightful Queen Anne cottage (c. 1880). The street elevation plays off a narrow, spindly porch on one side and a narrow bay on the other. In a rather odd fashion, the projecting bay and the porch are drawn together into a symmetrical composition by two gabled dormers which, with their small lunette windows, project from the steeply pitched hipped roof.

Atlantic

The town is situated on a low hill just east of the Nishnabotna River. It was platted in 1868, and the following year it was connected to the Chicago, Rock Island, and Pacific Railroad. Atlantic's original plat laid out its principal street, Chestnut Street, with a 100-foot width. Two parks (one of which was for the county courthouse) were also established at the center of the town. For a community its size, Atlantic boasts an impressive array of buildings, ranging from the octagonal Duncan house of 1865 to the Streamline Moderne Coca-Cola Building of 1940.

MW001 Cass County Courthouse

1932–1934, Dougher, Rich and Woodburn. Chestnut St., between US 6 and Poplar St.

Described as "modernistic," the courthouse has been called "an office building rather than a pile of brick, stone, and mortar."[1] Its design is indeed PWA Moderne, a three-story block balanced on two sides by single-story wings. The light buff-colored brick walls are trimmed in Indiana limestone. There is characteristic Art Deco ornamentation—scrolls, sunbursts, sunflowers—throughout the building.

MW002 Soldiers Monument

1888, E. H. Prior. Chestnut St., between 6th and 7th streets

Within a heavily planted park is an impressive monument in marble. This Civil War monument was designed by E. H. Prior and was built in 1888. A bronze statue of Liberty surmounts a fluted Doric column that rises 50 feet high. On the second level of its double-tiered base are two smaller bronze statues, one of a soldier, the other of a sailor. Nearby, appropriately tucked away in a grove of trees, is a log cabin with an overscaled stone chimney on one of the gabled ends.

MW003 Atlantic City Hall

1916, J. P. Guth. Southwest corner of Walnut and 4th streets

From some distance one might suppose that this two-story brick building was a factory, or at least some type of commercial building. Close up, one discovers that its inlaid stone nameplate declares it to be City Hall. The one other element that signals its public purpose is its square corner tower. The base of the tower as it proceeds upward is realized only by walls that project a few inches from the walls of the building itself, but this reticent treatment stops when the tower emerges above the surrounding parapets. How would one explain it? Perhaps it resulted from an urge for the Gothic felt by a Prairie architect. The tower's most startling features are the four corner finials that project at right angles from the building. A thin streamer ornament in cast stone leads up to a cardboard-thin roof atop each finial. Between the finials, the tower's parapet exhibits a curved gable projection. Unfortunately, many of the windows have been filled in, so the building's pattern of fenestration is no longer as apparent as it should be.

MW004 Coca-Cola Bottling Company Building

1940. 2nd St., between Chestnut and Walnut streets

A dignified, reserved interpretation of the Streamline Moderne of the 1930s, this two-story light-buff brick building exhibits banding across the second floor. On the left side is a separate wing with its counteremphasis on the vertical. At the base of this wing is a bay entirely faced in glass brick; above, as part of a vertical panel of cast stone, is a large framed octagonal window. A large section of the lower wall to the right is of glass brick, and above this is the cast-concrete sign panel bearing the name Coca-Cola.

MW005 **Kuikendahl House**

1907. 103 14th St., end of Poplar St.

This two-story Colonial Revival house seems to have the pretense of being a mansion. Its centered two-story porch with Ionic columns announces the house to the street. On the first floor a smaller porch runs underneath and behind the columns. Many features of the house, such as the larger porch and the pedimented horizontal dormers, relate more to the then-current Craftsman movement than to a strict interpretation of the Colonial.

MW006 **Whitmare House**

1917. 108 9th St. (northeast corner of Locust St.)

This stucco-sheathed Prairie-style dwelling is capped by a hipped roof. The street facade centers on two horizontal bands of casement windows. Off to the left are a small entrance terrace, the entrance itself, and the stair hall.

MW007 **Whitney House**

c. 1916. South side of 8th St., between Spruce and Pine streets

This good-sized English Tudor house has been simplified and organized according to the Craftsman aesthetic. The center portion of the house is a simple and direct two-story rectangular block capped by a steeply pitched gable roof. An open living porch projects from the left side of the house, and enclosed wings are attached to the right side and the rear. The gable ends bear half-timbering, and the front of the roof contains a Craftsman-like shed-roof dormer. The front entrance has a curved roof similar to those in the work of George Maher.

MW008 **Haas House**

1862. Proceed 2.2 miles south of Atlantic on US 6, turn right (west) on route G35, after 18 miles turn north on gravel road, proceed 1.2 miles to first house on west side of road

Gerald Haas, the first owner of this house, built it from lumber and precut parts brought by wagon from Des Moines. The house is an excellent example of a Greek Revival dwelling modified by Italianate detailing. The entrance porch of this two-story clapboard house is vigorously Greek; its two columns are fluted and of the Ionic order, the porch's entablature cornice has dentils, and the end posts of the balustrade around the roof are abbrevi-

MW008 Haas House

ated Doric shafts. In contrast the molding carried on the lintels of the windows and partially down each side is a device usually associated with either the Gothic Revival or the Italianate. The brackets supporting the overhanging hipped roof are strongly Italianate.

MW009 **Duncan House**

1865. At the eastern city limits of Atlantic, .5 miles south of US 6 on a gravel road

This is one of Iowa's octagonal houses, inspired by (or taken from) the published designs of Orson Fowler. Although the roof of this octagon is almost flat, the central octagonal cupola is quite tall. The paired openings of the cupola are louvered, and a chimney projects from the center of the cupola's roof.

MW009 Duncan House

The double-hung windows on the first and second floors have small pediments over them. The projecting single-floor wing is not original to the house, nor is the present sheathing of this wood-frame structure.

MW010 **Hofmeister Round Barn and Silo**

c. 1921. Travel south of Atlantic on US6 to Lewis, then west .2 miles on route G43; drive south 2 miles on the gravel road; barn is on east side of road

One form of farm building that developed after 1910 was the low, round or many-sided barn from the center of which projects a tall

silo. A few examples of this type were built in Iowa and are recorded by Soike.[2] The Hofmeister barn has a moderately pitched roof, but the original conical roof of the silo is now missing. The walls of both barn and silo are of reinforced concrete that has been banded with steel rings. As a designed object, the Hofmeister barn is most abstract.

Audubon

The town's plan centers on a large, open park that is approached on one side by two blocks of commercial buildings. On the opposite side, two public buildings—one of them the Audubon County Courthouse of 1938–1939—look out onto the park. The courthouse was designed by the Des Moines architect Karl Keffer; in style it is PWA Moderne, with a central, somewhat raised section meant to be read as a pilastered pavilion. Leading between the two public buildings is a continuation of the town's main street; it is terminated two blocks farther on as the street turns past a church. At the southwest corner of Broadway and Division streets is a clapboard and shingled Queen Anne house (c. 1889) with a bay tower capped by a high segmented dome. A block farther down the hill, at the southwest corner of Division and Chicago streets, is another large Queen Anne dwelling (1890), this one sheathed in brick, with a slate roof. However, the "glory" of Audubon is "Albert the Bull," a large, colored sculpture of a bull. Albert is located south on US 71 as one approaches town.

Avoca

Within gently rolling terrain just east of the Nishnabotna River is the community of Avoca. In the downtown, on Elm Street south of Crocker Street, is a two-story commercial building now occupied by the Home Federal Savings and Loan (1900). On the second floor, two pediments are supported by pairs of rough, almost primitive brick columns. Contrasting with these columned pediments are two horizontal bay windows which have been thrust into the intervening wall surface. Up on the hill in a residential area overlooking the downtown is a large brick villa (c. 1878) at the northeast corner of Taylor and Chestnut streets. The designer's catholic taste brought together an Italianate tower and bays, accompanied by both Gothic Revival and Eastlake detailing.

Battle Creek

Noteworthy in Battle Creek is the bank building (1912) at the northwest corner of Main and First Street Southeast. This Beaux-Arts design looks to the Greek Hellenistic tradition rather than to Rome. The wide entablature contains triglyphs, and the pilasters of the wall below sit upon a rusticated base. As originally designed, the two-story limestone-sheathed building contained a bank at the corner, a retail store to the right (on Main Street), a second retail store at the side of the building facing First Street, and an adjoining entrance leading to stairs and offices on the second floor. The building is no longer used as a bank, and a number of the bank windows have been filled in with glass brick.

MW011 **Warnock House**

c. 1899, George F. Barber. 201 Maple St.

The prolific architectural "salesman" George F. Barber provided Francis B. Warnock with one of his designs. The design of the Warnock house comes close to design No. 41B (p. 58) in Barber's *New Model Dwellings and How Best to Build Them.* The focus of this Queen Anne/Colonial Revival building is the three-story corner bay tower in front of which projects a spire-roofed bay of the wraparound porch. The two principal wings of the two-story house contain Palladian windows with exaggeratedly vertical central sections. The house is now operated as The Inn at Battle Creek.

Brayton

The Brayton Town Hall (1940), at the northeast corner of Main Street and county road T, is one of the many WPA public buildings constructed in Iowa during the depression of the 1930s. Almost all of the designs for town halls in Iowa employ the PWA Moderne image. The Brayton Town Hall is a single-story building on a raised basement and was constructed of concrete block. Its main floor is approached via a pair of stairways parallel to the front wall of the building. These lead up to a platform containing an entrance to the lower floor. At the rear is an enclosed garage to house the fire truck. Decoration is minimal: three bands of bricks are carried around the center of the building. The upper and lower bands connect with the sills and headers of the windows. At the cornice is an indented horizontal pattern that remotely suggests dentils. The best decorative feature of the building is its Moderne lettering spelling out "Town Hall" over the entrance.

Carroll

Approaching Carroll from the east on US 30 (near Glidden), one sees an impressive, quite large corncrib made up of two semicircular masonry units; they are separated by a central wood section and held in place by a single roof with a gable-roofed monitor at the center of the ridge (for the lift machinery). The geometry of this building demonstrates how effectively abstract are many of the Midwest's agricultural buildings.

In Carroll itself is the Public Library building (1905) by Thomas R. Kimball, located at the northwest corner of Sixth Street (US 30) and Court Street. The general flavor of the library design is Italian Renaissance, but the architect has gone far beyond his historical source in modifying and simplifying this image. On each side of the entrance are three vertical bands containing windows; below each of these is a terracotta panel displaying an open book. A low-pitched hipped roof projects far out over the walls, holding the small box in place.

At the southwest corner of North West Street and West Fifth Avenue is the Chicago and Northwest Railroad Station (c. 1900). The station, with a stone base and brick walls, appears medieval, though the actual details are classical. The roof forms are what matter, and they are projected far out from the walls, creating a horizontal sheltered area below.

Carson

The small town of Carson is located on the east bank of the West Nishnabotna River. By the end of the nineteenth century the community was a stop on the north-south Chicago, Burlington, and Quincy Railroad. Currently it lies just west of the intersection of US 59 and Iowa 92.

MW012 **Lewood T. Osler House**
1911–1912. 304 Broadway

The Osler house unites some Craftsman detailing with an essential Prairie box. The walls of the lower section of the house (up to the second-floor window sills) are covered in shingles; above, the walls are stucco, which is carried out onto the boxed roof eaves. To the left on ground level is an entrance and a porte-cochère. The roof of the entrance porch is a simple extension of one side of the gable roof over the porte-cochère. Supporting this entry roof is a pair of dramatic curved brackets. There is a rectilinear pattern of mullions within each casement window. Although the solar collector panels on the roof may be practical, they certainly have added little aesthetically to the house.

MW013 **Hillman House**
1917. 214 High St.

A second Prairie house in Carson is the James Hillman house. As is the case with several other Prairie style houses, this one creates the impression that a smaller box with a hipped roof has been placed atop a somewhat larger box with the same type of roof. This is due mainly to the high pitch of both roofs and is accentuated by the covering of the lower floor in brick and the upper floor in narrow clapboard. At the front of the house to the left on ground level is the entrance (easy to miss); then at the center of the front is an open porch whose roof is supported by brick piers. The second-floor windows (in this instance, all of the windows are double hung) are grouped quite close to the corners of the building.

MW014 Way House

1894, George F. Barber. 316 Broadway

Farther down Broadway at the northwest corner of Broadway and Dye streets is the W. J. Way house, a Queen Anne dwelling built according to a design by the Knoxville, Tennessee, architect George F. Barber. The second-floor porch over the entrance has a gable roof supported by a single turned wood column in the middle, a design feature that Barber seems to have favored. As with many Queen Anne houses, the exuberant porches, bays, and towers, and the luxury of wood ornamentation is basically confined to the street facade. The sides and rear are relatively plain, except for the decoration of the roofscape, particularly the gable ends.

Carter Lake (near Council Bluffs)

Carter Lake, although part of Iowa, is situated within a bend in the Missouri River that is now within the northern suburbs of Omaha, Nebraska. At 301 Locust Street is the Old Dutch Mill (now Carter Lake Bait and Tackle) (c. 1931). Here one is confronted with a former service station that is a sophisticated version of a late-twenties Art Deco building. The salient feature of the design is its central tower with an Art Deco (very sharp and angular) windmill. The Old Dutch Mill can be "discovered" by proceeding across the river from Council Bluffs to Omaha on US 6, then north on route 165 to Locust Street and west to 301 Locust.

Casey

At the southeast corner of Logan and McPherson streets is the Abram Rutt National Bank building (1915), now the Security State Bank. This was one of an array of smaller bank buildings designed throughout the upper Midwest by the Lytle Company of Sioux City. Generally the bank designs from the firm are well done, and in a few instances, such as this bank in Casey, the company produced a really outstanding building. The design of this forceful box looks toward a mannered version of the Georgian. This Prairie example is rendered in the usual brick, glazed brick, and terracotta. The cream-colored glazed brick and terracotta dominate the walls of the building, with the red bricks forming strange pilasters supporting an attic story. Over the entrance, in terracotta, is a multicolored cornucopia overflowing with abundance. If you look closely at the pattern within the upper row of terracotta panels (in the attic story), you will discover Abram Rutt's initials.

Cherokee

Proceeding up the hill to 801 West Main Street, one will find a magnificent Queen Anne dwelling visible through a thick grove of shrubs and trees. The building's ground floor is sheathed in stone; above, the walls are divided into a variety of repeated and connected geometric patterns. The best feature of the building is the very high corner tower topped by a conical roof. To the side, the porte-cochère is treated as an independent pavilion with two segmental arches gently breaking through and into the roof. The thick, turned columns supporting the porte-cochère roof are placed on raised masonry walls, and along the side is a delicate, lacy, turned balustrade.

The community also boasts a Prairie dwelling reminiscent of the work of George Maher. This is the Cantine house (1925) at 1110 Main Street. The house is formed of the usual brick-sheathed box covered by a hipped roof with a wide overhang. A large porch runs across the front of the house, and a gabled dormer projects from the center of the roof. The upper sashes of the double-hung windows have a pattern of two horizontal bands with two vertical bars placed near each end. The enclosed second-floor sleeping porch to the rear, with its continuous band of glass windows, is the most overt Prairie-style feature of the building.

Council Bluffs

The city of Council Bluffs was platted in 1854 on a wide bend of the Missouri River. To the east was a series of high bluffs cut into by deep, narrow valleys. As the city grew, it spread farther out onto the river plain to the west, and at the same time its residential districts developed on the bluffs and hills to the east.

It was the railroad that established the importance of both Council Bluffs and neighboring Omaha, Nebraska, just across the river. In 1863 President Lincoln selected Council Bluffs as the eastern terminus for the transcontinental Union Pacific line. The first train crossed the Missouri on a temporary bridge in 1867.

While the city has lost its wonderful nineteenth-century courthouse and many of its older business blocks, it has been able to retain a large number of its nineteenth-century houses. Council Bluffs is home to several of the state's major monuments, including the Lewis and Clark Monument and Daniel Chester French's well-known *Angel of Death*. Other community assets are the public parks, especially the 45-acre Fairmount Park; it occupies a high point of land with views over the city, the river, and Omaha in the distance.

Council Bluffs

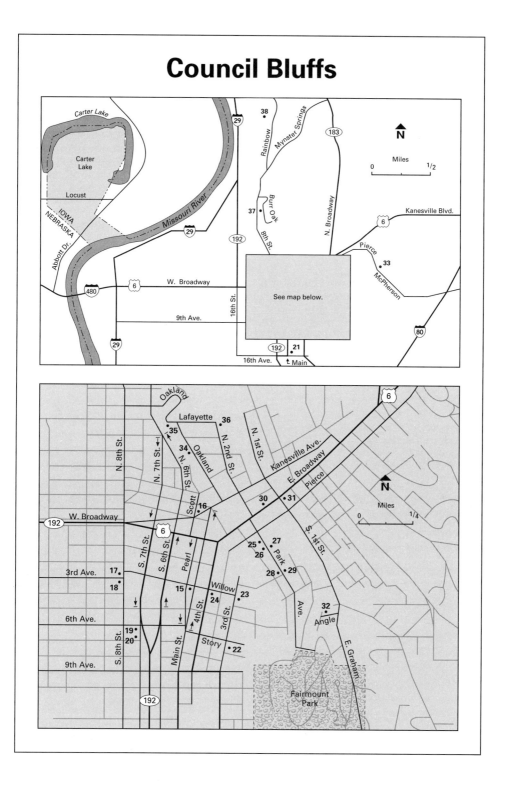

MW015 Council Bluffs Public Library

1904–1905, Patton and Miller. Southwest corner of Willow Ave. and Pearl St.

The library's prominent location and large size provide a good indication of the important place it has occupied in the community. The long, low Beaux-Arts structure built of brick with stone trim appears strong and assertive at its entrance portico. At this point in the design, the architect introduced a screen of Ionic columns set slightly in front of three arched openings.

MW016 Wickham Block

c. 1885. Northeast corner of W. Broadway and Scott St.

This four-story Richardsonian Romanesque commercial block turns the corner with a thin, pencil-like bay turret. The upper section of the little turret has a band containing the building's name, and above this is a tile-clad conical roof.

MW017 Hancock Cottage

1880. 803 3rd Ave.

A Gothic Revival one-and-a-half-story cottage was made grander by the addition of a square Italianate tower and a wide Eastlake-inspired shed-roof wall dormer.

MW018 House

c. 1910. 224 S. 8th St.

A characteristic classical palazzo, two and a half stories tall, has been placed upon a balustraded terrace. Though the design was certainly meant to convey authority, the delicate fenestration of the house brings it into the realm of the domestic.

MW019 House

c. 1878. 608 S. 7th St.

This is a typical post-Civil War Italianate dwelling. The narrow end of the two-story brick-sheathed box provides its main entrance; its long side, interrupted by a two-story bay, faces the side street. Present are the usual pronounced stone lintels over the windows (quite brittle in outline) and brack-

eted eaves supporting a low-pitched hipped roof.

MW020 Wickham House

1882, O. P. Wickham, contractor. 616 S. 7th St.

The patterns of the wood detailing, posts, and capitals of this large brick Queen Anne dwelling indicate that elements of the earlier Eastlake style continued on into the middle to late 1880s. The local contractor and builder O. P. Wickham constructed the house for his own use.

MW021 Rock Island Railroad Station

c. 1900. 16th Ave. at S. Main St.

If one arrived by train at Council Bluffs, this station's Châteauesque tile roof tower would have captured one's attention. The tower rises out of a long, low brick structure whose walls are sheltered by a roof supported by wide brackets.

MW022 Grenville M. Dodge House

1869, W. W. Boyton. 605 S. 3rd St.

A high blufftop location provides a commanding position for this house, designed in 1869 for the city's leading citizen, a railroad builder and Civil War general. Though the mansard roof places the house safely within the French Second Empire style, much of the detailing is late Italianate. The interior was modified over the years, reflecting changes of taste from the mid-1870s on. The present entrance veranda is also of a later date.

MW023 **Jennings House**

c. 1902, Cox and Schoentgen. 201 S. 3rd St.

This Colonial Revival house has a two-story semicircular Ionic porch. There are classical broken pediments over the pair of first-floor windows. Though pedimented, the two dormers seem more Craftsman than Colonial.

MW024 **Bennett House**

1884. 333 Willow St.

A two-story brick Italianate house, now painted, this dwelling features a central bayed pavilion capped by a tiny towerlike roof with a single dormer.

MW025 **Baumeister House**

c. 1901. 126 Park Ave.

The Baumeister house is a miniaturized clapboard dwelling poised stylistically somewhere between the Eastlake and the Queen Anne. The most assertive feature of the house is a small octagonal tower that dominates one corner of the dwelling.

MW026 **House**

1878. 150 Park Ave.

The designer of this two-story brick dwelling introduced a most unusual window detail above the entrance porch. Here he placed a window within a wide Gothic arch, and then he attached another on one side only.

MW027 **Lysander Tulleys House**

1875, P. E. Hale. 151 Park Ave.

The form of this large, two-story brick house is that of an Italian villa, but the window patterns and the wood detailing are Eastlake. The solidity of the brick walls provides a contrasting background to the lightness of the Eastlake woodwork. Tulleys engaged the Chicago architect P. E. Hale to design the house; it was constructed by Wickham Brothers of Council Bluffs.

MW028 **House**

c. 1905. 228 Park Ave.

A broad verandalike porch suggests both entrance and a place for outdoor living during the summer months. The porch and the one-and-a-half-story dwelling behind it are rendered in the turn-of-the-century American Colonial Revival style.

MW029 **Thomas Hart Benton, Jr., House**

1857. 231 Park Ave.

Except for a slight hint at verticality, this Federal-style house might have been built in upstate New York around 1820. The central entrance door is surrounded by side lights and a rectangular transom. The house was built by Brig. Gen. Thomas H. Benton, nephew of Sen. Thomas H. Benton of Missouri.

MW030 **Commercial Buildings**

mid-1870s and later. 100 block of E. Broadway

This is an excellent example of a late nineteenth-century streetscape composed of small commercial buildings. The strongest of the group is the brick building with Eastlake ornament at 144–146 Broadway.

MW031 **Broadway United Methodist Church**

1892. Corner of 1st St. and E. Broadway

One can assume that the source for this church (most likely indirect) was southern French

Romanesque architecture. Whatever the inspiration, the bold massing, the fenestration, and the thin, curved spire roof on the corner tower have been handled with great freedom.

MW032 Cottage

c. 1880. 110 Angle St.

This small cottage shows a wide range of design features of the 1880s and later. A tiny entrance porch disappears alongside an oversized bay tower.

MW033 Iowana Motel

1943–1945. 1414 McPherson

Each of the little white clapboard cabins with gable roofs is trimmed in red and each is separated from the next by an open space for cars. The obligatory wagon wheel and metal shell chair sit out in front of each one.

MW034 Cottage

c. 1880. 528 Oakland Ave.

This Eastlake/Queen Anne cottage exhibits splendid Gothic Revival detail. Aggressive horizontality seems to be the theme of the one-and-a-half-story cottage, though much of the sawed and cutout wood detailing provides a counterpoint of verticality.

MW035 Lincoln Monument

1911. Oakland Ave. at Lafayette St., at bluff's end

A tall, narrow shaft of granite commemorates the visit of Lincoln to Council Bluffs in the year 1859.

MW036 *Angel of Death*

1916–1918, Daniel Chester French. N. 2nd St. at Lafayette St., southeast corner of Fairview Cemetery

The winged figure of the Angel of Death holds a basin of water, symbolizing eternal life. She stands on the prow of a boat that sails toward the viewer. The cast-bronze figure was commissioned as a memorial to Ruth

MW036 *Angel of Death*

Anne Dodge, the wife of the railroad builder Grenville M. Dodge. The accompanying landscape design is as impressive as the sculpture itself. Steps lead up to a forecourt defined informally by shrubs. The figure has been placed at one end of the forecourt, with a backdrop of large hardwood trees.

MW037 Peterson House

1971, Dan R. Fox. 317 Burr Oaks Dr.

The image of the rural wood barn has been played off against the precise geometry of the cut-into box. The axis of the living room is directed to a view of Omaha, across the river.

MW038 Lewis and Clark Monument

1935; Harry Stinson, sculptor; George L. Horner, architect. North end of Rainbow Rd.

This monument was erected in the mid-1930s to commemorate the 1804 meeting of Lewis and Clark with members of the Otoe and Winnebago tribes, the "council" referred to in the city's name. Figures in low relief have been cut into the front and back of two curved stone slabs, suggesting a fine line drawing.

Denison

The town site was platted by the Providence Western Land Company, and it was named for one of its agents, the Reverend Jesse W. Denison. The site selected was close to the geographic center of the county, and it had the advantage of being located between the Boyer and East Boyer rivers. The community was laid out in 1856, and the town plat—some 700 acres—was a large one for the time. The plan of the town had several unusual features, including major streets 100 feet wide and, as Andreas noted, "handsome and eligible blocks . . . reserved for public parks and other purposes."[3] In addition to the usual full blocks set aside for the future county courthouse and high school, two public parks were planned—one circular, the other octagonal—and an oval scheme of streets and open space was established on Prospect Hill for an anticipated college. By the early 1870s a branch of the Chicago and Northwestern Railway had traversed the community, and by 1900 four additional railroads entered the town.

MW039 **Crawford County Courthouse**

1904, G. A. Berlinghoff. Corner of 12th St. and Broadway

The scale and detailing of this Beaux-Arts courthouse fits in beautifully with the size of the town and the small square within which the building has been placed. The building is reminiscent of an eighteenth-century English Georgian country house. The principal facade has a tripartite scheme, with slightly projecting pavilions on each side and a pedimented portion at the center. Small, low, octagonal drums with low domes surmount each of the building's four corner pavilions. The two principal floors of the building are set on the usual Georgian raised basement.

MW040 **McHenry House**

1885, Luman A. Sewell, builder and designer. 1426 1st Ave. N.

When the term "Queen Anne" was applied to a building in the 1880s and 1890s, it meant different things in different instances. But certainly one of the constant qualities of the style was its essential variety and picturesqueness. At times the variety and richness seemed quite mad; on other occasions, such as in the McHenry house, the picturesque was handled with reserve, even great subtlety. The surfaces of this house, varied in form, provide a wonderful sequence of different materials:

clapboard and shingles. This concern for geometric patterning continues even in the surfaces of the brick chimneys.

MW041 **House**

c. 1900. 1316 2nd Ave. N.

This strong Colonial Revival design has just a touch of the picturesque quality found in the Queen Anne. The central gable of this two-and-a-half-story house contains an overscaled Palladian window; to each side of the gable are large-scaled dormers with gable roofs. The open front porch has now been enclosed and the walls have been painted a strong teal blue with contrasting cream trim.

MW042 **House**

c. 1889. 1104 2nd Ave. S.

The central gable of this two-story Eastlake dwelling displays a fanlike pattern in turned and sawed wood. The building's T-shape plan includes porches on the first floor, one of which still has its original sawed and turned work.

MW043 **House**

c. 1895. 1516 2nd Ave.

The Queen Anne/Colonial Revival design of this dwelling features an extensive veranda, a broad porte-cochère, and a semicircular second-floor porch. The columns of the veranda and porte-cochère are grouped in pairs and are thin and delicate. The roof of the corner open tower changes pitch at the eaves, becoming almost flat. Thin classical brackets support the soffit of all the roofs.

MW044 Harts Haven House

c. 1890. Northeast corner of Broadway and 17th St.

The picturesque roofscape of this classic Queen Anne dwelling consists of a spired bay tower on one side, an oversized dormer in the center of the roof, and on the other side an extension of the open second-floor porch, which has a semicircular front and its own spire roof. A large porch runs across the front of the house at the first-floor level and extends out to the side as a circular open pavilion covered by yet another spired roof. The usual sawed and turned work one associates with the Queen Anne is found in most parts of the house, except on the gabled ends of the porch and of the upper dormer; here the theme is Colonial Revival. The house is sited on a hill, so that its verticality is accentuated.

Dow City

MW045 Dow House

1872–1874. South end of Princes St., off US 30

The town was named for its founder, Simeon E. Dow, and his house was sited like a feudal castle, visually dominating the community below. Dow was a land speculator and promoter, and he entertained high hopes for his new city. His grand two-story brick house shares a number of qualities with a similarly sited house, Montauk (1874), in Clermont. Both are Italianate in style, both are strong and aggressive designs, and both are situated on high eminences overlooking their respective communities. The bracketed roof of the Dow house is broken in the front by a central curved gable that contains a circular window. The principal windows and doorways of the

MW045 Dow House

house have segmental curved lintels that project from the surrounding brick walls.

Elk Horn (and Kimballton)

Elk Horn and nearby Kimballton are the self-proclaimed capitals of the Danish settlement in Iowa. A Danish windmill (MW046) is a landmark there.

The local house museum, the Bestemors House, is situated at the southeast corner of Union Street and College Avenue. If the date (1908) given for the construction of this one-and-a-half-story Queen Anne dwelling is correct, then it certainly represents the realization of an architectural image far out of then current fashion. The character of this house is expressed through the use of gables; these include the pair of wall gables at the front, those on the sides, one on the roof of the entry porch, and finally—the best one of all—a windowless gabled dormer set high in the center of the roof. The walls of the house are patterned with bands of shingles, and within the various gables there are sunrise patterns in cutout wood.

In nearby Kimballton, facing Iowa 173, is a miniature version of the famous "Little Mermaid" in Copenhagen. However, Kimballton's most interesting building is not Danish in style. It is the PWA Moderne Kimballton Town Hall (1941) built directly alongside commercial buildings facing onto the town's main street (Iowa 173). The two-story town hall was built by the WPA; its most powerful design feature is the entrance, with its surround of receding layers of brick, and its signage. The building has recently been brought up to date by the addition of little shingled shed roofs over each of the side windows on the ground floor.

MW046 **Windmill**

1848. 1976, moved and reassembled. 4038 Main St.

In 1976 the community of Elk Horn obtained and reassembled a 60-foot-high windmill that had originally been built in Norre Snede, Denmark, in 1848. The mill is an eight-sided building, and the blades span 67 feet.

Emerson

MW047 **Runnels House**

1882. 3 miles east of Emerson on route H34; south on route M37 1 mile to the crossroads of Hawthorne; take the gravel road west .3 miles; the house is on the south side of the road

Iowa is dotted here and there with deserted dwellings and farm buildings, but few if any can equal the romantic and melancholy atmosphere presented by the B. F. Runnels house. This large, elegant French Second Empire house stands alone on a barren knoll. Its wood porches are gone, which accentuates the vertical thrust of the building. The house has ashlar block stone walls of a light color; a darker, more finely cut stone was used for

MW047 Runnels House

quoining and for banding at the basement level, midway up the walls, and below the entablature cornice. Many of the lintels over the windows and doors form 45-degree an-gles at the corners, while others are gabled or formed of segmental curves. The house is now deserted and in partial ruin.

Exira

The tiny town of Exira is situated at the confluence of the East Nishnabotna River and Davids Creek, 8 miles north of Interstate 80.

MW048 Exira City Hall

1921. 108 Washington St.

As with a number of municipal buildings in the Midwest, this one is treated as a storefront structure. The designer sought to establish the building's public identity by placing its name in the upper section of the light-tan brick facade, and by creating a central pediment that projects above the name. The public purpose is also conveyed by the reserved dignity of the facade treatment. Pilasters are suggested through two vertical rows of brick that terminate in a horizontal row (the cornice). Between these pilasters are entrance doors with pedimented lintels. The lintel to the right bears the words "Fire Truck," and the one to the left, "Council Room." Between these paired pilasters and the doors and lintels is the large garage opening for the fire truck (now closed in). The design is in the realm of the late Prairie style, somewhat akin to the designs of the 1920s of George Grant Elmslie and Barry Byrne.

MW049 House

c. 1890. 214 Kiallworth St.

The designer of this Queen Anne-style house focused his interest on the housetop. At the

MW049 House, c. 1890

center, a steeply pitched gable roof ascends almost three floors. Beneath this gable, at a lower level to the front, is a central gable, and then a pair of gables at a 45-degree angle to each corner of the building. Each of the many gables is treated with a variety of patterns. At the very front, in the center, is a small entrance porch with a shed roof and, of course, its own small gable over the steps leading onto the porch. The house represents an effective essay in the play of volumes, roof forms, and linear surface ornament.

Glenwood

The community was originally settled by the Mormons in 1846 and 1847. "This little city," Andreas wrote in 1875, "is romantically embowered in one of the finest groves in the valley of Keg Creek."[4] In 1853 the town became the seat for Mills County, and a central park was provided as a location for the projected courthouse. The siting of the town's business district is on the flatlands, with the residential district placed on the surrounding hills.

The community's most notable building is the Davis Amphitheater (1979–1980), situated in Glenwood Lake Park (across Keg Creek from the downtown on US 275 East). The architect, Dennis W. Stacy, provided a Modernist structure of exposed steel "unistrut space frames" that play off the brick walls and volumes. Though assertive, the structure has been carefully fitted into the sloping contours of the park.

Grand Junction

One mile east of the central Iowa community of Grand Junction (and .5 miles north on route P46) is one of the most well known true-round barns in Iowa. As Lowell J. Soike has pointed out, the barn—constructed by Beecher Lamb in 1911 for Henry A. and Martha Frantz—was based on a plan prepared and circulated by the Illinois Experimental Station (in its *Bulletin*).[5] W. E. Frudden, in his 1916 publication *Farm Buildings, How to Build Them*, illustrated the barn along with its plan and included a discussion of it (p. 15). The Frantz barn has walls of concrete block and is covered by a double-pitched gambrel roof. It is 55 feet in diameter. Within it is a central silo measuring 16 feet in diameter and 60 feet high. A raised basement was provided, and a ramp originally led to the large doors on the main level. At the peak of the building was a louvered round cupola (now gone) and a small gabled dormer (still in place). The Frantz barn sits within a farm complex, and from a distance it arises majestically from the surrounding flat fields.

Greenfield

The town was established in 1856, and because of its central location it became the county seat in 1875. The downtown is oriented around a large public square that contains the Adair County Courthouse. This brick and stone-trim Richardsonian Romanesque courthouse was erected in 1891–1892, and was designed by S. E. Maxon, a Council Bluffs architect who designed several of Iowa's county courthouses. Like so many of these buildings, this one has lost its high, assertive central tower, so that the building now reads more as a school building than a courthouse.

Across from the courthouse, at 156 Public Square, is the Warren Opera House (1896), now an apartment building. For this commission the architects Bell and Kent (of Council Bluffs) provided a two-story block built of brick with stone trim; there are retail stores below, the opera house above, and a small playful bay tower at one corner. Its style is somewhat Queen Anne. The entrance to the opera house is emphasized by a pediment that projects from the parapet and contains the words "Opera House." Next door is the smaller two-story Hetherington Building with its own small central pediment.

Griswold

Within the western Cass County community of Griswold are two pairs of interesting houses, across the street from one other. At 407 Fifth Street is the two-story Gude house (MW050). Next door, at 411 Fifth Street, is the stucco-sheathed two-story Olson house. Each house has a red tile roof, but there the similarity ends. The Olson house has the appearance of a Craftsman dwelling with Prairie-style features, the most pronounced of these the living porch. It is covered by a low hipped roof and is supported by a pair of thick, square, stuccoed piers. The roof of the house is gabled, but with the ends hipped, and the same treatment was used for the garage. This house is also given a date in the early 1930s, but it has all of the characteristics of a house built between 1910 and 1919.

Across the street are two Craftsman California bungalows, the Busse (MW051) and Rabe houses. The Rabe bungalow at 406 Fifth possesses a wonderful stucco screen wall that spreads out onto the landscape and then projects upward in a series of tiers to support a single-gabled roof of thin profile. The plans of the two houses are mirror images, and both were built in 1920.

Turning to Griswold's downtown, at the northeast corner of Main and Montgomery streets one encounters the Whitney Bank (1880). Here is another of those "Victorian" buildings that command attention. The two-story red brick building with stone trim, though not large, is richly detailed in stone and metal. The metal entablature/cornice is particularly rich, with finials projecting above and even a suggestion of crenellation on the parapet of the corner, which is at a 45-degree angle to the main block. The lower part of the entablature/cornice has a wealth of brackets and other details. Below, the crenellation is repeated in the entrance to the bank, as well as in the entrance to the second-floor offices. The stone lintels of the windows form segmental curves, and project forward as hoods.

MW050 **Gude House**

c. 1910. 407 5th St.

Here we encounter as pure an example of the Mission Revival as could be found in Southern California. The front porch has a row of three arches facing the street; its parapeted gable end contains a false window in the form of an elongated quatrefoil, and there are similar windows (some containing vents) elsewhere in the house. The walls of the dwelling are roughcast stucco, and the red tile roof has eaves supported by Craftsman-like beams and struts. Though a later date has been suggested for the house (1932), it is much more likely that it was built c. 1910.

MW051 **Busse House**

1920. 408 5th St.

The plan of the Busse house, and of its neighbor the Rabe house, is typical of the bunga-

low. Bedrooms and bath are located on one side; living room, dining room, and kitchen are on the other. Instead of a single gable roof, as in the Rabe bungalow, the Busse house has a second gable facing the street; below this gable is the similarly pitched gable roof of the porch. The stucco walls of the front porch of the bungalow are low and curve up to the double wood posts supporting the porch roof.

Guthrie Center

The John W. Foster house is most appropriately located on Prairie Street (at 706), for it is a version of the large brick-sheathed Prairie houses popularized by the Chicago architect George W. Maher. In the Foster house the architect Henry K. Holsman, also of Chicago, borrowed from the classical tradition while working within the avant-garde Prairie movement. The house has a number of points of similarity to Frank Lloyd Wright's 1892 Winslow house in River Forest, Illinois. A projecting band of brick connects the window sills of the upper windows and is carried around them. The windows are all horizontal double-hung units that appreciably help to suggest the horizontality of the prairie. The pier-supported entrance porch has a simple rectangular cornice with dentils.

Eight miles northeast of Guthrie Center is Spring Brook State Park, established in 1926 and now containing 786 acres. This is a park that should be experienced for its rustic architecture. The principal picnic shelter (c. 1930) is a stone structure whose rear wall contains a segmental arched fireplace. The side walls step down to the ground, and the front of the building is supported by log posts. The posts at the sides have a pair of large struts; those in the middle, only one. Spring Brook State Park may be reached by traveling 6.2 miles north of Guthrie Center on Iowa 25; then right (east) for 1 mile on Iowa 384.

Harlan

Harlan was founded in the mid-1850s on a site near the West Nishnabotna River close to the geographic center of Shelby County. The offices and court of the county were transferred to the town shortly after it was established. The usual courthouse square and a block for a public school were included within the conventional grid scheme. By the late 1890s two north-south railroads ran through the town.

MW052 **Shelby County Courthouse**

1892, C. E. Bell. Court St., between 6th and 7th streets

This gaunt, rather tight version of the Richardsonian Romanesque style seems to mirror the starkness of its open site. The building has a sense of incompleteness, due in part to the removal in 1899 of its dominant central tower. The building's fenestration of arched openings running across all four facades still conveys great strength, even though most of the windows have been reduced in size and in many cases filled in with glass brick.

MW053 Shelby County Bank

c. 1892. Northwest corner 6th and Market streets

The eye-catching feature of this two-story commercial block on a raised basement is the dramatic round tower on the second floor. This corner bay tower culminates in a pointed domed roof and is Queen Anne in flavor, but the building itself, with its arched openings, is mildly Richardsonian Romanesque in its presentation.

MW054 Saint Paul's Episcopal Church

1898–1900, Proudfoot and Bird. 712 Farnham St.

This is one of the gems among Iowa's churches. The architects brought together a wide range of design approaches prevalent at the turn of the century. The late Queen Anne-Shingle style generally dominates, accompanied by Gothic Revival details; however, the massing of the building relates to the Colonial Revival, and a number of the wood details are from the Arts and Crafts movement. As in many Episcopal churches, there has been a dramatic reduction in scale; everything (including the central tower) seems miniaturized.

MW055 House

c. 1887. 2102 7th St.

The format of this two-story house with a corner bay tower is Queen Anne, though the delicate spindle and sawed work of its porches and gable ends is more related to the Eastlake tradition. The corner bay starts out on the first floor as a rectangular bay with a large plate-glass window; then on the second floor it becomes a "real" hexagonal tower proceeding upward to a tall, pointed roof.

MW056 Leland Log Cabin and McIntosh Log Cabin

1856, 1857. Potter's Park, corner of Pine and Morse streets

The one-and-a-half-story McIntosh log cabin was moved from its original site in nearby Galland's Grove to Potter's Park in 1971. The smaller, single-story Leland cabin was moved there a few years later. Both cabins have walls of split logs; the gable ends of the McIntosh cabin are shingled.

MW057 Conoco Service Station

1918. Portsmouth; travel 9 miles west of Harlan on Iowa 44; the station is 1 block north of the junction of Iowa 44 and Iowa 191

This is an early form for a service station; a rectangular single-story block with an open cut-in corner facing onto the junction of two streets. The station, built originally for Leo Monahan, is of concrete block that imitates cut stone. Contrasting red brick has been used as trim around the automobile entrances.

Hartley

One of the most effective ways of updating a motion picture theater was to change its marquee, especially in the 1930s and later. Since the prime time for a theater was in the evening, the lighted marquee in many cases "became" the building. The name of the theater could be seen up and down the street, and as one neared it, the viewer was informed as to what movie was currently showing. The marquee of the Capitol Theater in Hartley dates from the late 1930s. It was applied to a two-story nondescript brick building. The two wedge sides of this marquee bear the theater's name in horizontal modern letters. The end of the marquee has a vertical pattern of V's and a stack of horizontal disks in the center. All of this, together with its neon lights and banks of incandescent lights, conveyed to the citizens of Hartley that the modern age was coming, if it wasn't here at this very moment. The theater is situated at the northwest corner of South Central and Second streets.

Hawarden

This community situated on the east bank of the Big Sioux River contains two buildings by William L. Steele, the Prairie architect from Sioux City. These are the Hawarden City Hall (1918), and the First National Bank and Masonic Hall building (1907). The bank building is located at the southeast corner of Central Avenue and Eighth Street. It is a two-story brick block, extremely simple in fenestration. The most pronounced feature is the round-arched entrance, with banding of light-colored stone carried alongside the door. This entrance is slightly Richardsonian Romanesque, somewhat abstracted, as Frank Lloyd Wright interpreted it around 1900.

The city hall, at the southwest corner of Central and Ninth streets, is a structure on a raised basement that is approached by a solid brick-walled staircase. The entrance is housed in a lower projecting wing. The entrance door is arched, as are the five large windows on the side of the building. A double garage at the rear of the building houses a fire truck. The general treatment of the building conveys a no-nonsense practicality. Shutters have recently been added to several of the windows to help Colonialize it.

Another building relating to the Colonial Revival is the 1940–1941 Hawarden post office, designed by Louis A. Simon. As with many other small post office buildings of the late 1930s, this one looks back to the Federal style, but the architect simplified it to convey a feeling of modernity. The post office is located at 900 Central Avenue.

Hospers

Usually, naive sculptural monuments, or follies, are created on a personal level, and although they are almost always meant to be on view, their location and stance are not public. Here in Hospers, a small town on the Floyd River in northwestern Iowa, one will come across a group of follies produced by a single individual, Frederickus Reinders, and sited to be public monuments. Located right in the middle of the intersection of Main Street and Second Avenue, south of Iowa 60, is a 20-foot-high World War I memorial statue (1921) fashioned in concrete. The piece consists of the figure of a soldier placed on a high base; at the base is a nude female figure. Moving on to the northeast corner of Main Street and Third Avenue, one will be able to experience the World War II Memorial Park (MW058).

The creator of these public monuments, Frederickus Reinders (1874–1959), was born in Groningen, the Netherlands, and came to the United States in 1893. He settled in Hospers around 1900. There he practiced as a mortician and also ran a furniture store. Folk follies are not generally crafted for a long life, and this is true of Reinders's work in Hospers. Fortunately, both of the memorials were restored as a United States bicentennial project in 1976.

MW058 **World War II Memorial Park**

1945, Frederickus Reinders. Corner of Main St. and 3rd Ave.

This area is filled with a wonderful array of sculpture and other fragments. One should enter the park through the ceremonial concrete archway labeled "Memorial Park." Among the decorative elements on the face of the arch are large-scale depictions of corn-on-the-cob (painted concrete renditions of green-and-yellow husked corn). To your left, on the white painted brick wall of an adjoining building, are five brightly colored plaques. Their subjects are *Indians, The Emigrants, Farmers and Settlers, Threshing in 1890,* and

Speed Era (note the V-2 rocket). At the center of the park, near a second arch (in this case of stone), is a layered monument on a rectangular base. The first layer is a ring with what looks like ice cream cones placed through it; then there is a cone-shaped form in white painted stone. Next comes a second ring on top of which is a spiral column, and on top of this is the third and final ring, with a crenellated edge. Also within the park are two figures on pedestals of rough stone and random brick. These personify Victory (as a Greek goddess) and Liberty (a version of the Statue of Liberty). Both of these figures are brightly painted. The next attraction is the Iwo Jima Memorial. This consists of a four-sided pyramid with a standing female figure looking on. One face of the pyramid contains a version of the well-known flag-raising scene, with the profile head of an Indian above; other scenes cover the remaining three sides of the pyramid. Finally, there is the band shell, with eight scenes painted on the interior of the shell.

Ida Grove

Though founded in the late 1850s on the southeast bank of the Maple River, Ida Grove has the atmosphere of a town that evolved between the 1960s and the present. The person responsible for its contemporary form is Byron Godbersen, the owner of Midwest Industries, a company that manufactures farm and marine equipment.[6] Godbersen has acted essentially as both designer and client for these buildings at Ida Grove. He has apparently garnered his design ideas from popular magazines, as well as from travels to Mexico and Europe. As one drives into the town from the east on Iowa 175, one encounters a new single-family housing development composed of large parcels of land. Dominating this landscape is Godbersen's own house (1976), presumably a version of a Spanish Mediterranean house. Joined to this composition of tile roofs, stucco walls, and arches is a theme that recurs again and again in Ida Grove— the lighthouse. This image is repeated at the gated entrance to the development, accompanied by a low arch that springs directly from the ground.

On the other side of Iowa 175 is Lake LaJune (created in 1969 and named for Godbersen's wife, LaJune). Floating tranquilly in the water is a half-scale replica of HMS *Bounty*. (Godbersen obtained the plans for the ship from the MGM movie studio, and it was launched in 1970.) At the end of this manmade lake is a second form that fascinated Godbersen, the castellated medieval castle. Here castellated towers protect and enclose a convention center (1974). Adjacent to the center is an airplane runway and a hangar (1967); it too is in the castellated style (note that a large tile mosaic depicting the voyage of the *Bounty* is on the floor of the hangar).

Proceeding into town one will come across a castle tower as the "city marker" (1971). Within the town other buildings carry on the idiom—the castellated medieval castle appears on a lonely bridge in the middle of a golf course, in small and large shopping centers, and in the Ida County Courier / Reminder Building (MW059). Other medieval and Hispanic structures are the Midway Industries Factory Building (1954–1956), the Skate Palace (1982), and Legion Park (1983). Don't miss the community's medieval McDonald's.

On one of the highest hills in Ida Grove is the Ida County Courthouse (1880–1883), at 401 Moorehead Street. The architects, J. P. Bryant, D. W. Townsend, and J. M. Starbuck, provided the community with a tall, narrow, brick Italianate design modified with Eastlake details. The principal entrance is at the base of a hundred-foot square tower, topped by a double-pitched spirelike roof.

Perched on the side of a hill at the southwest corner of Burns and Fourth streets is a large two-story Craftsman house enshrouded by trees and shrubs. The first floor, encased in brick, presents a glassed-in arcade; above, the many bedroom windows are arranged as a horizontal band within the clapboard walls. The third-floor gable is treated in stucco and half-timbering with accompanying large-scaled brackets supporting the overhang of the roof.

MW059 Ida County Courier / Reminder Building

1974, Byron Godbersen. Northeast corner of Moorehead and 2nd streets

Near the center of town, at the northeast corner of Moorehead and Second streets, the Ida County Courier / Reminder Building, "The Castle" (1975), is reminiscent of the Spanish medieval style.

Jefferson

Jefferson's grid plan, with the usual provision of a courthouse square, was laid out in 1854. The site was a high tableland located between the North Raccoon River and Hardin Creek. Two mills, the Eurel Mill and the Jefferson Mill, were situated on the nearby river. The town was first reached by the Chicago and Northwestern Railroad, and later by the north-south Chicago, Milwaukee, and Saint Paul Railroad. In the 1920s Jefferson became an important stop-off point on the east-west US 30.

MW060 Farmers Coop Elevators

c. 1960. Northeast edge of town, next to US 30

This is an effective image of high-tech agricultural storage and processing. A tall bank of cylindrical storage elevators is connected to a high rectangular tower sheathed in metal. Projecting above and out of the elevators and tower is an array of metal piping, walkways, and conveyor belts.

MW061 Home State Bank, North Highway 4 Office

1973–1974, Charles Herbert and Associates. Southeast corner of N. Elm (Iowa 4) and Stanford streets

Located on the developing commercial strip leading into town is this well-detailed excursion into High Art architecture. The building's basic shape, that of a bisected triangular volume, is in many ways typical of low commercial buildings of the late 1960s and 1970s; but what aren't typical are the cherry-red walls, effectively set off against the thick green lawn.

MW062 Greene County Courthouse

1917, Proudfoot, Bird and Rawson. Courthouse Square, off Lincoln Way

The Beaux-Arts Greene County Courthouse is quite close to Norman T. Vorse's contemporaneous courthouse at Boone (CE036, p.

169). The north and south elevations of the two-story Greene County building are identical, each with a windowed pediment supported by a row of engaged Ionic columns. The east and west facades are again the same, with recessed porticoes defined by Ionic pilasters. The facades are divided according to the classic tripartite scheme, and light-colored Bedford limestone has been used for the walls and detailing. The building is on a raised basement. Inside the courthouse, the space centers on a rotunda that rises through all of the floors of the building to a stained glass ceiling. Within the rotunda are four murals by William Peaco of the Andreas Decorating Company. The titles of these murals are *The Buffalo Hunt, The Pioneers, The Emigrants*, and *The Modern Farm*. The murals were reworked in the 1950s by John Pritchard, who replaced *The Buffalo Hunt* with a contemporary farm scene showing a modern city in the background.

MW063 **Group of Commercial Blocks**

c. 1890. South side of Lincoln Way at Courthouse Square

Though altered on the street level, these brick commercial blocks exhibit the usual wide array of designs used in the 1890s through the early 1900s. The three-story block, with its three sets of bay windows, looks to the classical tradition, while the others seem to be versions of the late Italianate in style.

MW064 **House**

c. 1905. 408 W. Lincoln Way

A two-story gabled portico with paired Ionic columns effectively declares the Colonial heritage of this house, and it also reflects the social prestige of its original client. Especially impressive is the composition of the entrance, which has its own pair of columns, side lights, lunettes, and balcony above carried on paired consoles.

MW065 **House**

c. 1888. 307 W. State St.

A calm Queen Anne design was given some zest by the delicately turned columns of the veranda and by the patterns of curved boards in the gables which render an all-wood version of half-timbering.

Larchwood

About 8 miles northwest of Larchwood, at the extreme northwestern point of Iowa, is the Gutchie Manitou State Monument. This 48-acre park situated on the east bank of the Big Sioux River was originally a stone quarry worked by state prison laborers. It was one of the state's early parks, having been acquired in 1919. The stone quarried here was Sioux quartzite, a material often used in construction. The architectural triumph of the park is its stone picnic shelter (c. 1930). The shelter will please anyone enamored of the "picturesque garden," for it is almost a grotto, partially sunken into a low rise of ground. The front has three openings placed between two thick piers. At the back of the shelter is a large fireplace. The shelter is a perfect example of the rustic image used for park architecture. To reach Gutchie Manitou State Monument, proceed west 5.3 miles from Larchwood on route A18 and turn north on route K10; the park entrance is 4.3 miles farther.

LeMars

The town of LeMars was established in 1869 and became the seat of Plymouth County in 1872. The grid plat of the town was laid out on the flat prairie southeast of the junction of the Floyd River and Deer Creek. By the mid-1870s the town was connected by rail to Sioux City to the southwest. The community's first period of growth occurred in the late 1870s and early 1880s, when it was the center of extensive colonization by the English-owned Iowa Land Company.

MW066 Plymouth County Courthouse

1901–1902, Kinney and Detweiler. Corner of 3rd Ave. S.E. and 2nd St. S.E.

The Austin, Minnesota, firm of Kinney and Detweiler also designed the similar Clay County Courthouse (1900–1901) at Spencer (NO273, p. 433). Both are Beaux-Arts designs, with a projecting pavilion or portico repeated on each of the four facades. The Plymouth County Courthouse is raised almost a full floor above the ground, thus providing a high, grand stairway leading up to its principal entrance with Corinthian columns. The building is sheathed in Portage-entry red sandstone, which provides a warm salmon-rose color. The building is now regrettably devoid of its high central tower and dome, which were removed in 1932.

MW067 Service Station (now Jimbo's Bait and Tackle)

c. 1930. Corner of 5th Ave. N.W. and 6th St. N.W.

The body of this former gasoline service station is reminiscent of a somewhat flattened milk carton with eight sides. The canopy covering the pump area is supported by two truncated piers. Its prime eye-catching feature is the small windmill projecting from the upper neck of the "milk carton."

MW068 Clark Public School

c.1938, Beuttler and Arnold. Northeast corner of 2nd St. N.W. and 2nd Ave. N.W.

This PWA Streamline Moderne school building of the late depression years has a design realized in light-colored brick, with a darker brick used for horizontal banding. The essential ingredients of the Streamline Moderne are present in this one-floor building, including dramatic rounded corners and glass brick.

MW069 Bungalow

c. 1912. 127 3rd Ave. S.E.

A commodious Craftsman bungalow and its separate garage are sheathed in river stones.

The stone walls are banded horizontally with patterns of brick and exposed concrete lintels. The piers of the wide entrance porch are also of river stones, with contrasting brick used to define the corners.

MW070 Charles Flaugher House

1890, Zack Eyres. 32 6th St. S.W.

This is a highly refined interpretation of the late Queen Anne. In this instance the earlier picturesque exuberance is held in check by a classical (Colonial Revival) restraint. This large-scale dwelling seems to spread gently over the surrounding broad lawn; the building's centerpiece is a corner domed pavilion over an expansive porch.

MW071 House

c. 1885. 611 Central Ave. S.

At the front and on each side of this dwelling are cantilevered gable ends with a slightly protruding pattern of bargeboards delineated below the projecting roof soffits. Sections of the walls of this two-story clapboard house exhibit crisscross patterns, and the thin vertical windows are joined together at the lintels and sills by horizontal banding. It all adds up to a well-carried-out version of the Eastlake (Stick) style.

MW072 House

c. 1892. 800 Central Ave. S.

A wide, seemingly "well-fed" bay tower with a bell-shaped roof is clearly visible as one walks up toward the house. There is a stylistic mixture here: a Queen Anne format is held in check through Colonial Revival simplicity and classical details. The porches on each side of the corner bay tower have Tuscan columns, and there are Palladian windows on the third-floor gable ends.

MW073 **House**

c. 1885. 135 2nd Ave. N.W.

Here is a delightful and inventive oddity that defies any effort to pinpoint its style. The lower section of the house is somewhat French Second Empire in style, with a mansard roof for the second floor; but on top of this has been placed a second gable roof which dramatically extends out over the mansard roof below. Other unusual features are the mansard-roofed dormers with their small-scaled gabled pediments; the mildly Italianate entrance porch; and then, as a finale, the louvered Palladian window placed in the center of the top gable roof.

MW074 **Tonsfeldt True-Round Barn**

1919. County Fairgrounds, east side of LeMars

The original site for the Tonsfeldt barn was off Iowa 3, at the west side of LeMars. It was moved to the county fairgrounds in 1981. The barn was built to show Hereford cattle. The distinctive feature of the building is the steeply pitched bell-shaped roof, surmounted by a metal aerator. Within is a central wood-stave and plastered silo, 18 feet in diameter.

Lewis

MW075 **Hitchcock House**

1856. On the south, .3 miles west of Lewis, on an unpaved road that leads from the northwest corner of town

In 1856 the Reverend George Hitchcock built a handsome two-story stone house just west of the town of Lewis. The walls of the house are laid in local dark-brown stone; the joints are irregular, but the faces of the stone are smooth. Larger, more finely cut stones were employed for the lintels and for the edges of the building. The general proportions of the house, the symmetry of the windows on three facades, and the low hipped roof attest to its inheritance of the Federal style. The entrance, with side lights and transom window,

MW075 Hitchcock House

is sheltered by a small cantilevered hipped roof.

Logan

The architectural centerpiece of Logan is the Harrison County Courthouse (1910), designed by the Detroit architect J. E. Mills. The architect produced a conventional Beaux-Arts design in its detailing, although its form and proportions—linear, sharply angular, and vertical—are really nineteenth century. Instead of the usual drum and dome, Mills created a low cupolalike form with angled corners and a segmental roof. The courthouse is located at the intersection of Seventh Street and Fifth Avenue. Nearby on Seventh Street, just east of Third Avenue, is the community's most handsome building, a small two-story commercial building now occupied by the Harrison Mutual Insurance Apartment Building agency (c. 1915). The windows, entrance, and cornice are sumptuously and beautifully ornamented in delicate classical motifs carefully cast in glazed terracotta.

Marcus

MW076 Emdens House
1917, Howard B. Burr. 607 E. Anhurst St.

Howard B. Burr of Waterloo utilized a wide range of elements derived from the Prairie school. The two-story brick-clad box that forms the core of the dwelling is covered by a low-pitched red tile hipped roof, which is cantilevered out to an extreme degree. In the front center of this roof is a wonderfully overscaled gable dormer. A gable roof projects over the entrance, and the gable theme reappears on the dormer on the front of the roof and on the accompanying one-and-a-half-story garage building. The boxlike form of the house is, as one often finds in Prairie houses, countered by an emphasis on the horizontal. In the Emdens house the contrast is accomplished through the low walls of the raised brick terrace in front, as well as by the porte-cochère on one side and the living porch on the other. The designer seems to have expressed his delight in playing with the horizontal by introducing bands of different widths across the facades of the house. He has even added horizontal bars in the upper units of the double-sash windows. All in all, it is a remarkable example of the Prairie mode.

Massena

The Dygdrt house, just east of Massena, is a good illustration of how the Streamline Moderne style of the thirties continued into the immediate post-World War II years. The house was designed and built by its owner, Harold Dygdrt, and supposedly based upon a 1930s house he had seen in Des Moines, probably one of the late thirties houses of Kraetsch and Kraetsch. The single-floor house that Dygdrt built is faced in light cream brick. The projecting wing is curved back into the house by means of a curved glass window. There is glass brick in a curved wall on one side of the recessed entrance, and a porthole window pierces the right side of the front elevation. The whole design is carried out well, and if one came across this house by accident, one would indeed assume that it has been built in the middle to late 1930s.

Menlo

Within Menlo are two attractions well worth a detour north of I-80. Situated among trees on Fifth and Sheridan streets is the Methodist Episcopal Church (MW077). Menlo's other noteworthy monument is in front of the Socony Mobile Gas Station (MW078).

MW077 Methodist Episcopal Church

1913–1914. Southeast corner of 5th and Sheridan streets

The building hardly fits our conventional image of a midwestern church. Rather it has all of the atmosphere of a miniaturized Moorish castle. At one corner is a crenellated tower; crenellations occur around the roof, and a low segmented dome pops up in the center of the building. All of the walls are richly articulated in ashlar block patterns that contrast with decorative areas of pilasters, lintels, and a strongly projecting false cornice. This has been realized not in stone, but in varied patterns of concrete block.

MW078 Socony Mobile Gasoline Station

1935. Northeast corner of US 6 and Sherman St.

The cut-out metal, over-life-size automated figure of a gasoline dealer, which has become faded over time, is located at what was originally a White Rose Gasoline Service Station.

Missouri Valley

Three miles northeast of the community of Missouri Valley, on Iowa 30, is the Harrison County Historical Village. A number of buildings have been moved to this site, among them an 1853 log cabin, an 1856 stage depot, a schoolhouse, and a small chapel. The village is open to the public during the summer months.

To the west of Missouri Valley is a section of the extensive Missouri River floodplain. Off Iowa 30, 5 miles west of town, is the DeSoto Wildlife Refuge. The refuge centers on a wide oxbow of the river that is no longer the major channel. Within the refuge is the Bertrand Steamboat Museum and Visitors Center. The museum houses artifacts recovered from the steamboat *Bertrand*, which struck a snag and sank at this site on April 1, 1865. The museum building was designed by Astle Ericson and Associates, and it was opened to the public in 1981. Since the building is located in the floodplain, it was placed on clustered pilings that mirror the verticality of the surrounding tree trunks. The interior exhibition spaces are open and airy, and they provide continuous views of the adjacent water and landscape.

Moville

Moville is situated on the West Fork of the Little Sioux River, some 20 miles due east from Sioux City. Much of Woodbury County, including the region of Moville, is an open and gently rolling prairie. Since the late 1860s, Moville has been connected to Sioux City by road; presently US 20 passes through the southern limits of the city. When one is visiting the public buildings of down-town Moville, one might also wish to look at two examples of the Craftsman aesthetic in the residential area. These are the Lause House (c. 1913) at 320 Miller Street, a two-story brick building with a green tile roof, and the brick and stucco bungalow (c. 1912) at 411 South Street.

MW079 Moville City Hall

c. 1922. 326 Main St.

The small city hall presents a wonderful combination of its designer's utilitarian concerns and his interest in imagery. As first encountered, the building has the appearance of a converted service station. It is brought right up to the street, and it has a large garage door to the right side. But then there is the name of the building, "City Hall," emblazoned in cast stone right in the center of the upper facade. The medieval image is suggested by two bays developed into crenellated towers; between the towers is a lower section of a crenellated wall. Finally, the brick of the facade seems to have been treated almost as a woven oriental rug, with a repeated pattern of variously colored brick and occasional squares of cream-colored terracotta.

MW080 Garage and Service Station

c. 1924. Northeast corner of Main St. and Iowa 140

For a downtown area, one of the sensible forms given a combined garage and service station was a rectangular single-floor building situated on a corner, with the building's corner opened up as a covered area for the pumps. In this example the brick box is kept basic, its strongest decorative element being a false cornice with dentils and brackets below realized in the same brick as the walls of the building itself.

MW081 First Trust and Savings Bank

c. 1916, attrib. The Lytle Company. 245 Main St.

Moville's citizens have the choice of doing their banking business in a traditional Beaux-Arts Classical bank building at 246 Main Street, or they can cross the street and advance into the modern world of the midwestern Prairie school, in the First Trust and Savings Bank. The two street facades of this dark red-brown brick building feature the usual pilaster sys-tem, with windows between and the piers articulated by square capitals (in this case with a T-motif extending down from the capital into the pilaster). Above is a brick entablature band and then a false cornice. The corner pilasters are doubled, and because of their depth, they almost become piers.

MW082 Bank Building

c. 1917, attrib. The Lytle Company. 246 Main St.

The Beaux-Arts Classical concept of design is effectively realized in this small corner building. This bank is one of the most inventive interpretations of the Beaux-Arts to be found in Iowa. As with almost all small-town banks, this one is essentially a rectangular box that makes its statement by its fenestration and through its varied parapet. The design has the feeling of the delicate Renaissance forms one associates with northern Italy in the early fifteenth century. But when one examines how pilasters, the building's base, its entablature, cornice, and parapet have been handled, it is apparent that the building has little to do with a revival of early Renaissance architecture. The entablature, for example, with its pattern of triglyphs, seems to take us back to Greece, not Florence, and there is a suggestion of crenellation above the parapet, which seems (at least at first glance) to be medieval, rather than classical. If this building was conceived of as a Beaux-Arts answer to the upstart modernism of the Prairie school, it certainly succeeded in its aim.

MW083 Jim's Barber Shop

c. 1935. 141 Main St.

This small shop building in the popular Moderne mode of the 1930s combines a little bit of the Art Deco with the Streamline Moderne. The decoration of the facade is carried out through patterns of glazed brick in black and white. A wainscot is in black glazed tile, and above this within the white tile is a pattern of black bricks suggesting, in a highly abstract fashion, a pilaster. The capital of the pilaster reaches a horizontal band that suggests a cornice. Above is additional decoration, including the usual pattern of triple horizontal bands at each corner. In a sympathetic fashion, the lower section of the showcase window has been painted with a multicolor "V" pattern. This is an excellent example of the way the surface of a building can function as a sign.

MW084 Everhart Motors (Ford Dealership) Building

c. 1941. Northeast corner of Main and N. Pearl streets

The street corner holds a two-story block, and single-floor sections project off to each side. The building is sheathed in cream-colored glazed brick, with dark brown glazed tile used for decoration. The darker tile forms bands around the windows, as well as creating a number of horizontal bands reaching from the ground to the parapeted cornice. In style, the building is late Streamline Moderne. The present signage on the building and the pole sign are of a later vintage.

MW085 Public School Building

1923. South side of 4th St.

The format of this two-story brick building is characteristic of the designs for school build-

ings that one encounters across the country. In this example, however, the Prairie tradition was carried into the 1920s in a somewhat abstract manner. The two front entrances are contained within pavilions that project from the body of the building. These pavilions each have a pair of Prairie-style pilasters with capping and horizontal banding in brick. Between these pilasters, on the wall below the parapet, is a rectangle of vertical lines formed of projecting and receding bricks. The lines can be read as a pattern as well as an abbreviated assertion of small, stylized pilasters. A similar but larger pattern is repeated toward each end of the main building.

MW086 Holly Springs Gymnasium and Auditorium

1941. Holly Springs is located 14.5 miles south of Moville on route K64 at its junction with Iowa 141

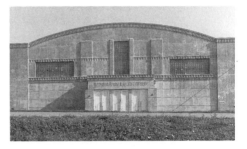

This is one of a number of auditorium and gymnasium buildings that were constructed in Iowa during the depression years. In style the building is PWA Moderne—a mixture of the earlier Art Deco and the Streamline Moderne. In structure it is of reinforced concrete, with the pattern of form boards left visible. The low curve of the hooped roof is contained at each side by wide pierlike devices. There are other, smaller piers toward the center of the building, and a pair of thin piers defines the central vertical glass-block window. A motif of abstracted dentils frames the tops and bottoms of the horizontal glass-brick windows that appear toward each end of the facade. All of these elements suggest a traditional classical composition played off against the modern style.

Oakland

Oakland presents a classic example of a restored turn-of-the-century downtown that one might find anywhere in the Midwest (MW087). The town is sited into a hill, its main street running at the base of the hill.

On the hill above the downtown and in the flatlands to the northwest, one will discover a number of modest as well as substantial Queen Anne and Colonial Revival dwellings. One of these is the Vieths cottage (1892), just opposite where Mulberry Street ends at Linden Street. The front of the cottage has a gable end at each side, with an entrance porch between them. The end gables have patterned bargeboards, and within the gabled ends are shingles that curve out over the windows. The gable wing to the left projects a corner bay at a 45-degree angle to the adjacent walls. The entrance has a flat roof with cornice and a pair of fluted columns, and leans heavily to the Colonial Revival. Above the porch, in the center of the house, is a second-floor dormer whose walls curve down and out onto the porch roof. It all adds up to an unusual Queen Anne cottage, accompanied by Colonial Revival details.

MW087 **Main Street Commercial District**

1880s-early 1900s. Main Street

The two-story commercial buildings along the main street of Oakland date from the 1880s through the early 1900s. The most assertive of these buildings is the Spalti Block (c. 1890), with its strong detailing and contrasting colors. To the left and around the corner from the Spalti building is the bay-windowed S. S. Rust building of 1898. On the other side of the Spalti Block is a turn-of-the-century exercise in well-mannered classicism, the Oakland Savings Bank Building (c. 1910).

MW088 **Hanley House**

1910. .5 miles south of Oakland on the west side of US 59 and US 6

South of Oakland is the Hanley house, which on one side is Edwardian/Colonial Revival,

MW087 Main Street

but to the left suddenly becomes a romantic medieval castle with a large, three-story crenellated tower. Working into the tower at the first-floor level is a beautifully detailed Colonial Revival porch with paired Tuscan columns set on a solid stone railing. The delicacy of the porch is repeated in the low-pitched attic gable with a swayed roof and small-scaled casement window; the window is surmounted by a projecting lintel supported at each side by brackets. Despite the varied, even opposing images used, the house still manages to hang together remarkably well as a design.

MW088 Hanley House

Onawa

The town of Onawa was platted in 1857 some 5 miles east of the Missouri River. In the following year the community became the seat of Monona County. The Monona County Courthouse (1891–1892) is a picturesque rendition of the Richardsonian Romanesque, due largely to a varied roofscape. A tall tower with a pyramidal roof looks down on the main roofs, which are broken up by gables and wall dormers, many with finials. This two-and-a-half-story brick building with stone trim was designed by S. E. Maxon. It is located within the Courthouse Square north of Iowa Avenue.

Close to the courthouse is the Iowa Theater (c. 1937), whose marquee and street facade assert both the Art Deco and the Streamline Moderne styles. In addition to the eye-catching design of the V-shaped marquee with projecting lettering and neon bands, there is to the right of the marquee a set of three narrow ascending windows of glass brick, each with its own hooded top. These and the marquee provide visual excitement at night.

MW089 **Onawa Public Library**

1908–1909, Patton and Miller. Corner of Iowa and 7th streets

A little outside of the downtown area, is the Carnegie public library (1908–1909), designed by Patton and Miller of Chicago. The format of the building is not at all usual for small public libraries within the state. The two-story brick building covered by a hipped roof with a wide overhang appears like a recreational building one could find in the parks around Chicago, or as one of the houses of George W. Maher. There is a Maher-like entrance with a projecting curved roof, while the first-floor windows are arches that have been filled in with glass or in some cases with wood paneling. On the second floor the architects have created and repeated a pattern of horizontal Chicago-like windows. Because of the size and number of the windows on both floors, the interior is well lighted.

Orange City

Named for Prince William of Orange, the town was established as a predominantly Dutch colony in 1869. The community celebrates its Dutch heritage through pageants, extensive gardens of tulips, and, of necessity, numerous windmills.

MW090 **Windmills**

c. 1950s and later

At the corner of Central Avenue Northwest and West Second Street is what every Dutch city needs, a telephone booth in the form of a windmill (c. 1975). On Iowa 10, a half mile east of route K64, is a half-sized windmill atop what appears to be a California ranch house with a shake roof (c. 1970). The ranch house turns out to be a small office building located within a new industrial park. Also suburban in location (off route K64, a half mile south of Iowa 10) is the Northwestern State Bank, Windmill Office (c. 1975). In this instance the windmill is full sized.

MW091 **Sioux County Courthouse**

1902–1904, Wilfred Beach. Southwest corner of Central Ave. and W. 2nd St.

From the point of view of fashion, this vigorous, muscular version of the Richardsonian Romanesque should have been built in the late 1880s, not after 1900. At the base of the central six-story tower is a deep rusticated Richardsonian arch that serves as the principal entrance to the building. Windows and doors are deeply cut into the dark sandstone walls of the courthouse, and they appear even more pronounced because of their light buff-colored stone trim. Atop the steeply pitched hipped roof of the tower is a statue of Justice.

MW092 **Orange City National Bank**

c. 1916. Central Ave. north of 1st St.

The bank's facade is that of a temple with two fluted Doric columns in antis. Though this is not a large building, it does manage to dominate the street. The play of flat and sculptural details gives this Beaux-Arts design the feel of the Colonial Revival style.

MW093 **Cambier Brothers Garage Building**

1919, Beuttler and Arnold. 103 3rd St.

This single-story brick garage building is part pure industrial, part Prairie-style, and part Beaux-Arts. A suggestion of the Prairie style lies in the inverted triangular ornament projecting above the parapet of the roof, while an entrance surmounted by a classical pediment leads into the showroom of the building. In front of the building is a tile-roofed canopy that provides shelter for the pump area.

MW094 **House**

c. 1910. Northeast corner of Arizona Ave. and 2nd St.

The street facade of this long, low Craftsman bungalow is sheathed in small river stone. The stone piers of the wide porch extend out to one side to provide a pergola for an auto entrance. This house has certainly captured the nature of the horizontal Prairie landscape.

MW095 **House**

c. 1915. 2202 2nd Ave.

This Craftsman bungalow has a slightly Japanese flavor. Apronlike piers contain the horizontal lower band of green-stained shingled walls and the narrow white clapboard above. The motif of the open-gabled entrance porch is matched by a similarly designed garage.

MW096 **Zwemer Hall, Northwestern College**

1894. South end of Central Ave.

This two-and-a-half-story structure on a raised basement terminates the vista down Central Avenue. In the springtime the avenue is lined with beds of colorful tulips. Like the courthouse, Zwemer Hall is Richardsonian Romanesque, only it is a much more linear and vertical version of the style. A narrow eight-sided tower projects forward from the lower entrance with a Richardsonian arch. The building's brick walls seem thin, an impression reinforced by the light-tan stone trim that projects out in front of the walls. The grounds of the college (founded in 1882) are, as with the other public and private gardens of Orange City, beautifully planned and maintained.

Panora

Quite often in the settlement of Iowa towns the first public building constructed was a school building. Throughout the nineteenth century, town histories mentioned the school buildings within a community as proudly as the railroad stations, banks, and manufacturing enterprises. Very few of these nineteenth-century school buildings remain. One that has survived is the Panora-Linden High School (1897), situated at the corner of Main and Vine Streets. This brick two-and-a-half-story building has slightly projecting pavilions at each corner, and on each of the side elevations is a central pavilion with a somewhat higher roof. The general feeling of the building is French academic, but with little specific reference to the classical tradition. The building ceased to be used as a school in 1930; it is now used as a memorial and a museum.

Primghar

O'Brien County was organized in 1860, and Primghar, which lies almost exactly in the center of the county, became the county seat. The present O'Brien County Courthouse, located at the junction of US 59 and route B40, is the third within Primghar. It is a particularly strong example of the Beaux-Arts Classical tradition of the second decade of this century. The Des Moines firm of Smith and Keffer devised a variation on the theme of a building on a podium with classical columns in their 1916–1917 courthouse. The center section of the entrance facade contains a row of six thick Tuscan columns forming a porch which is contained on each side by narrow ends defined by pilasters. The architects emphasized horizontality by treating the ground floor (the podium base) and the entablature/cornice area on top as two bands that act as a beginning and conclusion for the central section. The building is sheathed in limestone, and there are polished marble and bronze details inside.

Remsen

MW097 Saint Mary's Roman Catholic Church

1903. 1910, school building. Between 3rd and 4th streets

This Gothic Revival church with a central tower and spire has all the appearance of a late nineteenth-century cast-iron toy church that has been magically enlarged, but its enlargement is insufficient to take it completely out of fairyland and into the real world. The interior is plain, except for lush reredos and two elaborately carved

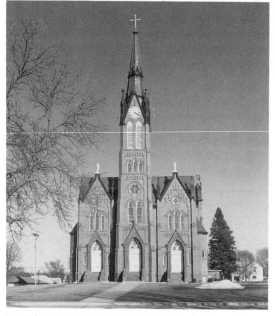

MW097 Saint Mary's Roman Catholic Church

golden oak confessionals. The accompanying two-story school on a raised basement is Renaissance in image, and in contrast to the church, it suggests stern reality and harsh seriousness.

Rock Rapids

The northwestern section of Iowa was settled in the late 1860s, Rock Rapids itself in 1868–1869. The town's grid was established just south of the Rock River at its juncture with Tom and Kanaranzie creeks. The community became the county seat with the establishment of Lyon County in 1871.

MW098 **Lyon County Courthouse**

1916–1917, Joseph Schwartz. Corner of 3rd and Story streets

As the architect of the courthouse, Joseph Schwartz of Sioux Falls, South Dakota, presented the county and town with a well-informed exercise in Beaux-Arts Classicism. The rectangular block is broken into on all four sides by porches with Doric columns, while the four corners of the building are defined by wide, solid-appearing pilasters. The limestone surface is treated with horizontal rustication on the ground-floor level; the surfaces above are smooth, with appropriate ornamentation. The entrance, which projects from the main block, is surmounted by a fierce seated lion.

MW099 **First (United) Methodist Episcopal Church**

1895–1896, Joseph Schwartz. 302 S. Carroll

This picturesque, rambling church of blue-gray quartzite and red sandstone has a tall entrance tower at one corner. In style the building is Central European Romanesque. Here, as well as in the design of the 1916–1917 Lyon County Courthouse, Schwartz demonstrated a knowledge of historic forms and current fashion as well as an ability to realize these designs in an original manner.

MW100 House

c. 1915. 511 S. Carroll St.

A loose, easy-going example of the Colonial Revival of the teens, this two-and-a-half-story dwelling has parapeted gable ends; it has a gambrel roof, and its three front dormers also have gambrel roofs. The entrance hall is lighted by a broad fanlight together with side lights; along one side is an extensive living porch. The white shutters (bearing a cut-out moon pattern) and trim contrast with the dark stained shingle walls.

MW101 House

c. 1890. 109 S. Carroll St.

The basic style of this two-story cruciform dwelling is Queen Anne, modified in this case by Eastlake details in the gable ends and by Colonial Revival porches with thin columns and balustrades.

MW102 Cottage

c. 1875. 305 S. Boone St.

The format of this cottage is derived from the earlier Gothic Revival—there is a symmetrical facade with a central gable and a porch below; in this instance, however, the turned and sawed wood detailing is Eastlake.

MW103 House

c. 1937. 202 S. Tampa St.

The concrete block walls of this Streamline Moderne cottage are painted white. The parapet displays a series of thin horizontal bands similar to those then being used on automobiles and radios. The obligatory curved corner leading into the recessed entrance has glass block windows; on the other side of the entrance is a single porthole window.

MW104 "Melan" Bridge

1893, Fritz von Emperger, engineer. Sater Park, north side of Iowa 9; eastern edge of Rock Rapids

A bridge of reinforced concrete with elliptical arches and a 30-foot span, this was one of the first reinforced concrete bridges for highway use to be constructed in the United States. The design of the bridge was based on a system developed by the Austrian engineer Joseph Melan. In 1964 it was moved to its present site from its former location over Dry Creek, 3 miles to the south.

Sheldon

Rising thin and tall at the southwest corner of Third Avenue and Ninth Street is the Sheldon Bank building (1888). The walls of this two-story commercial block on a raised basement are of warmly colored but sharp and brittle quartzite laid in an irregular pattern. Exterior steps lead up to a pair of arched doorways, between which is a single glass window with a transom. On the second floor, two pairs of arched windows have been remodeled into two tripartite windows with flat lintels.

If Saint Patrick's Roman Catholic Church (1911) were stuccoed instead of being of brick, we would most likely respond to it as an example of the Mission Revival. Its entrance facade, facing onto the southeast corner of Fourth Avenue and Tenth Street, centers on a pediment with a scalloped parapet between towers with domes and lanterns. The flanks of the building have a repeated pattern of shallow buttresses and small arched windows. The church is covered with a gable roof.

In early 1906 a Carnegie grant of $10,000 was made to the community for a library building. The architect P. O. Moratz of Saint Louis was engaged to design the building, which was completed in 1908. The scale of the structure fits in well with its residential location at the northwest corner of Fourth Avenue and Tenth Street. Its public nature is declared by its Beaux-Arts Classical entrance, by a one-and-a-half-story porch defined by horizontally grooved piers at the corners, and by a pair of Tuscan columns between the piers. The Carnegie Public Library building is now used as a museum.

Near the library is the United States Post Office building (1935), designed in the Washington office of Louis A. Simon. Built of red brick and trimmed with buff-colored terracotta, it is a Beaux-Arts product that has been highly abstracted. The slightly projecting center entrance pavilion presents a linear pattern of pilasters, cornice bands, and medallions.

Proof that the Queen Anne mode could and did go off in various directions is offered in the two-and-a-half-story house at 602 Sixth Avenue. This dwelling (c. 1890) brings together a Moorish cusped arch, a classical pediment, and stubby Tuscan columns. To the side, a rounded stair bay projects from the corner of the house; within the third-floor gables and dormers are pairs of roundheaded windows.

Sibley

Sibley was the first town laid out in Osceola County. It was platted by the Sioux City and Saint Paul Railroad in 1872. Three blocks were set aside for public use: a courthouse square, a public park, and a site for a schoolhouse. The present brick-and-stone Osceola County Courthouse was designed by F. W. Kenney of Austin, Minnesota, and was constructed in 1902–1903. His classically inspired design has the atmosphere of an English manor building of the late seventeenth century. Such historical references had been surfacing in English architecture in the 1890s and early 1900s, and this imagery had also entered the American architectural scene. The building's central and corner pavilions emphasize the horizontal joinery of the masonry, and in a number of instances the pattern of this joinery becomes the voussoirs around the arched windows. The attic section of the entrance pavilion has a set of large round windows, their surrounds pulled out quite far from the surface of the building. Originally there was a dramatic layered, open clock tower topped by a dome, and within the tower was a large statue of Justice. The tower and dome have been removed, and other changes also occurred in remodelings that took place in 1925 and 1961. The courthouse is located in the public square off of routes L40 and A22.

Sidney

Sidney, the seat of Fremont County, was established in 1851. Now occupying the southeast corner of Illinois and Filmore streets, at the courthouse square, is the Fremont County Courthouse (1889). The architect, S. E. Maxon, rendered the Richardsonian Romanesque in brick and stone. The building's entrance porch, its two side arches and great arch supported by short columns, is the most telling Romanesque Revival feature of the building. The body of the building and its entrance tower rely on simple rectangular volumes and surfaces, realized in brick with only a small number of horizontal bands of stone. The tower with dormers capped by hipped roofs seems abbreviated, as if waiting for a belfry and spire roof.

Also within the downtown is the former Fremont County Savings Bank of 1914, designed and built by the Lytle Company of Sioux City, a firm that specialized in the design and construction of small banks throughout the upper Midwest. Most of its designs were within the Beaux-Arts Classical tradition, but some, such as the one for the Sidney bank, were in the Prairie style. The building is an elongated brick box, with the center portion of the facade articulated by a gable front. The most striking quality of this building is the high-contrast checkerboard pattern created by the brick and the creamy white glazed tile. A cream-colored terracotta cornice is carried around the pediment and parapets of the building.

Sioux Center

Facing one another across the town's main street (US 75) are two small bank buildings, both of which have the quality of Beaux-Arts design as well as the many variations possible within this classical approach. Both of the banks were designed by the Saint Paul firm of A. Moorman and Company, a Midwestern firm specializing in the design of small-town banks. The First National Bank building (c. 1916), located at the southeast corner of Main Street and US 75, presents an Indiana limestone portico with Ionic columns which is set slightly in front of a simple brick box. The building as initially planned had a heavy limestone entablature and cornice, and limestone quoins, but these were deleted from the final design—and in this case the elimination helped the design. Diagonally across the intersection is the Sioux Center State Bank (MW105).

MW105 **Sioux Center State Bank**

c. 1915, A. Moorman and Company. Northwest corner of Main St. and US 75

The architects themselves described the design of this building as "striking." The design is unusual in that it has a Colonial or Georgian quality. The body of the building is of brick, and the trim is in limestone. Three arched openings are presented on the principal facade, while a single arched entrance placed off-center occupies the other street facade. The scale of the building is domestic, and the fenestration and layout are similar to the Prairie-style banks designed by Louis H. Sullivan and by Purcell and Elmslie.

Sioux City

The wide, deep Missouri River provided a natural transportation corridor for the northwestern section of Iowa. This region was a lush, rich prairie just waiting for cultivation and husbandry. Two of Iowa's cities sought to exploit the potential of the waterway and its surrounding fertile land: Council Bluffs and Sioux City. To the south, Council Bluffs ended up sharing a portion of its economic pie with Omaha, Nebraska, just across the river. But Sioux City enjoyed the fruits of its favorable location alone, even though there is indeed a South Sioux City on the Nebraska side of the river. Sioux City had another advantage: being farther up the river than Council Bluffs, its hinterland eventually extended into the adjoining states of South Dakota and Nebraska, and even into Minnesota, some 75 miles to the north.

Sioux City's initial grid was platted in 1854–1855. The site was a broad, flat river plain situated between the Missouri River and the much smaller Floyd River. To the west of the future downtown was a 200-foot-high bluff called Prospect Hill, and behind the town to the north were gently undulating hills eminently situated, as Andreas observed, to "furnish many fine sites for residences."[7] A year after its platting, in 1856, the first steamboat arrived at the site of the town, carrying as part of its cargo "ready-framed houses."[8] Early in its development, the city expended its own revenues to develop docking facilities along the river. The community was equally aggressive and successful in promoting the development of several rail lines to and through the community. The Sioux City and Pacific Route was completed in 1868, and by the 1890s Sioux City had developed as a major hub for a number of national and regional railroad systems.

The usual wide variety of industries developed in the city, but its major industry (in addition to transportation) was comprised of its stockyards and meatpacking plants. With the improvement in Iowa's road system in the middle to late 1920s, the system of interstate highways leading into Sioux City permitted the growth of a trucking industry for transporting livestock and farm produce.

One of Sioux City's many architectural fantasies was a sequence of corn palaces.[9] The first of these was built in 1887. This was an exposition palace sheathed from top to bottom in corncobs—stems, leaves, and all. This first palace was followed in 1888, 1889, 1890, and 1891 by fairy-tale creations of increasingly elaborate design. Though each of the palaces was mentioned as being "Moorish," "Spanish," of "Composite Order," or "a Mohammedan Mosque with Iowa trimmings," they were in truth so delightfully extravagant and playful that no stylistic label could ever be attached to them. One of America's presidents, Grover

Sioux City, Outer Map (MW151–MW153)

Cleveland, remarked during his visit to the first of the corn palaces that this was the "first new thing he had seen on his trip."[10]

Architecturally, the city reflected the waves of taste expressed nationally and regionally.[11] Within this sequence of styles, from the late 1850s through much of the twentieth century, there were two somewhat unusual departures from the expected. One of these was a strong fascination with the Richardsonian Romanesque expressed in a large number of stone "mansions" built at the end of the 1880s and on into the early 1890s. For its population, Sioux City could boast more examples of these suggestions of medieval castles than any other city in the state. The availability of fine stone in this region was one reason for this popularity; another and probably more likely reason had to do with the economic closeness of this city to Chicago. Thus, Sioux City's stone castles closely mirrored what was then being built in Chicago by that city's great "captains of industry."

The second episode that was distinctive for a midwestern community of its size was Sioux City's acceptance of Prairie architecture during the years 1910 through the 1920s. Here one can identify a single individual responsible for the "progressive" outlook: Sioux City architect William L. Steele (1875–1949). Steele brought to the community one of the largest and finest Prairie buildings, the Woodbury County Courthouse. He was also responsible for a number of other Prairie-style buildings—libraries, churches, fraternal and commercial buildings, and houses—all built within the community.

In recent years the image of the modern skyscraper has been taken up in Sioux City for several buildings; especially visible is the ten-story Terra Center (BWBR Architects of Minneapolis, 1981–1983), with a skin of reflective glass. Contemporaneous are the designs of several bridging skywalks already built or projected, including an especially ill-conceived one which, if built, would penetrate one facade of the Woodbury County Courthouse. As with other midwestern cities, Sioux City's skywalks have worked best visually when they have been integral to a new building. When they plunge into an older building they have often come close to destroying the integrity of the original design. This is not a problem unique to this city, but one hopes that as the system is expanded, the city's major landmarks will not be violated in this fashion. In a way, a lesson can be learned by looking back to 1887 when one of the country's first elevated street railroads was built in Sioux City. This system lasted only ten years before it went bankrupt. The citizens of the community had been quick to adopt a new concept of elevated transportation, but like people in many other cities they gave little thought to the devastating effect the elevated tracks would have on livability of the streets and in adjoining buildings. With the care now being taken with a good number of historic buildings in the community, one hopes that similar care will be taken as new transportation elements are introduced into the community.

SIOUX CITY, DOWNTOWN

MW106 Sioux City Auditorium

1949–1950, K. E. Westerlind. South end of Douglas St.

Across the country there were a number of public and private buildings constructed between 1945 and the early 1950s for which architects continued to employ the imagery of the pre-World War II years. For the Sioux City Auditorium, K. E. Westerlind gathered together those design features associated with the PWA Moderne of the late 1930s. The massing, symmetry, proportions, and details were derived from the Beaux-Arts Classical tradition. Westerlind modernized the classical spirit of this building by emphasizing smooth brick walls, by having the openings essentially cut into the building, and by introducing rounded corners and patterns of horizontal lines. The Sioux City Auditorium was sited so that it functions as a terminus to Douglas Street. The post-World War II injection of a wide freeway (US 77) between the auditorium and the river has appreciably enhanced the building's visibility, thus relating its northern exposure to the city proper and revealing its southern exposure to people entering the city via the freeway.

MW107 Turner Octagon House

c. 1870s. 108 Kansas St.

A "do-it-yourself" single-floor octagon has been set on a masonry foundation which,

Inset 1, Sioux City, Downtown (MW106–MW124)

because of the slope of the land, is partially exposed as a full story. The house has acquired new siding, and the original narrow, vertical double-hung windows have been replaced by wide windows. The octagon's original detailing was Italianate, with segmental arched windows and lintels accompanied by a pronounced cornice.

ing exhibits a smooth surface that carefully establishes the simple rectangular volumes. The windows and their frames are brought right out to the surface of the building, and while they are arranged in horizontal bands, the brick wall intervenes between the windows. A counternote of a row of cut-in vertical rectangles suggests an abstracted portico.

MW108 Iowa Public Service Company Building

1978–1979, Rosetti Associates / Foss, Englestad, Heil Associates. Northwest corner of Douglas and 4th streets

This six-story brick box visually helps to anchor the western end of the Fourth Street Mall. In the fashion of the 1970s, this build-

MW109 First National Bank and Parking Structure

1982. Northeast corner of 5th and Douglas streets

This seven-level garage and banking facility functions as a neutral background to a grouping of five Ionic columns and an accompanying architrave situated within the small park

MW109 First National Bank and Parking Structure

across the street. These fragments were rescued from a 1905 bank building and were erected as a landscape folly.

MW110 United States Courthouse and Post Office

1932–1933; Beuttler and Arnold; James A. Wetmore. Southwest corner of Douglas and 6th streets

The PWA Moderne style is presented here in cut gray stone and brick. The symmetrical design centers on a four-story pavilion that projects slightly forward from the building's main three-story block. The architects employed the usual fenestration associated with the style—rows of pilasters with recessed windows and spandrels between. The interior harks back to the Art Deco of the twenties with many surfaces of polished bronze and marble.

MW111 City Hall

1893–1897. Northeast corner of Douglas and 6th streets

The dominant note of this limestone civic building is the corner tower, supposedly modeled after the Palazzo Vecchio in Florence. The building was constructed as the city's first United States Post Office and Federal Building. In 1948, it was revamped as a city hall.

MW112 Woodbury County Courthouse

1915–1918, William L. Steele, Purcell and Elmslie. Southeast corner of Douglas and 7th streets

In 1914 a decision was made to replace the 1876–1878 French Second Empire courthouse. The Sioux City architect William L.

MW112 Woodbury County Courthouse

Steele won a limited local competition for this building with a modernized Gothic Revival scheme. He then proceeded to convince the County Board of Supervisors that they should be thinking of a more contemporaneous image for the community. Having worked in the Chicago office of Louis H. Sullivan, under the direction of George Grant Elmslie, Steele was quite naturally thinking in terms of a Sullivanesque Prairie school image. He turned to the Minneapolis firm of Purcell and Elmslie to work with him on the design for the project. Initially what he desired from Elmslie was simply the design of the ornamentation for his building. What he obtained instead was the design for the entire building.

The concept of the building, that of a public boxlike volume on the street level coupled with an office skyscraper, was an approach that went back to the tower added by Peabody and Stearns to Ammi B. Young's Greek Revival Boston Custom House in 1913, and by the contemporaneous play on this theme by Henry Hornbostel in his 1914 city hall at Oakland, California. The largest and certainly the widest known variation on this concept was Bertram G. Goodhue's Nebraska State Capitol building at Lincoln (1920–1932).

The Woodbury County Courthouse was the largest public building realized by any of the Midwest Prairie architects, and without question it is one of the most successful. The proportional relationship between the lower cube and the tower would have been far more successful if the tower had been built several stories taller than was originally proposed. The center of the tower is composed of a solid narrow block from which project lower wings on two sides; V-shaped bay windows project from the other two sides. The architect sought to have the viewer experience the tower almost as a distinct building unconnected to its base. The west front of the building is composed of a row of narrow brick piers culminating in terracotta capitals. Over the entrance there is a figurative terracotta panel designed by Purcell and executed by the sculptor Alfonzo Iannelli of Chicago. Iannelli also produced the two figures over the entrance on the north side and the soaring eagle atop the west bay of the tower.

The interior public space revolves around a central rotunda sheltered by a luxuriously patterned stained glass dome. The rotunda and the adjacent lobbies overflow with Elmslie ornamentation, realized in terracotta, cast iron, and sawed wood. Around the lower balcony walls of the rotunda are four murals by the Chicago artist John Norton—a mural painter often engaged by Purcell and Elmslie, Frank Lloyd Wright, and other Prairie architects. The courtrooms are as impressive as the rotunda. Their walls are of warm-colored brick, with natural wood trim, and are lighted by a broad V-shaped skylight; the exterior large window walls of opaque colored glass are both domestic and public in scale, detail, and material.

The editor of the magazine *The Western Architect* wrote of the building in 1922, "Serene, almost impudent it stands there. You feel a sense of illusion about its reality which leaves you presently to be followed by the feeling that the building itself is the only reality and its surroundings are the phantoms."[12] Nothing much has changed, and one's impression is the same today.

MW113 **Firestone Tire Store**

1929. Southwest corner of Douglas and 8th streets

A commonplace brick commercial building became something distinct through its corner parapet, decorated in cast-stone automobile tires and wheels.

MW114 **Knights of Columbus Hall** (former Scottish Rite Temple)

1926, William L. Steele. Northwest corner of Douglas and 8th streets

The richness of the Prairie school is here

MW114 Knights of Columbus Hall

reduced to a light, linear pattern running across two of the building's street facades. The windows are all organized as tight groups broken by narrow intervening piers. Each of the upper piers displays slightly projecting cast-stone capitals.

MW115 **Willigos Building**

1930–1931, William L. Steele. 613 Pierce St.

Steele seems to have decided in this instance to look back to a more traditional version of the Prairie style. The second and third floors of this building have piers with terracotta capitals reminiscent of the work of George Elmslie. They support a thin, continuous terracotta lintel. The center of the brick parapet is raised in a low-pitched gable containing the company's name.

MW116 **Badgerow Building**

1929–1930, K. E. Westerlind. Southwest corner of Jackson and E. 9th streets

"In planning the Badgerow building," its architect wrote, "we realized we must start anew and create a free architecture."[13] The "free architecture" he had in mind was the then-modish Art Deco, with the exterior walls arranged as alternating vertical bands of piers and windows. The ornament is cast bronze and terracotta encrusted with the usual Art Deco patterns—triangles and rows of zigzags—and accompanied by stylized plant forms. Above its entrance and along the parapet of this twelve-story skyscraper is the repeated motif of an Indian head. The building's exterior is sheathed in light-colored terracotta; within, the lobby has walls of black Belgian marble contrasted by pink Tennessee marble and patterned terrazzo floors. The architect consciously sought to play off the past and the present in his design program for the building, which included "symbols of Indian days depicting the past history of our city, and presenting the present in the free lines of action in the spandrel at the second floor—lines typical of present-day dynamic energy."[14]

MW117 **Krummann Block**

1891, Charles B. Brown. Northeast corner of 4th and Court streets

This is one of four nineteenth-century commercial blocks located along East Fourth Street between Court and Iowa streets (one is MW118). This one is a three-story Richardsonian Romanesque block with a rounded corner. The engaged piers extend through and above the balustrade and cornice of the roof. The ground floor has been appreciably remodeled.

MW118 **Bay State Block**

c. 1891. 1107 E. 4th St.

In style, the Richardsonian Romanesque merges here into the Beaux-Arts Classical. The windows on the fourth floor are arched; those on the second floor are rectangular and are designed as fill-ins between the vertical stone piers. The ground floor has been altered.

MW119 **Call Terminal Building**

c. 1890. 1106 E. 4th St.

Four stories of Richardsonian Romanesque masonry have been piled up in this building. The rusticated stone walls have large-scaled arches on the second floor, and there are rows of small arched windows on the fourth floor.

MW120 **Northwest Bank Building**

1890–1891, Charles B. Brown. 1128 E. 4th St.

An arch resting on coupled columns was at one time the entrance to the banking room of this Richardsonian Romanesque design.

MW121 **Mike's Diner** (Dick's Diner)

1954. Northeast corner of W. 7th and Omaha streets

In this Streamline Moderne diner, glass brick is carried right around the curved corners and on either side of the entrance. The surface of the diner is of shimmering metal.

MW122 **Central High School**

1892–1893, F. S. Allen. 1912–1913, addition. 1212 Nebraska St.

Lake Superior brownstone was used to construct this Romanesque "pile." A seemingly stern but actually quite fairy-tale-like crenellated castle resulted. The north wing was added in the same style in 1912–1913. Within the building is a Federal Arts Project (WPA) mural, *Arrival of the First Teacher*, by Herbert O. Mayer.

MW123 **First Congregational Church** (now First Baptist Church)

1918, William L. Steele. Northwest corner of 13th and Nebraska streets

Though generally thought of as a Prairie-style design, this church seems to incorporate not only the Prairie mode, but also, with its pattern of round arches, the Beaux-Arts, and, in its white dome, the Byzantine.

MW124 United Orthodox Synagogue

1901, 1920. Southeast corner of 14th and Nebraska streets

This synagogue is a veritable forest of small-scaled towers and gables, essentially Queen Anne in style. William L. Steele added a classroom building to the side; it has the appearance of a railroad passenger car minus its wheel carriages.

SIOUX CITY, DOWNTOWN–NORTH

MW125 Smith Villa Branch Library

1924–1927, William L. Steele and George B. Hilgers. 1509 George St.

This Prairie-style building is a near duplicate of the Fairmount Park Branch Library (MW144).

MW126 House

c. 1892. 1525 Rebecca St.

An enlarged semicircular window placed in the principal front dormer is the assertive

Insert 2, Sioux City, Downtown–North (MW125–MW137)

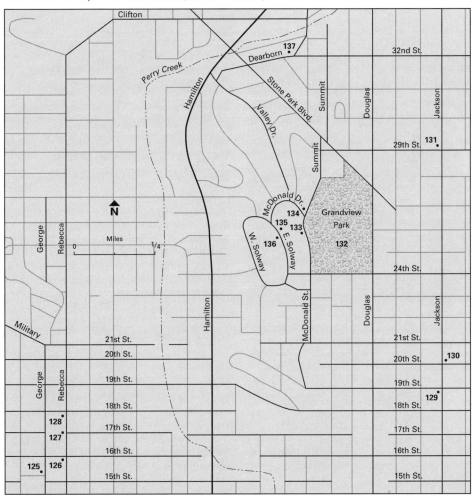

design element of this commodious Queen Anne/Colonial Revival dwelling. Classically inspired consoles support the cantilevered front gable.

MW127 Smith Villa School

1892–1893. 1623 Rebecca St.

Built originally as a private residence for Dr. William R. Smith, this building was purchased in 1899 by the Sioux City School Board to be used as a school. Additions were made in 1910 and 1914. The image of this pink quartzite building is medieval—not playful medievalism, but the sternly disciplined variety.

MW128 French House

1888–1889. 1721 Rebecca St.

This pink quartzite Richardsonian Romanesque house has a highly contrasting spindly veranda. A small stone-roofed turret joins the front gable to the rest of the house.

MW129 Ellemund House

1892. 1825 Jackson St.

The rough-cut stone Ellemund house rests close to the ground. From the street one sees a deep arched entrance leading into a porch; to each side of this porch is a balustraded terrace.

MW130 House

c. 1900. 2000 Jackson St.

A low stone wall and the terrace behind provide a platform for this large Queen Anne/ Colonial Revival dwelling. The lower walls of the house are of brick; there is a more tactile surface of small stones above. The roof towers and dormers are highly picturesque, especially the corner bay tower with its third-floor wall that slopes inward.

MW131 Pierce House (now Sioux City Public Museum)

1891–1893. 2901 Jackson St.

Generally, buildings in the Richardsonian Romanesque style tended to be more solid and sedate than wood-inspired American Queen Anne buildings. The Pierce house illustrates how stone could be treated relatively lightly, yet still retain its solid masonry quality. The varied roofscape of this house is as picturesque as one could desire.

MW132 Grandville Park

24th St. to Stone Park Blvd., between Douglas and McDonald streets

The centerpiece of the park is the Streamline Moderne band shell built in 1933–1935. The spherical shell was placed in a natural hollow and faced a spherical ellipse containing 6,000 seats. The architect, Henry L. Kamphoefner, had submitted the project to a competition sponsored by the Society of Beaux-Arts Architects. He was able to realize his design through federal depression funding (PWA).

MW132 Grandville Park Band Shell

MW133 **Hafter House**

1922. 2507 McDonald St.

Designs such as this—a Prairie house in brick with a tiled hipped roof—reflected the work in the early teens of such Chicago-based firms as Spencer and Powers. The house also conveys the ambience one associates with the period revival designs of the time. On the whole, however, the house projects a lukewarm image.

MW134 **Everist House**

1916–1917, William L. Steele. 27 McDonald Dr.

The extended hipped roofs of this Prairie-style house, coupled with the various porch roofs, virtually nudge the house into its hillside site. The hovering horizontality of the roofs is reinforced by the long bands of casement windows and by the brickwork.

MW135 **Baron House**

1935–1936. 2524 E. Solway Dr.

The drama of this Streamline Moderne house is created by the cantilevered semicircular canopy that extends out over its upper deck. Within are two 1930 murals by the Chicago artist Raymond Katz.

MW136 **House**

c. 1926. 2515 E. Solway Dr.

A stone entrance gable equipped with a second-floor oriel window suggests that this upper-middle-class suburban dwelling is a miniature English medieval manor house. The remainder of the house, which sits back from this frontispiece, is stone sheathed on the first floor, with stucco and half-timbering above.

MW137 **Lustron House** (Warren Gower House)

1950. 3300 Dearborn Ave.

This is a pale-yellow two-bedroom steel Lustron model. Another of the prefab Lustron houses, erected a year earlier (1949) for Melvin Gandy, is situated at 100 Medvale.

SIOUX CITY, NORTH

MW138 **Albertson House**

1927, K. E. Westerlind. 3927 Country Club Blvd.

The architect of this late Prairie-style house had worked in William L. Steele's office. With the Albertson house, he followed Steele's lead in providing a dwelling that emphasized the horizontal, but he was committed only in part to the visual language of the Prairie mode. His use of brick for the walls and green tile for the roof suggests a more staid, traditional domestic image.

MW139 **The Normandy**

c. 1931. Southwest corner of 38th St. and Hamilton Blvd.

A service station and a restaurant building were designed in the full-blown French Nor-

MW141 Jacobson House

man style. The service station has two small round towers with conical roofs which are placed one behind the other. The restaurant has a much larger, round three-story tower and a steeply pitched hipped roof. The two buildings have now been joined together.

MW140 Harold Brown House

1940. 4206 Country Club Blvd.

This two-story brick Colonial Revival house is distinguished by a handsome entrance com-

Inset 3, Sioux City, North (MW138–MW142)

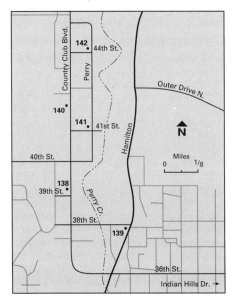

posed of a pedimented porch behind which is the entrance door with side lights and upper lunette window. Dentils and other "correct" details appear throughout the house.

MW141 Jacobson House

1928, William L. Steele. 4401 Perry Way

For the design of this house Steele took the theme of the Prairie-style bungalow and updated it by simplifying the fenestration of the volumes, and then by covering the forms by projecting gabled roofs of thin profile. The house now reads as an easygoing 1920s brick bungalow. One notes the brick gateposts, composed of layered rectangular volumes surmounted by tall, rectangular lamps. Behind the gateposts is the much-needed three-car garage which perfectly mirrors the gable roof forms of the house. The front porch, which was originally open, has now been enclosed.

MW142 Atherton House

1935. 4103 Perry Way

The Atherton house is one of the most important of the state's 1930s Moderne houses. A label such as "angular thirties Moderne" would probably come closest to characterizing it. The house is composed of interlocked cubes and rectangular volumes. At the center of the house is a three-story narrow volume that rises from the horizontal roof. Windows are treated as patterns moving across the surfaces, and of course these openings go around

MW142 Atherton House

corners. The entrance to the house is adjacent to the attached garage. As one would expect of a "futurist" house of the thirties, this building's mechanical plant is entirely electric.

SIOUX CITY, SOUTHEAST

MW143 Farmers Union GTA Terminal

c. 1917, later. N.E. 12th and Division streets

The gentle curve of the railroad tracks glides past what suggests a 1920s or 1930s "American Scene" painting of cylinders and rectangular towers accompanied by a pattern of lacy

metalwork of the storage and processing facility. This is a perfect image of industry on the prairie.

MW144 Fairmount Park Branch Library
(Greenville Neighborhood Center)

1924–1927, William L. Steele and George B. Hilgers. 220 S. Fairmount St.

The Fairmount Park Branch is one of three libraries designed by Steele and Hilgers. The plan, with its central pavilion, is characteristic of small library buildings of the late nineteenth and early twentieth century. The detailing is in the Prairie style: hovering hipped roofs, horizontal grouping of windows, and a horizontal stucco band carried above the brick walls and just below the roof's support.

MW145 Livestock National Bank, Exchange Building

c. 1920, William L. Steele. Cunningham Dr., south of Chicago Ave.

It is the Sullivan-inspired terracotta ornamentation that draws attention to what is otherwise a nondescript three-story brick office building. There are rectangular cartouches above the cornice on the parapet; the two terracotta signs inserted into the surrounding brick walls display letters intertwined within a field of naturalistic and geometric ornament. Most of the windows have now been filled in with glass brick.

MW144 Fairmount Park Branch Library (Greenville Neighborhood Center)

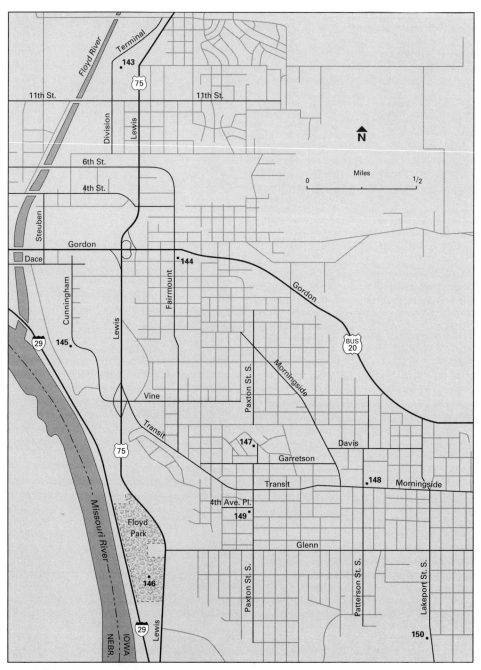

Inset 4, Sioux City, Southeast (MW143–MW150)

508

MW146 Floyd Monument

1912. Lewis Blvd., southwest of Glenn St.

A 100-foot-high white sandstone obelisk commemorates the burial site of Charles Floyd, a member of the Lewis and Clark Expedition (1804–1806), who died in 1804.

MW147 Poorbough House

1891. 1631 S. Paxton St.

The design of this Queen Anne house provides a street view of a large parapeted gable, within which is set a large arched window. On the ground level, matters change; there the center of attention is a long-arched stone porch that has been pulled across the front of the house and continued around the side.

MW148 Fire Station No. 6

1917. 4203 Morningside Ave.

A fire station is rendered in the guise of a midwestern brick bungalow, front porch and all.

MW149 White Eagle Oil Company Service Station

1930. 3232 4th Ave. Pl.

The image of this service station is medieval, with steeply pitched sweeping roofs, chimney,

and wall dormer. The design seems inspired more by historic examples from French Normandy than from the Cotswolds of England.

MW150 Graceland Cemetery Chapel

1912. 2701 S. Lake Port St.

The high gable ends of this miniature Gothic chapel are parapeted, containing the steep roofs.

MW151 Theophile Brughier Log Cabin

1849. Riverside Park; take Riverside Blvd. to Council Oaks Dr., then to southwest end of drive

This cabin was fortunately preserved by having been encased at a later time within a larger dwelling. It was originally located to the southeast of its present site. It was disassembled in the early 1930s and was subsequently reassembled and restored. The facade of the hewn-log cabin is symmetrical, with a central door balanced to each side by double-hung windows.

MW152 Tredway House (now Elmswood Inn)

1887, later. 3251 Floyd Blvd.

This dwelling began as a small, nondescript farmhouse, but its modest life was ended when a low mansard roof and porches with Ionic columns were added. The lower portion of the building has a light-handed Beaux-Arts quality about it. The small mansard roof set on the wide entablature and cornice seems almost to be the roof of a distant building.

MW153 Calvary Cemetery Mausoleum

1919, Anglaise Mausoleum Company. Casselman St., between Military Rd. and 28th St.

A central Egyptian pylon is balanced on each side by long wings which terminate in mastabalike tombs. At the entrance is a pair of lotus columns. The smooth dark granite walls and the closed nature of the design reinforce its funereal atmosphere.

Stuart

The post-Civil War railroad town of Stuart was laid out along the tracks of the east-west Chicago, Rock Island, and Pacific Railroad. For a number of years, until 1897, the town was the location for extensive railroad repair shops.

MW154 **Hollingsworth House**

1883. US 6, at western city limits

This large-scaled Italianate house has characteristics of the Eastlake in many of its details. The front of the house centers on a central two-story splayed bay, on each side of which are first-floor porches with elongated paired columns. As one often encounters in these late Italianate houses, the short, steep roof suggests a mansard roof. Visible behind the house is a large barn with cupola, designed entirely in the Eastlake style.

MW155 **Masonic Temple**

1894. Division St. west of 2nd St. N.

The connected, heavily arched windows of the third floor are certainly meant to be responded to as Romanesque Revival, but the remainder of this three-story brick structure seems almost classical. And then there is the tower that springs up from behind the stepped parapet of the roof. The walls of the tower with their clock faces and surrounds of curved ornamentation seem almost Georgian. Though an oddity in style, this building is very strong.

MW156 **First Congregational Church**

1903. Southwest corner of 3rd and Division streets

The low profile of this Gothic Revival church makes it appear as a distant object in relationship to its large corner tower. The tower asserts its presence not only by its size, but by a richness in the stone detailing which contrasts with the surrounding brick surfaces. The quoining, the surrounds of the pointed arched windows (and belfry), and the cornice are all rendered in light-colored stone.

MW157 **All Saints Roman Catholic Church**

1908. Fremont, between 3rd and 4th streets

The French Romanesque style was the inspiration for the design of this stone church.

MW157 All Saints Roman Catholic Church

The plan of the church comes close to being in the form of a Greek cross, with a pair of small round towers built into the juncture of the two sides of the cross toward the front. Everything about the design emphasizes the vertical, including the central dome on a high drum. The dome can be seen from all parts of town.

MW158 **Penn Township Methodist Episcopal Church**

1918. Proceed 10 miles east of town on I-80; take Redfield/Dexter exit, no. 100; follow routes G14 and P53 4 miles south

This brick and stucco church suggests a Prairie school interpretation of the Gothic Revival. The corner entrance tower is low and squat, made even more so by the wide overhang of its hipped roof. The windows above the entrance door are carried through the wood entablature right up to the soffit of the roof. One tends to read the pointed windows as horizontals, and the building's gabled ends are slightly cantilevered out over the brick foundation walls.

Tabor

This community, situated in the southwest corner of the state, 8 miles east of the Missouri River, contains a characteristic example of a Federal-style one-and-a-half-story dwelling. This is the Todd house of 1853, a clapboard house with a central chimney, located on Park Street in central Tabor. Later additions, such as a bay window at the side, have occurred, and changes to the rear wing have also been made. The house is closely associated with its original owner, the Reverend John Todd, an associate of John Brown in the antislavery movement. Also in town are a few remaining nineteenth-century buildings of Tabor College, which was founded in 1866 and closed in 1926.

Walnut

Just south of I-80 in Pottawattamie County is the community of Walnut. The town presents a nearly perfect assemblage of buildings that have come to characterize our mental picture of a small Iowa agricultural town. Iowa 83 runs due south from I-80, and as it enters town and becomes Central Street, the pavement becomes brick. The commercial buildings lining Central Street start abruptly, marking a sharp edge between the town and the surrounding country. Within town, at the northwest corner of Central and Highland streets, is an unlikely building to be encountered in Iowa: a shimmering white Mission Revival bank building straight from the streets of Los Angeles and Southern California. This two-story building, the Walnut State Bank (c. 1916), displays the appropriate Mission Revival ingredients: parapeted gables with arches, accompanied by tile roofs.

An added exotic note in the town is the house (c. 1890) located at 410 Central Street. The roof of this two-story clapboard house has been carried upward to form a peak at each of the two front corners of the dwelling; and each of these peaked second-floor corners has been cantilevered out over the lower floor to emphasize its presence. Part of the siding on this projecting second-floor section has been placed diagonally to mirror the slanted slope of the roof. There are drop finials at the peak of each of the corner roofs, and the roofs' edges exhibit lacy wood bargeboards.

Notes

INTRODUCTION

1. John Plumbe, Jr., "Sketches of Iowa and Wisconsin Taken during a Residence of Three Years in These Territories, 1839," *Annals of Iowa* 14, no. 7 (Jan. 1925): 484.
2. Grant Wood, *Revolt Against the City* (Iowa City: Clio Press, 1935), 23.
3. Thomas H. Benton, et al., *The Garden of the World, or the Great West*, 146.
4. Ibid., 145.
5. Plumbe, "Sketches of Iowa and Wisconsin," 484.
6. Marshall McKusick, *Men of Ancient Iowa* (Ames: Iowa State University Press, 1964), 98; Wilfred O. Logan, *Woodland Complex in Northeastern Iowa*, 181–84.
7. McKusick, *Men of Ancient Iowa*, 168–96.
8. J. B. Jackson, *American Space* (New York: W. W. Norton, 1972), 23.
9. Hildegard Binder Johnson, *Order upon the Land: The U.S. Rectangular Land Survey and the Upper Mississippi Country*, 40–49, 55–56.
10. Duane Anderson, *Eastern Iowa Archaeology*, 13–20.
11. Ibid., 26.
12. Logan, *Woodland Complex*, 178–89.
13. Peter Nabokov and Robert Easton, *Native American Architecture* (New York: Oxford University Press, 1989), 56–62.
14. Ibid., 63, 66–67.
15. Anderson, *Eastern Iowa Archaeology*, 34.
16. McKusick, *Men of Ancient Iowa*, 171–73; John and Margaret Hotopp, "Gathering the Past at Glenwood."
17. Anderson, *Eastern Iowa Archaeology*, 40.
18. McKusick, *Men of Ancient Iowa*, 106.
19. Cyrus Thomas, "Report on Mound Exploration," 99–103.
20. Ibid., pl. 5, fig. 49.
21. R. Clark Mallam, "The Mound Builders: An American Myth." *Journal of the Iowa Archaeological Society* 23 (1976): 145–75.
22. Charles R. Keyes, "A Unique Survey," *Palimpsest* 11:5 (1930): 214–27.
23. Thomas, "Mound Exploration."
24. Alfred Theodore Andreas, *Illustrated Historical Atlas of the State of Iowa, 1875*, 436.
25. Ibid., 440.
26. Ibid., 437.
27. Ibid., 445.
28. Clare C. Cooper, *The Role of the Railroads in the Settlement of Iowa* (Lincoln: University of Nebraska, 1958), 46; William H. Thompson, *Transportation in Iowa: A Historical Survey*, 18–26.
29. Frank P. Donovan, *"The Rock Island in Iowa," Palimpsest* 44 (September 1963): 384.
30. William J. Petersen, "Railroads Come to Iowa," 257.
31. Andreas, *Atlas of the State of Iowa*, 454.
32. M. Huebinger, *Atlas of the State of Iowa*, 293.
33. David C. Mott, "Abandoned Towns, Villages and Post Offices of Iowa," *Annals of Iowa* (3rd Series) 17 (October 1930): 435.
34. Ibid., 435.
35. George B. Ford and Ralph E. Warner, *City Planning Progress in the United States*, 49–51.
36. Charles Mulford Robinson, 1909 "Report with Regard to Civic Affairs in the City of Cedar Rapids, Iowa," (Cedar Rapids: City Commissioners, 1908). Ford and Warner, *City Planning*, 30–31.
37. Thomas P. Christensen, "The State Parks of Iowa," 332–33.
38. Ibid., 345.
39. Ibid., 348.
40. P. W. Elwood, Jr., "Work of Landscape Architect in Iowa State Parks."
41. Charles W. Roberts, "Poetry in Stone," 1976.
42. Daniel Harrison Jacques, *The House: A Pocket Manual of Rural Architecture*, 46.
43. Rita Goranson, "Sod Dwellings in Iowa."
44. Lowell J. Soike, *Without Right Angles: The Round Barns of Iowa*, 9–24.
45. Richard Pare, *Court House* (New York: Horizon Press, 1978); Paul K. Goeldner, "Temples of Justice: 19th Century County Courthouses in the Midwest and Texas."
46. Ginalie Swain, ed., "Iowa's Incredible Exposition Palaces," 4–9.
47. Betty Baldwin, "Flax Palaces,"; Ruth S. Beitz, "Swarthy King of the Palace Age"; John Ely Briggs, "Sioux City Corn Palaces"; Bruce E. Mahan, "The Blue Grass Palace," *Palimpsest* 44:12 (December 1931): 563–71. Swain, ed., "Exposition Palaces," 10–14.
48. James D. McCabe, *The Illustrated History of the Centennial Exposition . . .* (Philadelphia: The National Publishing Company, 1876): 605.
49. Iowa Columbian Commission, *Iowa at the World's Columbian Exposition, Chicago, 1893*, 10–26.
50. Loren N. Horton, *Iowa Planning, Growth and Architecture. In Selected Mississippi River Towns of Iowa, 1833–1860*, 233, 350.
51. Paul Kruty, "Patton and Miller: Designers of Carnegie Libraries."
52. Bowers and Klingensmith, 1980.
53. Alan M. Schroder, *Dictionary of 19th Century Iowa Architects.*
54. William T. Comstock, *The Architects' Directory and Specification Index for 1905–1906*, 43–44.
55. M. M. Hoffman, "John Francis Rague—Pioneer Architect of Iowa"; Betsy Woodman, *John*

Francis Rague: Mid-Nineteenth Century Revivalist Architect (1799–1877).

56. William Wagner, "William Foster—An Early Iowa Architect."

57. Barbara Beverly Long, *Iowa's Pre-Eminent Architectural Firm: the Architectural Legacy of Proudfoot and Bird, et al. in Iowa.*

58. William Elmer Frudden, *Farm Buildings.*

59. Soike, *Round Barns,* 51–56.

60. Keith E. Roe, *Corncribs: In History, Folklife, and Architecture* (Ames: Iowa State University Press, 1988).

61. Ibid., 27.

62. Frudden, *Farm Buildings,* 26–30.

63. E. G. Nourse, "Fifty Years of Farmer's Elevators in Iowa," *Bulletin* of the Agricultural Experiment Station, Iowa State College of Agriculture and Mechanic Arts, No. 221 (March 1923): 235–71.

64. John S. Gardner, "Tanks and Towers: Waterworks in America," Craig Zabel & Susan Scott Munshower, eds., *American Public Architecture; European Roots and Native Expression* (University Park: Pennsylvania State University, 1989), 211.

65. Gladys Hamlin, "Mural Painting in Iowa."

66. James M. Dennis, "The Mural Projects of Grant Wood," *The Iowan* 26 (Summer 1978): 22–26; Gregg R. Narber, "These Murals Were a New Deal," *The Iowan* 32 (Spring 1984): 8–17; Gregg R. Narber and Lea Rosson DeLong, "The New Deal Murals in Iowa," *Palimpsest* 63 (May/June 1982): 86–95; Mary L. Meixner, "Lowell Houser and the Genesis of a Mural," *Palimpsest* 66 (January/February 1985): 2–13.

67. Richard Guy Wilson and Sidney K. Robinson, *The Prairie School in Iowa.*

68. David Franklin Martin, "The Moderately Priced House and The Prairie School."

69. Katherine Cole Stevenson & H. Ward Jandl, *Houses By Mail: A Guide to Houses from Sears, Roebuck & Co..*

70. Lawrence McCann, "The World's Most Modern House," *American Magazine* 123 (March 1937): 50–51, 124–27.

MISSISSIPPI RIVER—EAST

1. William H. Thompson, *Transportation in Iowa: A Historical Survey,* 2–8, 18–27.

2. Alfred Theodore Andreas, *Illustrated Historical Atlas of the State of Iowa, 1875,* 458.

3. Lori Erickson, "Anamosa's Landmark in Stone," *Iowan* 38:3 (Spring 1990): 22–27.

4. Chuck Anderson, "Stone City."

5. Steven Brower, "The Durable Buildings of Burlington."

6. Willard Glazier, *Down the Great River,* 280.

7. William Peterson, "Railroads Come to Iowa," 515.

8. Ronald E. Schmitt, *Clinton, Iowa: An Architectural Heritage;* Katherine Long and Melvin Erickson, *Clinton: A Pictorial History.*

9. Andreas, *Atlas of the State of Iowa, 1875,* 484.

10. Arthur A. Hart, "M. A. Disbrow & Co.: Catalogue Architecture."

11. Schmitt, *Clinton, Iowa,* 80.

12. Marlys A. Svendsen, John Pfiffner, and Martha Bowers, *Davenport, Where the Mississippi Runs West: A Survey of Davenport History and Architecture;* Marlys A. Svendsen, *Davenport: A Pictorial History, 1836–1986.*

13. Thomas H. Benton et al., *The Garden of the World or the Great West,* 155.

14. Glazier, *Down the Great River,* 256.

15. Philippe Oszuscik, "A History of the Architecture and Urbanization of Nineteenth Century Davenport, Iowa."

16. Martha H. Bowers, *Davenport Architecture: Tradition and Transition;* Edmund H. Carroll, Jr., "Davenport's Golden Building Years."

17. "The First National Bank Building, Davenport, Iowa, Childs and Smith," *Architecture* 51:4 (April 1925): 125–26.

18. King's *Handbook of Notable Episcopal Churches* (1889), 241.

19. E. C. Hussey, *Home Building,* Pl. 33.

20. Benton et al., *Garden of the World,* 157.

21. Loren N. Horton, "Early Architecture in Dubuque," 144.

22. Gwen W. Steege, "The *Book of Plans* and the Early Romanesque Revival in the United States: A Study of Architectural Patronage," *Journal of the Society of Architectural Historians* (September 1987):221.

23. Horton, "Early Architecture in Dubuque"; Lawrence J. Sommer, *The Heritage of Dubuque: An Architectural View;* William E. Wilkie, *Dubuque on the Mississippi 1758–1988.*

24. Wilkie, *Dubuque on the Mississippi,* 105.

25. Fred Sloat, *Fort Madison: A Pictorial History.*

26. Glazier, *Down the Great River,* 297.

27. Raymond E. Garrison, *Tales of Early Keokuk Homes* (Hamilton, Illinois: The Hamilton Press, 1959).

28. Ibid., 80.

29. Andreas, *Atlas of the State of Iowa, 1875,* 488.

30. Melba Rae Widmen, *Victorian Home Architecture, Mt. Pleasant* (Mount Pleasant: 1989).

31. Melba Rae Widmen, "Nineteenth Century Home Architecture of Mount Pleasant, Iowa," 159.

32. Loren Horton, "Iowa Planning, Growth and Architecture," in *Selected Mississippi Rivertowns of Iowa, 1833–1860,* 139.

33. Glazier, *Down the Great River,* 273.

34. Lori Erickson, *Historic Architecture of Muscatine, Iowa* (1977).

35. Andreas, *Atlas of the State of Iowa, 1875,* 431.

36. William Gray Purcell, "Spencer and Powers, Architects," *Western Architect* 20:4 (April 1919):36.

CENTRAL

1. M. Huebinger, *Atlas of the State of Iowa,* 355.

2. Alfred Theodore Andreas, *Illustrated Historical Atlas of the State of Iowa, 1875,* 477.

3. Works Project Administration (Federal Writers Program), *Iowa: A Guide to the Hawkeye State*, 169.

4. Paul Venable Turner, *Campus: An American Planning Tradition*, 146.

5. Robert William Werle, *A Historical Review and Analysis of the Iowa State University Landscape, from 1858–1966*, 6.

6. James M. Dennis, "The Mural Projects of Grant Wood," *The Iowan* 26 (Summer 1978): 22–26.

7. Comprehensive City Plan for Cedar Rapids, Iowa (Cedar Rapids: Cedar Rapids Plan Commission, 1931), 9.

8. Joan Liffring-Zug, "The Armstrong House," 35.

9. Liffring-Zug, "Armstrong House," 34.

10. Kirk Blunck, "Iowa Museum Opens," *Architecture* 79 (February 1990): 24.

11. Montgomery Schuyler, "The People's Savings Bank of Cedar Rapids, Iowa," 78.

12. Huebinger, *Atlas of the State of Iowa*, 325.

13. Orin L.Dahl, *Des Moines: Capitol City*.

14. Andreas, *Atlas of the State of Iowa, 1875,* 429.

15. Harry B. Frase, "A Municipal Natatorium for Des Moines, Iowa," 453.

16. Ernest E.Clark, "Architecture in Iowa's Capitol City," 110–11.

17. Louise Rosenfield Noun, "The Iowa Soldiers' and Sailors' Monument," *Palimpsest* 67 (1986): 80–93.

18. Lawrence McCann, "The World's Most Modern House," *American Magazine* 123 (March 1937): 51.

19. McCann, "Modern House."

20. Scherrie Goettsch, *Terrace Hill*.

21. Charles W. Roberts, "The Saga of Salisbury House."

22. Eliel Saarinen and Robert F. Swanson, "Art Center in Iowa," *Architectural Forum* 91 (July 1949): 67.

23. Mickunas and Zingsheim, 30.

24. Martha B. Darbyshire, "Helfred Farms: The Estate of Mr. Fred W. Hubbell," *Country Life* 73 (April 1938): 63.

25. Dorothy Schwieder, *Patterns and Perspectives in Iowa History*.

26. Andreas, *Atlas of the State of Iowa, 1875*, 461.

27. Gerald Mansheim, *Iowa City: An Illustrated History*, 25–29.

28. Benjamin F. Shambaugh, ed., *Documentary Material Relating to the History of Iowa*, 142.

29. Shambaugh, *Documentary Material*, 149.

30. Huebinger, *Atlas of the State of Iowa*, 279.

31. Margaret N. Keyes, *Nineteenth Century Home Architecture of Iowa*, 114.

32. Glady Hamlin, "Mural Painting in Iowa," 255.

33. Henry-Russell Hitchcock and William Seale, *Temples of Democracy* (New York: Harcourt Brace Jovanovich, 1976), 107–10.

34. Robert K. Bower, "Frontier Stone: The Story of Iowa's Old Capitol," 107.

35. Bower, "Frontier Stone"; Keyes, *Home Architecture*.

36. Walter Netsch (S.O.M., Chicago), "Basic Science Building and Educational Research Building, University of Iowa, Iowa City, Iowa," *Progressive Architecture* 54 (April 1973): 82.

37. Gunnar Birkerts, 107.

38. Lowell J. Soike, *Without Right Angles: The Round Barns of Iowa*, 20.

39. Andreas, *Atlas of the State of Iowa, 1875*, 478.

40. Ibid., 438.

41. Huebinger, *Atlas of the State of Iowa*, 344.

42. Marshalltown Club, *In the Forefront as a City of Progress*.

43. Andreas, *Atlas of the State of Iowa, 1875*, 474.

44. Mike Whye and Charles W. Roberts, "A Connecticut Classic comes to Iowa," 1987.

45. Andreas, *Atlas of the State of Iowa, 1875*, 483.

46. Drake Hokanson, *The Lincoln Highway*.

47. Andreas, *Atlas of the State of Iowa, 1875*, 483.

48. Soike, *Round Barns*, 85.

SOUTH

1. H. Roger Grant, "Highway Commercial Architecture: Albia Iowa's 'Dutch Mill,'" 1977.

2. Leroy G. Pratt, *Discovering Historic Iowa*, 1975.

3. Lowell J. Soike, *Without Right Angles: The Round Barns of Iowa*, 78.

4. Alfred Theodore Andreas, *Illustrated Historical Atlas of the State of Iowa, 1875*, 500.

5. Bruce E. Mahan, "The Blue Grass Palace."

6. Andreas, *Atlas of the State of Iowa, 1875*, 498.

7. Ibid., 494.

8. Charles W. Roberts, "Liberty Hall, Showcase for Church's Heritage," 42.

9. Andreas, *Atlas of the State of Iowa, 1875*, 497.

10. Ruth S. Beitz, "Swarthy King of the Palace Age," 1962.

11. Ibid.

NORTH

1. Lowell J. Soike, *Without Right Angles: The Round Barns of Iowa*, 79.

2. Environmental Planning and Research, *Mason City, Iowa. An Architectural Heritage*, 1977.

3. C. R. Jones, "Floyd County is a Land of Limestone Landmarks."

4. Alfred Theodore Andreas, *Illustrated Historical Atlas of the State of Iowa, 1875*, 464.

5. Ibid., 434.

6. Ibid.

7. Leonard K. Eaton, *Landscape Architect in America: The Life and Work of Jens Jensen*, 179.

8. Betty Baldwin, "Flax Palace."

9. Karl F. Haugen and Atlee R. Loomis, *Historic Homes of Fort Dodge*, 1975.

10. Alfred Theodore Andreas, *Illustrated Historical Atlas of the State of Iowa, 1875*, 471.

11. M. Huebinger, *Atlas of the State of Iowa*, 338.

12. Andreas, *Atlas of the State of Iowa, 1875*, 462.

13. Ibid., 453.

14. Huebinger, *Atlas of the State of Iowa*, 337.

15. Andreas, *Atlas of the State of Iowa, 1875*, 470.
16. Environmental Planning and Research, *Mason City, Iowa. An Architectural Heritage*, 1976.
17. Walter Burley Griffin, "Town and Community Planning," 75.
18. Andreas, *Atlas of the State of Iowa, 1875*, 460
19. Soike, *Round Barns*, 75.
20. John Zug and John Liffring-Zug, "The Foster House," *Iowan* 23:3 (Spring 1973).
21. Kevin Boatright, ed., *Historic Tour, Black Hawk County, Iowa*, 74.
22. Andreas, *Atlas of the State of Iowa, 1875*, 443.
23. Huebinger, *Atlas of the State of Iowa*, 282
24. Herman J. Doscher, et al., eds., *History of West Union, Iowa* (West Union: Private printing, 1974), 40.
25. Soike, *Round Barns*, 78.

MISSOURI RIVER—WEST

1. Leroy G. Pratt, *The Counties and Courthouses of Iowa*, 59.
2. Lowell J. Soike, *Without Right Angles: The Round Barns of Iowa*, 79.
3. Alfred Theodore Andreas, *Illustrated Historical Atlas of the State of Iowa, 1875*, 490.
4. Ibid., 491.
5. Soike, *Round Barns*, 80.
6. Jolene Stevens, "Fantasy World in Ida Grove."
7. Andreas, *Atlas of the State of Iowa, 1875*, 457.
8. M. Huebinger, *Atlas of the State of Iowa*, 330.
9. Ruth S. Beitz, "Sioux City's Splendid Corn Palaces."
10. William J. Petersen, "In Quest of Tourists in 1887," *Palimpsest* 44:12 (December 1963): 580.
11. Marilyn Laufer, Edward Storm and Scott Sorensen, eds., *Sioux City Iowa: An Architectural View*, 1983.
12. *The Western Architect*, "Woodbury County Courthouse, Sioux City, Iowa," 14.
13. Jackson Street Building Company, *Badgerow Building, Monarch of the City* (Sioux City: Pritchard-Richardson Co., Printers, 1930), 10.
14. Ibid.

Suggested Readings

The readings listed here consist of only a small fragment of the material consulted for the writing of this guide. The many county histories issued over the years have been among the most valuable sources of information, but there are so many that we have not wished to encumber this reading list with them. We have also been perhaps too selective of the many articles published in the *Palimpsest* and the *Iowan*, for these two magazines contain a wealth of information about Iowa cities and towns, their architecture and history. For nineteenth-century Iowa architecture, the single most valuable volume is Alfred Theodore Andreas, *Illustrated Historical Atlas of the State of Iowa, 1875*. For Iowa at the turn of the century, M. Huebinger's *Atlas of the State of Iowa* (1904) is essential. The best guide to the state remains The Works Progress Administration's *Iowa: A Guide to the Hawkeye State*. The material gathered by the Historic American Building Survey in the depression years and later is also important, as is that compiled more recently by the Historic American Engineering Record. The people of Iowa, along with other states, have shown a strong interest in the state's history, especially within the past two decades. This is reflected in numerous publications of the Iowa State Historical Society (including historical and architectural surveys) and in the many active county and local historical societies. Post-World War II architecture has been well presented within the pages of the *Iowa Architect*, which in the past two decades has emerged as one of the best state journals in the country.

Agnew, Dwight L. "The Rock Island Railroad in Iowa," *Iowa Journal of History* 52:3 (July 1954): 203–22.

Allen, Richard Sanders *Covered Bridges of the Middle West*. (Brattleboro, Vt.: Greene, 1970).

American Institute of Architects, Iowa Chapter. *Architecture on Hand: Des Moines Architecture*. Des Moines: Acme Printing Co., 1990.

Anderson, Adrian Dale. "Preserving our Heritage," *Palimpsest* 53:10 (October 1972): 433–47.

———. "Historic Preservation in Iowa." *Palimpsest* 53:10 (October 1972): 448–68.

Anderson, Chuck. "Stone City." *Iowa Architect* 30:5. (September/October, 1983): 22–25.

Anderson, Duane. *Western Iowa Prehistory*. Ames: Iowa State University Press, 1975.

———. *Eastern Iowa Archaeology*. Ames: Iowa State University Press, 1981.

Andreas, Alfred Theodore. *Illustrated Historical Atlas of the State of Iowa, 1875*. Chicago: Andreas Atlas Co., 1875. Reprint, Iowa City: State Historical Society of Iowa, 1970.

Arden, Harvey. "Iowa, America's Middle Earth."

National Geographic Magazine 159:5 (May 1981): 602–29.

Baldwin, Betty. "Flax Palace." *Iowan* 13:1 (Fall 1965): 41, 52.

Barber, George E. *The Cottage Souvenir #2*. Knoxville, Tenn.: Newman, 1892.

———. *New Model Dwellings and How Best to Build Them*. Knoxville, American Home Publishing Co., 1895–1896.

Barrington, Lewis. "Iowa," in *Historic Restorations of the Daughters of the American Revolution*, pp. 185–87. New York: Richard R. Smith, 1941.

Beitz, Ruth S. "Sioux City's Splendid Corn Palaces." *Iowan* 9:3 (February/March 1961): 43–44.

———. "Swarthy King of the Palace Age." *Iowan* 10:4 (Summer 1962): 42–45, 51.

Benesh, Dick. "Train Depots: Our Architectural Heritage." *Iowa Architect* 35:6 (November/December 1986): 30–33.

Benton, Thomas H., et al. *The Garden of the World or the Great West*. Boston: Wentworth, 1856.

Blunck, Kirk V. "In Search of Recognition." *Iowa Architect* 28:6 (November/December 1981): 30–39.

———. "Sources: Pre-Modern to Post-Modern." *Iowa Architect* 28:5 (September/October 1981): 8–17.

Blunk, Mark E. "The Butler House." *Iowa Architect* 36:2 (March/April 1988): 38–41.

Boatright, Kevin, ed. *Historic Tour, Black Hawk County, Iowa*. Cedar Falls: Office of the Mayor, n.d.

Bobinski, George. *Carnegie Libraries: Their History and Impact on American Public Library Development*. Chicago: American Library Association, 1969.

Bonney, Margaret Atherton, ed. "Iowa Houses." *The Goldfinch* 2:4 (September 1981).

———. "The Town Builders of Iowa." *The Goldfinch* 3:3 (February 1982).

Bowers, Martha H. "Community Images in Iowa: Belle Plaine." *The Bracket* (Spring 1982): 4–10.

———. *Davenport Architecture: Tradition and Transition*. Iowa City: Dennett, Muessig and Associates, Ltd., 1984.

Bower, Robert K. "Frontier Stone: The Story of Iowa's Old Capitol." *Palimpsest* 57:4 (July/August 1971): 98–120.

Branch, E. Douglas. "Railroads Come to Council Bluffs." *Palimpsest* 10 (June 1929): 201–32.

Briggs, John Ely. *Iowa Old and New*. Lincoln: The University Publication Co., 1939.

———. "The Sioux City Corn Palaces." *Palimpsest* 44:12 (December 1963): 549–62.

Brooks, H. Allen. *The Prairie School*. Toronto: University of Toronto Press, 1972.

Brower, Katherine and Steven. "Heritage Hill, A New Historic District in Burlington." *The Bracket* (Spring 1982): 12–13.

517

Brower, Steven. "The Durable Buildings of Burlington." *Palimpsest* 61:2 (May/June 1980): 92–96.

Brown, Janet. "Pairing the Past with the Present." *Iowan* 32:3 (Spring 1984): 35–39.

Brown, Joseph K. "Iowa Jewel Boxes of Louis Sullivan." *Iowan* 6 (August/September 1958): 18–25.

Bruce, Edward and Forbes Watson. *Art in Federal Buildings*. Vol. I. Washington, D.C.: Art in Federal Buildings, Inc., 1936.

"Bute Cottage." *American Agriculturalist*. (November 1845): 345.

Cackler, Claudia. "Salisbury House: Quest for Perfection," *Iowa Architect* 36:2 (March/April 1988): 24–29.

Canine, Craig A. "Deco in Des Moines," *Iowan* (Fall 1980): 32–39.

Carpenter, Matthew. *Bibliography on Select Sources Available for Identification and Restoration of Iowa's Domestic and Commercial Architecture*. Iowa City: Iowa State Historical Society, 1989.

———. "Iowa Trolleys." *Bulletin* 114 of the Central Iowa Railfans Association, 1975.

Carroll, Edmund H., Jr. "Davenport's Golden Building Years." *Palimpsest* 63:2 (March/April 1982): 52–64.

———. *A Century of Farming*. Ames: Iowa State College, 1946.

Cheever, L. O. "Census of Covered Bridges." *Palimpsest* 51:11 (November 1970): 466–96.

Chappell, Sally Anderson. "Barry Byrne, Architect: His Formative Years." *Prairie School Review* 3:4 (1966): 5–23.

Chicoine, B. Paul. "A Dazzling Showplace for a Steamboat's Treasure." *Iowan* 31:2 (Winter 1982): 36–41.

Chicoine, B. Paul, and Scott Sorensen. "Iowa City Xanadou." *Iowan* 32:1 (Fall 1983): 36–43.

Christensen, Thomas P. "The State Parks of Iowa." *Iowa Journal of History and Politics* 26 (July 1928): 331–414.

Christian, Rebecca. "Glimpses of a Gilded Age." *Iowan* 33:4 (Summer 1985): 27–31.

———. "They Preserved a Treasure," *Iowan* 34:2 (Winter 1985): 4–14.

Clark, Ernest E. "Architecture in Iowa's Capital City." *Midland Monthly Magazine* 10 (August/September 1898): 110–20, 205–13.

Close, William B. *Farming in North-Western Iowa, United States of America: A Pamphlet for Emigrants and a Guide to Northwestern Iowa*. Manchester, 1880.

Coggeshall, John, and Jo Anne Nast. *Vernacular Architecture in Southern Illinois: The Ethnic Heritage*. Carbondale: Southern Illinois University Press, 1988.

Curtis, Peter H. *Fire Insurance Maps of Iowa Cities and Towns*. Iowa City: Iowa State Historical Dept., 1983.

Dahl, Orin L. *Des Moines: Capitol City*. Tulsa, Oklahoma: Continental Heritage Press, 1978.

Dawson, Patricia, and David Hudson. *Iowa History and Culture: A Bibliography of Materials Published Between 1952 and 1986*. Ames: Iowa State University Press, 1989.

De Jaho, Wayne A. "The Interurban Years." *Palimpsest* 62:2 (March/April 1981): 34–43.

Dennett, Muessig and Associates. "An Architectural and Historical Survey of Public Libraries in Iowa 1870–1940." Iowa City: Dennett Muessig and Associates, 1980, unpublished.

Des Moines Heritage, A Survey of Significant Architecture. Des Moines: Des Moines Planning and Zoning Commission, 1976.

Dikis, William Melvin. "Iowa's Architecture: An Historical Overview and Guide to Certain Cities." M. Arch. thesis, Iowa State University, 1967.

Dilts, Harold E., Katherine Dilts, Ann Dilts, and Linda Jo Dilts. *From Ackley to Zwingle. A Collection of the Origin of Iowa Place Names*. Ames: Carter Press, Inc., 1975.

Dondore, Dorothy Ann. *The Prairie and the Making of Middle America: Four Centuries of Description*. Cedar Rapids: Torch Press, 1926.

Donovan, Frank P. "Great Northern-Union Pacific-Santa Fe." *Palimpsest* 46:4 (April 1965): 193–224.

Drury, John. *Historic Midwest Houses*. Minneapolis: University of Minnesota Press, 1947.

Duffield, George C. "Frontier Mills." *Annals of Iowa* (3rd Series) 6 (July 1904): 425–36.

Eaton, Leonard K. *Landscape Architect in America: The Life and Work of Jens Jensen*. Chicago: University of Chicago Press, 1964.

Eckhardt, Patricia. *Historical Organizations in Iowa*. Iowa City: Iowa State Historical Society, 1982.

Eckhardt, Patricia, and Charles W. Roberts. "The Courthouse: Its Age of Grandeur." *Iowan* 29:1 (Fall 1979): 24–33.

Elwood, P. W., Jr. "Work of Landscape Architect in Iowa State Parks." *Parks and Recreation* 11:2 (December 1927): 93–96.

Environmental Planning and Research, Inc., (Chicago) *Charles City, Iowa: A Historical Inventory*. 1976.

———. *Historic Architecture of Muscatine, Iowa*. 1977.

———. *Mason City, Iowa: An Architectural Heritage*. 1977.

Evans, Cheryl Dreasta. "Ready Mades: A Unique Form of Vernacular Housing." *The Bracket* (Summer 1984): 4–9.

Fairall, Herbert S. *Iowa at the World's Industrial and Cotton Centennial, and the North Central and South American Exposition, 1884–1885*. Des Moines: State of Iowa, 1885.

Fishburn, Jesse J. "Octagon Place." *Palimpsest* 29:2 (February 1948): 33–38.

Fisher, Oneita. "A Homestead Preserved." *Iowan* 12:2 (January 1964): 18–21.

Fletcher, Margerie. "Grand Manor of an Elegant Age." *Iowan* 26:3 (March 1978): 4–10.

Ford, George B., and Ralph E. Warner. *City Planning Progress in the United States*. Washington, D.C.: American Institute of Architects, 1917.

Fox, Diana. *Checklist of Printed Maps of the Middle West to 1900*. Vol. 8, *Iowa*. Chicago: G. K. Hall, 1981.

Frederick, John T. "The Farm in Iowa Fiction," *Palimpsest* 32:3 (March 1951): 121–52.

Frudden, William Elmer. *Farm Buildings.* Charles City, Iowa: Frudden, 1916.

Gallaher, Ruth A. *Some Historical Markers in Iowa.* Iowa City: State Historical Society, 1943.

Garrison, Raymond E. *Tales of Early Keokuk Homes.* Hamilton, Ill.: Hamilton Press, 1959.

Gebhard, David. "William Gray Purcell and George Grant Elmslie and the Early Progressive Movement in American Architecture, 1900–1920." Ph.D. thesis, University of Minnesota, Minneapolis 1957.

Gebhard, David, and Tom Martinson. *A Guide to the Architecture of Minnesota.* Minneapolis: University of Minnesota Press, 1977.

Glazier, Willard. *Down the Great River.* Philadelphia: Hubbard, 1892.

Goeldner, Paul K. "Temples of Justice: 19th Century County Courthouses in the Midwest and Texas." Ph.D. thesis, Columbia University, 1970.

Goettsch, Scherrie. *Terrace Hill.* Des Moines: Wallace-Homestead Book Co., 1978.

Goranson, Rita. "Sod Dwellings in Iowa," *Palimpsest* 65:2 (March/April 1984): 124–34.

Gordon-Van Tine Co. *Gordon-Van Tine Co., Architectural Details 1915.* Davenport, Iowa. Republished, Watkins Glenn, N.Y.: The American Life Foundation, 1985.

Grant, H. Roger. "Iowa's Railroad Stations: A Pictorial Essay." *Palimpsest* 54:4 (July/August 1973): 16–25.

———. "Highway Commercial Architecture: Albia Iowa's 'Dutch Mill.'" *Palimpsest* 53:3 (May/June 1977): 84–87.

Grant, Jackie. "Life with Frank Lloyd Wright's House." *Iowan* 8:1 (October/November 1959): 24–28, 53.

Grant, Linda. "An Historic Octagonal House." *Iowan* 15:1 (October 1966): 43–47.

Greiner, Chuck. "Victorian Stenciling in Iowa's Statehouse." *Palimpsest* 69:4 (Winter 1988): 173–85.

Griffin, Walter Burley. "Town and Community Planning." *Western Architect* 19:6 (August 1913): 67–81.

Hair, James T. *Iowa State Gazetteer.* Chicago: Bailey and Hair, 1865.

Ham, Adrenne Camille. "The Iowa Residential Architecture of Frank Lloyd Wright." M.A. thesis, University of Iowa, 1972.

Hamlin, Gladys. "Mural Painting in Iowa." *Iowa Journal of History* 37:3 (July 1939): 227–307.

"A Handsome Heritage: The Homes of Keokuk." *The Iowan* 27:1 (Fall 1978): 4–18.

Hansen, Charles. "Iron Age in Architecture." *Iowan* 10:2 (Winter 1962): 42–48, 53–54.

Harland, Edgar R. "Proposed Improvements of the Iowa Capitol Grounds." *Annals of Iowa* 11:2 and 3 (July/October 1913): 96–114.

Hart, Arthur A. "M.A. Disbrow & Co.: Catalogue Architecture." *Palimpsest* 56;4 (July/August 1975): 98–119.

Haskins, Mary. "A Loving Revival: Kingman Place." *Iowan* 10:4 (July 1962): 38–41.

Haugen, Karl F., and Atlee R. Loomis. *Historic Homes of Fort Dodge, Iowa.* Fort Dodge: Messenger Printing Co. 1975.

Hedberg, Anderson. "Caretakers of the Classics." *Iowan* 37:3 (Spring 1989): 21–34.

Herman, Andrea. "Victorian Showcase." *Iowan* 23:3 (March 1975): 15–19.

Hermann, Patricia Broshar. "Stone Architecture of Stone City and Waubeck, Iowa." M.A. thesis, University of Iowa, 1966.

Hickman, C. Addison. "Barlow Hall." *Palimpsest* 22:10 (October 1941): 301–9.

Hirsch, Mary. "A French Farmhouse in Newton: Bill and Marilyn Vernon's Country French Home," *Iowan* 34:4 (Summer 1986): 14–17.

"Historic Plum Grove." *Iowan* 8:6 (August/September 1960): 32–37.

Hoffman, M. M. "John Francis Rague—Pioneer Architect of Iowa," *Annals of Iowa* 3 (October 1934): 444–48.

Hokanson, Drake. "The Lincoln Highway in Iowa." *The Bracket* (January 1983): 2–5.

———. *The Lincoln Highway.* Iowa City: University of Iowa Press, 1988.

Horton, Loren N. "Early Architecture in Dubuque." *Palimpsest* 55:5 (September/October 1974): 130–54.

———. "The Architectural Background of Trinity Episcopal Church." *Annals of Iowa* 43 (1977): 539–48.

———. "Iowa Planning, Growth and Architecture. In Selected Mississippi River Towns of Iowa, 1833–1860." Ph.D. thesis, University of Iowa, 1978.

———. "River Town: Davenport's Early Years." *Palimpsest* 60:1 (January/February 1979): 16–27.

———. "A Seven-Day Tour of Historic Iowa," *Journal of the West* (July 1982): 65–70.

———. "Through the Eyes of Artists: Iowa Towns in the 19th Century." *Palimpsest* 59:5 (September/October 1978): 133–45.

———. *Town Planning, Growth and Architecture in Select Mississippi River Towns.* Iowa City: University of Iowa Press, 1978.

Hotopp, John, and Margaret Hotopp. "Gathering the Past at Glenwood." *Iowan* 24 (Summer 1976): 41–46.

Houlette, William D. "Madison County's Wonderful Stone Houses," *Iowan* 2:6 (August/September 1954): 30–35.

Hubach, Robert R. "They Saw the Early Midwest: A Bibliography of Travel Narratives, 1727–1850." *Iowa Journal of History* 52:3 (July 1954): 223–34.

Huebinger, M. *Atlas of the State of Iowa.* Davenport: Iowa Publishing Co., 1904.

Hussey, E.C. (Elisha). *Home Building.* New York: Leader and Van Halsch, 1875.

Huttenlocher, Fae. "Victorian-Oriental Home." *Iowan* (June 1969): 44–48.

Indiana Limestone Bank Bldgs. Limestone Library, Vol. 4, Series B, 3rd Edition. Bedford, Indiana: Indiana Limestone Quarrymen's Association, August 1922.

Iowa Columbian Commission. *Iowa at the World's Columbian Exposition, Chicago, 1893.* Cedar Rapids: Republican Printing Co., 1895.

Iowa: The Home for Immigrants. Studies in Iowa History, vol. 1, no. 3. Iowa City: State Historical Society. 1970.

Iowa State Historical Department. *National Register of Historic Places in Iowa.* Iowa City, 1981.

"An Iowa Home From Iowa Stone." *Iowan* 1:6 (August-September 1953): 24–26.

"An Italian Villa." *American Agriculturalist.* (January 1850): 25.

Jaastad, Judy. "A Man and His Mansion." *Iowan* 28:2 (Winter 1980): 32–36.

Jackson, Marilyn. "A New Life for a Vintage Home." *Iowan* 19:3 (March 1970): 20–23, 50.

Jacques, Daniel Harrison. *The House: A Pocket Manual of Rural Architecture* (Designed by F. E. Graef, Architect, and others). New York: Fowler and Wells, 1859.

Johnson, Hildegard Binder. *Order in the Land: The U.S. Rectangular Land Survey and the Upper Mississippi County.* New York: Oxford, 1976.

Johnson, Jack T. *The Iowa Capitol: A Harvest of Design.* Des Moines: Plain Talk Publishing Co., 1989.

———. "Guides to Iowa Territory." *Palimpsest* 20:3 (March 1939): 65–76.

Johnson, Patty. "Colorful Houses That Cosmetics Preserve." *Iowan* 9:3 (February/March 1961): 16–17.

———. "From an Era of Elegance—The Purdy-Twaite House." *Iowan* 14:4 (July 1966): 14–17.

Jones, C. R. "Floyd County Is a Land of Limestone Landmarks." *Iowan* 13:2 (January 1965): 10–14.

Keehn, Jeanne. "Guttenberg." *Iowan* 12:4 (July 1964): 6–11.

Keyes, Margaret N. "He Left a Legacy of Landmarks." *Iowan* 20 (Fall 1971): 1–2.

———. "Iowa City's Prize 19th Century Houses." *Iowan* 16:1 (September 1967): 33–39, 52.

———. *Nineteenth Century Home Architecture of Iowa.* Iowa City: University of Iowa Press, 1966.

———. "Old Capitol, Iowa City, Iowa." *Antiques* 114 (July 1978): 120–31.

Kidder Smith, G. E. *The Architecture of the United States.* Vol. 3, *The Plains States and the West,* pp. 295–320. New York: Anchor Books 1981.

Kinne, Ann Spencer. "The Renselaer Russell House." *Annals of Iowa* 3rd Series, 42:4 (Spring 1974): 303–13.

Knudson, George E. *Self Guiding Tour of Decorah for Motorists and Cyclists.* Decorah, Iowa: Lutheran College Press, 1971.

Koch, Theodore W. *A Book of Carnegie Libraries.* White Plains, N.Y.: H.W. Wilson Co., 1917.

Kooi, Muriel. "Over the Threshold—Step Back to 1909." *Iowan* 8:3 (1959): 32–35, 53.

———. "Pella's Unusual Old Homes," *Iowan* 9:2 (December/January 1960–1961): 30–37, 50.

———. "A Touch of the Dutch." *Iowan* 22:3 (March 1979): 12–14.

Kruty, Paul. "Patton and Miller: Designers of Carnegie Libraries." *Palimpsest* 64:4 (July/August 1984): 110–22.

Kuebler, Nancy S. "Selected Rehabilitation of Old Buildings in Central and Eastern Iowa." M.A. thesis, University of Iowa, 1980.

LaFore, Laurence. *American Classic.* Iowa City: Division of the State Historical Society, 1975. Rev. ed., Iowa City: Division of the State Historical Society, 1979.

Lane, Pat Sonquist. "An Iowa Barn: Swedish Style." *Palimpsest* 64:5 (September/October 1983): 170–78.

Langholz, John D. *Architectural Survey Report Madison County, Iowa.* Iowa City: Iowa State Historical Department, Division of Historic Preservation 1975.

Larson, Elaine, and Warren Larson. "Old Barns: Facing a Perilous Future." *Iowan* 30:4 (Summer 1983): 28–35.

Laufer, Marilyn, Edward Storm, and Scott Sorensen, eds. *Sioux City Iowa: An Architectural View.* Sioux City: Sioux City Art Center Pub., 1983.

Leonard, L.O. "The Antoine-LeClaire House." *The Rock Island Magazine* 23:10 (October 1928): 11–12.

———. "The Bonnifield Home in Fairfield." *The Rock Island Magazine* 24:10 (October 1929): 15–16.

Liffring-Zug, Joan. "The Age of Elegance Recalled in Lisbon," *Iowan* 12:2 (January 1969): 34–41, 53.

———. *The Amanas Yesterdays: A Religious Communal Society.* Iowa City: Penfield Press, 1975.

———. "The Armstrong House." *Iowan* 11:4 (July 1963): 32–37.

———. "Woodbury County Courthouse." *Iowan* 152 (Winter 1966–67): 4–9, 51.

———. "A Heritage Dating back to the Steamboat Era." *Iowan* 22:3 (March 1974): 37–50.

———. "Seminole Valley Farmhouse." *Iowan* 18:4 (June 1970): 41–45, 53.

———. "A Handsome Heritage." *Iowan* 27:1 (September 1978): 11–18.

Logan, Wilfred O. *Woodland Complex in Northeastern Iowa.* Washington, D.C.: National Park Service Publications in Architecture No. 15, 1976.

Long, Barbara Beverly. *Des Moines, Center of Iowa: Survey of Historic Sites.* Des Moines: Des Moines Planning and Zoning Commission, 1983.

———. *Hometown Architecture: Changing Central Iowa Towns and Farms* Des Moines: Des Moines State Historical Department, 1981.

———. *Iowa's Pre-Eminent Architectural Firm: The Architectural Legacy of Proudfoot and Bird, et al. in Iowa.* Iowa City: Iowa Office of Historic Preservation, 1987.

Long, Katherine, and Melvin Erickson. *Clinton: A Pictorial History.* Rock Island: Quest Publishing, 1983.

Loomis, Allen R. *Historic Homes, Fort Dodge, Iowa.* Fort Dodge: Blanden Federation of Arts, 1975.

Lufkin, Jack, and Sheila Hainlin. *Des Moines Heritage: A Survey of Significant Architecture, Phase II.* Des Moines: Des Moines Planning and Zoning Commission, 1977.

"The Lytle Company." *Common Clay* (Chicago) (January 1921): 2–11.

Macy, Harriet P. *Sketches of Historic Iowa.* Ames: Carten Press, 1969.

Mahan, Bruce E. "The Blue Grass Palace." *Palimpsest* 12:12 (December 1963): 563–71.

Mansheim, Gerald. "A Preserve of Prairie School Architecture." *Iowan* 24:2 (Winter 1975): 37–44.

———. "Louis Sullivan in Iowa." *Palimpsest* 61:2 (March/April 1980): 54–64.

———. "William Steele's Silent Music." *Palimpsest* 62:2 (March/April 1981): 44–55.

———. "Prairie School Architecture in Mason City: A Pioneering Venture in City Planning." *Palimpsest* 65:3 (May/June 1984): 94–105.

———. *Iowa City: An Illustrated History.* Norfolk, Va.: Donning, 1989.

Marshalltown Club. *In the Forefront as a City of Progress.* Marshalltown: Marshalltown Printing Co., 1916.

Martin, David Franklin. "The Moderately Priced House and the Prairie School." M.A. thesis, University of Iowa, 1978.

Martin, Dick. "Paradise Valley," *Iowan* 13:2 (January 1965): 41–45, 54.

Massey, James C., and Shirley Maxwell. "Planbook Houses: Architecture by Mail." *Old House Journal* 17:6 (November/December 1989): 40–45.

May, George S. "Getting out of the Mud," *Palimpsest* 46 (February 1965): 80–122.

———. "Recent Industrial Developments." *Palimpsest* 37:5 (May 1956): 229–88.

Morgan, William T. "Strongboxes on Main Street: Prairie-Style Banks." *Landscape* 24:2 (1980): 35–40.

Niles, C. J., and Debbie Felton. "He Promised Her a Mansion." *Iowan* 34:2 (Winter 1985): 52–57.

Oszuscik, Philippe. "A History of the Architecture and Urbanization of Nineteenth Century Davenport, Iowa." Ph.D. thesis, University of Iowa, 1979.

Pelzen, Louis. "Early Burlington." *Palimpsest* 15:7 (July 1934): 225–54.

Petersen, Dorothy. "A New Life for an Old Show-Place." *Iowan* 20:1 (September 1971): 32–35.

Petersen, William J. "The Beginnings of Davenport, Iowa." *Palimpsest* 20:8 (August 1939): 241–80.

———. "Transportation By Land." *Palimpsest* 27:10 (October 1946): 301–16.

———. *Iowa: Rivers of Her Valleys.* Iowa City: Iowa State Historical Society, 1941.

———. *The Story of Iowa.* New York: Lewis Historical Co., 1952.

———. *Iowa History Reference Guide.* Iowa City: Iowa State Historical Society, 1952.

———. "Industry in 1840." *Palimpsest* 38:5 (May 1956): 225–28.

———. "The Harlin-Lincoln House." *Palimpsest* 41:3 (March 1960): 173–76.

———. "Railroads Come to Iowa." *Palimpsest* 41:4 (April 1960): 177–260.

———. "The Pioneer Log Cabin." *Palimpsest* 41:11 (November 1960): 485–517.

———. "Some Historic Sites in Iowa." *Palimpsest* 48:5 (May 1967): 209–48.

Pierick, Judi. "Tale of Two Mansions." *Iowan* 22:2 (December 1973): 15–19.

Plowden, David. *A Sense of Place.* New York: Norton, 1988.

Plumbe, Jr., John. "Sketches of Iowa and Wisconsin Taken During a Residence of Three Years in These Territories, 1839." *Annals of Iowa* 14:7 (January 1925): 483–619.

Plymat, William. *The Victorian Architecture of Iowa.* Des Moines: Elephant Eye, 1976.

Polk, R. L., & Co., *Architects, Builders and Carpenters Directory of the United States.* New York: Polk & Co., 1886.

Powell, Johnnie. "The Harker House." *Iowan* 15:2 (January 1967): 44–49.

Powers, Samuel C. E. "The Iowa State Highway Commission." *Iowa Journal of History and Politics* 29:1 (January 1931): 42–103.

Pratt, LeRoy G. *Discovering Historic Iowa.* Des Moines: Iowa Department Public Instruction, 1975.

———. "Iowa Counties and Courthouses." *Annals of Iowa* 43:6 (Fall 1976): 459–75.

———. *The Counties and Courthouses of Iowa.* Mason City: Klipto, 1977.

Preston, Howard H. *History of Banking in Iowa.* Iowa City: Iowa State Historical Society, 1922.

Prior, Jean Cutler. *A Regional Guide to Iowa Landforms.* Iowa City: Iowa Survey Educational Series, State of Iowa, 1976.

Purcell, William Gray. "Walter Burley Griffin, Progressive." *Western Architect* 9 (September 1912): 93–94.

Raabe, Sylvia I. *Court Avenue Historic Area Study (Des Moines).* Des Moines: Des Moines Development Corp., 1983.

———. "They Crown the Hill." *Iowan* 30:1 (Fall 1980): 4–13.

Randall, G. P. *A Handbook of Designs. . . . .* Chicago: Church, Goodman and Donnelley, 1868.

Riley, Robert B. "Grain Elevators: Symbols of Time, Place and Honest Building." *Journal of the American Institute of Architects* 66:12 (November 1977): 50–55.

Rinehart, Frank A.. *Trans-Mississippi and International Exposition.* Omaha, Neb.: Trans Mississippi and International Exposition, 1898.

Roalson, Louise. "Cornell College." *Iowan* 33:1 (Fall 1984): 4–12.

Roberts, Charles W. "Poetry in Stone." *Iowan* 25:1 (Fall 1976): 1–22).

———. "The Saga of Salisbury House." *Iowan* 25:3 (March 1977): 4–26, 48–52.

———. "Cedar Rock: Frank Lloyd Wright Home in Quasqueton." *Iowan* 32:1 (Fall 1983: 48–51).

———. "Liberty Hall, Showcase for Church's Heritage." *Iowan* 32:4 (Summer 1984): 38–43, 52.

Robinson, Sidney. "Three Prairie Houses." *Iowa Architect* 35:6 (November/December 1986): 20–24.

Rosendahl, Rose. *Lake City: A Blueprint of Its History.* Lake City: Lake City Preservation Commission, 1987.

Ross, Earle D. "The Evolution of the Agricultural Fair in the Northwest." *Iowa Journal of History and Politics* 24 (July 1926): 445–80.

———. *Iowa Agriculture: An Historical Survey.* Iowa City: Iowa State Historical Society, 1951.

Rouse, Clara B. *Iowa Leaves.* Chicago: Illinois Printing & Binding Co., 1891.

"Rural Architecture." *American Agriculturalist.* (March, 1843): 367–68.

Sage, LeLand L. *A History of Iowa.* Ames: Iowa State University Press, 1974.

Sayre, Robert F. *Take This Exit: Rediscovering the Iowa Landscape.* Ames: Iowa State University Press, 1989.

Schaffer, James. "Historic Montauk." *Iowan* 16:2 (December 1967): 10–19.

———. "Mississippi Mansion." *Iowan* 22:1 (September 1973): 27–33.

Schmidt, John F. *A Historical Profile of Sioux City, Iowa.* Sioux City: Sioux City Stationery Co., 1969.

Schmitt, Ronald E. *Clinton, Iowa An Architectural Heritage.* Clinton: Clinton Department Community Development, 1980.

Schroder, Alan M. *Directory of 19th Century Iowa Architects.* Iowa City: Iowa State Historical Society, 1982.

Schultz, John E. "Return to Covered Beauty." *Iowan* 27:1 (September 1978): 30–35.

Schuyler, Montgomery. "The People's Savings Bank of Cedar Rapids, Iowa." *Architectural Record* 31 (January 1912): 44–56.

Schwieder, Dorothy. "Historic Sites in Council Bluffs." *Annals of Iowa* 41:1 (Winter 1973): 1148–52.

———. *Patterns and Perspectives in Iowa History.* Ames: Iowa State University Press, 1973.

Shafer, Mark. *Fairfield at the Turn of the Century.* Fairfield: privately printed, 1976.

Shambaugh, Benjamin F., ed. *Documentary Material Relating to the History of Iowa,* 3 vols. Iowa City: Iowa State Historical Society, 1897–1901.

Shank, Wesley I. "Hugh Garden in Iowa." *Prairie School Review* 5:3 (1968): 43–47.

———. "The Residence in Des Moines." *Journal of the Society of Architectural Historians* 29:1 (March 1970): 56–59.

———. *Historic American Building Survey: The Iowa Catalogue.* Iowa City: University of Iowa Press, 1979.

———. *Studies of Historic Iowa Architecture.* 10 vols. Ames: Engineering Research Institute, Iowa State University, 1972.

———. *Studies of Historic Iowa Architecture.* Pt. 2, 12 vols. Ames: Engineering Research Institute, Iowa State University, 1975.

Short, C. W., and R. Stanley-Brown. *Public Buildings: A Survey of Architecture.* Washington, D.C.: Government Printing Office, 1939.

Sissel, Dewey Kent. *The Octagonal Form in Nineteenth Century Domestic Architecture in Iowa.* M.A. thesis, University of Iowa, 1968.

Sloat, Fred. *Fort Madison: A Pictorial History.* Saint Louis: G. Bradley, 1987.

Smith, Frederick C. "The Gate City of Iowa." *Palimpsest* 32 (October 1951): 380–408.

Smith, John Calvin. *The Western Tourist, or Immigrant's Guide Through the States of Ohio, Michigan, Indiana, Illinois and Missouri, and the Territories of Wisconsin and Iowa.* New York: J. H. Colton, 1884, 1853, 1857.

Soike, Lowell J. *Without Right Angles: The Round Barns of Iowa.* Des Moines: Iowa State Historical Dept., 1983.

Sommer, Lawrence J. *The Heritage of Dubuque: An Architectural View.* Dubuque: Tel Graphics, 1975.

Stanek, Edward J., and Jacqueline W. Stanek. *Iowa's Magnificent County Courthouses.* Des Moines: Wallace-Homestead, 1975.

Stegmaier, Mark. "Davenport Homes: Eight from an Elegant Age." *Iowan* 34:1 (Fall 1985): 27–33.

Stevens, Jolene. "Fantasy World in Ida Grove." *Iowan* 21:4 (Spring 1973): 42–45.

Stevenson, Katherine Cole, and H. Ward Jandl. *Houses By Mail: A Guide to Houses from Sears, Roebuck & Co.* Washington, D.C.: Preservation Press, 1986.

Stimmel, Stephen John. "Potential Utilization of Underused Portions of Central Business District in Boone, Iowa." M.A. thesis, University of Iowa, 1975.

Sutcliffe, Judy. "Sutcliffe, A Historic Holiday House." *Iowan* 25:2 (December 1976): 42–43.

Svendsen, Marlys A. *Davenport: A Pictorial History, 1836–1986.* Davenport: G. Bradley, 1987.

Svendsen, Marlys A., John Pfiffner, and Martha Bowers. *Davenport, Where the Mississippi Runs West: A Survey of Davenport History and Architecture.* Davenport: City of Davenport, 1982.

Swain, Ginalie, ed. "Iowa's Incredible Exposition Palaces." *Goldfinch* 6:1 (October, 1984): 2–14.

Swanson, Leslie C. *Covered Bridges of Illinois, Iowa and Wisconsin.* Moline, Ill.: Swanson, 1970.

Swisher, Jacob A. "Iowa State Parks." *Palimpsest* 12 (June 1931): 201–53.

———. "Some Historical Sites in Iowa." *Iowa Journal of History and Politics* 32:2 (July 1934): 195–259.

Taylor, John W. *The West: Description of Iowa.* Dubuque: Daily Times and Job Printing, 1860.

Thomas, Cyrus. "Report on Mound Exploration." *Annual Report* of the Bureau of American Ethnology, No. 12 for 1890–1991. Washington, D.C.: U. S. Government Printing Office, 1894.

Thomas, Richard H. "From Porch to Patio." *Palimpsest* 56:4 (July/August 1975): 120–27.

———. "The Changing Architectural Landscape of the Lincoln Highway as Seen in Select Iowa Communities." *The Bracket* (Summer 1983): 6–8.

Thompson, William H. *Transportation in Iowa: A Historical Survey.* Des Moines: Iowa Department of Transportation, 1989.

Tjernagel, Nehemias. "Pioneer Iowa Homes," *Annals of Iowa* 31:2 (October 1951): 146–51.

Turk, Carl. "A Home in An Orchard," *Iowan* 1:1 (October–November, 1952): 28–35.

Turner, Paul Venable. *Campus: An American Planning Tradition.* Cambridge: MIT Press, 1984.

Van Zanten, David. *Walter Burley Griffin; Selected Designs.* Palos Park, Ill.: Prairie School Press, 1970.

Vest, Richard. "Vanishing Show Places in Iowa." *The Bracket* (Spring 1985): 7–11.

———. "The Last Picture Show." *Iowan* 34:2 (Winter 1985): 15–21.

Vexler, Robert I. *Chronology and Documentary Handbook for the State of Iowa.* Dobbs Ferry: Oceana, 1978.

Viggers, Ruth, "Blair House—Washington's Terrace Hill." *Annals of Iowa* 42:3 (Winter 1974): 237–39.

Vogel, Virgil J. *Iowa Place Names of Indian Origin.* Iowa City: University of Iowa Press, 1983.

Wagner, William. "Sketches of Iowa Landmarks." *Iowan* 7:4 (May 1959): 43–50.

———. "William Foster—An Early Iowa Architect." *Annals of Iowa* 36:5 (Summer 1962): 345–53.

———. "Preserving the Grandeur of Victorian Architecture." *Iowan* 12:4 (July 1964): 36–37.

———. "The Estes Home: Reflection of the Past." *Iowan* 12:4 (July 1964): 38–43.

———. *Sixty Sketches of Iowa's Past and Present.* West Des Moines: Brown and Wagner, 1967.

Wall, Joseph Frazier. *A Bicentennial History.* New York: Norton, 1978.

Walsh, Robert Andrew. "Louis Sullivan in Iowa." M.A. thesis, University of Iowa, 1969.

Watson, Clair Benjamin. "The Architecture and Minor Arts of the Amana Society." MFA thesis, University of Colorado, 1946.

———. "The Amana Style in Architecture." *Iowan* 7:5 (June/July 1959): 19–22.

Weingarden, Lauren S. *Louis H. Sullivan: The Banks.* Cambridge: MIT Press, 1987.

Weitz, Rudolph W. "Pioneer Building Industry in Polk County." Des Moines, 1969.

Welsch, Roger. "Sod Construction on the Plains." *Pioneer America* 1 (1969): 13–17.

———. *Sod Walls.* (Broken Bow, Neb.: Purcells, 1968.

Werle, Robert William. "A Historical Review and Analysis of the Iowa State University Landscape, from 1858–1966." M. A. thesis, Iowa State University, 1966.

———. "Shelter on the Plains." *Natural History* 26 (May 1977): 48–51.

Whye, Mike. "A Connecticut Classic Comes to Iowa." *Iowan* 35:3 (Spring 1987): 18–22.

Widmen, Melba Rae. "Nineteenth Century Home Architecture of Mount Pleasant, Iowa." University of Iowa, 1969.

Wilkie, William E. *Dubuque on the Mississippi 1758–1988.* Dubuque: Union-Hoermann Press, 1988.

Willard, John. "The Village People," *Iowan* 30:2 (Winter 1981): 4–16, 54.

———. "River Center." *Iowan* 33:3 (Spring 1985): 11–13.

Wilson, D. Ray. *Iowa: Historical Tour Guide.* Carpenterville, Ill.: Crossroad Communications, 1986.

Wilson, Richard Guy, and Sidney K. Robinson. *The Prairie School in Iowa.* Ames: Iowa State University Press, 1977.

Witt, Bill. "Pride of Parkersburg." *Iowan* 24:4 (June 1976): 38–41.

———. "Terrace Hill—Proud Treasure for the People." *Iowan* 28:2 (December 1979): 4–23.

Witt, Sandra L. "Vintage Elkader." *Iowan* 26:3 (March 1978): 27–35.

Wood, Grant. *Revolt Against the City.* Iowa City: Clio Press, 1935.

"Woodbury County Courthouse, Sioux City, Iowa." *Western Architect* 30:2 (February 1927).

Woodman, Betsey. "John Francis Rague: Mid Nineteenth Century Revivalist Architect (1799–1877)." M.A. thesis, University of Iowa, 1969.

Works Project Administration (Federal Writers Program). *Iowa: A Guide to the Hawkeye State.* New York: Viking 1941.

"The World's Most Modern Home." *American Magazine* 123 (May 1937): 50–51, 124–28.

Wright, Luella M. "Views and Reviews of Iowa." *Palimpsest* 27:2 (August 1946): 240–53.

Yates, Carole Shelley, and Charles W. Roberts. "Heritage in Stone." *Iowan* 31:2 (Winter 1982): 24–35.

Yenser, J. Kelly. "They've Ground to a Halt." *Iowan* 31:3 (Spring 1983): 24–30.

Zalaznik, David. "New Melleray Abbey." *Iowan* 34:4 (Summer 1986): 26–31.

Zook, Nancy Gibbons. "Mills That Turned with a Right Good Will." *Iowan* 4:4 (April/May 1956): 48–49.

Glossary

AIA See AMERICAN INSTITUTE OF ARCHITECTS.

abacus The top member of a column capital. In the Doria order, it is a flat block, square in plan, between the echinus of the capital and the architrave of the entablature above.

Academic Gothic see COLLEGIATE GOTHIC.

acroterium, acroterion (plural: acroteria) **1** A pedestal for a statue or similar decorative feature at the apex or at the lower corners of a pediment. **2** Any ornamental feature at these locations.

Adamesque A mode of architectural design, with emphasis on interiors, reminiscent of the work of the Scottish architects Robert Adam (1728–1792) and his brother James (1732–1794). It is characterized by attenuated proportions, bright color, and elegant linear detailing. Adamesque interiors, as one aspect of the broader Neoclassical movement, became popular in the late eighteenth century in Britain, Russia, and elsewhere in northern Europe. Simplified versions of these interiors began to be seen in the United States around the year 1800 in the work of Charles Bulfinch (1763–1844) and Samuel McIntire (1757–1811). Adamesque interiors, often emulating original Adam designs, were again popular in the 1920s. See also the related term FEDERAL.

aedicule, aedicular An exterior niche, door, or window, framed by columns or pilasters and topped by an entablature and pediment. Meaning has been extended to a smaller-scale representation of a temple front on an interior wall. Distinguished from a tabernacle (definition **1**), which usually occurs on an interior wall. See also the related term NICHE.

Aesthetic movement A late nineteenth-century movement in interior design and the decorative arts, emphasizing the application of artistic principles in the production of objects and the creation of interior ensembles. Aesthetic movement works are characterized by a broad eclecticism of materials and styles (especially the exotic) and by a preference for "conventionalized" (i.e., stylized) ornament, rather than naturalistic. The movement flourished in Britain from the 1850s through the 1870s and in the United States from the 1870s through the 1880s. Designers associated with the movement include William Morris (1834–1896) in England and Herter Brothers (1865–1905) in America. The Aesthetic movement evolved into and overlapped with the Art Nouveau and the Arts and Crafts movement. See also the related term QUEEN ANNE (definition **4**).

ambulatory A passageway around the apse of a church, allowing for circulation behind the sanctuary.

American Adam style See FEDERAL.

American bond See COMMON BOND.

American Foursquare See FOURSQUARE HOUSE.

American Institute of Architects The national professional organization of architects, established in New York in 1857. The first national convention was held in New York in 1867, and at that meeting, provision was made for the creation of local chapters. In 1889, the American Institute of Architects absorbed the independent Chicago-based Western Association of Architects (established 1884). The headquarters of the national organization moved from New York to Washington in 1898. Abbreviated as AIA.

American Renaissance Ambiguous term. See instead BEAUX-ARTS CLASSICISM, COLONIAL REVIVAL, FEDERAL REVIVAL.

Anglo-Palladianism, Anglo-Palladian An architectural movement in England motivated by a reaction against the English Baroque and by a rediscovery of the work of the English Renaissance architect Inigo Jones (1573–1652) and the Italian Renaissance architect Andrea Palladio (1508–1580). Anglo-Palladianism flourished in England (c. 1710s–1760s) and in the British North American colonies (c. 1740s–1790s). Key figures in the Anglo-Palladian movement were Colen Campbell (1676–1729) and Richard Boyle, Lord Burlington (1694–1753). Sometimes called Burlingtonian, Palladian Revival. See also the more general term PALLADIANISM and the related terms GEORGIAN PERIOD, JEFFERSONIAN.

antefix In classical architecture, a small upright decoration at the eaves of a roof, originally devised to hide the ends of the roof tiles. A similar ornament along the ridge of the roof.

anthemion (plural: anthemions) A Greek ornamental motif based upon the honeysuckle or palmette. It may appear as a single element on an antefix or as a running ornament on a frieze or other banded feature.

antiquity The broad epoch of Western history preceding the Middle Ages and including such ancient civilizations as Egyptian, Greek, and Roman.

apse, apsidal A semicircular or polygonal feature projecting as a major element from an important interior space, especially at the chancel end of a church. Distinguished from an exedra, which is a semicircular or polygonal space, usually containing a bench, in the wall of a garden or nonreligious building. A substantial apse in a church, containing an ambulatory and radiating chapels, is called a chevet. The terms apse and chevet are used to describe the *form* of the end of the church containing the altar, while the terms chancel, choir, and sanctuary are used to describe the liturgical *function* of this end of the church and the spaces within it. Less substantial projections in nonreligious buildings are called bays if polygonal or bow fronts if curved.

arbor 1 An openwork structure covered with climbing plants. Distinguished from a trellis, which is generally a simpler, more two-dimensional structure, often attached to a wall. Distinguished from a pergola, which is an openwork structure supported by a colonnade, creating a shaded walk. **2** A grouping of closely planted trees or shrubs, trained together and self-supporting.

arcade 1 A series of arches, carried on columns or piers or other supports. **2** A covered walkway, one side of which is part of a building, while the other is open, as a series of arches, to the exterior. **3** In the nineteenth and early twentieth centuries, an interior street or other extensive space lined with shops and stores.

arch A curved construction that spans an opening. (Some arches may be flat or triangular, and many have a complex or compound curvature.) A masonry arch consists of a series of wedge-shaped parts (voussoirs) that press together toward the center while being restrained from spreading outward by the surrounding wall or the adjacent arch.

architrave 1 The lowest member of a classical entablature. **2** The moldings on the face of a wall around a doorway or other opening. Sometimes called the casing. Distinguished from the jambs, which are the vertical linings perpendicular to the wall planes at the sides of an opening. Distinguished from surround, a term usually applied to the entire door or window frame considered as a unit.

archivolt The group of moldings following the shape of an arched opening.

arcuation, arcuated Construction using arches.

Art Deco A decorative style stimulated by the 1925 Exposition Internationale des Arts Décoratifs et Industriels Modernes, held in Paris. As the first phase of the Moderne, Art Deco is characterized by sharp angular and curvilinear forms, by a richness of materials (including polished metal, stone, and exotic woods), and by an overall sleekness of design. The style was often used in the commercial and residential architecture of the 1930s (e.g., skyscrapers, hotels, apartment buildings). Sometimes called Art Deco Moderne, Deco, Jazz Moderne, Zigzag Moderne, Zigzag Modernistic. See also the more general term MODERNE and the related terms MAYAN REVIVAL, PWA MODERNE, STREAMLINE MODERNE.

Art Moderne See MODERNE.

Art Nouveau A style in architecture, interior design, and the decorative arts that flourished principally in France and Belgium in the 1890s. The Art Nouveau is characterized by undulating and whiplash lines and by sensuous organic forms. The Art Nouveau in Britain and the United States evolved from and overlapped with the Aesthetic movement.

Arts and Crafts A late nineteenth- and early twentieth-century movement in interior design and the decorative arts, emphasizing the importance of hand crafting for everyday objects. Arts and Crafts works are characterized by rectilinear geometries and high contrasts between figure and ground, and the furniture often features expressed construction. The term originated with the Arts and Crafts Exhibition Society, founded in England in 1888. Designers associated with the movement include C. F. A. Voysey (1857–1941) in England and the brothers Charles S. Greene (1868–1957) and Henry M. Greene (1870–1954) in America. The Arts and Crafts movement evolved from and overlapped with the Aesthetic movement. For a more specific term, used in the United States after 1900, see also CRAFTSMAN.

ashlar Squared blocks of stone that fit tightly against one another.

atelier 1 A studio where the fine arts, including architecture, are taught. Applied particularly to the offices of prominent architects in Paris who provided design training to students enrolled in or informally attached to the Ecole des Beaux-Arts. By extension, any working office where some organized teaching is done. **2** A place where artworks or handicrafts are produced by skilled workers. **3** An artist's studio or workshop.

attic 1. The area beneath the roof and above the main stories (or story) of a building. Sometimes called a garret. **2** A low story above the entablature, often a blocklike mass that caps the building.

axis An imaginary center line to which are referred the parts of a building or the relations of a number of buildings to one another.

axonometric drawing A pictorial drawing using axonometric projection, in which horizontal lines that are perpendicular in an object, building, or space are drawn as perpendicular (usually at two 45-degree angles from the vertical, or at complementary angles of 30 and 60 degrees). Consequently, all angular and dimensional relationships in plan remain the same in the drawing as in the thing depicted. Sometimes called an axon or an axonometric. See also the related terms ISOMETRIC DRAWING, PERSPECTIVE DRAWING.

balloon frame construction A system of light frame construction in which single studs extend the full height of the frame (commonly two stories), from the foundation to the roof. Floor joists are fastened to the sides of the studs. Structural members are usually sawn lumber, ranging from two-by-fours to two-by-tens, and are fastened with nails. Sometimes called balloon framing. The technique, developed in Chicago and other boomtowns of the 1830s, has been largely replaced in the twentieth century by platform frame construction.

baluster One of a series of short vertical members, often vase-shaped in profile, used to support a handrail for a stair or a railing. Balusters that are thinner and simpler in profile are sometimes called banisters.

balustrade A series of balusters or posts supporting

a rail or coping across the top (and sometimes resting on a lower rail). Balustrades are often found on stairs, balconies, parapets, and terraces.

band course Ambiguous term. See instead BAND MOLDING or STRINGCOURSE.

band molding In masonry or frame construction, any horizontal flat member or molding or group of moldings projecting slightly from a wall and marking a division in the wall. Not properly a synonym for band course. Simpler horizontal bands in masonry are generally called stringcourses.

bandstand A small pavilion, usually polygonal or circular in plan, designed to shelter bands during public concerts in a garden, park, green, or square. See also the related terms GAZEBO, KIOSK.

banister 1 Corrupted spelling of baluster, in use since about the seventeenth century. Now occasionally used for balusters that are thinner and simpler in profile than classical vase-shaped balusters. 2 Improperly used to mean the handrail of a stair.

bargeboard An ornate fascia board that is attached to the sloping edges (verges) of a roof, covering the ends of the horizontal roof timbers (purlins). Bargeboards are usually ornamented with carved, turned, or jigsawn forms. Sometimes called gableboards, vergeboards. Less ornate boards along the verges of a roof are simply called fascia boards.

Baroque A style of art and architecture that flourished in Europe and colonial North America during the seventeenth and eighteenth centuries. Although based on the architecture of the Renaissance, Baroque architecture was more dynamic, with circles frequently giving way to ovals, flat walls to curved or undulating ones, and separate elements to interlocking forms. It was a monumental and richly three-dimensional style with elaborate systems of ornamental and figural sculpture. See also the related terms RENAISSANCE, ROCOCO.

Baroque Revival See NEO-BAROQUE.

barrel vault A vaulted roof or ceiling of semicircular or semielliptical cross section, forming a tunnellike enclosure over an apartment, corridor, or similar space.

Barryesque Term applied to Italianate buildings showing the influence of the English architect Sir Charles Barry (1795–1860), who introduced a derivative form of the Italian High Renaissance palazzo in his Travelers Club in London, 1829–1832. The style was brought to the United States by the Scottish-trained architect John Notman (1810–1865) and was popular from the late 1840s through the 1860s, especially for institutional and government buildings. Distinguished from the Italian Villa style, which has the northern Italian rural vernacular villa as its prototype. See also the more general term ITALIANATE.

basement 1 The lowest story of a building, either partly or entirely below grade. 2 The lower part of the walls of any building, usually articulated distinctly from the upper part of the walls.

batten 1 A narrow strip of wood applied to cover a joint along the edges of two parallel boards in the same plane. 2 A strip of wood fastened across two or more parallel boards to hold them together. Sometimes called a cross batten. See also the related term BOARD-AND-BATTEN SIDING.

battered (adjective). Inclined from the vertical. A wall is said to be battered or to have a batter when it recedes as it rises.

battlement, battlemented See CRENELLATION.

Bauhaus 1 Work in any of the visual arts by the faculty and students of the Bauhaus, the innovative design school founded by Walter Gropius (1883–1969) and an active force in German modernism from 1919 until 1933; 2 Work in any of the visual arts by the former faculty and students of the Bauhaus, or by individuals influenced by them. See also the related terms INTERNATIONAL STYLE, MIESIAN.

bay 1 The interval between two recurring members. A facade is frequently measured by window bays, a skeletal frame by structural bays. 2 A polygonal or curved unit of one or more stories, projecting from the wall and usually containing grouped windows (bay windows) on each story. See also the more specific term BOWFRONT.

bay window The horizontally grouped windows in a projecting bay (definition 2), or the projecting bay itself, if it is not more than one story. Distinguished from an oriel, which does not rise from the foundation and has a suspended rather than a rooted appearance. A semicircular or semielliptical bay window is called a bow window. A bay window with a central section of plate glass in a late nineteenth-century commercial building is called a Chicago window.

beam A structural spanning member of stone, wood, iron, steel, or reinforced concrete. See also the more specific terms GIRDER, I-BEAM, JOIST.

bearing wall A wall that is fully structural, carrying the load of the floors and roof all the way to the foundation. Sometimes called a supporting wall. Distinguished from curtain wall. See also the related term LOAD-BEARING.

Beaux-Arts Historicist design on a monumental scale, as taught at the Ecole des Beaux-Arts in Paris throughout the nineteenth century and early twentieth century. The term Beaux-Arts is generally applied to an eclectic Roman-Renaissance-Baroque architecture of the 1850s through the 1920s, disseminated internationally by students and followers of the Ecole des Beaux-Arts. As a general style term Beaux-Arts connotes an academically grounded discipline for historical eclecticism, rather than one single style, as well as the disciplined development of a *parti* into a fully visualized design. More specific style terms include Neo-Grec (1840s–1870s) and Beaux-Arts Classicism (1870s–1930s). See also the related terms NEOCLASSICISM, for describing Ecole-related work from the 1790s to the 1840s, and SECOND EMPIRE, for describing the work from the 1850s to the 1880s.

Beaux-Arts Classicism, Beaux-Arts Classical Term applied to eclectic Roman-Renaissance-Baroque architecture and urbanism after the Neo-Grec and Second Empire phases, i.e., from the 1870s through the 1930s. Sometimes called Classic Revival, Classical Revival, McKim Classicism, Neoclassical Revival. See also the more general term BEAUX-ARTS and the related terms CITY BEAUTIFUL MOVEMENT, PWA MODERNE.

belfry A cupola, turret, or room in a tower where a bell is housed.

bellcote A small gabled structure astride the ridge of a roof, which shelters a bell. It is usually close to the front wall plane of the building.

belt course See STRINGCOURSE.

belvedere 1 Any building, especially a pavilion or shelter, that is located to take advantage of a view. See also the related term GAZEBO. **2** See CUPOLA (definition **2**).

blind (adjective) Term applied to the surface use of elements that would otherwise articulate an opening but where no opening exists. Used in such combinations as blind arcade, blind arch, blind door, blind window.

board-and-batten siding A type of siding for wood frame buildings, consisting of wide vertical boards with narrow strips of wood (battens) covering the joints. (In rare instances, the battens may be fastened behind the joints. If the gaps between boards are wide and the back battens approach the width of the outer boards, the siding is called board-on-board.) See also the related term BATTEN.

board-on-board siding A type of siding for wood frame buildings, consisting of two layers of vertical boards, with the outer layer of boards covering the wide gaps between the boards of the inner layer.

bowfront A semicircular or semielliptical bay (definition **2**).

bow window A semicircular or semielliptical bay window.

brace A single wooden or metal member placed diagonally within a framework or truss or beneath an overhang. Distinguished from a bracket, which is a more substantial triangular feature, and from a strut, which is essentially a post set in a diagonal position.

braced frame construction A combination of heavy and light timber frame construction, in which the principal vertical and horizontal framing members (posts and girts) are fastened by mortise and tenon joints, while the one-story-high studs are nailed to the heavy timber frame. The overall frame is made more rigid by diagonal braces. Sometimes called braced framing.

bracket Any solid, pierced, or built-up triangular feature projecting from the face of a wall to support a projecting element, like the top member of a cornice or the verges or eaves of a roof. Brackets are frequently used for ornamental as well as structural purposes. Distinguished from a brace, which is a simple barlike structural member. Dis-

tinguished from the more specific term console, which has a height greater than its projection from the wall. See also the related term CORBEL.

Bracketed style A nineteenth-century term for Italianate..

brick bonds, brickwork See the more specific terms COMMON BOND, ENGLISH BOND, FLEMISH BOND, RUNNING BOND.

British colonial A term applied to buildings, towns, landscapes, and other artifacts from the period of actual British colonial occupation of large parts of eastern North America (c. 1607–1781 for the United States; c. 1750s–1867 for much of Canada). The British colonial period saw the introduction into the New World of various regional strains of English and Scotch-Irish folk culture, as well as high-style Anglo-European Renaissance, Baroque, and Neoclassical design. Sometimes called English colonial. Loosely called colonial or Early American. See also the related term GEORGIAN PERIOD.

Brutalism An architectural style of the 1950s through 1970s, characterized by complex massing and by a frank expression of structural members, elements of building systems, and materials (especially concrete). Some of the work of Paul Rudolph (born 1918) is associated with this style. Sometimes called New Brutalism.

bungalow A low one- or one-and-a-half-story house of modest pretensions with a low-pitched gable or hipped roof, a conspicuous porch, and projecting eaves. This house type was a popular builders' type from around 1900 to 1930. The term bungalow was also loosely applied to any vernacular building of a semirustic nature, including vacation cottages and lodges.

Burlingtonian See ANGLO-PALLADIANISM.

buttress An exterior mass of masonry bonded into a wall that it strengthens or supports. Buttresses often absorb lateral thrusts from roofs or vaults.

Byzantine Term applied to the art and architecture of the Eastern Roman Empire centered at Byzantium (i.e., Constantinople, Istanbul) from the early 500s to the mid-1400s. Byzantine architecture is characterized by massive domes, round arches, richly carved capitals, and the extensive use of mosaic.

Byzantine Revival See NEO-BYZANTINE.

campanile In Italian, a bell tower. While usually freestanding in medieval and Renaissance architecture, it was often incorporated as a prominent unit in the massing of picturesque nineteenth-century buildings.

cantilever A beam, girder, slab, truss, or other structural member that projects beyond its supporting wall or column.

cap A canopy, ledge, molding, or pediment over a window. Sometimes called a window cap. Distinguished from a hood, which is a similar feature over a door. See also the related term HEAD MOLDING.

capital The moldings and carved enrichment at the top of a column, pilaster, pier, or pedestal.

Carpenter's Gothic Term applied to a version of the Gothic Revival (c. 1840s–1870s), in which Gothic motifs are adapted to the kind of wooden details that can be produced by lathes, jigsaws, and molding machines. Sometimes called Gingerbread style, Steamboat Gothic. See also the more general term GOTHIC REVIVAL.

carriage porch See PORTE-COCHÈRE.

casement window A window that opens from the side on hinges, like a door, out from the plane of the wall. Distinguished from a double-hung window.

casing See ARCHITRAVE (definition 2).

cast iron Iron shaped by a molding process, generally strong in compression but brittle in tension. Distinguished from wrought iron, which has been forged to increase its tensile properties.

cast-iron front An architectural facade made of prefabricated molded iron parts, often markedly skeletal in appearance with extensive glass infilling. Prevalent from the late 1840s to the early 1870s.

castellated Having the elements of a medieval castle, such as crenellation and turrets.

cavetto cornice See COVED CORNICE.

cement A mixture of burnt lime and clay with water, which hardens permanently when dry. When a fine aggregate of sand is added, the cement may be used as a mortar for masonry construction or as a plaster or stucco coating. When a coarser aggregate of gravel or crushed stone is added, along with sand, the mixture is called concrete.

chamfer The oblique surface formed by cutting off a square edge at an equal angle to each face.

chancel 1 The end of a Roman Catholic or High Episcopal church containing the altar and set apart for the clergy and choir by a screen, rail, or steps. Usually the entire east end of a church beyond the crossing. In churches that have a long chancel space, the part of the chancel between the crossing and the apse, where the singers participate in the service, is called the choir. The innermost part of the chancel, containing the principal altar, is called the sanctuary. **2** In less extensive Catholic and Episcopal churches, the terms chancel and choir are often used interchangeably to mean the entire eastern arm of the church.

Châteauesque A term applied to masonry buildings from the 1870s through the 1920s in which stylistic references are derived from early French Renaissance châteaux, from the reign of Francis I (1515–1547) or even earlier. Sometimes called Château style, Châteauesque Revival, Francis I style, François Premier.

chevet In large churches, particularly those based upon French Gothic precedents, a substantial apse surrounded by an ambulatory and often containing radiating chapels.

Chicago school A diverse group of architects associated with the development of the tall (i.e., six-to twenty-story), usually metal frame commercial building in Chicago during the 1880s and 1890s. William Le Baron Jenney, Burnham and Root, and Adler and Sullivan are identified with this group. Sometimes called Chicago Commercial style, Commercial style. See also the related term PRAIRIE SCHOOL.

Chicago window A tripartite oblong window in which a large fixed center pane is placed between two narrow sash windows. Popularized in Chicago commercial buildings of the 1880s–1890s. See also BAY WINDOW.

chimney girt In timber frame construction, a major wooden beam that passes across the breast of the central chimney. It is supported at its ends by the longitudinal girts of the building and sometimes carries one end of the summer beam.

choir 1 The part of a Roman Catholic or High Episcopal church where the singers participate in the service. Usually the space within the chancel arm of the church, situated between the crossing to the west and the sanctuary to the east. **2** In less extensive Catholic and Episcopal churches, the terms choir and chancel are often used interchangeably to mean the entire eastern arm of the church.

Churrigueresque Term applied to Spanish and Spanish colonial Baroque architecture resembling the work of the Spanish architect José Benito de Churriguera (1665–1725) and his brothers. The style is characterized by a freely interpreted assemblage of such elements as twisted columns, broken pediments, and scroll brackets. See also the related term SPANISH COLONIAL.

cinquefoil A type of Gothic tracery having five parts (lobes or foils) separated by pointed elements (cusps).

City Beautiful movement A movement in architecture, landscape architecture, and planning in the United States from the 1890s through the 1920s, advocating the beautification of cities in the image of some of the most urbane places of the time: the world's fairs. City Beautiful schemes emphasized civic centers, boulevards, and waterfront improvements, and sometimes included comprehensive metropolitan plans for parks, parkways, and transportation facilities. See also the related term BEAUX-ARTS CLASSICISM.

clapboard A tapered board that is thinner along the top edge and thicker along the bottom edge, applied horizontally with edges overlapping to provide weathertight siding on a building of wood construction. Early clapboards were split (rived, riven) and were used for barrel staves and for wainscoting. The term now applies to any beveled siding board, whether split or sawn, rabbeted or not, regardless of length or width. (The term is sometimes applied only to a form of bevel siding used in New England, about four feet long and quarter-sawn.) Sometimes called weatherboards.

classical orders See ORDER.

classical rectangle See GOLDEN SECTION.

Classical Revival Ambiguous term, suggesting **1** Neoclassical design of the late eighteenth and early nineteenth centuries, including the Greek Revival; or **2** Beaux-Arts Classical design of the late nineteenth and early twentieth centuries. Sometimes called Classic Revival. See instead BEAUX ARTS CLASSICISM, GREEK REVIVAL, NEOCLASSICISM.

classicism, classical, classicizing Terms describing the application of principles or elements derived from the visual arts of the Greco-Roman era (seventh century B.C.E. through fourth century C.E.) at any subsequent period of Western civilization, but particularly since the Renaissance. More a descriptive term for an approach to design and for a general cultural sensibility than for any particular style. See also the related term NEOCLASSICISM.

clerestory A part of a building that rises above the roof of another part and has windows in its walls.

clipped gable roof See JERKINHEAD ROOF.

coffer A recessed panel, usually square or octagonal, in a ceiling. Such panels are also found on the inner surfaces of domes and vaults.

collar beam A horizontal tension member in a pitched roof connecting opposite rafters, generally halfway up or higher. Its function is to tie the angular members together and prevent them from spreading.

Collegiate Gothic **1** Originally, a secular version of English Gothic architecture, characteristic of the older colleges of Oxford and Cambridge. **2** A secular version of Late Gothic Revival architecture, which became a popular style for North American colleges and universities from the 1890s through the 1920s. Sometimes called Academic Gothic.

colonial **1** Not strictly a style term, but a term for the entire period during which a particular European country held political dominion over a part of the Western Hemisphere, Africa, Asia, Australia, or Oceania. See also the more specific terms BRITISH COLONIAL, DUTCH COLONIAL, FRENCH COLONIAL, SPANISH COLONIAL. **2** Loosely used to mean the British colonial period in North America (c. 1607–1781 for the United States; c. 1750s-1867 for much of Canada).

Colonial Revival Generally understood to mean the revival of forms from British colonial design. The Colonial Revival began in New England in the 1860s and continues nationwide into the present. Sometimes called Neo-Colonial. See also the more specific term GEORGIAN REVIVAL and the related terms FEDERAL REVIVAL, SHINGLE STYLE.

colonnade A series of freestanding or engaged columns supporting an entablature or simple beam.

colonnette A diminutive, often attenuated, column.

colossal order See GIANT ORDER.

column **1** A vertical supporting element, usually cylindrical and slightly tapering, consisting of a base (except in the Greek Doric order), shaft, and capital. See also the related terms ENTABLATURE, ENTASIS, ORDER. **2** Any vertical supporting element in a skeletal frame.

Commercial style See CHICAGO SCHOOL.

common bond A pattern of brickwork in which every fifth or sixth course consists of all headers, the other courses being all stretchers. Sometimes called American bond. Distinguished from running bond, in which no headers appear.

Composite order An ensemble of classical column and entablature elements, particularly characterized by large Ionic volutes and Corinthian acanthus leaves in the capital of the column. See also the more general term ORDER.

concrete An artificial stone made by mixing cement, water, sand, and a coarse aggregate (such as gravel or crushed stone) in specified proportions. The mix is shaped in molds called forms. Distinguished from cement, which is the binder without the aggregate.

console A type of bracket with a scroll-shaped or S-curve profile and a height greater than its projection from the wall. Distinguished from the more general term bracket, which is usually applied to supports whose projection and height are nearly equal. Distinguished from a modillion, which usually is smaller, has a projection greater than its height (or thickness), and appears in a series, as in a classical cornice.

coping The cap or top course of a wall, parapet, balustrade, or chimney, usually designed to shed water.

corbel A projecting stone that supports a superincumbent weight. In medieval architecture and its derivatives, a support for such major features as vaulting shafts, vaulting ribs, or oriels. See also the related term BRACKET.

corbeled construction Masonry that is built outward beyond the vertical by letting successive courses project beyond those below. Sometimes called corbeling.

corbeled cornice A cornice made up of courses of projecting masonry, each of which extends farther outward than the one below.

Corinthian order A ensemble of classical column and entablature elements, particularly characterized by acanthus leaves and small volutes in the capital of the column. See also the more general term ORDER.

cornice The crowning member of a wall or entablature.

Corporate International style A term, not widely used, for curtain wall commercial, institutional, and governmental buildings since the Second World War, which represent a widespread adoption of selected International style ideas from the 1920s. See also the more general term INTERNATIONAL STYLE.

Corporate style An architectural style developed in the early industrial communities of New England during the first half of the nineteenth century. This austere but graceful mode of construction was derived from the red-brick Federal architecture of the early nineteenth century and is characterized by the same elegant proportions, cleanly cut openings, and simple refined detailing. The term was coined by William Pierson in the 1970s. Not to be confused with Corporate International style.

cottage 1 A relatively modest rural or suburban dwelling. Distinguished from a villa, which is a more substantial and often more elaborate dwelling. **2** A seasonal dwelling, regardless of size, especially one located in a resort community.

cottage orné A rustic building in the romantic, picturesque tradition, noted for such features as bay windows, oriels, ornamented gables, and clustered chimneys.

course A layer of building blocks, such as bricks or stones, extending the full length and thickness of a wall.

coved ceiling A ceiling in which the transition between wall and ceiling is formed by a large concave panel or molding. Sometimes called a cove ceiling.

coved cornice. A cornice with a concave profile. Sometimes called a cavetto cornice.

Craftsman. A style of furniture and interior design belonging to the Arts and Crafts movement in the United States, and specifically related to *The Craftsman* magazine (1901–1916), published by Gustav Stickley (1858–1942). Some entire houses known to be derived from this publication can be called Craftsman houses. See also the more general term ARTS AND CRAFTS.

crenellation, crenellated A form of embellishment on a parapet consisting of indentations (crenels or embrasures) alternating with solid blocks of wall (merlons). Virtually synonymous with battlement, battlemented; embattlement, embattled.

cresting. An ornamental strip or fencelike feature, usually of metal or tile, along the ridgeline or summit of a roof.

crocket. In Gothic architecture, a small ornament resembling bunched foliage, placed at intervals on the sloping edges of gables, pinnacles, or spires.

crossing In a church with a cruciform plan, the area where the arms of the cross intersect; specifically, the space where the transept crosses the nave and chancel.

cross rib See LIERNE.

cross section See SECTION.

crown The central, or highest, part of an arch or vault.

crown molding The highest in a series of moldings.

crowstep Any one of the progressions in a gable that ascends in steps rather than in a continuous slope.

cruciform In the shape of a cross. Usually used to describe the ground plans of buildings. See also the more specific terms GREEK CROSS, LATIN CROSS.

cupola 1 A small domed structure on top of a belfry, steeple, or tower. **2** A lantern, square or polygonal in plan, with windows or vents, which is located at the summit of a roof. Sometimes

called a belvedere. Distinguished from a skylight, which is a lesser feature located on the slope of a roof. **3** In historic English usage, synonymous with dome. A dome is now understood to be a more substantial feature.

curtain wall In skeleton frame or reinforced concrete construction, a thin nonstructural cladding of stone, brick, terracotta, glass, or metal veneer. Distinguished from bearing wall. See also the related term LOAD-BEARING.

cusp The pointed, roughly triangular intersection of the arcs of lobes or foils in the tracery of windows, screens, or panels.

dado A broad decorative band around the lower portion of an interior wall, between the baseboard and dado rail or cap molding. (The term is often applied to this entire zone, including baseboard and dado rail.) The dado may be painted, papered, or covered with some other material, so as to have a different treatment from the upper zone of the wall. Dado connotes any continuous lower zone in a room, equivalent to a pedestal. A wood-paneled dado is called a wainscot.

Deco See ART DECO.

dentil, denticulated A small ornamental block forming one of a series set in a row. A dentil molding is composed of such a series.

dependency A building, wing, or room, subordinate to, or serving as an adjunct to a main building. A dependency may be attached to or detached from a main building. Distinguished from an outbuilding, which is always detached.

diaper An overall repetitive pattern on a flat surface, especially a pattern of geometric or representational forms arranged in a diamond-shaped or checkerboard grid. Sometimes called diaper work.

discharging arch See RELIEVING ARCH.

dome A major hemispherical or curved roof feature rising from a circular, polygonal, or square base. Distinguished from a cupola, which is a smaller, usually subordinate, domical element.

Doric order An ensemble of classical column and entablature elements, particularly characterized by the use of triglyphs and metopes in the frieze of the entablature. See also the more general term ORDER.

dormer. A roof-sheltered window (or vent), usually with vertical sides and front, set into a sloping roof. Sometimes called a dormer window.

dosseret See IMPOST BLOCK.

double-hung window A window consisting of a pair of frames, or sashes, one above the other, arranged to slide up and down. Their movement is sometimes stabilized by a system of cords and counterbalancing weights contained in narrow boxing at each side of the window frame. Sometimes called guillotine sash.

double-pen In vernacular architecture, particularly houses, a term applied to a plan consisting of two rooms side by side or separated by a hallway.

double-pile In vernacular architecture, particularly houses, a term applied to a plan that is two rooms deep and any number of rooms wide.

drip molding See HEAD MOLDING.

drum 1 A cylindrical or polygonal wall zone upon which a dome rests. **2** One of the cylinders of stone that form the shaft of a column.

Dutch colonial A term applied to buildings, towns, landscapes, and other artifacts from the period of actual Dutch colonial occupation of the Hudson River valley and adjacent areas (c. 1614–1664). Meaning has been extended to apply to the artifacts of Dutch ethnic groups and their descendants, even into the early nineteenth century.

Dutch Colonial Revival The revival of forms from design in the Dutch tradition.

ear A slight projection just below the upper corners of a door or window architrave or casing. Sometimes called a shouldered architrave.

Early American See BRITISH COLONIAL.

Early Christian A style of art and architecture in the Mediterranean world that was developed by the early Christians before the fall of the Western Roman Empire, derived from late Roman art and architecture and leading to the Romanesque (early fourth to early sixth century).

Early Georgian period Not strictly a style term, but a term for a period in British and British colonial history approximately coinciding with the reigns of George I (1714–1727) and George II (1727–1760). See also the related term LATE GEORGIAN PERIOD.

Early Gothic Revival A term for the Gothic Revival work of the late eighteenth to the mid-nineteenth century. See also the related term LATE GOTHIC REVIVAL.

Eastlake A decorative arts and interior design term of the 1860s and 1880s sometimes applied to architecture. Named after Charles Locke Eastlake (1836–1906), an English advocate of the application of Gothic principles of construction and design, rather than mere Gothic elements. Characterized by simplicity and solidity of forms, which are sometimes embellished with chamfered, turned, or incised details. Sometimes called Eastlake Gothic, Modern Gothic. See also the related term QUEEN ANNE.

eaves The horizontal lower edges of a roof plane, usually projecting beyond the wall below. Distinguished from verges, which are the sloping edges of a roof plane.

echinus A heavy molding with a curved profile placed immediately below the abacus, or top member, of a classical capital. Particularly prominent in the Doric and Tuscan orders.

eclecticism, eclectic A sensibility in design, prevalent since the eighteenth century, involving the selection of elements from a variety of sources, including historical periods of high-style design (Western and non-Western), vernacular design (Western and non-Western), and (in the twentieth century) contemporary industrial design. Distinguished from historicism and revivalism by drawing upon a wider range of sources than the historical periods of high-style design.

Ecole, Ecole des Beaux-Arts See BEAUX-ARTS.

Egyptian Revival Term applied to eclectic works or elements of those works that emulate forms in the visual arts of ancient Egyptian civilization.

elevation A drawing (in orthographic projection) of an upright, planar aspect of an object or building. The vertical complement of a plan. Sometimes loosely used in the sense of a facade view or any frontal representation of a wall, whether photograph or drawing, whether measured to scale or not.

Elizabethan Manor style See NEO-TUDOR.

Elizabethan period A term for a period in English history coinciding with the reign of Elizabeth I (1558–1603). See also the more general term TUDOR PERIOD and the related term JACOBEAN PERIOD for the succeeding period.

embattlement, embattled See CRENELLATION.

encaustic tile A tile decorated by a polychrome glazed or ceramic inlay pattern.

engaged column A half-round column attached to a wall. Distinguished from a free-standing column by seeming to be built into the wall. Distinguished from a pilaster, which is a flattened column. Distinguished from a recessed column, which is a fully round column set into a nichelike space.

English bond A pattern of brickwork in which the bricks are set in alternating courses of stretchers and headers.

English colonial See BRITISH COLONIAL.

English Half-timber style See NEO-TUDOR.

entablature In a classical order, a richly detailed horizontal member resting on columns or pilasters. It is divided horizontally into three main parts. The lowest is the architrave (definition **1**), the structural part, and is generally an unornamented continuous beam or series of beams. The middle part is the frieze (definition **1**), which is generally the most freely ornamented part. The uppermost is the cornice. Composed of a sequence of moldings, the cornice overhangs the frieze and architrave and serves as a crown to the whole. Each part has the moldings and decorative treatment that are characteristic of the particular order, but modern adaptations often alter canonical details. See also the related terms COLUMN, ORDER.

entablature block A block bearing the canonical elements of a classical entablature on three or all four sides, placed between a column capital and a feature above, such as a balcony or ceiling. Distinguished from an impost block, which has the form of an inverted truncated pyramid and detailing typical of medieval architecture.

entasis The slight convex curving of the vertical profile of a tapered column.

exedra A semicircular or polygonal space usually containing a bench, in the wall of a garden or a building other than a church. Distinguished from a niche, which is usually a smaller feature higher in a wall, and from an apse, which is usually identified with churches.

exotic revivals A term occasionally used to suggest a distinction between revivals of European styles (e.g., Greek, Gothic Revivals) and non-European styles (e.g., Egyptian, Moorish Revivals). See also the more specific terms EGYPTIAN REVIVAL, MAYAN REVIVAL, MOORISH REVIVAL.

extrados The outer curve or outside surface of an arch. See also the related term INTRADOS.

eyebrow dormer A low dormer with a small segmental window or vent but no sides. The roofing warps or bows over the window or vent in a wavy line.

facade An exterior face of a building, especially the principal or entrance front. Distinguished from an elevation, which is an orthographic drawing of a building face.

false half-timbering A surface treatment that simulates half-timber construction, consisting of a lattice of broad boards and stucco applied as an exterior veneer on a building of masonry or wood frame construction. Most commonly seen in domestic architecture from the late nineteenth century onward.

fanlight A semicircular or semielliptical window over a door, with radiating mullions in the form of an open fan. Sometimes called a sunburst light. See also the more general term TRANSOM (definition 1) and the related term SIDELIGHT.

fan vault A type of Gothic vault in which the primary ribs all have the same curvature and radiate in a half circle around the springing point.

fascia 1 A plain, molded, or ornamented board that covers the horizontal edges (eaves) or sloping edges (verges) of a roof. Distinguished from the more specific term bargeboards, which are ornate fascia boards attached to the sloping edges of a roof. Distinguished from a frieze (definition 2), which is located at the top of a wall. **2** One of the broad continuous bands that make up the architrave of the Ionic, Corinthian, or Composite order.

Federal A version of Neoclassical architecture in the United States popular from New England to Virginia, and in other regions influenced by the Northeast. It flourished from the 1790s through the 1820s and is found in some regions as late as the 1840s. Sometimes called American Adam style. Not to be confused with Federalist. See also the related terms JEFFERSONIAN, ROMAN REVIVAL.

Federal Revival Term applied to eclectic works (c. 1890s-1930s) or elements of those works that emulate forms in the visual arts of the Federal period. Sometimes called Neo-Federal. See also the related terms COLONIAL REVIVAL, GEORGIAN REVIVAL.

Federalist Name of an American political party and the era it dominated (c. 1787–1820). Not to be confused with Federal.

fenestration Window treatment: arrangement and proportioning.

festoon A motif representing entwined leaves, flowers, or fruits, hung in a catenary curve from two points. Distinguished from a swag, which is a motif representing a fold of drapery hung in a similar curve. See also the more general term GARLAND.

fillet 1 A relatively narrow flat molding. **2** Any thin band.

finial A vertical ornament placed upon the apex of an architectural feature, such as a gable, turret, or canopy. Distinguished from a pinnacle, which is a larger feature, usually associated with Gothic architecture.

fireproofing In metal skeletal framing, the wrapping of structural members in terra-cotta tile or other fire-resistant material.

flashing A strip of metal, plastic, or various flexible compositional materials used at roof valleys and ridges and at chimney corners to keep water out. Any similar material used to protect door and window heads and sills.

Flemish bond A pattern of brickwork in which the stretchers and headers alternate in the same row and are staggered from one row to the next. Because this creates a more animated texture than English bond, Flemish bond was favored for front facades and more elegant buildings.

Flemish gable A gable whose upper slopes ascend in steps rather than in a straight line. These steps may be rectilinear or curved, or a combination of both.

fluting, fluted A series of parallel grooves or channels (flutes), usually semicircular or semielliptical in plan, that accentuate the verticality of the shaft of a column or pilaster.

flying buttress In Gothic architecture a spanning member, usually in the form of an arch, that reaches across the open space from an exterior buttress pier to that point on the wall of the building where the thrusts of the interior vaults are concentrated. Because of its arched construction, a flying buttress exerts a counterthrust against the pressure of the vaults contained by the vertical strength of the buttress pier.

foliated (adjective). In the form of leaves or leaflike shapes.

folk Not a style term in itself, but a descriptive term, applicable to all the visual arts and all styles and periods. Applied to **1** a regional, often ethnic, tradition in which continuities through the years in the overall appearance of artifacts (including buildings) are more important than changes in stylistic embellishment; **2** the work of individual artists and artisans unexposed to or uninterested in prevailing or avant-garde ideals of form and technique. Approximate synonyms include anonymous, naive, primitive, traditional. For architecture, see also the more general term VERNACULAR and the related term POPULAR.

four-part vault See QUADRIPARTITE VAULT.

foursquare house A hipped-roof, two-story house with four principal rooms on each floor and a symmetrical facade. It usually has a front porch across the full width of the house and one or more large dormers on the roof. A common suburban house type from the 1890s to the 1920s. Sometimes called American Foursquare, Prairie Box.

frame construction, frame Ambiguous terms. See instead BRACED FRAME CONSTRUCTION, LIGHT FRAME CONSTRUCTION (BALLOON FRAME CONSTRUCTION, PLATFORM FRAME CONSTRUCTION), SKELETON CONSTRUCTION, TIMBER FRAME CONSTRUCTION. Not properly synonymous with wood construction, wood-clad, or wooden.

Francis 1 style. See CHÂTEAUESQUE.

François Premier See CHÂTEAUESQUE.

French colonial A term applied to buildings, towns, landscapes, and other artifacts from the period of actual French colonial occupation of large parts of eastern North America (c. 1605–1763). The term is extended to apply to the artifacts of French ethnic groups and their descendants, well into the nineteenth century.

French Norman A style associated since the 1920s with residential architecture based on rural houses of the French provinces of Normandy and Brittany. While not a major revival style, it is characterized by asymmetrical plans, round stair towers with conical roofs, stucco walls, and steep hipped roofs. Sometimes called Norman French.

fret An ornament, usually in series, as a band or field, consisting of a latticelike interlocking of right-angled linear elements.

frieze 1 The broad horizontal band that forms the central part of a classical entablature. **2** Any long horizontal band or zone, especially one that has a chiefly decorative purpose, located at the top of a wall. Distinguished from a fascia, which is attached to the horizontal edge of a roof.

front gabled Term applied to a building whose principal gable end faces the front of the lot or some feature like a street or open space. Sometimes called gable front. Distinguished from side gabled.

gable The wall area immediately below the end of a gable, gambrel, or jerkinhead roof.

gableboard See BARGEBOARD.

gable front See FRONT GABLED.

gable roof A roof in which the two planes slope equally toward each other to a common ridge. Sometimes called a pitched roof.

galerie. In French colonial domestic architecture, a porch or veranda, usually sheltered by an extension of the hip roof of the house.

gambrel roof A roof that has a single ridgepole but a double pitch. The lower plane, which rises from the eaves, is rather steep. The upper plane, which extends from the lower plane to the ridgeline, has a flatter pitch.

garland A motif representing a rope of entwined leaves, flowers, ribbons, or drapery, regardless of its shape or position. It may be formed into a wreath, festoon, or swag, or follow the outline of a rectilinear architectural element.

garret See ATTIC (definition 1).

gauged brick A brick that has been cut or rubbed to a uniform size and shape.

gazebo A small pavilion, usually polygonal or circular in plan and serving as a garden or park shelter. Distinguished from a kiosk, which generally has some commercial or public function. See also the related terms BANDSTAND, BELVEDERE (definition 1).

General Grant style See SECOND EMPIRE.

Georgian period A term for a period in British and British colonial history, and not, in architecture or the other visual arts, a sufficiently specific style term. The Georgian period begins with the coronation of George I in 1714 and extends until about 1781 in the area that became the United States (and in Britain, until the death of George IV in 1830). See also the related terms ANGLO-PALLADIANISM, BRITISH COLONIAL.

Georgian plan See DOUBLE-PILE, DOUBLE-PEN.

Georgian Revival A revival of Georgian period forms—in England, from the 1860s to the present, and in the United States, from the 1880s to the present. Sometimes called Neo-Georgian. See also the more general term COLONIAL REVIVAL and the related term FEDERAL REVIVAL.

giant order A composition involving any one of the five principal classical orders, in which the columns or pilasters are nearly as tall as the height of the entire building. Sometimes called a colossal order. See also the more general term ORDER.

Gingerbread style See CARPENTER'S GOTHIC.

girder A major horizontal spanning member, comparable in function to a beam, but larger and often built up of a number of parts. It usually runs at right angles to the beams and serves as their principal means of support.

girt In timber frame construction, a horizontal beam at intermediate (e.g., second-floor) level, spanning between posts.

glazing bar See MUNTIN.

golden section Any line divided into two parts so that the ratio of the longer part to the shorter part equals the ratio of the length of the whole line to the longer part: $a/b = (a+b)/a$. This ratio is approximately 1.618:1. A golden rectangle, or classical rectangle, is a rectangle whose long side is related to the short side in the same ratio as the golden section. It is proportioned so that neither the long nor the short side seems to dominate. In a Fibonacci series (i.e., 1, 2, 3, 5, 8, 13, . . .), the sum of the two preceding terms gives the next. The higher one goes in such a series, the closer the ratio of two sequential terms approaches the golden section.

Gothic An architectural style prevalent in Europe from the twelfth century into the fifteenth in Italy (and into the sixteenth century in the rest of Europe). It is characterized by pointed arches and ribbed vaults and by the dominance of openings over masonry mass in the wall. The Gothic was preceded by the Romanesque and followed by the Renaissance.

Gothic Revival A movement in Europe and North America devoted to reviving the forms and the spirit of Gothic architecture and the allied arts. It originated in the mid-eighteenth century. Sometimes called the Pointed style in the nineteenth century, and sometimes called Neo-Gothic. See also the more specific terms CARPENTER'S GOTHIC, EARLY GOTHIC REVIVAL, HIGH VICTORIAN GOTHIC, LATE GOTHIC REVIVAL.

Grecian A nineteenth-century term for Greek Revival.

Greek cross A cross with four equal arms. Usually used to describe the ground plan of a building. See also the more general term CRUCIFORM.

Greek Revival A movement in Europe and North America devoted to reviving the forms and the spirit of Classical Greek architecture, sculpture, and decorative arts. It originated in the mid-eighteenth century, culminated in the 1830s, and continued into the 1850s. Sometimes called Grecian in the nineteenth century. See also the more general term NEOCLASSICAL.

groin The curved edge formed by the intersection of two vaults.

guillotine sash See DOUBLE-HUNG WINDOW.

HABS See HISTORIC AMERICAN BUILDINGS SURVEY.

HAER See HISTORIC AMERICAN ENGINEERING RECORD.

half-timber construction A variety of timber frame construction in which the framing members are exposed on the exterior of the wall, with the spaces between timbers being filled with wattle-and-daub (i.e., woven lath and plaster) or masonry materials, such as brick or stone. These masonry materials may also be covered with stucco. Sometimes called half-timbered construction.

hall-and-parlor house, hall-and-parlor plan A double-pen house (i.e., a house that is one room deep and two rooms wide). Usually applied to houses without a central through-passage, to distinguish from hall-passage-parlor houses.

hall-passage-parlor house, hall-passage-parlor plan A two-room house with a central through-passage or hallway.

hammer beam A short horizontal beam projecting inward from the foot of the principal rafter and supported below by a diagonal brace tied into a vertical wall post. The hammer beams carry much of the load of the roof trussing above. Hammer beam trusses, which could be assembled using a series of smaller timbers, were often used in late medieval England instead of conventional trusses, which required long horizontal tie beams extending across an entire interior space.

haunch The part of the arch between the crown or keystone and the springing.

header A brick laid across the thickness of a wall, so that the short end of the brick shows on the exterior.

head molding A molding or set of moldings designed to shelter and embellish the top of a door or window. Sometimes called a drip molding. See also the related terms CAP (for windows) and HOOD (for doors).

heavy timber construction See TIMBER FRAME CONSTRUCTION.

high style or high-style (adjective). Not a style term in itself, but a descriptive term, applicable to all the visual arts and all styles and periods. Applied to the works of the masters and their schools and disciples, usually reflecting a cosmopolitan awareness of traditions beyond a particular place or time. Usually contrasted with vernacular (including the folk and popular traditions).

high tech Term applied to architecture in which building materials and elements of building systems are used to celebrate contemporary technology. Elemental geometric forms, primary colors, and metallic finishes are used to heighten the technological imagery.

High Victorian Gothic A version of the Gothic Revival that originated in England in the 1850s and spread to North America in the 1860s. Characterized by polychromatic exteriors inspired by the medieval Gothic architecture of northern Italy. Sometimes called Ruskin Gothic, Ruskinian Gothic, Venetian Gothic, Victorian Gothic. See also the more general term GOTHIC REVIVAL.

hipped gable roof See JERKINHEAD ROOF.

hipped roof A roof that pitches inward from all four sides. The edge where any two planes meet is called the hip.

Historic American Buildings Survey A branch of the National Park Service of the United States Department of the Interior, established in 1933 to produce detailed documentation of American architecture. Such documentation typically includes historical and architectural data, photographs, and measured drawings and is deposited in the Prints and Photographs Division of the Library of Congress. Abbreviated HABS. See also the related term HISTORIC AMERICAN ENGINEERING RECORD.

Historic American Engineering Record A branch of the National Park Service of the United States Department of the Interior, established in 1969 to produce detailed documentation of sites and structures associated with industry, transportation, and other areas of technology. Abbreviated HAER. See also the related term HISTORIC AMERICAN BUILDINGS SURVEY.

historicism, historicist, historicizing A type of eclecticism prevalent since the eighteenth century, involving the use of forms from historical periods of high-style design (usually in the Western tradition) and, occasionally, from favored traditions of vernacular design (such as the various colonial traditions in the United States). Historicist influences are designated by the use of the prefix Neo-with a previous historical style (e.g., Neo-Baroque). Distinguished from the more general term eclecticism, which draws upon a wider range of sources in addition to the historical. See also the more specific term REVIVALISM.

hollow building tile A hollow terra-cotta building

block used for constructing exterior bearing walls of buildings up to about three stories, as well as interior walls and partitions.

hood A canopy, ledge, molding, or pediment over a door. Distinguished from a cap, which is a similar feature over a window. Sometimes called a hood molding. See also the related term HEAD MOLDING.

horizontal plank frame construction A system of wood construction in which horizontal planks are set or nailed into the corner posts of a timber frame building. There are, however, no studs or intermediate posts connecting the sill and the plate. See also the related term VERTICAL PLANK FRAME CONSTRUCTION.

hung ceiling See SUSPENDED CEILING.

hyphen A subsidiary building unit, often one story, connecting the central block and the wings or dependencies.

I-beam The most common profile in steel structural shapes (although it also appears in cast iron and in reinforced concrete). Used especially for spanning elements, it is shaped like the capital letter "I" to make the most efficient use of the material consistent with a shape that permits easy assemblage. The vertical face of the "I" is the web. The horizontal faces are the flanges. Other standard shapes for steel framing elements are Hs, Ts, Zs, Ls (known as angles), and square-cornered Us (channels).

I-house A two-story house, one room deep and two rooms wide, usually with a central hallway. The I-house is a nineteenth-century descendant of the hall-and-parlor houses of the colonial period. The term is commonly applied to the end-chimney houses of the southern and mid-Atlantic traditions. The term most likely derives from the resemblance between the tall, narrow end walls of these houses and the capital letter "I."

impost The top part of a pier or wall upon which rests the springer or lowest voussoir of an arch.

impost block A block, often in the form of an inverted truncated pyramid, placed between a column capital and the lowest voussoirs of an arch above. Distinguished from an entablature block, which has the details found in a classical entablature. Sometimes called a dosseret or supercapital.

in antis Columns in antis are placed between two projecting sections of wall, in an imaginary plane connecting the ends of the two wall elements.

intermediate rib See TIERCERON.

International style A style that originated in the 1920s and flourished into the 1970s, characterized by the expression of volume and surface and by the suppression of historicist ornament and axial symmetry. The term was originally applied by Henry-Russell Hitchcock and Philip Johnson to the new, nontraditional, mostly European architecture of the 1920s in their 1932 exhibition at the Museum of Modern Art and in their accompanying book, *The International Style*. Also called International, International Modern. See also the more specific term CORPORATE INTERNATIONAL

STYLE and the related terms BAUHAUS, MIESIAN, SECOND CHICAGO SCHOOL.

intrados The inner curve or underside (soffit) of an arch. See also the related term EXTRADOS.

Ionic order An ensemble of classical column and entablature elements, particularly characterized by the use of large volutes in the capital of the column. See also the more general term ORDER.

isometric drawing A pictorial drawing using isometric projection, in which all horizontal lines that are perpendicular in an object, building, or space are drawn at 60-degree angles from the vertical. Consequently, a single scale can be used for all three dimensions. Sometimes called an isometric. See also the related terms AXONOMETRIC DRAWING, PERSPECTIVE DRAWING.

Italianate 1 A general term for an eclectic Neo-Renaissance and Neo-Romanesque style, originating in England and Germany in the early nineteenth century and prevalent in the United States between the 1840s and 1880s, not only in houses but also in Main Street commercial buildings. The Italianate is characterized by prominent window heads and bracketed cornices. Called the Bracketed style in the nineteenth century. See also the more specific terms BARRYESQUE, ITALIAN VILLA STYLE, and the related terms RENAISSANCE REVIVAL, ROUND ARCH MODE, SECOND EMPIRE. **2** A specific term for Italianate buildings that are predominantly symmetrical in plan and elevation. Distinguished from Barryesque, which is applied to more formal institutional and governmental buildings.

Italian Villa style A subtype of the Italianate style (definition 1), originating in England and Germany in the early nineteenth century and prevalent in the United States between the 1840s and 1870s, mostly in houses, but also churches and other public buildings. The style is characterized by asymmetrical plans and elevations, irregular blocklike massing, round arch arcades and openings, and northern Italian Romanesque detailing. Larger Italian Villa buildings often had a campanile-like tower. Distinguished from the more symmetrical Italianate style (definition 2) by having the northern Italian rural vernacular villa as prototype.

Jacobean period A term for a period in British history coinciding with the rule of James I (1603–1625). See also the related term ELIZABETHAN PERIOD for the immediately preceding period, which itself is part of the Tudor period.

Jacobethan Revival See NEO-TUDOR.

jamb The vertical side face of a door or window opening, amounting to the full thickness of the wall, and usually enriched with paneling, moldings, or jamb shafts (which are engaged columns set into a splayed, or angled, jamb). In an opening containing a door or window, the jamb is distinguished from the reveal, which is the portion of wall thickness between the door or window frame and the outer surface of the wall. (In an opening without a door or window, the terms jamb and reveal are used interchangeably.) Also distinguished from an architrave (definition 2), which consists of the moldings on the face of a wall around the opening.

Jazz Moderne See ART DECO.

Jeffersonian A personal style of Neoclassicism identified with the architecture of Thomas Jefferson (1743–1826), derived in part from Palladian ideas and in part from Imperial Roman prototypes. The style had a limited influence in the Piedmont of Virginia and across the Appalachians into the Ohio River valley. Sometimes called Jeffersonian Classicism. See also the related terms ANGLO-PALLADIANISM, FEDERAL, ROMAN REVIVAL.

jerkinhead roof A gable roof in which the upper portion of the gable end is hipped, or inclined inward along the ridgeline, forming a small triangle of roof surface. Sometimes called a clipped gable roof or hipped gable roof.

joist One of a series of small horizontal beams that support a floor or ceiling.

keystone The central wedge-shaped stone at the crown of an arch.

king post In a truss, the vertical suspension member that connects the tie beam with the apex of opposing principal rafters.

kiosk Originally, a Turkish summer palace. Since the nineteenth century, the term has been applied to any small pavilion or stand, usually found in public gardens, parks, streets, and malls, where it serves some commercial or public function. Distinguished from a gazebo, which may be found in public or private gardens or parks, but which usually serves as a sheltered resting place. See also the related term BANDSTAND.

label 1 A drip molding, over a square-headed door or window, which extends for a short distance down each side of the opening. **2** A similar vertical downward extension of a drip molding over an arch of any form. Sometimes called a label molding.

label stop 1 An L-shaped termination at the lower ends of a label. **2** Any decorative boss or other termination of a label.

lancet arch An arch generally tall and sharply pointed.

lantern 1 The uppermost stage of a dome, containing windows or arcaded openings. **2** Any feature, square or polygonal in plan and usually containing windows, rising above the roof of a building. The square structures that serve as skylights on the roofs of nineteenth-century buildings—particularly houses—were also called lantern lights, and, in Italianate and Second Empire buildings, came to be called cupolas.

Late Georgian period Not strictly a style term, but a term for a period in British and British colonial history approximately coinciding with the reigns of George III (1760–1820) and George IV (1820–1830). In the United States, the Late Georgian period is now understood to end sometime during the Revolutionary War (1775–1781) and to be followed by the Federal period (c. 1787–1820). In Britain, the Late Georgian period includes the Regency period (1811–1820s). See also the related term EARLY GEORGIAN PERIOD.

Late Gothic Revival A term for the Gothic Revival work of the late nineteenth and early twentieth centuries. See also the more specific term COLLEGIATE GOTHIC (definition 2) and the related term EARLY GOTHIC REVIVAL.

lath A latticelike, continuous surface of small wooden strips or metal mesh nailed to walls or partitions to hold plaster.

Latin cross A cross with one long and three short arms. Usually used to describe the ground plans of Roman Catholic and Protestant churches. See also the more general term CRUCIFORM.

leaded glass Panes of glass held in place by lead strips, or cames. The panes, clear or stained, may be of any shape.

lean-to roof See SHED ROOF.

lierne In a Gothic vault, a short ornamental rib connecting the major transverse ribs and the secondary tiercerons. Sometimes called a cross rib or tertiary rib.

light frame construction A type of wood frame construction in which relatively light structural members (usually sawn lumber, ranging from two-by-fours to two-by-tens) are fastened with nails. Distinguished from timber frame construction, in which relatively heavy structural members (hewn or sawn timbers, measuring six-by-six and larger) are fastened with mortise-and-tenon joints. See the more specific terms BALLOON FRAME CONSTRUCTION, PLATFORM FRAME CONSTRUCTION.

lintel A horizontal structural member that supports the wall over an opening or spans between two adjacent piers or columns.

living hall In Queen Anne, Shingle Style, and Colonial Revival houses, an extensive room, often containing the entry, the main staircase, a fireplace, and an inglenook.

load-bearing Term applied to a wall, column, pier, or any vertical supporting member, constructed so that all loads are carried to the ground through the wall, column, or pier. See also the related terms BEARING WALL, CURTAIN WALL.

loggia 1 A porch or open-air room, particularly one set within the body of a building. **2** An arcaded or colonnaded structure, open on one or more sides, sometimes with an upper story. **3** An eighteenth- and nineteenth-century term for a porch or veranda.

Lombard A style term applied in the United States in the mid-nineteenth century to buildings derived from the Romanesque architecture of northern Italy (especially Lombardy) and the earlier nineteenth-century architecture of southern Germany. Characterized by the use of brick for both structural and ornamental purposes. Also called Lombardic. See also the related term ROUND ARCH MODE.

lunette 1 A semicircular area, especially one that contains some decorative treatment or a mural painting. **2** A semicircular window in such an area.

Mannerism, Mannerist 1 A phase of Renaissance art and architecture in the mid-sixteenth century, characterized by distortions, contortions, inversions, odd juxtapositions, and other departures from High Renaissance canons of design. **2** (not capitalized) A sensibility in design, regardless of style or period, characterized by a knowledgeable violation of rules and intended as a comment on the very nature of convention.

mansard roof A hipped roof with double pitch. The upper slope may approach flatness, while the lower slope has a very steep pitch, sometimes flaring in a concave curve (or swelling in a convex curve) as it comes to the eaves. This lower slope usually has windows, and the area under the roof often amounts to a full story. The name is a corruption of that of François Mansart (1598–1666), who designed roofs of this type, which were revived in Paris during the Second Empire period.

Mansard style, Mansardic See SECOND EMPIRE.

masonry Construction using stone, brick, block, or some other hard and durable material laid up in units and usually bonded by mortar.

massing The grouping or arrangement of the primary volumetric components of a building.

Mayan Revival Term applied to eclectic works or elements of those works that emulate forms in the visual arts of the Maya civilization of Central America. See also the related term ART DECO.

McKim Classicism, McKim Classical Architecture of, or in the manner of, the firm of McKim, Mead and White, 1890s–1920s. See BEAUX-ARTS CLASSICISM.

medieval Term applied to the Middle Ages in European civilization between the age of antiquity and the age of the Renaissance (i.e., mid-400s to mid-1400s in Italy; mid-400s to late 1500s in England). In architecture and the other visual arts, the medieval period included the end of the Early Christian period, then the Byzantine, the Romanesque, and the Gothic styles or periods.

Mediterranean Revival A style generally associated since the early twentieth century with residential architecture based on Italian villas of the sixteenth century. While not a major revival style, it is characterized by symmetrical arrangements, stucco walls, and low-pitch tile roofs. Sometimes called Mediterranean Villa, Neo-Mediterranean. See also the related term SPANISH COLONIAL REVIVAL.

metope In a Doric entablature, that part of the frieze which falls between two triglyphs. In the Greek Doric order the metopes often contain small sculptural reliefs.

Middle Ages See MEDIEVAL.

Miesian Term applied to work showing the influence of the German-American architect Ludwig Mies van der Rohe (1886–1969). See also the

related terms BAUHAUS, INTERNATIONAL STYLE, SECOND CHICAGO SCHOOL.

Mission Revival A style originating in the 1890s, and making use of forms and materials from the Spanish and Mexican mission architecture of the eighteenth and early nineteenth centuries. Not to be confused with Mission furniture of the Arts and Crafts movement. See also the more general term SPANISH COLONIAL REVIVAL.

Modern Ambiguous term, applied in various ways during the past century to the history of the visual arts and world history generally: **1** from the 1910s to the present. See also the more specific terms BAUHAUS, INTERNATIONAL STYLE; **2** from the 1860s, 1870s, 1880s, or 1890s to the present; **3** from the Enlightenment or the advent of Neoclassicism or the industrial revolution, c. 1750, to the present; **4** from the Renaissance in Italy, c. 1450, to the present.

Modern Gothic See EASTLAKE.

Moderne A term applied to a wide range of design work from the 1920s through the 1940s, in which aspects of traditionalism and modernism coexist and in which eclecticism (from a historical, exotic, or machine aesthetic) is inseparable from the urge for stylization. Sometimes called Art Moderne, Modernistic. See also the more specific terms ART DECO, PWA MODERNE, STREAMLINE MODERNE.

modillion One of a series of small, thin scroll brackets under the projecting crown molding of a classical cornice. It is found in the Corinthian and Composite orders. Distinguished from a console, which usually is larger and has a height greater than its projection from the wall.

molding A running surface composed of parallel and continuous sections of simple or compound curves and flat areas.

monitor An extensive shed-roofed feature on a roof, containing a band of windows or vents. It may be located along one of the roof slopes (a trap-door monitor) or along the ridgeline (a clerestory monitor), and it usually runs the entire length of the roof. Distinguished from a skylight, which is a low-profile or flush-mounted feature in the plane of the roof.

Moorish Revival Term applied to eclectic works or elements of those works that emulate forms in the visual arts of those parts of North Africa and Spain under Muslim domination from the seventh through the fifteenth century. See also the related term ORIENTAL REVIVAL.

mortar A mixture of cement or lime with water and a fine aggregate of sand used to secure bricks or stones in masonry construction.

mortise-and-tenon joint A timber framing joint that is made by one member having its end shaped into a projecting piece (tenon) that fits exactly into a hole (mortise) in the other member. Once joined, the pieces are held together by a peg that passes through the tenon.

mullion 1 A post or similiar vertical member dividing a window into two or more units, or lights, each of which may be further subdivided (by muntins) into panes. **2** A post or similar vertical member dividing a wall opening into two or more contiguous windows.

muntin One of the small vertical or horizontal members that hold panes of glass within a window or glazed door. Distinguished from a mullion, which is a heavier vertical member separating paired or grouped windows. Sometimes called a glazing bar, sash bar, or window bar.

mushroom column A reinforced concrete column that flares at the top in order to counteract shear stresses in the vicinity of the column.

National Register of Historic Places A branch of the National Park Service of the United States Department of the Interior, established by the National Historic Preservation Act of 1966, to maintain files of documentation on districts, sites, buildings, structures, and objects of national, state, or local significance. Properties listed on the National Register are afforded administrative—and, ultimately, judicial—review in instances where projects funded or assisted by federal agencies might have an impact on the historic property. Properties listed on the register may also be eligible for certain tax benefits.

nave. **1** The entire body of a church between the entrance and the crossing. **2** The central space of a church, between the side aisles, extending from the entrance end to the crossing.

Neo-Baroque Term applied to eclectic works or elements of those works that emulate forms in the visual arts of the Baroque style or period. Sometimes called Baroque Revival.

Neo-Byzantine Term applied to eclectic works or elements of those works that emulate forms in the visual arts of the Byzantine style or period. Sometimes called Byzantine Revival.

Neoclassical Revival See BEAUX-ARTS CLASSICISM.

Neoclassicism, Neoclassical A broad movement in the visual arts which drew its inspiration from ancient Greece and Rome. It began in the mid-eighteenth century with the advent of the science of archeology and extended into the mid-nineteenth century (in some Beaux-Arts work, into the 1930s; in some Postmodern work, even into the present). See also the related terms BEAUX-ARTS, BEAUX-ARTS CLASSICISM, CLASSICISM, and the more specific terms GREEK REVIVAL, ROMAN REVIVAL.

Neo-Colonial See COLONIAL REVIVAL.

Neo-Federal See FEDERAL REVIVAL.

Neo-Georgian See GEORGIAN REVIVAL.

Neo-Gothic Term applied to eclectic works or elements of those works that emulate forms in the visual arts of the Gothic style or period. The cultural movement that produced so many such works in the eighteenth, nineteenth, and twentieth centuries is called the Gothic Revival, though that term covers a wide range of work.

Neo-Grec An architectural style developed in connection with the Ecole des Beaux-Arts in Paris during the 1840s and characterized by the use of stylized Greek elements, often in conjunction with cast iron or brick construction. See also the more general term BEAUX-ARTS.

Neo-Hispanic See SPANISH COLONIAL REVIVAL.

Neo-Mediterranean See MEDITERRANEAN REVIVAL.

Neo-Norman Term applied to eclectic works or elements of those works that emulate forms in the visual arts of the eleventh- and twelfth-century Romanesque of Norman France and Britain.

Neo-Palladian See PALLADIANISM.

Neo-Renaissance Term applied to eclectic works or elements of those works that emulate forms in the visual arts of the Renaissance style or period. The mid- to late nineteenth-century cultural movement that produced so many such works is called the Renaissance Revival, though that term covers a wide range of work.

Neo-Romanesque Term applied to eclectic works or elements of those works that emulate forms in the visual arts of the Romanesque style or period. The mid-nineteenth-century cultural movement that produced so many such works is called the Romanesque Revival, though that term covers a wide range of work.

Neo-Tudor Term applied to eclectic works or elements of those works that emulate forms in the visual arts of the Tudor period. Sometimes called Elizabethan Manor style, English Half-timber style, Jacobethan Revival, Tudor Revival.

New Brutalism See BRUTALISM.

New Formalism A style prevalent since the 1960s, characterized by symmetrical arrangements, rich materials (marble cladding, metal grillework), and stylized classical (even Gothic) detailing. Architects associated with this style include Philip Johnson (born 1906), Edward Durell Stone (1902–1978), and Minoru Yamasaki (1912–1985).

newel post A post at the head or foot of a flight of stairs, to which the handrail is fastened. Newel posts occur in a variety of shapes, in profile and cross section, and are generally more substantial elements than the individual balusters that support the handrail.

niche A recess in a wall, usually designed to contain sculpture or an urn. A niche is often semicircular in plan and surmounted by a half dome or shell form. See also the related terms AEDICULE, TABERNACLE (definition 1).

nogging Brickwork that fills the spaces between members of a timber frame wall or partition.

Norman French See FRENCH NORMAN.

octagon house A rare house type of the 1850s, based on the ideas of Orson Squire Fowler (1809–1887), who argued for the efficiencies of an octagonal floorplan. Sometimes called octagon mode.

oculus A circular opening in a ceiling or wall or at the top of a dome.

ogee arch A pointed arch formed by a pair of opposing S-shaped curves.

order The most important constituents of classical architecture are the orders, first developed as a structural-aesthetic system by the ancient Greeks.

An order has two major components. A column with its capital is the main vertical supporting member. The principal horizontal member is the entablature. The Greeks developed three different types of order, the Doric, Ionic, and Corinthian, each distinguishable by its own decorative system and proportions. All three were taken over and modified by the Romans, who added two orders of their own, the Tuscan, which is a simplified form of the Doric, and the Composite, which is made up of elements of both the Ionic and the Corinthian. The Romans often used the orders as a structural system in the same manner as the Greeks. Unlike the Greeks, however, they also applied them as decoration to the surfaces of walls that were supported by other means. Sometimes called classical orders. See also the related terms COLUMN, ENTABLATURE, GIANT ORDER, SUPERPOSITION (definition 1).

oriel A projecting polygonal or curved window unit of one or more stories, supported on brackets or corbels. Sometimes called an oriel window. Distinguished from a bay window, which rises from the foundation and has a rooted rather than a suspended appearance. However, a multistory projection in a tall building, whether cantilevered out or built from the foundation, is called a projecting bay or a unit of bay windows.

Oriental Revival Ambiguous term, suggesting eclectic influences from any period in any culture in the "Orient," or Asia, including Turkish, Persian, Indian, Chinese, and Japanese, as well as Arabic (even the Moorish of North Africa and Spain). Sometimes called Oriental style. See also the related term MOORISH REVIVAL.

orthographic projection A system of visual representation in which all details on or near some principal plane, object, building, or space are projected, to scale, onto the parallel plane of the drawing. Orthographic projection thus flattens all forms into a single two-dimensional picture plane and allows for an exact scaling of every feature in that plane. Distinguished from pictorial projection, which creates the illusion of three-dimensional depth. See also the more specific terms ELEVATION, PLAN, SECTION.

outbuilding A building subsidiary to and completely detached from another building. Distinguished from a dependency, which may be attached or detached.

overhang The projection of part of a structure beyond the portion below.

PWA Moderne A synthesis of the Moderne (i.e., Art Deco or Streamline Moderne) with an austere late type of Beaux-Arts Classicism, often associated with federal government buildings of the 1930s and 1940s during the Public Works Administration. See also the more general term MODERNE and the related terms ART DECO, BEAUX-ARTS CLASSICISM, STREAMLINE MODERNE.

Palladianism, Palladian Work influenced by the Italian Renaissance architect Andrea Palladio (1508–1580), particularly by means of his treatise, *I Quattro Libri dell'Architettura (The Four Books of Architecture)*, originally published in 1570 and disseminated throughout Europe in numerous translations and editions until the mid-eighteenth century. The most significant flourishing of Palladianism was in England, from the 1710s to the 1760s, and in the British North American colonies, from the 1740s to the 1790s. Sometimes called Neo-Palladian, Palladian classical. See also the more specific term ANGLO-PALLADIANISM.

Palladian motif A three-part composition for a door or window, in which a round-headed opening is flanked by lower flat-headed openings and separated from them by columns, pilasters, or mullions. The flanking sections, and sometimes the entire unit, may be blind (i.e., not open).

Palladian Revival See ANGLO-PALLADIANISM.

Palladian window A window subdivided as in the Palladian motif.

parapet A low wall at the edge of a roof, balcony, or terrace, sometimes formed by the upward extension of the wall below.

pargeting Elaborate stucco or plasterwork, especially an ornamental finish for exterior plaster walls, sometimes decorated with figures in low relief or indented. Found in late medieval, Queen Anne, and period revival buildings. Sometimes called parging, pargework. See also the more general term STUCCO.

parquet Inlaid wood flooring, usually set in simple geometric patterns.

parti The essential solution to an architectural program or problem; the basic concept for the arrangement of spaces, before the development and elaboration of the design.

patera (plural: paterae) A circular or oval panel or plaque decorated with stylized flower petals or radiating linear motifs. Distinguished from a roundel, which is always circular.

pavilion 1 A central or corner unit that projects from a larger architectural mass and is usually accented by a special treatment of the wall or roof. **2** A detached or semidetached structure used for specialized activities, as at a hospital. **3** In a garden or fairground, a temporary structure or tent, usually ornamented.

pediment 1 In classical architecture, the low triangular gable end of the roof, framed by raking cornices along the inclined edges of the roof and by a horizontal cornice below. **2** In Renaissance and Baroque and later classically derived architecture, the triangular or curvilinear culmination of a prominent part of a facade. **3** A similar but smaller-scale feature over a door or window. It may be triangular or curvilinear.

pendentive A concave surface in the form of a spherical triangle that forms the structural transition from the square plan of a crossing to the circular plan of a dome.

pergola A structure with an open wood framed roof, often latticed, and supported by a colonnade.

It is usually covered by climbing plants, such as vines or roses, and provides shade for a garden walk or a passageway to a building. Distinguished from arbors or trellises, which are less extensive accessory structures lacking the colonnade.

period house Term applied to suburban and country houses in which period revival styles are dominant.

period revival Term applied to eclectic works—particularly suburban and country houses—of the first three decades of the twentieth century, in which a particular historical or regional style is dominant. See also the more specific terms COLONIAL REVIVAL, DUTCH COLONIAL REVIVAL, GEORGIAN REVIVAL, NEO-TUDOR, SPANISH COLONIAL REVIVAL.

peripteral (adjective). Surrounded by a single row of columns.

peristyle A range of columns surrounding a building or an open court.

perspective drawing A pictorial drawing representing an object, building, or space, as if seen from a single vantage point. The illusion of three dimensions is created by using a system based on the optical laws of converging lines and vanishing points. See also the related terms AXONOMETRIC DRAWING, ISOMETRIC DRAWING.

piano nobile (plural: *piani nobili*) In Renaissance and later architecture, a floor with formal reception, living, and dining rooms. The principal and often tallest story in a building, usually one level above the ground level.

piazza 1 A plaza or square. 2 An eighteenth- and nineteenth-century term for a porch or veranda.

pictorial projection A system of visual representation in which an object, building, or space is projected onto the picture plane in such a way that the illusion of three-dimensional depth is created. Distinguished from orthographic projection, in which the dimension of depth is excluded. See also the more specific terms AXONOMETRIC DRAWING, ISOMETRIC DRAWING, PERSPECTIVE DRAWING.

picturesque An aesthetic category in architecture and landscape architecture in the late eighteenth and early nineteenth centuries. It is characterized by relationships among buildings and landscape features that evoke the qualities of landscape paintings, in which the eye is led past a variety of forms and spaces into the distance and the mind is led to contemplate a sense of age (by means of ruins, fallen trees, weathered rocks, and mossy surfaces on all of these). In actual settings, asymmetrical and eclectic buildings, indirect approaches, and contrasting clusters of plantings heighten the experience of the picturesque.

pier 1 A freestanding mass, supporting a concentrated load from an arch, a beam, a truss, or a girder. While generally rectilinear in plan, piers in buildings based upon medieval precedents are often curvilinear in plan. 2 An upright portion of a wall that performs a columnar function. The pier may be continuous with the plane of the wall,

or it may be distinguished from the plane of the wall to give it a columnlike independence.

pier and spandrel A type of skeletal wall organization in which the vertical metal columns (and their square-cornered cladding) project in front of the plane of windows and their spandrel panels. The spandrel panels may be exposed structural spanning members. More often they provide decorative covering for the structure.

pilaster 1 A flattened column, with or without fluting, that is attached to a wall. It is usually finished with the same capital and base as a freestanding column. 2 Any narrow, vertical strip attached to a wall. Distinguished from an engaged column, which has a convex curvature.

pillar Ambiguous term, often used interchangeably with COLUMN, PIER, or POST; see instead one of those terms. (Although the term pillar is sometimes applied to columns that are square in plan, the term pier is preferable.)

pinnacle In Gothic architecture, a small spirelike element providing an ornamental finish to the highest part of a buttress or roof. It has a slender pyramidal or conical form and is often articulated with crockets or ribs and is topped by a finial. Distinguished from a finial, which is a smaller feature appearing by itself.

pitched roof See GABLE ROOF.

plan A drawing (in orthographic projection) representing all or part of an object, building, or space, as if viewed from directly above. A floor plan is a drawing of a horizontal cut through a building, usually at the level of the windows, showing the configuration of walls and openings. Other types of plans may illustrate ceilings, roofs, structural elements, and mechanical systems.

plank construction General term. See instead the more specific terms HORIZONTAL PLANK FRAME CONSTRUCTION, VERTICAL PLANK CONSTRUCTION.

plate 1 In timber frame construction, the topmost horizontal structural member of a wall, to which the roof rafters are fastened. 2 In platform and balloon frame construction, the horizontal members to which the tops and bottoms of studs are nailed. The bottom plate is sometimes called the sill plate or sole plate.

Plateresque Term applied to Spanish and Spanish colonial Renaissance architecture from the early sixteenth century onward, in which the delicate, finely sculptured detail resembles the work of a silversmith *(platero)*. See also the related term SPANISH COLONIAL.

platform frame construction A system of light frame construction in which each story is built as an independent unit and the studs are only one story high. The floor joists of each story rest on the top plates of the story below, and the bearing walls or partitions rest on the subfloor of each floor unit or platform. Platform framing is easier to construct and more rigid than balloon framing and has become the common framing method in the twentieth century. Structural members are usually sawn lumber, ranging from two-by-fours to two-by-tens, and are fastened with nails. Sometimes called platform framing, western frame, western framing.

plinth The base block of a column, pilaster, pedestal, dado, or door architrave.

Pointed style A nineteenth-century term for Gothic Revival.

polychromy, polychromatic, polychrome A many-colored treatment, especially the combination of materials in various colors or the application of surface color, to articulate wall and roof planes and to highlight architecture.

popular A term applied to vernacular architecture influenced by such publications as books of the orders, builders' guides, style books, pattern books, mail-order catalogs, architectural periodicals, and household magazines. Architecture in the popular tradition may be built according to commercially available plans or from widely distributed components; or it may be built by local practitioners (architects, builders, contractors) emulating buildings that are represented in publications. The distinction between popular architecture and high-style architecture by lesser-known architects depends on one's point of view with regard to the division between vernacular and high-style. See also the more general term VERNACULAR and the related term FOLK.

porch A structure attached to a building to shelter an entrance or to serve as a semienclosed sitting, working, or sleeping space. Distinguished from a portico, which is either a pedimented feature at least one story in height supported by classical columns or a more extensive colonnaded feature.

porte-cochère A porch projecting over a driveway and providing shelter to people leaving a vehicle and entering a building or vice versa. Also called a carriage porch.

portico 1 A porch at least one story in height consisting of a low-pitched roof supported on classical columns and finished in front with an entablature and pediment. **2** An extensive porch supported by a colonnade.

post A vertical supporting element, either square or circular in plan. Posts are the integral vertical members of a frame or truss, whether of wood or metal. Posts may also carry fences or gates, or may serve as freestanding markers (e.g., mileposts).

post-and-beam construction. A structural system in which the main support is provided by vertical members (posts) carrying horizontal members (beams or lintels). Sometimes called post and girt construction, post and lintel construction, trabeation, trabeated construction.

Postmodernism, Postmodern A term applied to work that involves a reaction against the ideas and works of various twentieth-century modern movements, particularly the Bauhaus and the International style. Postmodern work makes use of historicism, yet the traditional elements are often merely applied to buildings that, in every other

respect, are products of modern movement design. The term is also applied to works that are attempting to demonstrate an extension of the principles of various modern movements.

Prairie Box See FOURSQUARE HOUSE.

Prairie school, Prairie style A diverse group of architects working in Chicago and throughout the Midwest from the 1890s to the 1920s, strongly influenced by Frank Lloyd Wright and to a lesser degree by Louis Sullivan. The term is applied mainly to domestic architecture. An architect is said to belong to the Prairie school; a work of architecture is said to be in the Prairie style. Sometimes called Prairie, for short. See also the related terms CHICAGO SCHOOL, WRIGHTIAN.

pre-Columbian Term applied to the major cultures of Latin American (e.g., Aztec, Maya, Inca) that flourished prior to the discovery of the New World by Columbus in 1492 and the Spanish conquests of the sixteenth century. Distinguished from North American Indian, which is generally applied to indigenous cultures within the area that would become the United States and Canada.

pressed metal Thin sheets of metal (usually galvanized or tin-plated iron) stamped into patterned panels for covering ceilings and exterior and interior walls or into molding profiles and other details for assembly into exterior and interior cornices. Loosely called pressed tin or stamped metal. Prevalent from the 1870s through the 1920s.

program The list of functional, spatial, and other requirements that guides an architect in developing a design.

proscenium In a recessed stage, the area between the orchestra and the curtain.

proscenium arch In a recessed stage, the enframement of the opening.

prostyle Having a columnar portico in front, but not on the sides and rear.

provincialism, provincial Term applied to work in an isolated area (such as a province of a cosmopolitan center or a colony of a mother country), where traditional practices persist, with some awareness of what is being done in the cosmopolitan center or the homeland.

purlin In roof construction, a structural member laid across the principal rafters and parallel to the wall plate and the ridge beam. The light common rafters to which the roofing surface is attached are fastened across the purlins. See also the related term RAFTER.

pylon 1 Originally, the gateway facade of an Egyptian temple complex, consisting of a truncated broad pyramidal form with battered (inclined) wall surfaces on all four sides, or two truncated pyramidal towers flanking an entrance portal. **2** Any towerlike structure from which bridge cables or utility lines are suspended.

quadripartite vault A vault divided into four triangular sections by a pair of diagonal ribs. Sometimes called a four-part vault.

quarry-faced See ROCK-FACED.

quatrefoil A type of Gothic tracery having four parts (lobes or foils) separated by pointed elements (cusps).

Queen Anne Ambiguous but widely used term. **1** In architecture, the Queen Anne style is an eclectic style of the 1860s through 1910s in England and the United States, characterized by the incorporation of forms from postmedieval vernacular architecture and the architecture of the Georgian period. Sometimes called Queen Anne Revival. See also the more specific term SHINGLE STYLE and the related terms EASTLAKE, STICK STYLE. **2** In architecture, the original Queen Anne period extends from the late seventeenth into the early eighteenth century. **3** In the decorative arts, the Queen Anne style and period properly refer to work of the early eighteenth century during the reign of Queen Anne (1702–1714, i.e., after William and Mary and before Georgian). **4** In the decorative arts, eclectic work of the 1860s to 1880s is properly referred to as Queen Anne Revival. See also the related term AESTHETIC MOVEMENT.

quoin One of the bricks or stones laid in alternating directions, which bond and form the exterior corner of a building. Sometimes simulated in wood or stucco.

rafter One of the inclined structural members of a roof. Principal rafters are primary supporting elements spanning between the walls and the apex of the roof and carrying the longitudinal purlins. Common rafters are secondary supporting elements fastened onto purlins to carry the roof surfacing. See also the related term PURLIN.

raking cornice A cornice that finishes the sloping edges of a gable roof, such as the inclined sides of a triangular pediment.

random ashlar A type of masonry in which squared and dressed blocks are laid in a random pattern rather than in straight horizontal courses.

recessed column A fully round column set into a nichelike space only slightly larger than the column. Distinguished from an engaged column, which appears to be built into the wall.

reentrant angle An acute angle created by the juncture of two planes, such as walls.

refectory A dining hall, especially in medieval architecture.

regionalism **1** The sum of cultural characteristics (including material culture, language) that define a geographic region, usually extending beyond a single state or province, and coinciding with one or more large physiographic areas. **2** The conscious use, within a region, of forms and materials identified with that region, creating an architecture that is in keeping with the historical architecture of the region, and even a distinctive new regional style.

register A horizontal zone of a wall, altarpiece, or other vertical feature. Usually synonymous with story, but more inclusive, allowing for the description of zones with no corresponding interior spaces.

relieving arch An arch, usually of masonry, built over the lintel of an opening to carry the load of the wall above and relieve the lintel of carrying such load. Sometimes called a discharging arch or safety arch.

Renaissance The period in European civilization identified with a rediscovery or rebirth *(rinascimento)* of classical Roman (and to a lesser extent, Greek) learning, art, and architecture. Renaissance architecture began in Italy in the mid-1400s (Early Renaissance) and reached a peak in the early to mid-1500s (High Renaissance). In England, Renaissance architecture did not begin until the late 1500s or early 1600s. The Renaissance in art and architecture was preceded by the Gothic and followed by the Baroque.

Renaissance Revival **1** In architecture, an ambiguous term, applied to (a) Italianate work of the 1840s through 1880s and (b) Beaux-Arts Classical work of the 1880s through 1920s. **2** In the decorative arts, an eclectic furniture style incorporating a variety of Renaissance, Baroque, and Neo-Grec architectural motifs and utilizing wood marquetry, incised lines (often gilded), and ormolu and porcelain ornaments. Sometimes called Neo-Renaissance.

rendering Any drawing, whether orthographic (plan, elevation, section) or pictorial (perspective), in which shades and shadows are represented.

reredos A screen or wall at the back of an altar, usually with architectural and figural decoration.

return The continuation of a molding, cornice, or other projecting member, in a different direction, as in the horizontal cornice returns at the base of the raking cornices of a triangular pediment.

reveal **1** The portion of wall thickness between a door or window frame and the outer face of the wall. **2** Same as jamb, but only in an opening without a door or window.

revival, revivalism A type of historicism prevalent since the eighteenth century, involving the adaptation of historical forms to contemporary functions. Distinguished from a more pervasive historicism by an ideological conviction that sought to rationalize the choice of a historical style according to the values of the historical period that produced it. (The Gothic Revival, for instance, was associated with the Christianity of the Middle Ages.) Revival works, therefore, tend to invoke a single historical style. More hybrid works are manifestations of a less dogmatic historicism or eclecticism. See also the more general terms HISTORICISM, ECLECTICISM.

rib The projecting linear element that separates the curved planar cells (or webs) of vaulting. Originally these were the supporting members for the vaulting, but they may also be purely decorative.

Richardsonian Term applied to any work showing the influence of the American architect Henry Hobson Richardson (1838–1886). See the note under the more limiting term RICHARDSONIAN ROMANESQUE.

Richardsonian Romanesque Term applied to Neo-Romanesque work showing the influence of the American architect Henry Hobson Richardson (1838–1886). While many of Richardson's works make eclectic use of round arches and Romanesque details, many of his works show a creative eclecticism that transcends any particular historical style. The term Richardsonian, therefore, is a more inclusive term for the work of his followers than Richardsonian Romanesque—a term that continues to be widely used. Sometimes called Richardson Romanesque, Richardsonian Romanesque Revival.

ridgepole The horizontal beam or board at the apex of a roof, to which the upper ends of the rafters are fastened. Sometimes called a ridge beam, ridgeboard, ridge piece.

rinceau An ornamental device consisting of a sinuous and branching scroll elaborated with leaves and other natural forms.

rock-faced Term applied to the rough, unfinished face of a stone used in building. Sometimes called quarry-faced.

Rococo A late phase of the Baroque, marked by elegant reverse-curve ornament, light scale, and delicate color. See also the related term BAROQUE.

Romanesque A medieval architectural style which reached its height in the eleventh and twelfth centuries. It is characterized by round arched construction and massive masonry walls. The Romanesque was preceded by the Early Christian and Byzantine periods in the eastern Mediterranean world and by a variety of localized styles and periods in northern and western Europe; it was followed throughout Europe by the Gothic.

Romanesque Revival Ambiguous term, applied to 1 *Rundbogenstil* and Round Arch work in American as early as the 1840s and 2 Richardsonian Romanesque work into the 1890s. Sometimes called Neo-Romanesque.

Roman Revival A term, not widely accepted, for a version of Neoclassicism involving the use of forms from the visual arts of the Imperial Roman period. Applied to various works in Italy, England, and the United States, where it is most clearly visible in the architecture of Thomas Jefferson. See also the related terms FEDERAL, JEFFERSONIAN, NEOCLASSICISM.

rood screen An ornamental screen that serves as a partition between the crossing and the chancel or choir of a church.

rosette A circular floral ornament similar to an open rose.

rotunda 1 A circular hall in a large building, especially an area beneath a dome or cupola. 2 A building round both inside and outside, usually domed.

Round Arch mode The American counterpart of the German *Rundbogenstil,* characterized by the predominance of round arches, whether these are accentuated by Romanesque or Renaissance detailing or left as simple unadorned openings. See also the related terms ITALIANATE, LOMBARD, RUNDBOGENSTIL.

roundel A circular panel or plaque. Distinguished from a patera, which can be oval shaped.

rubble masonry A type of masonry utilizing uncut or roughly shaped stone, such as fieldstone or boulders.

Rundbogenstil. Literally, "round arch style," a historicist style originating in Germany in the 1820s and spreading to Britain and the United States from the 1840s through the 1860s. It is characterized by an eclectic combination of Romanesque and Renaissance elements. See also the related term ROUND ARCH MODE.

running bond A pattern of brickwork in which only stretchers appear, with the vertical joints of one course falling halfway between the vertical joints of adjacent courses. Sometimes called stretcher bond. Distinguished from common bond, in which every fifth or sixth course consists of all headers.

Ruskin Gothic, Ruskinian Gothic See HIGH VICTORIAN GOTHIC.

rustication, rusticated Masonry in which the joints are emphasized by narrow recessed channels or grooves outlining each block. Sometimes simulated in wood or stucco.

sacristy A room in a church where liturgical vessels and vestments are kept.

safety arch See RELIEVING ARCH.

sanctuary 1 The part of a church that contains the principal altar. Usually the innermost space within the chancel arm of the church, situated to the east of the choir. 2 Loosely used to mean a place of worship, a sacred place.

sash Any framework of a window. It may be movable or fixed. It may slide in a vertical plane (as in a double-hung window) or may be pivoted (as in a casement window).

sash bar See MUNTIN.

Secession movement The refined classicist Austrian (Viennese) version of the Art Nouveau style, so named beause the artists and architects involved seceded from the official Academy in 1897. Josef Hoffmann (1870–1956) is the architect most frequently mentioned in association with this movement.

Second Chicago school A term sometimes applied to the International style in Chicago from the 1940s to the 1970s, particularly the work of Mies van der Rohe. See also the related terms INTERNATIONAL STYLE, MIESIAN.

Second Empire Not strictly a style term but a term for a period in French history coinciding with the rule of Napoleon III (1852–1870).Generally applied in the United States, however, to a phase of Beaux-Arts governmental and institutional architecture (1850s-1880s) as well as to countless hybrids of Beaux-Arts and Italianate forms in residential, commercial, and industrial architecture

(1850s-1880s). Sometimes called General Grant style, Mansard style, Mansardic. See also the related terms BEAUX-ARTS, ITALIANATE (definition 1).

section A drawing (in orthographic projection) representing a vertical cut through an object, building, or space. An architectural section shows interior relationships of space and structure, and may also include mechanical systems. Sometimes called a cross section.

segmental arch An arch formed on a segmental curve. Its center lies below the springing line.

segmental curve A curve that is a segment (i.e., less than half the circumference) of a circle or an ellipse. The base line of the curve is a chord measuring less than the diameter of the larger circle from which the segment is taken.

segmental pediment A pediment whose top is a segmental curve.

segmental vault A vault whose cross section is a segmental curve. A dome built on segmental curves is called a saucer dome.

setback 1 In architecture, particularly in the design of tall buildings, a series of upper stories that are stepped back to allow more sunlight to reach the streets. 2 In planning, the amount of space between the lot line and the perimeter of a building.

shaft The tall part of a column between the base and the capital.

shed roof A roof having only one sloping plane. Sometimes called a lean-to roof.

Shingle style A term applied primarily to American domestic architecture of the 1870s through the 1890s, in which broad expanses of wood shingles dominate the exterior roof and wall planes. Rooms open widely into one another and to the outdoors, and the ample living hall or stair hall is often the dominant feature of the interior. The term was coined in the 1940s by Vincent Scully for a series of seaside and suburban houses of the northeastern United States. The Shingle style is a version of the Anglo-American Queen Anne style. See also the related terms COLONIAL REVIVAL, STICK STYLE.

shouldered architrave See EAR.

side gabled Term applied to a building whose gable ends face the sides of a lot. Distinguished from front gabled.

side light A framed area of fixed glass alongside a door or window. See also the related term FANLIGHT.

sill course In masonry, a stringcourse set at windowsill level, usually differentiated from the wall by its greater projection, its finish, or its thickness. Not applicable to frame construction.

sill plate See PLATE (definition 2).

skeleton construction, skeleton frame A system of construction in which all loads are carried to the ground through a rigid framework of iron, steel, or reinforced concrete. The exterior walls are curtain walls (i.e., not load-bearing).

skylight A window in a roof, specifically one that is flush with the roof plane or only slightly protruding. Distinguished from a cupola (definition 2), which is a major centralized feature at the summit of a roof. Distinguished from a monitor, which is an extensive roof feature containing a band of windows or vents.

soffit The exposed underside of any overhead component, such as an arch, beam, cornice, or lintel. See also the related term INTRADOS.

sole plate See PLATE (definition 2).

space frame A series of trusses placed side by side and joined to one another by triangulated rods, tubes, or beams, so that the individual planar trusses are united into a three-dimensional structural framework. Often used in roof structures requiring long spans.

spandrel 1 The quasi-triangular space between two adjoining arches and a line connecting their crowns, or between an arch and the columns and entablature that frame it. 2 In skeletal construction, the wall area between the top of a window and the sill of the window in the story above. Sometimes called a spandrel panel.

Spanish colonial A term applied to buildings, towns, landscapes, and other artifacts from the various periods of actual Spanish colonial occupation in North American (c. 1565–1821 in Florida; c. 1763–1800 in Louisiana and the Lower Mississippi valley; c. 1590s–1821 in Texas and the southwestern United States; c. 1769–1821 in California). The term is extended to apply to the artifacts of Hispanic ethnic groups (e.g., Mexicans, Puerto Ricans, Cubans) and their descendants, even into the early twentieth century. See also the related terms CHURRIGUERESQUE, PLATERESQUE.

Spanish Colonial Revival The revival of forms from Spanish colonial and provincial Mexican design. The Spanish Colonial Revival began in Florida and California in the 1880s and continues nationwide into the present. Sometimes called Neo-Hispanic, Spanish Eclectic, Spanish Revival. See also the more specific term MISSION REVIVAL, and the related term MEDITERRANEAN REVIVAL.

spindle A turned wooden element, thicker toward the middle and thinner at either end, found in arch screens, porch trim, and other ornamental assemblages. Banisters (i.e., thin, simple balusters) may be spindle-shaped, but the term spindle, when used alone, usually connotes shorter elements.

spire A slender pointed element surmounting a building. A tall, attenuated pyramidal form with any number of thin triangular faces that are unbroken or articulated only with crockets, pinnacles, or small dormers. Distinguished from a steeple, which is divided into stages and which may be topped with a spire.

splay The slanting surface formed by cutting off a right-angle corner at an oblique angle to one face. A reveal at an oblique angle to the exterior face of the wall.

springing, springing line, springing point The line or point where an arch or vault rises from its supports and begins to curve. Usually the juncture between the impost of the support below and the springer, or first voussoir, of the arch above.

squinch An arch, lintel, or corbeling, built across the interior corner of two walls to form one side of an octagonal base for a dome. This octagonal base serves as the structural transition from a square interior crossing space to an octagonal or round dome.

stair A series of steps, or flights of steps connected by landings, which connects two or more levels or floors.

staircase The ensemble of a stair and its enclosing walls. Sometimes called a stairway.

stair tower A projecting tower or other building block that contains a stair.

stamped metal See PRESSED METAL.

Steamboat Gothic See CARPENTER'S GOTHIC.

steeple 1 A tall structure rising from a tower, consisting of a series of superimposed stages diminishing in plan, and usually topped by a spire or small cupola. Distinguished from a spire, which is not divided into stages. 2 Less commonly used to mean the whole of the tower, from the ground to the top of the spire or cupola.

stepped gable A gable in which the wall rises in a series of steps above the planes of the roof.

stereotomy The science of cutting three-dimensional shapes from stone, such as the units that make up a carefully fitted masonry vault.

Stick style A term applied primarily to American domestic architecture of the 1850s through the 1870s, in which exterior wall planes are subdivided into bays and stories outlined by narrow boards called "stickwork." The term was coined by Vincent Scully in the 1940s for a series of houses with clearly articulated wall panels and sticklike porch supports and eaves brackets. Sources include the English and German picturesque traditions, as well as the French rationalist tradition. See also the related terms QUEEN ANNE, SHINGLE STYLE.

story (plural: stories). The space in a building between floor levels. British spelling is storey, storeys. Sometimes called a register, a more inclusive term applied to horizontal space on vertical plane zones that do not correspond to actual floor levels.

Streamline Moderne A later phase of the Moderne, popular in the 1930s and 1940s and characterized by stucco surfaces with rounded corners, horizontal banding, overhangs, and window groupings, and by other details suggestive of modern Machine Age aerodynamic forms. Sometimes called Streamline Modern, Streamline Modernistic. See also the more general term MODERNE and the related terms ART DECO and PWA MODERNE.

stretcher A brick laid the length of a wall, so that the long side of the brick shows on the exterior.

stretcher bond See RUNNING BOND.

string In a stair, an inclined board that supports the ends of the steps. Sometimes called a stringer.

stringcourse In masonry, a horizontal band, generally narrower than other courses, extending across the facade of a building and in some instances encircling such features as pillars or columns. It may be flush or projecting; of identical or contrasting material; flat, molded, or richly carved. Not applicable to frame construction. Sometimes called a band course or belt course. More elaborate horizontal bands in masonry or frame construction are generally called band moldings.

strut A column, post, or pole that is set in a diagonal position and thus serves as a stiffener by triangulation. Distinguished from a brace, which is usually a shorter bracketlike member.

stucco 1 An exterior plaster finish, usually textured, composed of portland cement, lime, and sand, which are mixed with water. 2 A fine plaster used for decorative work or moldings. See also the more specific term PARGETING.

stud One of the vertical supporting elements in a wall, especially in balloon and platform frame construction. Studs are relatively lightweight members (usually two-by-fours).

Sullivanesque Term applied to work showing the influence of the American architect Louis Henry Sullivan (1856–1924).

sunburst light See FANLIGHT.

supercapital See IMPOST BLOCK.

supercolumniation See SUPERPOSITION (definition 1).

superimposition, superimposed See SUPERPOSITION.

superposition, superposed 1 The use of an ensemble of the classical orders, one above the other, as the major elements articulating a facade. When this is done, the Doric, considered the simplest order, is used on or near the ground story. The Ionic, considered more complex, comes next; and the Corinthian, considered the most complex, is used at the top. Sometimes the Tuscan order or rusticated masonry may be used for the ground story beneath the Doric order, and the Composite order may be used above the Corinthian order. Sometimes called supercolumniation, superimposition. See also the related term ORDER. 2 Less commonly, any vertical relationship of architectural elements (e.g., windows, piers, colonnettes) in any style or period.

superstructure A structure raised upon another structure, as a building upon a foundation, basement, or substructure.

Supervising Architect The Supervising Architect of the United States Treasury Department, whose office was responsible for the design and construction of all major federal government buildings (such as courthouses, customhouses, and post offices) from the 1850s through the 1930s. The Office of the Supervising Architect was formally established by Congress in 1864 and lasted until 1939, when its functions were absorbed into the

Public Buildings Administration (and in 1949, into the General Services Administration).

supporting wall See BEARING WALL.

surround An encircling border or decorative frame around a door or window. Distinguished from architrave (definition **2**), a term usually applied to the frame around an opening when considered as a series of relatively flat face moldings.

suspended ceiling A ceiling suspended from rod-like hangers below the level of the floor above. The interval between the floor slab above and the suspended ceiling often serves as a space for ducts, utilities, and air circulation. Sometimes called a hung ceiling.

swag A motif representing a suspended fold of drapery hanging in a catenary curve from two points. Distinguished from a festoon, which is a motif representing entwined leaves, flowers, or fruits, hung in a similar curve. See also the more general term GARLAND.

tabernacle **1** A niche or recess, usually on an interior wall, framed by columns or pilasters and topped by an entablature and pediment. Distinguished from an aedicule, which more often occurs on an exterior wall. See also the related term NICHE. **2** In the Jewish religion, a portable sanctuary. **3** In Protestant denominations, a large auditorium church.

terracotta A hard ceramic material used for **1** fireproofing, especially as a fitted cladding around metal skeletal construction; or **2** an exterior or interior wall cladding, which is often glazed and multicolored.

tertiary rib. See LIERNE.

thermal window A large lunette window similar to those found in ancient Roman baths (*thermae*). The window is subdivided into three to five parts by vertical mullions. Sometimes called a *thermae* window.

three-hinged arch An arch in two major segments anchored with cylindrical "hinge" pins at either end and at the crown. Movement within the arch, caused by temperature changes, the torsion of wind movements, or other forces, can be absorbed by the movement of the arch around the pins, thereby avoiding stresses that would occur in the structural frame if the arch were fixed.

tie beam A horizontal tension member that ties together the opposing angular members of a truss and prevents them from spreading.

tier A group of stories or any zone of architectural elements arranged horizontally.

tierceron In a Gothic vault, a secondary rib that rises from the springing to an intermediate position on either side of the diagonal ribs. Sometimes called an intermediate rib.

tie rod A metal rod that spans the distance between two structural members and, by its tensile strength, restrains them against tendencies to collapse outward.

timber-frame construction, timber framing A type of wood frame construction in which heavy timber posts and beams (six-by-sixes and larger) are fastened using mortise and tenon joints. Sometimes called heavy timber construction. Distinguished from light frame construction, in which relatively light structural members (two-by-fours to two-by-tens) are fastened with nails.

trabeation, trabeated construction See POST AND BEAM CONSTRUCTION.

tracery Decoration within an arch or other opening, made up of narrow curvilinear bands or more elaborately molded strips. In Gothic architecture, the curved interlocking stone bars that contain the leaded stained glass.

transept The lateral arm of a cross-shaped church, usually between the nave (the area for the congregation) and the chancel (the area for the altar, clergy, and choir).

transom **1** A narrow horizontal window unit, either fixed or movable, over a door. Sometimes called a transom light. See also the more specific term FANLIGHT. **2** A horizontal bar, as distinguished from a vertical mullion, especially one crossing a door or window opening near the top.

transverse rib In a Gothic vault, a rib at right angles to the ridge rib.

trefoil A type of Gothic tracery having three parts (lobes or foils) separated by pointed elements (cusps).

trellis Any open latticework made of strips of wood or metal crossing one another, usually supporting climbing plants. Distinguished from an arbor, which is generally a more substantial yet compact three-dimensional structure, and from a pergola, which is a more extensive colonnaded structure.

triforium In a Gothic church, an arcade in the wall above the arches of the nave, choir, or transept and below the clerestory window.

triglyph One of the slightly raised blocks in a Doric frieze. It consists of three narrow vertical bands separated by two V-shaped grooves.

triumphal arch **1** A freestanding arch erected for a victory procession. It usually consists of a broad central arched opening, flanked by two smaller bays (usually with open or blind arches). The bays are usually articulated by classical columns, supporting an entablature and a high attic. **2** An similar configuration applied to a facade to denote a monumental entryway.

truss A rigid triangular framework made up of beams, posts, braces, struts, and ties and used for the spanning of large spaces. The major horizontal or inclined members are called chords. The connecting vertical and diagonal elements are called the web members.

Tudor arch A low-profile arch characterized by two pairs of arcs, one pair of tight arcs at the springing, another pair of broad (nearly flat) arcs at the apex or crown.

Tudor period A term for a period in English history coinciding with the rule of monarchs of the house of Tudor (1485–1603). Tudor period architecture is Late Gothic, with only hints of the Renaissance. See also the more specific term ELIZABETHAN PERIOD for the end of this period, and the related term JACOBEAN PERIOD for the succeeding period.

Tudor Revival See NEO-TUDOR.

turret A small towerlike structure, often circular in plan, built against the side or at an exterior or interior corner of a building.

Tuscan order An ensemble of classical column and entablature elements, similar to the Roman Doric order, but without triglyphs in the frieze and without mutules (domino-like blocks) in the cornice of the entablature. See also the more general term ORDER.

tympanum (plural: tympana). **1** The triangular or segmental area enclosed by the cornice moldings of a pediment, frequently ornamented with sculpture. **2** Any space similarly delineated or bounded, as between the lintel of a door or window and the arch above.

umbrage A term used by Alexander Jackson Davis (1803–1892) as a synonym for veranda, the implication being a shadowed area.

vault An arched roof or ceiling, usually constructed in brick or stone, but also in tile, metal or concrete. A nonstructural plaster ceiling that simulates a masonry vault.

Venetian Gothic See HIGH VICTORIAN GOTHIC.

veranda A nineteenth-century term for porch. Sometimes spelled verandah.

vergeboard See BARGEBOARD.

verges The sloping edges of a gable, gambrel, or lean-to roof, usually projecting beyond the wall below. Distinguished from eaves, which are the horizontal lower edges of a roof plane.

vernacular Not a style in itself, but a descriptive term, applicable primarily to architecture, covering the vast range of ordinary buildings that are produced outside the high-style tradition of well-known architects. The vernacular tradition includes the folk tradition of regional and ethnic buildings whose forms (plan and massing) remain relatively constant through the years, in spite of stylistic embellishments. The term vernacular architecture is often used as if it meant only folk architecture. However, the vernacular tradition in architecture also includes the popular tradition of buildings whose design was influenced by such publications as books of the orders, builders' guides, style books, pattern books, mail-order catalogs, architectural periodicals, and household magazines. Usually contrasted with high-style. See also the more specific terms FOLK, POPULAR.

vertical plank construction A system of wood construction in which vertical planks are set or nailed into heavy timber horizontal sills and plates. A building so constructed has no corner posts and no studs. Two-story vertical plank buildings have planks extending the full height of the building,

with no girt between the two stories. Second-floor joists are merely mortised into the planks. Distinguished from the more specific term vertical plank frame construction, in which there are corner posts.

vertical plank frame construction A type of vertical plank construction, in which heavy timber corner posts are introduced to provide support for the plate, to which the tops of the planks are fastened. See also the related term HORIZONTAL PLANK FRAME CONSTRUCTION.

vestibule A small entry hall between the outer door and the main hallway of a building.

Victorian Gothic See HIGH VICTORIAN GOTHIC.

Victorian period A term for a period in British, British colonial, and Anglo-American history, and not, in architecture or the other visual arts, a sufficiently specific style term. The Victorian period extended across eight decades, from the coronation of Queen Victoria in 1837 to her death in 1901. See instead EASTLAKE, GOTHIC REVIVAL, GREEK REVIVAL, QUEEN ANNE, SHINGLE STYLE, STICK STYLE, and other specific style terms.

Victorian Romanesque Ambiguous term. See instead RICHARDSONIAN ROMANESQUE, ROMANESQUE REVIVAL, ROUND ARCH MODE.

villa 1 In the Roman and Renaissance periods, a suburban or rural residential complex, often quite elaborate, consisting of a house, dependencies, and gardens. **2** Since the eighteenth century, any detached suburban or rural house of picturesque character and some pretension. Distinguished from the more modest house form known as a cottage.

volute 1 A spiral scroll, especially the one that is a distinctive feature of the Ionic capital. **2** A large scroll-shaped buttress on a facade or dome.

voussoir A wedge-shaped stone or brick used in the construction of an arch. Its tapering sides coincide with radii of the arch.

wainscot A decorative or protective facing, usually of wood paneling, applied to the lower portion of an interior partition or wall. Distinguished from a dado, which is the zone at the base of a wall, regardless of the material used to cover it. Wainscot properly connotes woodwork. Sometimes called wainscoting.

water table 1 In masonry, a course of molded bricks or stones set forward several inches near the base of a wall and serving as the cap of the basement courses. **2** In frame construction, a ledge or projecting molding just above the foundation to protect it from rainwater. **3** In masonry or frame construction, any horizontal exterior ledge on a wall, pier, or buttress. Often sloped and provided with a drip molding to prevent water from running down the face of the wall below.

weatherboard See CLAPBOARD.

weathering The inclination given to the upper surface of any element so that it will shed water.

web 1 The relatively thin shell of masonry between the ribs of a ribbed vault. **2** The portion of a truss between the chords, or the portion of a girder or I-beam between the flanges.

western frame, western framing See PLATFORM FRAME CONSTRUCTION.

winder A step, more or less wedge-shaped, with its tread wider at one end than the other.

window bar See MUNTIN.

window cap See CAP.

window head A head molding or pedimented feature over a window.

Wrightian Term applied to work showing the influence of the American architect Frank Lloyd Wright (1867–1959). See also the related term PRAIRIE SCHOOL.

wrought iron Iron shaped by a hammering process, to improve the tensile properties of the metal. Distinguished from cast iron, a brittle material, which is formed in molds.

Zigzag Moderne, Zigzag Modernistic See ART DECO.

Index

Pages with illustrations appear in bold.